WOMEN, POPULATION
AND GLOBAL CRISIS

ABOUT THE AUTHOR

Asoka Bandarage is Associate Professor and Chair of the Women's Studies Program at Mount Holyoke College, South Hadley, Massachusetts, USA. She has published widely in the fields of women's studies, population, ecology, international politics and economics. Her work has often paid close attention to the experiences of Sri Lankan and South Asian women. A member of the editorial board of the *Bulletin of Concerned Asian Scholars* she also sits on the coordinating committee of the Committee on Women, Population and the Environment.

WOMEN, POPULATION AND GLOBAL CRISIS

A Political-Economic Analysis

ASOKA BANDARAGE

ZED BOOKS
London & New Jersey

Dedicated to Maithri

Women, Population and Global Crisis was first published in 1997 by
Zed Books Ltd, 7 Cynthia Street, London N1 9JF, UK, and
165 First Avenue, Atlantic Highlands, New Jersey 07716, USA.

Second Impression 1998

Typeset in Monotype Baskerville by Lucy Morton, London SE12
Printed and bound in Canada

A catalogue record for this book is available from the British Library

Library of Congress Cataloging-in-Publication Data
Bandarage, Asoka, 1950–
    Women, population and global crisis : political-economic analysis
/ Asoka Bandarage
      p. cm.
    Includes bibliographical references (p.   ) and index.
    ISBN 1–85649–427–6 (cloth). — ISBN 1–85649–428–4 (pbk.).
    1. Population.   2. Birth control.   3. Population policy.
    I. Title
    HB871.827   1997   96–36915
    304.6—dc21   CIP

ISBN 1 85649 427 6 (Hb)
ISBN 1 85649 428 4 (Pb)

Contents

Figures and Tables   vii

Abbreviations   ix

Acknowledgements   xii

Introduction   1

Dominant Perspectives 4
An Alternative Political-Economic Analysis 12
Paradigm Shift 19
Outline of the Book 19

Part I   Malthusianism: Theory and Practice

1   Malthusian Analysis of Global Crisis   27

Malthusian Doctrine 27
Population and the Environment 30
Population and Poverty 39
Population and Political Instability 44
Population and Women 51

2   Politics of Global Population Control   63

The 'Contraceptive Revolution' 65
Sterilization 68
Non-Surgical Methods 80
Contraceptive Promotion and Distribution 88
Women's Health and Human Rights 92
Democracy or Authoritarianism? 101

Part II   Political-Economic Analysis

3   Historical Evolution of Socio-Demographic Relations   115

Population in Pre-capitalist Societies 116
Capitalism, Patriarchy and Population 122
Imperialism and Socio-Demographic Transformation 126
Population Growth in the Neo-Colonial Era 140
Demographic Trends into the Future 143
Demography and Democracy 149

4 Social Structural Determinants of Fertility 157

Social Class and Fertility 157
Gender and Fertility 169
Social Justice and Fertility 175
Worsening Inequality and Fertility 180

5 Political Economy of Poverty 187

Widening Inequality 187
Economic Imperialism 191
Structural Adjustment 198
The Arms Trade 205
Restructuring in the North 211
Women's Poverty and Global Crisis 217

6 Political Economy of the Environment 228

Unequal Consumption 228
Capitalist Production 238
Ecological Imperialism 239
Agriculture, Poverty and the Environment 241
Industrial Manufacturing 252
Militarism and the Environment 257

7 Political Economy of Violence and Insecurity 270

Inequality and Insecurity 270
Imperialism and Militarism 272
The New World Order 276
Women, Children and War 284
Ethno-Nationalism and Fundamentalism 287
Insecurity and Violence in the North 291
Democracy or Fascism? 295

Part III Paradigm Shift: From Domination to Partnership

8 Towards Psycho-Social Transformation 307

Resistance against Domination 307
From Domination to Partnership 314
Towards Democratic and Sustainable Development 324
Empowerment of Women 335

Appendix 1 Women, Population and the Environment:
Call for a New Approach 345

Appendix 2 The Seville Statement on Violence 348

Appendix 3 Responsible Wealth: A Call to Action 351

Appendix 4 Networks and Organizations 354

Bibliography 358

Index 389

Figures and Tables

Figures

1	Paradigm shift: psycho-social transformation	3
2	World population growth, 1750–2100	5
2.1	Global population control: hierarchy of financial and technological aid disbursement	67
2.2	Sex ratios at birth in China, 1970–1987	98
3.1	The demographic transition: developed and developing countries	125
3.2	Population growth rates and population size with and without AIDS	145
5.1	Reversing resource flows: North to South net transfers, 1980–1988	197
5.2	US government's proposed 1997 spending for key programs	213
8.1	Global psycho-social revolution	314
8.2	Paradigm shift: from domination to partnership	315
8.3	Levels and strategies of psycho-social transformation	320
8.4	Buddhist well-being curve, equilibrium and diminishing returns	331

Tables

1	Widening global income disparity, 1960–1991	13
2	World's 200 largest corporations, 1985 and 1995	14
1.1	Global population and health expenditures, 2000 and 2015	54
2.1	Contraceptive users by method, 1989	68
2.2	Estimated deficits in female populations due to excess female mortality, 1981–1991: selected areas	99
3.1	Estimated average annual growth rates of population, 1750–1950	130
3.2	World population by continent, 1650–1950	131
3.3	World survey of tribal depopulation, 1780–1930	132
3.4	Population growth rates 1950–2020, medium-variant projections	141
3.5	Declining global fertility rates (per woman), 1950–2020	147
4.1	Physical quality of life and fertility, 1990–1995	165
4.2	High rates of infant and child mortality: selected countries, 1960 and 1991	166
4.3	Female/male ratios, infant and child mortality rates, selected countries, 1986/1993	173
4.4	Socio-demographic indicators: India, Kerala and Sri Lanka, early 1990s	178
5.1	Inequality in the distribution of landholdings: selected countries, 1980–1987	188
5.2	Widening income disparity in the US, 1980 and 1993	190

5.3	Corporate control of global commodity trade, 1988	194
5.4	Countries with IMF/World Bank programs which have experienced increasing rates of infant or child mortality, and falling ratios of primary school enrollment, 1980–1985	201
5.5	Countries with IMF/World Bank programs which have experienced a deterioration in female nutrition or health, 1980–1985	204
5.6	The 25 leading suppliers of major conventional weapons, 1990–1994	206
5.7	Population in poverty before and after public benefits: selected industrialized countries, 1984–1987	216
6.1	Annual per capita consumption: meat, automobile travel, energy, steel and paper, 1987–1990	230
6.2	Unequal contributions to greenhouse effect, 1987	232
6.3	Fuel consumption and estimated air pollutant emissions of military aircraft: selected countries and world, late 1980s	258
7.1	Quantity of weapons exported during 1994	278
7.2	Military strength of nations, 1994–1995	280
7.3	PACs' (Political Action Committees') contributions, 1994 and 1996: US congressional elections	296

Abbreviations

AIDS	Acquired Immune Deficiency Syndrome
AFDC	Aid to Families with Dependent Children
AFSC	American Friends Service Committee
Alt-WID	Alternative Women in Development
API	Associated Press International
ARP	Agricultural Rehabilitation Program
AVSC	Association for Voluntary Surgical Contraception
BBC	British Broadcasting Corporation
BCCI	Bank of Credit and Commerce International
CARASA	Committee for Abortion Rights and Against Sterilization Abuse
CCN	Carrying Capacity Network
CDC	Center for Disease Control
CEDPA	Center for Development and Population Activities
CFCs	chlorofluorocarbons
CIA	Central Intelligence Agency
CNN	Cable News Network
CPI-M	Communist Party of India–Marxist
CSM	Contraceptive Social Marketing
CWPE	Committee on Women, Population and the Environment
DAWN	Development Alternatives with Women for a New Era
DBCP	dibromochloropropane
DDT	Dichlorodiphenyltrichloroethane
DHEW	Department of Health, Education and Welfare
EDA	Excess Defense Articles
ESF	Economic Support Fund
EZLN	Zapatista Army of National Liberation
FAIR	Federation for American Immigration Reform
FAO	Food and Agriculture Organization
FAS	Federation of American Scientists
FBI	Federal Bureau of Investigation
FHI	Family Health International
FMS	foreign military sales
G7	Group of 7 countries
GAD	Gender and Development
GAO	General Accounting Office
GATT	General Agreement on Tariffs and Trade

GDP	gross domestic product
GEF	Global Environmental Facility
GOBI	Growth monitoring; Oral rehydration therapy; Breast-feeding and improved weaning practices; Immunization
GNP	gross national product
HIV	Human Immunodeficiency Virus
HRP	Human Reproduction
ICDDR	International Center for Diarrhoeal Disease Research
ICPD	International Conference on Population and Development
IEC	information–education–communication
ILO	International Labour Organization
IMET	International Military Education and Training (Program)
IMF	International Monetary Fund
INSTRAW	United Nations International Research and Training Institute for the Advancement of Women
IPPF	International Planned Parenthood Federation
IPS	Inter-Press Service
ITTO	International Tropical Timber Organization
IUCNNR	International Union for the Conservation of Nature and Natural Resources
IUD	intrauterine device
IUF	Indigenous Uranium Forum
IVF	in-vitro fertilization
IWHC	International Women's Health Coalition
JVPC	Janata Vimukti Peramuna– People's Liberation Front
LTTE	Liberation Tigers of Tamil Eelam
MAP	Military Assistance Program
MCH	maternal and child health
MDBs	multilateral development banks
MIC	mid-intensity conflict
MRCs	Major Regional Contingencies
NACLA	North American Congress on Latin America
NAFTA	North American Free Trade Agreement
NARAL	National Abortion Rights Action League
NCHS	National Center for Health Statistics
NGOs	Non-Governmental Organizations
NIEO	New International Economic Order
NOW	National Organization of Women
NRR	net reproduction rate
ODA	Overseas Development Aid
PACs	Political Action Committees
PCBs	polychlorinated biphenyls
PCC	Population Crisis Committee
PDA	Population, Community and Development Association
PEG	Political Ecology Group
PND	prenatal diagnostic (techniques)
PPE	poverty, population growth and environmental stress
PSI	Population Services International

SALs	structural adjustment loans
SAPs	structural adjustment policies
SIDA	Swedish International Development Association
SIPRI	Stockholm International Peace Research Institute
STDs	Sexually Transmitted Diseases
TCE	trichloroethylene
TNCs	transnational corporations
TFAP	Tropical Forest Action Plan
UBINIG	Policy Research for Development Alternatives
UNCED	United Nations Conference on Environment and Development
UNCTAD	United Nations Conference on Trade and Development
UNDP	United Nations Development Programme
UNFPA	United Nations Fund for Population Activities
UNHCR	United Nations High Commission for Refugees
UNICEF	United Nations Children's Fund
UNIFEM	United Nations Development Fund for Women
UPI	United Press International
USAID	United States Agency for International Development
USFDA	United States Food and Drug Administration
VGF	Vulnerable Group Feeding Program
WEDO	Women's Environment and Development Organization
WGNRR	Women's Global Network for Reproductive Rights
WHO	World Health Organization
WHO-HRP	WHO Special Program for Research Development and Research Training in Human Reproduction
WID	Women in Development
WTO	World Trade Organization

Acknowledgements

I am grateful to all the individuals and circumstances in my life that enabled me to write this book. While I am not able to thank all those who helped individually, I would like to acknowledge at least some of them here.

The work of several generations of scholars and activists in the areas of peace, justice, ecology and women's rights has provided the intellectual and political foundation for this book. Of the many individuals and organizations I have worked with, the Committee on Women, Population and the Environment (CWPE) has had the greatest impact on the conceptualization and development of this work. My thanks to all the members of the CWPE Coordinating Committee, especially Betsy Hartmann, Judy Norsigian, Gabriela Canepa, Marlene Gerber Fried, April Taylor, Pat Hynes, Nalini Visvanathan, Norma Swenson and Ynestra King, who have shared ideas, information and materials relevant to this work. Thanks also to Betsy Hartmann for her valuable comments on Chapter 2.

My thanks to family members, friends and colleagues who have provided information or access to information relevant to this work. Among them, I wish particularly to thank my father, Dr D.S. Bandarage, sister Wasantha Bandarage, husband James (Jaime) Babson and friend Mr Hewage Jayasena.

Thanks to Karin Aguilar-San Juan, Bobbie Lewis, Tom Neilson, Nancy Fulton, among others, whose commentary on different drafts helped shape and improve the manuscript. Thanks also to editors Louise Murray and Robert Molteno, copyeditor Justin Dyer and Anne Rodford of the Production Department of Zed Books for their patient assistance in producing this work. My gratitude also to students in my seminar on Women, Population and Global Crisis at Mount Holyoke College who read the draft manuscript and provided valuable feedback for revisions.

Without the support of many Mount Holyoke students who have worked as my research assistants over the years, this book could not have been written. I am grateful to Srijana Dhakwa, Radharani Ray, Gail Scanlon, Penny Marston, Kathleen Kim, Michelle Dolson, Wen-Hua Yang and others whose help with data collection and manuscript preparation was essential to this work. I am indebted to Lale Uner and Siby Thomas for their incredible help in the final stages of completing the book. I would also like to express my appreciation to the Faculty Grants Committee for funds to pay my student assistants, to the reference librarians at Mount Holyoke for their patience and help with my extensive requests for information, and to Cindy Legare at the College's Computer Services for technological assistance.

My thanks to family and friends who have provided loving care for my son during the times I have been at work on this book. My deepest gratitude is to my mother, Mrs Tilaka Bandarage, for her tremendous support during the post-partum months. Thanks also to Mollie Bunnell and Debbie Vanderpoel for child-care support and to Danushi Wijewardene for her help with both the baby and library work on the book

My gratitude to my teachers, especially at Visakha Vidyalaya, Bryn Mawr College and Yale University, for their encouragement during different stages of my intellectual development. My gratitude also to the great meditation teacher S.N. Goenka for his teaching and spiritual inspiration. Very special thanks to Sister Clare Carter and Rev. Gyatso Kato at the Leverett Peace Pagoda for their friendship and continuing support of my work.

Thanks to my husband Jaime for his patience and support during the ups and downs of what has seemed like an endless project. And, last but not least, thanks to my son Maithri for his love and joy which inspired me to complete this work and to whom the book is dedicated.

Introduction

We are at a critical juncture in the history of human and planetary evolution. As humanity moves towards the twenty-first century and the next millennium, we are caught in a relentless spiral of violence and self-destruction. The ecosystem is rapidly collapsing around us; millions of people are dying of hunger, disease and war; nation states, communities and families are breaking apart, turning more and more people into migrants and refugees; and the ignorance, greed and hatred in our minds are aggravating fear and insecurity, damaging all our relationships.

Every year, about 4 million hectares of rainfed cropland are lost due to soil erosion and as much as 70,000 square kilometers of farmland are abandoned due to salinization, desertification, paving and other forms of environmental degradation.[1] Between 1950 and the year 2000, the world's tropical forests are expected to decline by 50% and as a result of the destruction of their habitats, nearly 140 species of plant or animal are condemned to extinction every day.[2] The destruction of coral reefs also wipes out myriads of ocean species, while eroding shorelines. Climatic and other environmental disturbances, such as the greenhouse effect, global warming, acid rain and ozone depletion, pose major threats to human and planetary health unlike any we have previously experienced.[3]

Like the natural environment, much of humanity is also faced with a crisis of survival. The world is said to be experiencing the worst unemployment crisis since the 1930s, according to the ILO: 30% of the global labor force, that is, about 820 million people, were unemployed at the beginning of 1994.[4] Of the 5.8 billion or so people in the world today (late 1996), nearly one billion go hungry every day. Almost one-third of the population in the South, nearly 1.3 billion people, live in absolute poverty, lacking access to essentials of life such as basic health care, sanitation and safe water.[5] Thirty-five thousand children under 5 years of age die every day due mostly to poverty-related causes in the Third World.[6]* In the

---

* The term 'Third World' is undoubtedly pejorative. In the absence of a 'Second World' (since the collapse of the Communist Bloc), it has even less meaning. Still, other

industrialized countries, including the former Soviet Union and Eastern Europe, about 200 million people lived below the poverty line in 1990. More than 20% of children in the United States currently live below the official poverty line.[7] Everywhere, women and children suffer the most due to the combined effects of environmental destruction, poverty and war. As much as 70% of the world's poor and almost 600 million of the world's one billion illiterate adults are estimated to be women.[8] Destruction of forests and the land, unemployment and increasingly limited access to other resources make it difficult for women to feed their families. Just as environmental pollution affects the earth's capacity to bear life, increased exposure to toxic chemicals damages women's health, threatening their ability to bear and nurture human life in the long term.

The current nuclear stockpiles in the world are estimated to contain 900 times more explosive power than was expended in World War II, including 10,000 nuclear warheads, each potentially more destructive than the bombs exploded in Hiroshima and Nagasaki.[9] Despite the end of the Cold War and the so-called 'peace dividend', global military expenditures continue to be extremely high: an estimated $767 billion for 1994, which is more than the total income of the poorest 45% of the world's population. 'Developing countries' themselves spent about $118 billion on defense in 1994.[10] The United States, the global military super-power, has allocated over $1.8 trillion for military spending for the 1996–2002 period.[11]

Between 1945 and 1992, there were 149 major wars in the world. In 1994, 164 armed conflicts, many of them ethnic wars, raged across the world.[12] According to 1995 estimates, there were 27 million refugees worldwide and a total of 50 million refugees including those displaced in their own lands. One out of every 115 people in the world today has been forced to flight due to war, violence and human rights abuses. Up to 75% of all refugees are estimated to be women or girls.[13] Ninety per cent of people killed in wars during the 1990s have been civilians, a large proportion of them being children. During the last decade, child victims of war have included "2 million killed, 4–5 million disabled, 12 million homeless, more than a million orphaned or separated from parents and some 10 million psychologically traumatized".[14]

In sharp contrast to the peaceful new world order envisioned by many analysts at the end of the Cold War, the world is now experiencing an intensification of violence. Events such as the Oklahoma City bombing and the Tokyo subway gas attack reflect deepening insecurity. 'Complex emergencies' combine armed conflicts with collapse of economic, political and social institutions, environmental destruction, poverty, displacement and massive

---

terms such as 'developing world', 'the South', and so on, do not capture the exploitative nature of the relations between the West and the neo-colonial nations of Asia, Africa and Latin America. Hence the term 'Third World' is retained along with the use of alternative terms in this book.

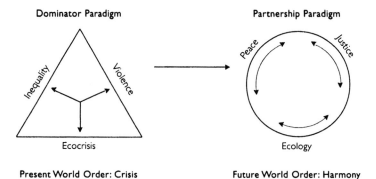

Figure 1 Paradigm shift: psycho-social transformation

slaughter. In countries such as Zaire and Sri Lanka, innocent women, men and children are massacred, and in Rwanda and Bosnia, hundreds of thousands of people have been exterminated due to barbaric policies of 'ethnic cleansing'. The 'holocaust' did not end in Nazi Germany; it continues in many shapes and forms. If humanity continues on this trajectory of ignorance, greed and hatred, we could extinguish ourselves from the face of the earth, sooner rather than later, just as we are wiping out hundreds of other animal and plant species every day. Indeed, we are moving into an extremely fluid and volatile period, now, when underlying tensions are erupting to the surface threatening the stability and security of the entire world.[15]

The exploding 'complex emergencies' have their roots in the worsening global political-economic crisis. The crisis now at hand in the entire global economic, political and cultural system has evolved over the last 500 or so years of European conquest and in particular the past 250 years of global capitalist development. The balance of the whole planetary organism and the survival of life itself are at stake. Indeed, environmental destruction, poverty and violence are not phenomena peculiar to the current period. But never have social problems been as thoroughly interconnected as they now are within the increasingly integrated and homogenized global economy and the military–industrial complex. Today, in order to resolve the seemingly separate environmental and social problems in different locations, we must necessarily take a global approach in addition to individual and local approaches.

A time of crisis can be described as one when the old is dead but the new is not yet born. In the original Greek usage, 'crisis' refers to 'decision': a point in a process when a critical decision has to be made.[16] In Chinese, 'crisis' can be interpreted to mean that in danger there is also opportunity. It is now time for a fundamental shift towards a new vision of social and psychological development and towards a path of unity and peace in the world. To help identify the old and envision the new: these are the broad objectives for writing this book (Figure 1).

Unfortunately, however, the world seems to be moving towards greater conflict, destruction and despair instead of peace, justice and ecological renewal at this time. This is also a time of intellectual and ideological confusion when many self-serving doctrines and extremist, violent social movements are presenting themselves in the guise of truth and wisdom. However, dominant analyses and solutions are narrow and oriented to the short term. Not only are they inadequate for comprehending the roots of modern dilemmas, but they also block the development of more comprehensive analyses and peaceful solutions.

Dominant Perspectives

Malthusianism

A dominant ideology that seeks to directly address the global crisis and provide solutions is Malthusianism, which derives its name from the doctrine articulated by Thomas Malthus in 1798.[17] This doctrine attributes virtually all major social problems to human population growth and advocates population control as the solution to those problems. Just as the Malthusian doctrine came into prominence during the turmoils of the Industrial Revolution, it has aligned itself with dominant class as well as race and gender interests and repressive social movements during subsequent social crises.

As the current global crisis worsens, calls for stringent Malthusian solutions are intensifying in the highest echelons of academia and policy making in the North. This study begins, therefore, with a critical examination of the controversial question of population and Malthusian policies as a useful starting point. From there, it develops an alternative and broader analysis of the global crisis and offers a vision for radical social change.

Since the time of Malthus, global population has grown exponentially. However, population estimates are subject to a great deal of variation and error as evident, for example, in the United Nations' low, medium and high projections and undercounting of racial 'minorities' in the US Census. As such, population estimates must be treated with caution. According to widely used estimates, global population increased from 1 billion in the mid nineteenth century to 2 billion between 1918 and 1927; 4 billion in 1974 and 5 billion in 1987. United Nations' medium variant projections estimate world population to increase to 6 billion by the turn of the twenty-first century and over 8 billion by 2025. Population growth in the so-called 'developing' countries or the Third World accounts for about 90% of current global growth. It is estimated that by the year 2025 about 85% of the global population will be there (Figure 2). However, according to recent

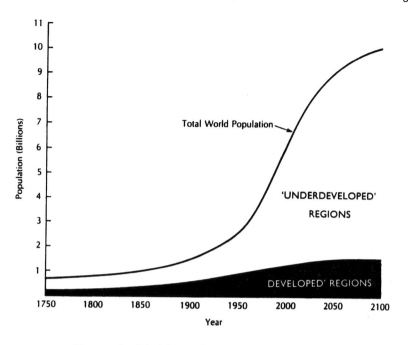

Figure 2 World population growth, 1750–2100

Source: A Citizen's Guide to the International Conference on Population and Development, Washington, DC: Population Reference Bureau, 1994, p. 8

UN estimates, world population is stabilizing much faster than earlier predicted.[18]

Malthus himself opposed abortion and deliberate birth control on moral grounds; nevertheless, his doctrine has become closely associated with the provision of contraception and abortion for purposes of population control. Despite the difference between the original doctrine and subsequent neo-Malthusian positions on the question of artificial contraception, they share a common social philosophy which identifies population growth as the root cause of, and population control as the major solution to, social problems. Blaming global environmental destruction, poverty, hunger and political instability on massive and unprecedented increase in human population in the Third World, neo-Malthusian policy makers look to what they call the 'contraceptive revolution' as the most urgent remedy for these problems.

The current resurgence of Malthusianism is not a phenomenon restricted to the dominant world institutions such as the US government, the World Bank (International Bank for Reconstruction and Development) and the United Nations system. Liberal social change movements such as the environmental movement and feminist movement in the North are also increasingly accepting fertility control and population stabilization as prerequisites for sustainable development and women's reproductive freedom and empowerment. In the South, too, most governments as well as nongovernmental organizations (NGOs) seem to accept this position imported from the North. However, Malthusian arguments cannot be taken simply at face value. The origin and evolution of Malthusian thinking and the international population control movement must be understood in the context of increasing concentration of economic and political power and widening global social inequalities. As this book demonstrates, the fear of unequal reproduction across classes, races and regions and the desire to control the fertility of poor women underlie Malthusianism.

With the emergence of the US as the world's leading military and economic power after World War II and the 'explosion' of population in the Third World, US leaders began to see the deepening global disparity between global demographic and economic power as a threat to US hegemony in the world. George Kennan, author of the Cold War 'containment' theory, spelled out the true rationale for the Cold War in a secret US State Department memorandum in 1948, when he stated:

> We have about 50 per cent of the world's wealth, but only 6.3 per cent of its population. In this situation, we cannot fail to be the object of envy and resentment. Our real task is ... to devise a pattern of relationships which will permit us to maintain this position of disparity without positive detriment to our national security.[19]

The vast amounts of money given by private foundations and the US government for population research, program design and implementation have created a "powerful cult of population control" within US as well as global academic and policy planning circles.[20] Like Malthus, contemporary Malthusian analysts who work within the population control paradigm advocate population stabilization as a substitute for social justice and political-economic transformation.

However, Malthusianism is fundamentally flawed in both its theory and its practice. Instead of a comprehensive explanation of the global population 'explosion', it gives a narrow, compartmentalized view extricating population growth from all other issues of human reproduction and the broader historical processes of societal evolution. Population control by itself does not lead to the alleviation of poverty, environmental destruction, political unrest or other social problems. On the contrary, as this book shows, population control without poverty alleviation, environmental restoration and demilitarization results in the exacerbation of the existing problems and the victimization of poor women.

The Malthusian position has resulted in targeting the bodies of poor women of color both in the South and in the North as the solution to the global crisis. The expansion of family planning programs based on extensive use of demographic targets, economic incentives, forced sterilization and experimental contraceptive methods involve coercion and dangers to the health and well-being of poor women and their children. The magnitude of these dangers becomes especially evident in the context of deepening poverty, especially the feminization of poverty, and other forms of violence against women.

The 'new' women's agenda

Adopting the feminist tenet of individual choice in reproduction, neo-Malthusian analysts in recent years have increasingly emphasized women's reproductive rights as the reason for family planning interventions. The Programme of Action adopted in Cairo in September 1994 at the International Conference on Population and Development (ICPD) was put forward as a global 'consensus' on a new and broader reproductive rights approach that is fundamentally different from the prevailing family planning and demographic approach to population.[21]

Despite the ICPD agenda's claim that empowerment of women should be an end in itself, the overriding commitment to quantitative goals persists. The ICPD Programme of Action states that "the long-term success of population programmes" requires improvement of the status of women, thus revealing an instrumentalist approach to women's rights.[22]

As liberal feminist activists form alliances with population control advocates and depend on the latter's monetary and institutional support, they, too, come to accept the neo-Malthusian position which reduces 'women's rights' to 'reproductive rights', which in turn are equated with 'population policies'.[23] As this book reveals, subsuming women's issues within the neo-Malthusian framework leads to a neglect of the social structural roots of women's subordination.

The focus on fertility control and sexual and reproductive rights in the ICPD consensus has also diverted attention from the fact that everywhere it is women who take care of children and hold families and communities together, especially during this period of global social crisis and turmoil. The lack of recognition given to women's nurturing and caring labor in the new agenda has produced a discourse that equates women's freedom with individual reproductive choice and which sees 'women's rights' as separate from that of children and family. As Indian feminist activists Vandana and Mira Shiva have argued, not only does this allow the right wing to appear as the only ones concerned with family and community, but it also contributes to 'disempowering' rather than empowering women in the long run.[24]

These observations do not negate the fact that birth control and reproductive self-determination provide an essential material basis for the liberation of women. Malthusianism, however, is inherently limited in its ability to understand the complexity of women's lives and the global crisis or to provide democratic and sustainable solutions. A truly feminist stance on reproductive freedom can be built only upon a broader political-economic analysis of the global crisis and an ethic of human caring and nurturance which simultaneously empowers women, their families and communities. The development of such an analysis is one of the objectives of this book.

A feminist analysis of reproduction must necessarily distinguish itself from both antinatalist Malthusian population control as well as right-wing pronatalism, especially religious fundamentalism. While a thorough examination of the escalating right-wing backlash against women's reproductive rights is beyond the scope of this study, some developments pertaining to the controversial issue of abortion and women's rights are addressed briefly in this Introduction.

Right-wing fundamentalism

Religious fundamentalism and certain forms of ethno-nationalism rely frequently on patriarchal authority to invoke a stable and secure past. In challenging the forces of cultural modernization and in advancing their own solutions to the problems of social disintegration and insecurity, many such movements seek to relegate women to the private sphere, defining them solely by their wife and mother roles. Thus, in many contexts, in both the North and the South, religious fundamentalism opposes abortion and reproductive choice for women, and often it does so violently.

International population control advocates have considerably softened their stance on abortion in recent years in order to accommodate their conservative opponents, especially the Christian fundamentalists in the US and the Vatican. At the 1984 Mexico City World Population Conference, the Reagan administration, due to lobbying by so-called 'pro-life' groups, asserted that population is at best a neutral phenomenon in the process of economic development; and the US abruptly cut off funding for family planning agencies assisting abortions overseas. The influence of conservative neo-classical economists like Julian Simon, who see population as a resource rather than an impediment to economic and market growth, also played a role in this decision.[25]

According to population control organizations, the loss of US funds since the Mexico City decision resulted in hundreds of thousands of 'unwanted pregnancies', births, illegal abortions and maternal deaths in the world. It is estimated that worldwide approximately 200,000 women are killed every year due specifically to complications from illegal abortions. The actual number of deaths may be even higher given that only about half of the countries in the world report maternal mortality statistics to the WHO, which itself is an indication of the low status of women in those countries.[26]

There is continued pressure from fundamentalist religious groups around the world to stop funding for all artificial methods of birth control. Recent developments in Germany and Poland indicate that women are losing their previously held rights to abortion and reproductive choice in those countries.[27] If the right-wing backlash and the power of the Vatican are not challenged, the worldwide trend towards abortion liberalization which took place in the 1970s and 1980s could be reversed.

Both the ICPD Programme and the Beijing Platform for Action adopted at the 1995 UN Fourth World Conference on Women in Beijing recognize unsafe abortions as a major health issue. But the absence of references to women's right to terminate pregnancies in these agendas represents a victory for the global anti-abortion and religious fundamentalist movements and a defeat for the global women's struggle for decriminalizing abortion and for reproductive self-determination.

Through the Vatican's vast access to money and the media and the special status of the Holy See as a Non-Member State Permanent Observer at the United Nations (a status not accorded any other religious body), it succeeded in excluding references to women's right to abortion from the ICPD Programme of Action.[28] It also refused to support a clause in the Beijing Platform for Action calling on governments to review laws that punish women who undergo illegal abortions.[29]

Appropriating the language of leftist, Third World and feminist critics, the Vatican charged family planning programs with western cultural and biological imperialism during the deliberations on the ICPD agenda. The Vatican's interest, however, is not in economic or cultural liberation of the Third World but the restriction of the reproductive freedoms of women and the augmentation of its own authority in the world.[30] For the Vatican, as for Islamic fundamentalists, abortion and contraception represent a threat to patriarchal power. The export around the world of religious fundamentalism, especially evangelical Christianity and militant Islam, poses serious threats to women's freedom and cultural survival as well as to the evolution of secular, democratic political institutions.

Women and social minorities are increasingly the victims of fundamentalist forces fighting in the name of the traditional family and morality and against the sexual permissiveness represented supposedly by adolescent sexuality, homosexuality, non-traditional families and the AIDS epidemic. Much of the opposition of the religious right to the ICPD Programme of Action came during attempts to address such issues. The translation of such opposition into social policy exacerbates social conflicts and insecurity, especially the insecurity of women.

Increases in teenage pregnancy, illegal abortions and even abortion-related deaths among poor women have been frequently attributed to withdrawal of federal funding for abortion in the US. Election of anti-abortion activists to school boards and legislatures, lobbying for so-called fetal protection policies which subordinate women's rights to 'fetal rights', and opposition to the introduction of the new non-surgical abortion method – RU486 – are commonplace in the US. Bombing of abortion clinics and attacks on doctors and patients by 'pro-life' activists have also resulted in deaths in recent years. As funds for reproductive health and social programs in the US and overseas are slashed by the Congress under the influence of the conservative Christian Coalition, women's access to abortion and modern contraceptives are further undermined. In January 1996, the US House of Representatives cut funding for international family planning programs from $550 million to $360 million.[31]

The organized and increasingly violent opposition to women's reproductive choice makes neo-Malthusian population control appear as a liberal and enlightened social movement. Yet it is important to recognize that despite their differences with regard to fertility control, both Malthusianism and right-wing fundamentalism are inherently conservative social forces serving dominant gender, race and class interests and the repression of progressive social change. Like many international population control organizations and conservative anti-environmental networks such as the 'Wise Use Movement' in the US, some ethnic and religious fundamentalist movements in the South and the North may well be efforts funded by self-serving corporate business interests.[32] The common objective of all these efforts is to prevent radicalization of the masses by distracting consciousness and conserving dominant economic and political interests.

Liberal–right-wing convergence

Notwithstanding its opposition to secular modernism and rationality as represented by neo-Malthusianism, religious fundamentalism shares with Malthusianism a basic acceptance of capitalism. Religious fundamentalists and the Malthusian 'demographic fundamentalists' who attribute all problems to 'overpopulation' share many organizational strategies. They both use sophisticated funding techniques and media; they both adapt indigenous culture to change consciousness and win converts: souls in the case of the religious fundamentalists and 'contraceptive acceptors' in the case of the neo-Malthusians.[33]

Sophisticated fund-raising, lobbying and media management have been cornerstones in the origin and evolution of the international population control establishment. As reproductive rights activist Betsy Hartmann has pointed out, these tactics were utilized by a few powerful actors such as the Pew Charitable Trust's Global Initiative, the US State Department, the United Nations Fund for Population Activities (UNFPA), the Turner Broadcasting System and CNN in 'manufacturing' the so-called 'landmark consensus' of the ICPD.[34] The Vatican, like other conservative religious groups in turn, utilizes powerful fund-raising, media and advertising techniques to infuse public consciousness with their own self-righteous messages. Indeed, antipathy towards modernity and globalism has not prevented many extremist fundamentalist groups from embracing the latest technology in mass media and modern weaponry to further their causes.

Ultimately, both the Malthusians and their right-wing opponents attempt to wrest reproductive decisions and power from women and hand them to external authorities, whether they be patriarchal religious entities or state and medical hierarchies. In this regard, it is interesting to note that both the pronatalist Vatican and the antinatalist Chinese government interfered in the planning of the Women's Conference in Beijing, seeking to control the event to suit their own interests, China having taken extreme measures to control the women's gathering itself.[35]

As in the past, the collusion between religious and ethnic fundamentalism and neo-Malthusian scientific interests could again produce fascist movements and governments based on eugenic ideologies of gender, race and class hierarchy and new policies for genetic engineering. The media attention given in the US to recently published books such as *The Bell Curve* and *The Decline of Intelligence in America* help legitimize eugenicist thinking.[36] The growing alliance of the conservative eugenics and the anti-immigration movements with the more liberal population control and environmental organizations in the US, for example, is contributing to a shift of the entire political spectrum more and more to the right and 'free trade' economic fundamentalism.

Capitalist growth ideology

Although the contemporary global crisis is largely attributable to unbridled growth of technology and capital, capitalist growth doctrine remains sacrosanct. In fact, all the dominant ideologies, whether the Malthusian doomsday predictions of Paul Ehrlich and Lester Brown, the cornucopian free market scenarios of Julian Simon and Greg Easterbrook, the utopian futurism of Alvin Toffler and Newt Gingrich, the liberal reformism of Al Gore and Paul Hawken or the religious fundamentalist visions of Pat Robertson and the Pope – all of them futurist visions of privileged white males – seek solutions to the current crisis within the paradigm of market growth and technological expansion.[37]

The Agendas of the recent United Nations conferences – such as the 1992 Rio Earth Conference (UNCED); the World Conference on Human Rights in Vienna in 1993; the 1994 Cairo Population Conference (ICPD); the 1995 Copenhagen Social Development Conference; and the 1996 World Food Summit in Rome – have also sought solutions to the global crisis within the framework of economic growth and technological expansion. Despite its calls for ending the violence against women, gender justice and women's economic empowerment, the Platform of the 1995 Beijing

Women's Conference also fails to challenge the global economic and technological growth paradigm and its contradictory effects on women.[38]

The language of environmental sustainability, social equity, human rights and women's empowerment have been adopted by dominant world institutions such as the US Agency for International Development (USAID), the World Bank, the United Nations and even transnational corporations. The incorporation of such language does reflect the influence of progressive social forces on the status quo. Yet, at the same time, the adoption of progressive language by the liberals has marginalized radical analyses that focus on the contradictions of capitalism and the dialectics of gender, race and class.

In making alliances with corporate interests (especially funding establishments), liberal feminist, environmental and peace groups have tended to neglect demands for radical change and social justice made by grassroots environmental, human rights and women's groups. In the US, many liberal environmental and women's groups have jumped onto the population control bandwagon while ignoring such critical issues as overconsumption in the North, corporate weapons testing, the arms trade and toxic waste and weapons dumping in the communities of poor people of color both in the US and in the Third World.

As the right-wing conservative onslaught discredits liberalism more and more, radical analyses have disappeared from mainstream discourse. Even as the main ingredients of fascism – the growing power of the extreme right wing, the merging of business and the state, ideologies of belligerent nationalism, racism and patriarchy – come together on a global scale, radical analyses seem to be largely absent. However, radical change represents the yearnings of the masses of silenced and oppressed women and men in the world. Radical analysis – that which goes to the roots of problems – is needed more than ever. This book is written with the aim of addressing the urgent need for comprehensive and critical analyses of the global political economy at this time.

An Alternative Political-Economic Analysis

This analysis begins with the premise that growing global economic inequality, not population growth, is the main issue of our time. The economic gap between the rich and poor has been steadily increasing over the last three decades. The richest 20% of the world's population saw an increase of their income from 70.2% to 85.0% between 1960 and 1991. In the same period, the poorest 20% of the world's population saw their share of global income decline from 2.3% to 1.4%. Thus, for the world at large, the Gini coefficent, which is a statistical measure of inequality (measured on a scale where zero represents perfect equality and 1.00 total inequality), rose from 0.67 in 1960 to a staggering 0.87 in 1989 (Table 1).

Table 1 Widening global income disparity, 1960–1991 (% of global income)

Year	Poorest 20%	Richest 20%	Richest to poorest	Gini coefficient
1960	2.3	70.2	30 to 1	0.69
1970	2.3	73.9	32 to 1	0.71
1980	1.7	76.3	45 to 1	0.79
1989	1.4	82.7	59 to 1	0.87
1991	1.4	85.0	61 to 1	n/a

Sources: UNDP, *Human Development Report 1992*, New York: Oxford University Press, 1992, p. 36; UNDP, *Human Development Report 1996*, New York: Oxford University Press, 1996, p. 13.

Today, the nearly 80% of the global population who live in the South earn 15% of the global income, while the 20% or so of the world's population in the North earn 85% of the global income.[39] According to 1995 estimates, of the $39 trillion global economic output, about $16 trillion consisted of 'invisible', unpaid or underpaid work. A total of $11 trillion of that unrecognized and unrecompensed work is done by women. As the global crisis worsens, many of these regional, race, class and gender inequalities are predicted to widen in the years ahead.[40]

Increasing concentration of global economic and political power in the hands of transnational corporations (TNCs) underlies the problem of increasing global inequality. A few hundred TNCs, the vast majority of them based in the North and the US in particular, dominate nearly every sector of global economic production, exerting more power over people's lives than most national governments. TNCs continually augment their power through mergers and acquisitions, expanding their reach into the remotest corners of the world and wider areas of economic activity.

The value of aggregate sales of the top 200 private sector firms in the world increased from 17% of gross national product (in the non-socialist world) in 1960 to over 30% of global GNP in 1988. Between 1985 and 1995, the total sales revenue of the top 200 corporations nearly doubled from over $3 trillion to over $6 trillion (Table 2). As the corporations continue to develop more sophisticated technologies and financial networks, they will further wipe out local producers and small entrepreneurs, controlling even larger shares of global resources and wealth. They will be the "world empires of the 21st century", if they are not that already.[41] Multilateral agreements such as the General Agreement on Tariffs and Trade (GATT) and the newly established World Trade Organization (WTO) could also help widen and deepen the authoritarianism of the transnational corporations. Serious consideration of any of the major issues facing the world

Table 2 World's 200 largest corporations, 1985 and 1995*

Country	1985			1995		
	No.	Sales ($ bn)	Sales (%)	No.	Sales ($ bn)	Sales (%)
USA	104	1,615.9	52.8	77	2,030.7	33.5
Japan	38	704.1	23.0	51	2,142.2**	35.4
FRG	15	176.6	5.8	18	543.7	9.0
UK	11	158.1	5.1	12	351.6	5.8
Netherlands/UK	2	103.3	3.4	–	–	–
Canada	8	67.5	2.2	2	44.8	0.7
Korea, Rep. of	5	53.2	1.7	3	49.0	0.8
Israel	3	39.2	1.3	–	–	–
South Africa	3	29.8	1.0	–	–	–
Switzerland	2	24.6	0.8	4	91.4	1.5
Australia	–	–	–	2	27.2	0.4
Netherlands	2	24.2	0.8	4	162.1	2.7
Italy	2	21.6	0.7	6	173.3	2.9
Brazil	2	15.1	0.5	–	–	–
Sweden	1	10.0	0.3	3	55.8	0.9
Belgium	1	9.8	0.3	1	17.6	0.3
France	1	9.4	0.3	15	333.6	5.5
Spain	–	–	–	2	31.7	0.5
Total	200	3,062.4	100.0	200	6,054.7	99.9

* Private-sector firms.
** Increase of Japan's sales partly attributable to appreciation of the yen in relation to the US dollar.
Sources: Frederic Clairmont and John Cavanagh, "The Rise of the TNC", *Third World Resurgence*, No. 40, 1993, p. 19; Datastream International, New York, 1995.

today must take into account the global political-economic control of monopoly capitalism.

The critique of the Malthusian perspective and policies in this book must not necessarily be taken to mean that the population 'explosion' is not a serious issue calling for social structural transformations and humane interventions. Demographic dynamics bear upon practically every aspect of life: the magnitude and speed of global population increase or decrease will have a major impact upon political-economic as well as environmental evolution in the twenty-first century.

Obviously, people and the natural environment are closely intertwined. But this relationship is not a simple, static, mathematical one that can be extricated from socio-historical contexts. Rather, it is a complex and dynamic relationship shaped by the choice of technologies of production and reproduction, patterns of consumption, and so on. It is not sufficient, then, to look only at the overall population size and growth, as do the Malthusians; the differential relationships of regions (for example, the North vs the South), social classes, race and ethnic groups and the sexes to the social and natural environments must be taken into account. Indeed, human population is not a uniform and monolithic category.

This study demonstrates that population growth is not the root cause of the contemporary global crisis. It is not an inevitable long-term phenomenon, but an epiphenomenon. Each of the major social crises facing the world – environmental destruction; worsening poverty; violence and insecurity – as well as the population dilemma result largely from contradictions within the twin forces of modern technology and the social relations of capitalism. They represent a crisis of global capitalism.

Marxism is overwhelmingly discredited today. Yet an analysis of social class and the worldwide expansion of capitalism remains more important than ever for understanding widening global socio-economic inequality. Population growth and economic inequality are not separate issues; as this book demonstrates, socio-economic inequality underlies unequal population dynamics between classes and regions (Figure 2 and Table 1).

In attempting to develop an integrated critique of both capitalist social relations and technology of production, this study seeks also to transcend the tendency of some environmentalists to conceptualize industrialism as an entity separate from capitalism. Rather, this analysis is built upon the historical observation that from the very outset capital accumulation and technological expansion have reinforced each other; they constitute a single, global social–political process.[42] As such, the many separate struggles today to move the world towards greater social justice and environmental sustainability, must also be linked to a unified movement for global socio-political transformation.

Crisis of capitalism

While taking a historical overview of the entire span of the modern era, this book addresses the questions of women, population and the global crisis specifically in the context of global economic restructuring since the early 1970s. Corporate restructuring constitutes a set of political-economic responses to the crisis in capital accumulation, competition and workers' struggles implemented by the transnational corporations in conjunction with the Group of Seven (G7) countries (USA, Japan, Germany, France, Canada, Britain and Italy) and the two Bretton Woods institutions – the International Monetary Fund (IMF) and the World Bank – which were created to facilitate free movement of capital globally after World War II.

The main features of restructuring include increasing economic concentration, monopoly and mergers; speculation over productive investment; dismantling previous gains of labor through massive lay-offs and shift of production from the North into low-wage areas in the South; intensification of incorporation of regions and countries into the global market economy through agreements like GATT and NAFTA and policies like structural adjustment and management of the debt; wage restraints and squeezing of workers across the world; lifting of environmental regulations and restrictions on natural resource use.[43]

As this book discusses, the costs of corporate restructuring have been borne by the environment and the poor and overwhelmingly by women and children. The extension of Malthusian solutions at this time must be seen in terms of the crisis of accumulation and the search of capital for quick-fix solutions in place of fundamental changes in the world economy, including changes in the global financial system and capital–labor relations.

With the collapse of Communism, capitalism has become victorious the world over; no visible alternatives exist at this time. All countries and regions are forced to compete ever more fiercely in attracting investment, technology and trade simply to survive in the world economy. Everywhere, liberal capitalism which favors market regulation and state social welfare is giving way to neo-liberal, conservative capitalism which promotes privatization of state sectors and opposes state support for social programs. In the US, Democrats and Republicans are competing with each other to slash social programs and to tie whatever is left of Aid to Families with Dependent Children (AFDC) payments to limiting the number of children borne by poor women. Given pressures for deficit reduction, even European countries, such as Sweden, known for their generous social support systems in the past are now dismantling those programs.[44]

With increasing corporate control of the global economy and intensifying trade wars between the economically dominant countries, especially the US and Japan, the assaults against people and the environment will widen, deepening the global crisis. As more and more countries in the South, especially Asian countries such as China and India, fully embrace industrial capitalism and militarism, they are casting aside concerns of environmental and human health and well-being in order to compete globally. In the absence of efforts to alleviate worsening inequality and poverty, they are likely to undertake still more repressive policies, such as stringent population control efforts, aggravating the violence against women.

The 1992 riots in Los Angeles, labor strikes in France and South Korea, the rebellion in Chiapas, Mexico, illegal mafia activities in the former Soviet Union and various neo-fascist ethno-nationalist movements around the world all demonstrate that as the contradictions of the 'growth first' developmental model sharpen and social and ecological degradation worsen, resistance to those conditions will arise in many different forms. This resistance will face mounting military repression, thereby heightening the level of fear, hatred and violence and the generalization of Third World conditions throughout the world.

Subordination of women

Unlike classical Marxist theory and its Third World variants, the political analysis of this book does not focus merely on modes of production and class relations.[45] It views female subordination in relation to women's restricted access to and control of the means of both production and reproduction in the private and public spheres.[46] In other words, patriarchy is not seen simply as a phenomenon restricted to male dominance in the family; rather, it is viewed as an organizing principle of the entire global political-economic system.

Rejecting the narrow gender analysis adopted by neo-Malthusianism to justify its own objectives of population stabilization, this study develops a dialectical analysis wherein women's lives are placed in relation to race and class dynamics in the evolution of global capitalism, patriarchy as well as white supremacy. In demonstrating the divergent and often conflictual interests among women, this analysis seeks to move beyond the common depiction of women as a homogeneous category and liberal feminism as a sufficient response to women's subordination. As a statement issued by the Indigenous Women's Network at the 1995 Beijing Women's Conference points out, we need to move away from the narrow gender justice approach to a broader feminist approach which challenges existing politico-economic structures:

> 'Gender equity' is a narrow concept which focuses on sex-based discrimination and which has been manipulated by nation states to avoid issues of racial, environmental, civil, political and cultural inequities. It fails to acknowledge or challenge racism, economic disparity, and environmental injustices....[47]

Focusing on the feminization of poverty as the central issue linking women, population and global crisis, this book calls for women's economic empowerment as the key to redressing women's subordination as well as the population dilemma and the global crisis. Unlike liberal feminist analyses which seek women's economic empowerment within the status quo, this analysis questions if, in fact, women, humanity and the environment can be preserved as global capitalism moves in its present increasingly destructive direction. The book demonstrates that policies of current global restructuring such as the feminization of manufacturing, structural adjustment policies, the growth of the service sector, including sexual and reproductive services, and population control policies have not improved women's lives, but changed the form and manner of women's oppression.

Without infusion of ethical, social and environmental criteria into economic planning, the increasing polarization of wealth and poverty, the eco-crisis and attendant problems of violence and insecurity cannot be halted. The band-aid solutions put forward by dominant world institutions such as population stabilization could exacerbate gender, race and class repression, contributing to new forms of technological and bureaucratic authoritarianism in the volatile years ahead.

The intensification of gender-, race- and class-based violence and the violence against the environment make it clear that we need new, sustainable and democratic models of development. We need models that put the needs of human and planetary survival and reproduction before the needs of capital accumulation and technological expansion. We need a global society that honors the essential oneness of life and equality of all human beings. Such a social structural transformation rests on a fundamental psychological transformation in our understanding of life.

While class analysis is essential for understanding the global crisis, the solution to the crisis does not necessarily lie at the level of class analysis or Marxist fundamentalism. Marxist solutions of proletarian revolution and state authoritarianism have proved themselves to be élitist and violent. Many nationalist and even feminist solutions advocating narrowly based identity politics and separatist solutions also feed into the divisive ideologies and competitive ethic of the status quo. In place of either the Malthusian 'contraceptive revolution' or violent left- or right-wing revolutions, we need a non-violent psycho-social revolution built on a strong, universal moral and ethical framework.

This book draws upon feminist perspectives and struggles of the last two decades, especially important alternative statements issued in conjunction with recent international conferences such as the Alternative Treaty on Population, Environment and Development adopted at Planeta Fêmea, the women's tent at the Rio Earth Summit in 1992; the Call for a New Approach circulated by the Committee on Women, Population and the Environment prior to both the Earth Summit and the Cairo Population Conference in 1994 (Appendix 1); and the alternative NGO Beijing Declaration and the Beijing Declaration of Indigeneous Women issued at the Beijing Women's Conference in 1995.[48]

The voices of women of color represent the yearnings of the majority of the world's people. The world needs desperately to hear and listen to their visions for the next millennium.[49] This book hopes to add yet another voice to the growing calls and visions of women of color for peace, justice and global survival. The book argues that all forms of domination, whether the domination of human over non-human nature, or class, race and gender dominance, must be seen as inter-related forces operating within a single 'dominator paradigm'. The examination of the political-economic structures of the dominant world order is the main focus of this book. However, in the concluding chapter it also seeks to envision the shift from what feminist theorist Riane Eisler has termed the prevailing 'dominator' paradigm towards a future 'partnership' paradigm of human relations (Figure 1).[50] In so doing, the book takes inspiration from the words of nineteenth-century ex-slave and abolition activist Sojourner Truth, who said:

Now if the first woman God ever made was strong enough to turn the world upside down, these women together ought to be able to turn it back and get it rightside up again...[51]

Paradigm Shift

A new global ethic and spirituality that is based on universal rights and social justice must replace the self-serving interests of dominant ideologies and the military–industrial complex. It is only then that the problems of poverty, environmental destruction and violence can be resolved and we can move towards greater peace, justice and ecology in the world. But the ethical and spiritual foundation needed at this time cannot come from the patriarchal ideology and violent tactics of religious fundamentalism, neo-Malthusianism or capitalism.

We need to move beyond the western materialistic, reductionistic worldview that assumes that all phenomena are governed by inviolable scientific and quantitative laws. We need to accept and live by the more accurate and organic worldview which sees the inherent interconnectedness of all phenomena. We need to strengthen qualitative development – the moral basis and compassion in all our relationships – if, indeed, we are to resolve the crisis facing us at this time.

This book concludes that it is only with such a radical psycho-social transformation – a paradigm shift[52] – that we can seriously develop social strategies for greater economic equality, rational allocation of natural resources and socially and environmentally appropriate technologies of production and consumption. The global crisis challenges us to move away from cynicism, fear and apathy towards hope, courage and action. It is within such a revolutionary social and psychological framework, far different from the Malthusian framework and the current policies of economic restructuring, that reproductive rights, women's empowerment and human freedom can successfully be addressed.

Outline of the Book

Part I focuses on Malthusianism and its contemporary resurgence. Chapter 1 presents a summary of recent neo-Malthusian analyses of the global crises of environment, poverty, insecurity as well as women's subordination. Chapter 2 discusses the modern family planning strategies and their harmful effects on women's health and human rights.

Part II provides an alternative historical and sociological perspective on population and the global crisis. Chapter 3 examines population growth in the context of the evolution of industrial capitalism and western imperialism. Chapter 4 examines the relationship between high fertility and social class and gender relations with an emphasis on women's poverty. Chapter 5 addresses widening economic inequalities and deepening poverty in relation to such issues as the Third World debt, structural adjustment policies and military expenditures. Chapter 6 explores environmental destruction in relation to economic and technological expansion and unequal patterns of consumption. Chapter 7 examines global conflicts and insecurity in relation to global militarism and the forces of repression and resistance.

Part III focuses on the need for a paradigm shift, from domination to partnership. Chapter 8 considers strategies for developing democratic and sustainable solutions to the global crisis and women's subordination. The appendices provide three important organizational statements on population policy, the psychology of peace and wealth distribution in the United States as well as a resource list of organizations and networks engaged in non-violent social change activism.

Notes

1. UNDP, *Human Development Report 1995*, New York: Oxford University Press, 1995, p. 14.

2. John C. Ryan, "Conserving Biological Diversity", in *State of the World 1992*, Washington, DC: World Watch Institute, W.W. Norton and Co., 1992, p. 9.

3. Edward Goldsmith, *The Way: An Ecological World-View*, Boston: Shambala, 1993, p. xi.

4. "The Worst Global Unemployment Crisis", ILO, excerpted in *Hunger Notes*, Vol. 20, No. 4, Spring 1995, p. 15.

5. UNDP, *Human Development Report 1995*, p. 16; UNDP, *Human Development Report 1992*, New York: Oxford University Press, 1992, p. 14.

6. UNICEF, *The State of the World's Children 1993*, New York: Oxford University Press, 1993, p. 5.

7. UNDP, *Human Development Report 1991*, New York: Oxford University Press, 1991, p. 25; US Bureau of the Census, *Statistical Abstract of the United States: 1995*, 115th edition, Washington, DC, 1995, p. 480.

8. UNDP, *Human Development Report 1995*, p. 4; UNDP, *Human Development Report 1992*, p. 14.

9. Daniel U.B.P. Chelliah, "Violence and Militarism", in *Hunger 1995: Causes of Hunger, Fifth Annual Report on the State of World Hunger*, Bread for the World Institute, Silver Spring, MD, October 1994, p. 38.

10. Ibid., p. 39; UNDP, *Human Development Report 1994*, p. 48.

11. "The Clinton Administration Plan For Future Military Spending", prepared by Martin Calhoun, Senior Research Analyst, Center for Defense Information, Washington, DC, March 27, 1996.

12. UNICEF, *The State of the World's Children 1996*, New York: Oxford University Press, 1996, p. 13; Steven Hansch, "An Explosion of Complex Humanitarian Emergencies", *Hunger Notes*, Vol. 21, No. 3, Winter 1996, p. 4.

13. UNDP, *Human Development Report 1994*, p. 35; UNHCR, *UNHCR at a Glance*, UNHCR Public Information, December 30, 1995, UNHCR Liaison Office, New York, p. 1; UNFPA, *The State of the World Population 1993*, New York, 1993, p. 31.

14. UNICEF, *The State of the World's Children 1996*, p. 13.

15. Ibid., p. 29; Hansch, "An Explosion", p. 4.

16. Diane Elson, "From Survival Strategies to Transformation Strategies: Women's Needs and Structural Adjustment", in Lourdes Beneria and Shelley Feldman, eds, *Unequal Burden: Economic Crises, Persistent Poverty and Women's Work*, Boulder, CO: Westview Press, 1992, p. 26; "Introduction", in R.J. Johnston and P.J. Taylor, eds., *A World in Crisis; Geographical Perspectives*, Oxford: Basil Blackwell, 1986, p. 2.

17. Thomas Robert Malthus, *An Essay on the Principle of Population*, ed. Philip Appleman, New York: W.W. Norton, 1976.

18. UNFPA, *The State of the World Population 1995*, p. 67; Steven A. Holmes, "Census Plan for 2000 Is Challenged on 2 Fronts", *The New York Times*, June 6, 1995, p. A21. UN estimates released in November 1996 suggested that world population is stabilizing much faster than earlier predicted. During 1990–95 the worldwide fertility growth rate was 1.48% a year, which is much lower than the 1.57% estimated earlier. Barbara Crossette, "World is Less Crowded than Expected, the U.N. Reports", *The New York Times*, November 17, 1996, p. 3.

19. George Kennan, Head, Planning Staff, US Department of State, cited in *Unconventional Warfare and the Theory of Competitive Reproduction: U.S. Intervention and Covert Action in the Developing World*, Working Paper No. 2, Information Project for Africa, Inc., Washington, DC, 1991, p. 4.

20. Betsy Hartmann, *Reproductive Rights and Wrongs: The Global Politics of Population Control*, Boston: South End Press, 1995, p. 104.

21. David L. Marcus, "Women's Issues High on U.S. Agenda", *The Boston Globe*, December 10, 1996, pp. A1, 18; Charlotte Bunch and Roxanna Carrillo, "Gender Violence: A Development and Human Rights Issue", Center for Women's Global Leadership, Rutgers University, New Brunswick, NJ, 1991, pp. 1–41.

22. United Nations Programme of Action, Report of the International Conference on Population and Development (ICPD), Cairo, September 5–13, 1994, paras 1:4, 3 and 6:1, pp. 25, 35; IPPF, *Open File*, London, November 1994, p. 1; Lori S. Ashford, "New Perspectives on Population: Lessons from Cairo", *Population Bulletin*, Vol. 50, No. 1, March 1995, p. 2; Adrienne Germaine and Rachel Kyte, *The Cairo Consensus: The Right Agenda for the Right Time*, New York: International Women's Health Coalition, 1995.

23. *Women's Voices '94: Women's Declaration on Population Policies*, New York: International Women's Health Coalition, 1994; "A Critical Appraisal of the Women's Declaration of Population Policies", *WGNRR Newsletter* 42, January–March 1993, p. 28; Vandana Shiva and Mira Shiva, "Was Cairo a Step Forward for Third World Women?", *Third World Resurgence*, No. 50, 1994, pp. 13–15.

24. Shiva and Shiva, "Was Cairo a Step Forward", p. 14.

25. Jonathan Lieberson, "Too Many People?", *New York Review of Books*, June 26, 1986, p. 36; Julian Simon, *The Ultimate Resource*, Princeton: Princeton University Press, 1981.

26. Jodi L. Jacobson, "The Global Politics of Abortion", World Watch Paper, No. 97, July 1990, p. 38; Jodi L. Jacobson, "Women's Reproductive Health: The Silent Emergency", *World Watch Paper*, No. 102, June 1991, p. 53; see also Rosalind Pollack Petchesky, *Abortion and Woman's Choice: The State, Sexuality and Reproductive Freedom*, New York: Longman, 1984, Chap. 7.

27. "Reinforcing Reproductive Rights", A Special Report of International Conference, May 5–8, Madras, India, *WGNRR Newsletter*, No. 43, April–June 1993.

28. *WGNRR Newsletter*, No. 47, July–September, 1994, p. 9.

29. Beijing Declaration and Platform for Action, UN Fourth World Conference on Women, Beijing, China, September 4–15, 1995, paras 96–98.

30. Barbara Crossette, "Vatican Holds Up Abortion Debate at Talks in Cairo", *The New York Times*, September 8, 1994, p. A1; Henry Miller, "Population Disagreement", Letter to Editor, *The New York Times*, June 29, 1994, p. B6; Interview with Frances Kissling, *Terra Viva*, IPS-ICPD Issue, September 6, 1994, p. 16.

31. Katha Pollitt, "A New Assault on Feminism", *The Nation*, March 26, 1990, pp.

409–418; "Restrictions on Funding for Abortion Services", Center for Reproductive Law and Policy, New York, n.d.; Barbara Crossette, "U.S. Aid Cutbacks Endangering Population Programs, UN Agencies Say", *The New York Times*, February 16, 1996, p. A14; Colum Lynch, "UN Population Efforts Under Question", *The Boston Sunday Globe*, June 16, 1996, p. 6.

32. Stephanie Kaza, "Wise Use vs. The Green Menace", *Turning Wheel*, Publication of Buddhist Peace Fellowship, San Francisco, Fall 1995, p. 9.

33. Shiva and Shiva, "Was Cairo a Step Forward", passim; Sara Diamond, "How To Win a Kingdom", *The New York Times*, September 16, 1995, p. 15; see also, Sara Diamond, *Roads to Dominion: Right-Wing Movements and Political Power in the United States*, New York: Guilford Press, 1995.

34. Hartmann, *Reproductive Rights and Wrongs*, p. 148.

35. "The Vatican and China Seek to Bar Opponents", *The New York Times*, March 17, 1995, p. A6.

36. Richard Herrnstein and Charles Murray, *The Bell Curve: Intelligence and Class Structure in American Life*, New York: Free Press, 1994; Seymour Itzkoff, *The Decline in Intelligence in America: A Strategy for National Renewal*, Westport, CT: Praeger, 1994.

37. Paul and Anne Ehrlich, *The Population Bomb*, New York: Ballantine Books, 1968; Lester Brown, *Who Will Feed China? Wake-up Call for a Small Planet*, New York: W.W. Norton and Co., 1995; Simon, *The Ultimate Resource*; Gregg Easterbrook, *A Moment on the Earth: The Coming Age of Environmental Optimism*, New York: Viking, 1995; Alvin Toffler, *The Third Wave*, New York: Morrow, 1980; Newt Gingrich, *To Renew America*, New York: HarperCollins, 1993; Al Gore, *The Earth in the Balance: Ecology and the Human Spirit*, Boston: Houghton Mifflin and Co., 1992; Paul Hawken, *The Ecology of Commerce: A Declaration of Sustainability*, New York: HarperCollins, 1993; Pat Robertson, *The Collected Works of Pat Robertson: The New Millennium, The New World Order, The Secret Kingdom*, New York: Inspirational Press, 1994; His Holiness John Paul II, *Crossing the Threshold of Hope*, New York: Alfred A. Knopf, 1994.

38. United Nations, Earth Conference, "Agenda 21: Programme of Action from Rio", United Nations Department of Public Information, 3–4 June 1992; United Nations Vienna Declaration and Programme of Action, World Conference on Human Rights, Vienna, June 14–25, 1993; ICPD, Programme of Action; United Nations World Summit for Social Development, Copenhagen, March 6–12, 1995; FAO, Rome Declaration on Food, Security and World Food Summit Plan of Action, Rome, 13–17 November 1996; Beijing Platform.

39. UNDP, *Human Development Report 1991*, p. 23; UNDP, *Human Development Report 1996*, p. 13.

40. UNDP, *Human Development Report 1995*, p. 97; see also Beijing Platform, para A.49.

41. Frederic Clairmont and John Cavanagh, "The Rise of the TNC", *Third World Resurgence*, No. 40, 1993, p. 19; Richard Barnet and John Cavanagh, "The World the Transnationals Have Built", *Third World Resurgence*, No. 40, 1993, p. 21; Canadian University Student Organization (CUSO), Education Department, *Here to Stay: Part Two A Resource Handbook Linking Sustainable Development and Debt*, Ottawa, November 1990, p. 5.

42. Joe Weston, *Red and Green: A New Politics of the Environment*, London: Pluto Press, 1986; Keith Buchanan, "Delineation of the Third World", in Ingolf Vogeler and Anthony R. de Souza, eds, *Dialectics of Third World Development*, Montclair, NJ: Allanheld, Osmun and Co., 1980, pp. 28–51; see also Eric R. Wolf, *Europe and the People Without History*, Berkeley: University of California Press, 1982; Immanuel Wallerstein, "The Rise and Future Demise of the World Capitalist System: Concepts for Comparative Analysis", *Comparative Studies in Society and History*, Vol. 16, 1974.

43. Joyce Kolko, *Restructuring the World Economy*, New York: Pantheon Books, 1988; Elson, "From Survival Strategies to Transformation", passim.

44. Richard W. Stevenson, "A Deficit in Sweden's Welfare State", *The New York Times*, February 2, 1995, pp. A1, 10.

45. Karl Marx, *Capital*, New York: Modern Library, 1906, p. 693; Mahmood

Mamdani, *The Myth of Population Control: Family, Caste, and Class in an Indian Village,* New York: Monthly Review Press, 1972; Luis A. Serron, *Scarcity, Exploitation and Poverty: Malthus and Marx in Mexico,* Norman: University of Oklahoma Press, 1980; David Harvey, "A Marxian Analysis of the Population-Resource Problem", in Vogeler and de Souza, eds, *Dialectics of Third World Development,* pp. 202–226.

46. Deborah Fahey Bryceson and Ulla Vurovela, "Outside the Domestic Labor Debate: Towards a Theory of Human Reproduction", *Review of Radical Political Economics,* Vol. 16, Nos 2–3, 1984, pp. 137–66; Mary O'Brien, *The Politics of Reproduction,* Boston: Routledge and Kegan Paul, 1981, pp. 137–166.

47. "The NGO Declaration of Indigenous Women", *Third World Resurgence,* Nos 61–62, double issue, 1995, pp. 37–43.

48. Ibid.; Alternative Treaty on Population, Environment and Development, Planeta Fêmea, United Nations Conference on the Environment and Development, Rio de Janeiro, Brazil, June 1992.

49. Vandana Shiva, *Staying Alive: Women, Ecology and Development,* London; Zed Books, 1988; Rigoberta Menchú, *I, Rigoberta Menchú: An Indian Woman in Guatemala,* London: Verso, 1984; Audre Lorde, *From a Land Where Other People Live,* Detroit: Broadside Press, 1973; Aung San Suu Kyi, *Freedom from Fear and Other Writings,* London: Penguin Books, 1991; *Woman of Power,* Issue on "Women of Color: A Celebration of Power", No. 4, Fall 1986; *Woman of Power,* Issue on "Women of Color: A Celebration of Spirit", No. 21, Fall 1991.

50. Riane Eisler, *The Chalice and the Blade: Our History, Our Future,* San Francisco: Harper and Row, 1988; Asoka Bandarage, "In Search of a New World Order", *Women's Studies International Forum,* Vol. 14, No. 4, 1991.

51. Soujourner Truth, "Women", in Daniela Gioseffi, ed., *Women on War: Essential Voices for the Nuclear Age,* New York: Simon and Schuster, 1988, p. 358.

52. Thomas S. Kuhn, *The Structure of Scientific Revolutions,* Chicago: University of Chicago Press, 1970.

PART I

Malthusianism: Theory and Practice

Malthusian Analysis of Global Crisis

Malthusian Doctrine

According to the principle of population put forward by English clergyman turned economist Thomas Malthus in his 1798 *Essay on the Principle of Population*, population increases geometrically (1, 2, 4, 8, 16, etc.); but, given the scarcity of natural resources, the food supply increases only arithmetically (1, 2, 3, 4, 5, 6, etc.) by a constant amount. The resulting 'overpopulation', Malthus argued, leads inevitably to natural resource depletion, poverty and social disorder and he called for stringent methods of population control to avert these problems.[1]

Malthus claimed that the disparity between the rates of increase in population and food supply and the inevitable food shortages it creates itself acts as the ultimate 'positive check' on overpopulation. While Malthus was against deliberate birth control, in the rewritten and enlarged second edition of his *Essay* he advocated 'preventive checks' such as prolonged celibacy and late marriage.[2]

Malthus's *Essay*, especially its first edition, was wrong on many basic estimates of population size and growth rates besides its overall theses. Yet it became immediately popular among the ruling classes, who were terrified by the French Revolution and were looking for justifications of the existing social order. Malthus's writing was directed specifically against the rising popularity of utopian socialist and anarchist thinking which opposed unequal ownership of property and tyrannical government and called for social justice and a rejection of the state.[3]

Malthus put forward his arguments during the so-called 'mortality revolution' when death rates were falling in Europe due to improvements commonly attributed to progress in medicine and hygiene. He reacted against the growing ranks of the unemployed and the disaffected, especially those displaced by the enclosures of the common lands, but who were unabsorbed by the urban factories.

Like his predecessor, the conservative English philosopher Thomas Hobbes (1588–1679), Malthus held a pessimistic attitude towards human nature; he believed in the primacy of individual self-interest and an in-evitable competition and struggle for existence. Malthus's arguments also rested on a deep-seated acceptance of the division of society into haves and have-nots, that is, a propertied class which has a moral right to its inher-itance and the propertyless whose duty it is to serve the wealthy as expend-able laborers. Indeed, Malthus never questioned whether the right to live should rest on the concept of property.[4]

These beliefs led Malthus to argue that the institution of private property and the fear of losing social position contributed to 'prudence' in procrea-tion among the wealthy, while the lack of property militated against such prudence by the poor. However, Malthus did not seek to alleviate poverty. He argued that the poor were a drain on society and that public assistance and health provisions merely encourage indolence and fertility. Malthus vehemently opposed the Poor Laws, the system of welfare provided by the state in England during his time. Warning the richer classes that too much sympathy for the poor would lead to disaster for all, he argued that nature must be allowed to take its toll and let the poor die.[5]

His diatribes against the poor notwithstanding, Malthus was not entirely oblivious to the effects of the industrial capitalist economy and wasteful consumption patterns of the rich on natural resource depletion and the poverty of the masses. He also had some awareness of the possibilities for decreasing scarcity through technological innovation.[6] Yet Malthus did not include social structural factors such as affluence and technology in formu-lating his universal law of population. His class interests prevented him from doing so. While Malthus went on to win academic prestige, his publication contributed to the repression of revolutionary ideas. Critical thinkers like William Godwin and Condorcet who put forward optimistic views of human nature and a vision of social justice and democracy had to bear the brunt of that political and intellectual repression.[7] Malthusian ideology, mean-while, has been invoked throughout the modern industrial capitalist age, especially during economic downturns and social crises.

Evolution of Malthusianism

As quantitative reasoning and statistics became the *lingua franca* during the course of industrial capitalist expansion, the term 'population' lost its active usage and relationship to real people. As feminist historian of science Barbara Duden has noted, over time the concept 'population' came to represent an inanimate 'totality of objects' instead of real live human beings.[8] Furthermore, as the field of demography and the study of func-tions and factors such as census, distribution, survey, and so on, expanded, people came to be viewed as a dependent variable to be managed and controlled by a class of scientific and bureaucratic professionals, many of whom became closely identified with Social Darwinism and its progenitor,

Malthusianism. Malthusianism provided the 'matrix' of Charles Darwin's natural selection theory – survival of the fittest – expounded in *The Origin of Species* in 1859, and subsequent Social Darwinist theories. In language highly reminiscent of Malthus, Social Darwinists like Herbert Spencer admonished the 'superior' classes – the rich – against protecting the biologically 'weaker' classes – the poor.[9]

The confluence of these ideological and political developments contributed to the emergence of eugenics as a dominant political movement in Europe and the US by the turn of the twentieth century. Eugenics is the belief in the betterment of the human genetic stock through selective breeding, that is, encouraging childbearing by the genetically 'fit' (positive eugenics) and preventing procreation by the 'unfit' (negative eugenics).[10] While eugenic population control policies will be explored in the next chapter, in this chapter we present a summary of leading neo-Malthusian analyses of the current global crisis.

Most neo-Malthusian formulations continue to subscribe to a simple people vs resources perspective, but some have attempted to develop a broader social analysis which identifies the complex and mutually reinforcing interaction of population, poverty, environment and other factors.[11] Over the course of its historical evolution, Malthusianism has been compelled to engage in a dialectical discourse not only with socialism but also with feminism, Third World nationalism and other social movements committed to social justice. As noted in the Introduction, the influence of feminism on Malthusianism is particularly evident in the repudiation of the language of population control and the current emphasis on reproductive rights and women's empowerment. Many feminist, Third World and environmental activists working within mainstream population organizations continue to work towards broadening the Malthusian analysis and humanizing its policy prescriptions.

The neo-Malthusian gender analysis is an improvement over other Malthusian formulations which ignore the specific concerns and needs of women. When compared with earlier neo-Malthusian formulations and with growing right-wing fundamentalist opposition to women's reproductive autonomy, the new gender approach seems to be compatible with feminist demands for reproductive choice and individual freedom. Many international women's rights activists and organizations such as the Women's Environment and Development Organization (WEDO), the International Women's Health Coalition (IWHC) and the Centre for Development and Population Activities (CEDPA) fought long and hard to include the broader reproductive health and women's concerns into the ICPD agenda.[12] Many of them have continued to take an active role in monitoring the enforcement of the ICPD Programme of Action and in infusing ICPD language into subsequent UN debates and ducuments such as the 1996 Rome Declaration on World Food Security.

Despite some of the advances represented by these feminist efforts, the neo-Malthusian analysis remains narrow and doctrinaire. It cannot provide a historical, sociological explanation for the demographic 'explosion' or fundamental solutions to the global crisis. Like Malthus, his contemporary followers are unwilling to challenge existing social class relations and global capitalist development. As such, despite the new reproductive rights language, neo-Malthusian analysis and solutions remain confined within the population control paradigm.

Given the deep entrenchment of Malthusian thinking in academic and policy planning circles and the extensive publicity given to fears of 'overpopulation' in every imaginable medium of communication, most educated people in the world tend to be predisposed toward a Malthusian view of the world. Indeed, it can be argued that Malthusianism has shaped modern consciousness, determining the moral spirit of our age. Many people pursuing the neo-Malthusian population control agenda are genuinely concerned about global dilemmas and the alleviation of human suffering. But many of them have not been challenged to look at the biases of their own thinking and the dangers of neo-Malthusian solutions for the well-being of the majority of the world's people.

The remaining sections of this chapter provide brief overviews of contemporary neo-Malthusian thinking on the problems of environmental destruction, poverty, the global security crisis as well as women's subordination. The objective here is to demonstrate that in spite of recent attempts to broaden and soften the Malthusian agenda, population control thinking continues to dominate global policy making.

While a thorough critique of neo-Malthusian analyses is not undertaken here, the limitations of the Malthusian logic will be made more apparent in later chapters which present an alternative political-economic analysis of women, population and the global crisis.

Population and the Environment

As noted earlier, the starting point of Malthusian analysis is the fixed, natural limit upon human action stemming from the scarcity of natural resources and the exponential nature of population growth. Accordingly, Malthusian analysts fear that unless controlled quickly, the global population explosion will deplete the earth's natural resources, steadily pushing the earth towards its maximum 'carrying capacity'.[13]

In the field of biology, 'carrying capacity' generally refers to the maximum number of a given species that a limited habitat can support indefinitely. Malthusians have applied this concept to human population, arguing that when the maximum sustainable population limit is surpassed, the planetary resource base declines, leading to ultimate population decline.

According to biologists Paul and Anne Ehrlich, "if the long term carrying capacity of an area is clearly being degraded by its current human occupants, that area is overpopulated".[14]

Applying the carrying capacity concept on a global scale, the influential report *Limits to Growth*, published by the Club of Rome in 1972, argued that rapid population growth will 'overshoot' the limit of carrying capacity, exhausting non-renewable natural resources. It further claimed that the pace of technological change would be insufficient to overcome diminishing returns from limited supplies of essential resources and that falling standards of living and increasing levels of pollution would lead to a population collapse within 100 years.[15]

Limits to Growth did admit that its world simulation models did not calculate inequalities in resources, capital and food distribution across national boundaries, world trade balances, migration patterns and other global political processes.[16] However, an updated version in 1992, *Beyond the Limits*, reproducing the computer simulation models used in *Limits to Growth*, reiterates the earlier conclusions. It warns that if global population and industrial production continue to grow without major policy changes, natural resource constraints will be exacerbated, resulting in increased pollution, falling food and health services, decreasing life expectancy and increased death rates.[17]

Seeing every human being born as a 'draft on all aspects of the environment', neo-Malthusian analysts attribute the major environmental problems – deforestation, desertification, topsoil loss, depletion of the ozone layer, accumulation of greenhouse gases, loss of biodiversity, acid rain and pollution – to increased population pressures.[18] According to some estimates, if current trends in resource use and population growth continue, then, between 1990 and 2010, the global per capita irrigated land will drop by 12%; cropland by 21%; rangeland and pasture by 22%; forests by 30%; and the fish catch by 10%.[19] Apparently, between 1990 and 2025, the number of persons dependent on one cubic meter of water will increase from 1,650 to 3,290 in North Africa, from 140 to 360 in Sub-Saharan Africa and from 300 to 530 persons in Southern Asia.[20]

Population, poverty and the environment

Although resource depletion and environmental destruction are much more attributable to the production and consumption patterns of the rich than the poor, it is the poor who receive much of the blame. A 1991 UNFPA publication entitled "Population, Resources and the Environment: the Critical Challenge" claims categorically that in the 'developing' countries, the 'bottom billion' people "impose greater environmental injury than the other three billion of their fellow citizens put together".[21]

A Round Table of 35 international experts convened by the International

Academy of the Environment in Geneva in 1993 also argued that since the poor have higher birth rates, they are often "forced by immediate need into short-sighted, environmentally unsustainable management of resources".[22] Slash and burn agriculture, overcropping, over-irrigation in rural areas and overcrowding in urban areas are some of the environmentally harmful practices commonly attributed to population pressure and poverty. Small farmers are called 'predatory' and the increasing numbers of shifting cultivators in the Third World are identified as the greatest threat to tropical forests.[23]

Despite the lack of reliable evidence and inconsistencies in some of its own figures, the 1990 UNFPA *State of the World Population* report blames overpopulation for global deforestation, claiming that population growth is far more responsible for deforestation than commercial logging or ranching. It says that much of cleared forest in 'developing' countries becomes cropland for growing populations and that population growth may account for 85% of the loss of forest cover.[24] Deforestation resulting from population pressure is also identified as a major culprit in soil erosion and global warming and as the most important cause in the loss of wildlife species.[25] The World Bank has also attributed alarming rates of soil erosion and land degradation in countries such as Bangladesh and the Philippines to population pressure and the migration of the poor in search of land; cultivation of upland slopes; loss of topsoil to typhoons; the silting of rivers downstream; and related factors.[26]

Population, affluence and technology

Malthusian environmentalists argue that as population pressure increases the need for agricultural land and fuelwood, it also contributes to the build-up of greenhouse gases such as CO_2 and methane which threaten the stratospheric ozone layer and contribute to global warming. It is said that between 1950 and 1985, population growth was responsible for two-thirds of the increase in CO_2 emissions, "holding everything else constant".[27]

In reality, it is not possible to isolate the effects of population increase from the social environment within which people live their lives. Neo-Malthusian analysts now admit that industrialized countries with their affluent lifestyles are more responsible for the build-up of greenhouse gases and CFCs (chlorofluorocarbons) than the poor in 'overpopulated' countries. But they hasten to add that if current trends in population growth and energy use continue, then by 2020 developing countries will be emitting half of all CO_2 emissions annually.[28]

Being committed to preserving the status quo, neo-Malthusian environmentalists are not advocating any serious strategies to limit industrial growth and overconsumption. This is apparent in some recent attempts to broaden the Malthusian environmental analysis such as the I = PAT equation put forward by Paul Ehrlich. This equation identifies affluence and technology as variables impacting upon the environment in addition to population:

Environmental Impact (I) = P (population size) × A (affluence) × T (technology)

However, the I = PAT equation does not help identify which particular institutions and social groups are most responsible for overconsumption and use of environmentally damaging technologies. As feminist environmentalist Patricia Hynes has demonstrated, I = PAT is a "power-blind" and "agent-less" equation.[29]

The same limitations exist in the so-called 'PPE Spiral' presented in UNICEF's *The State of the World's Children 1994*. Moving beyond the exclusive focus on population growth, this diagram schematizes the synergism between poverty, population growth and environmental stress (PPE) which reinforces global crises. Despite the sophistication of this presentation, it provides no room for understanding the historical, social evolution of these crises or for redressing global power imbalances that lie beneath them. The emphasis still remains on family planning.[30]

Today, Malthusian environmentalists are compelled to recognize the effects of overconsumption and harmful technologies on the environment. Yet, when it comes to providing solutions, they invariably advocate population stabilization over consumption control or the development of environmentally appropriate technologies. In *The Population Explosion*, Paul and Anne Ehrlich argue that "because of time lags involved, first priority must be given to achieving *population control*" (emphasis in original).[31]

Even in their later work, *The Stork and the Plow*, which seeks to address the issue of global inequity, the Ehrlichs and co-author Gretchen Daly fail to explore specific strategies to achieve equity, warning instead that "leveling down" of inequities would "be completely unacceptable to the wealthier segments, which would feel robbed". Yet as far as population control is concerned, they advocate timetables for reaching replacement-level fertility.[32]

A joint statement issued by the US National Academy of Sciences and the Royal Society of London in 1992, warning the world of the dangers of uncontrolled population growth, also recognizes that conservation of resources and energy in the developed world are necessary for environmental protection. However, identifying population growth as "the fundamental environmental issue" and population control as the "most promising field of action", the joint statement goes on to claim that "unlike many other steps that could be taken to reduce the rate of environmental changes, reductions in rates of population growth can be accomplished through voluntary measures".[33]

Not only do such statements place the responsibility of environmental sustainability on the poor, but they also dismiss coercion in family planning programs and the contradictions of the global economy which lie at the root of environmental and population dilemmas. As the global crisis worsens, prominent international agencies, scientific bodies, environmental and population control lobbies and world leaders have all been issuing increasingly alarmist declarations equating environmental sustainability largely with population stabilization.

Calls for population control

More than 70 leading population and environment organizations in the US signed a "Priority Statement on Population" in 1991 claiming that "there is no issue of greater concern to the world's future than the rapid rise in human population" and that "the United States and all nations of the world must make issues of human population growth a leading priority in this decade".[34]

A 'Population Summit' represented by 58 national scientific academies in New Delhi in October 1993 reinforced scientists' commitment to population stabilization and called for "prodigious planning efforts" to achieve "zero population growth within the lifetime of our children". After many years of being lobbied by population control advocates, the International Union for the Conservation of Nature and Natural Resources (IUCNNR) has also accepted a strong position on population control.[35]

Prominent leaders in the North, including Britain's Prince of Wales, former Norwegian Prime Minister Gro Harlem Brundtland and US President Bill Clinton have declared strong commitment to population stabilization. In his best-selling book, *Earth in the Balance*, US Vice President Al Gore also identified population stabilization as the "first strategic goal" to save the global environment.[36]

The major environmental organizations in the US, such as the Sierra Club, the Audobun Society and the National Wildlife Federation, have embraced the population control agenda in a big way. The Sierra Club, for example, is circulating a tree diagram identifying overpopulation as the "root of the problem" and population stabilization as the "real solution" to all the major environmental and social problems. Other big environmental lobbies in the US are also engaged in campaigns to train 'population activist leaders', mobilize middle-class (that is, mostly white) constituencies, influence the media and lobby Congress for funding for population control. The National Wildlife Federation is helping develop a constituency for global population stabilization in Japan as well.[37]

While they have forged a strong alliance with population control groups, liberal environmental groups in the United States have not challenged transnational corporate expansion or overconsumption in any significant manner. Despite recognition of increasing environmental damage caused by unbridled economic growth, many of these organizations ended up supporting NAFTA and GATT. Many liberal feminist activists and organizations speaking on the environment, including prominent Christian feminists in the North, seem also to have accepted the population control paradigm without much attention to gender, race and class contradictions within the world political economy.[38]

Despite their public criticisms of overconsumption of resources by the North, Third World governments and elites are also pursuing the same model of capitalist technological growth as the North. Working in collusion with their Northern counterparts, they, too, are vigorously promoting fertility control as a substitute for redistribution of wealth and resources and the adoption of appropriate technologies of production and patterns of consumption. Although the United Nations Conference for Environment and Development in 1992 did not assert a strong position on population control due to opposition by some delegations (especially the Vatican), 90% of the 'developing' countries at the Rio Earth Summit identified rapid population growth "as a major obstacle to achieving sustainable development".[39] Today, ruling classes in the North and the South, including many environmentalists in the North, are advocating increasingly drastic measures of population control.

'The disaster ethic'

In the late 1970s, US demographers Bernard Berelson and Stanley Lieberson called for a 'stepladder approach' to population ethics, arguing that population control programs should begin with less severe methods and ascend to harsher methods as the situations warrant them. Berelson proposed the addition of temporary sterilants to drinking water or the food supply, marketing of licenses to have children, temporary sterilization of all girls with time-capsule contraceptives, compulsory sterilization of men who have three or more living children, and mandatory induced abortions for all 'illegitimate pregnancies' as final solutions to the population problem, if voluntary methods were to fail![40]

At the time Berelson and Liberson put forward their 'stepladder approach' they hoped that a 'disaster ethic' requiring measures such as randomizing medical care might not arise since the 'disease' of overpopulation would be cured in the years ahead.[41] Certainly, not all neo-Malthusians support triage and other harsh and involuntary population control policies. But, as the global crisis intensifies, calls for triage and stringent fertility and immigration control policies are, again, increasing.

Triage

Biologist Garret Hardin is well known for popularizing the Malthusian 'lifeboat ethic' which claims that all the people on the planet cannot be saved and that the drowning poor and the weak should be allowed to die for the sake of the survival of the planet and the survival of the fittest. To Hardin, the fittest explicitly means "us Americans".[42] Hardin is now closely affiliated with Carrying Capacity Network (CCN) and Population–Environment Balance, two hard-line population control groups, and the Federation for American Immigration Reform (FAIR), a hard-line anti-immigration lobby in the US. In *Living Within Limits*, a book published in 1993, Hardin advocates such measures as reduction of food and development aid to poor countries and tighter immigration laws in the North in order to force the South to bring down population growth rates.[43]

Jonathan Stone, Professor of Anatomy at the University of Sydney in Australia, and Maurice King, Professor of Public Health at Leeds University in Britain, have also invoked the disaster ethic. Stone has argued that the contemporary "biological reality" of people destroying the environment make it necessary to see humans as "a plague" on earth.[44] Maurice King has taken this view still further, calling for removal of oral rehydration and other human life-sustaining methods from public health programs in the Third World as a means to control population growth and ensure environmental sustainability. In an article published in the authoritative journal *The Lancet* in September 1990, King sounds very much like his predecessor, Malthus, when he writes:

> The demographic and ecological implications of public health measures must be understood at all levels.... If these are desustaining (sustainability reducing), complementary ecologically sustaining measures, especially family planning and ecological support, must be introduced with them. If no adequately sustaining complementary measures are possible, such desustaining measures as oral dehydration should not be introduced on a public health scale, since they increase the man-years of human misery, ultimately from starvation.... Mother Theresa has reminded us that the world's poorest need our love and compassion; tragically, such programmes may not necessarily be part of that love.[45]

Associating his callous suggestions with morality and compassion and calling it "HSE 2100 – Health in a sustainable ecosystem for the year 2100" – King exhorts the WHO to sacrifice the health of some people for the sake of planetary health.[46] The biocentric perspective of King and other upper-class, white environmentalists fails to recognize that poor people are also an aspect of the planet and of nature. Moreover, this perspective fails to see that high mortality, especially high infant mortality, promotes high fertility. As we shall discuss in Chapter 4, one of the most powerful factors in voluntary fertility reduction for couples is the assurance of their children's physical survival.

The doctrine of triage refers to the process of sorting victims to determine medical priority in order to increase the number of survivors. Medical triage involves abandoning those who are both weak and mortally wounded in emergency situations such as battlefields to die. This doctrine has been invoked in discussions of food and famine in recent decades. Some policy makers in the US have advocated a development assistance policy which would ration aid only to countries that are willing and able to reduce population growth and overcome food scarcity with US help.[47]

The US government, under the Republican right-wing onslaught, has actually been cutting development assistance to poor countries in recent years. In 1995, it cut its yearly pledge of food aid nearly in half, from 4.47 million tonnes to 2.5 million tonnes.[48] Harsh immigration policies in the North such as the return of Haitian refugees coming to the US back to the high seas, and the relative neglect of HIV/AIDS and extensive deaths occurring in war zones in the Third World like Zaire and Rwanda also have Malthusian implications.

In the US, even individuals and groups critical of the mainstream corporate, managerial approach to the environment are nevertheless in agreement on the urgency for population stabilization. For example, the radical environmental group Earth First! is known for its Malthusian statement that famines in Africa and the AIDS epidemic are nature's mechanisms for dealing with the population explosion.[49] Echoing the sentiments of many western environmentalists, ecologist Kirkpatrick Sale is reported to have said that "if we don't try to save the trees before we can save all the children, we'll never save either".[50] Deep ecologist Bill Deval echoes this sentiment when he states that the flourishing of human and non-human life on earth requires a decrease in the human population.[51] Such thinking makes it easier for many environmentalists in the North to take up issues of animal rights over those of human rights and social justice.

If the environmental movement and global policy making move increasingly in a Malthusian direction, we are likely to see more and more racist triage policies that sacrifice the human rights of poor people of color. However, unlike Malthus's original doctrine, the main emphasis of neo-Malthusianism is not on mortality increase but fertility decrease. Thus, drastic fertility reduction measures are hastily being promoted as the key to global environmental sustainability.

Fertility control

Many population control advocates who attempt to cultivate a liberal, non-coercive approach to fertility control seem nevertheless to subscribe to the 'disaster ethic'. For example, Paul and Anne Ehrlich write in the *Population Explosion*, "One must always keep in mind that the price of personal freedom in making childbearing decisions may be the destruction of the world in which your children or grandchildren live".[52] In a laudable move, the Ehrlichs have recently left CCN's board of advisors. However, a number of other well-known US environmentalists like Herman E. Daly, Robert Constanza and Hunter Lovins, continue to be closely affiliated with the Carrying Capacity Network, which advocates the use of strong incentives and disincentives in population control programs. CCN sees incentives as a moral necessity to avoid the impending 'ecological disaster':

> ...if incentives and disincentives for a two child family are not instituted now, the only policy option remaining would be a desperate, last ditch use of coercive mandatory sterilization or other such programs. Where is morality if we wait until Nature makes an even more undesirable decision? The longer the delay in making necessary but hard choices, the harder the choices become.[53]

As we shall discuss in the next chapter, the 'disaster ethic' has been guiding Third World family planning programs from their inception. While upper-class, white environmentalists campaign to change reproductive behavior of poor women of color in the name of environmental sustainability and morality, they are doing very little, if anything, to change their own consumption patterns and the military–industrial expansion of their economies. Instead, many environmentalists in the US are choosing to join the anti-immigration movement as an alleged strategy to protect the environment.

Immigration control

Population control lobbies like Negative Population Growth in the US assert direct links between the massive increase in immigration into the US (from 530,639 in 1980 to 904,292 in 1993) and worsening environmental problems such as acid rain, the greenhouse effect, urban crowding, traffic congestion, ground water contamination, nuclear waste, toxic waste and garbage, vanishing farmlands and wetlands. FAIR claims that 75% of new immigrants settle in the ecologically fragile coastal areas of the US, creating a settlement pattern of 'coastal cramming'.[54]

It is the global forces of capital, technological expansion and militarism that are destroying the environment and human survival mechanisms, forcing enormous numbers of people from the South to seek emigration to the North. Instead of addressing these complex realities, anti-immigration movements in both Europe and the US are demanding drastic measures to restrict immigration and curtail benefits to immigrants and refugees.[55] The removal of a clause from the ICPD draft Programme of Action on the right of migrants to family reunification also represents a victory for the anti-immigration agenda in the North.[56]

A host of population and environmental lobbies in the US such as Carrying Capacity Network, Population–Environment Balance and Zero Population Growth have joined forces with growing right-wing anti-immigration groups to curb immigration.[57] FAIR among other organizations has called for a moratorium on immigration to the US and slashing of basic social services to illegal immigrants. The draconian California Immigration Act (Proposition 187) severely curtails public services including education and non-emergency health care to children of 'illegal aliens'. Recent legislation passed in the US House of Representatives also allows states to bar 'illegal aliens' from public schools.[58]

Following internal debate, the Sierra Club has recently disassociated itself from the neo-Malthusian anti-immigration position.[59] However, if other liberal environmentalist groups and individuals in the North continue to make alliances with right-wing, anti-immigration groups, they will further distance themselves from poor communities of color and their twin struggle against social inequality and environmental destruction, which we shall address in later chapters.

Although environmental sustainability has been the most frequently used justification for population stabilization in the 1990s, in the period since World War II, and particularly in the 1960s and 1970s, economic development and poverty alleviation were the more common arguments given by policy makers for population control interventions. In the next section, we shall present some of the currently popular neo-Malthusian views on the relations between population growth, economic development and poverty.

Population and Poverty

Like the Malthusian analysis of environmental destruction, the Malthusian analysis of poverty also rests on the notion of scarcity and the belief that technology is limited in its ability to provide for increasing numbers of people in the face of dwindling natural resources.

Lester Brown of the World Watch Institute states that while the world population growth rate was about 1.8% in the late 1980s, the annual growth rate in grain production was only 1% between 1984 and 1993. Arguing that "easy options" for yield increases may be running out and calling for greater efforts towards population control, Brown concludes that "Achieving a humane balance between food and people now depends more on family planners than on farmers".[60]

Henry Kendall, a Nobel laureate in physics at MIT and David Pimentel, a professor of insect ecology at Cornell University, concur that earlier increases in food production associated with the Green Revolution are slowing down and that an adequate level of food production might be achieved only if global population is stabilized at 7.8 billion instead of letting it increase to 13 billion by 2050.[61]

In Chapter 6 of this book, we shall demonstrate that hunger and poverty are not so much an outcome of population growth as a result of corporate policies of food production and distribution. However, in the next sections of this chapter, we shall look at further arguments of the neo-Malthusian school which attribute increasing global poverty to relatively higher levels of fertility in the South.

Fertility and poverty

In the 'developing world' (outside of China), approximately 40% of the population is estimated to be under the age of 15. Neo-Malthusian analysts claim that the resultant high dependency ratios (a large proportion of the population being dependent on adult breadwinners) tend to depress domestic savings and reduce per capita incomes, thus contributing to poverty.[62] Neo-Malthusian analysts assume that, unlike in traditional agrarian societies, large families are no longer a key to survival for urban and landless and near-landless families in the Third World. In a fairly typical western middle-class explanation of how the fertility–poverty relationship gets played out at the household level in poor countries like the Philippines, the Washington, DC-based Population Crisis Committee (now called Population Action International) states:

> a family of three could meet its daily food requirements with about 40% of the present minimum daily wage. But a family of 7 would need to spend 100% of that amount on food with nothing left over for shelter and clothing, much less for education, or other investments in the family's future.[63]

Such arguments ignore the fact that survival patterns tend to differ greatly across social classes and that in poor families in the Third World children are not necessarily dependants. They start to work at very early ages, contributing significantly to family incomes, although this leads to a perpetuation of the cycle of poverty and high fertility that we discuss in Chapter 4.

Neo-Malthusian analysts fail to examine how widening inequality between social classes within regions and between the North and the South contributes to poverty at the familial level. Rather, they attribute increasing social class and North–South disparities also to population growth.

Population vs economic growth

Many economists tend to approach 'overpopulation' as a 'developmental problem' which threatens market expansion, rather than simply a resource scarcity problem.[64] According to a report of a Consultative Meeting of Economists on Population Growth and Economic Development convened by the UNFPA in 1992, "long-term population growth endangers sustainable economic development since it drives economic agents to adopt short-term planning horizons".[65] The Report also states that as high fertility is concentrated among the poor, it tends to widen the distribution of income between the rich and poor. On the basis of these arguments, the Report stresses the urgency of lowering population growth rates.[66]

Malthusian theorists assert that to the extent that population growth 'frustrates' economic growth in the Third World, it contributes to the widening income gap between the North and the South and the increasing dependence of the South on the North, ultimately threatening the stability of the entire global economic and financial system. *Beyond the Limits*, the updated version of *Limits to Growth* cited earlier, elaborates upon these arguments by linking high rates of population growth with low capital formation, reduced per capita GNP and poverty. It claims that poor countries like Indonesia, Pakistan, India and Bangladesh, which together constitute half the global population, are barely able to increase their GNP per capita, especially when compared to the wealthier nations like Japan, the US and the former USSR, which have much lower population growth rates. *Beyond the Limits*, explains the apparent paradox of global wealth and poverty in the following way:

> ...the most common behaviour of the world system is the one captured in the old saying 'the rich get richer and the poor get children'.... Poverty perpetuates population growth by keeping people in conditions where they have no education, no health care, no family planning, no choices, no way to get ahead except to have a large family and hope the children can bring in income or help with family labor.[67]

The above analysis, which captures the complex and circular nature of the poverty–high fertility relationship, is an improvement on the more common Malthusian formulations which simply assert a unilinear relationship between high fertility and poverty. It also acknowledges that a sustainable society cannot be achieved within existing inequitable patterns of distribution and poverty. Yet *Beyond the Limits* makes no attempt to examine either the global political-economic forces which have produced inequality and poverty or the strategies necessary to achieve social justice.[68]

The limitations, if not the dangers, of the neo-Malthusian framework are particularly evident in current policies of institutions such as the World Bank, USAID and the UNFPA. They seek increasingly to substitute population stabilization for poverty alleviation and social equality in the South.

Population control vs development

The argument that Third World delegations put forward at the 1974 World Population Conference in Bucharest – that development itself is the best contraceptive – is increasingly being cast aside by neo-Malthusian analysts as an old theory which has little validity in the contemporary period of population explosion and worsening global crisis. They suggest that while fertility reduction may have been a result of social improvements in the European demographic transition, the Third World no longer has the time to wait for economic and social development to bring down birth rates. Increasingly, population control itself is seen as "the most cost-effective investment possible in development assistance".[69]

Arguing that rapid population growth "consumes all other economic gains", USAID under the Clinton Administration has sought to increase support for family planning as the most "cost-effective intervention" to foster sustainable development.[70] Claiming that all the efforts that have been put into social programmes has not been sufficient "to move upwards in numerical terms", the UNFPA *State of the World Population 1990* report also concludes that massive increase in family planning spending is the surest way to a better global future.[71]

Applying the cost–benefit analysis to fertility reduction in India, the UNFPA *State of the World Population 1991* report claims that where the cost of providing education and health care for a child from infancy to adulthood is approximately $7,000 in India, success in averting 106 million births since 1979 has saved the country $742 billion. The uncounted gains accruing to general development prospects and the global environment from this population reduction, it is argued, are much higher.[72]

This analysis fails to acknowledge that whatever costs are averted by birth reduction are not necessarily translated into social development and environment protection. It also overlooks the fact that averting births in the North and among the richer classes in the South may yield far higher gains given the magnitude of their per capita expenses, compared to the meagre $7,000 per capita life-time education and health care expenses of the average Indian citizen.

Some World Bank studies themselves have admitted that faster fertility decline among the poor does not necessarily lead to alleviation of poverty. They reveal that fertility decrease is often correlated with increases of income of the poor rather than of the rich. Despite these findings, the Bank has consistently and vigorously opposed income redistribution.[73] This is specially evident in current efforts by some demographers and the World Bank to promote the so-called Bangladesh 'success' story.

Bangladesh 'success'

Although for many years Bangladesh was referred to as a 'basket case' in terms of social development, it is now being held up as a 'perfect example' of how fertility can be brought down without poverty alleviation and social transformation. In a 1993 article published in *Scientific American*, demographers Bryant Robey, Shea O. Rutstein and Leo Morris point out that although Bangladesh continues to be a poor country with a predominantly agricultural economy and a conservative Muslim culture, fertility rates in the country came down 21% between 1970 and 1991, that is, from seven to five children per woman. They attribute this rapid fertility decline to family planning education and the expansion of contraceptive use from 3% to 40% among married women of reproductive age.[74]

The World Bank is especially interested in Bangladesh as an example of how fertility decline can be achieved without socio-economic development, that is, simply through family planning programs providing contraceptive information, supplies and services. An internal World Bank Operations Evaluation Study on 'Population and the World Bank', published in 1992 stated,

> ...it is possible for fertility to decline and contraceptive use to increase without much change in those social, economic, and health variables generally believed to be crucial pre-conditions for demographic change. This makes Bangladesh an especially important case to study in view of the great interest in whether similar demographic changes are possible in many other poor countries in which there is no obvious sign of the onset of fertility decline.[75]

Despite decline in population growth, the numbers of people living in poverty in Bangladesh in both rural and urban areas have been rising in recent years. Infant mortality continues to be high (at 108 per 1,000 in the 1990–1995 period) and female literacy continues to be low (at 22% of adult females in 1990). Indeed, the notion that family planning can succeed "in the absence of extensive socio-economic development" has involved great costs to the health and well-being of the poor.[76]

The 'success' of Bangladesh has been built upon extensive reliance on sterilization and on economic incentives and disincentives. As we shall discuss in Chapter 2, these practices have contributed to widespread abuses of the rights of poor women. The use of new high-tech hormonal contraceptives like Norplant in a country such as Bangladesh which lacks a basic health care infrastructure also raises serious questions about the safety and ethics of drastic family planning efforts.

The World Bank acknowledges the widely accepted fact that as people's incomes improve, they tend to have fewer children. But the Bank's approach, calling for population control over poverty alleviation, seems to be built on the assumption that below the poverty threshold, increases in income are associated with increases in fertility.[77] Thus, the Bank, like the UNFPA and other leading agencies in the population and development fields, is bent on reducing the fertility of the 20% of the global population living beneath the poverty level rather than improving their incomes and standards of living.

Indeed, as far as most policy makers are concerned, the 'bottom billion' are the source of poverty, environmental and political stresses in the world. There is a widespread belief that if the bottom billion, the mostly uneducated, unemployed and resourceless, the so-called 'excess people', 70% of whom are women, did not exist, poverty, environmental stress and global political turmoil would disappear. The Bank is not pursuing a deliberate strategy of exterminating the teeming millions of people of color who live beneath the poverty threshold, but, as we discuss in subsequent chapters, its policies of structural adjustment, promotion of export production, and so on, are contributing to crisis and poverty-induced Malthusian mortality increases and fertility declines. Within some groups in the Third World, however, the social and health care crisis seems also to be having pronatalist effects.

The World Bank anticipates that it is likely that in the difficult years ahead the Bangladesh model will be expanded to more and more areas in both the South and the North. While deadly viruses like AIDS and Ebola are blamed on population pressure in the Third World, the push for population control over famine relief and AIDS prevention could intensify, especially in Africa.[78] As policy makers assert close links between such phenomena as teenage pregnancy, poverty and urban violence, population control is increasingly promoted in lieu of broader social welfare programs and economic revival for the poor in the US as well.[79]

US involvement in global population control first emerged as a national security concern in the post-World War II era. In the highly volatile post-Cold War era, when containment of Communism is no longer the main objective of US foreign policy, 'overpopulation' has reemerged as a "top post-Cold War national security concern".[80]

Population and Political Instability

As in the case of environmental destruction and poverty, Malthusian analysis attributes global political conflicts and instability to scarcity of resources resulting from expanding population.

According to a study commissioned by the University of Toronto and the American Academy of Arts and Sciences, Thomas Homer-Dixon, Jeffrey Boutwell and George Rathjens argue that in regions such as Mauritania, the Philippines and Central America population growth has led to reduction of natural resources, degradation of the quality of renewable resources and increased inequalities in resource distribution within countries. They warn that in the years ahead worsening environmental degradation and resource scarcity could lead to greater conflicts and violence across the world:

> Scarcities of renewable resources are already contributing to violent conflicts in many parts of the developing world. These conflicts may foreshadow a surge of similar violence in coming decades, particularly in poor countries where shortages of water, forests and, especially, fertile land, coupled with rapidly expanding populations, already cause great hardship.[81]

In a February 1994 article in the *Atlantic Monthly* entitled "The Coming Anarchy", journalist Robert Kaplan has given a sensationalized version of the Malthusian scenario presented by Homer-Dixon and other academic analysts. Arguing that the environment, is a "hostile power" and "*the* national security issue of the early 21st century", Kaplan says that most other foreign policy challenges will emanate from the core challenge of surging populations and related problems of environmental destruction (emphasis in original).[82] Kaplan presents West Africa as a premonition of the utterly destructive and hopeless future that awaits much of humanity: overpopulation, scarcity, resource wars, population displacements, refugee flows, disease and hunger, border tensions, ethnic conflicts and regional destabilization. He concludes that in the Third World these stresses are already leading to totalitarianism, fascism, road-warrior cultures and other forms of 'criminal anarchy'.[83]

Population analysts in the US are concerned that political instability induced by population pressure in the Third World could block US access to strategic resources and raw materials. For example, they point out that Sub-Saharan Africa and the Middle East, which have both high rates of annual population growth (3.0 and 2.8% respectively) and strategic mineral resources, have experienced much political instability and warfare in recent years.[84] These analysts fear that unless high population growth rates in such regions are brought down quickly, the resultant migration, urbanization, youth unrest and ethnic and religious conflicts will threaten political stability, endangering the entire global economy.

Population, urbanization and migration

Millions of landless and other disenfranchised rural people, especially the young, are flocking to urban areas, creating rates of urbanization far higher than overall population growth rates in most Third World countries. According to the UNFPA, by the year 2000, more than half the world's population will be living in urban areas. By then, most of the world's largest 'megacities' will be in the Third World: Mexico City (25.6 million), São Paulo (22.1 million), Shanghai (17 million), Calcutta (15.7 million), Bombay (15.4 million), Beijing (14 million) and Jakarta (13.7 million) (population estimates for year 2000 in parentheses above).[85]

Population analysts point out that as these megacities cannot provide employment and social services for all, most migrants end up as squatters in shantytowns, which become the locus of diseases as well as of urban unrest. Demographer Nathan Keyfitz claims that politicians' attempts to appease urban dwellers with social services and food subsidies result in attracting more rural migrants into the cities and in exacerbating the foreign debt and poverty of Third World countries.[86] But, as we discuss in Chapter 5, the Third World debt and adjustment loans have been spent more on the rich than on the poor in the Third World; besides, debt and adjustment aggravate poverty rather than alleviate it.

Foreign policy analysts also point out that as Third World nations become less and less able to absorb the rapidly expanding numbers within their economies and as international communication and transportation become easily accessible, more and more people will opt to migrate across national borders. David Smith, a US State Department policy analyst, has estimated that between 1990 and 2010 the labor force in Central America and the Caribbean will grow from 56 to 93 million and that about 5 million migrants will arrive in North America during this period.[87]

According to the Programme of Action of the ICPD, all international migrants, including refugees, totalled over 125 million in 1994 and half of them were in the 'developing' countries. The main recipient countries took in approximately 1.4 million immigrants annually, about two-thirds from the South.[88] Such massive flows of population, neo-Malthusian analysts argue, contribute to increasing scarcities of natural resources and economic opportunities leading to ethnic and racial tensions and political conflicts in the recipient countries. The surging problems of immigration have prompted at least some analysts to also warn that if the outlets for surplus labor migration are closed off, "the population tread-mill effect" could generate political instability and violence in labor-sending countries.[89]

Yet the popular response of both liberals and conservatives in the North to the challenge of immigration is curtailment of immigration. Fuelling the divide and conquer mentality, the anti-immigration lobby in the US blames new immigrants for aggravating the poverty of the already existing 'underclass' in the country. It says that Hispanics and Asians take away jobs from Blacks and compete with them for affirmative action and social service benefits. Anti-immigration advocates also claim that new immigrants "glorify" separatism and reject "a common, shared American identity and culture" which contribute to the unity of the nation.[90] Despite evidence to the contrary, they also attribute major incidences of crime and violence in the US, such as growing hate crimes and the 1992 Los Angeles riots, mostly to immigration.[91]

Largely as a response to lobbying by anti-immigration groups, educational, language and family requirements for legal immigration have been tightened and employer sanctions, physical barriers, border patrol and other strong 'interior enforcement' measures to prevent illegal immigration have been adopted by both federal and state governments in the US.[92]

Although the number of immigrants is much smaller in Western Europe than in the US (about 15 million between 1980 and 1992), immigration there is considered an even graver crisis.[93] The immigration policies of the European Union have been tightened so severely that it has become a virtual 'Fortress Europe'. In Britain, France and Germany, politicians conveniently blame immigration for eroding their respective European ways of life without paying much attention to transnational corporate expansion and the spread of American culture which threaten economic and cultural integrity everywhere. The scapegoating of immigrants in Europe has incited widespread violence by white supremacist neo-Nazi groups, mostly unemployed white youth, against people of color.[94]

Malthusian analysts identify a relationship between the rise of racist and fascist political movements and such factors as population pressure, migration and differential fertility rates between ethnic groups.[95] But, as the political-economic analysis developed in later chapters of the book reveals, the very failure of Malthusianism and other mainstream analyses to grapple with the politico-economic causes of the global crisis contributes to the rise of racism, xenophobia and anti-democratic social movements and regimes both in the North and in the South.

Population, youth unrest and violence

Neo-Malthusian analysts frequently describe the largely young unemployed population in the Third World, as "a social and political time bomb ready to explode".[96] Thus, a common explanation given for the ethnic conflict and carnage in Rwanda is 'overpopulation': a fertility rate of 8.3 children per woman (the highest in the world) and 69% of population in the under-25 age group. Within the US and Europe too, the young and the poor of Third World origin are often seen as the cause of escalating urban violence and political instability.[97]

Yale historian Paul Kennedy, author of *Preparing for the Twenty First Century*, argues that historically revolutions and other forms of political unrest have occurred more often in countries with young populations, especially those with an excess of "energetic, frustrated, young men".[98] Applying this argument to regions experiencing severe unrest, Kennedy observes that in all these different regions there are "fast-growing, youthful populations with pent-up social and economic expectations". Kennedy cites the example of the Palestinian *intifada*, which he describes largely as a war waged by teenage youth against the Israeli occupying forces. He emphasizes that the Gaza Strip, where the *intifada* began, has a population density of 4,206 persons per square mile in comparison with 530 persons per square mile in Israel. Kennedy concludes that while ideological rivalries, racial and religious hatreds, and other factors also have their roles to play in these civil and regional wars, "the social effects of a population explosion appear to form the context within which such bitter struggles swiftly escalate".[99]

Western analysts frequently attribute the embrace of Islamic fundamentalism by many young North Africans also to population pressure, youth frustration and disillusionment with western culture. Robert Kaplan states that, at current growth rates, the population in many Arab states will double during the next 20 years and that, like many of the African countries, the Arab countries will become less and less governable through rational secular ideologies. Kaplan goes on to say that as central governmental control weakens and as environmental and demographic stresses increase, "'hard' Islamic city-states or shantytowns are likely to emerge", giving rise to more "Saddam Husseins of the future".[100] Asserting that political stability and democracy are necessarily correlated with lower levels of population pressure, the Population Crisis Committee has also called for population stabilization as a prerequisite for global security and democracy.[101]

Neo-Malthusians argue that inter-ethnic and cultural conflicts have greater potential for igniting in contexts of high population growth rates and differential fertility rates between groups. In a paper entitled "Population Change and National Security" presented to the US Army Conference on Long Range Planning, political scientist Nicholas Eberstadt has pointed out that differential fertility levels between ethnic groups in the Middle East, for example between Jews and Palestinians in Israel, and between ethnic Russians and Asians in the former Soviet Union, could have major political repercussions in the future.[102] Such fears are reflected in efforts by the Israeli government and ultra-orthodox political parties to boost the fertility of Jewish women in Israel and the eugenic policy encouraging educated women to bear more and uneducated women to bear fewer children in the authoritarian city-state of Singapore.[103]

In the US, where the fear of white supremacists of 'race suicide' is on the rise, policy makers are observing both immigration patterns and differential fertility rates among races and ethnic groups with alarm. It is commonly assumed that immigrants have larger families, although data on this issue are not readily available. As we shall note in Chapter 3, it is estimated that fertility rates among whites may be increasing slightly while rates among most non-white groups in the US may be decreasing by the beginning of the next century.

However, anti-immigration advocates fear that due to currently unequal birth rates between whites and non-whites and the large influx of 'non-white' immigrants, there will be a 'browning' of the US population, making non-Hispanic whites a racial minority during the twenty-first century. Underlying the calls for immigration control, then, is a deep fear on the part of many whites of losing their racial and cultural dominance. English-only legislation, attacks against multiculturalism and attempts to pit minority groups against each other stem from the fear of losing the dominant position of European-Americans.[104] This fear of demographic imbalance is a global phenomenon.

Demographic imbalance

Fertility per woman has fallen below replacement level in most industrialized countries (1.5 in Japan; 1.2 in Australia; 1.9 in Canada; 1.5 in Western Europe). The relatively high fertility rate of 2.1 children per woman in the US is generally attributed to immigration. As noted in the Introduction, 90% of global population growth is now taking place in the Third World, and by the year 2025 the 'developed' world will make up 15% of the total global population while the 'developing world' will account for 85%. According to neo-Malthusian analysts, the 'demographic imbalance' between the rich and poor countries constitutes the 'backdrop' to all other important forces of change taking place in the world today.[105]

According to United Nations projections, by the year 2000, the 'less developed countries' will have 52.7% in the 0–14 age category and 8.3% of their populations in the above 65 category. In contrast, the 'more developed' countries will have 31.6% in the 0–14 category and 20.1 in the over 65 category.[106] Western analysts see this relative youthfulness of the population in the South and the 'greying' of population in the North as an increasing source of global instability. In a 1990 document entitled "Youth Deficits: An Emerging Population Problem", the United States Central Intelligence Agency has explored some of the implications of 'youth deficit' (defined as less than 15% of 15- to 24-year-olds in the total population) in terms of shortages in the labor force, immigration and other demographic issues in the industrialized countries.[107]

Neo-Malthusian policy analysts in the West assert that the relative decline of western populations poses a threat to the survival of values associated with democracy such as individual rights, private property, rule of law and orderly government. Jessica Tuchman Mathews, a senior fellow at the US Council on Foreign Relations, has argued that as population growth and migration pressure lead to the "continuing use of excess people as a weapon" in foreign policy (as in the case of immigrants from Haiti and Cuba to the US), it will force representative governments in the West to compromise their "most cherished" democratic values.[108]

In "The Clash of Civilizations", a highly celebrated article published in *Foreign Affairs* in 1993, Harvard political scientist Samuel Huntington predicted a diminution of western influence in world affairs in the context of unequal population trends and competition between western and non-western civilizations.[109] For many western analysts, the so-called 'Islamic threat' represents the greatest challenge to global peace and security in the post-Cold War era.[110] Paul Kennedy has also voiced his anxiety over the possible decline of western power as a concern with the fate of global democracy:

> This relative diminution of their share of world population presents the industrial democracies with their greatest dilemma over the next thirty years. If the developing world manages to raise its output and standards of living, the West's proportion of economic output, global power, and political influence will decline steadily, simply because of the force of numbers; which in turn has raised the interesting question of whether 'Western values' – a liberal social culture, human rights, religious tolerance, democracy and market forces – will maintain their prevailing position in a world overwhelmingly peopled by societies which did not experience the rational scientific and liberal assumptions of the Enlightenment.[111]

As we elaborate in later chapters, however, desire for global democracy is not the fundamental motivation of policy makers in the West. As noted earlier, since World War II, they have been much more concerned with the fact that unequal global population dynamics could shift the geopolitical balance in the world to the detriment of the western countries, particularly the US.

Geopolitical imbalance

According to many contemporary western analysts, current population and economic growth trends could produce a global situation "even more menacing to the security prospects of the Western alliance than was the Cold War for the past generation".[112] Gregory Foster, a sociologist at the Industrial College of the Armed Forces, National Defense University, has suggested that low fertility rates of the US, and its NATO allies (as well as of the former Soviet Union and its Warsaw Pact allies) would make it difficult for them to maintain military forces at Cold War levels. Foster claims that, in contrast, if the high fertility rates in the Third World are not matched with commensurate growth in jobs, they could contribute to the expansion of Third World militaries as a "productive alternative to unemployment".[113] How arms exports from the North to the South fuel militarism and related subjects to be taken up in Chapter 7, however, are completely missing from neo-Malthusian analyses of the global security crisis.

Western analysts fear that whether the Third World surpasses the West in terms of economic and political power or whether it remains caught in the poverty trap continuing the migrant and refugee flows into the North, "the results are likely to be painful for the richest one-sixth of the earth's population that now enjoys a disproportionate five sixths of its wealth".[114] Identifying with the fears and potential 'pain' of the world's richest, former US National Security Advisor Zbigniew Brezinski observes that economic inequality between the North and the South which is exacerbated by Third World population growth could create further alienation, ideological confusion and irrational ethnic sentiments leading to forms of quasi-fascism severely threatening the global social order and US hegemony.[115]

Rather than advocating greater global economic equality, arms control and other fundamental solutions, the neo-Malthusian experts look to population stabilization in the poor countries as the major solution to the global security crisis. Giving voice to eugenicist beliefs, some analysts are calling explicitly for antinatalist policies in the South and pronatalist policies in the North. Paul Kennedy claims that in order to move the world towards a "better demographic balance", fertility rates in poor countries should be lowered while they should be raised in the richer ones.[116]

The fear of demographic imbalance has produced a demand for severe control of fertility from women in the South and a demand for increased fertility from women in the North. The irony of this is evident in corporate-scientific development of stronger contraceptives for the South and new reproductive technologies for fertility enhancement such as IVF (in-vitro fertilization) largely for the North and white upper-class women.[117] Concerned with population 'implosion' (as opposed to 'explosion' in the South), many governments in the North such as France and Sweden have been pursuing pronatalist policies for many decades, encouraging women to have more children. These policies, however, have received little worldwide attention in the contemporary population discourse.[118]

Differential demographic emphases for the North and the South, are apparent in the ICPD population agenda for the twenty-first century. The Japanese government, which is a leading funder of the ICPD agenda (in 1994, Japan agreed to contribute $3 billion for global population and AIDS issues), is at the same time providing economic incentives and exhorting Japanese women to bear more children in order to avert a domestic population 'implosion'.[119] While the ICPD Programme of Action has been focused on population stabilization in the Third World, the Report of the European Population Conference for the ICPD explicitly called for such measures as tax incentives, low-cost or free child and maternal welfare services and other supports to encourage childbearing and childrearing in Europe.[120] Social support for childbearing and childrearing must not be taken away from people in the North; rather, as we shall argue in later chapters, such support needs to be extended to all people everywhere as a basic universal human right.

Contemporary Malthusian thinking represents an extremist ideological response to the vast social upheavals taking place in the world. Like Malthus's doctrine, its modern variants are also built upon the deep-seated acceptance of the division of global society into haves and have-nots and the maintenance of this inherent inequality. Paul Ehrlich vividly expressed the primordial fear of the 'other' in his Malthusian classic *The Population Bomb*, in which he described how the sight of masses of people in "one stinking hot night in Delhi" "frightened" him into knowing the "*feel* of overpopulation" (emphasis in original).[121] Strong self-interest and overwhelming fear of the 'other' have always been and continue be the guiding forces of Malthusianism. Close examination reveals that the fear of the 'other' also underlies the neo-Malthusian gender analysis, even the much celebrated 'new' reproductive rights approach.

Population and Women

Despite its concerns for the well-being of women, the neo-Malthusian gender analysis tends to blame the victims, that is, poor Third World women and their fertility, for the global crisis. It is argued that in the process of trying to feed their large families from already damaged fragile natural environments, poor women cause further environmental destruction.

In a UNFPA publication entitled, "Investing in Women: The Focus of the '90s", Nafis Sadik, the Director General of the UNFPA, expresses concern and fear when she says:

> Land hunger, scarce fuel, pollution and migration deepen women's sense of uncertainty about their future. Already many are being forced into actions that they know are likely further to jeopardize their security. In countries with a shortage of firewood, for example, women use manure as fuel instead of fertilizer, mortgaging tomorrow's food to cook today's.[122]

Placing women at the center of what it calls the "population–environment–development triangle", a 1992 UNFPA publication shows that the social status of women affects each point in the triangle and that these points in turn affect women's status, creating a powerful synergy which can deter or help sustainable development.[123] Still, the primary focus on population tilts this analysis into identifying population as the root cause of women's subordination as well as environmental and development problems and to advocate control of women's fertility as the most important solution.

The World Resources Institute Report for 1994–1995 argues that in many regions in the South population pressures have resulted in deforestation and reduced access to fuel, water and other resources. As a result, women now have to spend more time walking to collect water and gather fuelwood. The report recognizes that these factors in conjunction with persistent high infant and child mortality make large families desirable for poor people. It also points out that in many places women have been and continue to be the protectors of the natural environment.[124] Despite the complexity of this analysis, here, too, the Malthusian emphasis on 'overpopulation' as the determinant factor in the chain of environmental destruction, poverty and high fertility persists.

Just as environmental destruction is attributed to women's fertility, global poverty and women's poverty in particular are also associated with women's fertility by neo-Malthusian analysts. Applying to the situation of women the basic Malthusian assumption that population growth increases poverty, neo-Malthusian analysts argue that pregnancy leads to suffering, powerlessness and the low status of women and that improvement of women's status is a direct consequence of the acceptance of modern family planning.

"Poor, Pregnant and Powerless", a chart developed by the Population Crisis Committee ranking countries according to the status of women, is instructive in this regard. According to this chart, women's social status is strongly correlated with their fertility: the lower the number of births per woman the higher her status, and the higher the number of births the lower her status. This chart suggests that pregnancy is a fundamental cause of women's poverty and powerlessness and that fertility control is the primary means for poverty alleviation and women's empowerment.[125] Similar thinking underlies the UNFPA publication "Food for the Future: Women,

Population and Food Security", released prior to the World Food summit in 1996. It argues that the first step to world food security is women's reproductive rights, by which is meant fertility control.[126]

The UNFPA *State of the World Population 1993* also states that for female migrants and refugees 'unwanted pregnancies' pose even more problems than for women who live in traditional community settings, and that expanded family planning and reproductive health services are urgently needed.[127] Women make up almost half of all international migrants today and in the years ahead many more women will be forced to flee their homes due to worsening environmental problems, poverty and political turbulence. Birth rates among women in the growing refugee camps of the world are said to be higher than 'traditional birth rates prior to flight', due to a variety of reasons, including lack of access to family planning and desire of refugees to compensate for significant numbers of children they have lost by rebuilding their populations.[128]

Not addressed in the growing calls for extending family planning services, however, are global militarism, sexual violence of men and the dangers of modern family planning methods which further victimize vulnerable migrant and refugee women around the world. The new reproductive rights approach to family planning promoted by the ICPD has not addressed these concerns either.

The new reproductive rights agenda

The new reproductive rights agenda calls for women's choice, health and human rights and improved quality of services. It emphasizes family planning as a precondition for gender equality and advocates the expansion of reproductive health interventions beyond fertility control to include maternal and child health, prevention of STDs (sexually transmitted diseases), HIV/AIDS, and so on.[129]

However, fertility control will continue to be the main focus of the new agenda despite the deterioration of basic health care in many regions and the rapid spread of HIV/AIDS and projections of massive population losses as a consequence. This focus is evident in the relative expenditures proposed by the ICPD Programme of Action, which favors family planning over reproductive health and the prevention of STDs (Table 1.1). Moreover, the focus on reproductive health also overlooks the fact that in many regions in the South disease, ill-health and female mortality are attributable largely to poverty, an issue we shall return to in later chapters.

The ICPD Programme, like most United Nations plans, is non-binding and no regulatory mechanisms exist to enforce its implementation. Many analysts have pointed out that as financial resources and foreign assistance from the North to the South become more limited, women's rights and reproductive health may receive even less priority than family planning in

Table 1.1   Global population and health expenditures, 2000 and 2015
(US$ billions)

Item	2000	2015
Family planning	10.2	13.8
Reproductive health	5.0	6.1
HIV/AIDS and other STDs prevention	1.3	1.5
Research and data of population and development policy analysis	0.5	0.3
Total	17.0	21.7

Source: United Nations, *Report of the International Conference on Population and Development,* Cairo, September 5–13, 1994, p. 98.

the future.[130] This is particularly visible in the Beijing Platform for Action, which makes no specific financial commitments whatsoever to carrying out its proposals to improve women's lives.[131]

The interest in population stabilization over socio-economic development is evident in foreign aid allocations of industrialized countries which have championed the ICPD agenda. Although very few countries in the North have complied with the internationally agreed upon foreign aid disbursement of 0.7% of GNP, almost all these countries, including the European Union, Britain, Australia and Japan, have substantially increased their funding for global population stabilization.[132] US funding for international and domestic family planning which increased significantly in the early years of the Clinton administration has steadily been slashed by the Republican Party-led Congress in recent years.

However, population, health and nutrition is the fastest growing area of World Bank operations, with Bank spending in this sector rising to $2.5 billion in 1995.[133] Within the United Nations, too, spending for family planning accounts for the greatest growth rate among all programs. While funding for all other programs including peacekeeping and socio-economic development are being severely slashed, spending by the UNFPA rose from $47 million in 1993 to $104 million in 1994.[134]

Family planning over development

As noted earlier, neo-Malthusians attempt to adapt feminist language to suit its own purpose of population control. This is evident in the 1994 UNFPA *State of the World Population 1994* which states:

> Individual choice in the size and spacing of the family is a human right: the extension of choice is the foundation of development at all levels of society. It is essential to achieving balance between populations and the resources to sustain

them. If barriers to free choice are removed, the overall result is smaller families and slower population growth.[135]

This analysis restricts the meaning of choice and human rights to the number and spacing of children. Choice is not extended to the right to the survival of children and the quality of their lives, let alone the survival of the environment, of families, communities and cultures. It does not address the gender, race and class politics of genetic engineering or the ethical dilemmas inherent in the spread of new reproductive technologies. Despite recognition of the improvement of women's education as a key for lowering fertility, the ICPD Programme of Action does not include women's education or employment generation within its proposed expenditures.[136]

Even when money is specifically allocated for the improvement of women's health and economic survival, it is frequently justified as best serving the goal of population stabilization. In an article published in *Conservation Digest*, a newsletter providing information to environmental grantmakers, Robert B. Wallace from the Wallace Gentic Foundation observes that "with modest adaption", Women in Development (WID) programs providing small-scale credit for self-employed women could be turned into a powerful force "in progress towards the small family norm and in reducing environmental degradation".[137] This kind of thinking is influencing the imposition of family planning as a condition for receiving micro-loans in some Third World settings. As we point out in the next chapter, the result could be increasing subsumption of WID programs within family planning and the so-called 'contraceptive revolution'.

Denouncing the increasing identification of social development with fertility control by population control advocates and liberal feminists from the North, more radical feminist activists, especially those from the South, have called for a broader development approach to women's empowerment. Many scholars and activists and NGOs from the South who participated in the 1994 Cairo Population Conference, in particular, demanded attention to the 'D', that is development, left out of the ICPD agenda.[138] Indeed, as we shall explore in later chapters of this book, if 'choice' is to be expanded to be meaningful for most people, especially poor women, the 'new' agenda would have to move far beyond family planning to focusing on poverty alleviation and structural changes in the global political economy.

In the absence of such broader social changes required for the empowerment of women and the poor, the 'new' reproductive rights approach will become another example of the capitulation of liberal feminism to the Malthusian interest in controlling the numbers of the poor. The next chapter demonstrates that alarmist Malthusian analyses, like those discussed in this chapter, necessarily lead to the adoption of stringent population control policies harmful to the health and well-being of the poor, especially poor women of color.

Notes

1. Thomas Robert Malthus, *An Essay on the Principle of Population*, ed. Philip Appleman, New York: W.W. Norton and Co., 1976, pp 21–26.

2. Ibid., p. 132.

3. A.B. Wolfe, "Population Theory", in *Encyclopaedia of the Social Sciences*, Vol. 12, 1934, p. 249; Roland Pressat, "Neo-Malthusianism", in Christopher Wilson, ed., *The Dictionary of Demography*, New York: Basil Blackwell Inc., 1985, p. 134; Nathan Keyfitz, "Population Theory", *International Encyclopaedia of Population*, Vol. 2, 1982, p. 539.

4. Klaus M. Leisinger and Karin Schmitt, *All Our People: Population Policy With a Human Face*, Washington, DC: Island Press, 1994, p. 48; Richard Hofstadter, *Social Darwinism in American Thought*, Boston: Beacon Press, 1955, passim.

5. Malthus, *An Essay*, pp. 99–100.

6. Ibid., p. 107.

7. Serron, *Scarcity, Exploitation and Poverty*, p. 7; Gilles-Gaston Granger, "Condorcet", in David L. Sills, ed., *Encyclopedia of the Social Sciences*, Vol. 3, Crowell Collier and Macmillan Inc., 1968, pp. 213–15.

8. Barbara Duden, "Population", in Wolfgang Sachs, ed., *The Development Dictionary*, London: Zed Books, 1992, p. 148.

9. Hofsdater, *Social Darwinism in American Thought*, pp. 56, 91.

10. Stephen Jay Gould, "The Smoking Gun of Eugenics", *Natural History*, December 1991, p. 12; Sharon Kingsland, "Evolution and Debates over Human Progress From Darwin to Sociobiology", in Michael S. Teitelbaum and Jay M. Winter, eds, *Population and Resources in Western Intellectual Traditions*, Cambridge: Cambridge University Press, 1989, p. 184; Linda Gordon, *Woman's Body, Woman's Right: A Social History of Birth Control in America*, New York: Grossman Publishers, 1976, p. 276.

11. Cited in Frances Moore Lappe and Rachel Schurman, "The Missing Piece in the Population Puzzle", Food First Development Report No. 4, San Francisco: Institute for Food and Development Policy, September 1988, p. 13; Alex de Sherbinin, "Population Issues of Concern to the Foreign Policy Community", Literature Search and Bibliography Prepared by the Population Reference Bureau for the Pew Charitable Trust's Global Stewardship Initiative, October 1993, p. 2.

12. Women's Environment and Development Organization (WEDO), 355 Lexington Avenue, 3rd floor, New York, NY 10017; International Women's Health Coalition (IWHC), 24 East 21st Street, New York, NY 10010; The Center for Development and Population Activities (CEDPA), 1717, Massachusetts Avenue, NW, Suite 200, Washington, DC 20036.

13. Garett Hardin, "Living on a Lifeboat", *Bioscience*, Vol. 24, No. 10, 1974, pp. 564–568; Sandra Postel, "Carrying Capacity: The Earth's Bottom Line", in Laurie Ann Mazur, ed., *Beyond the Numbers: A Reader on Population, Consumption and the Environment*, Washington, DC: Island Press, 1994, p. 49.

14. Paul R. Ehrlich and Anne H. Ehrlich, *The Population Explosion*, New York: Simon and Schuster, 1990, p. 19.

15. Donnela H. Meadows, Dennis L. Meadows, Jorgen Randers and William W. Behrens III, *The Limits to Growth: A Report for the Club of Rome's Project on the Predicament of Mankind*, New York: Universe Books, 1972, pp. 91–92, 126, 142.

16. Ibid., p. 94.

17. Donnella H. Meadows, Dennis L. Meadows and Jorgen Randers, *Beyond the Limits: Confronting Global Collapse, Envisioning a Sustainable Future*, Post Mills, VT: Chelsea Green Publishing Co., 1992, p. 132.

18. National Audubon Society and the Population Crisis Committee (PCC), *Why Population Matters: A Handbook for the Environmental Activist*, Washington, DC, 1991, pp. 3–4; see also Advertisement by Negative Population Growth in *The Progressive*, December 1988, p. 32; "Easing Population Pressures: Key to a Sustainable Planet", *Conservation Digest*, Vol. 13, No. 1, February 1991, p. 1.

19. Postel, "Carrying Capacity", p. 57.

20. "Population and Water Resources: A Delicate Balance", *Population Bulletin*, Vol. 47, No. 3, November 1992, p. 20.

21. UNFPA, *Population, Resources and the Environment: The Critical Challenge*, New York, 1991, pp. 18–19, 3; see also Malini Karkal, "Why the Cairo Document is Flawed", *Third World Resurgence*, No. 50, 1994, p. 19.

22. Cited in Mary Barberi, *Issues in Sustainable Development: Population, Poverty and the Environment, Population Reference Bureau, ICPD Newsletter*, No. 12, February 1994, p. 5; see also, UNFPA, *State of the World Population 1992*, p. 21; Alex de Sherbinin, "Population and Consumption Issues for Environmentalists", Literature Search and Bibliography Prepared by the Population Reference Bureau for the Pew Charitable Trust's Global Stewardship Initiative, October 1993, pp. 18–20.

23. Cited in Marianne Schmink and Charles H. Wood, "The 'Political Ecology' of Amazonia" in Peter D. Little and Michael M. Horowitz with A. Endre Nyerges, eds, *Lands at Risk in the Third World: Local Level Perspectives*, Boulder, CO: Westview Press, 1987, pp. 45, 47.

24. UNFPA, "Pushing the Limits", 1990, (news feature distributed to media and journalists to promote the UNFPA *State of the World Population 1990* report), p. 3; compare with UNFPA, *State of the World Population 1990*, pp. 10–11.

25. UNFPA, *State of the World Population 1990*, p. 10; UNFPA, *State of the World Population 1992*, p. 28; Sherbinin, "Population and Consumption", p. 15.

26. Attila Karaosmanoglu, "Environment, Poverty and Growth: The Challenge of Sustainable Development in Asia", an address to the Nieman Fellows at Harvard University, MA, February 9, 1989, in *Poverty and Prosperity: The Two Realities of Asian Development*, Address of Vice President for Asia, The World Bank, Washington, DC, 1989, p. 42.

27. F. Landis Mackellar and David E. Horlacher, "Population, Living Standards and Sustainability: An Economic View", in Mazur, ed., *Beyond the Numbers*, pp. 91–92.

28. National Audobon Society and the Population Crisis Committee, *Why Population Matters*, p. 9.

29. H. Patricia Hynes, *Taking Population Out of the Equation*, North Amherst, MA: Institute on Women and Technology, 1993, pp. 1, 11; Ehrlich and Ehrlich, *The Population Explosion*, p. 58.

30. UNICEF, *The State of the World's Children 1994*, New York: Oxford University Press, 1994, pp. 24–25, 48–49.

31. Ehrlich and Ehrlich, *The Population Explosion*, p. 190.

32. Paul R. Ehrlich, Anne H. Ehrlich and Gretchen C. Daly, *The Stork and the Plow: The Equity Answer to the Human Dilemma*, New York: G.P. Putnam's Sons, 1995, pp. 265, 279–280.

33. US National Academy of Sciences and the Royal Society, *Population Growth, Resource Consumption and a Sustainable World*, Washington, DC, and London, 1992.

34. "Priority Statement on Population", Population Communications International, January 10, 1991.

35. Cited in Norman Myers, "Scientists Reinforce Population Policies", *WGNRR Newsletter*, No. 45, January–March 1994, p. 4; "Science Academies Urge 'Incisive Action' on Population and Development", *ICPD '94, Newsletter*, ICPD Secretariat, No. 10, November–December 1993, pp. 2–3; see also 'A Call to Reason', August 30, 1994, *The New York Times* advertisement, op.-ed.; Keynote Address by Ralph O. Slater to IUCN General Assembly in 1990, cited in "The Most Urgent Task of All", *Earthwatch*, No. 41, 1991, p. 19.

36. Office of the Press Secretary, "Remarks by the President to the National Academy of Sciences", The White House Washington, DC, June 29, 1994; Gore, *Earth in the Balance*, pp. 305, 307; IPPF, *Open File*, London, May 1992, p. 1.

37. Tree diagram, in *Population Stabilization – The Real Solution: Overpopulation the Root of the Problem*, Sierra Club, International Population Program, Washington, DC, n.d.; "Japan Supports Population Stabilization Program", *Beyond Just-U.S., Newsletter*, International

Affairs Department, National Wildlife Federation, Vol. 1, No. 2, Summer 1994, p. 3; see also *Population Newsletters* of the Population Program, National Audubon Society, Washington, DC, 1994; also participant observation, Sierra Club population action group, Pioneer Valley, MA, 1992–93.

38. Andy Smith, "Christian Responses to Population Control", *Political Environments*, No. 3, Winter/Spring 1996, pp. 28–30.

39. IPPF, *Open File*, London, July 1992, p. 1; see also "The South Commission Report on Population and Population Policy", *Population and Development Review*, Vol. 16, No. 4, December 1990, pp. 795–798; *IPPF Briefing*, "Population and Environment", London, June 1992, p. 1.

40. Bernard Berelson and Jonathan Lieberson, "Government Efforts to Influence Fertility: The Ethical Issue", *Population and Development Review*, Vol. 5, 1979, pp. 581–613; Bernard Berelson, "Beyond Family Planning", *Science*, Vol. 163, February 1969, p. 533.

41. Berelson and Lieberson, "Government Efforts", p. 603.

42. Hardin cited in Barry Commoner, "Poverty Breeds 'Overpopulation'", in Vogeler and de Souza, *Dialectics of Third World Development*, p. 187; see also Garret Hardin, "The Tragedy of the Commons", *Sanctuary*, Vol. 27, No. 5, February–March 1988; Hardin, "Living on a Lifeboat", pp. 561–568.

43. Garret Hardin, *Living Within Limits: Ecology, Economics and the Population Taboo*, New York: Oxford University Press, 1993; see also Sherbinin, "Population and Consumption Issues for Environmentalists", p. 5.

44. Cited in Janice Jiggins, *Changing the Boundaries: Women-Centered Perspectives on Population and the Environment*, Washington, DC: Island Press, 1994, p. 43; Maurice King, "Health is a Sustainable State", *The Lancet*, Vol. 336, September 15, 1990, pp. 666–667.

45. King, "Health is a Sustainable State", p. 667.

46. Ibid.

47. Nicholas J. Demerath, *Birth Control and Foreign Policy: The Alternatives to Family Planning*, New York: Harper and Row, 1976, p. 13; William and Paul Paddock, *Famine – 1975!, America's Decision: Who Will Survive?*, Boston: Little, Brown, 1967.

48. Steven Greenhouse, "U.S. to Cut Overseas Food Aid by Nearly Half", *The New York Times*, April 2, 1995, pp. 8, 15.

49. Cited in Carolyn Merchant, *Radical Ecology: The Search for a Livable World*, New York: Routledge, 1992, p. 175.

50. "Eco-Symposium", *Springfeld Advocate*, Massachusetts, October 31, 1991.

51. Bill Deval, "Overpopulation and Deep Ecology", *Clearinghouse Bulletin*, Carrying Capacity Network, Washington, DC, Vol. 3, No. 1, January/February 1993, p. 2; see also Michael Tobias, *World War III: Population and the Biosphere at the End of the Millennium*, Santa Fe, NM: Bear and Company, 1994, p. 417.

52. Ehrlich and Ehrlich, *The Population Explosion*, p. 207.

53. "Q: Will Family Planning Alone Stop the Population Explosion? A: No", *Clearinghouse Bulletin*, Carrying Capacity Network, Washington, DC, Vol. 2, No. 10, December 1992, p. 3.

54. US Bureau of the Census, *Statistical Abstract of the United States: 1995*, p. 10; Sherbinin, "Population Issues", p. 5; FAIR, *Backgrounder*, "Immigration Issues in Congress – 1993", n.d., p. 5; Advertisement by Negative Population Growth, *The Progressive*, December 1988, p. 32; see also *Newsletters* of the Negative Population Growth Inc., Vol. 18, No. 1, Fall 1992, p. 4; Donald Mann, "A Negative Population Growth – Position Paper", Negative Population Growth, Washington, DC, 1992, p. 3.

55. "Coming to America: The Immigrants and the Environment", *Environmental Action*, Takoma Park, MD, Summer 1994, p. 23.

56. Alan Cowell, "Cairo Parley Hits a New Snag on Migrants: Latin America vs. the U.S. on Immigration Rights", *The New York Times*, September 11, 1994, p. 10.

57. Luke Cole, "The Anti-Immigration Environmental Alliance: Divide and Conquer at the Border", *Race, Poverty and the Environment*, Earth Island Institute, San Francisco, Spring 1992, pp. 13, 20.

58. Advertisement by FAIR, *Atlantic Monthly*, June 1994, p. 133; George J. Borjas, "Punish Employers, Not Children", *The New York Times*, July 11, 1996, p. A23.

59. "News Briefs", *Political Environments*, No. 3, Winter/Spring 1996, p. 45; Political Ecology Group (PEG) Immigration and Environment Campaign "Position Statement", in *Political Environments*, No. 3, Winter/Spring 1996, pp. 42–43; Immigration and Environment Campaign – Political Ecology Group (PEG) (Appendix 4).

60. Lester R. Brown, "Facing Food Insecurity", *State of the World 1994*, Washington, DC: World Watch Institute, 1994, p. 178; Lester R. Brown, "The New World Order", *State of the World 1991*, Washington, DC: World Watch Institute, 1991, pp. 13, 16; Lester R. Brown, *Full House: Reassessing the Earth's Carrying Capacity*, New York: W.W. Norton, 1994, pp. 22, 223; "10 Billion For Dinner, Please", *U.S. News and World Report*, September 12, 1994, p. 58.

61. Henry W. Kendall and David Pimentel, "Constraints on the Expansion of the Global Food Supply", *Ambio: A Journal of the Human Environment*, Royal Swedish Academy of the Sciences, 1994, pp. 198–205. The argument that population stabilization is a prerequisite to global food security is reinforced in a joint statement issued by US organizations working in the areas of population, environment, food security and women's issues prior to the Rome Food Summit in November 1996: "Population is a Food Security Issue", Johns Hopkins Center for Communication Programs, Baltimore, MD and Population Action International, Washington DC, October 1996. The Rome Declaration from the Food Summit also echoes this position: United Nations, FAO, Rome Declaration on Food Security.

62. Sherbinin "Population Issues", p. 7.

63. Population Crisis Committee, "Food and Population: Three Country Case Studies", Briefing Paper No. 18, Washington, DC, April 1987, p. 1.

64. World Bank, *World Development Report 1984*, New York: Oxford University Press, 1984, p. 51; Sherbinin, "Population Issues", p. 4.

65. UNFPA, *Population Growth and Economic Development*, Report of Consultative Meeting of Economists, New York, 1992, p. 35.

66. Ibid., pp. 35, 51, i.

67. Meadows et al., *Beyond the Limits*, p. 39.

68. Ibid., pp. 38–39; 210–211.

69. Steven W. Sinding and Sheldon Segal, "Birth-Rate News", *The New York Times*, December 19, 1991, p. A31; William K. Stevens, "Green Revolution Is Not Enough", *The New York Times*, September 6, 1994, p. C11.

70. USAID, "Stabilizing World Population Growth and Protecting Human Health: USAID's Strategy", USAID Strategy Papers, Draft, May 10, 1993 p. 29; USAID, "Strategy for Sustainable Development: An Overview", USAID Strategy Papers, Draft, May 10, 1993, p. 7; Keynote Address of J. Brian Atwood, Administrator, USAID, Meeting of the Office of Population Cooperating Agencies, Washington, DC, February 22, 1994, p. 5.

71. Cited in UNFPA, *State of the World Population 1990*, pp. 7–8.

72. UNFPA, *State of the World Population 1991*, p. 1.

73. World Bank, *World Development Report 1984*, pp. 83, 184.

74. Bryant Robey, Shea O. Rutstein and Leo Morris, "The Fertility Decline in Developing Countries", *Scientific American*, Vol. 269, No. 6, December 1993, pp. 60–68; see also William K. Stevens, "Poor Lands' Success in Cutting Birth Rate Upsets Old Theories" *The New York Times*, January 2, 1994, pp. 1, 8.

75. World Bank, Operations Evaluation Department, *Population and the World Bank: Implications from Eight Case Studies*, Washington, DC, 1992, pp. 40, 6.

76. John F. Burns, "Bangladesh, Still Poor, Cuts Birth Rate Sharply", *New York Times*, September 13, 1994, p. A10; UNFPA, *State of the World Population 1993*, pp. 49, 52; Betsy Hartmann and Hilary Standing, *The Poverty of Population Control: Family Planning and Health Policy in Bangladesh*, London: Bangladesh International Action Group, 1989, p. 67.

77. World Bank, *World Development Report 1984*, p. 109.

78. Betsy Hartmann, "Dangerous Intersections", *Political Environments*, No. 2, Summer 1995, p. 6.

79. Thomas L. Friedman, "Cold War Agency Looks at Problems Back Home", *The New York Times*, June 26, 1994, pp. 1, 18.

80. Peter J. Donaldson, *Nature Against Us: The United States and the World Population Crisis, 1965–1980*, Chapel Hill: University of North Carolina, 1990, p. 24; Office of the Press Secretary, "Remarks by the President to National Academy of Sciences", p. 2; "Administration Redefining 'National Security' Says Wirth", *Global Stewardship*, Vol. 1, No. 3, March 1994, p. 1; USAID, "Revitalizing A.I.D's Role in the Post-Cold War Era", Report of the Task Force to Reform A.I.D. Development Assistance, Draft No. 14, June 1993.

81. Thomas F. Homer-Dixon, Jeffrey H. Boutwell and George W. Rathjens, "Environmental Change and Violent Conflict", *Scientific American*, February 1993, p. 38.

82. Robert D. Kaplan, "The Coming Anarchy", *Atlantic Monthly*, February 1994, pp. 54, 58.

83. Ibid., passim; see also Sherbinin, "Population Issues", pp. 9, 11.

84. Sherbinin, "Population Issues", pp. 8–9; see also Donaldson, *Nature Against Us*, pp. 18, 24; Population Crisis Committee, "World Population Growth and Global Security", Briefing Paper No. 13, September 1983, pp. 6–7.

85. UNFPA, *State of the World Population 1993*, p. 4.

86. Cited in Sherbinin, "Population Issues", p. 13.

87. Cited in ibid., p. 5.

88. ICPD Programme of Action, p. 67; UNFPA, *State of the World Population 1993*, p. 7.

89. Howard J. Wiarda and Ieda Siqueira Wiarda, "Population, Internal Unrest, and U.S. Security in Latin America", in John Saunders, ed., *Population Growth in Latin America and U.S. National Security*, Boston: Allen and Unwin, Inc., 1986, p. 170; also cited in Sherbinin, "Population Issues", p. 8.

90. Cited in Cole, "The Anti-Immigration", p. 20; Vernon Briggs, Jr, "Political Confrontation With Economic Reality: Mass Immigration in the Post-Industrial Age", NPG Forum, *Negative Population Growth*, Washington, DC, February 1, 1990, pp. 1–5; see also George R. LaNoue, "The Demographic Premises of Affirmative Action", *Population and Environment: A Journal of Interdisciplinary Studies*", Vol. 14, No. 5, May 1993.

91. Cole, "The Anti-Immigration", p. 13; William Hamilton, "Harvest of Blame: Californians Turn on Illegal Immigrants", *The Washington Post*, June 4, 1993, pp. A1, A4.

92. FAIR, "A Legislative Agenda for U.S. Immigration Reform", n.d.

93. UNFPA, *State of the World Population 1993*, p. 16.

94. William Miller, "Major Raps Churchill Kin for Remarks on Asians", *The Boston Sunday Globe*, May 30, 1993, p. 5; Alan Riding, "New Law in France Allows Random Identity Checks", *The New York Times*, June 12, 1993, p. 2.

95. Nicholas Eberstadt, "Population Change and National Security", *Foreign Affairs*, Summer 1991, Vol. 70, No. 3, pp. 120–125.

96. Sherbinin, "Population Issues", p. 12; Population Crisis Committee, *Population Pressures – Threat to Democracy: Demographic Factors and Their Implications on Political Stability and Constitutional Government*, 1989, p. 1.

97. John R. Bermingham, Letter to the Editor, *The New York Times*, May 17, 1994, p. A18; Claudia Dreifus, "Jocelyn Elders", *New York Times Magazine*, January 30, 1994, p. 16.

98. Sherbinin, "Population Issues", p. 12; Paul Kennedy, *Preparing for the Twenty First Century*, New York: Random House, 1993, p. 34.

99. Kennedy, *Preparing*, p. 35.

100. Kaplan, "Coming Anarchy", pp. 70, 66.

101. Population Crisis Committee, "World Population Growth and Global Security", p. 3.

102. Eberstadt, "Population Change", p. 129.

103. Don Peretz, "Israeli Jews and Arabs in the Ethnic Numbers Game", *Ethnicity*, Vol.

8, No. 3, September 1981, pp. 233–255; Ruchama Marton, MD, "International Update", *The Fight for Reproductive Freedom: A Newsletter for Student Activists*, Hampshire College, Civil Liberties and Public Policy Program, Vol. VII, No. 3, Spring 1993, p. 6; Chee Heng Leng, "Babies to Order: Official Population Policies in Malaysia and Singapore", Bina Agarwal, ed., *Structures of Patriarchy: State, Community and Household in Modernising Asia*, London: Zed Books, 1988, p. 170; J. John Palen, "Population Policy: Singapore", in Godfrey Roberts, ed., *Population Policy: Contemporary Issues*, New York: Praeger, 1990, pp. 167–178.

104. Cole, "Anti-Immigration", passim.

105. Kennedy, *Preparing*, p. 46.

106. United Nations, "World Population Trends and Policies: 1987 Monitoring Report", New York, 1988, p. 33.

107. "The CIA on Youth Deficits", *Population and Development Review*, Vol. 16, No. 4, December 1989, pp. 801–807.

108. Eberstadt, "Population Change", p. 129; Jessica Mathews, "Demographic and Environmental Forces", cited in "Sources of Conflict: Highlights from the Managing Chaos Conference", *Peaceworks*, No. 4, United States Institute for Peace, Washington, DC, August 1995, p. 11.

109. Samuel P. Huntington, "The Clash of Civilizations", *Foreign Affairs*, Vol. 72, No. 3, Summer 1993, p. 32.

110. "The Red Menace is Gone: But Here is Islam' *The New York Times*, January 21, 1996, Section 4, pp. 1 and 6.

111. Kennedy, *Preparing*, pp. 45–46; see also Anthony Lake, "The Reach of Democracy", *The New York Times*, op.-ed. September 23, 1994.

112. Eberstadt, "Population Change", p. 129.

113. Gregory D. Foster, "Global Demographic Trends to the Year 2010: Implications for U.S. Security", *The Washington Quarterly*, Spring 1989, p. 6.

114. Kennedy, *Preparing*, p. 46.

115. Zbigniew Brezinski, *Out of Control: Global Turmoil on the Eve of of the Twenty First Century*, New York: Charles Scribner and Sons, 1993, pp. 51–52; de Sherbinin, "Population Issues", p. 15.

116. Kennedy, *Preparing*, p. 343; see also Sherbinin, "Foreign Policy", p. 15; Ben J. Wattenberg, *Birth Dearth*, New York: Pharos Books, 1987.

117. Sultana Kamal, "Seizure of Reproductive Rights? A Discussion on Population Control in the Third World and the Emergence of New Reproductive Technologies in the West", in Patricia Spallone and Deborah Lynn Steinberg, eds, *Made to Order: The Myth of Reproductive and Genetic Progress*, Oxford: Pergamon Press, 1987, pp. 146–153.

118. Michael S. Teitelbaum and Jay M. Winter, *The Fear of Population Decline*, New York: Academic Press, 1985; Kingsley Davis, Mikhail S. Bernstam, and Rita Ricardo-Campbell, eds, *Below Replacement Fertility in Industrial Societies: Causes, Consequences, Policies*, Cambridge: Cambridge University Press, 1987; Jan M. Hoem, "Social Policy and Recent Fertility Change in Sweden", *Population and Development Review*, Vol. 16, No. 4, December 1990, pp. 735–748.

119. Okuda Yuki, "A Move to Outlaw All Abortions – Revision of the Eugenic Protection Act", *Asian Women's Liberation*, No. 2, 1980, p. 4.

120. United Nations Economic and Social Council, Report of the European Population Conference, Geneva, March 23–26, 1993, p. 7 (Item 4 of the Provisional Agenda); see also United Nations, Report of the ICPD, p. 35.

121. Paul R. Ehrlich, *The Population Bomb*, New York: Ballantine Books, 1968, p. 16; see also Alfred Sauvy, "The World Population Problem: A View in 1949", *Population and Development Review*, Vol. 16, No. 4, December 1990, p. 765.

122. Nafis Sadik, "Investing in Women: The Focus for the 90s", UNFPA, New York, n.d., p. 13.

123. UNFPA, *Women, Population and the Environment*, March 1992, p. 2.

124. World Resources Institute, Washington, DC, *World Resources, 1994–1995*, New

York: Oxford University Press, 1994, Chap. 3, pp. 43, 47, 51.

125. Population Crisis Committee, "Country Rankings on the Status of Women – Poor, Pregnant and Powerless", *Briefing Paper*, No. 20, 1988.

126. UNFPA, "Food for the Future: Women, Population and Food Security", New York, 1996, pp. 1, 14.

127. UNFPA, *State of the World Population 1993*, p. 27.

128. Susan Forbes Martin, "Women Refugees Face Special Health Problems", *People*, IPPF, Vol. 18, No. 4, 1991, pp. 13–14.

129. United Nations, ICPD Programme of Action, p. 98.

130. *Earth Negotiations Bulletin*, Vol. 6, No. 33, September 14, 1994, International Institute for Sustainable Development, p. 12.

131. United Nations, Beijing Platform for Action, Chap. VI.

132. ESCAP (Economic and Social Commission for Asia-Pacific) *Population Headliners*, No. 232, July 1994, p. 4; "UK Wants Democratic Decision in Cairo", *ICPD Special Issue*, ICPD Secretariat, August 1994, pp. 4–5; "Australia Plans Increase in Population Funding", ESCAP, *Population Headliners*, No. 230, May 1994, p. 8.

133. Thalif Deen, "World Bank Cash Exists for Population Projects", *Terra Viva*, IPS-ICPD Issue, September 7, 1994, p. 3; *WIDLINE*, World Bank, Population and Human Resources Department, No. 4, May 1992, p. 2.

134. Lynch, "UN Population Efforts under Question", *The Boston Sunday Globe*, June 16, 1996, p. 6.

135. UNFPA, *State of the World Population 1994*, p. 1.

136. United Nations, ICPD Programme of Action; see also Asoka Bandarage, "Statement on Women, Population and the Environment", presented at the NGO Forum on the ICPD, Bureau for Refugee Programs, US Department of State, Washington, DC, April 29, 1993, reprinted in *Hunger Notes*, Issue on "Population: Broadening the Debate", Vol. 19, No. 4, Spring 1994, p. 10.

137. Robert B. Wallace, "Might Access to Credit for Poor Women Help Reduce Population Growth and Environment Degradation?", *Conservation Digest*, Washington, DC, Vol. 3, No. 1, February 1991, p. 8; see also Jael Silliman, "Women, Population, and Development", *Conservation Digest*, Vol. 3, No. 1, February 1991, p. 3.

138. "Collective Declaration on Development and Economic Issues from the Cairo NGO Forum 1994", United Nations, September 12, 1994; Sue Tibballs, "Northern Governments Hiding Behind the Cairo Agenda", *Terra Viva*, IPS-ICPD Issue, September 12, 1994, p. 11; Fawzy Mansour, "World Overpopulation or an Overpowering World Order?" *Al-Ahram*, Cairo, Egypt, ICPD Extra, September 8–14, 1994, p. 5; Evelyn Hong, "ICPD Under Fire for Sidelining Development Issues", *Third World Resurgence*, No. 50, 1994, p. 18.

2

Politics of Global Population Control

Contraception has the potential to contribute greatly to human health and welfare. It allows greater control over timing and spacing of births and prevention of early first births which can be detrimental to maternal and child health. The timing of the first birth in particular can have a lifelong socio-economic impact on mothers. Prevention of early first births allows women to gain valuable educational and employment experience necessary to succeed in the modern world.[1] However, contraception also has the potential to be harmful to health and welfare, especially of women, if it is promoted and used without regard to safety and ethical considerations. These concerns and a broader assessment of the practices of neo-Malthusian population control are the subjects of this chapter.

In the US, birth control emerged as a radical social movement led by socialists and feminists in the early twentieth century. The anarchist Emma Goldman promoted birth control not only as a woman's right and worker's right, but also as a means to sexual freedom outside of conventional marriage. However, as birth control became increasingly medicalized and associated with science and corporate control, the radicals lost their leadership of the birth control movement to professional experts, mostly male doctors, by the 1920s. As a result, birth control, which refers to voluntary and individual choice in control of reproduction, became transformed into population control, that is, a political movement by dominant groups to control the reproduction of socially subordinate groups.[2]

During the influx of new immigrants in the 1920s and 1930s and during the Depression when the ranks of the unemployed were swelling, eugenicist ideology and programs for immigration control and social engineering gained much ground among the ruling classes in the US. The rational scientific guise of eugenics allowed intellectuals – including some socialists and anarchists – to attribute social problems like unemployment and poverty to 'heredity' and to call for controlling 'breeding' among the 'genetically unfit' as the solution to those problems.[3] Many privileged women sought birth control for themselves as a route to higher education and careers. However, they wanted poor women to adopt birth control so that they and their families would not become a drain on the state and charity of the rich. Even the birth control pioneer Margaret Sanger and suffragists like Julia Ward and Ida Husted Harper surrendered to ruling-class interests and eugenics calling for birth control among the poor, Blacks and immigrants as a means for counteracting the declining birth rates of native-born whites.[4]

Influenced by eugenicist thinking, 26 states in the US passed compulsory sterilization laws and thousands of persons, mostly poor and Black, deemed 'unfit' were prevented from reproducing. By the 1940s, eugenicist and birth control interests in the US were so thoroughly intertwined "as to be almost indistinguishable".[5] Eugenic sterilizations were also carried out throughout Canada.[6]

Racism and science converged in producing eugenic sterilizations and exterminations in Nazi Germany. As medical historian Paul Weindling has observed, "demography and racial surveys of populations were preconditions for the Holocaust".[7] Nazi atrocities discredited eugenics. But eugenic beliefs and policies did not disappear in the post-World War II period when population in the Third World experienced an unprecedented and phenomenal increase.

Third World demographic transition

Much of neo-Malthusian policy making today is directed towards fitting the Third World into the model of demographic transition derived from the historical experience of European countries. According to the demographic transition theory, all countries pass through four distinct stages of demographic evolution: in the first, pre-industrial stage, both birth and death rates are high and population growth is slow, if not static; in the second stage, death rates fall due to technological and social improvements, but as birth rates remain high, a 'population explosion' takes place; in the third stage, birth rates fall due to socio-economic changes and population expansion slows down; in the fourth stage, both birth and death rates are low and population is stable or moves below replacement level (see Figure 3:1).[8]

According to neo-Malthusian demographers, in the Third World, the second stage of the demographic transition, that is, rapid decline in mortality, was achieved through technological imports, such as antibiotics, immunization and insecticides, rather than socio-economic development. Accordingly, the third stage in the demographic transition, that is, fertility decline in the Third World, can similarly be achieved through bio-medical management rather than improvements in standards of living.[9]

Apparently, contraceptive use in the 'developing world' has increased from less than 10% of couples in reproductive age in the 1960s to more than 50% (42% excluding China) in the 1990s. Neo-Malthusians attribute rapidly falling birth rates in the Third World to the 'contraceptive revolution' represented by expanding use of modern contraceptives.[10] However, as we discuss in subsequent chapters, other theorists attribute fertility decline largely to socio-economic development rather than family planning.[11]

Population control advocates insist that the 'contraceptive revolution' has been achieved through purely voluntary measures and that coercive methods that some advocates once thought necessary have not had to be used.[12] However, a closer look at the history and current strategies of population control reveals widespread abuses and human rights violations.

The 'Contraceptive Revolution'

From the dominant western perspective, contraceptive delivery appears to be the simplest, quickest and easiest solution to Third World problems. It allows external institutions to intervene without much attention to local socio-economic situations and cultures. Some population control zealots, like Reimer Ravenholt, MD, who headed the USAID Office of Population between 1967 and 1980, took this position to an extreme, arguing that "ordering contraceptives is like ordering bullets for a war. You don't want to run out." Indeed, military metaphors that 'declare war', 'target' and 'attack' 'overpopulation' with an 'arsenal' of new drugs have become the standard language of global population control.[13]

However, given its political sensitivity, the US government has tried to hide its direct involvement in population control whenever possible. Since the late 1960s, the US has sought to pass on the leadership of international population control to multilateral institutions such as the UNFPA and the World Bank. A primary reason for this was to "minimize charges of an imperialist motivation behind its support of population activities", particularly the Third World charge that US population programs sought to "limit the growth only of nonwhite populations".[14]

Although the role of multilateral organizations in international family planning has greatly expanded since the 1960s, the US and other governments in the North have continued to dominate these institutions through funding and political influence. The World Bank uses its leverage over finance, especially structural adjustment loans (SALs), to impose strong population control policies on the Third World. In Senegal, for instance, the Bank has required that the government adopt a Population Policy and Action Plan containing 60 measures of action, including explicit targets, as a condition for receiving adjustment loans.[15] As a result of such policies, governments in the South, let alone individual women and men, have not been able to exercise much influence in developing birth control solutions more appropriate to their own needs.

Today, global population control constitutes a vast establishment of governmental and non-governmental organizations whose financial, technological and ideological power emanates from Washington, DC, and New York to the far corners of the Third World. Within individual countries, this hierarchical model is reproduced, with control spreading from rulers in capital cities to professionals and elites in regions, communities and villages. (In India alone, there are an estimated 250,000 family planning workers.) Poor women are at the very bottom of the population control pyramid: they are the ultimate objects of numerical targets, economic incentives/disincentives and 'high-tech' contraceptives which are the quick-fix solutions to the problem of 'overpopulation' (Figure 2.1).[16]

Numerical targets

From its inception, global population control has relied on numerical targets. In 1989, the Amsterdam Declaration, adopted by governments and NGOs worldwide, set a global contraceptive prevalence target of 56% (for married women of childbearing age) to be achieved by the year 2000. Seeking to reduce population growth rates within the shortest time possible, the UNFPA increased this target to 59% in 1991, which would mean more than 2 billion male and female contraceptive users by the end of the century.[17]

Departing from earlier positions and upholding voluntary choice in family size, the 1994 ICPD Programme of Action states that demographic goals in the form of targets and quotas for the recruitment of clients should not be imposed on family planning providers and expresses disapproval of the use of incentives and disincentives. It acknowledges the setting of demographic goals as a legitimate subject of state development strategies to be "defined in terms of unmet needs for family planning information and services". But, as human rights and health activists concerned with abuses in family planning programs point out, there is still a long way to go in establishing policies and ethical standards to ensure that these objectives are achieved.[18]

Despite the ICPD position, many Third World family planning programs have not disavowed demographic targets. Nigeria's target is to reduce fertility from 6.5 children per woman in the 1980–1985 period, to 4.0 by the year 2000; Nepal's target for the same duration is a reduction from 6.1 to 2.5; India's a reduction from 3.9 to 2.1; and Tunisia's from 3.4 to 1.15.[19]

From health ministries and family planning bureaucracies of capital cities, targets continue to be extended to districts, villages (also to workplaces in China) and individuals, mostly poor women. Contraceptive prevalence targets are usually set for different methods, with greater emphasis on recruiting acceptors for long-term methods with the greatest emphasis on female sterilization. In some family planning programs, as in India and China, health workers are often assigned specific quotas of contraceptive

67

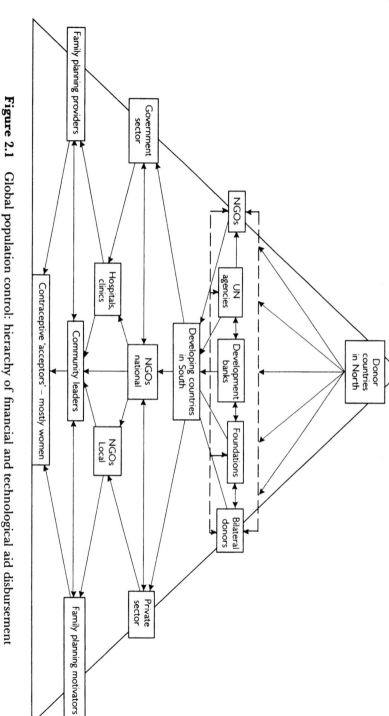

Figure 2.1 Global population control: hierarchy of financial and technological aid disbursement

Source. Adapted partly from Figure 2 in Jennifer Zeitlin, Ramesh Govindaraj and Lincoln C. Chen, "Financing Reproductive and Sexual Health Services", in Gita Sen, Adrienne Germaine and Lincoln C. Chen, eds, *Population Policies Reconsidered: Health, Empowerment, and Rights*, Cambridge, MA: Harvard University Press, 1994, p. 243.

Table 2.1   Contraceptive users by method, 1989 (% distribution)

Method	Developed countries	Developing countries	World
Female sterilization	10	33	26
Male sterilization	5	12	10
IUD	8	24	19
Hormonal pills	20	12	15
Condom	19	6	10
Hormonal injectables	–	2	1
Vaginal barrier methods	3	1	2
Rhythm	13	5	7
Withdrawal	20	3	8
Other methods	2	3	2
Total	100	101	100

Source: United Nations, 1989, as cited in Mahmoud F. Fathalla, "Fertility Control Technology: A Woman-Centered Approach to Research", in Gita Sen, Adrienne Germaine and Lincoln C. Chen, eds, *Population Policies Reconsidered: Health, Empowerment, and Rights*, Cambridge, MA: Harvard University Press, 1994, p. 226.

acceptors they must win on an annual, monthly, weekly and in some cases even a daily basis.[20]

Notwithstanding massive spending and extensive family planning promotion over three decades, many poor people in the Third World are still reluctant to use modern contraception. As we discuss in Chapter 4, the attitudes and need for children among the poor are often quite different from that of family planning enthusiasts. Even when poor people use modern contraceptives, their continuation rates are often low due to lack of access to health care, side-effects of contraceptives, and socio-economic and cultural reasons.[21] Given this reality and their urgency to meet targets, population control programs have increasingly resorted to the use of economic incentives and disincentives as well as highly effective, provider-controlled, female methods. These features are clearly evident in the case of sterilization, the one method that is irreversible.

Sterilization

Sterilization (male and female) accounts for 36% of contraceptive use worldwide: 15% in the 'developed' world and an astonishing 45% in the 'developing' world (Table 2.1). Exceptionally high rates of sterilization prevail among contraceptive users in some countries: 85.5% in Nepal; 69.7% in India; 66.1% in the Dominican Republic; 49.2% in China; 47.9% in Sri Lanka; 44.0% in Brazil; 41.3% in Thailand; 37.7% in Mexico.[22]

Although male sterilization (vasectomy) is a much simpler operation than female sterilization (tubectomy), female sterilization is the most favored method of family planners and the most widely used method of fertility control in the world. In 1990, 46.8% of married women of childbearing age in Puerto Rico, 36.8% in China, 31.4% in Sri Lanka, 31.3% in India, 30.4% in Brazil and 30.4% in Thailand were sterilized.[23] Female sterilization constitute 33% and male sterilization 12% of all contraceptive use in the developing countries (Table 2.1)

In terms of the numbers, sterilization is an increasing success and for many women and men in the North and the South it represents a choice to be free of biological reproduction. But closer examination of conditions under which most women have consented to be sterilized shows that sterilization abuse is a pervasive problem for poor women. While outright force has been used on some occasions, in most cases the abuses involved are more subtle. They stem from poverty and adverse social conditions, including lack of information and access to other methods of birth control, threats of discontinued social benefits and economic constraints.[24]

Sterilization abuse in the US

Sterilization has long been a strategy of eugenic population control in the US. In the 1950s and 1960s, white women in the US were still fighting for the right to have access to voluntary sterilization while many women of color were being sterilized without their consent and often their knowledge. In the United States, people as diverse as Margaret Sanger, H.L. Mencken and William Shockley have also suggested bonus schemes and monetary incentives for sterilization.[25]

Although these suggestions did not become law, there has been a long history of doctors and welfare officials coercing poor women to undergo sterilization in order to receive welfare payments. Involuntary sterilization of poor women and women of color was widespread in Department of Health, Education and Welfare-funded birth control clinics from the late 1960s to the mid-1970s. The Social Security Act of 1966, which made sterilizations widely available to Medicaid recipients, in conjuction with pre-existing eugenic sterilization laws, gave impetus to doctors and welfare officials to seek indiscriminate sterilizations of women on welfare. One doctor, Clovis Pierce, a former army physician and the sole obstetrician in the small town of Aiken, South Carolina, in the early 1970s, "consistently sterilized Medicaid recipients with more than two children", collecting some $60,000 of taxpayers' money for the sterilizations he performed.[26]

The justifications used for punitive sterilizations of poor women in the past as in the present are both economic ("rising costs of welfare services") and moral ("alarming rise in the rate of illegitimacy").[27] According to estimates of 1979, out of a total of 800,000 Native Americans, as much as 42% of women of reproductive age and 10% of the men were sterilized.[28]

Well-established liberal feminist organizations in the US like the National Abortion Rights Action League (NARAL) and the National Organization of Women (NOW) chose not to join the struggle for stricter federal sterilization guidelines led by more radical feminist organizations like the Committee to End Sterilization Abuse (CESA) and (The Committee for Abortion Rights and Against Sterilization Abuse (CARASA) in the 1970s. Not only were liberal feminists narrowly focused on abortion and individual choice, but they also did not want to lose the financial and political support of the population control organizations which opposed sterilization reforms. However, in so doing, white, liberal feminist groups not only distanced themselves from the interests of poor women of color, who suffered most due to sterilization abuse, but they also provided political space for 'pro-life' groups to appear as champions of sterilization reform and women's concerns.[29]

Federal sterilization guidelines passed in 1974 and 1978 helped reduce sterilization abuses of poor women, especially Medicaid patients. Still, due to the absence of mechanisms to enforce those regulations, sterilization abuses of poor women and women of color have persisted. In the context of continued government funding of sterilizations of Medicaid recipients, the cut-off of Medicaid funds for abortion (by the 1977 Hyde Amendment) resulted in sterilization becoming the most readily available fertility control method for poor women in the US.[30]

In the current political climate in the US, where welfare and child support are being severely slashed and fertility control is being promoted for economic and punitive purposes, sterilization abuses could increase taking new and diverse forms. An example is the controversial 'fetal protection policies' introduced by some US employers like Johnson Control Company which led some women to have themselves sterilized in order to protect their jobs. Later, some of those women won a law suit against Johnson Control for violating their reproductive rights.[31]

Sterilization abuses, especially eugenicist sterilizations, also exist in other countries of the industrialized North. Britain and Germany still require involuntary sterilization of the 'disabled' and the 'mentally incompetent'.[32] If sterilization abuses continue in the Northern industrialized countries where regulations and legal recourse generally exist, it is not hard to imagine how pervasive abuses could be in the South where such guidelines are rare and where poverty is rampant.

Sterilization abuse in the Third World

Targets and economic incentives/disincentives have defined the operation of many Third World population control programs from their inception. In other realms of social policy targets and incentives are not inappropriate.

But the pressure to meet targets and the offer of economic incentives in family planning programs have resulted in a highly techno-bureaucratic and monetarist approach obsessed with numbers of acceptors and financial rewards. Within such a quantitative approach, the complex psychological and sociological dimensions of sexuality and reproduction are easily overlooked.

Not only do poor people lack all relevant information, but, in many cases, the desperation of poverty drives them to agree to accept contraception or sterilization in return for payments in cash or kind. In such situations, choice simply does not exist. Direct force has reportedly been used in population control efforts in some countries, including China, India, Bangladesh and Indonesia.[33] However, coercion does not pertain simply to the outright use of force. More subtle forms of coercion arise when individual reproductive decisions are tied to sources of survival like the availability of food, shelter, employment, education, health care, and so on.

Since September 1988, when the new Brazilian Constitution granted 120 days maternity leave to female workers, many employers have been asking for certificates of sterilization from women employees so as to avoid providing maternity benefits. In a context of high unemployment and economic pressure, women have little choice but to get sterilized or lose their jobs. As Brazilian reproductive rights activist Sonia Corrêa has shown, in Brazil, sterilizations have tended to increase with the deepening of the foreign debt and cut-backs in public services and social programs. About 70% of female sterilizations are performed in public hospitals or are financed through welfare. In some of the poorest Black communities in northeastern Brazil, for example Maranhão state, 80% of the women are sterilized.[34]

While incentives are also used in population programs in other countries of the South, it is in Asia that they are most elaborate and routine. As Stephen Isaacs from the Columbia University School of Public Health has elaborated, practically all family planning programs in Asia supplement the salaries of family planning providers – physicians, nurses, paramedical staff and family planning recruiters. Payments to providers range from a certain amount per sterilization to additional monthly stipends. Payments in cash or kind are given to acceptors of different methods, especially sterilization. In most cases, these payments are justified as 'compensation' for wages lost, transportation and other incidental expenses.[35] In some countries, especially China, economic and social benefits are provided for families under a specified size, and in some cases rewards are given to communities that meet or exceed national population reduction targets.[36]

In the following pages, we shall take a brief look at some of the controversies associated with the use of targets and incentives in population control programs in Bangladesh, India and China. As Bangladesh is often cited as a population control success story, the historical basis of its success needs close examination. The experiences of India and China also deserve close examination. They are the world's most populous countries (935.7 million in India and 1.2 billion people in China in mid-1995) and their experiences with sterilization have global implications.

Bangladesh

Following Independence, population control was declared to be the number one priority of Bangladesh. The first Five Year Plan (1973–1978) stated that "no civilized measure would be too drastic to keep (the) population on the smaller side of 15 crores (150 million) for sheer ecological survival of the nation". However, concerned that the government's efforts were not effective enough, USAID, the World Bank and UNFPA pressured Bangladesh to take strong actions to meet national population control objectives 'on time'.[37]

Being heavily dependent on foreign aid, the military government of Bangladesh responded to donor pressure. In 1983, the government increased economic incentives for sterilization acceptors and disincentives against family planning workers failing to meet their monthly sterilization targets. It also equalized sterilization payments for both men and women at TK 175 (until then payments for men were lower). Women acceptors were also given a sari worth Rs.100 and men a lungi worth Rs.50. Violating the 1982/83 US Foreign Assistance Act which prohibits use of US funds as incentives for sterilization, USAID financed 85% of the sterilization incentives and referral fees as part of a $25 million annual contribution to the Bangladesh family planning program during the early 1980s.[38]

After the incentive payments were increased, the number of sterilizations in Bangladesh increased dramatically. Between the 1982–1983 period and the 1983–1984 period, vasectomies increased from 88,000 to 214,000 and tubectomies from 275,000 to 334,000.[39] However, a number of reports by international and Bangladesh reproductive rights activists as well as a World Bank-sponsored 1987 study on compensation payments have revealed that the Bangladesh incentive program resulted in a wide range of abuses and human rights violations.[40] Sterilization 'acceptors' were overwhelmingly poor people for whom a 'major reason' for undergoing sterilization was the compensation payment. This is further borne out by the fact that the number of sterilizations performed increased between the 'lean inter-harvest period' when employment and money were both scarce.[41]

The lack of choice inherent in this link between poverty and sterilization was accentuated by the manner in which the sterilization program was implemented. As reproductive rights activists Betsy Hartmann and Hillary Standing have noted, the clinical conditions under which the sterilizations were carried out were extremely poor and post-operative care was non-existent in most cases. Under the incentive schemes, a sterilization acceptor merely represented an additional number for the profiteers; after the operation, they served no useful purpose. Even the saris and lungis given to sterilization 'acceptors', which were justified as 'surgical apparel', were handed out only after the operation was performed![42]

Some poor people did not even receive the compensation promised them. Emergency food assistance was promised by some local officials working within the Vulnerable Group Feeding Program (VGF) in exchange for sterilization, but some of the desperately poor who underwent the operation were denied the wheat or other promised benefits by corrupt officials.[43] Apparently in one poor tribal community the army carried out forced sterilizations of women with more than three children after making them sign 'informed consent' papers.[44]

Referral payments also resulted in fostering a large array of unofficial, self-employed agents specializing in recruiting sterilization acceptors among poor, uninformed people. Some were not even told that sterilization is an irreversible procedure. As the World Bank studies on compensation payments later admitted, these agents pushed sterilization at the expense of other contraceptive methods, thus violating the principles of informed consent and reproductive choice.[45]

Despite these problems, the UNFPA resident Director in Bangladesh, Walter Holzhausen ,supported sterilization payments. In a confidential letter written to then Deputy Director General of the UNFPA, Nafis Sadik, in 1984, Holzhausen argued that the issue of human rights in family planning calls for different interpretations in different countries. He suggested that in some situations 'drastic actions' that may be considered as 'infringement' of human rights may have to be used in the interest of population control. He claimed that donors need to adopt a more lenient interpretation of the concept of voluntarism in promoting family planning in countries like Bangladesh.[46]

However, owing to widespread abuses and agitation by the Bangladesh International Action Group and threats to withdraw funding by donors such as the Swedish International Development Association (SIDA), the World Bank commissioned the earlier mentioned study on compensation payments in Bangladesh. The report of this study affirmed that the main reason for the strong "link between poverty and sterilization" was the "attraction of the compensation payment".[47] It also noted that among sterilization 'acceptors' interviewed, sterilization regret was highest among the very poor and the illiterate, who were induced to accept sterilization through offers of incentives. Of women interviewed, one-quarter who had been sterilized when they had only two children later regretted their decision. Ten percent of the women in the rural sample study had experienced the death of a child since sterilization, an experience which underlines ethical dilemmas in promoting sterilization in a country with high levels of infant and child mortality.[48]

Despite the presence of coercive elements, the World Bank study recommended the continuation of incentive payments on the ground that they have been proven successful in motivating the poor to be sterilized. Nevertheless, partly due to the World Bank report, referral payments to providers were stopped. In 1987 USAID withdrew from directly funding payments to sterilization acceptors, thereby shifting the responsibility of incentive payments on to the Bangladesh government. In 1988, the government also decided to discontinue payments to family planning referrers.[49]

The decision to continue payments to sterilization clients was accepted by Britain, the Netherlands and Norway, who were among the donors who had initially called for the World Bank study. They concurred with the Bank study that abolition of payments would "discriminate" against the poor by "raising a financial barrier". However, as Hartmann and Standing have pointed out, this narrowly defined concept of choice completely overlooks the fact that the poor are also "discriminated against in their access to reversible methods of contraception, to medical care and to education and training, because of cost".[50]

According to 1990 estimates, 34.0% of all contraceptive users were still relying on sterilization, although the World Bank has argued that sterilization rates in Bangladesh have declined in recent years.[51] Nevertheless, the Bangladesh 'success' in population control continues to be built on violations of women's rights and health and economic needs of the poor. Basic health care and women's choices continue to be neglected.[52] Indeed, as discussed in Chapter 1, the goal of the population control establishment is not socio-economic development, but the achievement of the demographic transition without social transformation in poor countries like Bangladesh. In India, too, aggressive family planning has pursued a similar course.

India

During the Emergency Rule imposed by Indira Gandhi in 1975, when civil liberties were suspended and all 'development' efforts were subordinated to population control interests, sterilization practices became unprecedentedly brutal. During the Emergency, population control became virtually "the dominant component of *all* government departments rather than the primary responsibility of the health and medical authorities" (emphasis in original).[53]

As Davidson Gwatkin, Marika Vicziany, and other analysts of the Emergency have observed, the techniques used during the Emergency in India, such as targets and incentives, were not new: rather it was the vigor with which they were used that was the novelty. School teachers, labor contractors, agricultural extension workers, and so on, were all made to give priority to meeting family planning targets over carrying out their normal work responsibilities. Central government financial assistance to state governments was made partly conditional on family planning performance and state governments were permitted to enact and implement compulsory sterilization.[54]

In terms of sheer numbers, the sterilization program under the Emergency was a great success. In the 1975–1976 period, when population control was most vigorously pursued, more than 8 million sterilizations took place. However, the single-minded pursuit of numbers led to the removal of all 'logical and ethical constraints' in the use of force. Most of the sterilizations carried out were vasectomies; the men rounded up for sterilization were almost always poor and many died from infections associated with the mass sterilizations. According to a subsequent Commission of Inquiry appointed by the government, the sterilization program under the Emergency resulted in 1,774 deaths around the country.[55]

Despite critical press coverage of sterilization abuses during the Emergency, international population control agencies and advocates upheld the Indian government's efforts. During the Fifth Five Year Plan of the Indian government (1974–1979), allocations for family planning increased, with the leading donors, the UNFPA, the World Bank and SIDA, continuing their support. Dr. Joseph van Arendonk of the UNFPA, who went to India to investigate the situation in 1976, concluded that forced sterilizations did not exist "except for a few abuses" and Robert McNamara, chief of the World Bank and population control enthusiast who was visiting India at the time, applauded "the political will and determination shown by the leadership at the highest level in intensifying the family planning drive with a rare courage of conviction". Paul Ehrlich also upheld the Indian sterilization effort under the Emergency. Arguing that it was "coercion in a good cause", he said that "we should have volunteered logistic support in the form of helicopters, vehicles and surgical instruments". In 1983, during her second term of office, Prime Minister Indira Gandhi (along with China's Family Planning Minister Qian Xinzhong) was given the United Nations award for "the most outstanding contribution to the awareness of population questions".[56]

However, resistance to the forced sterilization program was widespread in India and it became an important factor in bringing down the first Indira Gandhi government in 1977. The sterilization program became as unpopular as it did because it targeted mostly men. In a highly patriarchal and predominantly agricultural society where male status is derived from the control of women and offspring, forced vasectomies were a direct assault on male authority. Consequently, under the subsequent Janata Party government, the family planning program was given a new name – the family welfare program. Direct forms of compulsion were eliminated and the program came to concentrate on the politically more acceptable strategy of female sterilization.

Since 1977–1978, female sterilizations have sharply increased, constituting over 80% of all sterilizations carried out in India. Factors behind this situation include: the higher 'compensation' paid to women – now approximately $24 as opposed to the $15 paid to men; women's greater need for birth control; promotion of sterilization at the expense of non-terminal methods in family planning programs; and women's social subordination and poverty. For a poor woman leading a hand-to-mouth existence, the $24 payment (from the government) for sterilization is hard to resist, especially during times of drought or famine.[57] But, as in the case of Bangladesh discussed earlier, the coupling of incentives and targets has given rise to sterilization abuses and violation of human rights.

Sterilization targets sent down from Delhi and continuing pressures exerted by superiors has led to a race among health care workers to meet their targets as quickly as possible. Use of targets has resulted in frequent over-reporting of contraceptive acceptance rates and other fraudulent practices. For example, some health workers eager to meet their targets and collect their fees have recruited the same person for sterilization several times or sent both husband and wife or old men and post-menopausal women for sterilization.[58]

A recent example of coercion associated with sterilization comes from the Lingaredipalli village in Andhra Pradesh, where people allocated land were not allowed to harvest unless they underwent sterilization. Those refusing surgery apparently had flags placed in their fields.[59] As village midwives are absorbed into family planning programs, they begin to concentrate on winning sterilization acceptors rather than providing basic health care services to women and their families. In their research in Uttar Pradesh, India, anthropologist Patricia Jeffery and colleagues found that auxiliary nurse midwives no longer routinely visit pregnant or lactating women or attend deliveries; they only come to persuade women to be sterilized. Given the higher incentives attached to sterilization, midwives do not always inform women of non-terminal methods.[60] A reporter from the West, Elizabeth Bumiller, found a similar situation in the villages of Gujarat she visited.[61] The result is increasing distrust and manipulation in the relationship between clients and health providers and violations of the principles of informed consent and choice.

'Target fever' has given rise to the emergence of 'speed doctors' competing against each other to increase the pace with which they can perform sterilizations. Dr S.P. Khandawala, general secretary of the Indian Association of Gynecological Endoscopists, has expressed alarm about 'speed doctors' performing 300 to 500 female laparoscopic sterilizations in 10 hours in a single day, when, according to him, even if one does not get tired, the maximum possible is only 50.[62] An Indian gynecologist, P.V. Mehta, has even entered the *Guinness Book of World Records* for sterilizing more than 350,000 women in one decade. Dr Mehta boasts that he can do up to 40 sterilizations in one hour and that women can go home after two hours and work in the fields the following day. Dr Mehta is celebrated by the international population control establishment for "quality, non-coercive female sterilization".[63]

However, evidence shows that mass sterilizations in India are performed under unhygienic and sometimes dangerous conditions leading to debilitating effects on women. An Indian newspaper reported in 1988 that in a sterilization camp in Rajasthan an ordinary bicycle pump was used to pump air into women's bodies. Forty-four women had died from operations at this camp in the two years prior to the newspaper report. The documentary film *Something Like a War*, produced by Dheepa Dhanraj, portrays the dismal conditions under which sterilizations are performed.[64] Upon seeing mass sterilization camps in India first hand, Elisabeth Bumiller, an advocate of population control, was moved to comment:

> Before I saw [the] ... laparascopy camp, it was easy for me to sit in New Delhi and think that part of the answer to India's population problem was to sterilize more people. But, once I saw the operation for myself, my reaction was that treating women as if they were cattle could not possibly be the most humane or even the most effective method of population control.[65]

Sterilized women rarely have access to post-operative care and many are unable to return to their hard physical labor for months after the operation. A random survey of a family planning project funded by the British Overseas Development Administration in a slum resettlement project in Viskhapatnam, India, found that some women had not fully recovered from post-operative side-effects even three years after the operation. For many women, disabilities from sterilization meant destitution since temporary work requiring hard physical labor was the only employment available to most people in the area.[66]

If recent population policy recommendations in India are illustrative of developments to be expected in the twenty-first century, there is much to fear from increased use of coercive strategies and human rights violations. The draft national population policy of the Expert National Committee appointed by the Indian government recommends use of extensive economic disincentives and pressures to help bring down the birth rate. These include: restricting the number of children in order to qualify as candidates for contesting elections and employment in the organized sector; barring those entering child marriages from employment in the organized sector; and using the army and paramilitary forces in population control efforts.

Twelve leading women's groups have sent a joint letter to the Expert Committee demanding that it disassociate itself from these recommendations. However, there are powerful international actors behind the new Indian population policy. It is sponsored by the World Bank and pressures of economic liberalization and IMF/World Bank conditionalities are some of the factors pushing the Indian government to drastic actions to achieve population stabilization.[67]

In a June 1995 report on family planning, the World Bank calls on the Indian government to shift from numerical targets and incentives towards a more client-centered approach as defined by the ICPD Programme of Action. This is a laudable change. But, as we discuss later in this chapter, this new reproductive health approach still does not address the problems of poverty that underlie disease and maternal mortality in the country.[68]

China

The goal of Chinese population control policy is not zero population growth but negative population growth. In 1979 the Chinese government set a target to reduce average fertility to one child per couple and to bring down the country's population, then about 1 billion, to 700 million by 2070. To achieve the one-child family, the government introduced an elaborate system of incentives, including priority in housing, health subsidy, extra work points, bonuses, additional maternity leave and old age subsidies for the parents, and free medical care, priority in schooling, university enrolment and employment for the single child. In the rural areas, single children were also given an adult grain ration and an extra large plot of land for the private use of the family. An elaborate system of disincentives were also introduced to deter couples from having more than one child, including denial of additional housing space, extra plots of land, promotions, bonuses, medical and educational expenses. Parents having an 'excess' child or children were required to pay back benefits given to the first child and pay levies amounting to between 5 and 10% of their total income for 10 to 16 years.[69]

However, as incentives and disincentives were not sufficient to enforce China's stringent policy, the government has established an efficient and widespread 'reproductive policing operation' in all family and work units of the society. In China childbearing is a publicly controlled decision with publicly enforced consequences. Women cannot have children without official authorization and tremendous pressures are placed on them not to have more than one child. Although the Chinese government has denied use of compulsion in its efforts to enforce the one-child family policy, there are reports of various types of force placed on women. Forced abortions usually take place in the countryside and forced sterilizations usually take place immediately after a woman has given birth.[70] In 1988 the one-child policy was 'relaxed' in many rural areas, allowing parents to try for another child if the first was a girl.

A major aspect of forced sterilizations in China is eugenic sterilizations of those labelled 'mentally retarded'. A number of provinces in China have adopted eugenic laws since 1988 requiring sterilizations of the 'mentally retarded' who wish to be married. The justification commonly given is that by 'raising the quality of the population', poverty could be eradicated.[71]

Owing largely to criticisms from abroad, the eugenic sterilization program in Gansu Province was temporarily suspended in 1991. However, since then, eugenic sterilizations laws have been extended to five other provinces. A new family law effective since January 1995 forbids couples carrying serious genetic diseases to have children. Such laws are open to grave abuses and corruption in a highly authoritarian society such as China. People who may be considered simply neurotic or idiosyncratic in other societies could easily be classified as mentally 'deficient' and 'retarded' and forcibly sterilized if they wish to marry. The pressures placed on local officials to meet their family planning quotas could exacerbate the dangers inherent in such a situation.[72]

Eugenic sterilization seems also to be an aspect of genocide and the cultural destruction of Tibet. Population transfer and settlement of ethnic Chinese in Chinese-occupied Tibet has already led to Tibetans becoming a minority in their own land. Owing to the closed-door policy in Tibet, the atrocities of the population control program there have received little international coverage. However, the few accounts available paint a horrific picture. Dr Blake Kerr, who worked in Lhasa hospital in 1987, has reported that women who refuse to 'volunteer' for abortion or sterilization are later 'coerced' into doing so and are subjected to 'inhumane surgery' without anesthetics or pain killers.[73] Journalist John Aveden has also confirmed that it is typical for a woman who arrives at a hospital for childbirth without a pass granting permission to have a child to awake after labor to find that her child is dead and that she has been sterilized.[74] In *Tibet: The Facts*, Paul Ingram has argued that widespread forced abortions and sterilization in Tibet, in conjunction with the "master race" mentality of the Chinese, "provoke many striking parallels between Chinese occupied Tibet and Nazi occupied Poland or Russia".[75]

Despite the abuses and authoritarianism of China's policies, many international population control organizations uphold China as a model of population control for other countries, privately if not publicly. In the confidential letter to Dr Nafis Sadik, from Walter Holzhausen, UNFPA Director in Bangladesh, supporting sterilization payments, which was mentioned earlier in this chapter, Holzhausen wrote that most donor representatives in Bangladesh "greatly admire" the Chinese "success" in population control, brought about with "massive direct and indirect compulsion", thus upholding China as a model for emulation.[76] A 1989 confidential report of the World Bank also remarked that the population problem in Nepal calls for a Chinese-type solution "although something less than this is probably the best that can be expected".[77]

Malthusians fear that if China, the world's most populous country, fails to win its fight against population increase, there is little hope for resolving the global population problem or the crisis of planetary survival (India is expected to surpass China in population size in the twenty-first century). Condoning the authoritarianism of China's population control program, J. Mayone Stycos of the Population and Development Program at Cornell

University has argued that since one in five passengers in the global lifeboat is Chinese, "The remaining passengers should be grateful to their travelling companions for their unusual efforts to stop population growth".[78]

Sterilization as political control

When the success of family planning programs is determined by contraceptive prevalence rates and the number of 'births averted', contraceptive effectiveness tends to be valued over contraceptive safety, user control and satisfaction and ethical considerations. However, contraceptive effectiveness, technological advancement and corporate profitability are not the only reasons why population experts and medical professionals favor one method of fertility control over another at a given time. As Rosalind Petchesky and other feminist reproductive rights scholars and activists have observed, securing control, political legitimacy and the absence of vocal resistance to a given method are also determining factors.[79] High rates of sterilization in the Third World have to be understood in this context.

Contraceptives are not simply technical means to prevent pregnancy: they are also political tools of dominant groups to control their subordinates. This is clearly evident in the priorities of research, development and distribution with regard to both surgical and non-surgical contraceptive methods. While there is greater access to user-controlled barrier and other methods such as the condom and the diaphragm in the 'developed' countries, in the 'developing' countries, the use of provider-controlled methods is more commonplace.

Non-Surgical Methods

The lion's share of money for contraceptive research is spent on long-acting, provider-controlled surgical, hormonal and immunological methods which promote a bio-medical approach to fertility control. Relatively little money is allocated to safety assessments despite high risks associated with these methods. In the late 1970s, only about 2.2% of all public sector contraceptive research funds were spent on barrier methods (like the condom), which provide users with greater control and protection against sexually transmitted diseases, including HIV.[80]

Many representatives of drug companies participate in working groups and steering committees of the WHO, in particular the Special Programme for Research Development and Research Training in Human Reproduction (WHO-HRP), which coordinates, promotes, conducts and evaluates international research in human reproduction. There is a deepening partnership of drug company officials, technical and scientific experts and population control advocates in HRP committees. As Indian feminist health researcher Sumati Nair has observed, this partnership has resulted in an increasingly lenient and hasty approach to drug testing in the Third World, where the kinds of pre-marketing testing criteria, liability insurance and costly legal mechanisms that exist in the West are absent.[81]

Contraceptive manufacturing is a billion dollar business controlled by oligopolistic corporations. Overseas markets far exceed the US domestic market, with oral and injectable contraceptives being the most lucrative. USAID as well as private voluntary organizations such as the IPPF and multilateral organizations like the UNFPA buy contraceptives in large quantities from the corporations and provide them mostly without charge to Third World countries. In justifying US government involvement in population control, USAID documents point out that family planning services tend to support the private sector more than other components of its population programs.[82] In many countries where USAID has been exporting contraceptives, the problem has often been over-supply, not under-supply. Inundated with contraceptives and faced with problems of storage facilities, Nepal, Bangladesh and Mexico have had to destroy contraceptives worth millions of dollars and Bangladesh and the Philippines have had to request moratoriums on contraceptive imports from the US. Auditors for USAID have also found that the federal Contraceptive Procurement Project had lost or has had to destroy contraceptives worth millions of dollars purchased at the US taxpayers' expense.[83]

Contraceptive research is conducted and implemented by scientists, researchers, physicians, drug company vendors and government officials who are predominantly men. As feminist health researchers point out, these men, who push technological–scientific management of women's bodies, "never have to subject themselves to the very pills, devices, implants and injections they are promoting".[84] Thus, relatively little is done to promote contraceptive use among men and the patriarchal belief that birth control is solely a female responsibility continues to be affirmed.

The 'contraceptive revolution' has had differential effects upon different classes and races of women. While more privileged classes of women are able to exercise greater caution and choice in the use of contraceptives, poorer women and women of color are frequently the victims of experimental contraceptives and unethical and coercive promotional strategies. This seems to be the case with regard to practically all modern contraceptives, ranging from the pill to the non-surgical sterilant quinacrine.

The pill

The pill, the first contraceptive to be used on a mass scale, was initially tried out on poor women in Haiti and Puerto Rico who were given doses and combinations of estrogen that are now considered to be extremely hazardous. When the market for the pill levelled off in the industrialized countries in the 1960s, due to consumer concern about cancer and other risks, pill manufacturers turned increasingly to the Third World. After four of the biggest pill manufacturers, Searle, Syntex, Ortho and Parke-Davis, began supplying USAID with free pills, USAID began to buy larger and larger quantities of pills from them for distribution in the Third World.[85]

Women health activists have shown that indiscriminate use of the pill in the Third World increases risks and severity of side-effects such as circulatory disorders, changes in body metabolism, risks of cancer and birth defects.[86] Yet, population control advocates continue to urge heavy promotion and deregulation of the marketing of the pill. While they do not necessarily deny the risks involved, they tend to defend its use with cost–benefit arguments. According to Dr Frederick Robbins, a researcher of the contraceptive pill: "The dangers of overpopulation are so great that we may have to use certain techniques of contraception that may entail considerable risk to the individual woman".[87]

The IUD

The story of the development and distribution of the intrauterine device (IUD) is similar to that of the pill. The Dalkon Shield IUD was tested on poor women in the United States without much attention to research protocols or proper consent, and was marketed by its manufacturer, A.H. Robbins, in spite of the Shield's association with serious injuries, including pelvic infection, tubal pregnancy, infertility and even deaths. When lawsuits against A.H. Robbins began to mount in the 1970s and US sales dropped, the company turned increasingly to the Third World. As a promotional strategy, it offered USAID a 48% discount on bulk packages of unsterilized IUDs. Consequently, by the early 1980s, A.H. Robbins and USAID had together dumped 1.7 million Dalkon Shields abroad.[88]

Unlike the pill, which a woman has to remember to take every day, the insertion and removal of the IUD lies in the hands of a health care provider. However, poor health conditions, including inadequate training of health care workers in IUD insertion and removal, increased risks from infections and sexually transmitted diseases, septic abortions and untreated ectopic pregnancies, make IUD use especially dangerous in Third World countries. The mortality rate resulting from IUDs in the Third World is double the rate in the West. The National Women's Health Network in the US noted that in 1988 500,000 Shields sold abroad still remained unaccounted for.[89]

The population control objective has prevailed over women's health and safety in the heavy promotion of the IUD in countries such as India. While recognizing that "IUDs are horrible things [which] ... produce infection", some physicians, like Dr Robert Willson of the University of Michigan, have defended their widespread use. Willson has argued that "Perhaps the individual patient is expendable in the general scheme of things, particularly if the infection she acquires is sterilising, but not lethal."[90]

Injectables

The problems of women forgetting to take pills or trying to remove their IUDs are more easily averted with the injectable contraceptives such as Depo-Provera (depot progestogen) and Net-En. Once these long-acting hormonal contraceptives are injected into women's bodies, they cannot be reversed. A single Depo-Provera shot prevents pregnancy for three to six months and Net-En up to two months; pregnancy rates are said to be less than one per one hundred users.

The United States Food and Drug Administration (USFDA) banned the use of Depo-Provera as a contraceptive in the United States because studies in beagle dogs had shown increased incidences of cancer.[91] This ban was lifted in 1992 following years of persistent lobbying by its manufacturer, the US multinational Upjohn. Long before the USFDA lifted the ban, however, it was tested and used on minority women in the US and thousands of poor women in the Third World.

Depo-Provera was experimented on Black women in the Grady Clinic in Georgia without informed consent in the 1970s and it was also used among Hispanic women in Los Angeles County at the University of Southern California health services.[92] In 1987 the Indian Health Service revealed that it had prescribed the drug for 150–200 Native American women and was continuing to prescribe it as a contraceptive despite the government ban.[93] Before the ban was lifted, the USFDA had also allowed limited use of Depo-Provera on retarded women and drug addicts, thus demonstrating the drug's potential as a weapon of eugenicist population control.

In other Northern countries, too, Depo-Provera has been given to poor women of color without their knowledge or consent. In Canada, where Depo-Provera is not approved for use as a contraceptive, doctors still prescribe it "where they feel the benefits outweigh the risks", for example among "Aborginal women, women with disabilities, teenagers, women of color, women living in poverty, and substance abusers".[94]

Five years before the results of the beagle studies were known, a Christian missionary doctor named Ed McDaniel working in Chiang Mai province of Thailand volunteered the tribal women in his parish as subjects for trials of Depo-Provera. Apparently, about 56% of women in Chiang Mai were injected with the drug. A study carried out in 1979 in that region revealed a marked increase in cancer of the cervix and breast among women admitted to hospitals. However, in seeking to defend Depo-Provera, WHO officials who prepared the study report attributed the high cancer rates to increasing hospital admissions and cancer screening in Chiang Mai rather than to widespread use of the drug.[95]

As with the pill and the IUD, the potential risks of using Depo-Provera are greater in the South than in the North due to lack of routine medical care and long-term follow up. The potential long-term adverse effects associated with Depo-Provera include: risk of birth defects due to women taking the drug during pregnancy; negative impact on infant development due to ingestion of hormones in breast milk; breast, endometrial and cervical cancers. The most common side-effects are said to be menstrual disorders, skin disorders, fatigue, headaches, nausea, depression, hair loss, delayed return to fertility, weight change and loss of libido. Although Depo-Provera has been proved to be an effective male contraceptive, it has not been promoted among men because of male complaints about loss of libido. But, as feminist health researchers have pointed out, women's complaints about the same have not been taken seriously at all.[96]

The implicit trust in injections as safe, reliable modern medicine and the cleanliness and ease associated with injections also make both users and providers prefer them to the older methods. Besides, a woman can be given a shot during a quick visit to a clinic without her husband's knowledge. While this is considered an important factor in many cultures where males oppose women's control of their fertility, surreptitious use of contraceptive injections or vaccines by women does not necessarily contribute to greater male responsibility in sexuality and reproduction.[97]

At the height of the Depo-Provera controversy in the 1980s, SIDA refused to supply Depo-Provera to the Third World despite the drug's approval for limited use in Sweden. However, according to Dr Malcolm Potts, medical director of the International Planned Parenthood Federation (IPPF) who was responsible for millions of shots of Depo-Provera given in Thailand, Sri Lanka, Kenya, Jamaica and other Third World countries between 1969 and 1978, "We are not going to know whether Depo-Provera is safe until a large number of women use it for a very long time.... You cannot prove a drug is safe until you use it."[98]

Following this line of thinking, the Medical Boards of the WHO and the IPPF approved Depo-Provera for use in the Third World while the drug was still banned in the US. Justifying the ethical double standard involved at the time, many population control advocates argued that the problem of overpopulation requires "an entirely new set of medical standards for developing countries", and that use of experimental contraceptives is less problematic than the risks of pregnancy and death in childbirth in the Third World.[99]

Women's health groups in India like Stree Shakti Sanghatana have opposed government-sponsored trials of the injectable Net-En manufactured by German pharmaceutical company Schering. They have pointed out that where basic medical care is not available, the preconditions of safety cannot be guaranteed and that poor women 'volunteer' to be guinea pigs only because informed consent protocols are widely violated. They also observe that the tremendous pressures placed on health personnel to achieve population control targets also lead to the abuse of trial methods.[100]

Norplant

The hormonal implant Norplant, developed by the Population Council and manufactured by the Finnish multinational Leiras, consists of six silicone rods inserted under the skin of a woman's upper arm. It is considered highly effective because it prevents pregnancy for five years and is entirely provider-dependent. By 1990, clinical and pre-introductory trials of Norplant had been carried out in 44 developed and developing countries and over half a million women (three-quarters of them in Indonesia) had been implanted with it.[101]

In Brazil Norplant trials were stopped in 1986 due to concerns raised by women health activists regarding the ethics and safety of drug experimentation on very poor and uninformed women.[102] A Population Council Report on Norplant use in Indonesia revealed that user choice of contraceptive methods, information on side-effects, quality of care and removal on demand are serious problems.[103] Norplant has to be removed after five years; failure to do so could lead to life-threatening complications like ectopic pregnancy. However, in many countries women are unaware of this fact and Norplant users are frequently 'lost to follow up', the figure being as high as 29% in Indonesia.[104]

The WHO, in collaboration with the Population Council and Family Health International (FHI), has conducted a post-market surveillance survey to study long-term effects of Norplant use in multiple centers in Bangladesh, Chile, China, Egypt, Sri Lanka and Thailand. Side-effects have been reported by 64.7% of Norplant users. But, as health researchers like Anita Hardon, Lenny Achthoven and Daksha Hathi have pointed out, when surveys are carried out by the advocates of the drug, they are more interested in finding out reasons for discontinuation of Norplant and in convincing women to accept some of the side-effects such as irregular bleeding. They are not very interested, then, in providing alternative birth control methods.[105]

Despite the many warnings of serious problems and infringements of women's rights associated with Norplant use in the Third World, the USFDA approved its use in the US in December 1990. Since its approval, thousands of women in the US have used Norplant and many have suffered its adverse side-effects such as painful and excessive bleeding, depression, weight gain and even strokes and heart attacks. Claiming that they were not properly warned about these side-effects, many women have joined lawsuits against Wyeth-Ayerst Laboratories, the US manufacturer of Norplant. In 1995 there were 200 lawsuits including 50 class action suits against the company.[106] However, the legal attention to Norplant has not necessarily taken into account the eugenicist use of this drug.

Two days after Norplant use was approved in the US, the *Philadelphia Inquirer* newspaper carried an editorial advocating that Norplant be used as a "tool in the fight against Black poverty".[107] Although the paper later carried an apology in response to protests received, the eugenicist argument that women on welfare, especially teenage mothers, should be given Norplant is gaining wide acceptance in the US. Economist Sybil Sawhill has suggested that girls be started on Norplant at a young age in order to avoid unplanned pregnancies.[108] Indeed, Norplant seems to fit the bill for a time-capsule contraceptive to temporarily sterilize all girls, as envisioned by leading US demographer Bernard Berelson three decades ago. In recent years, a number of state legislators, including David Duke of Ku Klux Klan infamy from Louisiana, have introduced bills providing economic incentives to women on welfare to have Norplant inserted.[109]

Although these bills have not been passed, Norplant has been introduced into health clinics of public high schools in cities like Baltimore, Maryland and Norplant use seems to be increasingly commonplace among Black teenagers.[110] Native American activists have also charged that the Indian Health Service in South Dakota had given Norplant to women medically at risk, violating informed consent procedures.[111] Norplant is also amenable to direct punitive use. In December 1991 a California judge ordered that Norplant be implanted in a Black woman who had pleaded guilty to beating two of her children. The woman, Darlene Johnson, is a diabetic, was pregnant at the time, had no knowledge of Norplant, but agreed to have the implant rather than go to jail![112] The case later went to appeal and Darlene Johnson did not have Norplant implanted.

As women health activists argue, Norplant is a drug with unknown consequences, and features such as long-term effectiveness and provider control make it easy for Norplant to be abused. They especially stress the fact that, like many other modern contraceptives, Norplant is inappropriate for use in the Third World, where basic health facilities necessary for proper insertion, follow-up and removal are lacking, and where doctors might not adequately inform women of the side-effects such as menstrual disturbance or provide a choice of alternative methods. As the National Black Women's Health Project points out, like poor women in the Third World, poor minority women in the US also lack the kind of high-quality responsive health care that is essential for the proper use of Norplant.[113] Still, population control advocates promote Norplant as modern and safe – a 'magic capsule' for the problem of 'overpopulation' – despite concerns raised by health activists and new studies.[114]

The results of a recent 1996 study (involving rhesus monkeys) indicates that hormonal contraceptives which contain progestins may cause vaginal changes that could increase the risk of infection in women exposed to HIV. These findings further validate the concerns of health activists that while hormonal methods may be efficient as tools of population control, they do not protect women against HIV and other STDs.[115]

Anti-fertility 'vaccines'

The so-called 'vaccines' or new immunological contraceptives treat pregnancy as if it is a disease. They prevent pregnancy by manipulating the body's immune system to 'attack' hormones necessary to maintain pregnancy. In 1992, 10% of worldwide public spending on contraceptive research and 16% of annual contraceptive research spending of the WHO–HRP was allocated to the development of immunological contraceptives. A variety of organizations, such as the World Bank, UNFPA, USAID and the Rockefeller Foundation as well as pharmaceutical firms such as Sandoz from Switzerland, are funding this research.[116] Several groups around the world engaged in 'vaccine' research, including the WHO and the Population Council, are now competing against each other in a race to produce the perfect vaccine.

Clinical trials of the 'vaccines' have been carried out on women in several countries since 1974. The vaccine developed by Dr G.P. Talwar, Director of the National Institute of Immunology in India, has been tried on hundreds of women and is considered to have reached an advanced stage of testing. Its proponents, like the Family Planning Association of India, claim it to be "safe, devoid of any side effects and completely reversible".[117]

However, women health researchers have raised serious health and ethical concerns regarding the contraceptive 'vaccines'. They note that the 'vaccines' are actually not that efficient given the difficulty of determining when the contraceptive effect begins. They argue that as the potential for serious immunological disorders exists, it is unethical to do large trials. They state that poor women who participate in drug trials do not have access to basic health care and must at least be warned of the risks such as allergy, auto-immunity and irreversibility of the anti-fertility 'vaccines'. They fear that the vaccines carry "enormous potential for political coercion and abuse".[118]

These concerns have led to the organization of an international campaign to stop research on anti-fertility 'vaccines' and to redirect research towards safer methods which give women greater control over their bodies. By November 1994, the Campaign Call had been signed by 399 groups and organizations from 38 countries and 40 individuals (Appendix 4).[119] Still, the promoters of the method defend their work, arguing that the 'vaccine' is a highly effective weapon against global population expansion.[120]

The fact that the goals of population control, technological advancement and corporate profitability prevail over the health and well-being of women is also evident in current testing of the non-surgical sterilization method, quinacrine.

Quinacrine

Pellets made from the anti-malaria drug quinacrine have been tested on more than 80,000 women around the world and over 30,000 in Vietnam.

A field study conducted in Vietnam and reported in the prestigious scientific journal *The Lancet* in 1993 gives quinacrine its stamp of approval as a safe, efficient, cost-effective and simple method to use.[121] Although trials have since been stopped in Vietnam because an of international outcry, promoters of the drug are calling it the "most revolutionary birth control development since the pill".[122]

Critics point out that quinacrine appears to have a high rate of failure, despite claims made by promoters about its efficiency. Health activists are concerned that the chemical has not passed toxicological tests by the WHO and that it could also cause cancer, tubal pregnancies and other health problems. In a September 1993 report, the Association for Voluntary Surgical Contraception (AVSC) concluded that despite *The Lancet's* recommendation, quinacrine pellets are not a safe and effective female sterilization method. Judy Norsigian of the Boston Women's Health Book Collective has urged women's groups and health activists to protest use of quinacrine, especially given the lack of animal studies which are needed before further testing is done on women.[123]

Health activists are also concerned that quinacrine could be used coercively and that information about irreversibility could be withheld by providers eager to bring down population growth rates.[124] A Vietnamese publication called *The Woman* has revealed that more than 100 women who participated in the field study reported in *The Lancet* had quinacrine pellets inserted into the uterus without consent during pelvic check-ups. The authors of that study have denied the charge. Meanwhile, representatives of the population control establishment like Dr Tim Black, Director of Marie Stopes International, defend the drug, arguing that "the relative risk of having a baby in a rural area is much higher than anything quinacrine presents".[125]

Hasty drug development and lenient testing are only some of the health and human rights problems underlying the modern 'contraceptive revolution' Aggressive and unethical promotional strategies and unregulated marketing practices are some other major problem areas.

Contraceptive Promotion and Distribution

'IEC: information–education–communication'

Much of the literature in the field of family planning emphasizes the existence of 'unmet' need for contraceptives and the urgency of meeting that need. At the same time, population control advocates also believe that the poor are ignorant and irrational about their own needs and that they need to be educated and motivated to use modern contraceptives. Thus, from the earliest stage of international population control, large amounts of funds have been spent on motivating people to become contraceptive 'acceptors' (Figure 2.1).[126]

Both 'interpersonal channels' and mass media are utilized as tools to change attitudes and behavior related to fertility in the Third World.[127] Through extensive use of economic incentives, indigenous leaders as well as 'peer motivators' are incorporated into the global population control network. For example, in Thailand, the Population, Community and Development Association (PDA), founded by the population control zealot Mechai Viravaidya, has extended a range of 'community incentives' to shopkeepers, farmers, teachers, youth peer counsellors and even taxi cab drivers, policemen and Buddhist monks to become family planning 'motivators'. Viravaidya's objective is to permeate Thai culture at a deep psychological level with fertility control messages and to make family planning a 'part of everyday life'.[128]

However, the attempt to shape consciousness is not peculiar to family planning promotion in Thailand: it is a global undertaking.[129] Population control organizations search continuously for more effective and sophisticated public relations strategies to institutionalize population control in the Third World. A 1993 World Bank report entitled *Effective Family Planning Programs* states

> Promotional activities (also referred to as information–education–communication, or IEC) are an integral part of family services. Like any new product, contraceptives have to be brought to the attention of potential users, made attractive, and shown to be safe. This effort is essentially educational – aimed at producing satisfied and effective users willing to encourage others – but has to be accomplished with all the skills and techniques of modern public relations and advertising, so that family planning messages resonate in the public consciousness.[130]

Although the impact of media efforts on increasing contraceptive use is difficult to determine, population control organizations like the World Bank attribute increasing contraceptive prevalence in countries such as Brazil, Nigeria and Turkey to "aggressive use" of the mass media.[131] Family planning promotion is an expanding global enterprise with hundreds of publications, computer software and data systems and employing a vast array of professional population control advocates. Annual United Nations Population awards such as Media awards for "Excellence in Population Reporting" and population poster competitions for children are just a few examples of efforts to spread the population control message throughout the world.[132]

Mass media campaigns supported by USAID, IPPF, UNFPA and other major funders are intensifying in many regions of the Third World. They use print, radio, cinema and TV in sophisticated, ways to encourage the poor to have smaller families. But the tactics being used in promoting contraceptives are not always ethical. An example is a new program developed by Population Services International (PSI), a population communications group based in Washington, DC. In rural areas which lack electricity and mass media outlets, it promotes family planning through mobile film units, thereby subverting the need for regular access to electricity.[133] The problem here is not the creative use of film and video to disseminate information on birth control, but the use of advanced technology only for population control purposes. Why are the basic material needs of the poor and their need for modern services such as electricity neglected, while family planning services are pushed on them in countless ways?

Another example of questionable family planning promotion is a program launched by the Population Communications Services Center at Johns Hopkins University called Enter-Educate, which uses Third World entertainers to promote family planning messages. The program spent $350,000 from USAID on an album by King Sunny Adé, the famous Nigerian musician, in which he sings two songs urging Nigerians to have small families. However, the source of the funding is not revealed. When questioned about the ethics of promoting this album without revealing the source of funding to the consumer, a USAID official declared that it would have been "counterproductive". Phyllis Piotrow, Director of the Population Communications Center at Johns Hopkins, also defended the Enter-Educate program, saying, "Good health promotion can be personal, popular, persuasive and sometimes even profitable."[134]

In the contemporary information age, influencing public opinion is increasingly a 'fight for the media'. In this fight, the population control establishment, with its access to money and technology, is able to inundate the public with population control messages, producing what some critics have called a form of "psychological warfare" against the Third World.[135] These tactics help turn public attention away from problems inherent in the 'contraceptive revolution' such as its unregulated contraceptive marketing techniques.

Contraceptive marketing

In their urgency to expand contraceptive use in the Third World, pharmaceutical companies and population control organizations often distribute contraceptives without prescription, and with little screening or medical follow-up. For example, following the recommendation of the IPPF in 1973 that birth control pills be distributed without prescription, at least eight countries (the Philippines, Pakistan, Bangladesh, Antigua, Chile, Fiji, Jamaica, South Korea) withdrew the prescription requirement. But as some countries became hesitant to allow sales without prescription, birth control pill manufacturers like Syntex Laboratories increased their lobbying in the US Congress, demanding that USAID encourage Third World countries to drop the "pharmacy only requirement".[136]

Contraceptive Social Marketing (CSM) arose partly in response to such demands. CSM involves the sale of modern contraceptives donated by USAID, IPPF and other agencies at subsidized prices through 'already existing marketing channels' such as small shopkeepers and traders in Third World countries. PSI, the organization at the cutting edge of population control promotion, is also a leader in CSM. PSI, which is supported by major population control organizations and contraceptive manufacturers, upholds the virtues of social marketing in terms of cost effectiveness. However, PSI fails to question the ethics of distributing modern contraceptives to poor people who lack access to basic medical care when it says that "The shops ... cost us nothing. They are already there, serving every neighborhood. In contrast, clinics and health centers (aside from being relatively few in number) are very expensive to build and operate".[137]

Indeed, as health researchers like Cary LaCheen observe, wholesalers and retailers have very little knowledge of the products, but are motivated to promote contraceptive sales for their own profit. Not infrequently, family planning and contraceptives are promoted in deliberately deceptive ways among the poor. For example, in attempts to make women fear and avoid pregnancy and childbirth, marketing administrators for the contraceptive pill in Thailand tell women that the hormonal and related effects during pregnancy are the "size of an elephant", while the changes and side-effects caused by the pill are only the "size of an ant".[138]

Even in pharmacies, contraceptives and other drugs which should require prescription can frequently be bought without them. For example, health researchers have found that in Mexico, Depo-Provera is sold without prescription by pharmacists who have almost no knowledge of the drug and who tell customers that the drug has no contraindications.[139] In India too, soon after Depo-Provera marketing was approved in 1994, in spite of the prescription requirement and concerns raised by women health activists, the drug was being sold over the counter, without prescription or adequate identification of contradindications.[140]

The distribution of contraceptives without medical examination and prescription can only worsen the health care crisis in the Third World, not alleviate it, as argued by CSM promoters. Without medical follow-up, contraceptive users, especially those with high risk conditions, could experience unpleasant, if not dangerous, side-effects. In the long term, women's capacity to work and the already fragile health and well-being of women and the children they bear are greatly undermined.[141]

The 'Second Contraceptive Revolution'

Claiming the 'contraceptive revolution' to have been a major success, population control organizations are now declaring the launching of a 'Second Contraceptive Revolution' and a 'Contraception-21 agenda' for the next century.[142] Despite the current neo-Malthusian rhetoric on reproductive health and women's rights, the position that values maximum access to contraceptives over safety and ethical standards continues to guide the 'second contraceptive revolution'.

The 'new contraceptive revolution', like the 'new' reproductive rights agenda, upholds the bio-medical model of mass fertility management. Despite references to the importance of male contraceptive methods and greater male participation in family planning, the onus for fertility control will continue to be placed on women rather than on men. Despite talk of women-controlled methods, the emphasis will continue to be on developing long-acting, provider-controlled high-technology methods over client-controlled barrier methods. As Mahmoud F. Fathalla, MD former director of the WHO–HRP and Chairman of the International Medical Advisory Panel of the Planned Parenthood Federation has observed, currently about 94 new contraceptive products are being pursued, of which many are "variants of existing methods or alternatives within existing contraceptives". Among these are four IUDs, seven hormonal implants, five hormonal injectables, five hormonal pills, six vaccines and six methods for female sterilization.[143]

The 'second' contraceptive revolution also envisages a greater role for private industry. As Fathalla notes, given the 'latent demand' for new contraceptives, liberalization of trade, privatization of state-run enterprises and other factors, contraceptive marketing in the Third World will be even more profitable for pharmaceutical companies than it has been in the past. The privatization of health sectors, increasing corporate mergers (such as Pharmacia of Sweden and Upjohn of the US) and extension of intensive contraceptive promotional and marketing strategies such as IEC and CSM will further augment the power and profits of transnational pharmaceutical companies in the South. US and European drug companies currently have total annual revenues of $90 billion and by 1999 these revenues are expected to grow by 9–10%.[144]

The USFDA is now exempting more and more drugs and medical devices from review before marketing, a move which could have detrimental repercussions across the world. The ICPD and its 'new' reproductive rights agenda does not address the need for strict guidelines to monitor contraceptive trials and marketing practices of the corporations. Calls for population stabilization in the context of GATT and other 'free trade' agreements could result in further easing of protocols for contraceptive trials. Feminist activists from the South fear increased corporate dumping of dangerous and experimental contraceptives on the bodies of poor women in the Third World.[145]

Women's Health and Human Rights

Modern family planning programs have provided many poor women with contraceptives and the ability to limit family size; but they have rarely given women genuine choice, control over their bodies or a sense of self-empowerment. As discussed above, the focus of Malthusianism is on population stabilization and the meeting of targets, rather than on the means or the processes to achieve its ends. Although neo-Malthusian population control advocates now call for women's reproductive rights, population control programs are actually moving in more authoritarian directions.

Article 16 of the Teheran Proclamation issued by the UN Conference on Human Rights in 1968 states: "Parents have a basic human right to determine freely and responsibly the number and spacing of their children".[146] This Article represented a major victory for the population control movement. Perhaps, the term "responsibly" was the real victory, because it can be interpreted in a more or less coercive way. Indeed, the overwhelming importance given by international donors and local governments to fertility control has led to a relative neglect of other aspects of reproductive and human rights such as the right of the poor to health and well-being, including the right to bear and sustain children.

The emphasis on family planning has undermined public health care and maternal and child health (MCH) in many countries. Many of the new hormonal and immunological contraceptives do not protect against HIV/AIDS. Targets and incentives direct health care personnel towards population control over provision of health care. Population agencies speak of integrating family planning within a broader health care framework in public. In private, however, some argue that family planning programs should not be 'held hostage' to strict health requirements and that maximum access to contraceptives should override safety and ethical concerns.

A letter written by James D. Shelton, Chief of the Research Division, and Cynthia Calla, Medical Officer of the Family Planning Division of the USAID Office of Population, reviewing a draft of the IPPF's "Medical and Service Delivery Guidelines" in August 1991, is instructive in this regard. Their confidential letter addressed to Carlos Huezo, Medical Director of the IPPF, states that introduction of medical barriers to family planning services hinders effectiveness and impact of contraceptives, especially hormonal contraceptives. Among the long list of "medical barriers" the USAID officials identify against inclusion in service delivery guidelines are: "unnecessary laboratory tests"; "excessive physical exams (e.g. pelvic and breast)"; "excessive follow-up schedules"; "excessive counselling". With regard to providing information on contraindications of contraceptives, the letter says, "we prefer not to use the term. It is a term which may have very negative connotations and a major inhibitory effect, especially when transmitted downward through the system".[147] Similarly, a 1989 World Bank staff appraisal report on population control efforts in India suggested that too much emphasis was being given to side effects and contraindications of contraceptives in the training of physicians. The report recommended that the strict standards set by the Indian Council for Medical Research be lowered for purposes of promoting contraceptive use in the country.[148]

Even when the population control organizations have taken efforts to address public health issues and women's rights, the population control objective has continued to be dominant. The Safe Motherhood Initiative and Women in Development (WID) programs are examples.

Safe Motherhood Initiative

While maternal mortality is less than 10 per 100,000 live births in the 'developed' countries, it ranges from 400 to 1,000 per 100,000 in the 'developing' countries. According to the WHO, nearly one million women die annually from complications associated with biological reproduction. About 585,000 die specifically from causes related to pregnancy and childbirth (including abortions) and about 99% of these deaths occur in the Third World.[149] Although illegal and botched abortions cause thousands of maternal deaths every year, perhaps as many as 200,000, most population control organizations push contraceptives, neglecting the need for safe and legal abortion as a back-up method.

The Safe Motherhood Initiative was launched in 1987 by the World Bank, the UNDP, UNICEF, the UNFPA and the WHO to reduce maternal mortality within a decade. In many cases, this Initiative has approached Safe Motherhood as simply a means to reduce childbearing; the assumption being that fewer childbirths will cause fewer maternal deaths. For example, a World Bank paper on the Safe Motherhood Initiative discusses "reducing exposure to pregnancy" and calls for greater efforts towards "pregnancy prevention". It argues that many women die from unwanted pregnancies and that if their "unmet need" for contraception is met and "all unwanted pregnancies are avoided, in many countries, one-fourth to two-fifths of maternal mortality would be averted".[150]

However, a 1992 World Bank evaluation of its population sector work admits that its foray into broader health initiatives has been motivated by the "political sensitivity" of population control and the need to dissipate Third World perception that "population control is really the Bank's strategic objective". The same report also states that the Bank is now explicitly focusing on reproductive health and Safe Motherhood rather than reducing population growth as rationales for family planning efforts in Latin America.[151] The report further notes that many countries which will not accept donor support for population control will nevertheless "accept support for family health and welfare programs with family planning components" and that the likelihood of family planning getting "lost in an MCH program" today is less because MCH is now better accepted as a "legitimate intervention for both health and demographic reasons".[152]

This instrumentalist approach to MCH has led to the Safe Motherhood Initiative being restricted to a few cost-effective technological interventions such as pregnancy risk screening and emergency referrals which do not interfere with family planning. Such an emphasis, however, can lead to increased contraceptive use without a corresponding increase in improved public health and the quality of life. For example, researchers from the International Centre for Diarrhoeal Disease Research Bangladesh (ICDDRB) who investigated integration of family planning and MCH services in the Matlab project area in Bangladesh found a dramatic increase in contraceptive use, but no significant decrease in infant or maternal mortality in the 1980s. Even the limited reduction in maternal mortality in this area has been attributed largely to a reduction in the absolute number of pregnancies and births rather than to a reduction of health risks associated with individual pregnancies and births. The Matlab experiment is frequently cited in the family planning literature as an example of how contraceptive use can be increased even in 'conditions of extreme poverty'.[153] Population policy makers argue that such poor countries do not have the time or money to establish better MCH services, and that "a population control program does not have to depend on a functioning primary health care system".[154]

As Indian demographer Malini Karkal has pointed out, the tendency of the Safe Motherhood Initiative and other such programs to attribute maternal mortality simply to pregnancy and childbirth leads to a relative neglect of causes of reproductive mortality which supersede maternal mortality. Deaths due to unsafe sterilization and hazardous contraceptives, as well as those associated with sexually transmitted diseases, cancer of the reproductive organs and unsafe treatment of infertility, also account for a large proportion of reproductive mortality.[155]

In a review of the World Bank report *India's Family Welfare Programme: Towards a Reproductive and Child Health Approach* published in 1995, Dr Mohan Rao of the Centre of Social Medicine and Community Health at the Jawaharlal Nehru University in India notes that "India is yet to undergo an epidemiological transition ... the profile of death and disease continues to be dominated by diseases caused by poverty". Rao points out that a very large proportion of maternal deaths in India are attributable to undernutrition, anemia, infectious and communicable disease,s and other poverty-related causes which are obscured by the "new" reproductive rights focus of the Bank report.[156]

Although Neo-Malthusian analysis attributes improvement of women's status to fertility reduction, in countries such as India, where births have been 'averted' due to family planning programs, the reproductive choices or conditions of women, or of the general population for that matter, have not increased as a result. In India, although birth rates have declined, infant mortality (at 72 per 1,000 births) and maternal mortality (at 460 per 100,000 live births) in 1995 continued to be relatively high. As Indian women's rights advocate Vina Mazumdar has argued, improvement of the status of women is not the consequence of family planning programs, as believed by the population planners; rather it is a more complex outcome resulting from rise in age of marriage, education, employment, better living conditions, general awareness among women, and so on.[157]

The health care crisis in the Third World cannot be reduced to the obsession with population control. What the World Bank tries to achieve through programs such as the Safe Motherhood Initiative is undermined by the greater effects of developments in the global political economy. Military spending, debt crisis, World Bank- and IMF-imposed structural adjustment policies and privatization have all contributed to cutbacks in social welfare expenditures, including basic health and MCH services, aggravating the health-care crisis in the Third World. While these issues will be explored in later chapters of this book, it should also be noted here that the neo-Malthusian attitude that treats pregnancies and babies as an epidemic "that has to be eradicated once and for all" also permeates some Women in Development (WID) programs.[158]

Women in Development

Associating the improvement of women's status and global crisis resolution with fertility reduction, organizations such as the World Bank and UNFPA have called for the integration of WID programs and family planning programs.[159] The integration of WID programs with population control programs, however, is not leading to the kinds of social transformations necessary for women's social and economic empowerment. Instead, it is leading to subsumption of WID programs within family planning. One example is the Working Women's Forum in Madras, India.

The Working Women's Forum is a well-known organization in the WID field considered to be a successful model for providing small-scale credit and income generation programs for poor women. However, critics claim that it is also a "callous population control effort". According to an account published by an anonymous source in the *Newsletter* of the Women's Global Network for Reproductive Rights, during three years of work in a particular slum area, the Working Women's Forum had achieved a 'successful' contraceptive prevalence rate of 70%. However, apparently, this great 'success' was achieved through utter disregard for safety and ethical concerns. According to the account, contraceptive pills were widely distributed although hepatitis was endemic in the area; women were persuaded to undergo sterilization after the first child and women with severe bleeding and other problems associated with the IUD were simply told to "bear it, because otherwise you would risk a pregnancy".[160]

Accusations such as the above need greater investigation from feminists and human rights activists working in the WID field. In undertaking such investigations, however, it is important to bear in mind that many development programs in the South such as the Working Women's Forum are dependent on foreign aid and therefore in constant danger of having to subvert their independent objectives to population control and other agendas coming from the North.

In this regard, feminists need also to be cautious of the new Gender and Development (GAD) approach exported from the North to replace the older WID approach which sought simply to integrate women into the existing paradigm of development. GAD originated as a sincere feminist attempt to challenge existing power relations, including male–female and North–South hierarchies, and to improve neglected areas of women's lives such as reproduction and sexuality. But, as some feminist researchers have cautioned, the GAD approach has already been appropriated by dominant world institutions such as the World Bank; GAD could then be used to adapt women to structural adjustment and other programmes from the North aimed at managing and controlling populations in the South.[161]

As shown earlier in this chapter, many population control programs have victimized, not empowered, many poor women. Sterilization, provider-controlled high-tech contraceptive methods and inadequate information have hindered women from developing greater awareness or control over their bodies. The use of experimental methods exposes women and their children to a host of risks, potentially damaging human capacity for future reproduction. The subversion of the work of local midwives and primary health programs by the needs of population control have robbed women of sources of support in pregnancy and childbirth and undermined the power and status historically associated with childbearing. Neither WID nor GAD has addressed these issues adequately.

In societies where women derive their social status from childbearing and -rearing, family planning programs which do not accompany substantial reductions in infant mortality threaten women's status. This was seen in the high levels of sterilization regret in Bangladesh among women who lost children after they had had themselves sterilized. The overwhelming emphasis on female methods of contraception and neglect of male methods has resulted in an accommodation of gender inequality rather than in challenging male authority. A recent study of family planning in Bangladesh concludes: "In its intensive focus on family planning services for women, the program fails to disturb and may even reinforce the patriarchal structures that keep women isolated and vulnerable."[162]

The confluence of the forces of patriarchy, high technology, profit making and population control can also be seen in the emergence of the phenomenon known as 'missing women' in South, East and West Asia.

'Missing women'

About 105 to 106 boys are born for every 100 girls around the world. While the biological reasons for this disparity are a matter of debate, in several Asian countries today the proportions of girls born and living seem

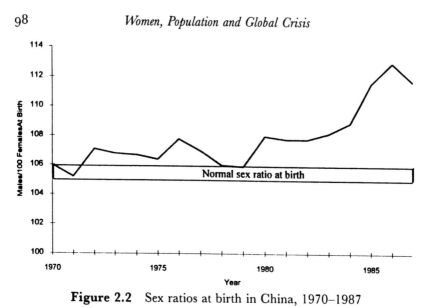

Figure 2.2   Sex ratios at birth in China, 1970–1987

Source: H. Yuan Tien, Zhang Tianlu, Ping Yu, Li Jingneng and Liang Zhongtang, 'China's Demographic Dilemmas', *Population Bulletin*, Vol. 47, No. 1, Washington, DC: Population Reference Bureau, 1992, p. 15.

to be steadily decreasing. In India, the ratio of women to men now is 929 females per 1,000 males whereas in 1901 it was 972.[163] In China, after the one-child policy was implemented in 1979, the sex ratio became more skewed (Figure 2.2). There were 94.1 women to 100 males in the 1982 census; in the 1990 census there were only 93.8 females per 100 males. Recent reports from South Korea also report 113 boys for every 100 girls.[164] Demographic data show that in China, India, Pakistan, Bangladesh, Nepal, West Asia and Egypt, 100 million or so women are currently unaccounted for by official statistics (Table 2.2).

Sex-selective abortions

One factor contributing to the problem of 'missing women' is sex-selective abortions. New technologies such as amniocentesis, ultrasound and chorionic biopsy which have been developed for purposes of pre-natal testing for birth defects are increasingly being used for the purpose of sex determination. In the patriarchal societies of China and India, where the preference for male children and the pressures to reduce family size are both very strong, abortion of female fetuses seems to be widespread.

Although use of these new technologies for sex selection is illegal in China, they are readily available even in rural areas.[165] With a small bribe like a carton of cigarettes, parents can easily find out the sex of the fetus and abort it if it is female, thus ensuring that the only child allowed by the state is a male. In China, in recent years, the number of induced abortions has risen significantly. It has been estimated that while induced abortions rep-

Table 2.2 Estimated deficits in female populations due to excess female mortality, 1981–1991: selected areas

Country or region	Ratio males/females (actual)	(expected)	No. of females (millions)	Females missing (%)	(millions)
China (1990)	1.066	1.010	548.7	5.3	29.1
India (1991)	1.077	1.020	406.3	5.6	22.8
Pakistan (1981)	1.105	1.025	40.0	7.8	3.1
Bangladesh (1981)	1.064	1.025	42.2	3.8	1.6
Nepal (1981)	1.050	1.025	7.3	2.7	0.2
West Asia (1985)	1.060	1.030	55.0	3.0	1.7
Egypt (1986)	1.047	1.020	23.5	2.6	0.6

Source: Ansley J. Coale, "Excess Female Mortality and the Balance of the Sexes in the Population: An Estimate of the Number of 'Missing Females'", *Population and Development Review*, Vol. 17, No. 3, September 1991, p. 522.

resented 31% of all births in 1978, by 1986 they had climbed to 53% of all births. As demographer Terrence Hull notes, "This means that increasing numbers of women have been resorting to pregnancy termination to achieve family-size targets".[166]

Demographers are reluctant to give precise estimates, but the increasingly skewed nature of China's sex ratio, the wide availability of sex determination tests, and at least one study reporting gender statistics concerning abortions make one suspect that a disproportionate number of abortions carried out in China are of females and that many abortions go unreported. The study reported in the *Chinese Medical Journal* in 1975 noted that in a hospital where chorionic biopsy was being used for sex determination at the time, of 30 abortions requested, 29 of the fetuses happened to be female.[167]

In India, too, sex-selective abortion is a thriving business. According to some estimates, between 1978 and 1983, 78,000 female fetuses were aborted after sex determination tests. Researchers have found that some poor districts in Uttar Pradesh, Maharashtra and Gujarat which do not have basic services like potable water and electricity have clinics doing a flourishing business in prenatal diagnostic (PND) techniques for sex selection.

Even poor farmers and landless laborers were willing to pay 25% compound interest on loans borrowed to pay for those tests. Given extreme social pressures to produce sons, many women, not only poor uneducated women, but also educated urban women, are resorting to abortion of female fetuses. In India some middle-class women justify these actions on grounds of choice and some medical doctors and intellectuals have also argued that it would prevent the suffering of women and that in the long run the shortage of women would lead to their improved status in society.[168]

Some nurses seeking to meet their family planning targets actively encourage 'scanning' for sex determination and abortion of female fetuses.[169] Some doctors also see sex-selective abortion as an effective method of population control that would allow the Indian government to achieve a Net Reproductive Rate (NRR) of one, that is, replacement of the mother with just one daughter, apparently the goal of an Indian government's Draft National Health Policy. But as the Campaign Against Sex Determination and Sex Pre-Selection in India has pointed out, it is a great irony that in a country where many medical professionals condone sex selection tests, amniocentesis was not made available to pregnant women in Bhopal who were exposed to toxic gases.[170]

Owing largely to agitation by feminist groups, state governments in Maharashtra, Punjab, Haryana and Gujarat have passed laws outlawing sex determination tests. In August 1994, the central government passed a draconian law banning the use of PND techniques for sex determination. But sex determination clinics are mushrooming and thriving: at least 100 tests are being conducted each day in a small town such as Sirsa in Haryana. As Madhu Kishwar, the editor of the Indian feminist journal, *Manushi*, has observed, outlawing these tests is not only ineffective but it can also lead to greater ethical abuses by doctors and the police in a society which is already beset with widespread inefficiency and corruption.[171] The eradication of sex-selective feticide requires that the deep-rooted preference for sons, soaring dowry demands for girls at marriage and population control pressures to limit family size be eliminated.

Female infanticide

Female infanticide is another factor contributing to the 'missing women' phenomenon. The Chinese government has either denied or condemned the practice and reliable data are not available. Female infanticide does have a long tradition in patriarchal societies like China and India. However, as Terrence Hull has noted, the "behavioral and emotional setting of infanticide in contemporary China" tends to be substantially different from the traditional pattern. The resurgence of infanticide in the early 1980s was at least partly related to the pressures of the Chinese family planning program and the infants killed at birth were overwhelmingly female.[172]

Most of the abandoned infants who end up in state-run orphanages are girls. Many of these girls as well as boys are subjected to starvation, torture and sexual assault. A recent report released by Human Rights Watch on a state-run orphanage in Shanghai claims that well over 1,000 children died between 1986 and 1992 alone due to the brutal treatment meted out at that orphanage.[173] *The Dying Rooms*, a documentary film produced by two British film producers, has also charged Chinese orphanages with widespread child abuse, although the Chinese government has vehemently denied these charges.[174] Large-scale abandonment of infants and malign neglect in child care work constitute some of China's "gravest human rights problems".[175] But, as researcher on China Kay Ann Johnson has pointed out, while the news reports on these problems attack the orphanages, they do not examine China's harsh population control policy which created the problems of abandonment in the first place.[176]

Female infanticide and sex-selective abortion in China could create a deficit of females in future generations, making it difficult for some men, especially poor men, to obtain wives. Such a situation could lead to a revival of the traditions of infant betrothal and the buying and selling of women, as well as new forms of female sexual and economic slavery.[177]

In India, too, analysts have linked the recent resurgence of female infanticide to new conditions, including increasing demand for dowry payments for girls and family planning promotion. In a study of high incidences of female infanticide in the Salem District in Tamil Nadu, Viji Srinivasan, the Director of the women's group Adithi, identified the "'internalization of the small family norm" due to family planning promotion as a source of female infanticide. Srinivasan's study raises questions about the ethics of aggressive population control in highly patriarchal societies and underscores the need for economic empowerment and elevation of women's status.[178]

Under-reporting of girls

The main reasons for the phenomenon of 'missing women' especially in China may be abandonment and concealment of girls rather than the sex-selective abortions or female infanticide.[179] In the Chinese countryside some parents bring up girl children surreptitiously so as to avoid violations of the one-child law and keep trying to have a male as their only child. Even after the relaxation of the one-child policy for rural couples in 1988, under-reporting of girls has continued due to stricter enforcement of the one-child policy. Unauthorized female children grow up as second-class citizens, 'black babies', without the social benefits usually offered to other children in the society.[180] While the long-term outcomes are hard to predict, it is most likely that women's status would not be enhanced by deliberate curtailment of female births or the abandonment and hiding of girls. These trends will only strengthen the forces of male dominance.

Democracy or Authoritarianism?

As noted at the beginning of this chapter, neo-Malthusian population control advocates and organizations claim that the modern 'contraceptive revolution' has been achieved without coercion, through 'purely voluntary means', with only 'minor disadvantages' to people in the Third World.[181] But a closer examination of the methods of contraception and strategies of family planning as undertaken in this chapter reveals widespread human rights violations and safety and ethical problems. In this regard, it is well to remember an argument put forward in the 1960s by the influential neo-Malthusian demographer Kingsley Davis. He stated that political will and strong measures need to be used in the fight against population growth and that democratic norms may have to be sacrificed for the sake of the greater good.[182]

Reproduction is a highly political issue and it is unlikely that in the long term either the problem of population stabilization or the global social crisis will be resolved by political repression or high technology. Questions pertaining to democracy and authoritarianism are embedded in the structures of the society. As noted earlier, the widespread protests against forced sterilizations in India under the Emergency was a major factor in the defeat of Indira Gandhi at the subsequent elections. Field researchers who have observed grass-roots reactions to coercive population control policies in India have warned that the situation is volatile and mounting dissatisfaction could again lead to conflict and violence as it did under the Emergency.[183]

In China, despite state authoritarianism, there have been outbursts and protests against the family planning policies and the government has had to soften its policies on a number of occasions. Reporters who have traveled in the Chinese countryside have observed that the government's population policy has caused "a mixture of anger, support, frustration, enthusiasm, deviousness and pain" and that the "desire to procreate" stirs more emotion than any desire for political democracy.[184]

Although a very crucial aspect, Malthusianism is only one particular expression of the ideology and social organization of the dominant world order. To understand the pervasiveness of Malthusian thinking and policies as well as the roots of the global crisis, we must examine Malthusianism in relation to domination/subordination, the central organizing principle of industrial capitalist society.

Malthusianism as domination

As demonstrated throughout this chapter, the neo-Malthusian approach is a quantitative, technical and bureaucratic approach. It is a frenzied approach driven by urgency and aggression to reduce the numbers of the human population in a race against the mechanical clock. Controlled by money and political influence, it has erected a vast global family planning enterprise far removed from the broader needs and interests of the masses whose numbers it seeks to control.

This hierarchical and often violent approach results in reinforcement of existing psycho-social structures of domination and subordination: humans over nature (anthropocentrism); men over women (patriarchy); capital over labor (capitalism); North over South (imperialism), white over people of color (white supremacy/racism), and so on (Figure 8.2).

Despite its veneer of scientific rationality, technological sophistication and bureaucratic efficiency, Malthusianism is founded ultimately on human ignorance, fear, hatred and greed. Dualistic thinking, the separation of self and other and of subject and object, lies at the root of the Malthusian approach. As such, it is unable to delve deeply to understand or see the connectedness between the self and other and subject and object or to see the inherent interdependence of human and planetary life (Figure 8.3). Fear of the unknown and desire for permanence and control, in this case the control of the global masses and their reproduction, underlies the dichotomous thinking of the Malthusians.

As a fragmented, top-down, homogeneous approach, Malthusianism leaves no room for more balanced, qualitatively oriented participatory and diverse approaches which incorporate, for example, indigenous and women's approaches to reproduction. Aggression and conquest rather than compassion and caring drive the population control establishment and the larger model of technological–capitalist development that it represents. Malthusianism cannot see the world from the point of view of those it objectifies as the mindlessly breeding, ignorant, teeming masses. Indeed, understanding and empathy require patience; but, according to its advocates, population control is urgent; it cannot lose time. Thus they see terminal and high-tech methods as being quicker, easier and more efficient to administer than women-controlled 'soft'-technology methods.

The aggressive, linear, quick-fix approach overlooks the interconnectedness between issues and the necessity for wholistic approaches to the global crisis and women's subordination. The underlying relationship between wealth and poverty, between the population decline in the North and population expansion in the South and other such historical social phenomena central to the understanding of the global demographic dilemma are neglected within the narrow, single-issue focus of Malthusianism. Myopic vision arising out of self-interest and fear leads to dangerous policies of gender, race and class oppression. If unchallenged and unchecked now, Malthusianism could become an even greater tool of authoritarianism and social engineering in the future than it has been in the past.

From its outset, Malthusianism has been challenged by a host of alternative views, including socialist, feminist and Third World perspectives.[185] Even when its assumptions and policies have been questioned and thoroughly discredited, Malthusianism has persisted; and it is likely that it will continue to do so in many forms and guises in the years ahead. Indeed, the ideological struggle between Malthusianism and alternative perspectives represents a broader historical power struggle, between the forces of domination and partnership.

A shift from population control to birth control, from external domination to greater individual control over reproduction, can only be achieved through changes in the industrial capitalist world order. What the world needs now is not a 'Second Contraceptive Revolution' but a psycho-social revolution. In Part II of this study, we move beyond the Malthusian population paradigm to developing a political-economic analysis of women, population and the global crisis. In Part III, we explore some of the criteria and strategies for a paradigm shift from domination to partnership and from population control to birth control.

Notes

1. Lant H. Pritchett, "Desired Fertility and the Impact of Population Policies", *Population and Development Review*, Vol. 20, No. 1, March 1994, p. 40.
2. Gordon, *Woman's Body*, p. 219, Chap. 10.
3. Ibid., p. 276; Gould, "The Smoking Gun of Eugenics", p. 12; Sharon Kingsland, "Evolution and Debates over Human Progress from Darwin to Sociobiology", in Teitelbaum and Winter, eds, *Population and Resources*, p. 184.
4. Angela Y. Davis, *Women, Race and Class*, New York: Random House, 1981, p. 210.
5. Ibid., p. 214, cited in Hartmann, *Reproductive Rights and Wrongs*, p. 99; Donaldson, *Nature Against Us*, pp. 20–21.
6. Canadian Women's Committee on Reproduction, Population and Development, "A Canadian Women's Report on Canadian Policies and Practices in the Areas of Reproduction", issued in preparation for ICPD, August 1994, p. 13.
7. Paul Weindling, "Fascism and Population in Comparative European Perspective", in Teitelbaum and Winter, eds, *Population and Resources*, p. 107; see also Allan Chase, *The Legacy of Malthus: The Social Costs of the New Scientific Racism*, New York: Alfred A. Knopf, 1977.
8. Anthony R. de Souza, *A Geography of World Economy*, New York: Macmillan, 1990, pp. 66–68.
9. Donald P. Warwick, "Bullying Birth Control", *Commonweal*, Vol. 102, No. 13, September 12, 1975, p. 394; Donald P. Warwick, *Bitter Pills: Population Policies and their Implementation in Eight Developing Countries*, Cambridge: Cambridge University Press, 1982, Preface, p. x; Paul Demeney, "Social Science and Population Policy", *Population and Development Review*, Vol. 14, No. 3, September 1988, p. 32.
10. Ashford, "New Perspectives on Population", p. 22; UNFPA, *State of the World Population 1991*, p. 7; "Reproductive Revolution Sweeps Developing World", *Open File*, IPPF, April 1993, p. 1; Sinding and Segal, "Birth-Rate News".
11. Pritchett, "Desired Fertility", p. 40.
12. UNFPA, *State of the World Population 1991*, pp. 1–4; Sinding and Segal, "Birth-Rate News".
13. Donaldson, *Nature Against Us*, pp. 85–86, 106; Sari Tudiver, "The Strength of Links: International Women's Health Networks in the 80s", in McDonnell, ed., *Adverse Effects: Women and the Pharmaceutical Industry*, Toronto: Women's Press, 1986, p. 192.
14. *Population Control and National Security: A Review of U.S. National Security Policy*, Information Project for Africa, Inc., PO Box 43345, Washington, DC, 1991, p. 17; Donaldson, *Nature Against Us*, p. 120.
15. Fred T. Sai and Lauren A. Chester, "The Role of the World Bank in Shaping Third World Population Policy", in Roberts, ed., *Population Policy*, p. 187; World Bank, *Population and the World Bank*, p. 62; Donaldson, *Nature Against Us*, p. 122.
16. Cary LaCheen, "Population Control and the Pharmaceutical Industry", in McDonnell, ed., *Adverse Effects*, p. 123; Peter J. Donaldson and Amy Ong Tsui, "The International Family Planning Movement", Population Reference Bureau, *Population Bulletin*, Vol. 45, No. 3, November 1990; Donaldson, *Nature Against Us, passim*; Amit Sen Gupta, "A Paradigm Shift", *Political Environments*, No. 4, Summer–Fall 1996, p. 20.
17. "Amsterdam Declaration", in UNFPA, *State of the World Population 1990*, p. 7; UNFPA, *State of the World Population, 1991*, p. 1.
18. United Nations, Report of the ICPD, p. 46, para 7:12; Stephen L. Isaacs,

"Incentives, Population Policy, and Reproductive Rights: Ethical Issues", *Studies in Family Planning*, Vol. 26, No. 6, November/December 1995, p. 363; Sen Gupta, "A Paradigm Shift", pp. 18–20.

19. Jodi L. Jacobson, "Gender Bias: Roadblock to Sustainable Development", *World Watch Paper*, No. 110, September 1992, p. 43; Malini Karkal, "Patriarchal Demography: Tracing India's History", *Political Environments*, No. 4, Summer–Fall 1996, pp. 31–32.

20. Elisabeth Bumiller, *May You be the Mother of a Hundred Sons*, New York: Random House, 1990, pp. 264–266; Marilyn Dalsimer and Laurie Nisonoff, "The Implications of the New Agricultural and One-Child Family Policies for Rural Chinese Women", *Feminist Studies*, Vol. 13, No. 3, Fall 1987, p. 594; Xiao Ling, "No Red Eggs: China's One Child Policy", *Sojourner*, Vol. 12, No. 8, April 1987, p. 15.

21. Donaldson, *Nature Against Us*, pp. 56–57; Mamdani, *The Myth of Population Control*, p. 42.

22. John A. Ross, "Sterilization: Past, Present, Future", Population Council Working Paper No. 29, 1991, pp. 4, 7.

23. Ibid., p. 8.

24. Adele Clarke, "Subtle Forms of Sterilization Abuse: A Reproductive Rights Analysis", in Rita Arditti, Renate Duelli Klein and Shelley Minden, eds, *Test Tube Women: What Future for Motherhood?*, London: Pandora Press, 1984, p. 189.

25. Julia R. Scott, "Norplant: Its Impact on Poor Women and Women of Color", National Black Women's Health Project, Washington, DC, n.d., p. 14; Thomas M. Shapiro, *Population Control Policies: Women, Sterilization and Reproductive Choice*, Philadelphia: Temple University Press, 1985, p. 188.

26. Angela Davis, "Racism, Birth Control, and Reproductive Rights", in Marlene Gerber Fried, ed., *From Abortion to Reproductive Freedom: Transforming a Movement*, Boston: South End Press, 1990, p. 23; Shapiro, *Population Control Policies*, Chap. 5; Philip Reilly, *The Surgical Solution: A History of Involuntary Sterilization in the United States*, Baltimore, MD: Johns Hopkins University Press, 1991, p. 148; Allan Chase, "Health News Commentary", *Medical News*, January 8, 1979.

27. Julius Paul, cited in Jack Slater, "Sterilization: Newest Threat to the Poor", *Ebony*, Vol. 28, No. 12, October 1973, p. 152.

28. "Growing Fight Against Sterilization of Native Women", *Akwesasne Notes*, Late Winter 1979, p. 29.

29. Shapiro, *Population Control Policies*, pp. 148–158; Susan E. Davies, ed., *Women Under Attack: Victories, Backlash, and the Fight for Reproductive Freedom*, Committee for Abortion Rights and Against Sterilization Abuse (CARASA) Boston, South End Press, 1988, p. 29; Testimony of Helen Rodriguez-Trias, MD, on Federal Financial Participation in Sterilization funded by Department of Health, Education and Welfare (DHEW), USA, draft submitted by the Committee to End Sterilization Abuse (CESA), n.d.

30. Howie Kurtz, "Some Doctors Are Critical of Sterilization Guidelines", *Washington Star*, June 22, 1980, p. 1; Diane Ainsworth, "Cultural Cross Fires", *Human Behaviour*, March 1979, pp. 53–55; Thomas M. Shapiro, William Fisher and Augusto Diana, "Family Planning and Female Sterilization in the United States", *Social Science Medicine*, Vol. 17, No. 23, 1983, pp. 1847–1855.

31. "Four Women Assert Jobs Were Linked to Sterilization", *The New York Times*, January 5, 1979, p. A21.

32. Theresia Degener, "Sterile Without Consent", *Connexions*, No. 25, Winter 1987, pp. 10–11, 28.

33. Hartmann, *Reproductive Rights and Wrongs*, pp. 78–80.

34. Sonia Corrêa, "The Rights of Reproduction in the Context of the Demographic Transition in Brazil", unpublished paper, 1992, pp. 4, 6, 8; "Brazil: The Price of a Vote", *Ms. Magazine*, January February 1992, p. 12; Fatima Vianna Mello, "International Update: Sustainable Development For and By Whom?", *The Fight for Reproductive Freedom*, Civil Liberties and Public Policy Program, Newsletter, Vol. VI, No. 2, Winter 1992, pp. 4–6; James Brooke, "Brazil Welcomes Drop in Population Growth", *The New York Times*, March 8, 1992, p. 18.

35. Isaacs, "Incentives, Population Policy and Reproductive Rights", p. 363; Stephen L. Isaacs, "Incentives for Family Planning – Ethical Considerations", presentation at Expert Round Table on Population Policy, UNFPA, New York, 1986; see also Hartmann, *Reproductive Rights and Wrongs*, pp. 66–72; LaCheen, "Population Control", pp. 120–124.

36. Ling, "No Red Eggs"; Dalsimer and Nisonoff, "The Implications", *passim*.

37. Betsy Hartmann and Hillary Standing, *Food, Saris and Sterilization*, London: The Bangladesh International Action Group, 1985, pp. 10–11.

38. Ibid., pp. 12–13; see also Farida Akhter, "Wheat for Statistics", in Spallone and Steinberg, eds, *Made to Order*, pp. 154–160.

39. Hartmann and Standing, *The Poverty of Population Control*, p. 80.

40. Ibid., *passim*; Hartmann and Standing, *Food, Saris*; Akhter, "Wheat for Statistics"; see also Sultana Kamal, "Seizure of Reproductive Rights? A Discussion on Population Control in the Third World and the Emergence of the New Reproductive Technologies in the West" in Spallone and Steinberg, eds, *Made to Order*, pp. 146–153; John Cleland and W. Parker Mauldin, "The Promotion of Family Planning by Financial Payments: The Case of Bangladesh", Working Papers, No. 13, World Bank, Washington, DC, 1990; see also J. Cleland and P. Mauldin, *Study of Compensation Payments and Family Planning in Bangladesh*, cited in Hartmann and Standing, *The Poverty of Population Control*, pp. 22–31.

41. Hartmann and Standing, *The Poverty of Population Control*, p. 25.

42. Hartmann and Standing, *Food, Saris*, pp. 13–16.

43. Akhter, "Wheat for Statistics", p. 160.

44. Hartmann and Standing, *Food, Saris*, p. 17.

45. Cleland and Mauldin, "The Promotion of Family Planning", p. 32.

46. Confidential UNFPA Letter from Walter Holzhausen to Nafis Sadik, January 18, 1984, reprinted in Hartmann and Standing, *Food, Saris*, Appendix 1, pp. 37–39.

47. Cleland and Mauldin, "The Promotion of Family Planning", p. 25.

48. Ibid., pp. 34, 38–39.

49. Ibid., pp. 37, 41–42; see also Hartmann and Standing, *The Poverty of Population Control*, pp. 25–27, 30.

50. Hartmann and Standing, *The Poverty of Population Control*, p. 30–31; Cleland and Mauldin, "The Promotion of Family Planning", p. 37.

51. Ross, "Sterilization", p. 7; Pastor B. Sisson, "Bangladesh Succeeds With Family Planning", Letter to Editor, *The New York Times*, October 6, 1994, p. A28.

52. Betsy Hartmann, "What Success Story?", *The New York Times*, op.-ed., September 29, 1994, p. A25.

53. Davidson Gwatkin, "Political Will and Family Planning: The Implications of India's Emergency Experience", *Population and Development Review*, Vol. 5. No. 1, 1979, p. 48.

54. Ibid., pp. 37–38, 52; Marika Vicziany, "Coercion in a Soft State: The Family Planning Program of India – Part 2: The Sources of Coercion", *Pacific Affairs*, Winter 1982–1983, pp. 557–589.

55. Gwatkin, "Political Will and Family Planning", pp. 29, 47, 52; see also Malini Karkal, "Compulsion: Political Will and Family Planning", collection of documents, 4 Dhake Colony, Andheri (W) Bombay 58, India, n.d., *passim*; Hartmann, *Reproductive Rights and Wrongs*, p. 252; Mohan Rao, "The World Bank's Prescription for India's Family Welfare Program", *Political Environments*, Special Double Issue, Winter/Spring 1996, p. 38.

56. Hartmann, *Reproductive Rights and Wrongs*, pp. 168, 252–253; Ramala Buxamusa, "The Price of Assistance: The Family Planning Programme in India", *Socialist Health Review*, March 1985, pp. 155, 157.

57. Hartmann, *Reproductive Rights and Wrongs*, p. 253; Bumiller, *May You Be*, pp. 258, 238–239.

58. Bumiller, *May You Be*, p. 264; Karkal, "Compulsion", *passim*.

59. Elisabeth Meloni Vieira, "Female Sterilisation", *WGNRR Newsletter*, No. 48, October–December 1994, p. 11.

60. Patricia Jeffery, Roger Jeffery and Andrew Lyon, *Labour Pains and Labour Power: Women and Childbearing in India*, London: Zed Books, 1989, p. 202.

61. Bumiller, *May You Be*, pp. 272–274.

62. "300 Sterilizations in 10 Hours? Rubbish", cited in Karkal, "Compulsion", p. 143.

63. Kalinga Seneviratne, "Method Behind Dr. Mehta's Guiness Record", *Terra Viva*, IPS-ICPD Issue, September 12, 1994, p. 16.

64. Milap Chand Dandia, "Sterilisation Drive Creates Terror in Rajasthan" cited in Karkal, "Compulsion", pp. 131–132; Dheepa Dhanraj, Director/Producer, documentary film: *Something Like a War*, D.N. Productions, India, in association with Equal Media Ltd., London, 1991.

65. Bumiller, *May You Be*, p. 259.

66. Anna Husson, "Integrated Development: Slum Resettlement and Sterilization Abuse in Visakhapatnam, India", *WGNRR Newsletter*, No. 34, January–March 1991, p. 10.

67. "Indian Women's Groups Protest Population Committee's Attitude", *WGNRR Newsletter*, No. 48, October–December 1994, pp. 6–7; Vandana and Mira Shiva, "World Bank Role in Unsafe Contraceptive Promotion", *Third World Resurgence*, No. 50, 1994, pp. 28–9.

68. Rao, "The World Bank's Prescription", pp. 38–39; Sen Gupta, "A Paradigm Shift", pp. 18–20.

69. Dalsimer and Nisonoff, "The Implications", pp. 586, 589, 594; Ling, "No Red Eggs", p. 13; Hartmann, *Reproductive Rights and Wrongs*, p. 162.

70. Dalsimer and Nisonoff, "The Implications", p. 597; Hartmann, *Reproductive Rights and Wrongs*, p.162; Sheryl WuDunn, "China, With Ever More to Feed, Pushes Anew for Small Families", *The New York Times*, January 16, 1992, pp. 1, 10; Ling, "No Red Eggs", pp.13–15.

71. Nicholas D. Kristof, "Chinese Region Uses New Law to Sterilize Mentally Retarded", *The New York Times*, November 21, 1989, pp. A1, A10.

72. "New Chinese Law Prohibits Sex-Screening of Fetuses", *The New York Times*, November 15, 1994, p. A5; Nicholas D. Kristof, "Some Chinese Provinces Forcing Sterilization of Retarded Couples to Marry", *The New York Times*, August 15, 1991, pp. A1, A8.

73. Cited in Clare Schnurr, "Family Planning or Population Control?", Shair: International Forum, Canada, March 1989, p. 4; Nicholas D. Kristof, "In Corner of Tibet, Chinese Now Predominate", *The New York Times*, September 9, 1991, pp. A1, A6.

74. Cited in Schnurr, "Family Planning".

75. Paul Ingram, *Tibet: The Facts*, Dharamsala, India: Tibetan Young Women's Buddhist Association, 1990, p. 51.

76. Cited in Hartmann and Standing, *Food, Saris*, Appendix 1, p. 37.

77. Cited in Betsy Hartmann, "Bankers, Babies, and Bangladesh", *The Progressive*, September 1990, p. 21.

78. J. Mayone Stycos, "The Second Great Wall of China: Evolution of a Successful Policy of Population Control", *Population and Environment: A Journal of Interdisciplinary Studies*, Vol. 12, No. 4, Summer 1991, p. 405; Stanley Johnson, "China, the United States and the United Nations", *Populi*, Vol. 15, No. 1, 1988, p. 67.

79. Rosalind Pollack Petchesky, "'Reproductive Choice'" in the Contemporary United States: A Social Analysis of Female Sterilization", in Karen L. Michaelson, ed., *And the Poor Get Children: Radical Perspectives on Population Dynamics*, New York: Monthly Review Press, 1981, p. 67; "Introduction", in Mintzes et al., eds, *Norplant Under Her Skin*, p. 5.

80. LaCheen, "Population Control", pp. 90, 102; Hartmann, *Reproductive Rights and Wrongs*, pp. 179–180.

81. Sumati Nair, "Imperialism and the Control of Women's Fertility", London and Amsterdam: The Campaign Against Long-Acting Contraceptives, 1989, p. 108; Hartmann and Standing, *The Poverty of Population Control*, Preface and pp. 20–21.

82. "Preventive Diplomacy: Revitalizing A.I.D. and Foreign Assistance for the Post-Cold War Era", Report of the Task Force to Reform A.I.D. and the International Affairs Budget, United States Agency for International Development, September 1993; "Blueprint for Development – The Strategic Plan of the Agency for International Development", United States Agency for International Development, n.d; see also Demerath, *Birth Control and Foreign Policy*, p. 47.

83. Jack Anderson and Dale Van Atta, "U.S. Blunders in Safe-Sex Crusade", *Washington Post*, January 16, 1990, p. D23; LaCheen, "Population Control", p. 108.

84. Kim Yanoshik and Judy Norsigian, "Contraception, Control and Choice: International Perspectives", in Kathryn Strother Ratcliff, ed., *Healing Technology: Feminist Perspectives*, Ann Arbor: University of Michigan Press, 1989, p. 71.

85. Yanoshik and Norsigian, "Contraception", pp. 67, 76–77; Hartmann, *Reproductive Rights and Wrongs*, pp. 191–192.

86. Canadian Women's Committee on Reproduction, Population and Development, "Canadian Women's Report", p. 16; Hartmann, *Reproductive Rights and Wrongs*, p. 190.

87. Yanoshik and Norsigian, "Contraception", p. 67.

88. Ibid., p. 74; Jack Anderson and Joseph Spear, "Dalkan Shield Still Poses Threat Abroad", *Washington Post*, July 6, 1985, p. D12.

89. Lezak Shallat, "Local Women File Suits Against Manufacturer", *The Tico Times*, November 27, 1987; Yanoshik and Norsigian, "Contraception", p. 75; Hartmann, *Reproductive Rights and Wrongs*, p. 218.

90. Cited in Hartmann, *Reproductive Rights and Wrongs*, p. 213; Vimal Balasubramanyan, "Towards a Women's Perspective on Family Planning", *Economic and Political Weekly*, Vol. XXI, No. 2, January 11, 1986, pp. 69–71.

91. Stephen Minkin, "Depo-Provera: A Critical Analysis, Institute for Food and Development Policy, San Francisco, 1981, p. 1.

92. *Ultimate Test Animal* (documentary film, produced by Karen Branan and Bill Turnley, New York, The Cinema Guild, 1985; "The Depo-Provera Debate", National Women's Health Network, March–April 1983, p. 9; "Depo-Provera: Loopholes and Double Standards", *Hastings Center Report*, October–November 1987, pp. 3–4.

93. "Indian Health Service Dispenses Banned Contraceptive Drug to 35", *The New York Times*, August 7, 1987, p. A19.

94. Canadian Women's Committee on Reproduction, Population and Development, "Canadian Women's Report", p. 15; Hartmann, *Reproductive Rights and Wrongs*, p. 204.

95. Stephen Minkin, "Nine Thai Women Had Cancer... None of Them Took Depo-Provera: Therefore Depo-Provera Is Safe", *Mother Jones*, November 1981, p. 54.

96. Yanoshik and Norsigian, "Contraception", p. 80; Hartmann, *Reproductive Rights and Wrongs*, pp. 202–203.

97. Yanoshik and Norsigian, "Contraception", pp. 79–80.

98. Cited in Minkin, "Nine Thai Women Had Cancer", p. 37; Lynn Duggan, "From Birth Control to Population Control: Depo-Provera in Southeast Asia", in McDonnell, ed., *Adverse Effects*, pp. 160–163.

99. "Marketing Abroad", *Multinational Monitor*, Vol. 6, February–March 1985, p. 11; "W.H.O. Can You Trust?", *Right to Choose*, No. 26, Autumn 1983.

100. Vimal Balasubramanyan, "Finger in the Dike: The Fight to Keep Injectabales Out of India", in McDonnell, ed. *Adverse Effects*, pp. 146–147; Hartmann, *Reproductive Rights and Wrongs*, p. 206.

101. Soheir A. Morsy, "Bodies of Choice: Norplant Experimental Trials on Egyptian Women", in Mintzes et al., eds, *Norplant Under Her Skin*, p. 96; Anita Hardon and Lenny Achthoven, "Norplant: A Critical Review", *Women and Pharmaceuticals Bulletin*, Health Action International, November 1990, pp. 14–15.

102. "Norplant Trials Stopped in Brazil", *WGNRR Newsletter*, July–September 1986, p. 4.

103. Sheila J. Ward, Ieda Poernomo Sigit Sidi, Ruth Simmons and George B. Simmons, "Service Delivery Systems and Quality of Care in the Implementation of Norplant in Indonesia", New York: Population Council, 1990, pp. 31–32, 34–35, 50–51.

104. Hardon and Achthoven, "Norplant: A Critical Review", p. 17.

105. Ibid., pp. 14, 17; Daksha Hathi, "Speaking Out on Norplant" (and Editor's Note), *Political Environments*, No. 4, Summer–Fall 1996, pp. 14–17.

106. "F.D.A. Backs Safety Aspect of Norplant", *The New York Times*, August 20, 1995, p. 11.

107. 'Norplant' *Vital Signs*, Newsletter from the National Black Women's Health Project, n.d.

108. Cited in Andrew Purvis, "A Pill That Goes Under the Skin", *Time*, December 24, 1990, p. 66.

109. Scott, "Norplant".

110. Mireya Navarro, "Threat of a Benefits Cutoff: Will it Deter Pregnancies?", *The New York Times*, April 17, 1995, pp. A1, B7.

111. Cited in Hartmann, *Reproductive Rights and Wrongs*, p. 212.

112. 'Norplant', *Vital Signs*; see also Scott, "Norplant", pp. 11–12.

113. Mintzes et al., eds, *Norplant: Under Her Skin*; "Norplant: Under Her Skin", letter regarding Norplant distribution from women attending the 6th International Meeting on Women and Health, to Duff Gillespie, USAID, November 1990; Daisy Dharamaraj, MD, "Critical Review of Norplant", *Prepare*, India Rural Reconstruction and Disaster Response Service, 1993; "The Price of Norplant is TK 2000! You Cannot Remove it", UBINIG, Bangladesh, n.d.; "Norplant", *Vital Signs*, .

114. Morsy, "Bodies of Choice", p. 96; Joint Memorandum [by Women's Organizations and Concerned Groups] to the Health Minister [Government of India] Against NORPLANT, *Political Environments*, No. 4, Summer–Fall 1996, pp. 16–17.

115. "Study Says Progesterone Might Boost HIV Risk", *Fax Bulletin*, American Health Consultants, Atlanta, GA, May 8 1996, p. 1; see also "Selected Bibliography of Scientific Studies and Reviews on Hormonal Contraceptives and STDs", Family Health International, Research Triangle Park, NC, 1996.

116. Judith Richter, *Vaccination Against Pregnancy: Miracle or Menace?*, London: Zed Books, 1996; "Immunological Contraceptives", *Sojourner: The Women's Forum*, March 1995, p. 5H; Ingrid Schneider, "Anti-Pregnancy Vaccines", Hamburg, Germany, unpublished ms, September 1991, p. 2.

117. *Planned Parenthood Bulletin*, Family Planning Association of India, Vol. XXXIX, November 5, 1991.

118. Anita Hardon, "An Analysis of Research on New Contraceptive Vaccines", *Women and Pharmaceuticals Bulletin*, Health Action International, November 1990, p. 24; Angeline Faye Schrater, "Contraceptive Vaccines: Promises and Problems", in Helen Bequaert Holmes, ed., *Issues in Reproductive Technology: An Anthology*, New York and London: Garland Publishing Inc., 1992, pp. 31–52.

119. "International Campaign for a Stop of Research on Anti-Fertility 'Vaccines'", *WGNRR Third Campaign Report*, November 1994.

120. Ulrike Schaz and Ingrid Schneider, *Antibodies Against Pregnancy* (film, 1994), available from Bleicherstr. 2, D2267, Hamburg, Germany; Hartmann, *Reproductive Rights and Wrongs*, pp. 280–281.

121. Do Trong Hieu, Tran Thi Tan, Do Ngoc Tan, Pham Thi Nguyet, Pham Than, Dao Quang Vinh, "31,781 Cases of Non-Surgical Female Sterilisation with Quinacrine Pellets in Vietnam", *The Lancet*, Vol. 342, July 24, 1993, pp. 213, 216.

122. Cited in Fawn Vrazo, "New Sterilization Tack: A Savior or a Menace?", *Seattle Times*, December 4, 1993, p. A3.

123. Association for Voluntary Surgical Contraception, *AVSC Technical Statement Quinacrine Pellets for Nonsurgical Female Sterilisation*, September 1993, p. 6; John M. DiConsiglio, "Risks and Rewards: Family Planners Weight Quinacrine", *Family Planning World*, January–February 1994, p. 20; Judy Norsigian, "Quinacrine Update", *Political Environments*, No. 3, Winter/Spring 1996, p. 26; Lezak Shallat, "Excerpts from: Business as Usual for Quinacrine Sterilization in Chile", *Political Environments*, No. 3, Winter/Spring 1996, p. 27.

124. DiConsiglio, "Risks and Rewards", p. 20; Verzo, "New Sterilization Tack", p. A18; Hartmann, *Reproductive Rights and Wrongs*, pp. 256–258.

125. Cited in DiConsiglio, "Risks and Rewards", p. 20.

126. LaCheen, "Population Control", p. 101; see also Mamdani, *The Myth of Population Control, passim.*

127. World Bank, *Effective Family Planning Programs*, Washington, DC, 1993, pp. 76–77.

128. Mechai Viravaidya, "Community Development and Fertility Management in Rural Thailand", *International Family Planning Perspectives*, Vol. 12, No. 1, March 1986; talk and slide show by Mechai Viravaidya, Harvard Institute for International Development, Cambridge, MA, April 10, 1989.

129. World Bank, *Effective Family Planning Programs*, passim; "Spreading the Word", *Al-Ahram*, September 15–21, 1994, p. 14; IPPF, *Open File*, January 1995, pp. 10–15.

130. World Bank, *Effective Family Planning Programs*, p.76.

131. Ibid., p. 78; see also Karen F. Forfeit, Marcos Paulo P. de Castro and Elaine F. Duarte Franco, "The Impact of Mass Media Advertising on a Voluntary Sterilization Program in Brazil", *Studies in Family Planning*, Vol. 20, No. 2, March–April 1989, pp. 107–116.

132. Economic and Social Commission for Asia and the Pacific (ESCAP), *Population Headliners*, No. 219, June 1993, p. 8.

133. IPPF, *Open File*, March 1995, pp. 3–4.

134. Betsy Hartmann, "International Update", *The Fight for Reproductive Freedom*, Newsletter, Civil Liberties and Public Policy Program, Hampshire College, Vol. V, No. 1, Fall 1990, p. 5; see also, Elisabeth Sobo, "Crooning for Contraceptives in Nigeria", *The Progressive*, September 1990, pp. 26–28.

135. Information Project for Africa, Inc., *Unconventional Warfare*, pp. 11, 16.

136. LaCheen, "Population Control", pp. 116–119.

137. Ibid., p. 116.

138. Ibid., p. 118.

139. "'No Problem': Buying Depo-Provera in Mexico", *Multinational Monitor*, Vol. 6, February–March 1985, p. 11.

140. Hartmann, *Reproductive Rights and Wrongs*, p. 205.

141. LaCheen, "Population Control", p. 116; see also Nair, "Imperialism", p. 98.

142. Mahmoud F. Fathalla, "Fertility Control Technology: A Women-Centered Approach to Research", in Gita Sen, Adrienne Germain and Lincoln Chen, eds, *Population Policies Reconsidered: Health, Empowerment, and Rights*, Cambridge, MA: Harvard University Press, 1994, p. 228–229.

143. Ibid., p. 229; Loes Keysers, "Reflections on Reproductive and Sexual Rights During the ICPD", *WGNRR Newsletter*, No. 47, July–September 1994, p. 4.

144. Fathalla, "Fertility Control", p. 233; see also Sonia Corrêa, *Population and Reproductive Rights: Feminist Perspectives from the South*, London: Zed Books, 1994, pp. 22–23, 58; Louis Uchitelle, "Aiming at H.M.O.'s Upjohn Agrees to a $13 Billion Merger", *The New York Times*, August 21, 1995, pp. A1.

145. Philip J. Hilts, "F.D.A. Takes Steps to Hasten the Marketing of New Devices", *The New York Times*, April 7, 1995, p. A22; Barbara Crossette, "Population Debate: The Premises Are Changed", *The New York Times*, September 14, 1994, p. A3.

146. United Nations, "Proclamation of Teheran", in *United Nations Action in the Field of Human Rights*, New York, 1974, p. 79.

147. Letter by James D. Shelton, MD, MPH, Chief Research Division and Cynthia Calla, MD, MPH, Medical Officer, Office of Population, USAID, to Carlos Huezo, MD, Medical Director, IPPF, August 21, 1991.

148. Cited in Vandana and Mira Shiva, "World Bank Role", pp. 28–29.

149. Barbara Crossette, "New Tally of World Tragedy: Women Who Die Giving Life", *The New York Times*, June 11, 1996, pp. A1, 12; Jacobson, "Women's Reproductive Health", pp. 5, 59; "Safe Motherhood Initiative at Midpoint", *WIDLINE*, Population and Human Resources Department, World Bank, May 1992, No. 4, pp. 1–2; Jodi L. Jacobson, "Anti-Abortion Policy Leads to ... More Abortions", *World Watch*, May–June 1988, p. 9.

150. Barbara Herz and Anthony R. Measham, "The Safe Motherhood Initiative", World Bank Discussion Paper, No. 9, Washington, DC, 1990, p. 9.

151. World Bank, *Population and the World Bank*, p. 48.

152. Ibid., p. 65.

153. Hartmann and Standing, *The Poverty of Population Control*, pp. 65–72; cited in Anrudh Jain and Judith Bruce, "A Reproductive Health Approach to the Objectives and Assessment of Family Planning Programs", in Sen, Germain and Chen, eds, *Population Policies Reconsidered*, p. 198; Deborah Maine, Murat Z. Akalin, Jyotsnamoy Chakraborty, Andres de Francisco, and Michael Strong, "Why Did Maternal Mortality Decline in Matlab?", *Studies in Family Planning*, Vol. 27, No. 4, July–August 1996, pp. 179–187.

154. Cited in Hartmann and Standing, *The Poverty of Population Control*, p. 64.

155. Karkal, "Why the Cairo Document is Flawed", p. 20.

156. Rao, "The World Bank's Prescription", pp. 38–39; see also "SAPs and Women's Health in India", *Political Environments*, No. 3, Winter/Spring 1996, pp. 39–40; Sen Gupta, "A Paradigm Shift", *passim*.

157. UNFPA, *The State of the World Population 1995*, p. 64; Vina Mazumdar, "Fertility Policy in India", in Scott Menard and Elizabeth W. Moen, eds, *Perspectives on Population: An Introduction to Concepts and Issues*, New York: Oxford University Press, 1987, p. 264.

158. Hartmann and Standing, *The Poverty of Population Control*, pp. 72–73.

159. World Bank, Population and Human Resources Department, *WIDLINE*, No. 5, August 1992; Report of the Expert Consultation on Women in Agricultural Development and Population in Asia, Penang, Malaysia, February 5–9, 1991, UNFPA and FAO; Joint Training Seminar on Women, Population and Development, UNFPA, INSTRAW (UN International Research and Training Institute for the Advancement of Women), May 22–26 1989, Santo Domingo, Dominican Republic.

160. "Women's Group in Madras Criticized", *WGNRR Newsletter*, No. 29, April–June 1989, p. 38.

161. Colette St. Hilaire, "Canadian Aid, Women and Development: Rebaptizing the Filipina", *The Ecologist*, Vol. 23, No. 2, March–April 1993, p. 1; see also Asoka Bandarage, "Women in Development: Liberalism, Marxism and Marxist-Feminism", *Development and Change*, Vol. 15, 1984, pp. 495–515.

162. Sidney Ruth Schuler, Syed M. Hashemi and Ann Hendrix Jenkins, "Bangladesh's Family Planning Success Story: A Gender Perspective", *International Family Planning Perspectives*, Vol. 21, No. 4, 1995.

163. Amartya Sen, "More Than 100 Million Women are Missing", *New York Review of Books*, Vol. 37, No. 20, December 20, 1990, p. 61; Vibhuti Patel, "Sex-Determination and Sex-Preselection Tests in India: Modern Techniques for Femicide", *Bulletin of Concerned Asian Scholars*, Vol. 21, No. 1, January–March 1989, pp. 2–10.

164. Nicholas D. Kristof, "Stark Data on Women: 100 Million Are Missing", *The New York Times*, November 5, 1991, p. C1; Where are the Missing Chinese Girls?", *WGNRR Newsletter*, No. 36, July–September 1991, p. 15; "Bad Year for Girls?", *Newsweek*, April 16, 1990, Vol. 115, No. 16, p. 81.

165. "New Chinese Law Prohibits Sex-Screening of Fetuses", *The New York Times*, November 15, 1994, p. 15; Patel, "Sex Determination".

166. Terrence Hull, "Recent Trends in Sex Ratios at Birth in China", *Population and Development Review*, Vol. 16, No. 1, March 1990, p. 75.

167. Ibid, pp. 74–75; see also Ling, "No Red Eggs".

168. Patel, "Sex-Determination", p. 4; 'Campaign Against Sex Selection Continues in India", *WGNRR Newsletter*, No. 29, April–June 1989, p. 38; Bumiller, *May You Be*, pp. 113–124.

169. Patel, "Sex-Determination", p. 4; Viji Srinivasan, "Death to the Female: Foeticide and Infanticide in India", *Third World Resurgence*, Vol. 29, No. 30, January–February 1993, p. 53.

170. Karkal, "Patriarchal Demography", p. 30; Patel, "Sex-Determination"; "Campaign Against Sex Selection", p. 38.

171. Madhu Kishwar, "When Daughters Are Unwanted: Sex Determination Tests in India", *Manushi: A Journal About Women and Society*, New Delhi, India, No. 86, January–February 1995, pp. 17–18.

172. Hull, "Recent Trends", p. 73.

173. Patrick E. Tyler, "U.S. Rights Group Asserts China Lets Thousands of Orphans Die", *The New York Times*, January 6, 1996, pp. 1, 4.

174. Cited in Patrick E. Tyler, "In China's Orphanages, a War of Perception", *The New York Times*, January 21, 1996, p. 31.

175. Tyler, "U.S. Rights Groups Asserts", p. 4.

176. Kay Ann Johnson, "Who is to Blame for High Death Rates in Orphanages?", unpublished ms., Hampshire College, Amherst, MA, 1996.

177. Hull, "Recent Trends", p. 79.

178. Srinivasan, "Death to the Female", pp. 53–56.

179. Hull, "Recent Trends", p. 76; Hartmann, *Reproductive Rights and Wrongs*, p. 166.

180. Hull, "Recent Trends", p. 79.

181. UNFPA, *State of the World Population 1991*, pp. 1–4; Sinding and Segal, "Birth-Rate News".

182. Kingsley Davis, "Wives and Work: The Sex Role Revolution and its Consequences", *Population and Development Review*, Vol. 10, No. 3, September 1984, p. 415.

183. Jeffery et al., *Labour Pains*, pp. 212–213.

184. WuDunn, "China With Ever More To Feed", p. 1.

185. David Harvey, "Population, Resources, and the Ideology of Science", *Economic Geography*, Vol. 50, July 1974, pp. 256–277; Bonnie Mass, *Population Target: The Political Economy of Population Control in Latin America*, Toronto: Women's Press, 1976; Mamdani, *The Myth of Population Control, passim*; Serron, *Scarcity, Exploitation and Poverty, passim*.

PART II

Political-Economic Analysis

3

Historical Evolution of
Socio-Demographic Relations

There is no universal law of population applicable everywhere to all people, as assumed by Malthus. Rather, population dynamics are defined by social structure. According to Marx, population laws vary in relation to modes of production, that is, the forces of production – control over nature and the technical processes of production – and the social relations of production – property relations and surplus appropriation.[1]

The laws of population cannot be understood merely at the level of modes of economic production; the modes of human reproduction need to be understood as well. As Marxist theorists have noted, mortality, fertility and migration, which constitute population dynamics, must be examined in relation to changing technical and social bases of production and reproduction and their inter-linkages, including ideologies and belief systems.[2]

Human reproductive patterns have seldom been completely at the mercy of sexual and environmental imperatives or levels of contraceptive development, as assumed by the neo-Malthusians. Throughout history, human beings have engaged in both pro- and antinatalist practices to "optimize rationalities" directed at enhancing social welfare. But such practices have rarely brought "equal or beneficial results to all".[3] As has been observed by anthropologists Marvin Harris and Eric Ross, who have studied population regulation in pre-industrial societies, "As power differentials increase, the upper and lower strata may, in fact, develop different or even antagonistic systems of population regulation."[4]

Gender dynamics constitute the core of biological reproduction. Being uniquely endowed with the capacity for reproduction, women of course have borne the costs of pregnancy, birth, lactation, as well as abortion and other stressful population regulation methods.[5] But male–female relations do not exist in isolation. They are shaped by patterns of human socialization and the reproduction of cultural and politico-economic institutions at the local, regional levels and increasingly at the global level. Class dominance over reproduction takes place through the control of lower-class women by upper-class men. The particular forms these controls take vary across historical periods and cultures, neo-Malthusian population control programs being a contemporary manifestation of this phenomenon.

To understand fertility and population dynamics, it is necessary to develop a dialectical, social-historical analysis. While such an analysis cannot be fully developed here, some general patterns relevant to understanding the contemporary population dilemma will be presented in this chapter. It should be mentioned at the outset that historical and cross-cultural data available on early social formations are often biased and inadequate. Many of the anthropological accounts of contemporary gatherer-hunters, pastoralists, and so on, have been shaped by the forces of western imperialism and social class and male dominance.[6]

Population in Pre-capitalist Societies

Foraging communities

In the technologically primitive early human societies there was little separation of humans from the rest of nature. The foraging economies were stagnant by modern technological and consumption standards. Yet our early ancestors seem to have enjoyed a well-fed existence with much leisure time at their disposal. For example, the diet of the !Kung of Southern Africa, who have been studied extensively in recent times, was "extremely low in salt, saturated fats, and carbohydrates, particularly sugar, and high in polyunsaturated oils, roughage and vitamins and minerals". The average intake of calories and proteins of the !Kung, in fact, exceeded the United Nations' recommendations for people of their size and stature.[7] As Marshall Sahlins noted in *Stone Age Economics*, gatherer-hunters lived in a kind of "original affluent society", with an abundance of materials necessary to meet their needs.[8]

As among many other animals, aggression was not uncommon among the early humans. Yet the low level of technological and material development among the gatherer-hunters both necessitated and resulted in co-operation and equality among the band members (Figure 8.1). Despite being at the mercy of the vagaries of nature, a sense of psychological freedom and emotional security seemed to have prevailed. The lack of material possessions and status aspirations probably contributed to low levels of conflict and stress. According to some anthropological accounts, many gatherer-hunter groups cited as exhibiting the worst forms of institutionalized violence and sexual antagonisms were relatively egalitarian and peaceful prior to contact with the Europeans and the imposition of capitalist institutions and western values.[9]

Foraging and population

Although control over the environment and biological reproduction was minimal in the gatherer-hunter societies, most of these small-band societies seemed to have retained a balance between population size and available resources. This balance resulted partly from egalitarian consumption patterns associated with the absence of a social surplus. Still, there is evidence that during crises some of these early societies turned to drastic measures such as abandonment of the elderly and the deformed, infanticide, and so on. Among some groups, female infanticide may have been widespread due to its "extreme effectiveness" as a population control mechanism.[10]

However, there is no consensus on the extensiveness of female infanticide among foraging bands. Some scholars believe that hunting gave men a higher status over women, who were mostly associated with gathering and childbearing.[11] Still, childbearing was treated with awe and respect and often revered. Among the Mbuti of Central Africa, for example, women were seen as closer to the forest than the men because of their possession of the ultimate power to give birth to life. To some extent, the esteem of childbearing was shared with Mbuti men, who, as 'male mothers', experienced some of the joys of mothering as children grew older.[12]

Yet, given general sexual promiscuity and absence of monogamy, paternity was probably not commonly known. Communities were centered on women and children and descent was traced matrilineally.[13] Women's contributions from gathering was perhaps more crucial to survival than the more sporadic contributions from hunting by men. Women were not dependent on men or children for survival and, given their nomadism, mobility was a great concern of both foraging men and women. There seems to have been little or no pressure on women to conceive and bear children: "children were neither a potential labour force nor an insurance against old age".[14]

Among Paleolithic gatherer-hunters, natural fertility levels have been estimated in the "neighbourhood of four to six live births". For the !Kung, anthropologists have calculated an average live birth rate of 4.7 per woman.[15] While it is not possible to make a definite conclusion as to whether fertility was low in the gatherer-hunter mode relative to later agricultural modes of production, what is clear is that a range of culturally mediated controls over both mortality and fertility existed among foraging peoples. These included abortion, infanticide, warfare, prolonged breast-feeding and child spacing. These contributed in different ways to population control.

Among the so-called 'post-Neolithic' pastoralists, too, a wide range of population regulation mechanisms existed. Studies of a pastoralist group, the Rendille camel herders of Kenya, have shown a tendency to synchronize population size with the reproductive potential of their animals, upon whom their lives depend. Given the scarcity of camels and the need to pay brideprice in them, celibacy was enforced on a large proportion of males in the 12 to 31 age group, thus ensuring population-resource balance within limited regions.[16] As a result of such practices and high mortality rates, the gatherer-hunter stage, where 99% of human history was spent, was characterized by a very low, if not stagnant, population growth rate. Estimated annual population growth rate for the entire Paleolithic period is 0.0015%.[17]

From foraging to agriculture

With technological advancement, especially the plow, and the evolution of settled agricultural societies – the Neolithic Revolution – humans developed greater control over nature. Even prior to European capitalist expansion, with the evolution of technology and social surplus, many societies came to be characterized by social dualisms and hierarchies including gender, class and ethnic inequalities and attitudes of domination towards nature. Pre-existing egalitarian communities were either absorbed within the dominant hierarchical forms or they struggled to maintain their autonomy outside of them (Figure 8.1).

'Overconsumption' among ruling classes and ecologically detrimental production methods were not entirely absent in pre-modern agricultural societies. Many pre-capitalist societies like the Sumer and Maya collapsed due to environmental degradation. Yet, unlike in the modern economy, such methods and practices usually had limited effects rather than global repercussions because of the small scale and relative autonomy of those societies.[18]

Although the surplus grew with the shift to sedentary agriculture, with increased workloads leisure time declined. The Neolithic economy did not necessarily improve the quality of life at the individual level; apparently it experienced a decline in dietary sources, especially quality protein, animal fats and iron.[19] Moreover, with the evolution of social class relations, specifically the emergence of a class of surplus-producing serfs and a class of surplus-appropriating lords, producers' control over their labor and surplus was undermined.

Many state-based agricultural societies became characterized by widespread external and internal violence. In the feudal agricultural societies, the patriarchal head of the family had power to mete out violence against women and children while the state had power to enforce violent control over subordinate social classes. The traditions of widow burning by families – *sati* – in India and beheading of criminals and dissidents by many feudal monarchies are just two examples. Similarly notions of ethnic and racial superiority, for example the placement of the lighter skinned European

Christians over the darker Islamic and other groups referred to as 'infidels' and Orientals, predated the modern era. In India, racial and color hierarchies and ethnic violence were firmly established, as evinced in the Aryan-Dravidian divide. In fact, the Sanskrit term for caste, *varna*, means color.[20]

Despite institutionalized state and family violence and caste, class, gender, age and ethnic oppression, feudal social arrangements were not without some redeeming features. Individuals and families could derive a certain sense of stability and security from knowing their place in the social hierarchy. Although they were required to pay taxes in kind and services to the state and the ruling classes, the peasants and artisans had access to the means of production and control over labor processes and technology. Feudal agricultural systems depended on peasants' cultivating the land and their customary rights to land had therefore to be guaranteed. These basic social and economic arrangements allowed the existence of strong community and family bonds and traditions of mutual support and social security.[21] Overall, the land-based peasant societies also maintained a basic congruence with and respect for the rhythms and cycles of nature.

Agriculture and population

With increased ability to produce a surplus, societies were able to support larger populations. Increased sedentarism and spread of agriculture translated into higher rates of population growth. Sedentarism undermined the need to transport neonates and toddlers and children's labor came to play an important role in agriculture and household craft production. In household modes of production where the role of children as a source of labor and old age security is important, high fertility norms tend to persist.[22] According to Penn Handwerker, who has studied children's work in agricultural communities, with the transition to agriculture some 10,000 years ago, children became "the most consistently and systematically exploited segment of humanity".[23]

Given the absence of modern forms of sanitation and technology, mortality rates, especially infant mortality rates, were and continue to be high in agricultural societies. Although a 'tremendous growth of population' was associated with the agricultural revolution and population growth rates exceeded those of the gatherer-hunter stage, over the long term agricultural societies maintained an equilibrium in population size. The estimated population growth rate during the Neolithic period is 0.1%.[24]

Like the foragers, many agriculturists also adopted strategies of population control in order to adapt to scarce resources and especially to maintain an optimal relationship towards land. For example, in the relatively egalitarian, self-sustaining communities in the Himalayan region of Ladakh, flexible social relationships such as polyandry (the custom of several men marrying one woman) in conjunction with Buddhist monasticism (involving large numbers of men and women living as celibate monks and nuns) have contributed to maintaining population equilibrium.[25]

Among the consequences of increased sedentarism and agriculture were greater social complexity, new problems of resource scarcity and in many societies increased competition between individuals and groups. In societies where the surplus was expropriated by the ruling class, the laboring classes had to bear the brunt of famines and other crises by reverting to foraging in the forest, infanticide and other survival mechanisms. In some cases, peasants found it rational to keep their numbers down despite the wishes of aristocratic lords. The widespread practice of polyandry in the Kandyan kingdom in Sri Lanka may have been a form of peasant survival and resistance against the tribute-exacting feudal state.[26]

But with labor, not land, being the scarce factor of production, feudal landowners took great efforts to keep the cultivators tied to the soil and to expand land under cultivation. Expansion of social surplus depended on the availability of labor: in this sense, labor was the 'ultimate resource' in agricultural societies. Indian writers of the early political–spiritual treatise the *Arthashastra*, Chinese writers during the time of Confucius and Roman writers all advocated marriage and reproduction so that population could be increased and the land cultivated and taxes paid to the state.[27] As pronatalism was institutionalized, pronatalist norms came to be "supported by popular values both sacred and secular and effectively enforced by a variety of societal sanctions".[28] Indeed, the development of agricultural modes of production and state societies and attendant rise in population were achieved with compulsion and gender-, class- and age-based exploitation.

'Creation of patriarchy'

Although women invented agriculture based on their knowledge of gathering, with technological advancement farming became predominantly a male vocation. Women's contributions to cultivation and craft production continued to be essential, but women came to be seen primarily as the producers of children. As the male role in human biological reproduction came to be better understood, men began increasingly to control women's sexuality and their children. Thus, matrilineality (descent traced through maternal line), matrilocality (residence with women's kin) and women and children-centered social organization gave way to patrilineality (descent through paternal line), patrilocality (residence with husband's kin) and patriarchy (the rule of family and tribe by men).

As the heads of households, men claimed ownership over both women and children and monogamy was enforced on women for this purpose. The control of women's sexuality became crucial, especially for dominant classes seeking to expand economic surplus and conquest in war. Thus, increased pressure was placed on women to reproduce and their social status came to be defined more and more by their role as mothers, particularly the mothers of sons.[29]

Evidence from around the world shows that women in agricultural societies came to enjoy a less favorable status than women in the band-organized gatherer-hunter societies.[30] Engels referred to the change of women's status associated with the transition from the communistic foraging societies to class- and state-based agricultural societies as the "world-historical defeat of the female sex" (Figure 8.1).[31]

Whereas foraging women had equal access to gathering and the fruits of their labor, in the settled agricultural societies property was controlled by men. With the shift to sedentarism women's work-load in food processing, cooking, childrearing, and so on, greatly increased while their access to food and nutrition was undermined. This is quite clear in the biased sex ratios of pre-industrial societies. As anthropologists Julio Divale and Marvin Harris point out in their article "Population, Warfare, and the Male Supremacist Complex",

> Demographic analysis of 160 band and village populations, censused prior to modern contact and while they still practiced warfare, shows an average sex ratio in the age group 14 or under of 128 boys per 100 girls. ... The average sex ratio of humans at birth is 105.5 males per 100 females. ... The only way in which sex ratios as high as 128:100 can be achieved is through postpartum selection... Infanticide involving strangling, blows to the head, exposure, and other direct acts, is correlated with the sex ratio. ... Nonetheless, preferential overt female infanticide must be reckoned as only the tip of the iceberg.[32]

While warfare was a distinct form of population control in the earlier band and village societies, in later state societies warfare became integral to territorial and demographic expansion. Divale and Harris argue that in such societies female infanticide was widespread. Female infanticide apparently was motivated by a preference for male warriors; warfare in turn was propelled by the scarcity of women and competition for women between opposing groups.[33] In this historical context, the implicit connection between male alienation from human reproduction, specifically inability to give birth to life, and male proclivity towards war and violence, is worth greater investigation.[34]

While the overall position of women was undermined, women from the poorer classes suffered the most. For example, upper-class women often turned over the burdens of household and child-care work to poorer women. In late medieval Europe, the demand for wet-nurses to breast-feed infants caused some "poor country women to destroy their own offspring".[35] While most poor women did not deliberately destroy their own children, their servitude to the upper classes led to the neglect of their own flesh and blood. There is plenty of evidence of this phenomenon across time and place. Black 'mammies' of US plantation society and contemporary migrant Asian 'nannies' in the Middle East are just two examples.[36]

As today, so too in the past, poor women have sought to relieve their own biological burdens by abortion, infanticide and abandonment of children. The witchcraft persecutions of women in Europe in the sixteenth and seventeenth centuries reflected some of these conflicting interests of the rulers and the ruled. Apparently many poor women of the time sought to limit their fertility while the ruling class sought to stimulate it. Among the 16 million or so women who were killed during the witch hunts in Europe, many were midwives who were also abortion providers. However, the witch hunt was not simply a patriarchal reaction supported by the state and the Christian Church against women's reproductive autonomy. As sociologist Maria Mies and other feminist scholars have argued, it was also a means for the economic dispossession of women and the accumulation of capital by men from the dominant social classes.[37]

While there is no consensus as to when and how male dominance originated, many feminist theorists see patriarchy as the original form of social hierarchy from which all other forms of stratification and domination have evolved.[38] Archaeologist Marija Gimbutas has linked the shift from matrilineality to patriarchy with nomadic invasions into Europe, the Near East and India and the replacement of earth-based Mother Goddess worship with worship of an omnipotent male Sky God about 5,000 years ago. Many contemporary ecofeminists also trace the origin of both patriarchy and the mechanistic worldview to this so-called Indo-European Revolution. Feminist theorist Riane Eisler observes in this shift the subordination of the female, partnership paradigm by a male, dominator paradigm of human relations. Historian Gerda Lerner has identified "the creation of patriarchy" specifically in the victory of Christianity over pre-existing earth- and women-based religions and in Christianity's justification of the domination of men over women as the will of God.[39]

With the victory of Judeo-Christian teleology over paganism and animistic practices, Europeans developed a concept of time as non-repetitive and linear and a dualism of human and nature, promoting the idea that it was God's will that man exploit nature for his benefit. Historian Lynn White Jr has argued that, despite the theories of Darwin, in their hearts westerners do not see themselves as part of nature; they feel contemptuous, superior to and separate from it. White also observes that the roots of human domination over nature and the modern ecological crisis lie in the rise of Christianity, "the most anthropocentric religion the world has seen".[40]

Capitalism, Patriarchy and Population

With the scientific revolution of the seventeenth century in Europe and the spread of the philosophies of Francis Bacon and René Descartes, the cyclical vision of life of earlier societies began further to give way to a linear, quantitative approach to life.[41] In sharp contrast to the veneration of nature and the Mother Goddess by early earth-based peoples, this mechanistic approach came to view life and the earth as an unruly force to be dissected into its separate parts and to be tamed and controlled by humans through technology. Thus a reductionist, positivist approach based on empiricism and mathematics became increasingly dominant. This hierarchical and mechanistic outlook was also applied to the female body and mind. Attributes such as nurturance and caring, defined as feminine, came to be increasingly subordinated to that which was defined as masculine and strong. Women were seen as overly emotional, unpredictable and weak, requiring control by males, who were associated with scientific rationality and technological superiority.[42] This rationalistic outlook laid the basis for the emergence of the intertwined forces of western science, the Industrial Revolution, the bureaucratic state and the capitalist mode of production.

In contrast to the relatively static pre-capitalist economies, capitalism is inherently dynamic. It is defined by expanded reproduction, that is, re-creation of itself through constant growth. Capitalism seeks to free individuals from the bondages of tradition and the limits of nature. It believes that pursuit of self-interest will result in the good of all. The accelerated technological and material advancements of the modern age are the results of this belief system.

Fuelled by competitive scientific and technological advancement and market expansion, capital expands to new frontiers subordinating all in its expansionary path. To maintain constant growth, consumption must be constantly encouraged and all barriers to competition and growth must be broken down. From the beginning, the engine for capital accumulation has been technological expansion. Technological and capital expansion, in fact, constitute a single process: 'technocapitalism'. It is through competitive advantage in technological know-how, as much as labor exploitation, that capital expands.

Worker discipline and control are essential for labor exploitation under capitalism. Christianity played a vital role in the psychological and physical regimentation of workers for this purpose. As sociologist Max Weber observed, the Protestant ethic in particular was crucial to the emergence of industrial capitalism.[43] Historian E.P. Thompson has also explained how Puritanism restructured human nature to suit the needs of factory production by inculcating new valuations of time, especially by teaching children "even in their infancy to improve every shining hour", saturating their minds "with the equation, time is money".[44]

Notwithstanding the ideology of democracy, freedom, prosperity and peace, the capitalist social order has been founded upon competition, hierarchy, violence and militarism. Unbridled growth pays no heed to ethical and ecological criteria. The very creativity and dynamism of capitalism and modern science are also exploitative and destructive of people and nature. The contemporary global population and social crisis and the unprecedented threats facing biological existence are largely attributable to the contradictions of industrialism and capitalism.

European demographic transition

As earlier noted, Malthus's concept of overpopulation is based on the assumption of inevitable population pressure on the means of subsistence. But Marx replaced this with what he called the "relative surplus population", arguing that what Malthus saw as a universal law is, in fact, a problem historically specific to the capitalist mode of production. Marx pointed out that subsistence is determined not by the relationship between population and food supply but by the relationship between population and employment/unemployment. He also noted that the dynamic of capital accumulation creates an industrial reserve army that weighs down on the active labor force. The capitalist mode of production inevitably dispossesses the laboring classes of the means of production; the laboring class in turn tries to accumulate the only marketable commodity it possesses, labor power, thus contributing to high population growth rates.[45]

Urban population growth in the European countries was not the product of improved standards of living as much as the result of powerful social and economic transformations that turned peasants into proletarians. Until well into the middle of the nineteenth century, mortality rates and birth rates among the working classes remained quite high (Figure 3.1). The reason for high fertility was not so much a lack of access to contraceptives as the differential needs of children across the social classes. Women and children constituted an important aspect of the industrial labor force and source of household income. Intensified labor exploitation through such methods as the 'putting out system' of cottage industry had pronatalist effects among the rural population.[46]

Emphasis on national averages has tended to obscure significant class differences in the timing of reductions in mortality and fertility in the European countries. As Harris and Ross point out, the demographic transition was achieved in the first half of the nineteenth century among the middle classes, who absorbed the greater measure of the benefits of the Industrial Revolution. In contrast, among the working classes, who bore much of the detrimental effects of industrialization, the third stage of the demographic transition was not achieved until well into the second half of the century, and in some cases even later.[47]

Divergent patterns in sexual relations probably also contributed to differences in fertility and the onset of the demographic transition across the social classes. Freedom from wage labor and availability of labor-saving devices and household help made many middle-class housewives economically redundant. The accessibility of working-class women for the sexual

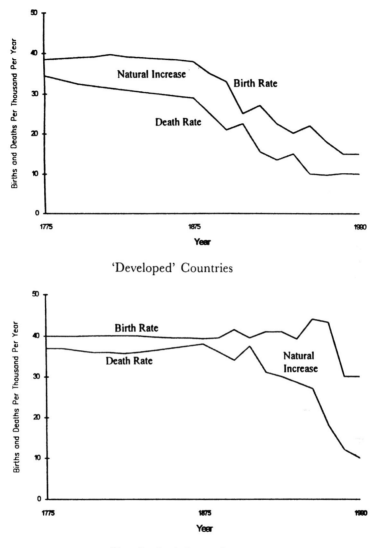

'Developed' Countries

'Developing' Countries

Figure 3.1   The demographic transition: developed
and developing countries

Source: A Citizen's Guide to the International Conference on Population and Development,
Washington, DC: Population Reference Bureau, 1994, p. 15.

exploits of middle- and upper-class men perhaps also minimized their wives' vulnerability to the risks of pregnancy and childbirth. As Harris and Ross note, to the extent that working-class women provided an outlet for the sexual inclinations of middle- and upper-class men through prostitution, it may have had an indirect effect on "dampening of middle class marital fertility".[48] This may also have bolstered working-class extra-marital fertility and need to resort to dangerous abortions and infanticide.

The delay in the demographic transition among the working classes can also be attributed partly to legal pressures brought by civil and church authorities against working-class efforts to curtail their fertility. These pressures persisted despite the growing popularity of Malthusianism among some segments of the ruling class during the course of the nineteenth century.[49]

Working-class fertility decline was the product of structural changes in the global economy as well as changes in the economic position of women. In the long run, the wealth extracted from the colonies contributed to improving standards of living of the European working classes, resulting in a lowering of their population growth rates. Fertility declined as childbearing was transformed from an investment into a consumption activity for parents, especially women. When compulsory education and laws prohibiting child labor were introduced in the 1870s, child labor lost its importance in industry and the household. It was then that contraceptive usage and the small family norm became common among the working classes. Legislation allowing property rights for married women, educational opportunities and well-paying employment for both men and women were crucial factors in this demographic transformation (Figure 3.1).[50]

Like its progenitor, modernization theory, neo-Malthusian demographic transition theory assumes a unilinear pattern of economic and demographic evolution for all societies and groups within societies. According to this Eurocentric and class- and gender-biased perspective, all societies will eventually follow the economic and demographic trajectories set forth by the West. Thus, wide variations of the demographic transition in European countries themselves are ignored and irrationality, ignorance and apathy of the poor, particularly that of women, are identified as obstacles in the path of a Third World demographic transition.[51]

In contrast, we show below that imperialism produced divergent population dynamics in the colonies and the metropolitan countries and that the so-called population 'explosion' in the Third World must be understood in relation to the impact of global capitalist development on pre-existing socioeconomic structures and gender, class and racial configurations.

Imperialism and Socio-Demographic Transformation

Even before the onset of the modern industrial age, long-distance trade created important links between diverse regions, cultures and peoples in the world. However, it was European conquest of the rest of the world beginning in the late fifteenth century and over two and half centuries of mercantile capitalism that set the stage for the emergence of a global capitalist economy centered on industrializing England from the middle of the eighteenth century.[52] Today, all regions and all people have been integrated within the capitalist market and the further spread of capitalist relations of production and modern technology is fast eroding what little is left of earlier tribal and peasant economies and cultures as well as unspoiled nature (Figure 8.1).

Imperialism has been a violent process from the beginning; it could not and still cannot survive without the backing of military force and collusion with local elites. Mercantilism was a process of pillage, plunder and rape of colonized lands and masses of men, women and children. The objective of the colonizers was to extract as much wealth – slaves, gold, raw materials – as quickly and cheaply as possible. The primitive accumulation of capital and political and cultural control consolidated by the Europeans during the mercantilist phase enabled the installation of the capitalist mode of production in the colonies during the course of the nineteenth and twentieth centuries. "Once 'pacification' was carried out and storehouses were emptied of gold and precious stones", the objective of the colonial nations shifted to obtaining primary products for export and manufactured products for import.[53]

The introduction of capitalist production produced a circuitous way of meeting basic needs, distorting ecosystems and the economic and social structures of colonized societies. Nature was privatized through the introduction of new individual property rights; land and labor were commoditized; and subsistence production was undermined by export production. Plantations and mines and roads and railways incorporated the colonies into the expanding global capitalist economy. But in the opening up of new lands and the development of mono-crop agriculture, mines, and so on, long-term ecological costs were woefully ignored. In the haste for capital accumulation and technological expansion, the traditional wisdom that human survival depends ultimately on the survival of the environment was cast aside.

Profits for western capital, rather than the survival of local populations, was the raison d'être of the new economic system. With clever use of theories and concepts such as 'comparative advantage', imperialism set in place a variety of mechanisms for the extraction of capital, profit, vital raw materials, food and even people and other resources from the colonies to the metropolitan countries and the 'New World'. The concept of 'carrying capacity', for instance, was first put into use by French and British colonial scientists and administrators seeking to estimate the minimum amount of land and labor needed by local people to meet their subsistence needs so that what was deemed in excess of that could be taxed by the colonial state and appropriated for export production. In other words, as ecologist Ben Wisner has pointed out, 'carrying capacity' is not a neutral, scientific term, as deemed by Malthusian analysts; rather it is a term which has carried a political agenda from its earliest usage.[54] As we point out in Chapter 6, this term must continue to be viewed in the geopolitical context of increasing economic dependency and the widening economic gap between the colonizing and colonized countries.

The commoditization of land and labor during the process of colonial capitalist evolution undermined peasant control over resources and production turning self-sufficient agriculturists and artisans into wage labor or surplus labor. The concentration of all energies on the supply of a single cash crop to the world market and the neglect of subsistence production made entire economies and societies vulnerable to the vicissitudes of the market. Thus, colonized lands such as Malaya (now Malaysia), Ceylon (now Sri Lanka) and Indonesia which had previously been self-sustaining became dependent on exports and imports for obtaining their basic rice supplies and daily survival. Fifty percent of the arable land in Malaya, 67% in Ceylon and 25% in Indonesia were turned over to cash crop production for export. By the late 1930s, exports constituted 75% of national income in Malaya, 48% in Ceylon and 25% in Indonesia, and each of these countries imported one-third of their rice in that decade.[55] Third World people began to develop a taste for the imported goods – refined rice, sugar and flour, and so on – although their nutritious value was much less than that of the natural foods they had previously been consuming. At every turn, colonial powers set higher prices for the manufactured goods imported into the colonies and lower prices for the raw materials and cash crops exported from them. Despite the rationale of comparative advantage, the terms of trade, that is, ratio of export prices to import prices, were unequal and biased in favor of the metropolitan countries. Moreover, exploitative wages paid to colonial labor brought wealth for the colonial masters and poverty for the colonized masses. According to historian Michael Barratt Brown's estimates for 1956, the value of annual output per worker in Northern Rhodesia, Southern Rhodesia, South Africa and Nigeria were £2450, £415, £700 and £205 (pounds sterling), respectively. In contrast, the annual wages paid per African worker in those four colonies the same year were £165, £47, £65 and £57, respectively.[56] As economist Harry Magdoff says, "A system built on inequality in the command of human and natural resources works in many ways not only to reproduce itself but to increase the extent of the in-built inequality".[57]

Unequal population dynamics

The demographic evolutions of the colonial and metropolitan countries were unequal but inherently interrelated. They continue to evolve dialectically within a single world socio-economic and demographic system. Anthropologist Steven Polgar argues that from a demographic point of view the period of direct European colonialism can be divided into two:

> In the first ... the population of colonizing peoples grew enormously (at average rates of 5 per 1,000), while the population of many subject societies was decimated through imported diseases, slavery, war and forcible removal. In the second ... in the metropolitan nations population increase slackened, while among subject peoples it generally surged...[58]

A defining feature of western imperialism was the expansion of the European population both within Europe and across the globe. For example, in England and Wales, the center of the Industrial Revolution, population increased from 6 million in 1750 to 9 million in 1800 and to 18 million in 1850. Although the rate of population growth declined after that, the absolute number of the population increased to 33 million by 1900. Between the sixteenth and early twentieth centuries, 20 million emigrated overseas from Britain while 60 million emigrated from other parts of Europe during the same period.[59] The relationship between this European emigration into the colonies and contemporary migration of peoples from the South to the North, however, is overlooked by anti-immigration movements in the North today.

What is also overlooked in conventional discussions of population is that natural population growth rates in the colonies were markedly less than those in the metropolitan countries during much of the colonial period (Table 3.1). By the end of the period of direct or classical colonialism around 1950, the population of European descent (in Europe and America) was over eight times the number it had been three centuries earlier compared to just a doubling of the population in Africa and an increase of about five times of the population in Asia (Table 3.2).

The "enormous demographic expansion" and global migration of the Europeans played a critical role in the consolidation of western control over the world. As Georg Borgstrom states in *The Food and People Dilemma*, white supremacy was achieved not on the basis of "superior mental or physical endowments", but on rapid population increase, in turn built on "grabbing and earmarking of vast land and soil resources" outside of Europe with "reckless and diligent" use of technology.[60]

Native depopulation

Colonial politico-economic expansion had diverse and enormous demographic consequences across the world. In many cases, colonial conquest decimated entire communities, depopulating entire regions. Apparently, most of the peoples who lived in the territory now known as the United States completely disappeared.[61] Even Charles Darwin observed that "Wherever the European has trod, death seems to pursue the aboriginal".[62]

Table 3.1   Estimated average annual growth rates of population, 1750–1950 (%)

Region	1750–1800	1800–1850	1850–1900	1900–1950
World	0.4	0.5	0.5	0.8
Africa	0.0	0.1	0.4	1.0
North Africa	0.2	0.5	1.2	1.4
Remainder	0.0	0.0	0.2	0.9
Asia	0.5	0.5	0.3	0.8
China	1.0	0.6	0.0	0.5
India and Pakistan	0.1	0.3	0.4	0.8
Japan	0.0	0.1	0.7	1.3
Remainder of Asia*	0.1	0.6	0.8	1.2
America	1.0	1.5	1.8	1.5
Latin America	0.8	0.9	1.3	1.6
North America	–	2.7	2.3	1.4
Europe*	0.4	0.6	0.7	0.6
USSR	0.6	0.6	1.1	0.6
Oceania	–	–	–	1.6

* Indicates figures excluding USSR

Source: Durand as cited in John G. Patterson and Nanda R. Shrestha, "Population Growth and Development in the Third World: The Neocolonial Context", in *Studies in Comparative International Development*, Vol. 23, Summer 1988, p. 17.

In many Caribbean islands, native depopulation was followed by Africanization, itself a result of slavery and the European plantation economy.[63]

The estimates of pre-contact population size and population decline associated with European conquest and expansion tend to vary widely.[64] According to some estimates, the total indigenous population in the Americas was reduced by 90% during the hundred years after the arrival of Columbus in 1492.[65] According to other estimates, the pre-contact population in the Americas (around 1492) was 20 times as large "on the average as the number of Indians at the population 'nadir'" (around 1900) (Table 3.3).[66]

According to estimates made on a global scale, during the 150 years between 1780 and 1930, world tribal populations were reduced by approximately 30 million due to conquest, the spread of new diseases by the Europeans and sometimes through outright extermination (Table 3.3). As demographer John Bodley argues, however, 50 million is a less conservative and more realistic estimate of the numbers of tribal people wiped out during that period. Bodley also suggests that population regulation mechanisms in the indigenous societies such as infanticide and abortion may have actually

Table 3.2 World population by continent, 1650–1950 (millions)

Region	1650	1750	1800	1850	1900	1950
Oceania	2	2	2	2	6	13*
Africa	100	100	100	100	120	199†
Asia	257*	437*		656*	857*	1,272*
	230†	479†	602†	749†	937†	
	250§	406§	522§	671§	859§	
America	8*	11*		59	144	338*
	13†	12.4†	24.6†	59	144	
	13§	12.4§	24.6§	59	144	
Europe	103*	144*		274*	423*	594*
(European Russia	100†	140†	187†	266†	401†	
included)	100§	140§	187§	266§	401§	
Totals *	470	694		1,091	1,550	2,416
†	445	733.4	915.6	1,176	1,608	
§	465	660.4	835.6	1,098	1,530	

Notes: * United Nations Bulletin, December 1951; † Carr Saunders; § Kuczvnski. Figures without a note are common to the three sources, as cited in Braudel.

Source: Fernand Braudel, *The Structures of Everyday Life: The Limits of the Possible*, Vol. 1, New York: Harper and Row, 1981, p. 42.

contributed to depopulation and even extinction when 'frontier' conditions created by European conquest elevated mortality rates drastically.[67]

This process of depopulation still continues, as can be seen for example from the rapid disappearance of indigenous populations and their tropical forest habitats across the world. Still other types of racial and cultural extinction have taken place and continue to take place through 'miscegenation', or evolution of new mixed races, such as the 'mestizos' in South America, and through continuing Christian proselytization and westernization. In European colonies throughout the world, many communities were often baptized en masse and Christian names imposed on people who had no idea what was being done to them. The introduction of Christianity, especially Catholicism, was coercive, frequently violent and bloody. As Chailang Palacios, a Chamorro woman activist from Saipan in the Northern Mariana Islands of Micronesia, recalls:

> The Spanish missionaries were blessing all the soldiers while the soldiers were cutting my ancestors into half, killing our men, raping our women. When they arrived we were about 40,000. And we ended up just 4,000 because they killed everyone that didn't want to embrace Christianity, which was the Catholic faith. So the Spanish stayed over 100 years. They came to do good work. And they did it very well, because today we are 97% Catholic.[68]

Table 3.3 World survey of tribal depopulation, 1780–1930

Region	Pre-contact population	Population low point	Depopulation
North America (US and Canada)	9,800,000	490,000	9,310,000
Lowland South America	9,000,000	450,000	8,550,000
Oceania			
Polynesia	1,100,000	180,000	920,000
Micronesia	200,000	83,000	117,000
Fiji	300,000	85,000	215,000
New Caledonia	100,000	27,000	73,000
Australia	300,000	60,500	239,500
Africa			
Congo			8,000,000
Estimated total depopulation			27,860,000*

* Total given by Bodley: the figures in fact only total 27,424,500. When moderate estimates are included for such areas as Melanesia, South Asia, South Africa, Southeast Asia and Siberia, total depopulation is estimated to be around 30 million

Source: John H. Bodley, "Demographic Impact of the Frontier", in Scott Menard and Elizabeth W. Moen, eds, *Perspectives on Population: An Introduction to Concepts and Issues*, New York: Oxford University Press, 1987, pp. 23, 24.

As Mexican scholar Sylvia Marcos has written in relation to the Americas, the colonization of the minds of natives was even more important to the success of the colonial enterprise than conquest and victory in the battle-field. 'Spiritual colonization' was built upon the claim that the identity of the natives had to be destroyed in order to 'save' them. As Marcos argues, this denial of the very being of the indigenous person came to affect the way they "saw their world, their people, the land, space, the sun, time, and the divine cosmic forces. Genocide and ethnocide were woven together."[69]

Continuing in the footsteps of their forebears, contemporary Christian missionaries seek to convert the entire world to Christianity in the twenty-first century.[70] Money and media tactics are often exported from the North to the South and great efforts are being taken to meet numerical targets (of Christian converts) through psychological manipulation and use of economic incentives among the poor. Notwithstanding current attempts by missionary forces to 'indigenize' Christianity by appropriating native cultural forms and appointing local clerics, Christianity continues to represent a force of spiritual colonization and destruction of indigenous cultures and self-identities. Moreover, historical experiences of much of Latin America, Africa and Asian countries like the Philippines show that conversion to Christianity does not necessarily lead to poverty alleviation or improvement in the quality of lives of the poor, as often promised by the proselytizers.

Like Christian domination, white supremacy, the assumed inherent superiority of whites over people of color, was integral to European imperialism from the very beginning. Quite often, the subjugated African, Indian and other natives were not even considered human by the European colonizers. A specific aspect of this was the differential values that came to be placed on white women and women of color. The elevation of the white woman into a 'sacred and idealized' figure and the denigration of the 'primitive' woman of color was a key element in the construction of the racial boundaries between the white colonizer and the colonized races. Feminist psychiatrist Jean Shindoa Bolen has observed that as the western civilization with its roots in Greek and Judeo-Christian values colonized the rest of the world, women of color came to be identified with nature and instinct and to be treated and abused as inferior, ignorant and dispensable.

> That which is 'earthly' or dark in color, female, instinctual, natural or physical in expression is repressed, considered inferior, dangerous, and in need of control or punishment – making it 'all right' to be abusive toward people so perceived. Women of color then become the recipient of 'dark' projections – forbidden passions and yearnings for earthy experience, for fulfillment of dependency needs. Intelligence is not ascribed to people who are darker or female in the Third World when the so-called First World makes this an attribute of individuals who are white and male.[71]

European men raped local women, used them as concubines and prostitutes, and in some cases even paid local women to bear mixed-race (for example, Eurasian), Christianized children, partly to increase their own numerical position. But rarely did European men take local women as wives: they did not want to upset colonial racial and property relations.[72] In many colonial contexts, the creation of mixed-race populations turned out to be politically and culturally advantageous to the Europeans because of the frequently greater allegiance shown by mixed-race populations to the colonizers than to the local masses.

White supremacy and the devaluing of native women underlie continuing policies of genocide and exploitation. For many tribal communities, survival is still the primary issue; not 'overpopulation'. In the US, uranium mining and testing of weaponry on native lands, introduction of alcohol and gambling into reservations, sterilization and the use of Depo-Provera and Norplant on women constitute new forms of extinction in the eyes of the indigenous peoples.[73] It is in the historical context of European economic, cultural and demographic expansion that the charge of genocide that native people make against western imperialism and population control programs needs to be considered. It is also in this context that the historical evolution of population dynamics in Africa and among people of African descent in the Americas needs to be addressed.

Physical anthropologists suggest that humanity may have originated in

Africa and the human race may have a common African ancestry. Yet in the global hierarchy of color that evolved with European imperialism, the 'Dark Continent', the black African and the African woman in particular came to be placed at the very bottom. The association of the African with the primitive in the forest in the minds of the European helped justify the savage enslavement of African people, the enslavement upon which much of the wealth and prosperity of Europe and the Americas was built.[74] As we discuss in Chapter 8, the mistaken notion of duality – self vs. other – underlies socio-psychological structures of global domination and oppression. The writing-off of Africa as the 'lost continent' and of poor African Americans as a hopeless 'underclass' by social analysts and policy makers in the contemporary period are expressions of continuing racism and denigration not only of that which is African but also of that which is primordial and human.

The African slave trade

The slave trade conducted by the Europeans in collusion with some native Africans, the importation of firearms and resultant conflicts and warfare destroyed and depopulated many communities in Africa. The estimates of the number of Africans taken forcibly as slaves during nearly four centuries of the slave trade vary greatly, anywhere from about 4 million to 15 million. According to Borgstrom, out of about 15 million Africans enslaved and taken out of Africa, only about half a million reached the United States, many having died en route on slave ships.[75]

Through emigration and death, slavery contributed to Africa's declining share of the world population. According to Patrick Manning's accounts in *Slavery and African Life*, the tropical African population was about 30% of the combined population of the New World, Europe, the Middle East and Africa in 1600.[76] According to Fernand Braudel's calculations, Africa's population had declined to about 22% of the global total in 1650 and further declined to about 12% in 1800 and less than 8% by 1900, rising slightly above 8% by 1950. What is most striking in these estimates is that while Africa and Europe each had about 100 million people in 1650, Europe's population had increased to about 600 million in 1950 while Africa's population had risen to only just under 200 million (Table 3.2).

The effects of the slave trade were not simply numerical. As Manning points out, slavery resulted in qualitative changes in African social life. For example, the declining ratio of men to women in slave-exporting regions affected marriage patterns and the domestic division of labor.[77] These changes probably reinforced patriarchy. While neo-Malthusian population control organizations like the World Bank and the UNFPA are greatly concerned about high fertility in African countries today, they have paid scant attention to the socio-historical roots of demographic change in Africa or other parts of the Third World.

The crisis of 'underpopulation'

Labor was essential for the growth of capital, but the Europeans found that most local people were reluctant to abandon their traditional agricultural, manufacturing and other work to become wage laborers. In other words, in the process of promoting export production, the Europeans experienced a crisis of 'underpopulation' rather than 'overpopulation'. These, however, are relational terms: a population is deemed sufficient, insufficient or excessive in relation to the labor requirements of capital at a given time and place. Experiencing 'underpopulation' crises, Europeans adopted all manner of coercive and subtle tactics, including slavery, forced labor, manipulation of prices, private property rights and so on to ensure cheap and regular labor supplies. Peasant lands were expropriated and 'head' taxes, 'hut' taxes, 'road' taxes, and so on, were imposed on local populations to turn them into wage laborers. Where these methods did not yield the necessary labor force, massive population transfers were undertaken across countries and regions without regard to cultural and ethnic boundaries to provide labor for plantations, mines, construction projects, and so forth. The origin and evolution of modern immigration lies not so much in 'overpopulation', as assumed by the neo-Malthusians, as in the uneven and unequal development of global capitalism.[78]

Colonial powers did not always seek complete destruction of subsistence economies. In many cases they preserved peasant subsistence sectors so that costs of labor reproduction would not have to be borne by capital. With the absorption of men into wage labor, women and children's unpaid labor in reproduction and subsistence production greatly increased. Reproduction of labor power lies at the core of social reproduction in capitalist society. Accumulation of capital requires both the expropriation of the means of economic production and control of the means of human reproduction. As philosopher George Caffentzis has put it: "primitive accumulation involves also the appropriation of the body, of sexual and reproductive powers, in so far as they are means for the accumulation of labour".[79] Given this reality, capitalist states have attempted to control demographic processes through control of women's sexuality and fertility using a variety of means. Current neo-Malthusian efforts, including the 'new' reproductive rights agenda, are a continuation of that historical legacy.

Many colonial states developed strong pronatalist policies to increase reproduction. In a study of colonial social policies in Uganda entitled "Intimate Colonialism", Carol Summers has discussed initiatives such as examination of women for sexually transmitted diseases and moral education promoting motherhood which were designed specifically to avoid labor shortages. She argues that these integrated bio-medical and ideological initiatives undertaken by the colonial state and Christian missionaries constituted a deliberate policy of 'social engineering':

In Uganda, the state ... worked to create new, colonial families ... designed specifically for the reproduction of an imperial structure threatened by reproductive failure. ... They were agencies of the state, cultivated for their effects on political stability and economic development. ... By promoting fertility, the administration sought to acquire taxpaying subjects and a labor force. By promoting new motherhood and attempting to reinforce social ties threatened through economic and political change, it endeavoured to make itself self perpetuating.[80]

Like some of the pre-existing hierarchical economies, colonial capitalism, too, had differential effects on different categories of people. Those class and ethnic groups who colluded with the colonial enterprise prospered over those who resisted it. Women's position in general was undermined. While a few colonial policies such as the abolition of *sati* or widow burning in India undermined pre-existing patriarchal traditions, colonialism introduced new forms of female subordination.

Even where women had been the primary economic producers, as in many parts of Africa, the new private property rights to land, access to credit, technology, trading privileges and education and employment training were generally given to men. The decline of village industry due to the competition from mass-produced imported goods eroded women's productive roles. With the introduction of commodity production, the entirety of women's work in subsistence production and reproduction became 'invisible'. The introduction of marriage registration strengthened the position of men as heads of households and controllers of family property.[81]

These changes undermined women's roles in economic production identifying women increasingly with the sphere of reproduction, notably childbearing and -rearing. Victorian notions of sexuality and concepts of the male breadwinner and dependent housewife that accompanied the expansion of colonialism and Christianity also contributed to the marginalization of women in colonial economies and cultures and their increasing economic and social subordination to men. As in the early manufacturing enterprises in industrializing Europe, in the colonies, too, women and children were incorporated in large numbers into the new sectors of production such as the plantations producing for export. Again, women and children were frequently paid lower wages than the men even when they did the same work. Moreover, the wages of women and children were often given to the men as family wages, thereby reinforcing male dominance over women and children.[82] In these many ways, colonialism set in motion a historical process that has come to be known as the 'feminization of poverty'.

However, women did not always accept colonial policies directed at them without resistance. In some cases, they refused to produce children for the hated colonial masters. After a rebellion of the Herero people in South West Africa had been brutally suppressed by the German colonialists there, Herero women went on a virtual 'birth strike'. Apparently, as a result, the

Herero population declined from 80,000 to 19,962 between 1892 and 1909.[83] There are also reports that slave women in the Caribbean went on similar strikes. Women who had internalized anti-motherhood attitudes as a form of resistance to slavery took bitter herbs to produce abortions or allowed their children to die after birth.[84] Nevertheless, the reaction of most colonized women has been to try to protect their young. For women living under the harsh conditions of imperialism and patriarchy, children are often the only source of joy and hope. Labor for the family, for their children if not their men, is the only labor of love.

How did colonized areas shift from being 'underpopulated' to being 'overpopulated'? Why did fertility and population growth rates begin to increase among some of the poorest sections of colonial populations? These transformations need to be understood in relation to the accumulation of wealth by the imperialist countries, the underdevelopment and poverty of the colonized countries, internal class disparities and the particular manner in which women were incorporated into the colonizing process.

From 'underpopulation' to 'overpopulation'

As noted earlier, population growth rates were lower in the colonies than in the metropolitan countries during much of the colonial era. Yet, as researchers John Patterson and Nanda Shrestha point out, "poverty, the principal measure of so-called Malthusian 'overpopulation', was no less a factor then than during the neo-colonial period (after World War II)".[85] In India, for example, population growth was slow during the centuries of British rule. Yet famines increased in intensity and frequency.[86] The problem of hunger and malnutrition, then, cannot be understood by mere references to population size; it must be viewed in relation to the socio-economic processes created and still maintained by imperialism.

Over time, the colonial transformation contributed to absolute increases in populations. While it may be erroneous to attribute all colonial efforts to improve transportation, health, education, and so on, only to profit maximization, colonial efforts to increase population were quite compatible with the interests of capital. As Polgar suggests,

> it should be apparent that as long as production for export in the colonies was labor-intensive, as long as these exports were essential to the metropolitan countries, and as long as the profits from international trade were not exceeded by the costs of maintaining hegemony, policies that led to increases in the labor force were not contradictory to the aims of economic colonialism.[87]

The connections between colonialism, the demand for labor and population growth could be observed across the colonized world. In Java, for example, under the Culture System introduced by the Dutch, the Javanese were required to maintain subsistence production of rice while simultaneously increasing their output of export crops such as sugar cane. As anthropologist Clifford Geertz and other scholars have noted, it was by increasing their family sizes that the Javanese were able to meet the escalating demands for cash crops and taxes by the Dutch.[88] Between 1830 and 1900, annual population increase was a 'fantastic' 20 per 1,000. The necessity for women's increasing participation in wage labor – in sugar cultivation and in sugar mills – may have led to a decline in breast-feeding. In Java, as in many other colonial contexts, the undermining of traditional methods of child spacing such as breastfeeding and post-partum sexual abstinence by the forces of modernization contributed to increased family size.[89]

Where populations were deprived of land and other means of subsistence, many people were left with children as their only source of wage labor and income. Marc Dawson has discussed accelerating population growth among the Kikuyu in Kenya during the 1930–1945 period by examining their integration into the capitalist world economy. He links increased fertility among Kikuyu women to transportation, urbanization, ecological and other social and economic changes brought forth by colonialism. Dawson points out that with emigration of adult and teenage men into the cities, the workload of the women in subsistence production increased. With increase in monogamy, potential help of co-wives and their children was also lost. The only help the women could then rely on was that of their own children. This, Dawson points out, was one contributory factor to increased fertility and population growth among the Kikuyu.[90]

Direct rule by a European power was not a necessity for the existence of economic colonialism and related population growth. For example, even before Egypt was annexed by the British, the country had been integrated within international trade and the Egyptian population grew rapidly during most of the nineteenth century. Japanese control of Taiwan from 1905 to 1945 was also characterized by a great expansion of export agriculture, "blocked socioeconomic mobility for the Taiwanese" and rapid population growth.[91]

Similarly, in southwestern Puerto Rico, poverty created by the evolution of the colonial plantation economy made it necessary for many families "to put everyone to work, males, females and children". As a study by James Wessman shows, economic and social insecurity contributed to high fertility. By the 1930s, unemployment and movement of seasonal laborers were so great that they were considered threats to economic and political stability of the island.[92] These conditions led to the introduction of a massive population control effort by the US in Puerto Rico in subsequent decades.

Fertility and 'internal colonialism'

Over the course of capitalist development, a poverty–fertility relationship also evolved among poor communities of color in the advanced capitalist societies in the North. The theory of 'internal colonialism' has some relevance to this evolution. It argues that just as imperialism created external colonies in the Third World, it created domestic colonies of people of color in the 'ghettoes', 'barrios', 'reservations' and 'Chinatowns' within the metropolitan countries, especially the US. The phenomenon of 'internal colonialism' is not simply the racial domination of whites over peoples of color; as elsewhere, it is also an expression of the inherently uneven and unequal nature of capitalist development and the dialectics of race, class and gender.[93] As discussed earlier, European expansion in the Americas resulted in widespread 'depopulation' of native communities. But, as in the Third World colonies, the need for labor and the refusal of indigenous people to become routine laborers also created crises of 'underpopulation' here. These crises were met with importation of African slave labor and indentured Asian labor as well as cheap European labor. The familial mode of production which persisted among many immigrants also relied on large pools of family labor. Even today, many Korean grocers, Chinese restaurant owners, Indian motel operators and even sweat-shop owners of different ethnic backgrounds in the US depend on family labor.

In the plantation South, slave owners encouraged slaves to reproduce and Negro slave women's social status was based largely upon their 'breeding power'. However, high fertility may also have been slave women's response to high mortality, particularly infant mortality, rather than obedience to slaveholders' demands. Black tenant farming in the South depended on large families. Adolescents' desire to marry early and leave patriarchal households led to parental–child conflicts because adults wanted to hold on to their labor supply. Thus, the Black tenant sharecropper's reproductive rationality in the southern United States was not very different from that of their counterparts in the colonies in Asia, Africa and South America. In the words of an old sharecropper interviewed by journalist Leon Dash for his study on contemporary Black teenage parents:

> If you were a small household, you couldn't get no farm ' cause there wouldn't be enough equity in the white farmer's pocket. The bigger the family, the better the white man would like that. So it was better off for you and better off for him, too, if you had a big family.[94]

According to African-American historian E. Franklin Frazier, out-of-wedlock births and high fertility among Black women were associated with poverty and family disintegration in the post-emancipation era. The relative lack of 'institutional and communal control' over Black women was carried over to the North, where, in the context of urban poverty and female-headed households, teenage mothering began to flourish.[95] While we shall return to this subject in Chapter 4, in the next section of this chapter, we shall discuss Third World population growth in the post-World War II, neo-colonial period.

Population Growth in the Neo-Colonial Era

While the Third World population 'explosion' began in the era between the two world wars, much of the population expansion in the Third World has taken place since World War II (Table 3.4). The roads, communications, engineering, agricultural and medical services introduced by the colonial powers to increase exploitation of labor and natural resources initiated the first phase of the demographic transition, that is, mortality decline. Imported public health technology, which included vaccines and insecticides against deadly diseases such as malaria, especially contributed to rapid declines in mortality in the Third World.[96]

As philosopher and public policy analyst Mark Sagoff has observed, "the engine of population growth" in the twentieth century has not been the increase in fertility as much as the steady decline in mortality. Infant mortality, an important determinant of overall mortality, declined from about 240 per 1,000 children (under 5 years) in the early 1950s to about 94 in the 1990s.[97] The overall mortality rate in the 'developing world', which was about 32 per 1,000 in the 1900–1950 period, fell to 17 per 1,000 in the 1960–1970 period and has been falling at an accelerated rate since then. It was estimated to be almost the same as the mortality rate of the 'developed' world in 1990: 10 per 1,000 in the 'developed' world and 9 per 1,000 in the 'developing' world.[98]

For the most part, advanced technology introduced into the Third World was an 'artificial transplant'. It did not emerge slowly within the Third World societies themselves. As a result, the drop in the death rate occurred rather suddenly, unaccompanied by improvements in general social conditions such as reduction in poverty, improvement of women's lives, and so on. The population 'explosion' in the Third World, then, is a product of the contradictions within the twin forces of modern technology and capitalism. Modern technology brought down death rates, but as capitalist social relations increased social inequality and undermined economic security and self-sufficiency of the masses, birth rates could not come down quickly. Consequently, the equilibrium between birth rates and death rates was disrupted and rapid population growth ensued (Figure 3.1).

Population growth in the Third World, then, cannot be blamed on the Third World poor, as the neo-Malthusians tend to do. Rather, as ecologist Barry Commoner has argued, the demographic explosion in the Third World must be seen as an "unresolved residue" of western imperialism. Commoner explains Europe's ability to make the demographic transition and the Third World's inability to achieve the same simultaneously by what he calls "demographic parasitism". He argues that it is imperialist exploitation which helped advance population balance in the dominant metropolitan countries while at the same time contributing to population imbalance in the subjugated colonies:

Table 3.4 Population growth rates 1950–2020, medium-variant projections: average annual rate of growth (%)

Region	1950–1960	1960–1970	1970–1980	1980–1990	1990–1994	1994–2000	2000–2010	2010–20
World	1.7	2.0	1.8	1.7	1.6	1.5	1.3	1.2
Developing	1.9	2.4	2.2	2.1	1.9	1.7	1.5	1.4
Developed	1.3	1.0	0.8	0.6	0.6	0.5	0.4	0.3
Africa	2.1	2.4	2.7	2.9	2.9	2.7	2.5	2.4
Sub–Saharan	2.0	2.4	2.7	2.9	3.0	2.9	2.6	2.6
North Africa	2.4	2.4	2.5	2.6	2.3	2.1	1.9	1.6
Asia	1.8	2.3	2.1	1.9	1.7	1.5	1.3	1.1
ex. Near East*	1.7	2.2	2.0	1.8	1.6	1.5	1.2	1.1
Near East	2.7	2.6	3.0	3.0	2.5	2.7	2.5	2.3
Latin America and Caribbean	2.7	2.7	2.4	2.0	1.7	1.5	1.2	1.1
North America	1.8	1.3	1.1	0.9	1.1	0.9	0.8	0.8
Europe	0.8	0.8	0.5	0.3	0.4	0.3	0.2	<0.05
(Former) Soviet Union	1.7	1.3	0.9	0.8	0.6	0.5	0.5	0.4
Baltics	0.9	1.2	0.8	0.7	0.7	0.6	0.6	0.6
Commonwealth of Independent States	1.8	1.3	0.9	0.8	0.6	0.5	0.5	0.4
Georgia	1.7	1.2	0.7	0.8	0.9	0.7	0.5	0.4
Oceania	2.3	2.1	1.6	1.6	1.5	1.3	1.1	0.9

Source: US Bureau of the Census, *World Population Profile: 1994*, Report WP/94, Washington, DC: US Government Printing Office, 1994, p. 64.

...the wealth produced in the colony was largely diverted to the advanced nation – where it helped that country achieve for itself the second phase of the demographic transition. Thus colonialism involves a kind of demographic parasitism: The second, population-balancing phase of the demographic transition in the advanced country is fed by the suppression of that same phase in the colony.[99]

With the rapid introduction of modern technology and capitalist social relations, local communities lost their relative economic and social independence and ability to regulate their numbers in relation to natural and social resources. The Third World population 'explosion' is a consequence of the destruction of self-sufficient communities, disempowerment of local people and disruption of pre-existing community population regulation mechanisms by external global political and economic forces.[100] It is also a result of the denial of access to property, education, credit and other resources to women and their need to view children as the only potential source of income.

In *Ancient Futures: Learning from Ladakh,* Helena Norberg-Hodge has demonstrated the demographic disequilibrium created by modernization in relation to Ladakh. With rapid integration into the global capitalist economy, Ladakh, which for centuries had remained an egalitarian, self-sufficient Buddhist society, has become an increasingly hierarchical, economically and culturally dependent, consumerist society. Norberg-Hodge's observations on changing male–female relations and social and economic disempowerment of women that has accompanied modernization and westernization in Ladakh are applicable globally. As women are not paid money for much of the work they do, they are no longer considered 'productive'. Thus, women, who held a highly esteemed place in the pre-capitalist society and were central to subsistence production, are now considered 'inferior' and they have internalized this view of themselves.[101]

In the process of capitalist development in Ladakh, people's relationship to their natural environment and each other weakened. Earlier familial arrangements and customs such as polyandry and monasticism declined, giving way to monogamy and the nuclear male-headed family; as a result, population soared. As Norberg-Hodge points out, "it is *after* contact with the modern world that population levels shoot up" (emphasis in original).[102]

In Europe, substantial emigration to the colonies in the past and wealth accumulated from them helped improve the living standards of the working classes, thereby contributing to their own achievement of the demographic transition. But for the masses of people in the Third World, such outlets and opportunities are not available. Improvements in the conditions of the poor require transformation of the poverty–wealth nexus that exists between the North and the South and within the South itself.

In this context, it is useful to recall the position taken by Third World delegates at the world population conference in Bucharest in 1974. Claiming that "development is the best contraceptive", they pointed out that rapid population growth in the Third World was a product of inequities in the global economy and emphasized the need for improving the position of the Third World vis-à-vis the First World. The Bucharest Conference Report stated:

> ...the present situation of the developing countries originates in the unequal processes of socio-economic development which have divided peoples since the beginning of the modern era. This inequity still exists and is intensified by lack of equity in international economic relations with consequent disparity in levels of living.[103]

As we shall discuss in later chapters, since the 1970s, global economic inequalities and poverty have greatly increased, not decreased. While the global political-economic forces underlying widening inequities and deepening poverty will be examined in Chapter 5, in the next section of this chapter we shall look at some contemporary demographic trends related to those broader socio-economic changes.

Demographic Trends into the Future

Mortality increase

Despite the fears and alarmist policies of the population control establishment, the demographic explosion has run its course. As Sagoff has noted, mortality rates will not continue to decrease indefinitely and the high population growth rates of the early 1970s are unlikely to be sustained over a long period of time (Table 3.4).[104] If current patterns of mortality related to poverty, AIDS and war and the worsening health care crisis continue, overall mortality rates could increase, bringing down population growth.

As we discuss in Chapter 5, the policies of free trade and structural adjustment have undermined social reproduction and survival of the poor across the Third World by slashing government employment, health, education and other benefits. As critics of the World Bank/IMF have also argued, the effects of debt crisis and structural adjustment policies (SAPs) in many Third World countries have been a reversal in the decline in mortality. Since the introduction of SAPs in the early 1980s, the crude death rate and infant mortality have risen and the increase in life expectancy has halted in a number of Sub-Saharan African countries.[105] Researcher Silvia Federici has demonstrated that the economic crisis and SAPs in Nigeria are operating as a means of population control. With the introduction of SAPs in Nigeria, malnutrition and poverty-related migration have increased; life expectancy fell, the death rate stagnated and the birth rate decreased during the 1981–1989 period.[106]

Almost everywhere, women and children have been the worst hit by these policies. Caffentzis argues that the overall effect of international policies has been a disaster-led demographic transition in Sub-Saharan Africa akin to the Malthusian scenarios that characterized the demographic transition among some poor populations in Europe:

> ...WB (World Bank) and other financial agencies have managed the debt crisis in such a way as to create a strikingly Malthusian situation, characterized by the presence of 'positive' and 'negative' checks: famines, war and disease, generated by falling incomes, reduced health services, and changes in land tenure and cropping. Indeed, the African body, especially the female body has been attacked by starvation, despair and plague rumours, in ways similar to those which the European proletariat in the 'transition to capitalism' was terrorized by witch hunts, plagues of syphilis, the 'price' revolution, famines and war....[107]

Despite the severity of the mortality related to AIDS as well as other diseases like the Ebola virus in Africa, the population control establishment continues to focus on Africa as the priority continent in terms of bringing down fertility. As noted in Chapter 1, some environmental activists in the North see the AIDS epidemic as a necessary Malthusian check against environmental decline. But diseases like AIDS and Ebola cannot be blamed on 'overpopulation'. Rather, the spread of AIDS in regions such as Central Africa may be largely attributable to poverty associated with global political and economic forces.[108]

A 1994 study by the US Bureau of the Census has estimated that owing to AIDS-related deaths, a doubling of the overall death rate in the African countries, Brazil and Haiti and a tripling of the death rate in Thailand are expected between 1985 and 2010. AIDS is also expected to lower life expectancy in many countries. In Uganda, life expectancy is expected to drop to 32 years by 2010, whereas without AIDS it would be 59. In Thailand life expectancy is expected to drop from 75 to 45 during the same period. The study has concluded that while the AIDS epidemic will not lower populations in most Third World countries, it will lead to large reductions in population growth in some of the worst affected countries. For instance, a 46.0% reduction in population growth rate in Uganda, 46.8% reduction in Zambia, 21.8% reduction in Thailand and 18.9% reduction in Haiti are expected by 2020 due to AIDS-related deaths. In Thailand population growth rate is expected turn negative (−0.8) owing to AIDS by 2010. There are 121 million fewer people expected in the 16 countries for which the Bureau of the Census study provides AIDS-adjusted mortality estimates (Figure 3.2).[109]

Increasing social dislocation and turmoil are also leading to increases in mortality rates in other regions and countries beyond the Third World. Russia, where mortality is increasing and fertility is decreasing, is perhaps an extreme case. In 1994, the mortality rate was 15.6 for every 1,000 people, a 30% increase from 1992. According to figures released in 1995, average male life expectancy in Russia declined from 67 to 57 in the

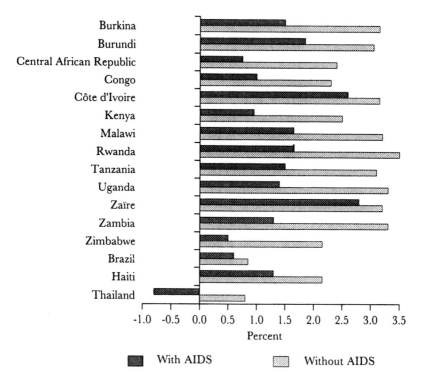

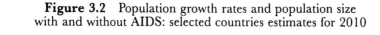

Figure 3.2 Population growth rates and population size
with and without AIDS: selected countries estimates for 2010

Source: US Bureau of the Census, *World Population Profile: 1994*, Report WP/94, Washington, DC:
US Government Printing Office, 1994, p. 64.

previous four years. Mortality and life expectancy rates in Russia today are less favorable than in many poor Third World countries.[110] Cutbacks in social programs and unemployment accompanying the transition to capitalism, spread of HIV and illnesses caused by environmental destruction may be some of the causes behind the demographic collapse in Russia.

Civil wars in regions like Bosnia and Rwanda and gang wars in inner cities in the US are also contributing to increasing mortality rates, although their effects on population growth rates have received little attention. It is estimated that half a million Tutsis, mostly men, were killed in the recent Rwandan war; 70% of the population in Rwanda today is female, and 60% of these women are said to be widows.[112] What will also be the long-term demographic consequences for countries such as Sri Lanka which are fast reaching replacement-level fertility while at the same time large segments of youth are getting killed in battlefields before they bear children? The North, which simultaneously exports population control agendas and weapons of war, holds a responsibility for possible population collapse in such countries. When mortality increases are combined with crisis-led fertility declines (to be discussed in Chapter 4), demographic collapse rather than explosion could be the long-term result for regions plagued with war, poverty and disease.

Despite increasing mortality in some regions, the expected drop in overall population growth in the years ahead is attributable more to falling fertility than to increasing mortality at this time.

Fertility decrease

A development that may have a significant impact on fertility rates in the future is the dramatic drop in sperm count in recent years. Although worldwide decline in sperm count may be an outcome of environmental disturbances resulting from overuse of chemical products, this issue has not yet received much attention in discussions of global population and human reproduction.[111]

Fertility decrease in the South

Fertility and population growth rates are now declining in all regions of Asia, Africa and Latin America (except for a slight increase expected for South-East Asia in the twenty-first century) (Table 3.5). Currently fertility is 1.71 children per woman in the 'developed' world and 3.38 in the 'developing world'.[112] In the latter, fertility has been falling far more rapidly than it did during the demographic transition in the West (Figure 3.1). It took 58 years in the United States (between 1842 and 1900) for fertility to decline from 6.5 children per woman to 3.5. In contrast, in recent times, Indonesia, Colombia, Thailand and China have undergone the same level of fertility decline over the course of 27, 15, 8 and 7 years, respectively.[113]

In Cuba, fertility has already fallen below replacement level of 2.1 children per woman; Thailand and Puerto Rico, which are at replacement level now, and countries like Jamaica and Sri Lanka, which are almost at replacement level, could also move below that level in the next few years.[114] As we discuss in the next chapter, in countries such as Sri Lanka and Cuba social improvements have been the determinant of the transition to low fertility, whereas, as we discussed in Chapter 1, in countries such as Bangladesh intensified family planning is considered to be the major force behind the transition to low fertility.

The poorest countries in the world have the highest fertility rates: in 1995, average fertility in the 'least developed countries' was 5.59.[115] But even in these countries, fertility levels are falling. It is estimated that in Africa, which currently has the highest fertility levels in the world, fertility

Table 3.5 Declining global fertility rates (per woman), 1950–2020

Region	1950–1960	1960–1970	1970–1980	1980–1990	1990–2000	2000–2010	2010–2020
World Total	4.94	4.94	4.15	3.54	3.03	2.78	2.53
Africa	6.70	6.76	6.59	6.33	5.58	4.70	3.91
Eastern Africa	6.82	6.92	7.00	6.69	6.23	5.26	4.30
Middle Africa	5.92	6.04	6.33	6.53	6.24	5.36	4.48
Northern Africa	6.92	6.97	6.19	5.38	3.96	3.11	2.56
Southern Africa	6.47	6.20	5.40	4.71	4.07	3.48	2.90
Western Africa	6.78	6.87	6.88	6.86	6.31	5.36	4.41
Asia	5.75	5.70	4.57	3.61	2.96	2.66	2.35
Eastern Asia	5.34	5.78	3.60	2.37	1.92	1.96	2.07
South-Eastern Asia	6.06	5.86	5.07	3.97	3.16	2.64	2.26
South-Central/Southern Asia*	n/a	n/a	n/a	n/a	3.95	3.23	2.51
Southern Asia	6.10	6.00	5.52	4.91	4.87	4.06	3.18
Western Asia	6.75	6.43	5.78	5.19	4.27	3.68	3.14
Europe	2.59	2.56	2.09	1.76	1.59	1.63	1.77
Eastern Europe	2.93	2.34	2.32	2.14	1.62	1.66	1.80
Northern Europe	2.43	2.59	1.95	1.83	1.85	1.89	2.01
Southern Europe	2.66	2.64	2.39	1.68	1.42	1.45	1.58
Western Europe	2.45	2.56	1.79	1.60	1.52	1.57	1.72
Latin America	5.89	5.74	4.68	3.66	2.96	2.53	2.27
Caribbean	5.17	5.24	3.93	3.07	2.71	2.59	2.56
Central America	6.78	6.74	5.77	4.24	3.32	2.67	2.32
South America	5.72	5.48	4.41	3.53	2.86	2.47	2.21
US and Canada	3.60	2.94	1.90	1.85	2.06	2.09	2.10
Oceania	3.95	3.75	3.02	2.57	2.48	2.39	2.33
USSR (Former)	2.82	2.48	2.39	2.39	n/a	n/a	n/a

Sources: United Nations, Department for Economic and Social Information and Policy Analysis, *World Population Prospectus, 1992 Revision,* New York: UN, 1993, pp. 216–221; United Nations, Department for Economic and Social Information and Policy Analysis, *World Population Prospectus, 1994 Revision,* New York, 1995, pp. 328–333.

will decline from 5.58 children per woman in the 1990–2000 period to 3.91 in the 2010–2020 period. In South Asia and West Asia, which have the highest fertility rates next to Africa, childbearing is estimated to fall rapidly during the same time-span: from 4.87 children per woman to 3.18 in South Asia and from 4.27 to 3.14 in West Asia (Table 3.5).

Currently, population increase in the world is attributable to 'population momentum' and exponential growth rather than high fertility. Population momentum refers to the sharp increase of population due to radical lowering of the age structure with a high proportion of people in the child-bearing age. Given that population momentum is already a part of the demographic process, even the most 'determined' population control efforts will require a generation or two before they can show results at the aggregate level. Thus, as Sagoff argues, between 1950 and 2050, "somewhere between a tripling and quadrupling of world population" is likely to take place (Figure 2).[116]

However, as Sagoff points out, as declining mortality rather than rising fertility underlies much of contemporary population growth, family planning programs are limited in their ability to curtail the global population 'explosion'.[117] Given already low and falling fertility rates, couples could be made to limit childbearing further only through coercive policies, such as China's one-child family policy, which has contributed to reducing the number of females in the population. In the years ahead, greater vigilance is required with regard to new technologies of reproduction and their eugenic gender, race and class implications.

Consider, for example, the $3 billion Human Genome Project sponsored by the US government to decipher all the 100,000 or more genes in the human body. This project will allow doctors to screen fetuses for a wide variety of physical and behaviour traits, including the ability to determine which "combinations affect kinky hair, olive skin and pointy teeth" and so on.[118] The ability to pre-determine such abilities, when combined with the increasing fear of 'overpopulation', could result in scientific attempts to reduce the size of the poor, 'non-white' masses in the world. These concerns must also be placed in the context of population policies and fertility trends in the North.

Fertility in the North

Notwithstanding the fears of the anti-immigration lobby regarding the relative increase in the number of 'non-whites' in the US, fertility among all people of color, including immigrants, is projected to fall slightly, while the fertility rate among the white population is expected to rise slightly by the first decade of the next century. For example, fertility per woman among whites is expected to rise from 1.97 in 1994 to 2.01 in 2010, while it is expected to decrease from 2.47 to 2.46 for Blacks, from 2.78 to 2.76 for American Indians, from 2.51 to 2.41 for Asian and Pacific Islanders and from 2.90 to 2.78 for Hispanics during the same period. Most recent data also reveal a significant drop in the teenage birth rate in the US: among 15–19 year olds the birth rate dropped by 8% between 1991 and 1995.[119]

Fertility is below replacement level in Europe and is expected to remain so in coming decades. However, despite fears of demographic decline in the North, in both North America and all regions of Europe fertility rates are expected to rise in the twenty-first century (Table 3.5). In Sweden, for example, largely due to state pronatalist policies, fertility rose consistently in the 1980s, reaching 2.02 in 1989, and is expected to surpass replacement level in the 1990s (in 1995 it was at the replacement level of fertility of 2.1) As demographer Jan Hoem argues, Sweden has often been a precursor of trends in Europe. As such, fertility increases in Sweden may represent what lies ahead demographically for other Scandinavian and European countries pursuing subtle but consistent pronatalist policies.[120] The dual policies of antinatalism for the South and pronatalism mostly for white populations in the North, in conjunction with disaster-led population declines in the South, may lead to the global demographic balance desired by policy makers in the North.

The fundamental issue facing the future, however, is not demography but democracy. To understand the global crisis, we need to move away from the narrow Malthusian focus on the size and growth rates of populations to examining changing social relations of reproduction and production within the global economy.

Demography and Democracy

As discussed in this chapter, the so-called population 'explosion' is not an independent variable but a dependent variable stemming from the contradictions of uneven and unequal global capitalist development. Global capital is still very much dependent on cheap Third World labor, although the form and manner of labor exploitation has undergone changes since the period of direct colonialism. For example, the transnational corporations rely on people in the Third World to labor in the free trade zones, agrobusinesses, tourist sectors, and so on. The US, Western Europe, Japan and the oil-rich Middle Eastern countries are also dependent on large pools of immigrant and migrant Third World labor to do low-paid menial work, especially in the growing service sectors of their economies. In addition, the Northern countries rely on the 'brain drain', particularly from countries such as India and China, to maintain their competitive edge in science and technology.

The existence of a 'reserve army of labor' is functional for capital since it keeps wages low and labor forces competing with each other globally rather than uniting against capital. Nevertheless, international capitalist interests also see global population as being excessively out of step with labor requirements at this historical juncture. While commodity production is displacing subsistence production and dispossessing more and more people of their lands and traditional means of livelihood, it is failing to provide employment for most people within the new sectors of global production. In the industrialized North too chief executive officers engaged in corporate mergers, hostile take-over of companies, and so on, pay themselves enormous salaries while laying off thousands of workers, including large numbers of professional, managerial staff.

As Frederic Clairmont, formerly senior economist at UNCTAD, points out, transnational corporations are one of the major liquidators of jobs. Downsizing, the euphemism for job destruction, not only introduces part-time, less secure employment, but also allows capital greater political control over the labor force. As Clairmont puts it: "This mass liquidation of working peoples by corporate capital is being done notwithstanding their Himalayan heights of profitability. This is the rationale of the bottom line".[121]

Still another source of growing corporate profitability and massive unemployment is the replacement of labor with new technology. As social analyst Jeremy Rifkin observes, human beings are becoming superfluous as capital moves increasingly towards labor-displacing technology:

> We are fast moving into a world where there will be factories without workers, and agricultural production without farms or farmers. ... Much of the global workforce could well be eliminated, replaced by information technology, robots, machines and biotechnology.[122]

As noted in the Introduction, 30% of the global labor force, that is, about 820 million people, were unemployed at the beginning of 1994 and the world is said to be faced with the worst employment crisis since the 1930s. Unemployment is particularly high among the youth, even those with a university education. According to the ILO, in Africa, "youth of all educational backgrounds represent between 60 and 75% of the region's unemployed".[123] The provision of education for girls for purposes of fertility reduction will not necessarily contribute to the alleviation of the global unemployment problem.

Indeed, as economist Richard Barnet observes, the vast majority of the 8 billion or so people expected to inhabit the earth in the first quarter of the next century will be neither producers nor consumers.[124] Instead, they will be a 'surplus population' living in poverty with no apparent usefulness to capitalism. The Malthusian 'overpopulation' problem, then, is fundamentally a crisis of capitalist social relations and technology of production. It is a crisis stemming from placing capital accumulation before the survival needs of people.

Nevertheless the dominant world institutions continue to promote economic liberalization as the solution to the very problems it has created.

The ILO's answer to the global unemployment crisis is further trade lib-eralization through such measures as the full implementation of GATT, export-led industrial development and stabilization of financial markets.[125] As noted in earlier sections of this book, recent major United Nations conferences have also sought solutions to different aspects of the global crisis within growth-oriented development.

The demographic crisis is a global political crisis between the 'haves' and the 'have-nots', particularly between the ageing white populations in the North and the youthful populations of color in the South as well as the North. The percentage of the elderly (those above 65 years) in the world is increasing sharply, especially in the North. In the US at least 20% of the total population is expected to be over 65 by the year 2025, with the numbers of people over the age of 75 and even 85 increasing the fastest.[126] This unprecedented demographic shift is already raising many fundamen-tal ethical, financial and socio-political issues. Should medical life support systems of the terminally ill, for example, be continued indefinitely, while infant mortality rates continue to be high among poor children in both the South and the North?

As noted in Chapter 1, population control enthusiasts tend to blame the increasing numbers of youth in the world for dwindling global resources, political turmoil and other major social problems. Yet, they have failed to pay much attention to the increasing demands placed on global resources by the elderly, especially those in the North, and the United States in particular, where medical costs for them are astronomically high. Appar-ently, in 1987, the US Congress spent $10,010 per capita on the elderly in contrast to $854 per child.[127]

While children cannot vote, the elderly in the US constitute a powerful voting bloc dedicated to their interests. As economist Lester Thurow points out, the elderly in the US tend to systematically vote against education levies or establish segregated retirement communities so that they do not have to pay any school taxes at all.[128] The negative impact of deteriorating public services is felt most immediately by poor children, especially immi-grant children of color, who cannot afford private education and health care. But in the long term the entire society suffers due to weakening commitment for nurturing and supporting the young. Thurow predicts that in the years ahead "class warfare is apt to be redefined as the young against the old, rather than the poor against the rich".[129]

The increasing global demand for social services like education, health care and housing originates not only from population growth but also from rising expectations and the democratic ideology of capitalism.[130] Masses of youth in the South lured by consumption patterns promoted by the global capitalist media are demanding the same opportunities and lifestyle as those in the privileged North. If their democratic impulse is curtailed and their demands are not met with global economic and social justice, the result could be increasing social rupture and intensified conflict and authoritarianism, including new forms of religious and ethnic fundamentalisms. The challenge of global democracy requires that we address social justice seriously. It is in this context that we address the poverty–fertility relationship in the next chapter.

Notes

1. Marx, *Capital*, p. 693.

2. Ibid.; Frederick Engels, *The Origin of the Family, Private Property and the State*, London: Lawrence and Wishart, 1973, p. 71.

3. Marvin Harris and Eric B. Ross, *Death, Sex and Fertility: Population Regulation in Preindustrial and Developing Societies*, New York: Columbia University Press, 1987, p. 1.

4. Ibid., p.19.

5. Ibid., p.18.

6. Talal Asad, *Anthropology and the Colonial Encounter*, Atlantic Highlands, NJ: Humanities Press, 1973; Asoka Bandarage, "From Universal Sexual Subordination to International Feminism: A Critical Assessment", paper selected for presentation at session on Feminist Critiques of Gender Theory, American Sociological Association Annual Meeting, Washington, DC, 1985.

7. Marjorie Shostack, *Nisa: The Life and Words of a !Kung Woman*, New York: Vintage Books, 1983, p. 15.

8. Marshall Sahlins, *Stone Age Economics*, New York: Aldine de Gruyter, 1972, pp. 1–32.

9. Eleanor Leacock, *Myths of Male Dominance: Collected Articles on Women Cross-Culturally*, New York: Monthly Review Press, 1981; Peggy Reeves Sanday, *Female Power and Male Dominance: On the Origins of Sexual Inequality*, Cambridge: Cambridge University Press, 1981; Asoka Bandarage, "From Universal Sexual Subordination", p. 11.

10. Harris and Ross, *Death, Sex and Fertility*, pp. 32–33; Bryceson and Vurovela, "Outside the Domestic Labor Debate", pp. 137–166.

11. Maurice Godelier, "The Origins of Male Domination", *New Left Review*, No. 127, May–June 1981, pp. 3–17.

12. Frances Dahlberg, "Introduction", in Frances Dahlberg, ed., *Woman the Gatherer*, New Haven: Yale University Press, 1981, p. 23.

13. Engels, *Origin*; see also Leacock, *Myths of Male Dominance*, passim.

14. F. Kajerby, "The Dynamic History of Subordination of women in Classless African Societies", BRAUP Workshop on Women's Studies and Development, Paper No. 35, University of Dar es Salaam, 1979, cited in Bryceson and Vurovela, "Outside the Domestic Labor Debate", p. 146; see also Steven Polgar, "Population History and Population Policies from an Anthropological Perspective", *Current Anthropology*, April 1972, pp. 205–206.

15. Harris and Ross, *Death, Sex and Fertility*, pp. 33–34.

16. Ibid., p. 46.

17. Ibid., p. 21; see also Roland Pressat, *Population*, Baltimore: Penguin Books, Inc., 1971, p. 10.

18. Gore, *Earth in the Balance*, p. 30; John Bellamy Foster, *The Vulnerable Planet: A Short Economic History of the Environment*, New York: Monthly Review Press, pp. 13, 36–39.

19. Harris and Ross, *Death, Sex and Fertility*, p. 43.

20. A.L. Basham, *The Wonder That Was India*, New York: Grove Press, 1954, p. 35.

21. John Isbister, *Promises Not Kept: The Betrayal of Social Change in the Third World*, West Hartford, CT: Kumarian Press, 1991, p. 87; Bandarage, *Colonialism in Sri Lanka*, Chap. 2.

22. Harris and Ross, *Death, Sex and Fertility*, pp. 39, 45; see also John C. Caldwell, *Theory of Fertility Decline*, London and New York: Academic Press, 1982.

23. W. Penn Handwerker, "Politics and Reproduction: A Window on Social Change",

in W. Penn Handwerker, ed., *Births and Power: Social Change and the Politics of Reproduction*, Boulder, CO: Westview Press, 1990, p. 10.

24. Harris and Ross, *Death, Sex and Fertility*, p. 22.

25. Helena Norberg-Hodge, *Ancient Futures: Learning from Ladakh*, San Francisco: Sierra Club Books, 1992, Chap. 5.

26. Harris and Ross, *Death, Sex and Fertility*, pp. 53–54; Asoka Bandarage, *Colonialism in Sri Lanka: The Political Economy of the Kandyan Highlands, 1833–1886*, Berlin: Mouton, 1983, Chap. 2.

27. Handwerker, "Politics and Reproduction", p. 12; Ester Boserup, *The Conditions of Agricultural Growth: The Economics of Agrarian Change under Population Pressure*, Chicago: Aldine Publishing Co., 1965, p. 41.

28. Michael S. Teitelbaum, "Relevance of Demographic Transition Theory for Developing Countries", in Menard and Moen, eds, *Perspectives on Population*, p. 29.

29. Ester Boserup, *Women's Role in Economic Development*, New York: St Martin's Press, 1970; Gerda Lerner, *The Creation of Patriarchy*, Oxford: Oxford University Press, 1986.

30. Bandarage, "From Universal Sexual Subordination"; Leacock, *Myths of Male Dominance*; Naomi Quinn, "Anthropological Studies on Women's Status", *Annual Review of Anthropology*, Vol. 6, 1977, pp. 181–225; Jane Manning Atkinson, "Review Essay: Anthropology", *Signs*, Vol. 8, No. 2, Winter 1982, pp. 236–258.

31. Engels, *Origin*; Lerner, *The Creation*.

32. William Julio Divale and Marvin Harris, "Population, Warfare and the Male Supremacist Complex", *American Anthropologist*, Vol. 78, No. 3, 1976, p. 525.

33. Ibid., pp. 527–532.

34. O'Brien, *The Politics of Reproduction*; Monica Sjoo and Barabara Mor, *The Great Cosmic Mother: Rediscovering the Religion of the Earth*, San Francisco: Harper and Row, 1987.

35. Harris and Ross, *Death, Sex and Fertility*, p. 90.

36. Judith Rollins, *Between Women: Domestics and their Employers*, Philadelphia: Temple University Press, 1985; Asoka Bandarage, "Women and Capitalist Development in Sri Lanka", *Bulletin of Concerned Asian Scholars*, Vol. 20, No. 2, 1988, pp. 69–72.

37. Maria Mies, *Patriarchy and Accumulation on a World Scale: Women in the International Division of Labour*, London: Zed Books, 1986, p. 81; Barbara Ehrenreich and Deidre English, *For Her Own Good: 150 Years of the Experts' Advice to Women*, New York: Anchor Books, 1979; see also Donna Read, director, *The Burning Times*, video Studio D, National Film Board of Canada, 1993.

38. Shulamith Firestone, *The Dialectic of Sex: The Case for Feminist Revolution*, New York: Bantam Books, 1970; Kate Millet, *Sexual Politics*, New York: Avon, 1969.

39. Marija Gimbutas, *The Language of the Goddess*, San Francisco: Harper and Row, 1989; Charlene Spretnak, "Ecofeminism: Our Roots and Flowering", in Irene Diamond and Gloria Orenstein, eds, *Reweaving the World: The Emergence of Ecofeminism*, San Francisco: Sierra Club Books, 1990, p. 11; Eisler, *The Chalice and the Blade*; Lerner, *Creation of Patriarchy*.

40. Lynn White, Jr. "The Historical Roots of Our Ecological Crisis", *Sanctuary*, February–March 1988, p. 5.

41. Carolyn Merchant, *Death of Nature: Women, Ecology and the Scientific Revolution*, San Francisco: Harper and Row, 1983, *passim*; Paul L. Wachtel, *The Poverty of Affluence: A Psychological Portrait of the American Way of Life*, Philadelphia: New Society Publishers, 1989, pp. 82–84.

42. Merchant, *Death of Nature*, pp. 155–163.

43. Max Weber, *The Protestant Ethic and the Spirit of Capitalism*, trans. Talcott Parsons, New York: Charles Scribner and Sons, 1950.

44. E.P. Thompson, "Time, Work-Discipline and Industrial Capitalism", *Past and Present*, No. 38, December 1967, p. 87.

45. Marx, *Capital*, pp. 692–694; see also Karen L. Michaelson, "Introduction" in Michaelson, ed., *And the Poor Get Children*; see also Martha E. Gimenez, "Population and Capitalism", *Latin American Perspectives*, Issue 15, Vol. IV, No. 4, Fall 1977, p. 41.

46. Polgar, "Population History", p. 207; Teitelbaum, "Relevance of Demographic

Transition Theory", p. 29; Pritchett, "Desired Fertility", p. 27.

47. Harris and Ross, *Death, Sex and Fertility*, pp. 119–121.

48. Ibid., p. 124.

49. Ibid., pp. 113–119, 124–125.

50. Handwerker, "Politics and Reproduction", p. 24.

51. Bandarage, *Colonialism in Sri Lanka*, Chap. 9; Souza, *A Geography of World Economy*, pp. 67–68; Mamdani, *The Myth of Population Control*.

52. Immanuel Wallerstein, *The Modern World-System: Capitalist Agriculture and and the Origins of the European World-Economy in the Sixteenth Century*, New York: Academic Press, 1974; Immanuel Wallerstein, *The Modern-World System II: Mercantilism and the Consolidation of the European World-Economy, 1600–1750*, New York: Academic Press, 1980; Wolf, *Europe and the People Without History*.

53. Polgar, "Population History" p. 207; Bandarage, *Colonialism in Sri Lanka*, Chapter 3.

54. Ben Wisner, "The Limitations of 'Carrying Capacity'", *Political Environments*, CWPE Newsletter, No. 3, Winter/Spring 1996, pp. 1, 3–6.

55. Rachel Heatley, *Poverty and Power: The Case for a Political Approach to Development and its Implications for Action in the West*, London: Zed Press, 1979, p. 21; Bandarage, *Colonialism in Sri Lanka*, pp. 276–277.

56. M. Barratt Brown, *After Imperialism*, cited in Heatley, *Poverty and Power*, p. 20.

57. Harry Magdoff, "Globalisation – To What End?", *Economic Review*, People's Bank Publication, Colombo, Sri Lanka, Vol. 18, No. 5, August 1992, p. 24.

58. Polgar, "Population History", p. 205.

59. Foster, *Vulnerable Planet*, pp. 14–15.

60. Georg Borgstrom, *The Food and People Dilemma*, North Scituate, MA: Duxbury Press, 1973, p. 2.

61. Gustavo Esteva, "Regenerating People's Space", *Alternatives*, Vol. 12, 1987, p 125; Fernand Braudel, *The Structures of Everyday Life: The Limits of the Possible*, Vol. 1, New York: Harper and Row, 1979, pp. 36–38.

62. Charles Darwin, cited in Foster, *Vulnerable Planet*, p. 14.

63. Kenneth F. Kiple and Brian T. Higgins, "Yellow Fever and the Africanization of the Caribbean", in John W. Verano and Douglas H. Ubelaker, eds, *Disease and Demography in the Americas*, Washington, DC: Smithsonian Institution Press, 1992, pp. 237–248.

64. Douglas H. Ubelaker, "North American Indian Population Size: Changing Perspectives", in Verano and Ubelaker, eds, *Disease and Demography*, pp. 169–176.

65. Foster, *Vulnerable Planet*, p. 14.

66. Polgar, "Population History", p. 207: Ubelaker, "North American Indian", p. 173.

67. John H. Bodley, "Demographic Impact of the Frontier", in Menard and Moen, eds, *Perspectives on Population*, p. 23; see also Verano and Ubelaker, eds, *Disease and Demography*.

68. Chailang Palacios, "The Colonization of Our Pacific Islands", in Gioseffi, ed., *Women on War*, p. 147; see also St Hilaire, "Canadian Aid, Women and Development".

69. Sylvia Marcos, "Clergy, Goddesses and Eroticism", trans. by Peter Bruce, in *Conscience*, September/October 1991, p. 11.

70. "Campus Crusade for Christ Head Given $1 Million Religion Prize", *The New York Times*, March 7, 1996, p. A16.

71. Gail Hanlon, "Living in a Liminal Time: An Interview with Jean Shinoda Bolen", *Woman of Power*, No. 21, Fall 1991, p. 24; see also Asoka Bandarage, "Women of Color: Towards a Celebration of Power", *Women of Power*, No. 4, Fall 1986, pp. 8–14, 82–83.

72. Abouali Farmanfarmaian, "Did You Measure Up? The Role of Race and Sexuality in the Gulf War", in Cynthia Peters, ed., *Collateral Damage: The 'New World Order' at Home and Abroad*, Boston: South End Press, 1992, pp. 118–119, 136.

73. *Akwesasne Notes*, "Growing Fight", p. 29.

74. Basil Davidson, *The African Genius: An Introduction to African Social and Cultural History*, Boston: Little, Brown and Co., 1969, pp. 28–29; E. Franklin Frazier, *Race and Culture Contacts in the Modern World*, Boston: Beacon Press, 1957, pp. 43–46.

75. Borgstrom, *Food and People*, p. 4; John Hope Franklin, *From Slavery to Freedom: A*

History of Negro Americans, New York: Alfred A. Knopf, 3rd Edition, 1967; Patrick Manning, *Slavery and African Life: Occidental, Oriental and African Slave Trades*, Cambridge, Cambridge University Press, 1990, p. 23.

76. Manning, *Slavery and African Life*, pp. 170–171.

77. Ibid., p.173.

78. Bandarage, *Colonialism in Sri Lanka*, Chap. 6; Polgar, "Population History", p. 207; Saskia Sassen, *The Mobility of Labor and Capital: A Study in International Investment and Labor Flow*, Cambridge: Cambridge University Press, 1988.

79. C. George Caffentzis, "The Fundamental Implications of the Debt Crisis for Social Reproduction in Africa", in Mariarosa Dalla Costa and Giovanna F. Dalla Costa, eds, *Paying the Price: Women and the Politics of International Economic Strategy*, London: Zed Books, 1995, p. 19; Mies, *Patriarchy*, p. 98; Boserup, *Women's Role*.

80. Carol Summers, "Intimate Colonialism: The Imperial Production of Reproduction in Uganda, 1907–1925", *Signs*, Vol. 16, No. 41, 1991, p. 807.

81. Bandarage, "Women and Capitalist Development"; Bandarage, *Colonialism in Sri Lanka*, pp. 242–245.

82. Bandarage, *Colonialism in Sri Lanka*, pp. 210–211; Summers, "Intimate Colonialism", *passim*.

83. Mies, *Patriarchy*, p. 99.

84. Ibid., p. 91; see also Mina Davis Caulfield, "Imperialism, the Family and Cultures of Resistance", *Socialist Revolution*, Issue 20, Vol. 4, No. 2, October 1974, pp. 67–85.

85. John G. Patterson and Nanda R. Shrestha, "Population Growth and Development in the Third World: The Neocolonial Context", *Studies in Comparative International Development*, Vol. 23, Summer 1988, p. 5.

86. Harris and Ross, *Death, Sex and Fertility*, p. 139.

87. Polgar, "Population History", p. 207.

88. Clifford Geertz, *Agricultural Involution*, Berkeley: University of California Press, 1963, p. 69.

89. Benjamin White, "The Economic Importance of Javanese Children", in Moni Nag, ed., *Population and Social Organization*, The Hague: Mouton, 1975; Polgar, "Population History", p. 207; Harris and Ross, *Death, Sex and Fertility*, p. 147.

90. Marc Dawson, "Health, Nutrition and Population in Central Kenya, 1890–1945", in Dennis Cordell and Joel W. Gregory, eds, *African Population and Capitalism: Historical Perspectives*, Boulder, CO: Westview Press, 1987, p. 217.

91. Polgar, "Population History", p. 207.

92. James W. Wessman, "Neo-Malthusian Ideology and Colonial Capitalism: Population Dynamics in Southwestern Puerto Rico", in Michaelson, ed., *And the Poor Get Children*, p. 216.

93. Robert Blauner, *Racial Oppression in America*, New York: Harper and Row, 1972; Donald J. Harris, "Capitalist Exploitation and Black Labor: Some Conceptual Issues", *Review of Black Political Economy*, Vol. 8, No. 2, Winter 1978, pp. 133–151.

94. Leon Dash, *When Children Want Children*, New York: Penguin Books, 1989, pp. 241, 243, 259.

95. E. Franklin Frazier, cited in Constance Willard Williams, *Black Teenage Mothers: Pregnancy and Child Rearing from their Perspective*, Lexington, MA: Lexington Books, 1991, p. 129.

96. Shirley Cereseto, "World Starvation: Causes and Solutions", *The Insurgent Sociologist*, Vol. 7, No. 2, Summer 1977, p. 37; Isbister, *Promises Not Kept*, p. 98.

97. Mark Sagoff, "Playing the Numbers", *Conscience*, Vol. 14, No. 3, Autumn 1993, pp. 15–16, 19.

98. UNFPA, *State of the World Population 1991*, p. 42.

99. Barry Commoner, *Making Peace With the Planet*, New York: The New Press, 1992, p. 160; see also Barry Commoner, "Rapid Population Growth and Environmental Stress", *International Journal of Health Services*, Vol. 21, No. 2, 1991, p. 226.

100. John Papworth, "Community Population Control", *The Ecologist*, Vol. 23, No. 2, March–April 1993, p. 79.

101. Norberg-Hodge, *Ancient Futures*, pp. 126–127.

102. Ibid., p. 151.

103. Report of the United Nations World Population Conference, 1974, cited in United Nations, Department of Economic and Social Affairs, "Interrelations Between Resources, Environment, Population and Development: Elements of Decisions of the World Conferences Held in the 1970's", in Pradip K. Ghosh, ed., *Population, Environment and Resources, and Third World Development*, Westport, CT: Greenwood Press, 1984, p. 86.

104. Sagoff, "Playing ther Numbers", p.19.

105. Ralph R. Sell and Stephen J. Kunitz, "The Debt Crisis and the End of an Era in Mortality Decline", *Studies in Comparative International Development*, Winter 1986–87, pp. 3–30.

106. Silvia Federici, "Economic Crisis and Demographic Policy in Sub-Saharan Africa: The Case of Nigeria", in Dalla Costa and Dalla Costa, eds, *Paying the Price*, p. 53.

107. Caffentzis, "The Fundamental Implications of the Debt Crisis", pp. 31–32.

108. Brooke Grundfest-Schoepf, "Women at Risk: Case Studies from Zaïre", in G. Herdt and Shirley Lindenbaum, eds, *The Time of AIDS: Social Analysis, Theory and Method*, Newbury Park, CA: Sage Publications, 1992.

109. US Bureau of the Census, *World Population Profile: 1994*, Report WP/94, Washington, DC: US Government Printing Office, 1994, pp. 63–65; see also "U.N.: HIV's Toll is Heavy", *Daily Hampshire Gazette*, November 29, 1996, pp. 1, 6.

110. Michael Specter, "Climb in Russia's Death Rate Sets Off Population Implosion", *The New York Times*, March 6, 1994, pp. 1, 18.

111. B. Seshadri, "Male Infertility and World Population", *Contemporary Review*, February 1995, Vol. 266. No. 1549.

112. Elizabeth Royte, "The Outcasts", *The New York Times Magazine*, January 19, 1997, pp. 37–38.

113. UNFPA, *The State of World Population 1995*, p. 67; *A Citizen's Guide to the Conference on Population and Development*, Washington, DC: Population Reference Bureau, 1994, p. 15.

114. UNFPA, *State of the World Population 1995*, pp. 68–69.

115. Ibid., pp. 67–70.

116. Sagoff, "Playing the Numbers", p. 16.

117. Ibid., p. 16.

118. Andrew Kimbrell, *The Human Body Shop: The Engineering and Marketing of Life*, San Francisco: Harper 1993, p. 25.

119. Hoem, "Social Policy and Recent Fertility Change in Sweden", pp. 735–736, 740–745; James Bennet, "Clinton Lauds Decline in Teen-age Pregnancy", *The New York Times*, January 5, 1997.

120. US Bureau of the Census, *Statistical Abstract of the United States, Projected Fertility Rates by Race and Age Group, 1994 and 2010*, Washington, DC, p. 76.

121. Frederic Clairmont, "The G-7 and the Spectre of Job Destruction", *Third World Resurgence*, No. 44, 1994, pp. 21–22.

122. Quoted in Martin Khor, "Worldwide Unemployment Will Reach Crisis Proportions Says Social Expert", *Third World Resurgence*, No. 44, 1994, p. 23; see also Jeremy Rifkin, *The End of Work: The Decline of the Global Labor Force and the Dawn of the Post-Market Era*, New York: G.P. Putnam's Sons, 1995.

123. "The Worst Global Unemployment Crisis", ILO, excerpted in *Hunger Notes*, p. 15.

124. Richard Barnet, "The End of Jobs", *Third World Resurgence*, No. 44, 1994, p. 19.

125. "The Worst Global Unemployment Crisis", p. 16.

126. Lester C. Thurow, "The Birth of a Revolutionary Class", *The New York Times Sunday Magazine*, May 19, 1996, p. 46; Kennedy, *Preparing*, p. 311.

127. Kennedy, *Preparing*, p. 312.

128. Thurow, "The Birth", p. 47.

129. Ibid., p. 47.

130. Philippe Fargues, "From Demographic Explosion to Social Rupture", *Middle East Report*, Issue on Gender, Population, Environment, Issue 190, Vol. 24, No. 5, March–April 1993, p. 7.

4

Social Structural Determinants of Fertility

Despite falling fertility rates everywhere, significant differences in birth rates still prevail across regions and social groups (Table 3.5). To understand divergent fertility rates, we need to look at the varying needs and desires of social classes as well as the sexes and cultural groups. In this chapter, we explore the social conditions that contribute to high fertility as well as to fertility decline by focusing on the dialectics of social class and gender relations in the contemporary period.

Social Class and Fertility

Affluence and low fertility

Among middle and upper social classes in the North today, children are economic liabilities not economic assets. In a context where familial kin and community networks are weak and where the provision of practically all goods and services is commoditized, the cost of raising a child from infancy to adulthood at upper middle-class consumption levels is staggering. Currently, annual tuition and board alone cost over $25,000 in many private colleges and universities in the US. Where each child adds a huge economic burden and where children are not expected to provide future support, adults opt for few or no children at all. Parents do not generally expect economic returns from their children; after children complete their education, they leave home to work, marry and start their own families. In this context, childbearing constitutes a consumptive, not an investment, activity. Historically, with the shift from large extended families to nuclear families, wealth flows from children to parents declined. As demographer John Caldwell has pointed out, in families where the net intergenerational wealth flow is from parents to children, fertility tends to be low.[1]

Such factors as high pressure on women to compete in the paid labor force and high divorce rates make it rational for couples and single women to delay childbearing and to have fewer children. This is reflected in declining birth rates in most industrialized countries in the North. The lack of social support systems makes it extremely difficult to raise large families. The individualism of capitalist culture and the excessively materialist and rationalist attitude towards children have resulted in a devaluation of motherhood. While women are compelled to take up paid employment outside the home, even while raising small children, men are not necessarily sharing in the domestic work. Parenting is not a rewarded occupation; everywhere, the burdens of raising children are borne overwhelmingly by women.

To succeed in the competitive, professional world, people have to develop the qualities of mobility, impatience, firmness, efficiency and total commitment to self. But these are often antithetical to qualities such as stability, patience, gentleness, a tolerance for chaos and commitment to others needed to succeed as a parent.[2] As both men and women are forced to value professional rationality and paid work outside the home before the work of childrearing, the emotional foundation of the entire society weakens. Children are frequently put out of the home in their infancy into 'day care' centers, which tend to regiment them within the mechanical clock and the bureaucratic life-style from a tender age.

For middle and upper classes everywhere, childrearing is increasingly an expensive undertaking. Since the beginning of colonialism, privileged classes in the colonies have emulated the values, consumption patterns and lifestyles of the West. In the Third World, as in Europe, privileged social classes that benefited from capitalism achieved the transition to low fertility first. The globalization of middle-class consumerism along with women's education and the necessity of their paid employment to meet rising aspirations have been decisive factors in the decrease in family size across the world. The expansion of education and employment and the availability of 'servants' have given some middle- and upper-class women in the South greater choices in their social and reproductive lives.[3]

Is childbearing a form of 'false consciousness', a relic of patriarchal tradition? Would liberated career women simply give up childbearing or hire younger, poorer women for the task? This seems to be the picture emerging in the 'brave new world' of artificial reproduction and 'surrogate mothering'. Even so, why do some educated career women in the North seek desperately to bear children late in their childbearing years when they expect no economic rewards from them? Is it because of the internalized social pressure, lack of fulfillment by careers or a biological urge guiding women to continue the chain of life?

Indeed, the fact that adults derive sensuality and joy from children, that children are intrinsically valuable and that women have borne children as a natural part of life to satisfy emotional and biological needs throughout history is rarely mentioned in Malthusian explanations of population growth. While the existential question of why women have children cannot be taken up here, we can seek answers to the more limited question of why relatively high fertility persists among poor women.

Poverty and high fertility

In many regions, a woman's social status is still linked almost entirely to her reproductive role; for many women, children are the only source of power. Failure to bear children, especially sons, is the cause of "ostracism, divorce and even brutality in areas of Africa and southern Asia".[4] Women in patriarchal agricultural societies who derive their only social status and self-esteem from their roles as mothers and mothers-in-law may be reluctant to give them up where better alternatives are not on the horizon. In this regard, one must be careful not to extend middle-class, western rationality and motivations to women living in all cultures and economic systems. As Germaine Greer reminds feminists in *Sex and Destiny*:

> ...Because motherhood is virtually meaningless in our society is no ground for supposing that the fact that women are still defined by their mothering function in other societies is simply an index of their oppression. We have at least to consider the possibility that a successful matriarch might well pity Western feminists for having being duped into futile competition with men in exchange for the companionship and love of children and other women.[5]

Children are often the only source of happiness and hope for poor people. But this is rarely understood by western experts or their Third World middle-class counterparts viewing the world from the basis of their own experiences. Consider the reaction of a middle-class woman in India to her maid's reluctance to accept family planning: "I have tried to persuade my servant to try it, but she replied 'It [having children] is the only pleasure we have.' I felt so sad there should be such *ignorance* in a citizen in India" (emphasis in original).[6]

A field survey of migrant households in Uttar Pradesh and Tamil Nadu in India conducted by demographic researcher Alaka Basu also revealed that in both regions and in all age categories the percentages of women who expressed happiness with life increased with the number of children. Basu found that although happiness is an "amorphous concept", the "consistent relationship between numbers of living children and general contentment with life" could not be dismissed.[7] In the light of Malthusian depictions of children as simply a drain on adults and the planet, such findings need greater consideration.

The links between poverty and population are varied and complicated. For most poor people in the Third World, children are not only a means of pleasure and hope, they are also a means of survival. Even by official accounts, which tend to underestimate the extent and value of child labor, in the 'developing world', anywhere from 4 to 20% of children in the 10–14 age group are currently working. According to ILO estimates, globally 250 million 5- to 14-year-olds are employed, 50% of them full-time.[8] To understand the conditions under which households voluntarily opt for large families, we must look at the social relations of production and reproduction, with particular attention to such factors as the economic value of children and the persistence of high levels of infant mortality.

Children as economic assets

Contrary to the assumptions of Malthusianism, higher fertility among the poor is not the result of ignorance, apathy, irrationality or lack of access to contraceptives. It is not the result of mere persistence of traditional reproductive patterns either. For most poor people, children are economic assets not liabilities. Caldwell's fertility transition theory shows that where wealth flows from children to the parents, fertility tends to be high.[9] The 1984 World Bank *World Development Report* observed that 80–90% of people surveyed in Indonesia, South Korea, Thailand and Turkey expected to rely on their children for support in their old age.[10]

A familiar story told in Brazil captures the rationality of high fertility for the poor particularly well. When asked why he has had nine children, a man replies, "Because three die when they are little; three migrate to São Paulo, Rio de Janeiro, or Brasília; and three stay here to take care of us when we get old."[11] Indeed, for many poor families in the Third World, having a large family is a rational economic calculation: children are poor people's source of power.[12]

Unlike in the middle classes, each additional child adds only a small marginal cost; in many cases, the economic returns they bring are far higher than the meagre expenses they incur to the parents. By his 15th birthday, a Javanese boy repays the entire investment his family has made in him through his labor. In Bangladesh, a son provides labor and/or income for the family by the age of 6 and by age 12 at the latest he contributes more than he consumes.[13] Caldwell also found that "the economic wellbeing of the Nigerian family does not change very much with family size and hence the social advantages of eight children outweigh those of four or completely eclipse the horrors of no-, one-, or two-child families."[14]

As noted in Chapter 3, since the emergence of settled agricultural societies, children have been an important and often exploited source of labor for adults. For women burdened with the tasks of domestic work and subsistence production, children's, especially girls', labor, is an indispensable and consistent source of support.[15] In many parts of the world, starting as early as 5, girls start helping with typically 'female tasks' such as caring for younger siblings, carrying water, and food production and preparation.[16] Not only is almost all of this labor unrecognized and unpaid, but also, as Handwerker argues, where parents' well-being is "heavily dependent" on children's labor, "the relationships between parents and children tend to be marked by clear hierarchy, exploitation and coercion even in agricultural societies that otherwise exhibit marked egalitarian characteristics".[17]

Political economist Asok Mitra has pointed out with particular reference to India that as long as the bulk of economic activity in the country depends on the extraction of economic surplus by the heads of households from the "pool of unrecompensed family labour", "the one- or two-child family will remain a far cry".[18] It is also for this reason that China's one child family law has faced most resistance from peasant households needing family labor for agricultural production.[19]

Differential reproductive rationality

The rationality of reproduction and fertility patterns varies significantly by social class, mode of production and time period. In a study of a birth reduction program in a village in Punjab – Manupur – that experienced the modernization of agriculture associated with the Green Revolution in the 1960s, population researcher Mahmood Mamdani discovered that the receptivity to birth control differed according to the labor needs of social classes. Landless agricultural laborers and small farmers with little access to either mechanization or hired labor opted for large families. Based on his conversations with a farmer, Gurdev Singh, the owner of medium-sized holdings, Mamdani reports:

> As he explained, if he had more sons, his labor costs would be significantly reduced and his household maintenance costs only marginally increased. Labor costs are the only variable part of a farmer's production costs, and they can be significantly lowered only by having a large family. Every farmer knows that the cost of having each child declines the more children he has. The benefits, on the other hand, increase. Gurdev Singh expressed the hope that his second son would be married and that his two daughters-in-law would bear him many grandsons so that in the near future they could accumulate enough savings to buy more land.[20]

In contrast, the smaller percentage of farmers with large landholdings in Manupur who could afford to buy tractors and hire laborers opted for smaller families. Similarly, non-agricultural middle-class employees such as school teachers also opted for smaller families. Children were not a source of livelihood for the latter; besides, their higher standards of living required education and other expenses for both male and female children.[21]

There is evidence from other regional contexts and time periods that wage laborers also opt for small families when the value of children as an employable economic asset declines. In the Indian state of Kerala, for example, the availability of universal primary education, the enforcement of minimum wage and child labor laws, better medical facilities and the likelihood of children surviving to adulthood have all contributed to reducing the economic advantages of large families. As anthropologist Joan Mencher has shown, under such circumstances, even poor agricultural labourers become "amenable to family planning".[22] We shall return to the Kerala case later in this chapter.

There is also evidence that for some urban wage laboring classes the economic advantages of children may be diminishing in ways that lead to fertility reductions. Thomas Merrick has argued that fertility declines in Mexico, Colombia and Brazil came in the wake of declining real wages in the 1980s. When faced with an economic squeeze, some families limited births in order to maintain their living standards despite those standards being already very low. Merrick also shows that the spread of education among women and their increased labor force participation were decisive factors in bringing down fertility in families pressured by inflation and rising consumer expectations.[23]

However, as social analysts Frances Moore Lappe and Rachel Schurman have emphasized, "before children can become a net drain on their wage-earning parents, those parents must have jobs".[24] In the burgeoning Third World cities vast numbers of urban people are unable to find regular wage employment. For many who are forced to survive in the so-called informal sector, children are still assets. Many urban slum communities are supported largely by 'street children'. In São Paulo and Bangkok, child prostitutes are often the sole supporters of families. Prostitution among young girls often leads to early childbearing, poverty and other problems such as the spread of AIDS. Still, for many thousands of poor young women in Third World cities, prostitution seems to be the only viable economic option. In a paper discussing the social class relations of human reproduction, Mamdani points out that:

> The marginal employment available to the appropriated masses is daily casual labor: in construction, in hawking, as restaurant waiters or cleaners – in what are euphemistically called the 'service industries'. But, most important, this employment is skewed in favor of child labor. Children shine shoes, open car doors or clean cars, and most of all they beg. In fact, begging becomes a regular occupation: it is organized. ... Once they grow up, these children may desert their families, but as long as they are young and physically unable to leave, these 'innocent ones' in fact support the adults.[25]

As we discuss in the next chapter, many poor countries like Bangladesh are using child labor more and more in export production in order to compete globally and achieve economic growth, for example in the garment sector. Poor children everywhere start working at an early age both within and outside the household. But this limits their educational achievements, making "the intergenerational propagation of class positions a fact of life despite an occasional rise by some members up the economic ladder".[26] The relationship between population growth and poverty is not unidirectional, as postulated in the traditional Malthusian thesis. This relationship is one of reciprocal causality, as has been demonstrated by many analysts in relation to different communities in the world.

Poverty–fertility cycle

In a study of population growth and capitalist development in a county of the state of Veracruz in Mexico, economist Nancy Folbre has demonstrated that many poor people see large families as serving their interests. However, she points out that these decisions do not imply the absence of ill effects. Population growth contributes to land fragmentation, the speed-up of the process of decomposition and proletarianization of the peasantry, the creation of a large reserve army of labor and downward pressure on wages.[27]

Benjamin White also found that in Java poor parents were aware that although high fertility brought benefits to themselves in terms of labor and income, the consequences of high fertility for "the welfare of their children are disastrous". Despite their anxiety for their children's economic future, however, many of these poor parents were powerless to break out of the cycle of poverty.[28]

Similarly, Helen Safa found that in conditions of extreme income inequality during the period of Brazil's 'economic miracle' in the 1970s the industrial working classes increased their fertility in order to have additional wage-earners in their families. However, Safa also observed that although high fertility levels appeared to be "functional from the perspective of the individual working-class family which has only its labor to sell", in the long run, it had 'contradictory' effects on the working class as a whole by increasing competition for jobs both among men and between men and women, keeping wages down.[29]

Poverty breeds anxiety, conflict and family violence. Yet without mutual support and without each other, the poor could not survive. The existence of non-monetary supports such as exchange of food and services often provides more security and satisfaction to people than meagre wages or state aid. Both in the Third World and in the West, extended kin networks are essential for the survival of the poor.[30]

Poverty and fertility in the North

In contrast to the assumptions of many upper-class people, meagre social welfare payments received from the state do not make children economic assets for poor parents in the US. Evidence does not support the common belief that state welfare is an incentive for high fertility.[31] Most welfare recipients have to rely on relatives and other sources of income to make ends meet. Why, then, do early childbearing, large families and extended households consisting of several generations persist among the poor, despite their lack of economic utility? What, in particular, explains the phenomenon of teenage pregnancy among poor, especially Black, communities?

About 33% of births outside of marriage in the US and 29% in the UK are to teenagers.[32] Malthusian analysts and policy makers usually attribute high birth rates among poor teenagers in the US to ignorance and lack of access to contraception, sexual promiscuity, male manipulation of females, and so on. In the period from 1993 to 2010, live births among 15- to 19-

year-olds in the US are expected to increase from 60.5 to 62.4 (per 1,000 women).[33] Restrictions on state Medicaid funding for abortion, 'gag rules' against abortion counselling, parental notification laws, and so on, have no doubt contributed to rising births among poor teenagers. But lack of access to abortion or contraception is not the only or the primary reason for teenage childbearing.

As many scholars and journalists have found, the causes of high teenage pregnancy in poor neighborhoods are social structural. In urban Black communities where poverty is the 'dominant factor' in the lives of teenagers, many young Black women and men consciously choose to bear children as a way of expressing their adult status in a harsh and racist world that denies their sense of being.[34] Given blocked economic opportunities, a young 'ghetto male' must affirm his manhood through peer-group interaction. He becomes a man when he is able to demonstrate that he has had casual sex with many women and has made one or more of them 'have his baby'.[35] Likewise, a girl becomes a woman by having a baby.

As Constance Willard Williams, author of a study on Black teenage mothers, has stated, in a world defined by declining neighborhoods and lack of economic opportunities, teenagers do not have strong reasons to delay 'having a baby'.[36] William Julius Wilson has also argued that unemployment, imprisonment and high mortality among Black men have reduced the numbers of marriageable Black men, thereby providing no incentives for young Black women to delay childbearing.[37] In the experience of the teenage girls interviewed by Williams for her study, the most secure emotional bonds are made between mothers and children, the ties between children and their fathers and women and the men who father their children not being very dependable.[38]

Despite poverty and the burdens of childbearing, many teenage Black as well as Hispanic mothers say that they are happy to have had babies and that they love them dearly.[39] As Williams points out, these teenage mothers exist in a sub-culture that places a high value on childbearing "without requiring that it occur only after marriage or when one can 'afford' to have children".[40] In fact, many teenage mothers are themselves the daughters of women who were teenage mothers and are female heads of households. As Leon Dash observed in his study of teenage childbearing in a Black community in Washington, DC, "The best predictor of a teenage mother's age at first birth is her adolescent mother's age at first birth."[41] But, as in the Third World, early childbearing and the burdens of child-rearing prevent these young people from furthering their education and improving their lives. It reinforces the culture of poverty and the continuation of the mutually reinforcing cycle of poverty and fertility.

The above observations of intergenerational transmission of poverty in the South and the North should not be taken to mean that population reduction alone will reduce poverty. As we have noted in earlier chapters,

Table 4.1 Physical quality of life and fertility, 1990–1995

Region	Life expectancy	Infant mortality (per 1,000 births)	Adult literacy rate[†] (male/female)	Fertility rate (per woman)
World Total	65	62		3.3
More developed regions	75	12	96.0/93.0	1.9
Less developed regions	62	69		3.6
Africa	53	95	60.9/42.0	6.0
Eastern Africa	49	108	66.7/47.5	6.8
Middle Africa	51	96	63.4/38.4	6.5
Northern Africa	61	69	64.3/39.3	4.7
Southern Africa	63	55	62.8/59.8	4.2
Western Africa	51	102	47.2/25.1	6.5
Asia	65	62	77.6/60.5	3.2
Eastern Asia[§]	72	26	94.2/83.6	2.1
South-Eastern Asia	63	55	82.9/67.6	3.4
Southern Asia	59	90	55.9/32.0	4.3
Western Asia[**]	66	54	77.3/58.6	4.7
Europe	75	10	96.5[*]	1.7
Eastern Europe	71	16	99.8/97.4	2.0
Northern Europe	76	7	99.1[*]	1.9
Southern Europe	76	12	93.2/85.2	1.5
Western Europe	76	7	99.0[*]	1.6
Latin America	68	47	85.1/81.1	3.1
Caribbean	69	47	87.5/84.2	2.8
Central America	69	39	77.6/73.0	3.5
South America	67	51	90.2/86.2	2.9
North America	76	8	97.0[*]	2.0
Oceania	73	22	90.8[*]	2.5
Australia–New Zealand[‡]	77	7	83.5[*]	1.9
USSR (former)	70	21	98.0[*]	2.3

[†] 1990 figure; all other columns are for the period 1990–1995.
[*] Total population literacy rates.
[§] Mongolia not included in the calculations of the adult literacy rates.
[**] Oman not included in the adult literacy rate for the region.
[‡] Melanesia not included in the adult literacy rate for the region.

Sources: UNFPA, *The State of World Population 1994*, New York, 1994, pp. 55–65; Central Intelligence Agency, *The World Factbook 1995*; United Nations, *The World's Women 1995: Trends and Statistics*, Social Statistics and Indicators, Series K, No. 12, New York, 1995.

Table 4.2 High rates of infant and child mortality: selected countries (per 1,000 live births), 1960 and 1991

Country	Infant mortality rate (under 1)		Under-5 mortality rate	
	1960	*1991*	*1960*	*1991*
Angola	208	170	345	292
Mozambique	190	170	331	292
Afghanistan	215	165	360	257
Sierra Leone	219	146	385	253
Guinea-Bissau	200	143	336	242
Guinea	203	138	337	234
Malawi	206	144	365	228
Mali	200	108	400	225
Niger	191	127	321	218
Chad	195	125	325	213
Ethiopia	175	125	294	212
Somalia	175	125	294	211
Mauritania	191	120	321	209
Bukina Faso	205	120	363	206
Bhutan	203	133	324	205
Zambia	135	112	220	200
Liberia	184	131	310	200
Uganda	133	110	223	190
Rwanda	150	112	255	189
Nigeria	108	86	212	188
Cambodia	146	120	217	188
Senegal	172	82	299	182
Yemen	214	110	378	182
Burundi	153	108	260	181
Zaïre	174	117	300	180
Central African Republic	174	106	294	180
Tanzania	147	112	249	178
Madagascar	219	113	364	173
Sudan	170	102	292	169
Gabon	171	97	287	161
Benin	184	89	310	149
Lao, PDR	155	101	233	148
Nepal	186	102	298	147
Togo	182	88	305	144
Iraq	117	111	171	143

Source: UNICEF, *State of the World's Children 1993*, New York: Oxford University Press, 1993, p. 68.

in poor countries like Bangladesh and India, reduction of population growth rates has not led to poverty alleviation. In the US, too, family planning, including sterilization and the introduction of Depo-Provera, Norplant and other modern contraceptives among the poor, has not alleviated the social and psychological structures of poverty.

Poor people tend to have relatively large families despite the dismal prospects for the children's future because they are forced to think in terms of immediate survival. High infant and child mortality rates among the poor contribute to short-term rationality and higher birth rates.

Infant mortality and high fertility

Although significant decreases in global mortality and infant mortality have taken place in recent decades, great disparities in mortality still persist between regions and social groups. Higher infant mortality and fertility rates can be observed in the poorer countries and poorer classes and racial groups across the world. The current infant mortality rate is 12 per 1,000 live births and the total fertility rate is 1.9 children per woman in the 'more developed regions'. In contrast, in the 'less developed regions', the infant mortality rate is 69 per 1,000 births and the fertility rate is 3.6 per woman. In regions such as Africa, infant mortality and fertility rates are much higher than in the rest of the South (Table 4.1).

Infant mortality rates account only for numbers of children who die in the first year of birth. But many more children die during their early years due to lack of health care, nutrition and other factors associated with poverty (Table 4.2). High levels of child mortality necessitate that women give birth to several children. Then at least a few will survive into adulthood, ensuring security for parents in their old age. For example, in India, out of the six or seven children that women gave birth to on the average, in the early 1980s only four were expected to survive into adulthood.[42]

Lactation has been a primary method of birth spacing and fertility reduction throughout history. In Africa, babies are still typically breast-fed for two or more years. But where infant mortality is high, breast-feeding periods are decreased, thereby contributing to more frequent births and high fertility.[43] The marketing of infant formula by transnational corporations in areas without sanitation and clean water harms infants' health and undermines breast-feeding, which is safer and more nutritious for infants. Despite the global campaign launched against the Nestlé Company and its unethical infant formula promotion in the Third World some years ago, cultural and market pressures to give up breast-feeding continue. As a result, breast-feeding rates are declining in the Third World and women are being deprived of their natural ability to nurture infants and of a natural means of fertility regulation (one that is not entirely reliable, however).[44]

When population control programs are introduced into contexts where child mortality is very high and AIDS and other diseases are wiping out entire populations, the charge of genocide does not seem entirely false. The explanation for high fertility in Sudan given by a woman doctor in that country in 1985 still has applicability in Sudan and many other regions in Africa and the South:

> In a country like ours where the infant mortality rate is 140 per 1,000 births, where infectious diseases kill so many children, where malnutrition affects about 30–50 percent of the people, where measles is a killer disease although it could be stopped by immunization, how can you tell us to stop having children? When a mother has twelve children, only three or four may live.[45]

High infant and maternal mortality, disease and malnutrition are reflections of the poverty in countries like Sudan. However, as we shall discuss later in this chapter, there are many examples from the South which show that in countries where poverty and infant mortality have been alleviated fertility has declined.

In the North, too, significant disparities in life expectancy and infant mortality can be observed across the races and social classes. For example, life expectancy at birth in 1991 for white males, white females, Black males and Black females was as follows: 72.7; 79.4; 64.5; 73.6 (violence is a major reason why life expectancy for Black males in the US is closer to the Third World rather than the US norm).[46] A 1995 study by the Center for Disease Control and Prevention in Atlanta revealed that while the infant mortality rate during the first year for women living above the poverty line was 8.3 (per 1,000), it was 13.5 among those below the line, that is, a 60% increase.[47] As we discuss in the next chapter, much larger percentages of Blacks and Hispanics live below the poverty line than whites. These socioeconomic differences underlie the currently higher fertility rates among Black and other 'non-white' groups relative to whites.

As Handwerker has put it, the neo-Malthusian assumption that the absence of modern contraception is the main reason for high fertility rates "is one of the great myths of our time".[48] In a recent paper, demographer Lant Pritchett has also demonstrated that family planning is only of "marginal relevance" to demographic change.[49] Contraceptive acceptance is not an independent variable; it is dependent on human needs and desires as conditioned by culture and socio-economic relations. The level of fertility in a society is especially dependent on such factors as women's nutrition and workloads, marriage arrangements, land tenure and inheritance patterns, and increasingly women's education.[50]

To understand the poverty–fertility nexus, then, women's roles in economic production and reproduction must be explored. While the politico-economic forces behind the exacerbation of global poverty and women's poverty will be examined in chapter 5, in the next section of this chapter we shall look at some aspects of women's socio-economic subordination that have a direct bearing on their reproductive rationality and fertility.

Gender and Fertility

Next to the African countries, Western Asia, constituting the prosperous oil-rich Middle East (Northern Africa and Western Asia), had the highest fertility rates in the world in the 1990–1995 period (Table 4.1). The persistence of relatively high fertility rates in this region is commonly attributed to Islam. As Carla Makhlouf Obermeyer suggests, however, the 'Islamic' explanation is not adequate for understanding high fertility in that region.[51] The benefits of prosperity and socio-economic development have not been adequately extended to women. Throughout the Middle East, the enrollment of girls in schools is less than boys; women's labor force participation is negligible and preference seems to be given to boys' health over girls. Obermeyer's conclusion that "demographic processes are less the direct product of religious rules ... and more the result of strategies and decisions reflecting the structure of power in society" is applicable to all regions across the world.[52]

As sociologist Kathryn Ward, has argued, lowered access to resources, conditions conducive to infant mortality and income inequality and other problems located within the world economic system, as well as the persistence of the high social and economic value of children, underlie the close relationship between women's poverty and high fertility.[53] Health researcher Jodi Jacobson, too, has pointed out that insufficient access to productive resources and family income and increased pressure on time and labor make women depend on children for social esteem and economic security.[54] Lacking alternative routes to survival, some women also have children to legitimate claims on income from men.[55] All these conditions contribute to the perpetuation of the cycle of low social status, poverty and high fertility of women.

When women cannot increase their own labor any more, they tend to rely more on the labor of their children, particularly girls. In many areas, women are increasingly keeping girls out of school to help with their work. As Phoebe Asiyo of the United Nations Development Fund for Women states, in Africa, "more and more girls are dropping out of both primary and secondary school or just missing school altogether due to increasing poverty".[56] This will contribute to continued illiteracy, poverty and high fertility in the future generation of women.

As noted in the last chapter and to be discussed further in the next chapter, in many Third World countries living standards have worsened during the 1980s and 1990s due to the debt crisis and structural adjustment policies (SAPs) imposed by the World Bank and the IMF. Many countries in the South which have Fund/Bank Adjustment programs, especially in Africa, have experienced a reversal of social improvements achieved in earlier decades. The result is increasing rates of infant and child mortality, deterioration of female nutrition and health, and falling rates of primary school enrollment, particularly for girls (Table 5.4). By inducing declines in female schooling and health as well as by increasing infant mortality, SAPs have in many places helped maintain conditions of high fertility. As Ingrid Palmer has stated in an ILO working paper for the World Employment Programme:

> What can be stated at once is that all the signs point to a pronatalist impact of structural adjustment policies in the short term. On every count – the value of children's assistance, the threat to women's personal income and the reduction in public expenditure on health-giving facilities – the outcome for fertility is forbidding. More will be expected of the household labour supply with its gender and age allocation.[57]

Evidence from different regions in the world that experience frequent famines also shows that in the long term famines do not lead to reduction of population growth rates; instead, the insecurity created by famines and the lack of other survival options induce the poor to maintain high levels of fertility.[58] There is also growing evidence, however, that absolute impoverishment may now be leading to crisis-led fertility declines in some parts of the Third World. We shall turn to this issue later in this chapter.

Externally imposed political and economic forces place contradictory pressures on women's fertility behavior. By increasing women's economic vulnerability, imperialist policies increase women's need for more children while at the same time making it difficult for women to take care of those children. Moreover, family planning programs demand that women reduce their fertility without providing any assurance whatsoever that the children who are born will be able to survive into adulthood.

Nevertheless, women's reproductive behavior cannot be attributed simply to poverty induced by the global economy. Material production and human reproduction in the world today are defined by the social and psychological structures of patriarchy as well as capitalism and racism. The subordination of women is a historical phenomenon that predates capitalism and imperialism. Neither women's poverty nor their fertility can be understood outside of patriarchy and the psychological and physical violence directed habitually against them.

Patriarchy and high fertility

Even in contexts where poor women may not necessarily perceive children to be economic assets and where their support for traditional fertility norms may be weak, they are often unable to make fertility decisions on their own. Fertility behavior is likely to reflect dominant social class, male and global interests.[59]

Many countries and international organizations are now beginning to recognize the existence of 'significant' forms of violence against women both within and outside the family, for example incest, rape, sexual harassment, battery, genital mutilation (removal of the clitoris or its parts in some Muslim societies). But what is not addressed by population control enthusiasts is the extent to which sexual violence and coerced sex results in pregnancy and childbirth around the world. For example, today, Rwanda is estimated to have between 2,000 and 5,000 children born through rape during the recent civil war.[60] Many women, especially young girls, including many teenagers in the North, are coerced or simply cajoled into having unprotected sex. As Martha Ward has noted in her study of adolescent pregnancy in the state of Louisiana, rape or incest may be a 'systematic' factor in 11-year-old girls conceiving.[61] While the compulsory implantation of Norplant may stop such girls from conceiving, it will not stop men from raping those girls. In fact, Norplant implantation could allow men, in the North or the South, to coerce or cajole young women into sexual intercourse without having to face the consequences of pregnancy and fatherhood.

A particular aspect of patriarchal thinking that has a direct bearing on fertility and mortality outcomes is the preference for sons, an issue raised earlier in relation to our discussion of declining female sex ratios. While son preference is a deep-rooted mentality that has its origin in agricultural societies, it continues to exercise a determining influence on reproductive behaviour in the contemporary era.

Preference for sons

Although women are increasingly active in the public sphere and are often the primary breadwinners of families, the ideology of female dependence continues to be strong. The persistence of such traditions as dowry, that is, the giving of wealth by the bride's family to the groom and his family at marriage in South Asia; the patrilocal custom of women living with the husbands' families after marriage; sons' roles at parents' funerals and in ancestor worship, make boys economic and social assets and girls liabilities. Son preference often contributes to high fertility since families continue to have children until they have enough sons, or at least one son.

In patriarchal societies where women receive social status only as the bearers of children, especially sons, women themselves may uphold high fertility norms. Although women bear children, they do not often make fertility decisions. These are usually made by the husbands and are enforced with psychological and sexual control and violence against women.[62] Surveys have found that even in the state of Kerala, where women have high social status and autonomy relative to other states in India, husbands' disapproval is a common reason for not using contraceptives on the part of women not wanting another child.[63]

Fertility decisions are made not only by the reproductive generation. Where extended family and kin relations continue to be strong, the older generation may encourage beliefs and customs hostile to fertility control and generally favorable to males.[64] A belief like one prevalent in Africa that the dead survive as spirits "only in so far as descendants remember them" contributes to the desire to have many descendants and large families.[65]

However, extreme preference for sons also leads to population reduction where female infanticide is widely practiced. As noted earlier in our discussion of population dynamics in foraging and agricultural societies, female infanticide has long been a population regulation mechanism. Even today in many villages of India and China it is fairly common. Ironically, it is the women, the mothers themselves, who often initiate 'putting a child to sleep', the euphemism for infanticide. Many believe that it is better to save a girl from a 'lifetime of suffering'. One woman in the Salem District of Tamil Nadu in India, where female infanticide and feticide are widely practiced, told Viji Srinivasan, who conducted a detailed study of the area:

> I had one daughter. I 'kept' her. I killed the second daughter. Now I am pregnant. I will kill this child if I have a girl. Why bring up girl children? How to prevent husbands from beating her up, from demanding 10 sovereigns and 20 sovereigns of gold? Erukkampal (the milk of the calotropis plant) is an easy killer. Sleeping tablets also. Otherwise the baby is suffocated with a wet towel and put upside down.[66]

As feminist activists point out, the issue of female infanticide is not an isolated one; it is an extreme expression of male supremacy and violence against women. In India, 999 registered cases of dowry deaths – the killing of brides by husbands' families over inadequate wealth transfers – were reported for 1985; 1,319 for 1986; and 1,786 for 1987.[67] Of course, the number of unreported cases is much greater.

Besides such outright killing of women, there are other more routine practices based on inequality and neglect that contribute to the lowering of the female population in countries such as India. As noted in Chapter 2, the disparity in the sex ratio could further widen in countries like China and India due to increased use of sex-selective abortions and other practices directed against female fetuses and baby girls.

There is evidence from around the world that after conception women tend to live longer where both sexes receive similar nutritional attention and health care.[68] However, in many Third World countries, owing to the reduced food and health care received by females, far more girls than boys die during the critical period from infancy until age 5.[69] In South Asia, for example, "females receive less care, fewer warm clothes, less medical attention (and that given belatedly) and, in spite of the drain of pregnancy and

Table 4.3 Female/male ratios, infant and child mortality rates, selected countries, 1986/1993

Region	Female/male ratio	
	infant mortality	child mortality
Developed regions (30 countries)	0.8	0.8
Developing regions (Northern Africa and Western Asia)		
Egypt	0.9	1.4
Jordan, Morocco, Tunisia, Yemen	0.9	1.1
Sub-Saharan Africa (17 countries)	0.8	1.0
Latin America and Caribbean (10 countries)	0.8	1.0
Asia		
China	1.2	1.0
Pakistan	0.8	1.6
Indonesia, Philippines, Sri Lanka, Thailand	0.8	1.0

Source: United Nations, *The World's Women, 1995: Trends and Statistics*, Social Statistics and Indicators, Series K, No. 12, New York, 1995, p. 69.

lactation, less food". They are also subjected to more food restrictions.[70] As John and Pat Caldwell argue, health beliefs and social customs favoring better health and nutritional care for boys must be seen in relation to "underlying material facts", such as men's greater income-earning capacity, girls' dowry costs and marrying out. Women themselves enforce food and health deprivations on their daughters. Women frequently justify their own misogyny with the claim that boys are inherently weaker than girls and need more food and attention than their sisters.[71]

These disparities are clearly reflected in differences in infant and child mortality rates between the sexes. In both 'developed' and 'developing' countries, females have a lower mortality ratio than males during the first year of life, with China being the exception for reasons such as female infanticide discussed in Chapter 2. However, for a number of 'developing countries' for which UN data are available, within the 1–4 age group, female child mortality is higher than male child mortality. Especially high female mortality rates exist in countries such as Egypt (1.4) and in Pakistan (1.6) (Table 4.3).[72] As noted above, unequal treatment of girls and boys in the areas of health and nutrition underlie the worsening death ratios of girls.

Economist Amartya Sen points out, "economic development is quite often accompanied by a relative worsening in the rate of survival of women (even as life expectancy improves in absolute terms for both men and women)".[73] Indeed, the phenomenon known as 'missing women' in Asia needs to be approached from within this broad social context of violence against women. Discrimination in health and nutrition, population control pressures, female infanticide, sex-selective abortions, dowry deaths in India, all contribute in different ways to this phenomenon.

As concluded by Patricia Jeffery, Roger Jeffery and Andrew Lyon, who conducted a case study of women and childbearing in a village in Northern India, the improvement of the position of women calls for "dramatic changes in patterns of landholding and employment, in women's work and access to property, in evaluations of their worth, and in the systems of kinship, residence and marriage which constrain them", in other words, changes in "the very basis of rural society". But these authors lament that there is "little on the local horizon that harbingers a better future" for the village women.[74]

In much of the Third World today, including villages such as the one studied by Jeffery and colleagues, Malthusian programs are being substituted for fundamental changes in the social relations of production and reproduction. The focus on women within such programs does not extend to alleviation of the structural roots of women's economic and social subordination. At best, they infuse family planning into income generation projects or public health services, which themselves are highly inadequate for improving the lives of women and their communities.

Many WID and GOBI (Growth monitoring, Oral rehydration therapy, Breast-feeding and improved weaning practices and Immunization) programs have often increased demands on women's time and resources and extended their traditional roles as mothers. WID programs, especially the WID Programme of the World Bank, which sets the ground rules for gender policy in much of the Third World, seek to integrate women more tightly into commodity production and to bring them under greater scientific and managerial control of external political-economic and cultural forces. However, this bureaucratic and market approach to gender fails to address the questions of land distribution, pricing and credit policies and other mechanisms that "reproduce and intensify inequalities within the agrarian sector".[75]

Fertility declines require alleviation of poverty and improvements in the living conditions of the poor, especially women. Where children's labor is not essential for family survival, where women and children have food and nutrition, education, health care and gainful employment, they are more likely to accept birth control and voluntarily lower their fertility. Across the world, a consistent correlation can be observed between female literacy/ schooling and reduced child mortality and fertility (Table 4.1). Education leads women to increase labor force participation, delay marriage and bear fewer children. In Thailand and Costa Rica, for example, improved health and educational resources for women were decisive factors in significant reductions in fertility during the 1960–1985 period.[76]

Where there are extreme social inequalities and concentration of resources and power in the hands of a small minority, poverty alleviation is not possible. Societies with highly unequal income distribution generally have high fertility whereas those with more equality have lower fertility.[77] There are many examples of countries and regions in the South where fertility has declined significantly due to the combined effects of income distribution, poverty alleviation and improvements in women's lives. These cases require greater attention than they have received within the neo-Malthusian literature. It is to some of those positive examples that we turn next.

Social Justice and Fertility

Studies show that the biggest reductions in fertility occur when the inequalities between economic sectors are reduced and particularly when the income of the poorest groups is increased.[78] A World Bank Staff Report of 1974 based on a study of 64 countries admitted that 50% of income accruing to the richest 15% of households is not as important in influencing overall population growth as the 50% of income received by the poorer 85% of households. This study also showed that when the proportion of income of the poorest group (that is, the bottom 40% of the population in terms of income) increased by just 1%, the overall fertility rate of the country dropped approximately 3%. The same study demonstrated that when literacy rate and life expectancy rates are added to the income analysis, these three factors account for 80% of the variation in fertility in the countries surveyed.[79] The 1984 World Bank World Development Report argued that above the poverty threshold, increases in income tend to be correlated with lower fertility levels.[80]

According to economist Robert Repetto, fertility decline in South Korea between 1960 and 1974, one of the fastest fertility declines in any nation in history, was due essentially to "improvement in the living standards and opportunities of the poor majority, and the absence of wide socio-economic disparities, rather than a particular political orientation of the government".[81] Land and educational reforms were important in the achievement of a high degree of social equality. When greater choices were made available, Korean households chose investments in land and their children's education over large families. In Taiwan too the demographic transition cannot be attributed only to public health measures and export-led industrialization. Agricultural reform, expansion of education, and so on, provided the social foundation for the eventual success of the country's family planning program.[82]

Frances Moore Lappe and Rachel Schurman have observed that by the 1980–1985 period, among the more than 70 poor countries in the world, only six had managed to cut their total fertility rates by a third or more since 1960 and reduce their population growth rates to less than 2%. These countries were China, Sri Lanka, Colombia, Chile, Burma and Cuba. Although not a country, Lappe and Schurman also include the Indian state of Kerala in this group because of its reductions in fertility and population growth rates.[83]

The experience of these countries and Kerala defies the conventional demographic transition theory in many ways. Unlike the European countries or the East Asian 'success' economies, these seven did not have very high levels of economic growth, per capita incomes, industrialization or urbanization. They also defy the neo-Malthusian population control theory in that they did not have strong family planning programs in common. What they did have in common were guarantees of basic necessities, especially access to a basic diet for all. Four of the seven – China, Kerala, Sri Lanka and Cuba – provided more extensive food guarantee systems than other Third World countries (few reliable data exist on Burma).[84]

Evidence also shows that in these six countries and Kerala fertility reduction was related not merely to improvements in general population, but also to improvements in the position of women. Patriarchy is far from being uprooted in these locations and family planning programs in many of them tend to use sterilization and high-tech contraceptives used elsewhere. However, increased health, education and economic opportunities for women have significantly improved women's lives in these countries.[85]

Sri Lanka is now in the third phase of the demographic transition, namely, declining fertility. The fertility rate of 2.39 children per woman in 1995 is expected to drop still further, reaching replacement-level fertility by the year 2000. The decline in fertility in Sri Lanka began before the country's family planning program had had much effect. Moreover, as Sri Lankan demographer Indralal de Silva has observed, a third of contraceptive users in Sri Lanka still rely on traditional methods of fertility control.[86] It is social development, more than the modern 'contraceptive revolution', that underlies Sri Lanka's demographic transition.

In Sri Lanka, advances made in women's health and education have been crucial factors in increasing women's life expectancy and age at marriage and decreasing infant mortality rates. These achievements in turn have contributed to fertility rates and population growth rates far lower than most Third World countries and the rest of South Asia. In Sri Lanka, despite low economic growth rates and per capita incomes during the 1960s and 1970s, benefits provided by the social welfare state such as universal education and health care and food subsidies helped improve the physical quality of life and lower mortality and birth rates. Women's literacy of

84%, average age at marriage of 24.4 (recent estimates even higher) and fertility per woman of 2.4 are unusual for a poor country (Table 4.4).[87]

The demographic transition in Kerala is even more instructive because it stands in sharp contrast to the rest of India, which has not achieved the same despite "massive and long-standing conventional western approaches" to family planning. Despite over forty years of population control efforts, the population growth rate did not decline significantly. Annual population growth has averaged 2.1% throughout this period. Although the tiny Indian state of Goa has also experienced a demographic transition similar to Kerala, the Goan case remains largely unexplored.[88]

Demographic transition in Kerala

While Kerala's population density is three times the average of India, and for many decades Kerala had been among the so-called 'lowliest' and most 'overpopulated' of Indian states, within a relatively short span, its population growth rate has sharply declined. Mortality declines have been "more rapid and substantial" in Kerala than other states in India (Table 4.4). According to social analysts, the size of the fertility decline in Kerala had not been previously seen in a state or nation at similar levels of income and economic growth. The Kerala birth rate declined from 30.5 per 1,000 in the 1971–73 period to 20.7 in the 1987–89 period, thus making it the lowest birth rate in India next to Goa's rate of 17.5.[89]

The demographic transition of Kerala was not the achievement of Malthusian population control strategies. Nor was it simply a "poverty-induced fertility transition" stemming from the inability of Kerala's wage-dependent poor to continue supporting several children, as argued by demographer Alaka Basu.[90] Rather, the increased receptivity to family planning even among some of the poorest landless laborers must be seen in the context of declining value of children as economic assets across the social classes.[91] The declining economic value of children was associated to a large degree with state-sponsored social reforms.

As John Ratcliffe and many other analysts have pointed out, the demographic transition in Kerala was the result of structural reforms that reduced social and economic disparities.[92] Transfer of resources to the poorest groups through a grain distribution system, pension funds, abolition of tenancy through land reform, enforcement of child-labor and minimum-wage laws, widespread health facilities, universal education, public work programs and expansion of agricultural labor unions have all contributed to the Kerala demographic transition.[93] These reforms led to an overall improvements in the Physical Quality of Life Index – infant mortality, life expectancy, literacy – as well as reduction in mortality and birth rates (Table 4.4).

The fertility declines in Kerala have to be seen in relation to women's status. Until recently, a large portion of the Kerala population followed

Table 4.4   Socio-demographic indicators: India, Kerala and Sri Lanka, early 1990s

Indicator	India	Kerala	Sri Lanka
Infant mortality (per 1,000 live births)	72	17	15
Under-5 mortality			
Male	104	–	24
Female	108	–	19
Life expectancy at birth (years)			
Male	62.6	70	70.9
Female	62.9	72	75.4
Literacy			
Male	64	94.4	93
Female	39	86.3	84
Female Age at 1st marriage	18.7**	22	24.4**
Sex ratio (females per 1,000 males)	929	1040	–
GDP per capita ($US c. 1992)	274	298	563
% below poverty line	40	27	–
Births per 1000 population	27.78	19	18.13
Deaths per 1000 population	10.07	5.9	5.78
Total fertility rate	3.56	1.8	2.39
Population growth rate (1995–2000)	1.8	1.3†	1.2
Population (millions)	936.5	29	18.4

Note: All data for early 1990 unless otherwise indicated.

† 1981–1991 figure.   ** 1980–1990 figure.

Sources: UNDP, *Human Development Report 1994*, New York: Oxford University Press, 1994, pp. 144–145; UNFPA, *State of World Population, 1995*, New York, 1995, pp. 64–70; Central Intelligence Agency, *The World Factbook 1995*, 1995, pp. 196–198; World Hunger Education Service, *Hunger Notes*, Vol. 18, Nos. 3–4, Winter/Spring 1993, p. 5, Washington, DC; B.A. Prakash, ed., *Kerala's Economy: Performance, Problems, Prospects*, New Delhi: Sage Publications, 1994, pp. 45, 47; also, communications to author from William M. Alexander, *Future of the Earth: Resources and People*, San Luis Obispo, CA, April 3, 1996.

matrilineal kinship in which women did not move to husbands' residences upon marriage and property descended along the female line. Although the matrilineal system has weakened, it has given Kerala women a higher social status compared to their counterparts in other states of India.[94] This is visible in the Kerala sex ratio, which, unlike in other Indian states, is favorable to women over men (Table 4.4).

The social reforms in Kerala increased access to health, education and labor force participation for women. These have been the most critical factors in Kerala's birth rate decline. Increased educational levels have led to higher age at marriage for women, making the Kerala female age at marriage at 22 the highest in India (Table 4.4). Fewer women in Kerala marry, a full 22% never do so, apparently "because of the attractive alternatives to marriage available to educated females".[95] For India as a whole the comparable figure was only 7% in the mid- to late 1970s. It is in the context of these social realities that higher 'contraceptive practice' in Kerala relative to the rest of India must be viewed.[96]

The social improvements in Kerala were the outcome of a confluence of historical developments unique in India. Kerala was home to an early educational movement launched by noted Hindu philosopher Sankaracarya between AD 788 and 820; it has long-established international trading and political contacts abroad; and has experienced extensive missionary activity in schooling (20% of the population is now Christian) during more recent centuries. But, as Amartya Sen points out, state-sponsored expansion of basic education, begun almost two centuries ago by the native rulers of the kingdoms of Travancore and Cochin (two kingdoms that defied annexation by the British), may have been the decisive factor in consolidating state efforts in education in recent years. In 1817, the young queen of Travancore, Gouri Parvathi Bai, expressed explicit support for state-funded education:

> The state should defray the entire cost of education of its people in order that there might be no backwardness in the spread of enlightenment among them, that by diffusion of education they might be better subjects and public servants and that the reputation of the State might be advanced thereby.[97]

It was this tradition of state-funded education that has been carried on by leftist governments in recent decades. The Communist Party of India–Marxist (CPI–M), which initiated many of the social reforms, has not been in power throughout. But, as Ratcliffe argues, even when it was out of power, as, for example, after it was 'removed from power' in 1959 (due to pressure from Kerala's large landholders), the CPI–M was able to influence the continuation of the social welfare policies due to its popularity with the poor. Peasant organization, strongest among all Indian states, put pressure on the state to enforce minimum wage and child labor laws and other progressive legislation and to carry out land reform, however imperfectly. Unlike in other Indian states, peasant organizations and labor unions in Kerala have ensured that progressive laws are implemented rather than ignored.[98]

The Kerala success, then, is not simply the result of top-down action from a benevolent state; without grass-roots organization and continued vigilance the achievements in Kerala could not have been sustained. In Sri Lanka, too, the welfare state was the product of very high levels of popular participation in electoral politics, as well as the historical strength of the Marxist parties.

The welfare state is not a panacea for all social problems or women's concerns. Certainly, the Kerala and Sri Lankan models have not been perfect. The lessons of these cases, however, is that if reduction of population growth rates is a priority, then social structural changes are essential. As Ratcliffe has pointed out, social equity concerns must take priority over aggregate growth concerns, and human needs must come before the 'needs' of externally imposed family planning and other institutional structures.[99] Similarly, as T.N. Krishnan, who has studied the Kerala case extensively, argues that increased education and employment opportunities for women must be made a "potent weapon for breaking the linkages between population growth and poverty".[100]

Analysts like Lappe and Repetto who have examined the poverty–fertility nexus in other Third World contexts have suggested national and international redistribution of wealth and income as the most effective response to the problems of poverty and rapid population increase.[101] National and international women's groups and networks such as the Committee on Women, Population and the Environment are calling specifically for an end to the feminization of poverty and a broader feminist social justice approach to population and development (Appendix 1).

The language and rhetoric of 'human development', reproductive health and women's rights have now been incorporated within institutions such as the World Bank. However, as these institutions represent the interests of transnational capital, they block policies towards social justice and economic democracy. Third World governments pay lip service to justice but their interests also lie in control of populations rather than redressing inequality and poverty.

Worsening Inequality and Fertility

North–South, class, gender and ethnic disparities are increasing and global crises of poverty, environmental destruction and repression are worsening. There is no guarantee that even a region like Kerala could withstand the penetration of international capital and policies of economic restructuring and hold on to its hard-won social improvements in the years ahead.

In Sri Lanka, for example, state expenditures on education, health and food subsidies have been slashed due to the confluence of economic liberalization, IMF/World Bank policies, dismantling of the welfare state and militarism. Income disparities have widened and hunger and malnutrition among the 'bottom' 20% of the Sri Lankan population have increased. According to 1995 United Nations estimates, 21% of Sri Lankan women were unemployed.[102] The long-term effects of these developments could be increasing class and gender inequalities and a reversal of earlier achievements in the quality of life of the people.[103]

As already noted, some of the World Bank's earlier studies have shown a close correlation between increases in income of the poorer groups and reductions in fertility. Notwithstanding those findings, the World Bank has continued to oppose income distribution. For example, the World Bank *World Development Report 1984* contradicts itself when it says:

> Raising the incomes of the rich (be it of rich countries or of rich groups within countries) reduces fertility less than does raising the incomes of the poor. There is, however, no good evidence that the distribution of income has an independent effect on fertility; it is influential only to the extent that poor households usually have higher absolute incomes if their share of the total is higher.[104]

Traditional demographic transition theory focuses on the decline of fertility and population growth rates resulting from socio-economic development and voluntary acceptance of contraception. However, in earlier chapters we discussed the growing interest of population control organizations such as the World Bank in bringing down fertility levels through intensified family planning efforts even in the absence of socio-economic development and poverty alleviation. There is now increasing evidence from the Third World of poverty-induced fertility declines as anticipated by the World Bank.

Poverty-led fertility decline

Extreme impoverishment in conjunction with aggressive family planning promotion may be leading to crisis- and poverty-led fertility declines among the so-called 'bottom billion' of the world's population.

A new study by anthropologists Patricia and Roger Jeffery based on extensive fieldwork in Uttar Pradesh in India shows that desired family size is declining among many poor peasants, especially women. However, this change does not seem to be associated with any significant improvement in standards of living or the position of women. Rather, with increasing land pressure, inflation, unemployment and so on, poverty, especially women's poverty, has increased.[105]

There is also evidence of poverty-induced fertility declines in a number of Latin American countries. As we pointed out in Chapter 2, sterilization has reached extremely high levels among the poorest women in Brazil, especially Black women in the northeastern region, who have been worst affected by the debt crisis and cutbacks in public services and social programs. In a study of the impact of recession and structural adjustment policies on women in Ecuador, Caroline Moser also found that 42% of women surveyed were sterilized.[106] Given the history of sterilization abuse worldwide and the poverty of these women, it is likely that many of them did not have genuine choice in accepting sterilization.

There is evidence that in many regions in Africa fertility may also be declining because of rising costs of childrearing and declining employment opportunities associated with the ongoing socio-economic and ecological crisis. In social climates where people are fearful of future survival and where state policy increasingly promotes family planning over social development, many people are compelled to delay or stop childbearing altogether.[107] As sociologist Ron Lesthaeghe has argued, although historically economic crises have only led to temporary fertility declines as opposed to sustained fertility transitions, the current situation in Africa may prove to be the exception.[108]

As discussed in Chapter 4, a number of countries in the Third World worst affected by structural adjustment, poverty, the AIDS epidemic and wars are experiencing significant mortality increases. Where crisis-led mortality increases are combined with crisis-led fertility decreases, as is potentially the case in a number of the poorest countries in Sub-Saharan Africa, population collapses could be the long-term result. This scenario does not seem entirely far-fetched when we consider how quickly the Third World and especially the African region have moved from depopulation and 'underpopulation' to 'overpopulation' and then to fertility declines due largely to imperialist policies during the course of global capitalist expansion. Indeed, the contemporary Third World population 'explosion' is a temporary phenomenon. It is important, then, to avoid alarmist fears and to approach changing demographic dynamics in a sober and humane way.

Poverty-induced fertility decline is not a cause for celebration, as assumed in discussions of the 'Bangladesh success' or cost-effectiveness of the 'contraceptive revolution'. Unlike the earlier European demographic transition, the contemporary Third World demographic transition involving crisis-led fertility declines is built not on democracy and choice, but on inequality and coercion. Similarly, the currently declining teenage pregnancy rate in the US may be a product of worsening poverty and stringent population control efforts rather than improvement in women's lives.[109]

To move the world towards a path of social justice and democracy, it is necessary to examine the social structural causes of the global crisis. To do so, we need to move beyond the Malthusian obsession with fertility and population growth reduction to examine the global political-economic forces which are widening economic inequality and exacerbating poverty, including the feminization of poverty. It is to these issues that we turn in the next chapter.

Notes

1. John Caldwell, *Theory of Fertility Decline*, New York: Academic Press, 1982.
2. Penelope Leach, *Children First: What Society Must Do – and Is Not Doing for Children Today*, New York: Vintage Books, 1994.
3. Hanna Papanek, "Class and Gender in Education-Employment Linkages", *Comparative Education Review*, Vol. 29, No. 3, 1985, p. 236.

4. United Nations, *The World's Women 1970–1990: Trends and Statistics*, Social Statistics and Indicators, Series K, No. 8, New York, 1991, p. 7.

5. Germaine Greer, *Sex and Destiny: The Politics of Human Fertility*, New York: Harper and Row, 1984, p. 29.

6. Quoted in Patricia Caplan, *Class and Gender in India: Women and their Organizations in a South Indian City*, New York: Methuen, 1986, pp. 202–203.

7. Alaka Malwade Basu, *Culture: The Status of Women and Demographic Behaviour: Illustrated with the Case of India*, Oxford: Clarendon Press, 1992, p. 240.

8. United Nations, *The World's Women 1995: Trends and Statistics*, Social Statistics and Indicators, Series K, No. 12, New York, 1995, p. 117; "U.N. Sharply Increases Estimate of Youngsters at Work Full Time", *The New York Times*, November 12, 1996, p. 6.

9. Caldwell, *Theory of Fertility Decline, passim.*

10. World Bank, *World Development Report 1984*, p. 52.

11. "Poverty Dooms the Planet: Now is the Time to Act", *World Press Review*, June 1992, p. 14.

12. Lappe and Schurman, "The Missing Piece", p. 27.

13. Ibid., p. 21; see also White, "The Economic Importance of Javanese Children", *passim.*

14. Caldwell, *Theory of Fertility Decline*, p. 26.

15. Handwerker, "Politics and Reproduction", p. 10.

16. United Nations, *The World's Women 1995*, p. 117.

17. Handwerker, "Politics and Reproduction", p. 11.

18. Asok Mitra, cited in Mazumdar, "Fertility Policy in India", p. 265.

19. Elisabeth J. Croll, "Production versus Reproduction: A Threat to China's Development Strategy", *World Development*, Vol. 11, No. 6, 1983, pp. 467–481.

20. Mamdani, *The Myth of Population Control*, p. 85.

21. Ibid., Chap. 5.

22. Joan Mencher, "The Lessons and Non-Lessons of Kerala: Agricultural Labourers and Poverty", *Economic and Political Weekly*, Special Number, October 1980, p. 1787; see also Alaka Malwade Basu, "Birth Control by Assetless Workers in Kerala: The Possibility of a Poverty Induced Fertility Transition", *Development and Change*, Vol. 17, 1986, pp. 265–282.

23. Thomas W. Merrick, "Recent Fertility Declines in Brazil, Colombia and Mexico", World Bank Staff Working Paper No. 692, Washington, DC, Population and Development Series, No. 1, 1985, pp. 34–35.

24. Lappe and Schurman, "The Missing Piece", p. 24.

25. Mahmood Mamdani, "The Ideology of Population Control" in Michaelson, ed., *And the Poor*, p. 48.

26. Patterson and Shrestha, "Population Growth and Development", p. 23.

27. Nancy Folbre, "Population Growth and Capitalist Development in Zongolica, Veracruz", *Latin American Perspectives*, Issue 15, Special issue on Population and Imperialism, Vol. IV, No. 4, Fall 1977, p. 50.

28. White, "The Economic Importance of Javanese Children", p. 145.

29. Helen I. Safa, "Women, Production and Reproduction in Industrial Capitalism: A Comparison of Brazilian and U.S. Factory Workers", New York: Women's International Resource Exchange Service, 1978, p. 10.

30. Oscar Lewis, *Five Families: Mexican Case Studies in the Culture of Poverty*, New York: New American Library, 1959; Carol B. Stack, *All Our Kin: Strategies for Survival in a Black Community*, New York: Harper and Row, 1974.

31. "Baby Boom Among Unwed", *Newsday* (New York), cited in *Daily Hampshire Gazette*, July 14, 1993, p. 1; see also Williams, *Black Teenage Mothers*, p. 25.

32. United Nations, *The World's Women 1970–1990*, p. 16.

33. US Bureau of the Census, *Statistical Abstract of the United States: 1995*, p. 76.

34. Dash, *When Children Want Children*, p. 31; see also, Katherine F. Darabi, Joy Dryfoos and Dana Schwartz, "The Fertility Related Attitudes and Behavior of Hispanic Adoles-

cents in the U.S.", Center for Population and Family Health, Working Paper No. 9, July 1985, Columbia University, New York.

35. Elijah Anderson, "Sex Codes and Family Life among Poor Inner-City Youths", *The Annals of the American Academy of Political & Social Science*, Vol. 501, January 1989; see also William Julius Wilson, "The Underclass: Issues, Perspectives, and Public Policy", ibid., p. 186.

36. Williams, *Black Teenage Mothers*, passim.

37. Ibid., p. 129; see also William Julius Wilson, *The Truly Disadvantaged: The Inner-City, the Underclass and Public Policy*, Chicago: University of Chicago Press, 1987, Chap. 3.

38. Williams, *Black Teenage Mothers*, p. 131.

39. *Newsday*, "Baby Boom", p. 1.

40. Williams, *Black Teenage Mothers*, p. 26.

41. Dash, *When Children Want Children*, p. 26.

42. Lappe and Schurmann, "The Missing Piece", p. 24.

43. Ibid., p. 25.

44. Evelyn Hong, "Women as Consumers and Producers in the World Market", *Third World Resurgence*, Nos 61–62, 1995, p. 49; Hartmann, *Reproductive Rights and Wrongs*, p. 11.

45. Cited in Lappe and Schurman, "The Missing Piece", p. 25.

46. US Bureau of the Census, *Statistical Abstract of the United States: 1995*, p. 87.

47. "Infant Deaths Tied to Poverty, Study Confirms", *The New York Times*, December 15, 1995, p. A32.

48. Handwerker, "Politics and Reproduction", pp. 20, 26.

49. Pritchett, "Desired Fertility", p. 40; see also Paul Demeney, as cited in Donaldson, *Nature Against Us*, p. 56.

50. Handwerker, "Politics and Reproduction", p. 20.

51. Carla Makhlouf Obermeyer, "Women, Islam and Population: Is the Triangle Fateful?", Working Paper Series No. 6, Harvard School of Public Health, Harvard Center for Population and Development Studies, July 1991, passim.

52. Ibid., p. 12.

53. Kathryn B. Ward. "Toward a New Model of Fertility: The Effects of the World Economic System and the Status of Women on Fertility Behavior", Working Paper No. 20 in Women in International Development, Michigan State University, March 1983.

54. Jodi L. Jacobson, "Women's Health: The Price of Poverty", in Marge Koblinsky, Judith Timyan and Jill Gay, eds, *The Health of Women: A Global Perspective*, Boulder, CO: Westview Press, 1993; see also Jodi L. Jacobson, "Closing the Gender Gap in Development", in *State of the World*, New York: W.W. Norton, 1993.

55. Handwerker, "Politics and Reproduction", p. 29.

56. Cited in Jacobson, "Women's Health", p. 11; see also *Engendering Adjustment for the 1990s*, Report of a Commonwealth Expert Group on Women and Structural Adjustment, London: Commonwealth Secretariat, 1989; United Nations, *The World's Women 1995*, p. 82.

57. Ingrid Palmer, "Gender Issues in Structural Adjustment of Sub-Saharan African Agriculture and Some Demographic Reflections", Working Paper No. 166, World Employment Programme, ILO, November 1988, cited in Jeanne Vickers, ed., *Women and the World Economic Crisis*, London: Zed Books, 1991, p. 22; see also Ingrid Palmer, *Gender and Population in the Adjustment of African Economies: Planning for Change*, Geneva: ILO, 1991, p. 146.

58. John Bongaarts and Mead Cain, "Demographic Responses to Famine", in Kevin M. Cahill, MD, ed., *Famine*, New York: Orbis Books, 1982.

59. Naila Kabeer, "Do Women Gain from High Fertility?", in Haleh Afshar ed., *Women, Work and Ideology in the Third World*, New York: Methuen, 1986, p. 104; see also Perdita Huston, *Message from the Village*, New York: Epoch B. Foundation, 1978.

60. United Nations, *The World's Women 1970–1990*, p. 19; Royte, "The Outcasts", pp. 37–38.

61. Cited in Handwerker, "Politics and Reproduction", p. 14; see also Matha C. Ward,

"The Politics of Adolescent Pregnancy: Turf and Teens in Louisiana", in Handwerker, ed., *Births and Power*, pp. 147–164.

62. Kabeer, "Do Women Gain from High Fertility?", *passim*; Caldwell, *Theory of Fertility Decline*, p. 26.

63. K.C. Zachariah, "The Anomaly of the Fertility Decline in India's Kerala State", World Bank Staff Working Paper, No. 700, Washington, DC, World Bank, 1984, p. 93.

64. Caldwell, *Theory of Fertility Decline*, p. 335.

65. Ibid., p. 26.

66. Srinivasan, "Death to the Female"; and Bumiller, *May You be*, p. 108.

67. United Nations, *The World's Women 1970–1990*, p. 19.

68. Amartya Sen, "More than 100 Million Women", p. 61.

69. United Nations, *The World's Women 1970–1990*, p. 60; also John C. Caldwell and Pat Caldwell, "Gender Implications for Survival in South Asia", Health Transition Working Paper, No. 7, 1990, The Australian National University, Canberra.

70. Caldwell and Caldwell, "Gender Implications", p. 17.

71. Ibid., p. 19.

72. United Nations, *The World's Women 1995*, pp. 67, 69.

73. Sen, "More Than 100 Million Women" p. 61; see also Lisa Leghorn and Mary Roodkowsky, *Who, Really, Starves?: Women and World Hunger*, New York: Friendship Press, 1977.

74. Jeffery et al., *Labour Pains and Labour Power*, p. 224.

75. Michel Chossudovsky, "The World Bank Derogates Women's Rights", *Third World Resurgence*, Nos 61–62, 1995, p. 47.

76. Lappe and Schurman, "The Missing Piece", p. 64; Robert A. Levine, Sarah E. Levine, Amy Richman, F. Medardo, Tapia Uribe and Clara Sunderland Correa, "Schooling and Survival: The Impact of Maternal Education on Health & Reproduction in the Third World", Working Paper Series, No. 3, May 1991, Harvard School of Public Health, Harvard Center for Population and Development Studies.

77. Lappe and Schurman, "The Missing Piece", p. 65.

78. Sally K. Gallagher, "Economic Disarticulation and Fertility in the Periphery", paper presented at American Sociological Association Meetings, Atlanta, GA, 1988; Scott Menard, "Inequality and Fertility", *Studies in Comparative International Development*, Spring 1985, p. 89; Lappe and Schurman, "The Missing Piece", *passim*; Patterson and Shrestha, "Population Growth and Development", p. 13; Robert Repetto, *Economic Equality and Fertility in Developing Countries*, Baltimore: Johns Hopkins University Press, 1979, *passim*.

79. Timothy King (coordinating author), *Population Policies and Economic Development, A World Bank Staff Report*, Baltimore: Johns Hopkins University Press, 1974, Appendix A, pp. 141, 147.

80. World Bank, *World Development Report 1984*, p. 109.

81. Repetto, *Economic Equality and Fertility*, p. 70.

82. Ibid., p. 69.

83. Lappe and Schurman, "The Missing Piece", p. 55.

84. Ibid., pp. 55–63.

85. Ibid.; see also "Working Women – Maternity Law", Ministry of Justice, Government of Cuba, 1975; Hugh Drummond, "And They Make House Calls", *Mother Jones*, May 1987, p. 16.

86. W. Indralal de Silva, "Ahead of Target: Achievement of Replacement Level Fertility in Sri Lanka Before the Year 2000", *Asia–Pacific Population Journal*, Vol. 9, No. 4, December 1, 1994, p. 14.

87. Bandarage, "Women and Capitalist Development"; John C. Caldwell, Indra Gajanayake, Bruce Caldwell and Pat Caldwell, "Is Marriage Delay a Multiphasic Response to Pressures for Fertility Decline? The Case of Sri Lanka", *Journal of Marriage and Family*, Vol. 51, No. 2, May 1989, pp. 337–351; UNFPA, *State of the World Population, 1993*, p. 49.

88. T.N. Krishnan, "Population, Poverty and Employment in India", *Economic and*

Political Weekly, November 14, 1992, p. 2480.

89. Ibid., p. 2481.

90. Basu, "Birth Control by Assestless Workers", *passim*.

91. Mencher, "The Lessons and Non-Lessons", p. 1787.

92. John Ratcliffe, "Social Justice and the Demographic Transition: Lessons from India's Kerala State", *International Journal of Health Services*, Vol. 8, No. 1, 1978, p. 123; Lappe and Schurman, "The Missing Piece", p. 59.

93. Ratcliffe, "Social Justice"; see also P.N. Mari Bhat and S. Irudaya Rajan, "Demographic Transition in Kerala Revisited", *Economic and Political Weekly*, September 1–8, 1990, p. 1963. The success of the South Indian state of Tamil Nadu in bringing down birth rates in recent years is also attributed to state-wide feeding programs for poor children which have improved child survival. See Sen Gupta, "A Paradigm Shift", p. 18.

94. Bhat and Rajan, "Demographic Transition", p. 1973.

95. Ratcliffe, "Social Justice", p. 139.

96. Bhat and Ranjan, "Demographic Transition", p. 1977.

97. Quoted in Sen, "More Than 100 Million Women", p. 66.

98. Ratcliffe, "Social Justice", pp. 128–132.

99. Ibid., pp. 141–142.

100. Krishnan, "Population, Poverty and Employment", p. 2496.

101. Lappe and Schurman, "The Missing Piece", Chap. 5; Repetto, *Economic Equality and Fertility*, p. 169; see also Serron, *Scarcity, Exploitation and Poverty*.

102. United Nations, *The World's Women 1995*, p. 122.

103. Bandarage, "Women and Capitalist Development", pp. 77–78; *Engendering Adjustment for the 1990s*, p. 81; S.W.R. de A. Samarasinghe, "Sri Lanka: A Case Study from the Third World", in David E. Bell and Michael R. Reich, eds, *Health, Nutrition and Economic Crises: Approaches to Policy in the Third World*, Dover, MA: Auburn House, 1988.

104. World Bank, *World Development Report 1984*, p. 109.

105. Patricia Jeffery, Roger Jeffery, and Andrea Lyon, *Don't Marry Me to a Plowman! Women's Everyday Lives in Rural North India*, Boulder, CO: Westview Press, 1996, *passim*.

106. Caroline Moser, "The Impact of Recession and Structural Adjustment on Women: Ecuador", *Development*, Vol. 1, 1989, p. 80.

107. Ron Lesthaeghe, "Social Organization, Economic Crises, and the Future of Fertility Control in Africa", in Ron J. Lesthaeghe, ed., *Reproduction and Social Organization in Sub-Saharan Africa*, Berkeley: University of California Press, 1989, pp. 477–478.

108. Ibid., p. 477.

109. James Bennet, "Clinton Lauds Decline in Teen-age Pregnancy", *The New York Times*, January 5, 1997, p. 15.

5

Political Economy of Poverty

Poverty cannot be eliminated by eliminating the poor; it is not a disease that stems from laziness or heredity. Poverty is a manifestation of social inequality; as such, poverty cannot be understood outside of unequal distribution of wealth within the global population. Increasing inequality in income and resource distribution is the main social issue of our time; it underlies the global crisis of poverty, environmental destruction, insecurity, as well as the population explosion. Gender inequality, and specifically the feminization of poverty, link women, population and global crisis, the subjects of this book.

Widening Inequality

As discussed earlier, with the transition from foraging to settled agriculture, women as a group were economically and socially subordinated. With the onset of the capitalist mode of production and the commoditization of labor, women were further disadvantaged in terms of access to land, credit, paid employment and earnings relative to men. Women and children's work in the home in child care and household maintenance as well as much of their work in subsistence production remain invisible and unpaid; it is not included in national income accounts such as the GNP. According to United Nations estimates of 1980, women accounted for two-thirds of the world's work hours but owned one-hundredth of the world's property and received one-tenth of the global income.[1]

Neither the issues of poverty nor the population explosion can be understood merely as resulting from gender inequality, as assumed by many liberal feminist theorists. Gender inequality needs to be understood in relation to increasing race and class disparities as well as global disparities between the North and the South. Although statistics are not widely available, in most regions and countries significant differences prevail in distribution of resources and income by race and ethnicity. In many regions and countries, such as South America and Mexico, indigenous people deprived of tradi-

Table 5.1 Inequality in the distribution of landholdings: selected countries, 1980–1987

Country	Year	Gini coefficient
Very high inequality (Gini above .75)		
Paraguay	1981	.94
Brazil	1980	.86
Panama	1981	.84
Uruguay	1980	.84
Saudi Arabia	1983	.83
Madagascar	1984	.80
Kenya	1981	.77
High inequality (.51 to .75)		
Colombia	1984	.70
Dominican Republic	1981	.70
Ecuador	1987	.69
Grenada	1981	.69
Chile	1987	.64
Honduras	1981	.64
Yemen	1982	.64
Sri Lanka	1982	.62
Peru	1984	.61
Nepal	1982	.60
Uganda	1984	.59
Turkey	1980	.58
Jordan	1983	.57
Pakistan	1980	.54
Philippines	1981	.53
Medium inequality (.40 to .50)		
Bahrain	1980	.50
Bangladesh	1980	.50
Morocco	1982	.47
Togo	1983	.45
Ghana	1984	.44
Low inequality (below .40)		
Malawi	1981	.36
Mauritania	1981	.36
Egypt	1984	.35
Niger	1981	.32
Korea, Republic of	1980	.30

Source: UNDP, *Human Development Report 1993*, New York: Oxford University Press, 1993, p. 29.

tional modes of living find themselves at the bottom of the class hierarchy with native women being among the worst off.[2]

In the extreme case of Brazil, the top economic quintile receives 32 times the income of the bottom quintile. In Chile, during its economic 'miracle', the economic growth rate has averaged 5% a year. While the income share of the richest fifth of the population was 44.5% and the poorest fifth 7.6% in 1969, by 1988 the percentages had changed to 54.6% and 4.4%. The percentage of Chileans living in poverty steadily increased from 28.5% in 1969 to 36% in 1979 and to 42% in 1989. Caloric intake of Chileans in the bottom 20% decreased more than 23% between 1969 and 1989.[3] Economic modernization in Mexico is also widening the gap between the rich and the poor. Half the population of Mexico – 45 million – are living in poverty today, with 17 million in extreme poverty; at the same time, the country is supposed to have more billionaires than the United States.[4]

Inequalities in wealth distribution are particularly great with regard to landholdings in many countries in the South. For example, in Egypt, 70% of the agricultural land is controlled by the richest 20% of landowners. Such disparities are revealed in the Gini coefficent, which shows extreme skewing of land distribution in favor of the rich: .94 in Paraguay, .86 in Brazil and so on (Table 5.1). In sharp contrast, very large percentages of agricultural households are either landless or near landless. Data for the mid 1970s show that 60% of all rural households in Brazil, 40% in India and 10% in Africa were landless. In addition, 10% of all rural households in Brazil, 13% in India and 30% in Africa were also near-landless at the time. Recent data reveals that these disparities may have increased in the 1980s and 1990s due to population growth as well as economic policies favoring the wealthy classes. According to United Nations estimates of 1993, in Bangladesh, small farmers (with less than 2.5 acres) held only 29% of the land, although they account for 70% of all farms.[5] In Mexico, due to pressures of free trade and structural adjustment policies, the government has put aside its land reform law, resulting in increased displacement of poor farmers and further augmentation of landholdings by wealthy ranchers.[6]

The US has also experienced a massive redistribution of income and wealth during the last 15 or so years. According to estimates of the US Bureau of the Census, between 1980 and 1993, the income share of the highest 20% of the population increased while the shares of all other groups declined (Table 5.2). According to still other estimates, in 1976, the top 1% of the population owned 19% of all private wealth; the top 10% owned 50%; while 90% of the population owned 50% of the wealth. By 1993, the share of the richest 1% nearly doubled to 37% and the share of the top 10% had increased to 68%, while the share of the rest of the population had declined to 32%.[7] By 1996, these disparities had further widened: the top 1% was said to be controlling 40% of all private wealth in the country (Appendix 3).

Table 5.2 Widening income disparity in the US, 1980 and 1993
(% of total income)

Year	Lowest 20% of pop.	Second 20% of pop.	Third 20% of pop.	Fourth 20% of pop.	Highest 20% of pop.	Top 5% of pop.
1980	5.2	11.5	17.5	24.3	41.5	15.3
1993	4.2	10.1	15.9	23.6	46.2	19.1

Source: US Bureau of the Census, *Statistical Abstract of the United States: 1995*, 115th edn, Washington, DC, 1995, p. 475.

At the global level, very sharp income and wealth cleavages exist across the social classes. As noted in the Introduction, in 1991, the percentage shares of the global income were as follows: the poorest 20%: 1.4%; the middle 60% (including second, third and fourth quintiles): 13.6%; and the richest 20%: 85.0% (Table 1). These disparities reflect inequalities in investment, savings and values attached to labor of the different social classes. These disparities in turn translate into wide differences in consumption patterns, a subject we shall turn to in Chapter 6 when we consider social class and differential environmental impact.

As noted in the Introduction, the income gap between the rich and the poor has been steadily increasing over the last three decades (Table 1). According to the United Nations Human Development Report for 1991, expressed in GNP per capita, the average annual income in the South was $710 whereas the average GNP per capita in the North was almost 18 times as much – $12,510. This gap is expected to widen due to decline in economic growth and increasing population in the South in the years ahead.[8]

To understand widening global inequality and consumption patterns, we must examine increasing concentration of property and resource ownership in transnational corporations and intensification of surplus appropriation (Table 2). In this regard, it is necessary to examine the mechanisms through which the resources and labor of the 'non-white' four-fifths of the population in the South is diverted towards the one-fifth (or less) white population in the North.[9]

An observation which casts serious doubts on the Malthusian proposition that 'overpopulation' causes poverty is that some of the wealthiest countries in the world have very high population densities while some of the poorest countries have very low population densities. Population per hectare in the Netherlands, Japan and Belgium is 4,349, 3,280 and 3,028, respectively, while population densities in Botswana, Brazil and Afghanistan are 23, 178 and 256, respectively. The European Community as a whole has a population density of 1,439 per hectare and Sub-Saharan Africa a density of 245.[10]

Furthermore, some countries like Japan, the Netherlands and Switzerland that lack significant natural resources and are dependent largely on imports to feed themselves have become some of the richest nations in the world while many countries in Africa, Asia and Latin America which have the resources and the potential for self-sufficiency have become some of the world's poorest countries. Despite increased exports in copper, diamonds, gold, bauxite, uranium and other minerals, nearly half the population in the thinly populated Sub-Saharan African region exists below the poverty level.[11] The answer to this paradox lies not so much in the Malthusian 'overpopulation'–scarcity–poverty thesis as in the political-economic analysis of imperialism.

Economic Imperialism

Global economic growth is increasingly dependent on 'constricting and depressing wages', that is, on increasing poverty as well as political and cultural repression.[12] Expansion of markets and economic growth in themselves do not guarantee poverty alleviation, as claimed by defenders of the status quo.[13] As discussed in Chapter 4, in the recent past, many countries and regions, including Sri Lanka and Kerala, have improved the physical quality of life despite low economic growth rates. Countries with high growth rates, such as South Korea and Taiwan, also improved standards of living through state-supported land reforms, education and other distributional programs. On the other hand, countries which experienced high rates of economic growth, for example Brazil during its 'miracle growth' period in the late 1960s and early 1970s, the Philippines in the 1970s and Sri Lanka in the post-1977 'economic liberalization' period, also experienced increasing income inequality and poverty.[14]

The terms 'free trade' and 'globalization' are euphemisms for increased penetration of transnational corporations into ever more areas of life across the world. As economist Herman E. Daly pointed out in his farewell address to the World Bank in 1994, not only does globalism weaken local economies and communities, but global competitiveness "reflects not so much a real increase in resource productivity as a standards-lowering competition to reduce wages, externalize environmental and social costs, and export natural capital at low prices while calling it income".[15]

The gap in economic production between the 'developed' market economies and the 'underdeveloped' economies has been increasing over the last three decades, along with widening gaps within regions in the South.[16]

GDP per capita of the 'underdeveloped' countries was 8.7% of the GDP per capita of the developed economies in 1960. By 1970 it had declined to 7.4% and by 1987 it had further dropped to 6.1%. Population growth partly explains this widening gap in per capita GDP. However, tightening 'chains of dependency' that bind the South to the North are the underlying factors in the widening North–South economic gap and exacerbation of poverty in the South.[17]

From the beginning of modern imperialism, international trade has been "one of the main mechanisms for perpetuating the gap between the core and periphery".[18] In the 1960s and 1970s, many Third World countries sought to develop their own industries through import substitution, expanded role of the state in the economy and experiments with socialism. In the 1970s, the Third World as a group led by UNCTAD demanded a New International Economic Order with better terms of trade and more equitable distribution of resources between the North and the South. It was also in this context that Third World delegates at the 1974 UN Population Conference in Bucharest called for economic development assistance over population control.[19] However, Third World efforts to develop new economic models were hampered by internal political corruption, bloated and inefficient bureaucracies and the external political and economic control of the North.

Instead of heeding to Third World calls for a New Economic Order, the North tightened terms of trade against the Third World in the 1980s. Between 1980 and 1988, terms of trade fell 16% for the Third World as a whole.[20] The costs of the sharp increase in world oil prices in the 1970s by Middle East countries and oil corporations was also borne largely by the Third World poor. As terms of trade continue to widen against them, Third World countries are forced to increase the volume of their exports, intensifying ecological and labor exploitation, and neglecting subsistence production.[21] The issues of global food production and hunger must be understood in this broader context.

Agriculture and food

Contesting the doomsday scenarios of the neo-Malthusians, Amartya Sen has pointed out that global food production has "significantly and consistently" outpaced global population growth during the recent decades.[22] According to the Food and Agriculture Organization (FAO) statistics, between the three-year averages of 1979–1981 and 1991–1993, global per capita food production increased by 3%. The most rapid rates of growth in food production took place in the most populous countries: per capita food production increased by 22% in Asia, including 23% in India and 39% in China. In contrast, in the industrialized regions with declining population growth rates, per capita food production increased more slowly or decreased: a 2% increase in Europe and almost a 5% decrease in North America during the above-noted period.[23]

During the same period, food production per capita decreased by 6% in Africa, and in some African countries like Malawi and Somalia even the absolute size of the output fell. Sen attributes the decrease in food production in the Sub-Saharan region not so much to population growth, which he sees as a "subsidiary factor", as to economic stagnation associated with political disruption, wars and military rule in the region.[24] The agrarian crisis in the Sub-Saharan region must also be seen historically in relation to the integration of the region into the global political economy.

As Sen notes, the growing commercialization of the Sahelian economy and collapse of traditional methods for fighting problems related to drought have been significant factors in famines in the Sahelian region.[25] Famines in the Sahel can be traced to the colonial period, when the region was turned over to monocrop export production of cotton and peanuts at the expense of food for the local people. Ethiopia was still exporting green beans to Britain during the famine of 1984–1985 which killed a million people, and in 1989, despite the threat of famine, the Sudanese government sold to the European Community 400,000 tons of sorghum in exchange for animal feed. Apparently, even at the height of famines in the Sahel, bumper cash crop exports were recorded while the local people, who once ate what was grown on their lands, were waiting for imported food and relief from the North. Import of food and food aid may have even contributed to the failure of domestic food production rather than help rejuvenate it.[26]

Arguing that the declines in world cereal output since 1984 were not "primarily the result of population growth", economist Tim Dyson has pointed out that the declines were influenced fundamentally by very low prices in the global market as well as by production policies aimed at reducing the amount of land cultivated with cereals. Dyson also fears that liberalization of international trading through GATT could lead to increased world food prices, aggravating the problem of market-induced hunger.[27]

Vandana Shiva and other feminist analysts have expressed the fear that new GATT rules which extend corporate control over biodiversity will further intensify the dispossession of women farmers in the Third World.[28] Women produce more than half the food grown in the Third World. In Africa, women's labor accounts for more than 80% of the food produced for local subsistence.[29] Yet the amount of land available to women food producers in Third World countries is declining. Work that poor women have depended on in the past is increasingly being done by men or machines.[30] In many parts of the Third World, especially South Asia, uneducated poor women have lost traditional income-generating activities due to changes associated with the imposition of agricultural developmental models from the North on farmers in the Third World.[31] These developments are contributing to

Table 5.3   Corporate control of global commodity trade, 1988

Commodity	% controlled by 3–6 largest corporations
Wheat	85–90
Sugar	60
Coffee	85–90
Cocoa	85
Tea	80
Bananas	70–75
Pineapples	90
Forest products	90
Cotton	85–90
Jute	85–90
Crude oil	75
Copper	80–85
Iron ore	90–95
Tin	75–80
Bauxite	80–85

Source: UNCTAD statistics cited in Canadian University Student Organization (CUSO) Education Department, *Here to Stay: A Resource Handbook Linking Sustainable Development and Debt*, Part 2, Ottawa, November 1990, p. 9.

economic dispossession, decreases in food security and increases in poverty among women and children.

As Frances Moore Lappe, Susan George and other writers have pointed out, scarcity of resources and shortages of food are not attributable to population growth as much as to the control of global food production and distribution within a few large corporations.[32] Corporate drive for profit underlies unequal consumption patterns and the hunger of the world's 'bottom' billion. For example, excessive meat consumption by the richer classes depends on the availability of vast amounts of land for cattle ranching. Meat production for hamburger chains requires that land be taken away from the cultivation of beans and other staple foods by local people in the Amazon, Africa and other parts of the world. As we discuss in the next chapter, modern methods of meat production are also much more harmful to the environment than subsistence cultivation.

While international commodity markets have been dominated by a few corporations since colonial times, in the post-World War II era, with increased horizontal and vertical integration of production and services within corporations, corporate dominance has been extended to all areas of life.[33] Between 85 and 90% of the global wheat trade and 90% of the trade in global forest products are controlled by three to six large corporations today (Table 5.3). Seven to ten transnational corporate giants, including Philip Morris, Coca-Cola, Unilever and Nestlé, dominate the growing beverage sector in the world. In fact, three to six transnational companies control an average of 75% of all exports from countries in the South for 21 of the main categories of commodity trade.[34]

Being more powerful than most Third World countries, the large transnational corporations which set prices and determine market conditions are able to set terms which are highly profitable to themselves. Take the case of bananas grown in Honduras. If bananas are sold at 20 cents per pound to the consumers, the breakdown would typically be as follows: 1.8 cents to Honduras in wages and taxes; 2.7 to transnational corporations in Honduras as expatriated earnings; 12 cents to TNCs outside Honduras as mark-up, freight, insurance, handling and service charges; and 3.5 cents as retail mark-up.[35] For practically every commodity produced by TNCs, comparable pricing structures prevail. This is especially apparent in the manufacturing sectors, which are increasingly relying on 'foreign sourcing' in the South.

Manufacturing

The Malthusian focus on population growth rates has diverted attention away from causes of poverty that are situated in the global political economy. The wage gap, for example, has been a fundamental cause of inequality between the North and the South from the early years of imperialism. This gap continues to grow, aggravating the disparities across countries. For example, between 1994 and 1995, hourly pay in the textile industry rose from $11.89 to $12.18 in the US and from $10.74 to $11.60 in Britain. But during the same period, the rate rose only from 26 to 28 cents an hour in Bangladesh while it dropped from $3.22 to $2.27 in Mexico. As long as such disparities continue, transnational corporations will move to whatever site offers them the most profit.[36] Economic liberalization measures such as the North American Free Trade Agreement will ensure that wages and living standards in countries such as Mexico will be further lowered for the benefit of corporations in the North.[37]

During the process of increased globalization and restructuring of production which has been taking place since the early 1970s, women's economic subordination and poverty have deepened. Even when women and children are given paid employment in export production, for example in lacemaking in India or carpet weaving in Iran, their labor has been considered domestic labor and has remained unpaid or terribly underpaid.[38] These developments reinforce the dualism of the male as the breadwinner and the female as the dependent housewife.

Although globalization of production is increasingly female-led and it is estimated that between 70 and 90% of new jobs in manufacturing are held by women, women's work in the formal labor force is relegated to relatively less paid, so-called 'women's work'. In South-East Asia, where feminization of manufacturing is most advanced, only 17% of administrative and managerial workers in 1990 were women.[39] With the increasing shift of manufacturing overseas and deindustrialization in the North, women in the North are being pushed more and more into the relatively low-paid, insecure service sector jobs in clerical work, domestic work, food service and retail work, the so-called 'women's jobs'.[40]

Even when women do the same work as men, on average they receive 30–40% less pay worldwide.[41] For example, in the 'newly industrialized countries' of Korea and Singapore, women's average wages in manufacturing in 1990 were 50% and 55% of men's wages, respectively. While women working for transnational corporations are paid higher wages than those working for local firms, the average wages for women workers in TNCs range from 50 to 75% of male wages in 'comparable occupations'. Indeed, the 'feminization' of manufacturing which has accompanied global economic restructuring has been built upon the 'flexibility' of women's labor, that is, lower wages and the supposed 'docility' of women.[42]

Corporate restructuring is built not only upon increased exploitation of women's labor, but also upon increasing exploitation of child labor. For example, in Bangladesh, 20% of the labor force in the garment industry is estimated to be children under 12 years of age, some as young as 7 or 8. These child workers are crucial for the country's export-led production and their families' survival. In Brazil, workers under the age of 18 represent 11.6% of the labor force and the use of child workers is still growing because employers want to avoid paying job benefits to adult workers.[43] The use of cheap child labor, whether it be by local employers or by transnational corporations, does not help improve the lives of poor children. It does not help bring down fertility rates in poor countries either. The suffering inflicted upon child export workers was recently brought to light by the case of the Pakistani child labor activist, Iqbal Masih, who received a Reebok human rights award, only to be brutally murdered soon thereafter.[44]

Notwithstanding low wages, exploitative working conditions, and absence of labor rights to organize, regular employment in the formal sector is considered a privilege in most countries. The reason for this is massive unemployment and underemployment. Unemployment is far greater among women as a group than men globally, and particularly so in the poorer countries.[45] As a result, large numbers of women are forced to migrate in search of work or attempt to survive in the informal sector doing poorly paid, menial work as petty traders, prostitutes, and so on. These issues will be discussed further later in this chapter in relation to the worsening global social crisis and new dimensions of women's poverty.

Since corporate restructuring of the global economy in the early 1970s, foreign investments in the South have shifted increasingly from traditional areas such as resource extraction and manufacturing to services such as finance, insurance, communications, advertising and the media.[46] This shift

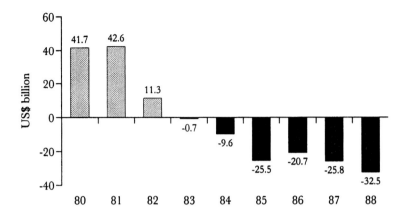

Figure 5.1 Reversing resource flows: North to South net transfers (US$ billions), 1980–1988

Source: UNDP, *Human Development Report 1990*, New York: Oxford University Press, 1990, p. 79.

greatly helped enlarge the net transfer of capital from the South, resulting in a massive debt crisis.

Banking and the debt crisis

During the last decade, the export income of the South fell sharply due to steadily declining commodity prices as well as trade protectionism in the industrialized countries. This, coupled with commercial banks' aggressive lending policies, led to increased borrowing by Third World countries. As investment markets in the North were saturated, banks looked to the Third World to recycle their petrodollars after the oil crisis in 1973.[47] While only 25% of US investments in the industrialized countries were in banking, finance and insurance, 40% of US investments in the Third World were in these areas. In 1990, US investments in finance, banking and insurance in the Third World were $43 billion, that is, one-third more than US investments in manufacturing.[48] But as financial analysts have pointed out, when overborrowing led to 'overheating' of Third World economies, the North cut off loans drastically in 1982, thus giving rise to the debt crisis.[49]

At the beginning of 1989, developing nations owed foreign creditors $1.3 trillion, that is, "just over half their combined gross national products and two-thirds more than their export earnings".[50] The annual debt service bill approximated $200 billion, and the debt and interest on it continue to grow.[51] In 1985 some African countries were spending as much as 50% of their export earnings on debt service payments. In 1990, Peru was being required to pay $100 million a month just to keep up with interest on the foreign debt.[52] According to the UN *Human Development Report* of 1992, the debt of Sub-Saharan Africa in 1992 was around $150 billion, that is, 100% of its GNP![53]

The percentage of foreign investment located in the 'underdeveloped' countries has also been declining: from 30.6% in 1967 to 26.1% in 1973 to 22.0% in 1980 to 19.2% in 1989.[54] Owing to these trends in investment and debt service, the South is today a net exporter of financial resources rather than a net recipient. While in the past the South received more from the North, since 1983, the resource flow has changed in the opposite direction (Figure 5.1)

The United States received over $60 billion in resource transfers from the developing world in 1990 alone, a substantial amount of these transfers being debt service payments to banks domiciled in the US.[55] According to the estimates of Susan George, between 1982 and 1990, the 'less developed countries' transferred $418 billion to the North, "the equivalent in today's dollars of some six Marshall Plans provided by the South to the North". As she points out, such a colossal "financial drain" was not achieved under direct colonialism; the Third World increasingly pays for its own oppression under neo-colonialism.[56]

As George also argues, although huge in comparison to the income of the Third World, the Third World debt is "relatively insignificant" when compared to the "Savings and Loans bailouts, BCCI scandals and astronomical federal budget and trade deficits in the United States itself – all numbering in the hundreds or thousands of billions".[57] Anne-Marie Beulink and other analysts have also pointed out that there is enough money in the world "to put an end to the debt crisis if the creditors were to see an advantage in that arrangement".[58] But the commercial and political advantages of the creditor countries, mostly the Group of 7 and the IMF and the World Bank working on their behalf, lie precisely in the continuation of the debt. In 1995, the Third World debt was estimated at $1.7 trillion and of this 17% or $278 billion was owed to the World Bank and the IMF.[59] Naturally, these institutions put enormous pressure on the Third World to pay back the debt.

Structural Adjustment

The responses of the North to the problem of Third World debt and worsening social crisis are population control and 'structural adjustment' – "a set of 'free market' economic policies imposed on countries by the IMF and the World Bank as a condition for receiving assistance". Structural adjustment policies seek to improve loan recipients' foreign investment climate by eliminating barriers to capital expansion and international trade.

trade. Thus adjustment loans come with stringent conditionalities attached to them. For example, they require trade liberalization, export promotion, devaluation of local currencies, curbs on import substitution industries, privatization of state sectors, deregulation of state controls, wage and salary freezes in the public sector, cutbacks on state social welfare expenditures and subsidies, and so forth.[60]

These adjustment loans must be seen in the historical context of aid received from the North. Despite alleged benevolence, bilateral and multilateral aid given by industrialized countries and international development agencies to the South to help with balance of payment difficulties and development programs have benefited the North.[61] Aid rarely consists of outright gifts but of loans requiring repayment with interest. Aid is almost always tied in that monies allocated are required to be spent on purchases of technology and services from corporations of the donor countries. As political economist Samir Amin states, adjustment provides the political conditions for the further expansion of capital.[62]

Over 70 countries have implemented adjustment measures over the last decade. Adjustment conditionalities greatly expand IMF and World Bank control over Third World economies, states and people. A 1985 World Bank policy study, for instance, indicated the Bank's interest in extending its economic authority to decisions over what countries under SAL programs should produce, so that export markets would not have too much of the same product.[63] As we noted in Chapter 2, the World Bank is also increasingly requiring that Third World debtor nations adopt stringent population control policies as a condition for receiving adjustment loans.

Adjustment conditionalities have been instrumental in widespread privatization of state-owned enterprises and social services. About 80 countries now have active privatization programs. During the last 12 years, approximately 8,500 state enterprises have been sold to the private sector worldwide.[64] While a narrow class of individuals have profited from privatization, the majority of people have found their access to previously state-provided health, education and other benefits curtailed as a result. Furthermore, as critics of the doctrinaire free market policies of the World Bank and IMF argue, privatization will "open the floodgates to foreign investment on a scale that is not consistent with the economic sovereignty in either the developing or the transnational economies".[65] Others who make a case for state activism in the economy also point out that the economic successes of countries such as Japan was due significantly to the government's active role in economic policy making and coordination.[66]

In contrast, adjustment policies have not achieved the stated objective of reducing the Third World debt; instead, they have contributed to the spiralling of this debt. The debtor countries are caught in a vicious cycle of loans and debts from which they are unable to extricate themselves. As a result, between 1983 and 1987, net "IMF transfers to developing countries turned from plus $7.6 billion to minus $7.9 billion" and World Bank transfers turned from plus $5.2 billion in 1984 to minus $1.7 billion in 1991.[67]

Economic liberalization associated with adjustment has not been able to prune corrupt and inefficient state bureaucracies or cut down on defense expenditures. Instead of stabilizing Third World economies, SAPs have destabilized, further distorted and weakened them. Currency devaluations have made exports cheaper and imports more expensive, thereby forcing debtor countries to turn further away from subsistence production towards export production and greater environmental and labor exploitation. Frequently, adjustment policies have intensified export production even in the face of shrinking export markets.[68]

As under formal colonialism, the poor and particularly women are the most tightly squeezed in the current economic strangulation of the South by the North. A growing body of data from around the world shows that pressures created by debt repayment and SAP targets have been disastrous on the Third World poor. Mandated cuts in government spending, freezing of wages, abolition of food subsidies, cutbacks in social expenditures, and so on, have increased unemployment and driven down wages, worsening the poverty and vulnerability of the 'bottom layers' of Third World nations.

Impact of debt and SAPs on the poor

Due to massive cuts in health budgets, per capita spending on health care declined by 50% in the 'least developed' countries during the 1980s, worsening the health care crisis.[69] In 42 of the poorest countries, spending on education fell by 25% during the 1980s, leading to decreased ratios of school enrollment, particularly among girls[70] (Table 5.4). According to a UNICEF study, following the removal of food subsidies in Sri Lanka, market prices rose by 158% for rice, 386% for wheat flour, 339% for bread and 345% for milk powder in the 1977–1984 period. Owing to the curtailment of food subsidies, the calorie consumption of the poorest 30% of the Sri Lankan population declined in the 1980s while that of the top 50% improved. With dismantling of the welfare state, per capita expenditure on education and health also declined.[71]

In Peru, in 1980, a minimum wage laborer worked approximately 17 minutes to buy one kilogram of rice. In 1984, he or she had to work ten times longer or more than two hours to make the same amount. The shock program introduced by the Peruvian government in August 1990 raised prices of basic consumer goods 'several thousand percent' overnight. In Chile, when educational coupons replaced state-sponsored education, the poor have had to survive by cashing in their coupons rather than spending on schooling. As the *World Economic Survey* has reported, in Nigeria, struc-

Table 5.4 Countries with IMF/World Bank programs which have experienced increasing rates of infant or child mortality, and falling ratios of primary school enrollment, 1980–1985 (% change)

Country	Rates of infant or child mortality		Ratios of primary school enrollment	
	(Children under 1)	(Children under 5)	(Total)	(Female)
Low-Income				
Ethiopia	+15.1	+18.8	−16.3	−6.7
Bangladesh			−3.2	+6.4
Mali	+13.0	+26.5	−14.8	−15.0
Mozambique			−9.7	−6.3
Tanzania	+6.8	+15.8	−30.8	−13.3
Togo			−18.1	−18.0
Somalia	+4.1	+3.1	−39.0	−37.9
Rwanda			−8.6	−6.0
Kenya	+4.6	+6.7	−13.0	−9.9
Sudan			−3.9	−4.7
Pakistan			−17.5	+6.7
Ghana			−4.3	−1.7
Guinea			−9.1	−13.6
Lao, PDR			−5.2	−10.2
Vietnam			−13.8	−13.8
Madagascar	+53.5	+90.9		
Uganda	+11.3	+16.7		
Haiti	+7.0	+22.2		
Nepal			−13.2	−11.3
Middle-Income				
Yemen, PDR			−8.3	−31.4
Philippines	+242.9		−3.6	−1.9
Nigeria			−6.1	n/a
El Salvador			−5.4	−5.4
Colombia			−8.6	−8.5
Chile			−6.8	−8.6
Costa Rica			−6.5	−5.7
Jordan			−8.3	n/a
Mexico			−4.2	−1.7
Portugal			−5.1	+2.6
Yugoslavia			−3.0	−2.0
Panama	+13.6		−7.1	−8.1
Argentina			−6.9	−6.9
Korea, Rep.			−10.3	+9.4
Romania			−3.0	−4.0
Indonesia	+3.2	+9.1		
Zimbabwe	+4.1	−41.7		
Jamaica	+25.0	n/a		
Peru	+6.8	+22.2		

Source: Report of a Commonwealth Expert Group on Women and Structural Adjustment, *Engendering Adjustment for the 1990's*, London: Commonwealth Secretariat, 1989, p. 83.

tural adjustment policies have markedly worsened income distribution in favor of the urban elite, leading to increased mortality, malnutrition and declining school enrollment ratios among the poor.[72]

In India, too, the adoption of the IMF/World Bank Programme in 1991 has increased economic impoverishment, social destitution and in some cases even the number of starvation-induced deaths. The combination of a 50% increase in the price of rice, removal of food subsidies and increase in the price of cotton yarn due to currency devaluation left many families of handloom weavers in Andhra Pradesh greatly impoverished. As a result, at least 73 starvation-related deaths were reported in two districts in Andhra Pradesh between August 30 and November 10, 1991. As economist Michael Chossudovsky notes, the IMF/World Bank Programme in India is "eliminating the poor" rather than "eliminating poverty".[73]

It has also been estimated that in the Philippines one child dies every hour due to the state's inability to curtail debt repayment. UNICEF has reported that "as many as 650,000 children die across the Third World each year because of the debt".[74] The Commonwealth Expert Group's study on structural adjustment has also shown that in many countries subjected to adjustment infant and child mortality have increased significantly (Table 5.4).

The World Bank itself has admitted that "standard of living in some adjusting countries has plummeted", and that "some adjustment programs have paid little attention to their effects on the poorest".[75] Despite talk of the social dimensions of adjustment, the Bank has not made basic changes in dealing with the debt crisis: instead, IMF/World Bank adjustment and stabilization policies are being extended to more and more countries, including the former USSR.[76]

Poverty constitutes a form of structural violence. As Brazilian labor leader Lula da Silva says: "The Third World War has already begun; it is a silent war fought over the foreign debt; interest is its main weapon and Third World children, unemployed and destroyed economies are its main victims."[77] The victims of adjustment are also largely women.

Impact of adjustment on women

According to the Report of the Commonwealth Expert Group on Women and Structural Adjustment and studies by feminist scholars, the effects of adjustment policies have been more severe on women as a group than on men.[78] SAPs aggravate women's poverty in many different ways: by limiting women's access to services; by decreasing food production; by reducing access to jobs; by shifting women into low-wage export sector jobs, and so on. The problem is not simply that SAPs ignore their effects on the conditions of women. Rather, as Peggy Antrobus of the international feminist network Development Alternatives with Women for a New Era

(DAWN) has argued, structural adjustment has been built upon the very exploitation of women:

> The problem with structural adjustment policies is not that they assume women are outside of development and need to be brought in (via accompanying compensatory programs) but that they are actually grounded in a gender ideology which is deeply, and fundamentally exploitative of women's time/work and sexuality.[79]

In the earlier periods of colonial capitalism, exploitation of women's labor was largely based on their roles as subsistence producers and reproducers of labor. However, in the contemporary period of global economic liberalization and restructuring, capital accumulation is built increasingly on both the subsistence and wage labor of women. As noted earlier, global manufacturing and the service economy increasingly favor the cheaper labor of women over that of men. WID programs also integrate women into commodity production while reinforcing their traditional unpaid work as wives and mothers in the home. Likewise, SAPs increase the double burden of women in the paid and unpaid sectors.

Cutbacks in social services have forced women, who are the primary nurturers and caretakers of families, to extend their own resources and that of their families. Slashes in health care have required that women spend more time in caring for sick and elderly family members, thus increasing their 'invisible' and unpaid labor. The shifting of resources into export production has threatened women's subsistence production and ability to feed their families. Adjustment has also aggravated women's already low economic position by decreasing their earnings and increasing their workloads. The jobs being cut in state services, such as teachers, nurses and administrative staff, are usually held by women. When dismissed or having their wages cut, women are forced to seek additional work, often in the informal sector as vendors, prostitutes, and so on, and to rely on the support of family and friends.[80] Where new jobs are available in the formal sector, they tend to be low-paid positions with little security or future, such as assembly-line work in free trade zones or migrant work as domestic workers.

As public resources become scarce and incomes fall, women tend to work harder to provide for families, putting their own food and health needs last. As the Report of the Commonwealth Expert Group on Women and Structural Adjustment revealed, due to IMF/World Bank adjustments, female nutrition and health have declined in many Third World countries, especially in Sub-Saharan Africa (Table 5.5).[81] As discussed in Chapters 3 and 4, in some cases, adjustment programs have exacerbated the conditions of high fertility by undermining women and children's health and education; in other cases, they have led to poverty-induced fertility transitions. Moreover, economic hardship induced by adjustment policies frequently leads to marital conflicts and violence against women by men.[82]

Table 5.5 Countries with IMF/World Bank programs which have experienced a deterioration in female nutrition or health, 1980–1985

	Female life expectancy (% change 1982–1985)	Daily calorie supply per capita (% change 1980–1985)
Countries experiencing a decline in life expectancy (1982–1985)		
Ethiopia	–4.1	–1.8
Ghana	–3.5	–9.1
Kenya	–5.1	+6.5
Liberia	–7.1	–0.7
Niger	–4.3	–2.2
Philippines	–1.5	–0.7
Countries experiencing a decline in calorie supply (1980–1985)		
Argentina	+1.4	–8.0
Bangladesh	+4.1	–8.0
Chile	+2.8	–8.8
Côte d'Ivoire	+12.2	–16.0
Ecuador	+4.6	–8.1
Guinea	+7.9	–16.4
Jamaica	+1.3	–1.8
Korea, Rep.	+1.4	–5.1
Madagascar	+8.0	–0.6
Mali	+2.1	–3.3
Nigeria	–	–17.6
Pakistan	+2.0	–0.2
Rwanda	+2.1	–18.1
Sierra Leone	+5.3	–13.1
Sudan	+2.0	–11.4
Uruguay	–	–3.6
Yugoslavia	+1.4	–1.9
Zaïre	+1.9	–1.3

Source: Report of a Commonwealth Expert Group on Women and Structural Adjustment, *Engendering Adjustment for the 1990s*, London: Commonwealth Secretariat, 1989, p. 83.

The vast system of global political and economic inequality created by imperialism is maintained by militarism. Arms exports (including military and police gear, intelligence systems, torture devices and related hardware) and military intervention constitute the ultimate bases for imperialist control of global resources and populations. As we discuss in the next chapter, the global arms trade is a main factor fuelling political instability and violence across the world. In this chapter, we show that while arms sales are vital to western economies, they exacerbate global income disparities, cut into social welfare expenditures, drive down living standards and aggravate the problems of poverty and insecurity.

The Arms Trade

Cold War rhetoric made defense the leading sector of the global economy with a trillion dollar annual allocation by the end of the 1980s. Despite declining military expenditures by both the 'developed' and 'developing' countries in the post-Cold War era, global military expenditures continue to be enormous. The total global military expenditure of $815 billion in 1992 equalled the income of almost half of the world's population. Notwithstanding expressions of intent to 'observe rules of restraint' in arms sales to volatile regions, all the five permanent members of the UN Security Council continue to be concerned more with protecting the comparative advantage of their respective arms industries and export markets than with preventing arms proliferation. These five countries – the US, Russia, France, Britain and China – together account for over 80% of all global arms trade. When Germany is added to this group, they account for 90% (Table 5.6). For the most sophisticated and expensive equipment, these five and Germany are the only exporters (Table 7.1).[83]

In the post-Cold War period, the US has been the world's leading arms exporter, accounting for nearly 50% of global conventional weapons exports. The rest of the arms sales distribution during the 1990–1994 period was as follows: the Soviet Union/Russia: 17.2%; the Federal Republic of Germany: 8.3%; UK: 5.2%; France: 4.9%; China: 4.7%; and all others combined 12.7% (Table 5.6). According to the latest estimates, in 1995, Russia overtook the US as the leading supplier of weapons to the Third World. Russian weapons sales to the Third World were $6 billion as compared to US sales, which were $3.8 billion, and French sales, which were $2.7 billion that year.[84]

Military procurement has long been the primary industrial sector in the US. Viewing the arms trade as a primary means for the US to maintain its technological supremacy and competitive edge in the global economy, the US government is increasingly taking a 'pliant' approach towards takeovers and mergers of giant defense companies like Lockheed and Martin Marietta. Both the federal government and individual states are also increasingly promoting US arms exports through such measures as loan guarantees and lobbying, while the Army, Navy and the Air Force are vigorously supporting US capture of more and more weapons sales. The US government approved the export of military equipment and military services valued at $38.5 billion to over 150 countries in the 1994 fiscal year. As the *Arms Sales Monitor*, published by the Federation of American Scientists, reported in February 1995, a number of 'surplus' items of US military equipment such as MIM–107 'Patriot' air defense missiles and F–16 fighter jets are now or in the near future will be produced solely for export.[85]

While Russian arms exports sharply declined after the collapse of the Soviet Union, lobbying groups in Russia are reviving arms exports in order

Table 5.6 The 25 leading suppliers of major conventional weapons, 1990–1994 (1990 US$ millions)

Suppliers	1990	1991	1992	1993	1994	1990–94	% of total 1990–94
USA	10,648	13,041	13,801	12,905	11,959	62,354	49.01
USSR/Russia	10,459	3,838	3,385	3,388	842	21,912	17.20
Germany, FR	1,656	2,505	1,487	1,726	3,162	10,536	8.27
UK	1,509	1,156	1,020	1,278	1,593	6,556	5.15
France	2,220	1,090	1,113	1,159	705	6,287	4.94
China	1,245	1,117	1,157	1,257	1,204	5,980	4.70
Netherlands	267	453	432	356	558	2,066	1.62
Italy	287	360	479	514	357	1,997	1.57
Czechoslovakia*	753	60	221	474	79	1,587	1.25
Switzerland	282	386	344	83	46	1,141	0.90
Korea, North	0	138	86	420	43	687	0.54
Sweden	248	121	129	56	91	645	0.51
Yugoslavia	60	543	21	0	0	624	0.49
Canada	67	15	131	161	208	582	0.46
Ukraine	–	–	400	23	0	423	0.33
Israel	74	93	39	73	87	366	0.29
Spain	87	65	57	39	116	364	0.29
Slovakia	–	–	–	145	150	295	0.23
Brazil	74	43	59	24	61	261	0.20
Germany, DR	245	–	–	–	–	245	0.19
Poland	152	63	0	1	0	216	0.17
Pakistan	62	129	0	0	2	193	0.15
Korea, South	53	53	0	48	38	192	0.15
Moldova	–	–	14	0	175	189	0.15
Norway	10	91	0	4	61	166	0.13
Others	433	168	399	316	188	1,504	1.18
Total	30,891	25,528	24,774	24,450	21,725	127,368	100.07

Note: Some errors in totals in the original source have been corrected in this Table.

* For 1990–1992 the data refer to the former Czechoslovakia; for 1993–1994 to the Czech Republic.

Source: SIPRI (Stockholm International Peace Research Institute), *Yearbook 1995: Armaments, Disarmament and International Security*, Oxford: Oxford University Press, 1995, p. 493.

to earn much-needed hard currency. Faced with financial difficulties, other states of the former Soviet Union, like the Ukraine, are stepping up their arms sales, magnifying the risk of nuclear, chemical and biological weapons proliferation.[86] Arms production and exports have become so vital to the economic survival of the industrialized countries that even a country such as Sweden, which is considered a leader in global disarmament, continues to maintain defense production and exports (Table 5.6). Kickbacks offered by the Swedish defense company Bofors to the Indian government also highlighted corruption inherent in the defense sector. As the UN *Human Development Report 1990* states:

> Defense assistance budgets of developed countries have often increased even when net economic assistance has declined. Defense industries in the industrial world have often aggressively sought willing clients in the Third World, offering soft credit and on occasion even illegal gratuities.[87]

Many countries in the Third World have also acquired arms producing capabilities, with Israel (sometimes counted as part of the Third World), Brazil, North and South Korea, India and Pakistan being some of the leaders in this group. These countries account for about 10% of global arms exports, producing mostly "small arms, artillery, mortars, armored personnel carriers and some light aircraft".[88] A number of these countries also possess nuclear, chemical and biological weapons. Many of the newly industrializing countries like Taiwan and South Korea are seeking to augment their growing economic power with advanced military capabilities. Asia now accounts for 35% of the world's imports of major weapons systems.[89]

Arms exports to the Third World jumped from $1.1 billion in 1960 to $35 billion in 1987, accounting for up to three-quarters of the global arms trade.[90] Under United States law, countries that do not pay interest on their military loans forfeit all US assistance. Thus, countries such as Egypt, owing huge interests on their military loans, must somehow meet their military debt obligations in order to qualify for further US loans.[91] According to the World Bank, the military-related debt constitutes more than one-third of the total debt of many large 'developing' countries.[92] Much of this debt went to helping maintain repressive regimes. Still, many of the published figures on arms sales may well be underestimates. Few governments make public their total military spending. Nor do various insurgent groups in the South nor expatriates living in the North who fund their arms purchases reveal their transactions. Indeed, the vast and lucrative illegal arms trade goes virtually unreported.[93]

Military spending by the 'developing' countries has risen nearly three times faster than in the industrialized countries during the last three decades. Between 1960 and 1987, military spending in the 'developing' world increased by 7.5% per year, from $24 billion to $173 billion.[94] The rise of countries like Iraq as regional military powers has also to be understood in the context of indiscriminate global arms sales. Using its vast oil wealth, Iraq became the largest retail buyer of arms, spending $43 billion by the end of 1987.[95]

The richest countries are not always the biggest arms spenders, however. Some of the highest spending on defense prevails in some of the poorest regions. Indeed, where inequalities are greatest and threats to governments high, military expenditures tend to be large as well. At the end of the 1980s, South Asia was spending $10 billion a year on the military, and

Sub-Saharan Africa, $5 billion.[96] While a small class of arms manufacturers, traders and buyers in the North and South benefit from the arms trade, military expenditures constitute a direct assault on social welfare, especially the welfare of the poor.

Military vs social expenditures

In many countries the average family struggles to pay for a twopenny loaf of bread while their governments spend billions of dollars on arms imports.[97] When countries increase spending on weapons and the armed forces, fewer resources remain for social welfare. For example, in 1990, there were eight times more soldiers than physicians in the Third World. In Sub-Saharan Africa, armed forces per thousand population increased from 0.5 to 1.8, while physicians per capita decreased from 0.04 to 0.08 between 1960 and 1986.[98]

The creation of a poverty-stricken 'surplus population' must be examined in relation to the military dominance in the global economy. A direct relationship can be observed between level of military expenditures and general living standards. In countries like Angola, Oman, Yemen and Pakistan, where military expenditures are nearly three times that of education and health, average life expectancy and literacy rates are relatively low. In contrast, in countries like Costa Rica, Venezuela, Jamaica and Botswana, where the health and education expenses are more than four times that of military expenditures, average life expectancy and adult literacy rates are considerably higher.[99]

As basic health care and other services are cut, the costs of food and transportation are increased and more and more men are recruited into armies, women have to make up the losses of income and labor by their own efforts. Whether they are occasioned by rising debt or military expenditures, fiscal cutbacks affect women disproportionately. According to *The World's Women*, a United Nations publication which examined trends and statistics in women's lives during the 1970 to 1990 period:

> When defense is a priority expenditure, domestic social programmes usually suffer. And cuts in education, food subsidies and health and family programmes tend to affect women disproportionately. Women are generally responsible for the family's health and nutrition and rely more heavily on food and health services. They also rely on educational programmes to redress long-standing inequities in their access to training and employment opportunities.[100]

As the UN *Human Development Report 1991* states, "The trend in social spending in developing countries over recent years is disturbing".[101] The combined effect of declining terms of trade, structural adjustment, debt, increasing military expenditures as well as population growth over the last decade has been a reduction in real social expenditures per person in many 'developing countries'. Half the African countries saw a fall in social spending while in most Asian and Arab countries the rate of increase in social spending was smaller in the 1980s than during the 1970s. In a number of Latin American countries, too, like Chile, Costa Rica, Mexico, Uruguay and Venezuela, GNP per capita allocated towards education and health declined significantly.[102] Demographic dynamics must necessarily be seen in this broad context of worsening social crisis caused largely by global political-economic forces. Indeed, as the late Richard Jolly, former head of UNICEF, observed, there was a "widespread and marked *deterioration* in the 'human condition' in the majority of countries during the 1980s" (emphasis in original).[103] However, resource transfers from the South to the North and the global social crisis have differential effects on different classes as well as the sexes and races. Financial and military collaboration with local elites continues to be a cornerstone of imperialism and militarism during the contemporary period of corporate restructuring as it has been from the very onset of European colonization 500 years ago.

Local collaboration

The appropriation of government funds for personal use is a common aspect of the corruption that pervades public life across the world. Aid is not always given to the most needy; a good portion is siphoned off at the top. While there has been a widespread decline in foreign aid from the North to the South in recent years, the shares of Overseas Development Aid (ODA) received by the richer groups in the Third World continue to be much greater than the shares of the poor. According to the UN *Human Development Report 1994*, 66% of the world's 1.3 billion poor who live in 10 countries receive less than one-third of all ODA. Arab states have more than six times the per capita income of South Asia, yet they receive more ODA, one reason for this being their strategic importance for oil export. Governments with high military spending are also 'rewarded' with high ODA.[104] According to a 1995 Report of the Secretariat on Sustainable Development appointed to monitor the implementation of Agenda 21 adopted at the Rio Environment Conference in 1992, only about 10% of ODA is actually being directed towards poverty alleviation.[105] Much of the aid from NGOs in the North may also be going to elites in the South, thus perpetuating existing global and local inequities.

Graham Hancock, author of *Lords of Poverty*, a critical study of aid and development to the South, has shown that a substantial amount of aid and debt service loans to the South goes towards maintaining the lavish and often corrupt lifestyles of technocrats and bureaucrats of the global development enterprise and their Third World allies, who are frequently the leaders of military regimes.[106] Much of the wealth appropriated by elites in the South is invested in the industrialized countries where profits rates are higher. According to some estimates, over $300 billion that left the South during the 1980s was deposited in private bank accounts in the US and Europe or invested in real estate.[107]

During his rule, President Ferdinand Marcos of the Philippines sent out more than the country's entire foreign debt, that is, $30 billion. In Haiti, during the regime of pro-American dictator Jean Claude Duvalier – Baby Doc – visiting IMF experts discovered that Baby Doc had withdrawn $20 million for his own use just two days after the IMF had given a $22 million stand-by credit to the poverty-stricken island. Apparently, Baby Doc's wife, Michele Duvalier, also drew $1.2 million annually from the Haitian Treasury for her own personal use. As Hancock points out, if President Mobutu Sese Seko of Zaire, who came to power in a CIA-backed coup, returned all the money he accumulated during 25 years in office, "then the country's foreign debt, estimated at $5 billion, would be reduced to an almost negligible sum". Instead of taking Mobutu to task, the IMF has continually provided generous loan rescheduling arrangements for him and others like him.[108] But it is not the dictators and government leaders alone who send their wealth abroad. Many other wealthy individuals and families also send their monies out, making capital flight from the South to the North "an intrinsic feature of the global economy".[109]

A common elite response, representing yet another mode of resource transfer from the South to the North, is the so-called 'brain drain'. This has greatly expanded with corporate restructuring and structural adjustment in recent decades. While the brain drain is an outcome of historical disparity between the North and the South, it exacerbates this disparity in turn.

The brain drain

Northern industrialized countries have shut their doors on poor immigrants like the so-called 'boat people'. Yet in order to maintain their economic competitiveness, they are at the same time encouraging selective immigration of high-level scientists and skilled professionals as well as extremely wealthy individuals. Between 1966 and 1986, the percentage of skilled immigrants from the 'developing world' to the USA increased from 45.7% to 75.1% and to Canada increased from 12.3% to 46.0%.[110]

While the immigration of skilled labor from the South to the North stems partly from overproduction of high-level university graduates, it results fundamentally from globalization of the economy and the inherently uneven and unequal nature of capitalist development. Just as capital gravitates to where profits are highest, labor moves to where wages and salaries are highest.[111] Political instability, difficult living conditions and lack of opportunities for career advancement and children's education are also factors motivating many people in the South to emigrate to the North.

In the case of women, patriarchal traditions such as arranged marriages and genital mutilation of females are also reasons for emigration.

Most of the high-level workers emigrating to the North have been trained in the South at great expense to those poor countries. Their emigration represents valuable wealth and much-needed services lost to the South. It has been estimated that in the early 1970s Third World countries as a whole lost an investment of $20,000 in each skilled migrant. Some of this is returned as remittances, although not on a scale to make up for the losses. Some 60% of all doctors trained in Ghana in the early 1980s were working abroad in the early 1990s, resulting in critical shortages in the health services. It is estimated that between 1985 and 1990, Africa as a whole lost "up to 60,000 middle and high-level managers".[112]

Immigrants from the South and the cultural diversity they represent are often subjected to racist derision and attacks in the North. However, immigrants infuse talent and vitality into the economies and cultures of the North, enabling them to remain dynamic and competitive. In contrast, loss of highly trained workers robs the poor countries of some of their most talented and energetic members. It also reduces the capacity of poor countries to train a new generation of professionals, forcing some of them to import highly expensive foreign experts. According to the UN *Human Development Report 1992*, there were about 30,000 such experts in Africa alone, which is more than there were before independence four decades ago.[113] These developments reinforce the vicious cycle of Third World debt and dependence on loans from the North.

The policies of corporate restructuring, slashing of social spending and increasing defense expenditures and even elite collaboration and the brain drain are not phenomena peculiar to the South; they represent the global evolution of capitalism and the military–industrial complex. So-called 'Third World' conditions are rapidly generalizing across the world, giving rise to widening gender, race and class disparities in practically all regions and countries. Next, we look at some of these developments in the North, with emphasis on the United States.

Restructuring in the North

Restructuring in the US

The restructuring of the global economy in the 1970s accompanied a decline in US manufacturing – 'deindustrialization' – and economic competitiveness. Increasing flight of corporate production into the Third World, a long-term shift into a service economy with a larger relative share of low-wage jobs, among other factors, led to a 'Third Worldization' of labor characterized by a slashing down of wages and union rights and an increase in structural unemployment. Real wages of US workers fell 16% between

1973 and 1995, leading to greater polarization of low- and high-income jobs and an increasing 'disappearance' of the middle class. This is evident in the declining income and wealth of the middle strata (Table 5.2).[114]

Policies of Republican presidents and Democrat-led Congress over the last 15 years have worsened income inequality and social conditions of the poor. The 'supply side economics' or Reaganomics of the 1980–1992 period, including privatization of state sectors, deregulation, social welfare cutbacks, tax reforms favoring the wealthy and the corporate sector, currency devaluations and so-called deficit reduction programs, was similar to IMF- and World Bank-financed stabilization and structural adjustment policies in the Third World.[115]

Corporate income taxes, which made up 17% of all tax receipts in 1970, fell to 12.5% in 1980 and 9% in 1985. Tax breaks to the wealthiest Americans 'stole' over $1.5 trillion from the federal treasury between 1981 and 1992, quadrupling the federal deficit.[116] In contrast, the percentage of income paid as payroll and income taxes by families at the poverty level increased significantly. Between 1978 and 1985, for example, the tax burden of a single person household went up by 4.8%; that of a family of four by 6.5% and a family of six by 5%.[117] Many large corporations, including defense companies like Boeing, Dow Chemical, ITT, General Dynamics and General Electric, paid no taxes at all; they received millions of dollars as tax rebates from the Internal Revenue Service.[118]

The national debt reached the statutory limit of $4.9 trillion in November 1995 and is now estimated to be over $5 trillion. According to the Congressional Budget Office, the Savings and Loan bailout alone will cost taxpayers a total of $1 trillion in debt over time.[119] The 'enormous tax bonanza' given to the corporations was used largely to increase executives' income and short-term speculation rather than to stimulate investment.[120]

While civilian sectors of manufacturing industries declined, military production and public funds, state subsidies and tax exemptions to the defense sector greatly expanded. US taxpayers have borne the costs of funding large military corporations. Between 1980 and 1995, the federal government increased defense spending by over a trillion dollars.[121] In contrast, over the last 15 years, state expenditures on the social sector were severely reduced: an 83% cut in anti-poverty programs, 59% cut in housing programs, 58% cut in job creation and training funds, 73% cut in community development funds, and so on.[122] According to estimates by consumer rights activist Ralph Nader, in 1994, corporate welfare spending, payments, grants and tax breaks amounted to $104 billion whereas AFDC payment to the poor was only $16 billion.[123]

Proposed defense spending by the federal government for 1997 at $254 billion amounts to more than the combined expenditures of all social sectors, including housing, education, job training, community development and environmental investment combined (Figure 5.2).[124] The US Con-

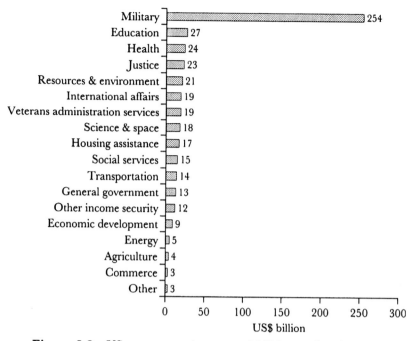

Figure 5.2 US government's proposed 1997 spending for key programs (US$ billions)

Source: Budget for the US Government, Office of Management and Budget, cited in *The Defense Monitor*, Vol. XXV, No. 4, April/May 1996, p. 5.

gressional budget for fiscal year 1996 cut $6 billion from child nutrition over seven years, paying 30 cents less per school lunch and cutting out one meal a day at child-care centers. In contrast, it gave the Pentagon $10 billion more than it asked for to build bombs and nuclear submarines![125] Could it not be argued, then, that the 'military–industrial complex' in the US rules the country, if not the whole world? The answer to this question will become even clearer in the light of information on US military intervention and its environmental record presented in the next two chapters.

Turning again to the US Congressional Budget for 1996, it must be noted that it cut admission of refugees into the US by half and denied access to most federal benefits even to legal immigrants. Underlying these policies is a lack of acknowledgment of the fact that the economic contributions that immigrants make through their hard work and taxes exceed the benefits they derive from state and federal programs in the US.[126]

As in the Third World, the combined effects of economic restructuring, new fiscal policies, increased military expenditures and social welfare cuts in the US have been increased income inequality (Appendix 3).[127] These developments have exacerbated the poverty among the most vulnerable social groups – especially people of color, women and children.

The increasingly unequal socio-economic structure in the US is maintained through tight corporate control of electoral politics and those elected into political office. Corporate contributions to political candidates have steadily increased over recent years. Political Action Committees (PACs) of large defense corporations are among the leading contributors: they gave $7.5 million to candidates from both the Democratic and Republican parties during the 1994 election cycle and over $7.8 billion in the 1996 election cycle.[128] Increasing PAC contributions to conservative electoral candidates have helped move the entire political agenda more and more towards right-wing conservatism.

The Republicans' Contract with America, which has also been embraced by the Democratic Party, involves further increases in privatization of services, redistribution of wealth to the rich, repeal of environmental and workplace safety laws, in addition to increases in the defense budget and cutbacks in already meagre public support for social services. But these measures could only worsen the social crisis, exacerbating poverty and crime and leading to the emergence of violent social movements and conflicts in the years ahead.

Impact on poor women and children

In the US poverty is closely correlated with both gender and race, with women of color being the poorest. African American women and their children constitute the largest single group living in poverty in the US.[129] The burden of budget deficits, growing militarism and social welfare cuts have been borne mostly by the poor. According to the US Bureau of the Census, in 1993, 33.1% of Blacks, 30.6% of Hispanics and 12.2% of whites fell below the poverty line (the poverty threshold was $14,763 for a family of four in 1993).[130] The percentage of children under the age of 18 living below the poverty line increased from 15.1% in 1974 to 22% in 1995. In 1993, 17% of white, 45.9% of Black and 39.9% of Hispanic children in the US lived in poverty.[131] These statistics alone should cause one to question whether the US is the most advanced and exemplary nation in the world. However, white male analysts like Patrick Moynihan have tended to blame the alleged matriarchy of women-headed households for poverty, crime and other problems in the Black underclass, while Malthusian analysts frequently blame these problems on teenage pregnancy.[132]

Feminization of poverty, female-headed households and homelessness are not problems peculiar to women in the Third World. They are global phenomena located in the expansion of the capitalist economy and patriarchal culture. Increasing numbers of educated career women in the North are also having children outside of marriage and creating alternative households. Evidence suggests that, globally, women heads of households provide better nutrition and education for children than do male heads of households.[133] Yet, owing to deep-rooted sexism, female-headed households tend to be disproportionately poorer than male-headed households across the world.

Although more and more women are working, they are in low-skilled, low-paying jobs and as such do not make enough to support themselves and their families adequately. According to a 'women's social health index' developed by the Fordham University Institute for Innovation in Social Policy, women's social health declined from 78 points in 1974 to 38 points in 1988. According to this index, which is based on poverty, violence, health coverage and the income gap between men and women, in 1988, one in seven women was poor; one in six was living without health coverage and one in three of all female-headed families lived below the poverty level.[134]

In some very poor urban and rural areas within the US, infant mortality actually increased during the early 1980s. Infant mortality rate is particularly high among the homeless population because 30% of homeless women do not receive prenatal care. Infant mortality among them is 25 deaths per 1,000 as compared to 17 per 1,000 for other poor women.[135] As noted earlier, poverty, infant mortality and high fertility are closely correlated. We can argue, then, that like IMF/World Bank policies in the Third World, 'adjustment' policies in the US, too, may have had a 'pro-natal impact' in that they have increased, poverty, especially the poverty of women. When income is lowered individuals and families attempt to survive by increasing the "number of family members in the labor force and by working longer hours".[136]

There are indications that as economic restructuring and 'free market' policies such as privatization, deregulation and dismantling of the welfare state advance across the North, more and more countries will experience increasing income inequality, worsening poverty and political turmoil. When women fall below the poverty line, children fall with them, and when children are turned into a 'surplus' population, they frequently turn to crime and violence as desperate attempts at survival.

Restructuring in Europe

The welfare state is not the ultimate answer to the problems of poverty and the global social crisis. Yet, it is important to recognize the important role that state social spending has played in reducing poverty in both industrialized countries and Third World countries and states such as Sri Lanka and Kerala, which we discussed in Chapter 4. In a number of industrialized countries, such as the UK, France, Germany and Sweden, public benefits have acted as a form of income redistribution and poverty alleviation. In these countries the percentage of the total population in poverty before public benefits is estimated to be greater than that in the US. It is the extensive provisions made available by the state in the form of health, education, labor and income security policies, and so on, that have helped

Table 5.7 Population in poverty before and after public benefits: selected industrialized countries, 1984–1987 (%)

Country	Total population in poverty before public benefits	Population in poverty after public benefits		
		Total	Elderly	Children
United States (1986)	19.9	13.3	10.9	20.4
Canada (1987)	17.1	7.0	4.7	9.3
Australia (1985)	19.1	6.7	4.0	9.0
Sweden (1987)	25.9	4.3	0.7	1.6
West Germany (1984)	21.6	2.8	3.8	2.8
France (1984)	26.4	4.5	0.7	4.6
UK (1986)	27.7	5.9	1.0	7.4

Source: Stephen J. Rose, *Social Stratification in the United States: The American Profile Poster Revised and Expanded*, New York: New Press, 1992, p. 14.

reduce the percentages of the populations in poverty in these countries much below the percentage of those living below the poverty level in the US (Table 5.7).

But now, as more and more European governments adopt conservative economic policies similar to those in the US, the social gains won through labor and other struggles are eroding. A close parallel can be observed between the policies starting with the Thatcher regime in the UK and the Reagan–Bush regime in the US in the 1980s. Due to privatization of state sectors, cutbacks in the social welfare state, harsh suppression of labor unions and increased spending on defense, and so on, income disparities and poverty increased in the UK. In 1989, 400,000 people in the UK were officially classified as homeless, of which 40% were single-parent families with young children.[137] As elsewhere in the world, most single-parent families in the UK tend to be headed by women. It is likely that the concentration of economic power within the European Community could strengthen the collective power of capital over that of individual states. This could result in a slashing of state benefits, a reduction of labor rights and increases in class, gender and racial inequalities in Europe.[138] The recent labor strikes in France and violence directed at immigrants in most European countries reflect growing economic insecurity and social discontent associated with rapid social changes taking place in contemporary Europe.

The social dislocations and economic inequalities associated with restructuring and integration of the former USSR into global capitalism seem to be even worse. As a number of analysts point out, while the IMF-imposed economic program upholds the narrow interests of the new, often corrupt, merchant class, it represents an instrument of 'Third Worldization' for the majority of people in the former Soviet Union.[139] Under the former Communist regime there was full employment and poverty was absent; now, open unemployment and poverty are said to be serious problems. In 1991, according to the UN *Human Development Report*, there were 100 million people below the poverty line in the USSR and Eastern Europe.[140]

Evidence from contemporary Eastern Europe and the former USSR indicates that economic restructuring may be leading to a process of feminization of poverty there as well. Although women in this region previously enjoyed the highest rates of female employment, as state social welfare supports are cut and women lose employment, they seem to be increasingly defined by their reproductive roles. As women get left out of jobs in the formal sector they become economically marginalized and forced to survive in the growing informal economy doing mostly odd jobs. As economic insecurity and poverty increase in Russia, more and more men are abdicating their parental obligations altogether and the number of women-headed households is soaring.[141]

As Noeleen Heyzer, the Director of UNIFEM, observes, as have many other feminist analysts and activists, the brunt of globalization and economic and social crises is borne disproportionately by women.[142] This is clearly visible in deepening poverty in the contemporary period and desperate survival strategies being adopted by the poor.

Women's Poverty and Global Crisis

Not only is women's work in the home unremunerated, but global economic growth and technological advancements, including the so-called 'contraceptive revolution', have not resulted in greater sexual equality or leisure time for women. In some of the countries in the South worst hit by the current economic crisis, some very poor women are now forced to work an average of 60 to 90 hours a week just to maintain their living standards of a decade ago. As United Nations and other studies show, the economic ravages of recent years have also contributed to widening the gap in hours worked by men and women. Almost everywhere, in their multiple roles as income earners, family caretakers, educators, health promoters, and so on, women work more hours a day than men.[143]

Gender inequalities in hours worked are greatest among the poor. In Nepal, for example, among men and women over the age of 15, women are estimated to work an average of 77 hours per week as opposed to 56 by men. In Bangladesh, in the same age group, women do an estimated average of 31 hours of housework per week as opposed to five hours by men.[144] As we shall discuss in Chapter 6, environmental destruction and the increasing scarcity of resources have increased the time women spend on household maintenance, obtaining water, fuelwood, and so on. Women of color are the beasts of burden in the world. Their social and economic subordination and the long hours worked affect health and nutrition, fertility patterns and the general quality of their lives.

The disparity in male and female lives is also evident in relation to personal expenditures. Evidence shows that even in the poorest households men tend to keep a personal allowance for such luxuries as cigarettes, alcohol, gambling and socializing outside the home. Just as most women are self-sacrificing, most men are selfish. Although women living alone or with other women may find a sense of relative freedom from the daily psychological and physical abuses of domineering men, evidence shows that in female-headed households women tend to be even poorer and more overworked. As economist Diane Elson has observed, "The core of gender subordination lies in the fact that most women are unable to mobilize adequate resources (both material and in terms of social identity) except through dependence on a man".[145]

Women are not counted as heads of households unless they are living alone or unless there is no adult male in the household. Male-biased data collection methods underestimate the extent of female-headed households. Still, these estimates show that up to 30% of households in the world today are headed by women. At least one-fourth of households not counted as female-headed also rely for more than 50% of their total income on women's earnings.[146]

More and more women are having children outside of marriage and the number of female-headed households is soaring across the world.[147] As increasing numbers of men move away from the role of providers, women are forced to play both the traditional male and female roles. This further increases women's burdens and their ability to compete in a labor market beset already with very high unemployment.

Although many women emigrate in order to avoid physical violence, it is the structural violence of poverty which most explains the rising numbers of women migrants across the world. (According to UN estimates, women outnumber men among foreign-born migrants in many countries, including many European countries and the United States.[148]) In many poor countries, like the Philippines and Sri Lanka, female labor export constitutes a main source of foreign exchange, if not *the* main source.[149] Many of the women who emigrate to work as nannies and housekeepers in the oil-rich countries in the Middle East and the newly industrializing countries in South-East Asia are mothers themselves, but they are forced to leave their own children behind in order to earn money to support them. This has been the sad reality for many poor women historically in class-based societies.

Migrant women workers have no labor rights or legal protection. Quite often, they are turned into virtual house slaves by their employers. Not only are many sexually exploited and physically attacked, but at least a few have died at the hands of their employers. The case of Flor Contemplación, a Filipina who was executed in Singapore for killing another Filipina maid and a Singaporean boy, brought to light the extremely difficult working conditions endured by many migrant women workers.[150] Still, many poor women 'choose' to emigrate for lack of alternatives in their own countries.

Emigration to the US or Europe does not always lead to social and economic improvement either. Many women and men find themselves working in thoroughly exploited jobs and living under oppressive conditions as 'illegal aliens'. Until recently, children provided a means for survival for immigrants in the North. But now, as children born in the US and Europe are not automatically given citizenship and as social benefits to children are cut, this survival option is being closed to many poor immigrant women.

As the migration option is closed, as the degraded natural environments can no longer provide subsistence, and as traditional community and family structures weaken in the process of capitalist development, more and more poor people are forced to turn to the informal sector in order to survive. Micro-enterprises in the informal sector such as small-scale production and petty trading tend to be glorified as the solution to poverty, especially women's poverty, by liberal theorists in the North.[151] But they fail to see that corporate expansion is inherently inimical to the long-term success of micro-enterprises and that illegal trades such as sex, drugs and weapons characterize the burgeoning informal sector.

Inequality and the skin trade

Constrained by the lack of viable economic options, many men, women and children are forced to adopt survival strategies ultimately destructive to themselves and their families and communities. With nothing but their bodies and the bodies of their children to sell, more and more poor people enter the expanding sectors of the global economy known as the global 'skin trade'.[152]

The skin trade, which constitutes the production and distribution of 'negative use values', is one of the most profitable and fastest growing sectors of the global economy. The global sex trade, which includes prostitution, sex tourism, mail order brides (the traffic in women as wives for foreign men) and pornography, is a billion dollar global enterprise.[153] Young women are typically the prostitutes. The number of masseuses and prostitutes in Bangkok alone is said to be in the range 100,000 to 200,000, which may be an underestimate. Child prostitution and prostitution of boys are also on the rise in many Asian countries.[154]

Malthusian analysts typically blame population density and growth for the spread of diseases such as AIDS and the Ebola virus in Africa. However, as many other analysts have shown, the spread of these diseases is 'socially determined'. The spread of AIDS is closely linked to poverty and sexism, especially male promiscuity and sexual irresponsibility in many countries and regions in the South like Thailand and Africa. Sex tourism in particular is considered to be a significant factor in the spread of AIDS in Thailand.[155]

Many poor Third World women among the so-called 'bottom billion' of the world's population are forced to participate in the global child adoption industry, which sells their infants, mostly baby girls, to wealthy couples in the North. Although this may seem to be a short-term solution to the problem of poverty and 'overpopulation' in the South and wealth and widespread infertility in the North, in the long term it is physically and psychologically destructive to women, their children and their communities. Despite the humane motivation of parents who adopt and the caring and prosperity experienced by many adoptees, it is difficult not to see international child adoption as a medium for appropriating the most precious resource – children – from the South by the North. While many couples in the North assert their right to adopt, they fail to look at such developments as stringent population control policies and widening global inequality which force many poor women to give up their children in the first place.[156]

In China, orphanages are said to be competing fiercely for western clients who pay thousands of dollars in hard currency to buy babies, most of them abandoned girls. Apparently, the prettiest and healthiest girls are groomed for adoption while the others are neglected and even allowed to die.[157] There have been reports of the existence of 'baby farms', joint local and foreign enterprises in Sri Lanka where poor, young women who are pregnant and often destitute are maintained only to have their infants taken from them soon after birth for sale to foreigners for large sums of money.[158] There are also designs underway by certain biogenetic corporations in the US to "supply" US clients with Mexican "surrogates" to bear them children.[159] The confluence of the forces of Malthusian population control and commoditization of children evokes a vision of a 'brave new world' where poor women are taught that they must bear children not for themselves but for sale to the rich. It represents an extreme form of labor alienation for women.

The expansion of the skin trade is not explainable by supply factors alone. There is an increasing demand for the services of the skin trade from the wealthier classes in the world and this demand is generated through the use of advanced technology. For example, pornography and the violent rest and recreation industry are promoted through advanced communications technology, just as 'surrogate mothering' (renting wombs) and other services in artificial reproduction are promoted through new reproductive technology. Indeed, capital and technology operate together in the skin trade as they do in all other sectors of the global economy.

As Andrew Kimbrell discusses in his book *The Human Body Shop*, the engineering and marketing of life, specifically human life, is one of the fastest growing sectors of world trade and scientific growth.[160] The buying and selling of body parts and fetuses for medical purposes is a major aspect of the growing skin trade. In poor countries such as India and Egypt the illegal trade in kidneys is booming. In Egypt, a poor, desperate person can make $10,000 to $15,000 by selling a kidney. In China, the trade in body organs forcibly removed from prisoners on death row is said to be a boom-ing business. World Health Organization officials have stated that the sale of bodily organs is "reaching alarming proportions in the Third World, especially as advanced medical technology proliferates".[161] Unless the un-derlying problems of global gender, race and class inequalities and poverty are addressed, the trade in sexual and reproductive services is likely to expand in the years ahead.

Just as prostitution is the most readily available employment for most poor women, soldiering, or taking up arms for armies, guerilla groups or gangs, is the most readily available employment for many poor young men and boys both in the South and in the North.[162] But as we shall discuss in Chapter 7, young women are also being recruited into armies in large numbers today. Here, too, both supply and demand factors prevail. The sex trade and soldiering offer higher remuneration than most other trades available to poor young women and men. The preservation of the unequal global social order and growth of the arms trade requires continuous wars and a large class of killers. As the global arms trade and wars expand across the world, militaries and armed groups are demanding that women keep supplying more children to fight their struggles.[163] An attitude of expendability towards those considered to be the world's 'excess people' underlies these developments. The ultimate outcome of the skin trade, however, is not the good life of freedom and prosperity promised by capi-talism, but utter devaluation of human life, disease, destitution and death.

A new development which has the potential to commoditize and cen-tralize all matters pertaining to life, including ethics, ecology, culture and knowledge, is the new trade rules adopted by the Uruguay round of GATT and the World Trade Organization (WTO) established on January 1, 1995.[164] As we shall discuss in Chapter 6, by increasing the penetration of transnational corporations into new sectors such as biotechnology and the services and by deepening resource exploitation and wealth transfers from the South to the North, GATT portends a future of increased global in-equality and human and environmental exploitation. In the next chapter, we shall show that the forces of global capitalist development which are destroying humanity are also largely responsible for destroying the natural environment.

Notes

1. Cited in Seager and Olson, *Women in the World: An International Atlas*, New York: Simon and Schuster, 1986, p. 101; Marilyn Waring, *If Women Counted: A New Feminist Economics*, San Francisco: Harper and Row, 1988.
2. Anthony De Palma, "For Mexico Indians, New Voices But Few Gains", *The New York Times*, January 13, 1996, pp. 1, 6.
3. UNDP, *Human Development Report 1996*, p. 12; Cathy Schneider, "Chile: The Underside of the Miracle", in *Report on the Americas*, NACLA (North American Congress on Latin America), Vol. XXVI, No. 4, 1991, p. 30; "Chile: A Success Story: But for Whom?", *Third World Resurgence*, No. 28, 1992.
4. "Partnerships for Change: Mexico", Grassroots International, Cambridge, MA, n.d.
5. UNDP, *Human Development Report 1993*, p. 29; Alan Durning, "Ending Poverty", *State of the World Report*, Washington, DC: World Watch Institute, 1990, p. 142; Shrestha and Patterson, "Population Growth and Development", p. 12; Lappe and Schurman, "The Missing Piece", p. 13.
6. "Partnerships for Change".
7. *Creating a Common Agenda: Strategies for Our Communities*, Executive Summary, A Citizens' Report on National Budget Priorities, Common Agenda Coalition, Washington, DC, 1994, p. 1.
8. UNDP, *Human Development Report 1991*, p. 23.
9. Jeremy Seabrook, "Re-examining the Lexicon of Development", *Third World Resurgence*, Nos 61–62, 1995, p. 12.
10. UNDP, *Human Development Report 1992*, pp. 170–203.
11. Lloyd Timberlake, *Africa in Crisis: The Causes, the Cures of Environmental Bankruptcy*, Philadelphia: New Society Publishers, 1986, p. 38; World Bank, *Sub-Saharan Africa: From Crisis to Sustainable Growth*, Washington, DC, 1989, p. 123.
12. Walden Bello, David Kinley and Elaine Elinson, *Development Debacle: The World Bank in the Philippines*, San Francisco: Institute for Food and Development Policy, 1982, p. 205.
13. Klaus Deinger and Lyn Squire, "A New Data Set Measuring Inequality", *The World Bank Economic Review*, Vol. 10, No. 3, 1996, pp. 565–591.
14. Bello, Kinley and Elinson, *Development Debacle*; Bandarage, "Women and Capitalist Development"; Charles H. Wood, "Infant Mortality Trends and Capitalist Development in Brazil: The Case of São Paulo and Belo Horizonte", *Latin American Perspectives*, Issue 15, Vol. IV, No. 4, Fall 1977, p. 58.
15. Herman E. Daly, "Farewell Lecture to World Bank", *Focus: Carrying Capacity Selections*, Vol. 4, No. 2, 1994, p. 8.
16. UNDP, *Human Development Report 1992*, p. 37.
17. Ibid.; Magdoff, "Globalisation", p. 11; Giovanni Arrighi, "World Income Inequalities and the Future of Socialism", *New Left Review*, No. 189, September–October 1991, pp. 39–65.
18. Magdoff, "Globalisation", p. 24.
19. United Nations Department of Economic and Social Affairs, "Interrelations Between Resources, Environment, Population and Development", cited in Ghosh, ed., *Population, Environment and Resources*, p. 86.
20. Magdoff, "Globalisation", p. 23.
21. Ibid., p. 32.
22. Amartya Sen, "Population: Delusion and Reality", *New York Review of Books*, Vol. XLI, No. 15, September 22, 1994; Tim Dyson, "Population Growth and Food Production: Recent Global and Regional Trends", *Population and Development Review*, Vol. 20, No. 2, June 1994, pp. 397–411.
23. Sen, "Population", p. 66.
24. Ibid., p. 24.
25. Amartya Sen, *Poverty and Famines: An Essay on Entitlement and Deprivation*, Oxford:

Clarendon Press, 1982, pp. 126–127.

26. Norman Myers, ed., *Gaia: An Atlas of Planet Management*, New York: Anchor Books, 1984, p. 51; see also Timberlake, "Africa in Crisis"; Walden Bello, "Population Control: The Real Culprits and Victims", *Third World Resurgence*, No. 33, 1993, p. 132; Dyson, "Population Growth", p. 404.

27. Dyson, "Population Growth", p. 407.

28. Vandana Shiva, "Beijing Conference: Gender Justice and Global Apartheid", *Third World Resurgence*, Nos 61–62, 1995, p. 23; Dzodzi Tsikata, "Effects of Structural Adjustment on Women and the Poor", *Third World Resurgence*, Nos 61–62, 1995, p. 59.

29. "Women and the Global Economy", *Global Exchange*, San Francisco, 1989, p. 3.

30. Jacobson, "Gender Bias", pp. 24–34; Bina Agarwal, "Rural Women, Poverty and Resources: Sustenance, Sustainability and Struggle for Change", *Economic and Political Weekly*, October 28, 1989, pp. 45–65.

31. "Food for Thought: Agriculture and the World Bank", World Sustainable Agriculture Association, World Bank/IMF: 50 Years Is Enough Campaign, n.d. (Appendix 3).

32. Frances Moore Lappe and Joseph Collins, *World Hunger: Ten Myths*, San Francisco: Institute for Food and Development Policy, 1979, p. 24; Susan George, *How the Other Half Dies: The Real Reasons for World Hunger*, Montclair, NJ: Allanheld Osmun and Co., 1977.

33. CUSO, *Here to Stay*, p. 5.

34. "An Indictment of the IMF and the World Bank", *Third World Resurgence*, No. 28, January 1992, pp. 21–22; Frederic Clairmont, "The Dynamics of Beverage Imperialism", *Third World Resurgence*, No. 40, 1993, p. 24.

35. James B. McGinnis, *Bread and Justice: Toward a New International Economic Order*, New York: Paulist Press, 1979, p. 71.

36. "Where the Jobs Go and Why", *World Press Review*, Vol. 42, No. 12, December 1995, p. 31.

37. *Partnerships for Change, passim.*

38. Maria Mies, *Lace Makers of Narsapur: Indian Housewives Produce for the World Market*, London, Zed Press, 1982; Haleh Afshar, "The Position of Women in an Iranian Village", in Afshar, ed., *Women, Work and Ideology.*

39. UN, *The World's Women 1995*, p. 124.

40. Hilda Scott, *Working Your Way to the Bottom: The Feminization of Poverty*, London: Pandora Press, 1984, pp. 32–33.

41. UN, *The World's Women, 1995*, p. 128; Peter F. Bell, "Capital and Gender in the Third World: Theoretical Analysis of the Current Crisis", in Joan Smith and Immanuel Wallerstein, eds, *Racism, Sexism and the World-System*, New York: Greenwood Press, 1980, p. 78.

42. Bell, "Capital and Gender in the Third World"; June Nash and Maria Patricia Fernandez-Kelly, eds, *Women and Men in the International Division of Labor*, Albany, NY: State University of New York Press, 1982; Cynthia Enloe, *Bananas, Beaches and Bases: Making Feminist Sense of International Politics*, Berkeley: University of California Press, 1990, Chap. 7.

43. Patricia McLaughlin, "Child-Labor Abuse Gains Notice", *Plain Dealer* (Cleveland), May 13, 1993, p. 5D; "Tragedy, Success and Precocity", *World Press Review*, Vol. 43, No. 1, January 1996, p. 10.

44. "Quincy Students Earn Award for Efforts", *Boston Globe*, December 1, 1995, p. 9.

45. UN, *The World's Women 1995*, p. 122.

46. Kolko, *Restructuring the World Economy*, Chaps 4 and 5.

47. "An Indictment of the IMF and the World Bank", pp. 21–22; CUSO, *Here to Stay*, p. 7.

48. Magdoff, "Globalisation", pp. 7–8.

49. "The Economics of Debt", An Interview with Lance Taylor, *Multinational Monitor*, Vol. 11, April 1990, p. 17.

50. "Structural Adjustment Programmes (SAPs): Questions and Answers", *Third World Resurgence*, No. 28, 1992, p. 20; UNDP, *Human Development Report 1990*, p. 79.

51. UNDP, *Human Development Report 1990*, p. 79; UNDP, *Human Development Report 1992*, p. 45.

52. John Lindsay-Poland, "Peru: On Desperate Terms", *Fellowship*, Fellowship of Reconciliation, December 1991, p. 13.

53. UNDP, *Human Development Report 1992*, p. 45.

54. Magdoff, "Globalisation", p. 6.

55. United Nations, *World Economic Survey*, Department of Economic and Social Affairs, New York, 1991, p. 72.

56. Susan George, "Debt as Warfare: Overview of the Debt Crisis", *Third World Resurgence*, No. 28, 1992, pp. 17–18.

57. Ibid., p. 16.

58. Anne-Marie Beulink, "Women and the Debt Crisis", *Development: Journal of the Society for International Development*, Vol. 1, 1989, p. 89.

59. "Debt", fact sheet, World Bank/IMF: 50 Years is Enough US Campaign, n.d., p. 1 (see Appendix 4).

60. "Structural Adjustment Programs", p. 20; United Nations, *World Economic Survey*, Department of Economic and Social Affairs, New York, 1990, pp. 30–31.

61. Graham Hancock, *Lords of Poverty*, London: Mandarin, 1992, p. 71.

62. Samir Amin, "Moving Beyond Structural Adjustment", *Third World Resurgence*, No. 28, 1992, p. 35.

63. Danilo Turk, "How World Bank–IMF Policies Adversely Affect Human Rights", *Third World Resurgence*, No. 33, 1993, p. 19; "Structural Adjustment Lending: An Evaluation of Programme Design", Staff Working Paper No. 735, World Bank, Washington, DC, 1985, cited in Hancock, *Lords of Poverty*, p. 65.

64. Inter Press Service, "UNDP Cautions against Indiscriminate Privatization", *Third World Economics: Trends and Analysis*, May 16–31, 1993, p. 4.

65. Ibid.

66. Chakravarthi Raghavan, "Japan's Study on State's Role Refutes Free-Market Myths', *Third World Economics: Trends and Analysis*, May 16–31, 1993, p. 5.

67. UNDP, *Human Development Report 1992*, p. 51.

68. Nancy E. Wright, "Disastrous Decade: Africa's Experience With Structural Adjustment", *Multinational Monitor*, Vol. 11, April 1, 1990, p. 21.

69. Turk, "How World Bank–IMF Policies Adversely Affect", p. 22.

70. Ibid., p. 17.

71. Diane Elson, "How Is Structural Adjustment Affecting Women?", *Development*, No. 1, 1989, p. 71; Giovanni Andrea Cornia, Richard Jolly and Frances Stewart, eds, *Adjustment with a Human Face: Protecting the Vulnerable and Promoting Growth*, Oxford: Clarendon Press and UNICEF, 1987, cited in Hancock, *Lords of Poverty*, p. 63; Commonwealth Secretariat, *Engendering Adjustment*, p. 81.

72. Beulink, "Women and the Debt Crisis", p. 91. John Lindsay-Poland, "Peru: On Desperate Terms", p. 13; Elson, "How is Structural Adjustment", p. 72; UN, *World Economic Survey*, 1990, p. 31.

73. Michael Chossudovsky, "Feeding on Poverty: India Under the IMF Rule", *Third World Resurgence*, No. 28, 1992, p. 26.

74. Chandra Muzaffar, "Western Global Domination and Human Rights", *Third World Resurgence*, No. 33, 1993, p. 24; see also Sell and Kunitz, "The Debt Crisis".

75. World Bank cited in CUSO, *Here to Stay*, p. 15; World Bank, *World Development Report*, New York: Oxford University Press, 1990, p. iii.

76. Yukon Huang and Peter Nicholas, "The Social Costs of Adjustment", *Adjustment with Growth: The Fund, The Bank, and Country Experiences*, IMF and World Bank, n.d.; African Development Bank, United Nations Development Programme and the World Bank, *The Social Dimensions of Adjustment in Africa*, 1990; see also Stephany Griffith Jones, "Debt Reduction with a Human Face: The IDB and UNICEF Initiative", *Development: Journal of the Society for International Development*, Vol. 1, 1989, pp. 50–53.

77. Cited in Noam Chomsky, "The Enemy is the Third World Itself", *Central American Reporter*, July–August, 1990, p. 6; see also George, "Debt as Warfare"; Oxfam America, *The Impact of Structural Adjustment on Community Life: Undoing Development*, Boston, April 1995.

78. *Engendering Adjustment for the 1990s*; see also Beneria and Feldman, eds, *Unequal Burden*.

79. *Alt-WID* (Alternative Women in Development), "Reaganomics and Women: Structural Adjustment U.S. Style, 1980–1992: A Case Study of Women and Poverty in the U.S.", Washington, DC, n.d., p. 28.

80. Jacobson, "Women's Health", p. 7.

81. Commonwealth Secretariat, *Engendering Adjustment*; Tsikata, "Effects of Structural Adjustment", pp. 56–59; CUSO, *Here to Stay*, p. 18; A. Lynn Bolles, "Surviving Manley and Seaga: Case Studies of Women's Responses to Structural Adjustment Policies", *Review of Radical Political Economics*, Special Issue on Women in the International Economy, Vol. 23, Nos 3–4, Fall–Winter 1991, pp. 20–36.

82. Palmer, "Gender Issues in Structural Adjustment", p. 22; Merle Hodge, "Women and Structural Adjustment", in "Women and the Global Economy", *Global Exchange*, San Francisco, 1989; Moser, "The Impact of Recession", p. 80; see also Ingrid Palmer, *Gender and Population*.

83. US Arms Control and Disarmament Agency, *World Military Expenditures and Arms Transfers, 1993–1994*, Washington, DC: US Government Printing Office, February 1995, p. 43; "Public Interest Report", *Journal of the Federation of American Scientists (FAS)*, Vol. 45, No. 6, November–December 1992, pp. 1, 10–11; "Hard Pressed Russia Seeks to Revive Global Arms Sales", *The Boston Globe*, July 29, 1992, pp. 1 and 4.

84. Philip Shenon, "Russia Outstrips U.S. as Chief Arms Seller to Developing Nations", *The New York Times*, August 20, 1996, p. A3; "France Leads in Arms Sales to Third World", *The New York Times*, August 8, 1995, p. 1.

85. "U.S. Approves Over $38 Billion of Exports in FY 1994", in *Arms Sales Monitor*, No. 29, March 1995, p. 3; "Surplus Arms Made for Export Only", *Arms Sales Monitor*, No. 28, February 1995, p. 2; "A 90's Military–Industrial Complex", *The New York Times*, January 21, 1996, p. E4: "Military Sales Logic", *Arms Sales Monitor*, No. 31, December 5, 1995, p. 6.

86. *Journal of the Federation of American Scientists (FAS)*, "Public Interest Report", pp. 3, 6.

87. UNDP, *Human Development Report 1990*, p. 78.

88. FAS, Public Interest Report, p. 11; *Arms Control Today*, Vol. 21, No. 5, 1990, p. 4.

89. "Asian Arms Binge", *World Press Review*, June 1992, p. 34.

90. Ian Anthony, "The Global Arms Trade", *Arms Control Today*, Vol. 21, No. 5, 1990; UNDP, *Human Development Report 1990*, p. 77.

91. "In Egypt – Two Penny Loaf is Family Heartbreak", *The New York Times*, July 9, 1990, p. A5.

92. World Bank, cited in UNDP, *Human Development Report 1990*, p. 77; UNDP, *Human Development Report 1992*, p. 57.

93. UNDP, *Human Development Report 1990*, p. 77.

94. UNDP, *Human Development Report 1991*, p. 82; United Nations, *World Economic and Social Survey*, 1995, Department for Economic and Social Information and Policy Analysis, New York, 1995, pp. 192–193.

95. Asoka Bandarage, "The Gulf War and the Crisis Facing Humanity", unpublished ms, January 1991, p. 3; Peters, ed., *Collateral Damage, passim*.

96. UNDP, *Human Development Report 1990*, p. 77.

97. UNDP, *Human Development Report 1994*, p. 48; "In Egypt", p. A5.

98. UNDP, *Human Development Report 1990*, p. 77; Ruth Sivard, *World Military and Social Expenditures* 1989, Washington, DC: World Priorities, 1989.

99. UNDP, *Human Development Report 1991*, p. 45.

100. UN, *The World's Women 1970–1990*, p. 36.

101. UNDP, *Human Development Report 1991*, p. 45.

102. Ibid.

103. Richard Jolly, "A UNICEF Perspective on the Effects of Economic Crises and What Can be Done", in Bell and Reich, eds, *Health, Nutrition and Economic Crises*, p. 81.

104. UNDP, *Human Development Report 1994*, p. 72; Hancock, *Lords of Poverty, passim*; Heatley, *Poverty and Power*, p. 27; Frances Moore Lappe and David Kinley, *Aid as Obstacle: Twenty Questions About Our Foreign Aid and the Hungry*, San Francisco, Institute for Food and Development Policy, 1980.

105. "Recent Developments in Southern Resource Flows", *Third World Resurgence*, No. 46, 1994, p. 17.

106. Hancock, *Lords of Poverty, passim.*

107. Ibid., pp. 71, 176.

108. Ibid., pp. 178–179.

109. UNDP, *Human Development Report 1992*, p. 53; Hancock, *Lords of Poverty*, p. 175; Elson "How Is Structural Adjustment", p. 89.

110. UNDP, *Human Development Report 1992*, p. 55.

111. Sassen, *The Mobility of Labor and Capital.*

112. UNDP, *Human Development Report 1992*, p. 57.

113. Ibid.

114. Barry Bluestone, *The Deindustrialization of America: Plant Closings, Community Abandonment, and the Dismantling of Basic Industry*, New York: Basic Books, 1982; Center for Popular Economics, *Economic Report of the People*, Boston: South End Press, 1986, p. 32; *Creating a Common Agenda*, p. 3.

115. *Alt-WID*, "Reaganomics and Women", p. 3.

116. *Creating a Common Agenda*, p. 6; Stephen J. Rose, *Social Stratification in the United States: The American Profile Poster Revised and Expanded*, New York: New Press, 1992, p. 149.

117. Ibid., pp. 149–150; see also *Annual Surveys of Corporate Tax Payers and Corporate Freeloaders*, Citizens for Tax Justice, Washington, DC, 1988, 1989; *Creating a Common Agenda*, p. 6.

118. Center for Popular Economics, *Economic Report of the People*, p. 147; see also *Inequality and the Federal Budget Deficit*, Washington, DC, Citizens for Tax Justice, September 1991.

119. *Alt-WID*, "Reaganomics and Women", pp. 6, 21–22; "Gingrich Promises Solution on Debt Ceiling", *The New York Times*, January 13, 1996, p. 9; see also "Responsible Wealth: A Call to Action" (Appendix 3).

120. *Alt-WID*, "Reagonomics and Women", p. 24; Rose, *Social Stratification*, pp. 149–150.

121. Letter to Editor, David Isenberg, Center for Defense Information, *The New York Times*, January 24, 1996, p. A18; *Creating a Common Agenda*, p. 5.

122. *Creating a Common Agenda*, p. 4.

123. Cited in ibid., p. 6.

124. Ibid., pp. 5–6.

125. "For the People", *STAND*, Massachusetts Human Services Coalition, Boston, December 15, 1995, p. 9.

126. Ibid., p. 9; Carey Goldberg, "Asian Immigrants Help Bolster U.S. Economy, New Report Says", *The New York Times*, March 31, 1996, p. 32.

127. US Bureau of the Census, *Statistical Abstract of the United States: 1995*, p. 475.

128. Cynthia McKinney and Caleb Rossiter, "It's Time the U.S. Stopped 'Boomerang' Arms Sales", *The Christian Science Monitor*, May 23, 1995, p. 19; see also Joshua Goldstein, *PACs in Profile; Spending Patterns in the 1994 Election*, Washington, DC, Center for Responsive Politics, 1995, p. 45; Larry Makinson, "The Price of Admission: Campaign Spending in the 1994 Elections", Center for Responsive Politics, Washington, DC, 1995.

129. Paul E. Zopf Jr, *American Women in Poverty*, New York: Greenwood Press, 1989.

130. US Bureau of the Census, *Statistical Abstract of the United States: 1995*, pp. 480–481.

131. Ibid., p. 480. See also Thérèse Funicello, "The Poverty Industry: Do Government and Charities Create the Poor?", *Ms, Magazine*, Vol., 1, No. 3, November–December, 1990, pp. 32–40.

132. Daniel Patrick Moynihan, "The Moynihan Report: The Negro Family – The Case for National Action", in Lee Rainwater and William L. Yancey, eds, *The Moynihan Report and the Politics of Controversy*, Cambridge, MA: MIT Press, 1967.

133. UN, *The World's Women 1995*, p. 6.

134. Marc L. Miringhoff, *The Index of Social Health, 1990: Measuring the Social Well-Being of the Nation*, Tarrytown, NY: Fordham Institute for Innovation in Social Policy, Fordham University, 1990, p. 5, cited in *Alt-WID*, "Reaganomics and Women", pp. 6–7, 10–11.

135. Center for Popular Economics, *Economic Report of the People*, pp. 28–29; "Hub Infants Deaths Up by 32%", *The Boston Globe*, February 9, 1987, p. 1; *Alt-WID*, "Reaganomics and Women", p. 14.

136. *Alt-WID*, "Reaganomics and Women", pp. 7, 10.

137. UNDP, *Human Development Report 1991*, p. 31; "Conservative Economics", *The Economist*, October 23–24, 1987, pp. 23–26.

138. Nicholas Hildyard, "Maastricht: The Protectionism of Free Trade?", *The Ecologist*, Vol. 23, No. 2, March–April 1993.

139. Michel Chossudovsky, "The 'Third Worldisation' of Russia Under IMF Rule", *Third World Economics*, June 16–30, 1993, pp. 14–16, 20; Guy Standing, ed., *The New Soviet Labour Market: In Search of Flexibility*, Geneva: ILO, 1991.

140. UNDP, *Human Development Report 1991*, p. 26.

141. "Russian Mothers From All Walks, Walk Alone", *The New York Times*, October 21, 1995, pp. 1, 5.

142. Cited in Dzodzi Tsikata, "Globalisation the Cause of Poor Women's Woes, Says Panel", *Third World Resurgence*, Nos 61–62, 1995, p. 35.

143. UN, *The World's Women 1970–1990*, p. 82; United Nations, *World's Women, 1995*, p. 108; Commonwealth Secretariat, *Engendering Adjustment*, p. 19.

144. UN, *The World's Women 1995*, p. 108.

145. Diane Elson, "From Survival Strategies to Transformation Strategies: Women's Needs and Structural Adjustment", in Beneria and Feldman, eds, *Unequal Burden*, p. 41.

146. UN, *The World's Women 1995*, p. 5; UN, *The World's Women 1970–1990*, p. 18; Jacobson, "Women's Health", p. 7.

147. Jacobson, "Women's Health", p. 7.

148. UN, *The World's Women 1995*, p. 45.

149. Bandarage, "Women and Capitalist Development".

150. Philip Shenon, "Outcry Mounts in Philippines over Hanging", *The New York Times*, March 22, 1995, p. A7.

151. "Microenterprise: On the Road to Success", *Hunger Notes*, Vol. 21, No. 2, Fall 1995.

152. Ann Danaiya Usher, "After the Forest: AIDS as Ecological Collapse in Thailand", in Vandana Shiva, ed., *Close to Home: Women Reconnect Ecology, Health and Development Wordwide*, Philadelphia: New Society Publishers, 1994, p. 29.

153. Kathleen Barry, *Female Sexual Slavery*, New York: New York University Press, 1984; Janice Raymond, "International Traffic in Reproduction", *Ms. Magazine*, May–June 1991, pp. 29–33.

154. Noeleen Heyzer, *Working Women in South-East Asia: Development, Subordination and Emancipation*, London: Open University Press, 1986; "For Girls, Few Choices – All Bad", *World Press Review*, Vol. 43, No. 1, January 1996, pp. 12–13; "Love for Sale", *Utne Reader*, January–February 1992, p. 37.

155. Usher, "After the Forest"; Grundfest-Schoepf, "Women at Risk: Case Studies from Zaire", in Herdt and Lindenbaum, eds, *Time of AIDS*, pp. 259–287.

156. Alessandra Stanley, "Anxious Vigil for Chinese Babies", *The New York Times*, January 18, 1996, pp. C1, 10.

157. Ibid.; Holly Burkhalter, "China's Horrific Adoption Mills", *The New York Times*, op-ed., January 11, 1996, p. A25.

158. Bandarage, "Women and Capitalist Development", pp. 74–75.

159. Cited in Raymond, "International Traffic". p. 34.

160. Kimbrell, *The Human Body Shop*, passim.

161. Cited in Chris Hedges, "Egypt's Desperate Trade: Body Parts for Sale", *The New York Times*, September 21, 1991, pp. 1, A8; and Radhakrishna Rao, "Illegal Kidney Trade Boom in India", *Third World Resurgence*, No. 17, 1991, p. 9.

162. Chris Hedges, "An Army of Angry Men, With Backs to the Wall", *The New York Times*, October 8, 1991; "Children in Bondage", *World Press Review*, Vol. 43, No. 1, January 1996, pp. 8–9.

163. "Children in Bondage", pp. 8–9; Mark Baker, "In the Forests of the Night", *The Island*, Colombo, Sri Lanka, December 31, 1995.

164. Vandana Shiva, "The Effects of WTO on Women's Rights", *Third World Resurgence*, Nos 61–62, 1995, p. 52.

6

Political Economy of the Environment

To understand the modern 'ecological crisis', it is essential to move beyond the Malthusian focus on population size and density and to examine the social determinants of the population–environment relationship. This requires investigation into the technology of production and social relations of production including unequal property relations and consumption patterns within the global political economy.

Carrying capacity of regions and the relationship between population and resources today are determined by the particular manner in which people and regions are integrated into the processes of capital accumulation and technological expansion. Lack of economic and political power may push the poor towards environmentally destructive behavior patterns. But the poor are only a small part of the problem. The fundamental reasons for reduction of sustainability and carrying capacity are inequality in resource and income distribution, ecologically faulty methods of production and militarism.

Unequal Consumption

Sharply different patterns of consumption exist among different social classes and regions as well as races and sexes with regard to all basic human needs – food, water, shelter, clothing, education, transportation. Affluent consumption patterns pose a far more serious threat to the survival of planetary life support systems than do less affluent ones. As environmental researcher Alan Durning has demonstrated, this can be clearly seen with regard to three ecologically important forms of consumption – diet, transportation and use of raw materials – by the three broad social classes in the world today.[1]

Food consumption

The 'bottom 20%' of the global population living in poverty do not have enough food to eat or clean water to drink. As a result, malnutrition and poverty-related illnesses are rampant among them. It is among this group that 35,000 children die a day due to hunger and it is also among this group that fertility rates tend to be the highest. As discussed earlier, it is also within this group that women and girls tend to receive less food and nutrition than men and boys. Clearly, this class, including girls and women, need to have their basic needs met before meeting family planning targets. Clearly also they need to increase their consumption, not decrease it.

On the next rung of the global food consumption ladder are about 3.4 billion grain eaters who consume the world's healthiest diet, consisting of sufficient calories and plant-based protein. This balanced, middle path of food consumption should become the global norm. Unfortunately, however, as more and more countries adopt the western model of 'development', people who have lived on grain-based diets traditionally are also shifting towards meat and processed foods.

On the topmost rung of the global food ladder are the 1.25 billion or so people who are meat eaters, who receive about 40% of their calories from the fat of the meat they consume (Table 6.1). The high-fat diet is associated with a number of so-called diseases of affluence, like heart disease, stroke and different types of cancer. But the fact that contemporary meat eating is inimical to planetary health as well as the survival of the poor is less well understood.

Indirectly, the meat eating quarter of the world's population consumes about 40% of the world's grain, that is, the grain used to fatten the livestock they eat. Not only does cattle ranching take land away from cultivation of beans and other staple food items of poor people, but modern methods of meat production are also one of the major causes of resource depletion and environmental destruction in the world. As Durning points out:

> Meat production is behind a substantial share of the environmental strains induced by the present global agricultural system, from soil erosion to overpumping of underground water. In the extreme case of American beef, producing two pounds of steak requires ten pounds of grain and the energy equivalent of a half a gallon of gasoline, not to mention the associated soil erosion, water consumption, pesticide and fertilizer run off, ground water depletion and emissions of the greenhouse gas methane.[2]

Transportation

At the bottom of the global transportation hierarchy are the billion or so people with a severe 'lack of transportation options' who must do most of their travelling by foot and an occasional animal or bus ride. Just as they need greater access to food, so the poor need to have increased access to reliable and safe methods of transport. On the middle rung of the global transportation ladder are some 3 billion global citizens, especially in China,

Table 6.1 Annual per capita consumption: meat, automobile travel, energy, steel and paper, 1987–1990

Country	Meat (kg)	Auto travel (km/capita)	Energy (kg/coal)	Steel (kg)	Paper (kg)
France	91	–	–	–	–
Italy	–	4030	–	–	–
Japan	41	2510	4032	582	222
Soviet Union	70	–	6546	582	36
United Kingdom	–	4730	–	–	–
United States	112	8870	10,127	417	308
West Germany	–	6150	5377	457	207
Brazil	47	–	798	99	27
Cameroon	–	120	–	–	–
China	24	–	810	64	15
Mexico	40	–	1689	93	40
Poland	–	710	–	–	–
South Korea	–	210	–	–	–
Thailand	–	190	–	–	–
Turkey	16	–	958	149	8
Bangladesh	–	–	69	5	1
Egypt	14	–	–	–	–
India	2	–	307	20	3
Indonesia	–	–	274	21	5
Nigeria	–	–	192	8	1
Philippines	16	–	–	–	–

Source: Alan Thein Durning, *How Much Is Enough? The Consumer Society and the Future of the Earth*, New York: W.W. Norton and Co., 1992, pp. 53, 67, 81, 91.

Latin America and the Middle East, who go most places by bus or bicycle. Although their mode of transport is both cheap and ecologically sound, there is increasing consumer pressure on this class to emulate the transportation habits of the richest group, who own cars and who also frequently travel in airplanes (Table 6.1).

As in the case of excessive beef consumption, in the case of excessive ownership of automobiles, too, the US does more damage to the global environment than most other countries in the world. The US lifestyle is dependent on individual ownership of cars: two or more vehicles are owned by one-fifth of US households, with more than 50% owning at least two. Some 65% of new American homes are built with two-car garages, and 90% of the cars have air conditioning.[3] Individual ownership of vehicles prevents development of public transit systems, disrupts community and earth-based lifestyles and alienates people from each other.

The UNFPA *State of the World Population 1990* report states that the world car fleet increased by seven times between 1950 and 1980 while human population only doubled during that period. The UNFPA estimates that the world car fleet will grow from 400 million (in 1990) to 700 million over the next 20 years – twice as fast as the human population – and that much of that growth will occur in the developing countries, which currently own only 12% of all cars. The UNFPA report attributes the increase in cars to increase in Third World populations, without questioning the logic of global economic growth which pushes all societies and individuals into adopting the environmentally faulty, affluent, western lifestyle.[4]

It needs to be seriously asked if cars, airplanes, refrigerators, air conditioning and the whole range of gadgetry and conveniences of the affluent in the North, as well as the South, are more of a threat to the environment than increases in the number of poor people. Today, the cars of the rich have a higher monetary value than the lives of poor human beings. A single car and its maintenance costs often exceed the upkeep of a poor person during an entire lifetime. In many cities in the United States, the hourly wage of an attendant at a parking garage, who is usually male, often exceeds the wage of a child-care worker, who is usually female.

Motor vehicles are directly responsible for about "13% of the carbon dioxide emissions from fossil fuels worldwide, along with air pollution, acid rain, and a quarter million traffic fatalities a year".[5] While automobile companies keep on promoting car sales, the planet's 'carrying capacity' for cars is running out. A 'population' control policy for cars is urgently called for!

Raw material use

As with diet and transportation, sharp class cleavages can be observed with regard to raw-material consumption in the world. About 1 billion rural people 'subsist on local biomass collected from their immediate environment' using about half a pound of grain, two pounds of fuel wood and fodder for their animals every day. Most of these come from self-replenishing renewable resources. But with increasing environmental destruction, poverty and population growth, even these minimal resource needs of this group, especially of women subsistence producers, are more and more threatened.[6]

As Durning points out, more than 2 billion people live in countries such as India and Indonesia where per capita consumption of steel, which is considered to be the basic modern material, falls below 50 kilograms a year. Per capita energy use, which is a good indirect indicator of overall use of materials, is relatively low. Contribution to forest destruction through use of paper is also minimal within this group (Table 6.1).

Table 6.2 Unequal contributions to greenhouse effect, 1987 (%)

Region	% of global population	CO$_2$ (fossil fuels)	CO$_2$ (land use)	CH$_4$	CFCs	Total
US/Canada	5.2	24	–	20	29	20
Europe/USSR	14.9	41	–	18	49	31
Japan	2.3	6	–	4	9	5
Asia (other)	56.5	21	31	41	7	23
Africa	12.1	3	14	7	3	6
Latin America	8.5	5	55	10	4	16
Other	0.5	–	–	–	–	–
Total	99.9	100	100	100	101	101

Note: Population figures are from 1990; greenhouse gases figures are from 1987.

CO$_2$ – Carbon dioxide from fossil fuels or changes in land use, such as deforestation.
CH$_4$ – Methane.
CFCs – Chlorofluorocarbons.

Sources: United Nations, *World Population Chart 1990 Revised*, Population Division, UN Secretariat 1990; World Resources Institute, *World Resources 1990–91*, Washington, DC, as cited in Ministry of Foreign Affairs Development Cooperation, Information Department, *A World of Difference: A New Framework for Development Cooperation in the 1990s*, The Hague, Netherlands, 1991, p. 73.

The 1.5 billion people living in countries such as Mexico and Turkey and who belong to the middle rung of the global raw-material consumption ladder use between 50 and 150 kilograms of steel, around 1,000 kilograms of (coal equivalent) energy and around 33 kilograms of paper a year (Table 6.1). People living in industrialized countries account for about 75% of the world's raw materials and energy use.[7] They constitute the 'throwaway class' responsible for much of resource depletion in the world. At the very top of the resource consumption ladder is the US, which consumes the bulk of the world's energy resources. To quote Durning, once again:

> A typical resident of the industrialized fourth of the world uses 15 times as much paper, 10 times as much steel, and 12 times as much fuel as a resident of the developing world. The extreme case is again the United States, where the average person consumes most of his or her own weight in basic materials each day – 40 pounds of petroleum and coal, 30 pounds of other minerals, 26 pounds of agricultural products and 19 pounds of forest products.[8]

Differential environmental impact

Differential use of resources by nations, regions, social classes as well as the sexes leads to uneven and unequal contributions to problems like ozone depletion and global warming and attendant environmental destruction. The industrialized nations have less than 25% of the global population, yet they account for about 75% of the world's energy use, two-thirds of greenhouse gases such as carbon dioxide and methane and over 90% of chlorofluorocarbons which damage the ozone layer that protects the earth (Tables 6.1 and 6.2).

Although industrialized nations in the North are responsible overwhelmingly for production of greenhouse gases, the effects are global; some of the worst effects are felt in some of the poorest countries. For example, Bangladesh produces only 0.3% of global greenhouse emissions; yet, as the UNDP *Human Development Report 1994* points out, because of a 1-meter rise in sea level partly attributed to global warming, the land area in Bangladesh could shrink by 17%.[9]

The unequal and uneven patterns in trade set in place during colonialism and continued during neo-colonialism allow the industrialized countries in the North to exceed local carrying capacities by importing carrying capacity from the Third World. The European Community, Japan and North America together imported $136 billion worth of crops and natural resources in excess of what they exported in 1989, thereby making 'developing nations' net exporters of these primary commodities. This massive export of carrying capacity from the South is increasingly depleting the energy of people and ecosystems in the South. Take the case of the Netherlands. It estimated to use up anywhere from three to seventeen times more land than that available within its own boundaries through agricultural imports largely from the Third World. Palm-kernel cake and cassava from deforested regions in Malaysia and Thailand and soybeans from pesticide-ridden lands in Brazil are fed to pigs and cows in the huge industrial farms of the Netherlands so that European consumers can enjoy their diets of high-fat meat and milk.[10]

The greatest threat to environmental sustainability comes from the top 20% of the global population in the North rather than the bottom 20% in the South. A citizen in the United States poses a far greater threat to the biosphere than a citizen in a Sub-Saharan African country. According to estimates revealed in UNICEF's *The State of the World's Children 1994*:

...the impact of the average American [US] citizen on the environment is approximately 3 times that of the average Italian, 13 times that of the average Brazilian, 35 times that of the average Indian, 140 times that of the average Bangladeshi, and more than 250 times that of a citizen born into one of the least developed nations of sub-Saharan Africa.[11]

The real population problem, then, exists in the affluent North with declining population growth rates rather than in the poor South where fertility and population growth rates are higher. The lesson here is that the world needs to move towards a more balanced redistribution and consumption of resources which is both socially and environmentally sustainable: the poor need to consume more and the rich need to consume less (Figure 8.4).[12] It is only then that the problem of 'overpopulation' can be redressed. In other words, overconsumption in the North and 'overpopulation' in the South are inextricably interlinked. Yet as discussed earlier in this book, policy makers in the North continue to push for population control in the South rather than control of environmentally harmful technologies of production and overconsumption in the North.

Among other factors, this apparent contradiction stems from the fact that the rich contribute to market expansion through their profligate consumption, while the poor, who lack purchasing power, are superfluous to capitalist growth. Despite disastrous consequences to the environment and human health, the technological–consumerist lifestyle and growth-oriented development continue to expand unabated.

The mechanistic-materialistic culture

Global advertising promoting individualist competitive consumption patterns is growing at faster rates than either global population or economic output. Between 1950 and 1990, global advertising increased approximately sevenfold, that is, three times faster than the growth of the world population.[13]

Global advertising expenditures rose from approximately $39 billion in 1950 to $237 billion in 1988, with per capita advertising increasing from $15 to $46. Advertising expenditures in the US increased from $198 per capita in 1950 to $498 in 1989. In the 1980s, India's advertising costs increased fivefold and South Korea's advertising industry grew by between 35 and 40%. The US sets the standards for global consumerism and advertising and in the United States itself life is permeated by advertising messages. It is estimated that:

> ...the typical American [US citizen] is exposed to between 50 to 100 advertisements each morning before nine o'clock. Along with their weekly twenty-two-hour diet of television, American teenagers are typically exposed to three to four hours of TV advertisements a week, adding up to at least 100,000 ads between birth and high school graduation.[14]

In the United States, where commoditization of life is more advanced than elsewhere, shopping is, perhaps, the primary cultural activity. It is estimated that US residents spend six hours every week on various kinds of shopping and some 93% of US teenage girls surveyed in 1987 identified shopping as their 'favorite pastime'.[15] But with rapid expansion of tele-marketing, mail order shopping, and so on, consumers around the world need no longer visit malls. They can buy 24 hours a day from the privacy of their homes or even their automobile or airplane seats.

Many countries in the South have called for reduction of over-consumption in the industrialized countries, for example as they did at the Earth Summit in Rio in 1992.[16] Yet these countries themselves are pursuing industrial capitalism and the affluent lifestyles associated with it. With the collapse of Communism in the Soviet Union and Eastern Europe, the model of competitive economic growth has emerged victorious the world over. As media advertising promotes the modern lifestyle based on individual consumption, a homogenized American culture is spreading with dizzying speed all across the world.

Just as the economic hegemony of the North has historically been built upon expropriation of natural resources and human labor power from the South, the cultural hegemony of the North is also increasingly built upon cultural appropriation from the South. Ancient healing traditions, music, dance and art forms such as ayurveda, yoga, tai chi, African dance and drumming, the Native American sweat lodge and other rituals are being commercialized and appropriated by the dominant global western culture. At the same time, the cultural foundations of ancient societies are being weakened and their capacity for autonomous development severely undermined by the onslaught of western commercial culture, the English language and Christianity.

Younger generations raised on corporate-controlled television know very little of life outside of consumerism, individualism and competition today. The global market economy discourages self-reliance and genuine creativity; instead, it promotes consumption as the primary means of self-expression as well as status maintenance. Everyone wants the same goods and material comforts – TVs, VCRs, refrigerators, cars and designer clothes – that are projected at them through the global media.

Technology, materialism and alienation

Despite global competition for material goods, all evidence shows that excessive consumerism does not necessarily empower people or make them any happier.[17] While the poor are dying of starvation, disease and war, the rich are being saturated with superfluous things that they have little time to enjoy. Although they have a comfortable lifestyle, individual citizens in the affluent North have little control over corporate domination of their societies. For example, finding healthier alternatives to 'junk' food or individually owned automobiles is so inconvenient and time-consuming that most people feel a lack of choice in these important areas of their lives.

The so-called privileged lifestyle is not only materialistic but it is also extremely competitive and mechanistic. Economic insecurity and the bureaucratic, hierarchical organization of work pit people against each other, forcing individuals to 'play the game' of self-aggrandizement. It encourages an instrumentalist approach to human relationships and maintaining appearances rather than fulfilling true creative potential or developing relationships based on honesty and justice.

The new technologies, especially communication technologies (such as electronic mail, voice mail, fax, Internet, etc.), have increased the speed and volume of human interactions while at the same time undermining leisure time and the quality of human relationships. As French philosopher Jacques Ellul observed, in the modern machine age, success is defined increasingly by a human being's ability to act as a cog – an extension of the machine:

> The human being who acts and thinks today is not situated as an independent subject with respect to a technological object. He is inside the technological system, he is himself modified by the technological factor. The human being who uses technology today is by that very fact the human being who serves it. And conversely, only the human being who serves technology is truly able to use it.[18]

Indeed, as we rapidly destroy the forest which is our original home, and live in urban concrete jungles and in cyberspace and virtual reality, trying so hard to keep up with the latest technology, we treat ourselves and each other more and more as if we are machines. In this process, we lose our emotional grounding in human relationships and our physical grounding on the earth. As these basic human needs are unmet, we become physically and psychologically unbalanced, sick and easily prone to anger and despair. The global environmental crisis needs to be addressed in the context of our alienation from nature, from the deeper aspects of ourselves and from each other and resultant numbing, stress and 'burn out'.

A primary reason for this stress is the almost total commodification and technological manipulation of time in modern industrial capitalist society and the experience of time and life itself in quantitative and monetary units. Hindi writer S.H. Vatsyayan observes that as we spend our lives within the restricted psychological and emotional space provided by the newspaper, the tabloid magazine, the radio and television broadcast, "Our time experience becomes thinner and more confined to the surface, actuality [reportage] replaces reality. More and more we live less and less". As modern technological society estranges us from our ecological evolutionary history, we are robbed of what Vatsyayan calls a "timeless order of experience" that is essential to our identity as human beings.[19] A complete disintegration of our primordial identity as a species in nature under the impact of technology and commoditization connotes not progress and development, but extinction.

As families and communities are scattered across the globe and human bonds weaken in the process of technological–capital expansion and quantitative growth, individuals feel increasingly fragmented, atomized and numbed. As a result, they seek to find comfort and security in still more material goods, including drugs, technology and commoditized therapeutic services. As psychologist Paul Wachtel and other analysts have pointed out, ultimately, capitalist growth and market expansion are built on human vulnerability and a view of human beings as inherently discontented and human desire as utterly inexhaustible.[20] Modern advertising and consumerism aggravate human ignorance, fear, greed and hatred, rather than help cultivate wisdom, generosity and compassion. This consumerism also takes distinct gender dimensions.

Consumerism and women

We have noted earlier that among the poor, girls tend to get even less food than do boys. Even in pre-capitalist feudal societies, the women of the dominant classes were the symbols of male economic power and conspicuous consumption while women of the subordinate classes were the beasts of burden. As Maria Mies has argued, with colonial capitalist expansion, a peculiarly exploitative transnational relationship was created between white women of the North as the consummate consumers and Third World women as the most exploited global producers.[21] However, some upper-class women in the South even outdo their Northern counterparts in emulating the extravagant lifestyle depicted in television shows such as *Dynasty* and *Dallas* exported from the US.

With the development of the consumer culture, women have been identified excessively with external beauty, and a homogenized western concept of beauty at that. As a result, women's other attributes, their capabilities and inner strengths, are less and less appreciated. Enormous industries in clothing, make-up, dieting, and so on, have been built by encouraging women to be insecure about their bodies. However, this over-identification with appearance and material consumption represents a form of disempowerment and patriarchal control of women: it takes women's minds away from the roots of oppression and ways to combat it. For example, it may prevent young privileged women in the North suffering from dieting disorders like anorexia and bulimia from seeing the very different geo-political reasons for the emaciation of many poor women in the South. These issues need to be addressed by the women's movement if feminism is to become a truly global political force.

The gender, class, racial and regional contradictions and the ecologically disastrous consumerist lifestyle cannot be changed by mere references to human values and appeals to human conscience, as some western environmentalists and New Age spiritualists attempt to do.[22] Rather, to understand the roots of overconsumption and environmental destruction, we need to examine the logic, or, more accurately, the illogic, of capitalist production and the ecological destruction resulting from unbridled growth.

Capitalist Production

As Marx showed, the tide of capital accumulation driven by competition always rises to new limits, making scarcity an endemic feature of the capitalist mode of production. Marx also observed that the imperative for short-term profit pushes capital to exploit the laborer as well as the environment: "all progress in capitalistic agriculture is a progress in the art not only of robbing the labourer, but of robbing the soil; all progress in increasing the fertility of the soil for a given time, is a progress towards ruining the lasting sources of that fertility."[23]

Ecologist Barry Commoner has argued that the "decisive factor" in determining environmental quality is the nature of the technology of production, rather than population growth or affluence.[24] Sociologist John Bellamy Foster also observes that industrial growth is the main enemy of the environment:

> A continuous 3% average annual rate of growth in industrial production, such as obtained from 1970 to 1990, would mean that world industry would double in size every twenty five years, grow sixteen fold approximately every century, increase by 250 times every two centuries, 4,000 times every three centuries, etc.... In order to generate profits, the treadmill relies heavily on energy-intensive, capital-intensive technology, which allows it to economize on labor inputs.[25]

The result of this increased throughput is rapid depletion of energy and other natural resources, massive dumping of wastes and pollution of the environment. Indeed, as Foster concludes, the world cannot "sustain many more doublings of industrial output under the present system without experiencing a complete ecological catastrophe ... we are already over-shooting certain ecological thresholds."[26] Yet the entire world seems to be pursuing industrial growth in an ever more competitive and frenzied fashion today. As Barry Commoner puts it, "the man-made 'technosphere' is at war with the 'natural ecosphere', the thin global skin of air, water and soil and the plants and animals that live in it."[27]

Violence against nature and ecocide are widening and deepening. Much ecological degradation in the North and the South today is attributable to social inequalities, power imbalances and corporate and governmental practices. As the environmental justice movement recognizes today, environmental protection and social justice are inherently interlinked issues. Furthermore, as environmental justice activists point out, immigration is not a fundamental cause of environmental degradation in the US. Rather, "agribusiness water consumption, auto-dependent transportation systems, rising levels of industrial and consumer waste, and deficient recycling programs" and other factors associated with unbridled economic growth are the more critical issues in environmental degradation in the US.[28]

The Soviet Union and Eastern Europe under the former Communist regimes also experienced some of the worst forms of ecological degradation. Socialism, defined as an economic system controlled by direct producers producing use values for human benefit rather than commodities for profit, does not necessitate such ecological depredation. However, like the capitalist economies, the Communist regimes pursued rapid industrialization and economic growth based on exploitation of natural resources and the development of environmentally faulty technologies such as nuclear power. It can be argued that the environmental record of Communism, especially that of the Soviet Union, was the result of state capitalism and a "hierarchical, state-directed war economy caught up in a protracted Cold War" rather than the product of a genuinely socialist mode of production.[29]

Be that as it may, the Cold War was largely a conflict between capitalism and Communism over the control of the Third World. 'Ecological imperialism' continues to be a determining aspect of the exploitative relationship between the North and the South. Ecological or environmental imperialism increasingly determines the relationship between the human population and natural resources and the population carrying capacity of regional ecosystems.

Indeed, more and more areas in the world have become what some analysts call 'Malthustans', that is, environmentally degraded regions where natural resources and population are out of balance, at least in the short term. Certain hill regions in South-East Asia, desertified areas across Sub-Saharan Africa and cleared rainforests in South America are examples of such areas.[30] While neo-Malthusians attribute the creation of such environmentally depleted areas to population pressure, they fail to explore how the confluence of commercial exploitation of forests, industrialized agriculture, debt and structural adjustment, widening social inequalities, poverty, militarism and other externally induced forces have contributed to the destruction of local ecosystems. We examine some of these forces in the remaining sections of this chapter.

Ecological Imperialism

Much of the environmental and social destruction today is attributable to transnational corporations, the biggest actors in the global economy. Transnational corporations are much greater predators of the tropical forests than the small farmers and shifting cultivators who are identified as the main destroyers of the forests by neo-Malthusian analysts.

This is clearly evident in the production of oil, the life-blood of the industrial world economy. For example, between 1972 and 1989, a pipeline constructed by Texaco to carry oil from the Amazon to the Pacific Coast ruptured at least 27 times, spilling some 17 million gallons of raw crude oil, that is, one-and-a-half times more than the *Exxon Valdez* spilled off the

Alaskan coast. As a result, "Rivers turned black, wildlife died in droves and ... humans experienced exceptionally high rates of illness and birth defects."[31] Arguably the indirect damage was worse. Roads Texaco built to open up the rain forest led to massive losses of plant and animal species and poverty and decline of indigenous tribes. Large numbers of poor peasants who poured in to colonize the newly opened areas found a choice only between "cleaning up oil spills with their bare hands ... or farming soil that was too poor and polluted to sustain decent crops and livestock".[32]

Still, the massive production of oil continues. In the Ecuadorian Amazon, for example, 300,000 barrels of crude petroleum are dredged up every day by oil companies. Upon refinement, half of it ends up in gas tanks in the United States as Regular, Unleaded and Super-gasoline. While US citizens drive around in their fancy automobiles, the oil workers each make about two dollars a day and the native Indians robbed of their lands are joining the ranks of the desperately poor.[33]

Much of global deforestation is also attributable to corporate giants such as Mitsubishi, Maxus and Georgia Pacific, who are tearing apart millions of acres of tropical rainforest to supply timber for Japan, North America and Europe.[34] Japan uses up almost one-third of the world's annual tropical wood export production, including 70% of the Philippines' output and 90% of Malaysia's output. In Burma, the Philippines and other countries too, local rulers in partnership with foreign capital are rapidly depleting forest reserves, extinguishing biodiversity in the process. Burma possesses many of the world's remaining teak trees, but due to logging, the country is now losing 800,000 hectares of forest every year. As a 1990 report by the environmental network Friends of the Earth notes, if the present rate of logging continues, then, in less than three years, Burma's teak forests will be "completely logged out".[35]

There is no inevitable relationship between population pressure and deforestation, as assumed by the Malthusians. Rather, as David Kummer has demonstrated in relation to the Philippines, deforestation is a "reflection of an entire socioeconomic system and the international context in which it is developing".[36] Studies of cattle ranching in the Amazon and of wood stock depletion in Sub-Saharan Africa also show that nationally and internationally imposed political and economic conditions including government policies and international lending were more significant causes of explosive rates in deforestation than demographic factors. These local-level studies demonstrate that, at best, population growth was one variable in a multiple feedback system and not the determining factor.[37]

A number of institutions and plans such as the International Tropical Timber Organization (ITTO) and the World Bank's Tropical Forest Action Plan (TFAP) have been put forward to safeguard the world's dwindling forests in recent years. But as Third World environmental activists have pointed out, these institutions and plans still place external commercial interests before environmental protection and the rights of local people. Apparently, the ITTO tends to act as a cover for rampant logging and the TFAP takes forestry away from the control of communities, making it a capital-intensive activity dominated by commercial plantations.[38]

Billions of dollars in financial capital and technical assistance have also been invested by TNCs, MDBs (multilateral development banks), the World Bank and USAID in the global beef industry. However, large-scale ranching for beef export leads to problems of severe deforestation and soil degradation. For example, in Botswana, an $18 million World Bank project designed to increase beef production for export by 50%, has exacerbated the country's already severe grazing problems. Over 25% of the entire land mass of Central America has also been converted into permanent pasture for beef export with the support of financial and technical assistance from the North. As a result, forests have dwindled and many major species of wildlife are threatened with extinction.[39]

Similarly, marine ecosystems, including coral reefs, mangroves and sea grasses in the tropics, are being rapidly depleted due to extremely destructive methods of fish farming and the explosive growth of tourism during the last two decades.[40] "Under an avalanche of pink-fleshed sun seekers", coral reefs have suffered some form of damage in more than 50 countries, increasing soil erosion, loss of biodiversity and other major ecological problems.[41] Most of the earnings from tourism are also exported out of the South by the multinational firms that dominate the industry.[42] The environmental and social destruction associated with capitalist growth is perhaps even more apparent in the case of modern agriculture than other sectors of capitalist production.[43]

Agriculture, Poverty and the Environment

Historical analyses reveal that the roots of contemporary famine and desertification lie in capitalist farming practices. While the desertification of the Sahel has often been blamed on population pressure, over-grazing of cattle and over-cultivation by the poor, it is large-scale monocrop cultivation for export that set in motion damaging processes of environmental degradation as well as poverty.[44] In Niger alone, the extent of land given to peanut cultivation tripled between 1954 and 1968, causing a large reduction in fallow land. Consequently nomadic pastoralists had to move to other lands less suited for grazing and farming. The result was the turning of "moderate-to-poor farmland into poor land, and poor land into useless land".[45]

In many areas where the Green Revolution took place, the confluence of mechanization and commercialization of agriculture has benefited the large farmers at the expense of the smaller farmers. In the Muda River region of Malaysia, for example, the rich farmers with disposable income began to buy up land from the poor farmers, driving the bottom sector of the community to take up tenant farming, be pressurized off the lands or resort to environmentally damaging practices such as slash and burn farming in the forests.[46]

A 1992 study by the World Resources Institute shows that in the Philippines, when unemployment and poverty were worsened by structural adjustment policies, millions of poor people went into the forested regions and marginal lands as migrants and began to eke out a subsistence livelihood as shifting cultivators. But their struggle to survive has "accelerated the degradation and deforestation of upper watersheds and the exploitation of coastal fisheries and mangroves", among other environmental problems.[47]

Another study by the World Resources Institute comparing the Philippines and Costa Rica shows that in Costa Rica, where population density is much lower than in the Philippines, soils have still been badly damaged due to widespread conversion of forest into cattle pasture and economic policies that depressed wages and increased unemployment. There, too, economic slumps "precipitated by the debt crisis" forced millions of unemployed or under-employed workers and their families "to migrate to forested areas, invading marginal lands that represented their last resort".[48] As areas ill-suited to agriculture were turned into cropland and pasture by poor migrants, forest and soil resources were lost.[49] These studies show that population density and natural resource depletion "cannot be correlated in any fixed way since such factors as poverty and land-tenure policies mediate what happens to the resource base".[50]

As export production continues to expand, restricting land and other resources available for the subsistence of the masses of people, the poor are forced to survive, often, by cultivating marginal lands and over-utilizing forest and ocean resources, thus destroying their own resource bases and the population carrying capacity of their environments.[51] The result is a continuing cycle of poverty, environmental destruction and population pressure. While the Malthusians blame this vicious cycle largely on 'overpopulation', they fail to examine how the forces of capital accumulation and technological expansion create the problems of overshooting carrying capacity, population–environment imbalance as well as women's poverty.

Women and the environment

As their environment becomes fragile, fuelwood, water, soil and other natural resources become more and more scarce. In such circumstances, the poor have to spend increasing amounts of time collecting fuelwood and fodder, fetching water, and so on. As these are generally considered women's work, the increasing work hours have also to be borne by women.

In a study of the interlinkages between gender, environment and poverty in India, economist Bina Agarwal has demonstrated that increasing appropriation of natural resources by the state and a small class of individuals has adversely affected poor rural women. The adverse effects include increasing time and energy put in by women and girls for fuel, fodder and water collection; decrease in women's earnings from agriculture and non-timber forest products; erosion of social support networks by women; decline in women's traditional knowledge of plants and species; and worsening of health and nutrition of household members and women in particular.[52] As ecologist Anil Agarwal has also observed in relation to India, women bear the brunt of 'eco-catastrophes'. "[Y]ear after weary year, fuel and fodder collection time periods increase. In many parts the women may have literally reached their carrying capacities".[53]

In Nepal, too, where the forests have receded to half their original extent over the last decade, women's daily journey to collect fuel and fodder has increased by more than an hour, their work day in the field has shortened as a result and family incomes and diets have deteriorated. Deforestation and childhood malnutrition rates are closely coupled. It has been reported that "In the hills of Nepal ... the health of a village's children can be read in the retreating tree line on surrounding slopes."[54] As earlier discussed, when women's workloads increase, their need for children to share the increased work burdens also intensifies. The social conditions of high fertility are further exacerbated by the existing high rates of infant mortality.[55]

As the main subsistence producers, women have historically been the protectors of forests and natural resources. In many regions in both the South and the North, they continue to be the main defenders of their resource bases and the environment against the onslaught of external forces. The case of the Chipko women in India who hug the trees to protect them from timber contractors is perhaps the most well-known example.[56]

Yet, at the same time, increasing poverty is also leading some women to over-exploit their resource bases and thereby to contribute to environmental destruction. But both the relatively high birth rates of poor women and any responsibility they bear towards environmental destruction need to be seen in the context of their increased economic marginalization. In other words, women's inevitable recourse to the 'natural' environment as a safety valve has to be understood in the context of the global political and economic forces that have produced the feminization of poverty.[57]

In exploring the politico-economic roots of environmental destruction, it is necessary to look at both the social relations of modern agriculture and its technologies of production.

Industrialized agriculture

While monocrop industrialized farming is profitable and increases food returns in the short term, in the long term it threatens the earth's capacity for food production. Large-scale monocrop cultivation developed by agribusiness corporations is more fragile and vulnerable than the older, more balanced complex multicrop systems of small farmers and shifting cultivators.[58]

The first Green Revolution of the 1950s and 1960s, for example, created a style of agriculture that is highly profitable to agro-chemical and bio-technology corporations. But the high-yielding varieties of seeds introduced increased farmers' dependence on mechanization and expensive imports such as petroleum-based fertilizers and pesticides as well as energy-intensive irrigation. Heavy use of such products led to steady and often irreversible deterioration of the soil resulting in famines, pest invasions, loss of bio-diversity and other disastrous consequences.[59] The extensive processing, packaging and transportation involved in the far-flung agribusiness food system are also major causes of resource depletion and environmental destruction.

World Bank support for export agriculture in the Third World has often aggravated these problems. For example, of $85 million allocated by the World Bank for its third Agricultural Rehabilitation Program (ARP) in Sudan in 1987, $50 million was earmarked for pesticides for the 1987–1988 cotton crop. As a report issued by the Bank Information Center, which watches World Bank activities, points out, the replacement of tradi-tional crop rotation methods with monocrop cotton production by external institutions like the World Bank has increased the costs of agricultural pro-duction. The cost of pesticide inputs alone amounted to a third of the value of the total cotton crop in Sudan in 1989.[60]

Farm workers around the world are routinely exposed to heavy doses of pesticides and other chemicals. Agribusiness companies from the North continue to use chemicals banned in the North in their plantations in the South due to lax environmental, legal and occupational protection in the latter. For example, owing to the use of the fumigant DBCP (dibromo-chloropropane), thousands of agricultural workers have been involuntarily sterilized; they also fear that the pesticide may have caused birth defects and cancer among workers and their families.[61]

Farm workers are not the only ones who suffer from the use of chemi-cals. Most of the food and drinks people consume in the world today carry health risks stemming from the 'circle of poison' created by high-tech agriculture. In some regions, even women's breast milk is contaminated due to proliferation of chemicals.[62] Some scientists have also warned that man-made chemicals are severely undermining the reproductive health of plants, animals and humans the world over. They fear that even though the use of DDT (dichlorodiphenyltricholroethane) and PCBs (polychlorin-ated biphenyls), which are suspected to lower sperm count, have been discontinued in the North, they are widely being promoted in the South, while still newer types of hormone-disrupting chemicals continue to be introduced across the world.[63] Indeed, as ecologist Edward Goldsmith warns us, "Just about every living creature on earth now contains in its body traces of agricultural and industrial chemicals – many of which are known or suspected carcinogens or mutagens."[64] New developments in the areas of biotechnology and global trade and environmental policies such as GATT further threaten rather than support ecological and human survival.

GATT and new developments

Current restructuring of global agriculture through the biotechnology revolution involves new forms of dependency on mechanical processes and agricultural chemicals as well as genetic manipulation. The new biotechnology and genetic engineering seek to alter the very structure of life by changing the genetic base of plants, animals and humans. Although these efforts are generally seen as examples of technological and economic growth and progress, they could unravel the web of life, causing irreversible damage to ecological balance. As critics like Indian physicist Vandana Shiva explain, among other problems, gene manipulation and the creation of more and more hybrid varieties threaten the survival of traditional seed varieties and biodiversity.[65]

Research centres and genetic resource centres established in the Third World with foreign assistance have become vehicles for extracting plant genetic resources to the gene banks of Europe, North America and Japan. For example, Union Carbide is said to be collecting germplasm of agricultural crops from the north-east regions of India and sending them to its headquarters in the USA.[66] Ultimately, the goal of high-tech agriculture is not merely corporate control of nature but its rejection. According to MIT economist Robert Solow, "The world can, in effect, get along without natural resources, so exhaustion is just an event, not a catastrophe." Vandana Shiva points out that Solow was awarded the Nobel Prize in Economics in 1987 for his theory of growth based on the dispensability of nature.[67]

The recently implemented GATT constitutes an important instrument in the intensification of natural resource extraction in the name of economic growth. The definitions of intellectual property rights advanced in GATT shift control and ownership of global biodiversity from Third World farmers and indigenous people to corporations in the North producing manufactured items using gene materials.[68] There have already been cases where GATT has determined environmental regulations to be 'illegal barriers to trade' and activists fear that GATT will further the trend of putting trade and the interests of corporations before that of the environment and of farmers and indigenous people. For example, owing to the new intellectual property rights and patents imposed on plants, farmers will no longer be able to save their seed for 'sowing in the next year'.[69]

Another cause for concern is the US approach to the Convention on Biological Diversity aimed at preserving endangered species of plants and animals, which was adopted at the UNCED in Rio in 1992. The Bush administration refused to sign it, fearing it would endanger US patents on biotechnology products. The Clinton administration later signed on to it, although the US has yet to ratify it. In signing the Convention, however, the US added its own 'interpretative statement' to ensure that US companies would not have to share patent rights with Third World countries that provide the genetic resources for their products. The task of implementing this important Convention is also hampered by the lack of financial support from the US and other industrialized countries in the North.[70]

Another development which could undermine global efforts towards ecological sustainability and democracy is the power given to the World Bank over the Global Environmental Facility (GEF), which was also put in place at the Rio Earth Summit in 1992. GEF is the mechanism for allocating funds to pay for the costs arising from the implementation of Agenda 21, the global action plan designed to protect the environment in the twenty-first century. However, as Third World environmental groups point out, authority given to the World Bank to approve GEF projects without any checks from any other body could only augment the ecological imperialism of the North over the South.[71]

Yet another controversial aspect of capitalist, high-tech agriculture that is of great concern to environmentalists is the building of massive infrastructural projects such as dams and highways, and massive population transfers to facilitate such developments. These projects are also funded by the North, frequently by the World Bank as the main lender.

Dams

All the major river valleys in the world are being lined with reservoirs. The World Bank is the largest single financing source for large dam projects: it has provided over $54 billion (in constant 1992 dollars) towards 530 dams in 92 countries.[72] Development of cheap hydropower, expansion of large-scale export agriculture, local rulers' desire for prestigious projects and western engineering companies' search for lucrative .contracts are some of the major reasons for undertaking these massive dams. By financing large dam projects, hailed as 'temples of development', the World Bank has been able to exercise control not only over rivers and water resources but also over Third World energy, agriculture, land and people in general.[73]

The Bank is increasingly using the language of "sustainable growth" in its publications and pronouncements. Despite this green coloring, the era of the World Bank's 'top-down' centralized economic planning 'secrecy' in project formulation and lack of economic accountability to local people is not over. Third World environmentalists point out that the mega-projects of the World Bank are planned by "short-sighted, self-interested technocrats and bureaucrats ... in distant boardrooms" without the participation of local women and men who are most affected.[74] As a result, projects have tended to fail, with disastrous consequences for the poor and the environment. Evidence from around the world shows that large dams lead to the wholesale destruction of agricultural land, forests, the ecology of riverine systems and economies and cultures of native people. Monies allocated have often been pilfered and dams have frequently been hastily constructed, even where geologists and others have warned of dire consequences.[75] Floods that have killed thousands in Bangladesh, the Philippines and other countries raise questions about the continuation of massive dam building in fragile ecosystems. Recent floods that hit areas in the Philippines never previously affected by floods have usually been attributed to deforestation caused by illegal logging and over-cultivation on fragile mountainsides by the poor.[76]

Mainstream media accounts tend to blame such problems on population pressure and poverty, which indeed do exacerbate them. But deeper investigation reveals that it is the forces of technological and capitalist expansion such as massive irrigation projects of the World Bank and structural adjustment policies that underlie many of these problems.[77]

Environmental activists also fear that the land in the Third World that is irrigated with large dams will be turned into salt deserts and that the increasing salinity of the water and the land may have already reduced crop yields in many Third World countries by as much as 50%.[78] In addition, it has been shown that pressure applied to fragile ecological structures by vast dams often gives rise to earthquakes. Major earthquakes have occurred in several large reservoirs in China, Rhodesia (Zimbabwe), Greece and India in the past.[79] A recent earthquake that killed hundreds of people in the Himalayas has led to demands for urgent reconsideration of World Bank-sponsored irrigation projects in Nepal and the building of the 850-foot Tehri Dam in India. In spite of protests by environmentalists (including long fasts by well-known activist Sunderlal Bahuguna), building of the controversial Tehri Dam continues.[80] However, owing to local and international protests against lack of proper environmental assessment and plans to resettle an estimated 200,000 whose lands were to be submerged by damming, the World Bank was forced to withdraw support for building the Sardar Sarovar Dam on the Narmada River in India in 1993.[81]

The Three Gorges Dam on the Yangtze river in China being planned by the Chinese government would construct the world's largest hydroelectric dam. It would flood large areas of fertile land, displace more than half a million people and may lead to increased state repression, among other problems. While the World Bank was involved in initial feasibility studies, neither the Bank nor the US government has committed funds for the Three Gorges Dam. However, Canada, Germany and Japan have committed export credit towards this project.[82]

It is a wise move on the part of the World Bank to withdraw support from controversial projects. A high-level team from the World Bank which conducted an internal investigation of its own projects concluded that 37.5% of Bank projects completed in 1991, especially projects in water supply and the agricultural sector, were failures. The team also concluded that 30% of the projects which were in their fourth and fifth years of implementation in 1991 also had major problems.[83]

In fact, some of the gravest failures have been made in World Bank-sponsored population transfers and population resettlement programs around the world. Malthusian analysts who attribute the massive increase in economic and 'environmental' refugees in the world to 'overpopulation' fail to see the extent to which the problems of homelessness and migration are attributable to World Bank-financed mega-projects such as irrigation and transportation projects, transmigration schemes, and so on.

Population displacement

The uprooting of thousands of poor people from traditional homelands and their relocation in alien territories in the name of development has resulted frequently in serious bureaucratic and technical failures, massive cultural disruptions, poverty and destitution as well as environmental destruction. As Leonard Sklar of the International Rivers Network has observed:

> Bank-funded large dams have turned millions of men, women and children into refugees on their own land, including 57,000 Tonga people flooded by the Kariba Dam on the Zambesi River, 70,000 Kuna Indians displaced by Panama's Bayno Dam, 24,000 Indonesian villagers, some of whom clung to their rooftops as the waters rose behind Kedung Ombo Dam, and the 80,000 farmers of the Volta River valley in Ghana, forced from their homes by the Akosombo Dam.[84]

Between 1979 and 1985, 750,000 poor people in the world were forcibly resettled by World Bank-sponsored projects. Between 1985 and 1993 this number increased to 2.5 million. New World Bank projects expected to be approved by 1997 are estimated to forcibly resettle 600,000 more people.[85] As anthropologist Thayer Scudder, who worked on several Bank projects, has concluded, "forced resettlement is about the worst thing you can do to a people, next to killing them".[86] Indeed, it can result in cultural genocide.

An example of a disastrous project is the World Bank- and Asian Development Bank-sponsored Transmigration Project in Indonesia, aimed specifically at solving the 'population problem'. It involved resettling 500,000 'surplus' Javanese every year from heavily populated Java into the outer islands sparsely populated by tribal peoples. The government's specific objective was to "integrate all ethnic groups into one nation" so that the "different ethnic groups will in the long run disappear". This program, begun in the 1970s, is considered to be history's most ambitious transmigration project. However, the forced integration of different ethnic groups, resettlement of migrants on poor soils and lack of compensation to tribal people for lost lands have created so much discontent that the project has had to be carried out by the Indonesian army.[87]

Lacking other survival options, the migrants in Indonesia have had to depend increasingly on clearing more and more rainforest for slash-and-burn cultivation. But, as the invasion of tribal lands continues, the tribal people and their way of life are rapidly disappearing. Furthermore, as Martha Belcher, the Rainforest Action Network's South-East Asia specialist has pointed out, transmigration in Indonesia has allowed the government and companies to work together to obtain cheap labor for logging concessions, creating a situation that is "tantamount to slavery".[88]

Another controversial World Bank project is the Polonoroeste Colonization Scheme in the Brazilian Amazon. This $1.6 billion project with $434 million in World Bank loans cut a 900-mile highway through the Amazon rainforest and resettled over 500,000 rural poor. Instead of the excellent farmland promised by the government, the settlers in Polonoroeste found only "poor soils unsuitable for agriculture, conflicts with indigenous people and rampant disease". Seeking land that would sustain them, the settlers here, like so many other forcibly resettled 'development refugees' elsewhere, have cleared more and more forest and, as a result, this area now has the highest rate of deforestation in the Brazilian Amazon. As elsewhere, deforestation here has resulted in the disappearance of hundreds of plant and animal species. Lacking resistance to diseases brought in by the settlers, the indigenous groups in the areas are also being rapidly extinguished.[89]

Still another example of a controversial irrigation cum resettlement project is the $1.5 billion Mahaweli River Project in Sri Lanka, funded by the World Bank and other donors and estimated to cover 39% of the whole island. While the Project was originally to be completed in 30 years, it was later telescoped into six years in the name of 'accelerated development'. However, as Sri Lankan researchers and journalists have pointed out, the ecological balance of the hill country and perhaps of the whole island is threatened due to faulty construction of dams and reservoirs. Among other problems, forest habitats of elephants have been diminished, resulting in elephant encroachment on peasant lands. The loss of habitats and attacks from peasants protecting their crops will hasten the extinction of elephants.[90]

Political patronage, caste and class politics associated with the Mahaweli Project have also given rise to a process of rapid class as well as gender differentiation. The powerlessness and anomie created by involuntary population transfers and resettlement of people in new regions have increased domestic violence and suicide. In addition, the government's leasing of thousands of newly irrigated Mahaweli lands to transnational corporations to cultivate export crops like tobacco, using peasants as contract labor, has made a mockery of the government and the World Bank's alleged commitment to national food self-sufficiency and the perpetuation of the smallholder peasantry.[91]

Women and population resettlement

Not only have resettlement policies privatized nature and extended capitalist class relations, they have also introduced norms of male authority even when they did not previously exist. For example, whereas traditionally in Sri Lanka a married woman could hold land, in the Mahaweli settlements only the husband is entitled to receive land; the family plot is always registered in his name. As Dutch researcher Ragnhild Lund observed in one of the early Mahaweli settlement areas, "if the woman wants to divorce her husband, she is deprived of the means of subsistence and she has no right to the family land. Consequently the woman is dependent on and subordinate to the husband."[92]

Lund also shows that despite women's work in all sectors of production in the Mahaweli settlements, credit and membership in farmers cooperatives are open only to those owning land – the men. In the provision of technology, skills and other services too, women's roles as co-producers are ignored by agricultural planners and administrators, who are almost always males. As a result, women's labor tends to be more tedious and less productive than men's labor. Much of the agricultural work women do is considered family labor and women do not receive wages for it. The earnings from the family farm generally go to the male, the head of the household and the property owner.[93]

The Mahaweli Program is not unusual. Other peasant resettlement schemes in the Third World, such as the Kano River Project in Nigeria and the Ai-Batang Hydroelectric Project in Malaysia, have also reversed earlier customs that guaranteed women certain economic and social securities.[94] As an internal Bank review of its resettlement projects has itself noted, women are often worse hit by resettlement than men because women tend to rely more on common property and to be engaged in home-based business ventures.[95]

The environmental and social destruction associated with dams and massive hydroelectricity projects is not restricted to the South. In Northern Quebec, near James Bay, a vast series of hydroelectric reservoirs are being built despite growing opposition by indigenous people and environmentalists. These projects will inundate the lands of the Cree, Naskapi and Inuit Indians, destroying their hunting and trapping way of life. As Winona LaDuke, native lands rights and environmental activist, says, when these projects arrive, "there are huge increases in domestic violence and suicide rates, as well as other social and economic problems. That's an example that is repeated across northern Canada, in Saskatchewan and all through the Arctic...."[96]

The debt crisis and IMF and World Bank stabilization policies introduced since the early 1980s have also exacerbated the twin problems of poverty and environmental degradation in the Third World. While the debt crisis and SAPs were discussed in relation to worsening global poverty in the last chapter, we shall consider the debt and SAPs as forms of ecological imperialism here.

Debt and structural adjustment

Adjustment-related pressures to increase exports have contributed to increasing deforestation and depletion of other natural resources in the Third World. There has been a 90% increase in global deforestation since 1981, and, as economist Richard Gerster has pointed out, "the accelerated deforestation that took place in the 1980s may ... not be an accident, but due, at least, in part, to the debt crisis".[97]

In Ghana, which is considered an exemplar of successful structural adjustment, timber exports nearly tripled between 1984 and 1987 due to adjustment pressures.[98] All the leading exporters of tropical woods, such as Brazil, Côte d'Ivoire and Indonesia, are highly indebted countries. As Brazilian labor leader Lula da Silva says, "If the Amazon region is the lung of the world, debt is a lung infection", in other words, unless the debt is remissed or alleviated, deforestation cannot be halted.[99]

Pressures to export shrimp in order to improve foreign exchange are also leading to destruction of ocean ecosystems and creating other problems such as flooding and soil salination. In Ecuador, 10,000 hectares of mangrove swamp have been cleared for commercial shrimp farming. As a result, unprotected agricultural land gets flooded during storms. In the island of Negros in the Philippines, too, shrimp farming for export has been introduced 'with commercial success'. But heavy demand for water by commercial farming poses many dangers, including lowering water tables and increasing soil salinity.[100]

IMF and World Bank policies promoting export-led growth undermine sustainable development in a number of indirect ways as well. Efforts by Third World nations to cut costs in order to make exports more competitive internationally frequently lead to removal of environmental protection regulations. Reductions in state spending due to stabilization policies also leave less money for enforcement of environmental protection laws. As natural resources continues to be undervalued and environmental destruction unaccounted in GNP calculations, the tremendous loss of future productive capacity continues to be disregarded in the calculations of economic growth and productivity such as the GNP.[101]

In recent years, 'debt-for-nature' swaps have been proposed as a means for relieving the Third World debt. These exchanges are based on the idea of 'purchasing the liabilities' of Third World countries at a reduced price and turning them over to Third World governments, on the understanding that they provide local currency, in turn, for financing environmental projects.[102] Admittedly, 'debt-for-nature' represents an important strategy to address both environmental protection and debt remission simultaneously. But, as the critics argue, illegitimate debts of corrupt business people or dictators in the Third World could be 'acknowledged instead of disallowed', compelling the poor to carry the costs of debt-for-nature transactions. Not only is the value of debt-for-nature transactions still very small in relation to the total Third World debt, but, as some critics point out, debt-for-nature could be used by the North to control the South, resulting in "one more instrument of domination of the North over the South, but this time with a green coloration".[103]

Malthusian policy makers blame Third World population growth and urban congestion for much of global soil, water and air pollution. However, closer examination shows that the shift of polluting industrial manufacturing plants, toxic wastes, military testing and wars by the North to the South is the crucial factor shaping the relationship between population and environmental pollution. Like modern agriculture, modern manufacturing is greatly responsible for the crash of ecosystems and reduction of sustainability and carrying capacity of habitats around the world.

Industrial Manufacturing

As discussed earlier, with global economic restructuring, transnational corporations have been increasingly shifting their production facilities to the Third World. The reason for this is not only the availability of cheap labor but also the laxity of environmental regulations. As noted above, structural adjustment policies that promote exports have frequently resulted in slashing of state environmental protection regulations. Policies promoting rapid economic growth have also undermined workers' right to organize and to demand healthy working and environmental conditions.

Most locally owned and foreign-owned industries using and producing toxic materials tend to be located in poor neighborhoods worldwide. As a result, it is the poor who suffer the most. The case of the US transnational chemical manufacturer Union Carbide in Bhopal, India, is perhaps the most well known. The Bhopal disaster in 1984, which killed thousands and injured several hundred thousands permanently when more than 40 tons of deadly toxic gases escaped into the atmosphere has been "misleadingly termed an accident".[104] But, as Bhopal-based journalist Raj Kumar Keswani warned three years prior to the event, given the deplorable conditions in the factory, the disaster was programmed to happen.[105] Many see Union Carbide's settlement with the Indian government for $460 million (much less than the $3.3 billion originally sought) as a "sellout", "hopelessly inadequate to deal with the needs of the victims". In 1989, five years after the disaster, the victims had not yet received financial compensation from any source at all.[106]

To date, there has been no scientific survey of the population affected by the disaster. As is usually the case, women have suffered disproportionate effects; but their needs have been neglected. Despite the requests made by some women's groups, ultrasound monitoring facilities and additional abortion services were not set up in Bhopal. Government officials told women who dared to ask about abortion that they were being unnecessarily 'alarmist'. While Union Carbide claimed that the gas exposure did not cause genetic or reproductive disorders, a survey by a Bombay women's medical group showed that among other fertility-related problems experienced by pregnant women in Bhopal the rate of spontaneous abortion soared from 9% in 1984 to 31% in 1985.[107] Given the deep-rooted patriarchy of the society, women maimed and blinded by the poisoning have not always received care and nurturing from their families either. In fact, the Bhopal disaster has led to a pattern of domestic violence, abandonment and divorce against women who have been left childless or infertile due to the poisoning.[108]

Since the disaster, Union Carbide has sold some of its least profitable divisions and has regained its status on the stock market. As one Union Carbide official has put it, "as far as the Company is concerned, the matter is over".[109] Despite its disastrous effects, the Bhopal case has not been used to challenge the development of petrochemicals that cause irreversible damage to the environment and people. The production, trade and use of toxic materials continue as before, thus ensuring that "Bhopal will continue to happen".[110]

Export production

One sector where extremely hazardous environmental and working conditions prevail is export manufacturing in the so-called 'free-trade zones', enclaves which produce mostly garments and electronics exclusively for export. Young women who are the labor force in these zones are frequent victims of exploitative working conditions and environmental hazards. Sweat shops in the US – most of them employing immigrant female labor – are beset with similar problems.

In some cases, the hazardous conditions have even led to deaths of women workers. Take the case of the Kader Company, a joint Thai and Taiwanese enterprise based in Bangkok, Thailand, manufacturing Bart Simpson and Cabbage Patch dolls, model trains, teddy bears and other toys for export to children in the North. Kader employed 2,000 workers, most of whom were young women from the rural areas. In May 1992, a fire killed 188 and injured 379 women when the Kader factory collapsed. Despite workers' charges, Kader claimed limited responsibility, arguing that it had no management control over the factory.[111] In July 1993, 10 more women workers between the ages of 14 and 21 were killed in a fire that occurred in a garment factory in a suburb of Bangkok.[112] In the absence of international environmental and legal regulations to control companies, such disasters are likely to increase.

Rarely does management inform workers of the dangers of chemicals they handle or provide them with protective equipment and facilities. As a result, chemical poisonings of women factory workers are fairly common. An example is the case of women workers of Bartleet Microdevices, a jointly owned Sri Lankan and Japanese company in Sri Lanka producing audio and video heads for export to Japan. In September 1991, women workers developed rashes, headaches and fainting attacks. The company was not charged or punished; only some 'corrective measures' were undertaken.[113]

However, women at Bartleet Microdevices continued to develop headaches, dizziness and nausea and in May 1992 many women had to be hospitalized. At first the company treated the whole incident as sabotage by the workers, dismissing 900 workers after 100 of them were sent to the hospital for chemical poisoning. Owing to worker protests, they were later reinstated and a medical investigation was conducted. Medical officers from the Occupational Health Division of the Sri Lankan Ministry of Labour noted that the workers were exposed to a number of different chemicals, including cyclomethalene, acetone and methyl ethyl ketone. While workers maintained that about 45 types of chemicals were used in the factory, only 15 types were shown to the medical officers.[114]

Despite all the dangers to human and planetary health, corporations and multilateral development agencies are seeking new ways to promote environmentally risky industries in the Third World. A confidential memo written by the chief economist at the World Bank, Lawrence Summers, on December 12, 1991, explicitly called for export of polluting industries to the Third World on the grounds of cost-effectiveness. Among his arguments were that the "demand for a clean environment for aesthetic and health reasons is likely to have very high income elasticity" and that a "given amount of health-impairing pollution should be done in the country with the lowest cost, which will be the country with the lowest wages".[115] Summers has since resigned from the World Bank, but he now serves as the Deputy Treasury Secretary of the US government.

Not only are corporations producing and using toxic materials without restraint in the Third World, but many transnational corporations based in the North have also begun to export their toxic wastes to the South. A close parallel can be observed here between industrial waste dumping and other types of corporate dumping, for example the dumping of dangerous contraceptives and cigarettes in the South. Toxic dumping is a new growth industry for the Third World and has disastrous implications for environmental sustainability and human health, especially women's reproductive health. However, the 'new' Malthusian reproductive rights agenda, which is narrowly focused on contraceptive choice, has not taken up these problems caused by transnational corporate expansion.

Toxic dumping

Owing to legal restrictions on toxic waste dumping and public opposition to this practice in the US and other western countries, waste management companies are seeking alternative dumping sites in the Third World. Many governments in western Africa as well as some islands in the Caribbean and the Pacific have been lured with offers of large sums of money by western companies to turn their lands into toxic waste dumping grounds.

For example, between August 1987 and May 1988, almost 4,000 tons of toxic wastes were dumped in Koko, Nigeria. As a result, there has been an increase in the number of cholera patients and premature births. In February 1988, a shipment of garbage and incinerator ash from Philadelphia was dumped on Kassa Island in Guinea. It reportedly "caused trees on the island to turn brown and die". American Cynamid exports 100 tons of mercury wastes each year to Thor Chemicals in Cato Ridge, South Africa. The mercury has contaminated the nearby marshes and Mngeweni River, which flows down into a valley where the local population uses the water for drinking, cooking and washing.[116] It is a great irony that while the South exports its most precious natural and human resources to the North, it receives from it in return debt, weapons and toxic wastes.

As in the Third World, polluting industries, including nuclear facilities, tend to be located in poor neighborhoods in the US. Hundreds of Native American tribes in the US are now being approached by the US government and waste disposal companies looking for new dumping grounds for toxic, nuclear, medical and solid waste. Established companies like Bechtel and Waste Tech (a subsidiary of Amoco oil), joined by 'fly-by-night operators', are seeking to make quick profits by converting the land still controlled by Native American people into "America's new dumping ground".[117] In 1991, there were a hundred proposals for introducing toxic waste incinerators (dumps, factories or facilities) on Native reservations throughout the US.[118] Agreements are signed between company officials and tribal official without the knowledge or approval of the tribal membership. It is in view of this relationship between race and the siting of toxic waste facilities that the term 'environmental racism' first came to be used.[119]

Lack of economic alternatives and political power also results in the neighborhoods of poor whites being chosen as dumping grounds for toxic wastes and radioactive materials as well as the location of polluting industries. For many poverty-stricken regions such as southern West Virginia, where wages are low and unemployment high, nuclear waste disposal facilities are being presented as a necessary evil. Corporations and their local business partners argue that these are growth industries with great potential for employment generation and community survival. Apparently, "even radioactive waste can seem attractive – if it has enough lures and bribes attached".[120]

The struggle over toxic dumping is growing both in the US and in other regions, and public opposition and protests have forced the rejection of some proposed dumping schemes.[121] Still, many 'sham recycling' schemes exist which involve exporting waste substances from the North for supposed 'reuse' in the Third World. For example a US firm, Stoller Chemical Company, has been exporting toxic waste disguised as fertilizer to Bangladesh as well as Australia in violation of US laws and without the knowledge and consent of either of the receiving countries. A Nigerian import firm has been soliciting toxic wastes from EC firms, suggesting that waste could be "disguised as 'edible oil'" to escape rigorous rules in the EC countries.[122]

International efforts taken against toxic dumping have not been adequate to deal with the problem. The Basel Convention on the Control of Transboundary Movement of Hazardous Wastes and their Disposal, which came into force in 1992, does not, for example, restrict the production of toxic wastes, but seeks to regulate its trade. The amendment to the Basel Convention, adopted in September 1995 by 91 countries, which bans the export of hazardous waste from OECD countries to 'developing' ones is an advancement over the previous amendments. The United States, one of the biggest exporters of hazardous and poisonous wastes to the Third World, has signed but not ratified the Convention.[123]

In a closely integrated global ecosystem, pollution cannot be prevented by export; the only lasting solution is to reduce producing pollution and for those doing it to be responsible for its safe disposal themselves. As the environmental activist group Greenpeace points out, "The price put on one ton of pollution – $120 to $450 – is a pittance when compared to the havoc a ton of pollution can wreak on our air, our water, our health – havoc we will eventually pay for."[124]

However, the corporations do not want to accept this basic ecological reality. Instead, they are devising various plans to develop a profitable trade in pollution. Already 'emissions trading' in the US allows utility companies who have not spent their total 'legal' allotments of air pollution to sell them to other companies who already have exhausted their 'rights' to pollute. Under this kind of 'free market environmentalism' the wealthier companies will be able to pollute as they like. The growth of this new industry, particularly the proposed trade in carbon dioxide emissions on the world market, would allow the rich corporations and nations to keep on pumping out pollution by paying poorer countries to pollute less. Although some Third World environmentalists support a trade in emissions as a mechanism for global justice, in the long term the expansion of such a trade will resolve neither the global ecological crisis nor the disparities in global income.[125] As Greenpeace warns, it could deepen the destruction of ecosystems and carrying capacity in the South by the North.

Under global CO_2 emissions trading, a corporation could cajole China or India into building a shoddy nuclear power plant instead of a coal-fired power plant for a few million dollars in emissions credits. While the global spreadsheet would register a 'saving' in CO_2 emissions here in the U.S., the poorer nation would be saddled with a reactor requiring expensive maintenance and potential meltdowns, radiation leaks and piles of radioactive wastes.[126]

Given that the global economy is predominantly a military economy, an examination of the relationship between industrial capitalist development and environmental destruction must be expanded to include militarism. Evidence shows that global expansion of weapons production and military activities may be far more responsible for resource depletion and environmental destruction than human population growth.

Militarism and the Environment

Protected by the rules of 'national security', armed forces and military contractors have generally been exempted from environmental regulations or they have simply ignored them.[127] Much of the available material comes from the United States, which is now the world's only military superpower. Although other nations publish less military-related information, their militaries have also been responsible for tremendous environmental destruction.

It is only after the Soviet armed forces began to withdraw from Eastern Europe that the enormous environmental destruction caused by the Soviet military was uncovered. Fuel, wastes and unexploded ammunition have been dumped in unmarked offbase locations; workers have been exposed to toxic materials; land and aquifers have been severely polluted. Some 6% of Czechoslovakia's territory is said to be despoiled, and in central Bohemia groundwater tests have revealed toxics in concentrations 30 to 50 times the allowable levels.[128]

Owing to the increasing size of armies and particularly the technological advances in weaponry, military requirements for land, air space and natural resources have steadily risen over the course of the twentieth century.[129] Nearly one-quarter of all jet fuel in the world, about 42 million tons per year, is used for military purposes. The Pentagon is considered to be the largest consumer of oil in the US and perhaps in the world (Table 6.3). One F–15 jet, at peak thrust, consumes 908 liters of fuel a minute; one B–52 bomber consumes 13,671 liters of fuel an hour; a Carrier battle group consumes 1,589,700 liters of fuel a day; and an armored division of 348 tanks consumes 2,271,000 liters of fuel a day. It has been estimated that the energy the Pentagon uses up annually is sufficient to run the entire US urban mass transit system for almost 14 years.[130]

Table 6.3 Fuel consumption and estimated air pollutant emissions of military aircraft: selected countries and world, late 1980s

Area	Fuel consumption		Emissions (thousand tons)*			
	Total (million tons)	Share (%)	CO	Hydro-carbons	NO$_x$	SO$_2$
USA	18.6	44.1	381	78	157	17.9
USSR	11.8	28.1	244	50	100	11.4
West Germany	1.5	3.5	31	6	13	1.4
World	42.2	100.0	865	178	357	40.6

* Emissions are given for carbon monoxide, nitrogen oxides and sulfur dioxide.

Source: Linda Starke, ed., *State of the World 1991*, World Watch Institute, New York: W.W. Norton and Co., 1991, p. 139.

The construction and deployment of weaponry require vast amounts of minerals besides fuel. A single land-based intercontinental missile requires 4,450 tons of steel, 1,200 tons of cement, 50 tons of aluminum, 12.5 tons of chromium, 750 kilograms of titanium and 120 kilograms of beryllium. In fact, the use of aluminum, copper, nickel and platinum for global military purposes seems to exceed the entire Third World's demand for these materials. As environmental researcher Michael Renner concludes, "the United States accounts for by far the largest share of military consumption of ... valuable raw materials".[131]

The production, maintenance and storage of conventional, chemical, biological and nuclear weapons generate enormous amounts of materials, such as "fuels, paints, solvents, heavy metals, pesticides, polychlorinated biphenyls (PCBs), cyanides, phenols, acids, alkalies, propellants, and explosives", that are inimical to human and environmental health. Military war games and other maneuvers also extend their devastation far beyond the limits of army bases by demolishing natural vegetation, disturbing wildlife habitats, eroding soil, causing flooding and damaging human health.[132]

Although little work has been done yet to calculate the military's contributions to global warming and ozone depletion, it has been estimated that total military-related carbon emissions could be as high as 10% of emissions worldwide. According to the Research Institute for Peace Policy in Starnberg, Germany, between 10 and 30% of all global environmental destruction can be attributed to military-related activities.[133]

The extent of pollution and environmental damage caused by the US Department's 375 bases (1991 figure) abroad remains 'shrouded in secrecy' because US military bases abroad are exempt from the US National Environmental Policy Act. Under basing agreements, they are also exempt from pertinent host-nation laws. Very little is known of conditions at US military installations in the Third World, although it is believed that contamination has been extensive as hazardous materials banned in the US have been used indiscriminately.[134]

In Guam, owing to the dumping of huge quantities of the solvent TCE and untreated antifreeze solutions onto the ground and into storm drains by the US Navy and the Air Force, aquifers supplying water for 75% of the island's population were contaminated. Tests have shown that at some points in the aquifer, TCE levels were six times the permissible limit.[135] A 1991 report of the General Accounting Office (GAO) stated that most US bases overseas have poor facilities for hazardous waste management. The US Navy has reported that the Subic base in the Philippines produced 500 metric tons of toxic waste annually in 1990 and 1991, but disposed of less than 20% each year. Scientists and researchers in the Philippines who have conducted on-site investigations have stated that the US has left a 'toxic legacy' at the Subic and Clark bases that they have now vacated.[136]

Although Malthusians blame overpopulation and poverty for destruction of ocean coral reefs, "the most complete and widespread destruction of coral reefs is now conducted by the U.S. military". The atoll Diego Garcia in the Indian Ocean, the "once fertile home of 2,000 people", is now almost completely covered in concrete and its biological productivity has been destroyed by US military activity.[137] Not only has militarism destroyed environmental sustainability and population carrying capacity of many regions in the world, but, like many World Bank-funded infrastructural projects, it has forcibly removed many native populations from their ancestral lands, resettling them in alien territories. These aspects of modern militarism are perhaps most apparent with regard to nuclear testing.

Nuclear testing and the environment

Nuclear war is the ultimate threat to the global environment. Nuclear weapons production alone has released radiation known to cause cancer, brain tumors, sterility, miscarriages, birth defects and a host of other human and environmental health problems. According to estimates made by anti-nuclear activist Dr Rosalie Bertell in 1988, casualties of the nuclear industry were about 16 million people worldwide.[138]

Recently released US government information shows that between the early 1940s and the early 1970s, the United States government, specifically its Department of Energy, was associated with a wide range of human radiation experiments on many different populations in the US. These included tests on pregnant women, fetuses and infants, including at least two Black women with thyroid disease and their breastfeeding infants.[139]

Hundreds of workers at nuclear sites, such as the Hanford nuclear weapons facility in Washington state (now closed), have absorbed quantities of plutonium "equal to the current lifetime limit" every six months. Apparently, the underground tanks at Hanford have released nuclear waste sufficient to produce more than 50 Nagasaki-size bombs.[140]

While the Chernobyl nuclear accident received worldwide coverage, other nuclear accidents and damage wrought on people and the environment in the former Soviet Union are less well known. Thousands of people have been exposed to radiation and rivers and the land have been severely contaminated. In Karaganda in the Soviet Union, where radiation was released during nuclear weapons testing, infant mortality is 44% higher than the Soviet average and incidents of cancer and blood diseases have sharply increased since the nuclear tests.[141]

Much of uranium (mineral used for nuclear power plants and weapons) mining and nuclear weapons testing around the world has taken place on lands stolen by major military powers and corporations from indigenous people – Native Americans and Native Canadians, Pacific Islanders, Kazakhs, Australian 'aborigines', and so on. Over 70% of all the uranium reserves in the world is estimated to lie underneath the lands of indigenous peoples. In Canada, uranium is believed to be located almost exclusively in native territories, and in the US two-thirds of the uranium, 30% of the unmined coal and an undisclosed amount of oil, copper, timber and other resources are located on Indian land.[142] In observing a close parallel between the attempt to control their lands and the widespread sterilization of native women, many native people charge the corporations as well as the population control agencies with genocide. As some Native Americans have put it: "By killing off the unborn ... [t]here will be no more Indians to hold the land."[143]

Globally, indigenous people have largely been the victims of uranium mining and the testing of nuclear weapons by global corporations and major powers.[144] Nuclear weapons testing by the US and France in the Pacific have contaminated water, the food chain and caused genetic defects and deformed births.[145] In 'French' Polynesia, for example, increases in the number of leukemia cases, brain tumors and thyroid cancers have been registered since the 1980s.[146]

In the Marshall Islands in the Pacific, where the US has been conducting nuclear tests, inhabitants of Bikini Atoll have been forcibly moved from island to island to make room for nuclear tests. As a result, the once self-sufficient islanders have led a rootless life for the past 45 years and have "ended up subsisting largely on surplus US Army food, living in grim barrack-like shelters on Ebeye" (a densely populated island).[147] The effects of the fallout from nuclear testing continue to be terrifying. One former inhabitant of Bikini, a woman named Darlene Keju-Johnson, has described the phenomenon known as 'jelly-fish babies':

...These babies are born like jelly-fish. They have no eyes. They have no heads. They have no arms. They have no legs. They do not shape like human beings at all. But they are being born on the labor table. The most colorful, ugly things you have ever seen. Some of them have hairs on them. And they breathe. This 'ugly thing' only lives for a few hours. When they die they are buried right away. A lot of times they don't allow the mother to see this kind of baby because she'll go crazy. It is too inhumane.[148]

Although the Cold War was ostensibly a conflict between the US and the USSR, it is Third World people, especially indigenous peoples like the Marshall Islanders, who have been its major victims. Yet even after the end of the so-called Cold War and protests by women activists like Darlene Keju-Johnson, the Pacific Islanders are continuing to be treated as easily disposable entities. For example, there are now reports that the United States is shipping its surplus chemical weapons from Europe to Johnston Atoll in the Pacific for incineration there.[149]

The attempts by the original nuclear powers – the US, Russia, Britain, France and China – to stop the spread of nuclear weapons are seen by some nuclear have-not nations as a case of 'nuclear imperialism' aimed at maintaining the military advantage of existing powers. The recently signed international Nuclear Non-Proliferation Treaty limits the emergence of new nuclear powers, especially among industrializing nations in the South; but it does not pay sufficient attention to the nuclear legacy and ongoing human and environmental devastation caused by the existing nuclear powers. As many non-nuclear weapons states point out, a comprehensive nuclear test ban treaty is urgently needed to control the spread of nuclear weapons and the possibility of nuclear holocaust.[150]

Warfare, environment and women's health

Virtually all of the 150 or so wars fought during the Cold War, many of them 'proxy wars' of the super-powers, took place in the Third World. Indeed, the Cold War was a period of 'hot' wars and tremendous violence, suffering and insecurity for millions of people in the Third World.[151] As we discuss in the next chapter, many of the wars in the post-Cold War period are also being fought in the South. In war-ridden areas, people are turned into corpses and refugees and the land itself is laid waste with mines and other lethal explosives. The effects on humans and on other animal and plant species are very long term.

The burning of oil wells in Kuwait during the 1991 Gulf War and extensive land-mines remaining in Afghanistan are examples of environmental destruction associated with armed conflict.[152] Afghanistan was self-sufficient in food before the Soviet military intervention. But during the intervention, villages were bombed, livestock shot and grain stores and irrigation systems destroyed. As a result, a third of the farms had to be abandoned; yields fell by up to a half; and the land cultivated by individual farms declined by approximately a third.[153]

The long-term effects of modern warfare can, perhaps, be best seen in Vietnam, where the United States fought a protracted war against Communism. During the course of the war, the US military dumped about 25 million gallons of defoliants and environmental toxins on Vietnam, including 4 million gallons of 'Agent Orange'. Between 1963 and 1968, the US Air Force dropped nearly 400,000 tons of napalm on Vietnam. Each bomb dropped blew away a "crater of precious topsoil; an estimated 25 million acres of farmland was destroyed".[154] Owing to the "bombs, napalm, defoliants and bulldozers", and so on, over half the coastal mangrove swamps were completely destroyed. As geographer Joni Seager notes, the mangrove swamps, a major stabilizer for the entire South-East Asian ecosystem, "will take more than a century to recover – if ever they do".[155] Due to degradation of farmland stemming from the war, farmers have been forced to push into the remaining forest to strip it for fuel and clear it for cultivation, thereby contributing to environmental destruction.[156]

The existence of military bases and wars has also turned many young women to prostitution. Lacking alternative modes of survival, thousands of young women in Saigon, as well as Bangkok and Manila, became prostitutes, serving the 'rest and relaxation' needs of US soldiers during the Vietnam War.[157] Many women associated with this industry have become the victims of HIV/AIDS. Wars have been waged on women's bodies in many different ways, although the neo-Malthusian reproductive rights agenda has been silent on many of those subjects.

Chemical and toxic materials released by wars threaten women's capacity for biological reproduction. For example, rates of miscarriages are elevated among Palestinian women regularly exposed to tear gas attacks in the West Bank and Gaza.[158] As Joni Seager points out, the illnesses that US veterans are now suffering due to exposure to Agent Orange "pale in comparison" with the legacy bequeathed to the Vietnamese people, especially the women and children. In Vietnam, reproductive disorders among women are extensive. Fetal death rates in pregnancy in Vietnam were 40 times higher in the early 1980s than they were in the 1950s. Vietnamese women still have the highest rate of spontaneous abortion and cervical cancer in the world and give birth to children with birth defects many years after the official end of the Vietnam War. Deformed fetuses and deformed children are the legacy of Agent Orange in Vietnam.[159] The ethics of testing new contraceptives like quinacrine on Vietnamese women must be considered in the light of continuing reproductive disorders associated with the Vietnam War.

The so-called 'Gulf War Syndrome' suffered by US and other soldiers – both men and women – who fought in the Gulf War has received some coverage in the mainstream media in the US.[160] However, the effects of the

Gulf War on the civilian population in Iraq has received scant attention. Medical experts such as Eric Hoskins, a Canadian physician who has visited post-war Iraq many times, fear that "mysterious post-war illnesses" and increasing cancers among Iraqi children may be due to exposure to nuclear waste contained in ammunition shells and radioactive bullets used by the coalition forces in the war. It is also feared that these bullets may have contaminated soil and drinking water.[161] The effects of these on Iraqi women and their reproductive health are yet to be studied.

The 'Peace Dividend' and improvements in the 'environmental performance' of the US military in the post-Cold War period has received much publicity. However, the bulk of the clean-up program of the US military has involved assessing the extent and nature of the military's contamination within the US rather than actual clean-up or evaluation of its damage across the world. Furthermore, current cutbacks in funds for the military's environmental clean-up program by the Republican-controlled Congress do not bode well for the future of this program even for the US.[162] Indeed, as will be noted in the next chapter, the claims made by the US military to be the protector of the environment in the post-Cold War era need close global scrutiny.

In the long term, the military–industrial system proves itself to be utterly irrational and based on a myopic vision of life. By weakening and destroying human and environmental reproduction, it destroys the basis of its own reproduction. In the next chapter we shall further demonstrate that the expansion of global capitalism and militarism, rather than population growth, underlie the worsening crisis of political instability and violence across the world.

Notes

1. Alan Thein Durning, *How Much is Enough? The Consumer Society and the Future of the Earth*, New York: W.W. Norton and Co., 1992, p. 27.

2. Alan Durning, "Asking How Much is Enough", *State of the World Report*, Washington, DC: World Watch Institute, 1991, p. 159.

3. Ibid., p. 158.

4. UNFPA, *State of the World Population 1990*, p. 12.

5. Durning, "Asking How Much", p. 158.

6. Ibid., p. 160; Durning, *How Much is Enough?*, Chap. 7.

7. "The Environment and Population Growth: Decade for Action", *Population Reports*, Series M, No. 10, p. 6, May 1992, Population Information Program, Johns Hopkins University; "Keynote – Green Justice", *New Internationalist*, No. 230, April 1992, pp. 4–7; Christopher Flavin, "Slowing Global Warming", *State of the World 1990*, World Watch Institute, Washington DC, 1990, pp. 17, 38.

8. Durning, "Asking How Much", p. 161.

9. UNDP, *Human Development Report 1994*, p. 36.

10. Durning, *How Much is Enough?*, pp. 56–57; see also Ehrlich et al.; *The Stork and the Plow*, p. 4; Janice Jiggins, "Don't Waste Energy? Fear of the Future", *Conscience*, Autumn 1993, p. 27; Walden Bello, "Population Control: The Real Culprits and Victims", *Third*

World Resurgence, No. 33, May 1993, pp. 11–14.

11. UNICEF, *The State of the World's Children, 1994*, p. 34; see also "Saints and Sinners", *New Internationalist*, No. 230, April 1992, p. 11.

12. Bello, "Population Control", pp. 11–14.

13. Hynes, *Taking Population Out of the Equation*, p. 15.

14. Durning, "Asking How Much", pp. 162–163.

15. Ibid., p. 163.

16. *Third World Resurgence*, Nos 14–15, Special Double Issue on the UNCED, 1991; Martin Khor, "A Year After Rio, the CSD Inches Forward...", *Third World Resurgence*, No. 36, 1993, pp. 12–13.

17. New Road Map Foundation, Seattle, Washington, *All-Consuming Passion: Waking Up From the American Dream*, 2nd edn, 1993.

18. Jacques Ellul, *The Technological System*, trans. Joachim Neugroschel, New York: Continuum, 1980, p. 325.

19. S.H. Vatsyayan, *A Sense of Time: An Exploration of Time in Theory, Experience and Art*, Delhi: Oxford University Press, 1981, pp. 32–33.

20. Wachtel, *The Poverty of Affluence*, p. 65; Norberg-Hodge, *Ancient Futures, passim*.

21. Mies, *Patriarchy and Accumulation*, pp. 232–233; see also Norberg-Hodge, *Ancient Futures*, p. 126.

22. Cited in H. Patricia Hynes, "The Pocketbook and the Pill: Reflections on Green Consumerism and Population Control", *Issues in Reproductive and Genetic Engineering*, Vol. 4. No. 1, 1991, pp. 47–52.

23. Karl Marx, *Capital*, Vol. 1, Moscow: Foreign Languages Publishing House, 1959, cited in David Pepper, *The Roots of Modern Environmentalism*, London: Routledge, 1986, p. 171.

24. Barry Commoner, "Rapid Population Growth", p. 199.

25. John Bellamy Foster, "Global Ecology and the Common Good", *Monthly Review*, Vol. 46, February 1995, p. 5.

26. Ibid.

27. Commoner, *Making Peace with the Planet*, p. 7.

28. Ann Bastian and Dana Alston, "An Update on Developments in the Environmental Justice Movements", An Open Letter to Funding Colleagues, January 1996, The New World Foundation, 100 E. 85th St., New York, N.Y 10028.

29. Foster, *The Vulnerable Planet*, pp. 101, 91.

30. Cited in Hartmann, "Dangerous Intersections", pp. 6–7.

31. Joe Kane, *Savages*, New York: Alfred A. Knopf, 1995, *passim*; Mark Hertsgaard, "What Time Is It in Huaroniland?", *New York Times Book Review*, October 15, 1995, p. 15.

32. Hertsgaard, "What Time Is It in Huaroniland?", p. 15.

33. Marc Cooper, "Rain Forest Crude", *Mother Jones*, March–April 1992.

34. *World Rainforest Report*, Vol. VII, No. 4, October–December 1991, p. 5.

35. Cited in Rainforest Action Network, "Thailand Resumes Logging in Burma", *Action Alert*, No. 85, June 1993, p. 2; see also Bello, "Population Control", p. 12.; *Greenpeace*, July–August 1990, p. 11.

36. David M. Kummer, *Deforestation in the Postwar Philippines*, Chicago: University of Chicago Press, 1992, p. 147.

37. S.B. Hecht, "Environment, Development and Politics: Capital Accumulation and the Livestock Sector in Eastern Amazonia", *World Development*, No. 13, 1985, pp. 663–664; D. Anderson, "Declining Tree Stocks in African Countries", *World Development*, No. 14, 1986, pp. 853–863.

38. "ITTO Promotes Deforestation Say Ecologists", *Third World Resurgence*, No. 31, 1993, p. 7; Vandana Shiva, "World Bank Cannot Protect the Environment", *Third World Resurgence*, Nos 14–15, 1991, p. 23; Dewi Sartika, "Indonesia Goes for Tree Plantations", *Third World Resurgence*, Nos 29–30, 1993, p. 14.

39. Daniel Faber, *Environment Under Fire: Imperialism and the Ecological Crisis in Central America*, New York: Monthly Review Press, 1993, pp. 121, 139–40; Patricia Adams, "All in the Name of Aid", *Sierra*, January–February 1987.

40. William K. Stevens, "A Food Fad's Ripple Effect on Reefs of Pacific: Cyanide", *The New York Times*, October 31, 1995, pp. 1, A6.

41. Nick Hanna and Sue Wells, "Tourism Time Bomb", *New Internationalist*, August 1992, p. 9.

42. Ibid., p. 10.

43. Marty Strange, *Family Farming: A New Economic Vision*, Lincoln: University of Nebraska Press; San Francisco: Institute for Food and Development Policy, 1988, p. 202.

44. Timberlake, *Africa in Crisis*, p. 69.

45. Myers, ed., *Gaia*, p. 51.

46. Ibid., p. 61.

47. Wilfrido Cruz and Robert Repetto, *The Environmental Effects of Stabilization and Structural Adjustment Programs: The Philippines Case*, Washington, DC: World Resources Institute, 1992, Washington, DC, pp. 57, 5.

48. Maria Concepción Cruz, Carrie A. Meyer, Robert Repetto and Richard Woodward, *Population Growth, Poverty, and Environmental Stress: Frontier Migration in the Philippines and Costa Rica*, Washington, DC: World Resources Institute, 1992, p. vii.

49. Ibid.

50. Ibid.

51. Richard Gerster, "Debt and the Environment – The Ecological Implications of the Debt Crisis in Developing Countries", *Third World Economics*, Penang, Malaysia, February 1–15, 1993, p. 15.

52. Bina Agarwal, "Gender, Environment and Poverty Interlinks in Rural India: Regional Variations and Temporal Shifts, 1971–1991", United Nations Research Institute for Social Development, Geneva, 1995, *passim.*

53. Anil Agarwal, "Women Bear the Brunt of India's Eco Catastrophes", *Habitat*, Australian Conservation Foundation, June 1988, p. 28; Agarwal, "Rural Women".

54. Agarwal, "Rural Women", p. 145; Durning, "Ending Poverty", p. 145.

55. World Bank, *Sub-Saharan Africa*, p. 69.

56. Shiva, *Staying Alive*; Agarwal, "Rural Women"; Agarwal, "Women Bear", p. 28; Anoja Wickramasinghe, "Forests in the Lives of Rural Women: A Case Study on A Forest Fringe Community", in *Conference on Women, Environment and Development*, Ruk Rakaganno and Environmental Foundation Ltd, Sri Lanka, February 22, 1992.

57. Michael Redclift, "Redefining the Environmental 'Crisis' in the South", in Weston, ed., *Red and Green*, p. 87; Jane L. Collins, "Women and the Environment: Social Reproduction and Sustainable Development", in Rita S. Gallin and Anne Ferguson, eds, *Women and International Development Annual*, Vol. 2, Boulder, CO: Westview Press, 1991.

58. Myers, ed., *Gaia*, pp. 64–65; Murray Brookchin, *The Ecology of Freedom: The Emergence and Dissolution of Hierarchy*, Palo Alto, CA: Cheshire Books, 1982, p. 24.

59. Vandana Shiva, *The Violence of the Green Revolution: Third World Agriculture, Ecology and Politics*, London and Atlantic Highlands, NJ: Zed Books, 1991; "The Need to Regulate and Control Genetic Engineering", *Third World Resurgence*, Nos 53–54, 1995, pp. 16–24.

60. "Sudan: Steady Economic Decline", in Bank Information Center, *Funding Ecological and Social Destruction: The World Bank and International Monetary Fund*, Washington, DC, 1989, p. 30.

61. Lori Ann Thrupp, "Sterilization of Workers from Pesticide Exposure: The Causes and Consequences of DBCP-induced Damage in Costa Rica and Beyond", *International Journal of Health Services*, Vol. 21, No. 4, 1991, pp. 731–757; Diana Jean Schemo, "U.S. Pesticide Kills Foreign Fruit Pickers' Hopes", *The New York Times*, December 6, 1995, p. A12.

62. "Sudan: Steady Economic Decline", p. 12; Ecumenical Institute for Study and Dialogue, *Integrity of Creation: How Humanity is Destroying the Environment*, Colombo, Sri Lanka, 1991, p. 53; Agarwal, "Rural Women", p. WS-57.

63. Mark Hertsgaard, "A World Awash in Chemicals", *The New York Times Book Review*, April 7, 1996, p. 25.

64. Goldsmith, *The Way*, p. xi.

65. Vandana Shiva, *Biodiversity: A Third World Perspective*, Third World Network, Penang,

Malaysia, n.d; *Third World Resurgence*, Nos 53–54, 1995, Double Issue on Biotechnology and Genetic Engineering, pp. 16–24.

66. Ecumenical Institute for Study and Dialogue, *Integrity of Creation*, p. 73.

67. Cited in Shiva, *Staying Alive*, p. 218.

68. Shiva, *Violence*; Shiva, *Biodiversity*.

69. "GATT – a Four-Letter Word", *Third World Resurgence*, No. 28, 1992, p. 39; "Karnataka Farmers Ransack Cargill Seeds", *Third World Resurgence*, Nos 29–30, 1993, p. 39.

70. Timothy Noah, "Clinton to Back International Accord on Environment That Bush Spurned", *Wall Street Journal*, April 22, 1993, p. B7.

71. Chee Yoke Ling, "Whither the GEF Restructuring?" *Third World Resurgence*, Nos 29–30, 1992, p. 8; "Recommended Reforms in World Bank Structure and Policy: Proposed by NGOs in 1987, 1988 and 1989", in Bank Information Center, *Funding Ecological and Social Destruction*, pp. 32–43; Khor, "A Year After Rio", pp. 12–13; "Environmentalist Calls for Closure of World Bank, IMF", Home News, *Bangkok Post*, Sunday, October 13, 1991.

72. "Damning the World's Rivers: A Fact Sheet on World Bank Lending for Large Dams", International Rivers Network, World Bank/IMF: 50 Years is Enough, US Campaign, n.d. (Appendix 4); Ecumenical Institute for Study and Dialogue, *Integrity of Creation*, p. 34; Steve Turner and Todd Nachowitz, "The Damming of Native Lands", *The Nation*, October 21, 1991, p. 473.

73. International Rivers Network, "Damning the World's Rivers", *passim.*

74. Ecumenical Institute for Study and Dialogue, *Integrity of Creation*, p. 42.

75. Ibid., pp. 33–44; Bandarage, "Women and Capitalist Development", p. 64.

76. Ecumenical Institute for Study and Dialogue, *Integrity of Creation*, pp. 36–37; Seth Mydens, "2,000 Are Killed as Flash Floods Swamp Towns in the Philippines", *The New York Times*, November 9, 1991.

77. Bello et al., *Development Debacle*, pp. 86–87; Farida Akhter, "New Reasons to Depopulate the Third World", *WGNRR Newsletter*, No. 42, January–March 1993, p. 11.

78. Ecumenical Institute for Study and Dialogue, *Integrity of Creation*, p. 35; Smitu Kothari and Rajni Bakshi, "On Dams and Protests", Editorial, *Lokayan Bulletin*, Vol. 7, No. 1, 1989, pp. 1–6.

79. Ecumenical Institute for Study and Dialogue, *Integrity of Creation*, p. 36; Sakunthala Perera, "Tremors Cause for Concern? Authorities Differ" *The Island* (Sri Lanka), December 17, 1995, p. 13.

80. Bharat Dogra, "Tehri Dam Struggle at a Crucial Stage", 1995, paper available from *Southlinks*, United Nations Volunteers, Palais des Nations, CH-1211 Geneva 10, Switzerland.

81. International Rivers Network, "Damning the World's Rivers"; Barbara Crossette, "Water, Water Everywhere? Many Now Say 'No'", *The New York Times*, October 7, 1989, p. 4.

82. Philip B. Williams and Haipei Xue, "World Bank Backs Unsound China Dam", *The New York Times*, Letter to Editor, February 7, 1992; Rainforest Action Network, "World Bank Must be Held Accountable", *Action Alert*, No. 80, January 1993, p. 11; communications to author from Patrick McCully, International Rivers Network, 1847 Berkeley Lane, Berkeley, CA 94703, January 6, 1997.

83. Pratap Chaterjee, "World Bank Failures Soar to 37.5% of Completed Projects in 1991", *Third World Economics*, Third World Network, Penang, Malaysia, No. 55, December 16–31, 1992, pp. 2–3.

84. Cited in "Damning the World's Rivers".

85. "Bankrolling Homelessness: A Fact Sheet on Resettlement and the World Bank", World Bank/IMF 50 Years is Enough, US Campaign, n.d. (Appendix 4).

86. Cited in ibid., p. 1.

87. Adams, "All in the Name of Aid", pp. 46–47; Survival International, "Banking on Disaster", *Index on Censorship*, Nos 6–7, 1989, p. 14.

88. Cited in "Earth Summit Backlash", *World Rainforest Report*, Vol. IX, No. 1, January-

–March 1993, pp. 4–5.

89. Survival International, "Banking on Disaster", p. 14; Adams, "All in the Name of Aid", pp. 47–48.

90. Ecumenical Institute for Study and Dialogue, *Integrity of Creation*, pp. 40–43; Bandarage, "Women and Capitalist Development", p. 64.

91. Ibid.; Kalinga Tudor Silva and W.D.N.R Pushpakumar, "Suicide, Anomie and Powerlessness among the Mahaweli Settlers in Sri Lanka", unpublished ms.

92. Ragnhild Lund, "A Survey on Women's Working and Living Conditions in a Mahaweli Settlement Area with Special Emphasis on Budgets and Household Surplus", Colombo, Sri Lanka: People's Bank Research Department, 1978, p. 78.

93. Ibid., pp. 49–52; Bandarage, "Women and Capitalist Development", p. 65.

94. Gita Sen and Caren Grown, *Development, Crises and Alternative Visions: Third World Women's Perspectives*, New York: Monthly Review Press, 1987, p. 43; Heyzer, *Working Women in South East Asia*, pp. 31–32; Barbara Rogers, *The Domestication of Women: Discrimination in Developing Countries*, New York: St Martin's Press, 1979.

95. "Bankrolling Homelessness"; see also Maurice Malanes, "Indigenous Women Victims of World Bank Policies", *Third World Resurgence*, No. 31, 1993, p. 33.

96. Gail Hanlon, "Supporting Our Front-Line Struggles: An Interview With Winona LaDuke about *Indigenous Women Magazine*", *Woman of Power*, No. 21, Fall 1991, p. 75.

97. Gerster, "Debt and the Environment", p. 13; *World Rainforest Report*, Vol. VII, No. 4, October–December 1991, p. 5;.

98. Gerster, "Debt and the Environment", p. 13.

99. Cited in ibid., p. 16.

100. Ibid., p. 14.

101. "Structural Adjustment Programmes", *Third World Resurgence*, p. 20.

102. Gerster, "Debt and the Environment", p. 16.

103. Ibid.

104. Indira Jaising and Dr C. Sathyamala, "Bhopal: A Test Case of Toxic Industries for UNCED", Briefing Paper No. 7 for UNCED, *Third World Network*, Penang, Malaysia, n.d., p. 1.

105. Ibid.

106. Ibid.

107. Joni Seager, *Earth Follies: Coming to Feminist Terms with the Global Environment Crisis*, New York: Routledge, 1993, p. 100.

108. Ibid.

109. Cited in ibid., p. 101.

110. Jaisingh and Sathyamala, "Bhopal", pp. 6, 1, 11; see also Joshua Karliner, "Bhopal: Setting the Record Straight", *Third World Resurgence*, Nos 53–54, 1995, pp. 13–15.

111. "Call to Boycott Kader Products", *Asian Women Workers Newsletter*, Hong Kong, Vol. 12, No. 3, July 1993, pp. 1–2.

112. Ibid., p. 2.

113. "Sri Lanka: Chemical Poisoning Among Women Workers", *Asian Women Workers Newsletter*, Hong Kong, Vol. 12, No. 3, July 1993, pp. 6 and 8.

114. Ibid., p. 6.

115. World Bank Office Memorandum by Lawrence H. Summers, Chief Economist, December 12, 1991, reprinted in "Let Them Eat Pollution", *The Economist* (London), February 8, 1992, p. 66.

116. Donovan Marks and N. Brown, "The Next Link in the Dumping Chain", in *We Speak for Ourselves: Social Justice, Race and Environment*, Washington, DC: The Panos Institute, 1990, pp. 32–33; *Toxic Terror: Dumping Hazardous Wastes in the Third World*, Third World Network, Penang, Malaysia, 1989.

117. Brad Angel, "Today's Conquistadors", *CrossRoads – Forward Motion*, Center for Democratic Alternatives, Jamaica Plain, MA, Vol. 11, No. 2, April 1992, p. 35.

118. Hanlon, "Supporting Our Front-Line Struggles", p. 75.

119. "Building Coalitions for Our Earth", Interview with Ellie Goodwin, *Woman of*

268   *Women, Population and Global Crisis*

Power, No. 20, 1991, p. 32; Richard Moore, "Confronting Environmental Racism", *Cross-roads – Forward Motion*, Center for Democratic Alternatives, Jamaica Plain, MA, Vol. 11, No. 2, April 1992, p. 6.

120. Frank Kuznik, "Wasted", *American Politics*, March 1988, p. 5.

121. Cate Collins, "Havasupais Battle against Uranium Mine to Preserve Their Land", *Navajo-Hopi Observer*, August 2, 1989; Marks and Brown, "The Next Link", p. 33; "Pacific Islanders send Back Toxic Soil to U.S.", *Third World Resurgence*, No. 31, 1993, p. 7.

122. Farhad Mazhar, "Dumping Toxic Waste in Bangladesh as Fertiliser", *Third World Resurgence*, Nos 29–30, 1993, pp. 18–19; Debra Percival, "EC Publicises Toxic Waste Trade", *Third World Resurgence*, Nos 29–30, 1993, p. 19.

123. Pablo Diaz, "Toxic Trade Remains Legal", *Third World Resurgence*, Nos 29–30, 1993, p. 10.

124. *Greenpeace*, July–September, 1993, p. 2.

125. "Saints and Sinners" p. 11.

126. Ibid., p. 2.

127. Michael Renner, "Assessing the Military's War on the Environment", *State of the World 1991*, New York: W.W. Norton, 1991, p. 133.

128. Ibid., p. 144.

129. *The Relationship Between Disarmament and Development*, New York: United Nations, Center for Disarmament, Disarmament Study Series, No. 5, 1982.

130. Renner, "Assessing the Military's War", p. 137.

131. Ibid., pp. 140–141.

132. Ibid., pp. 135, 142–143.

133. Renner, "Assessing the Military's War", p. 139.

134. Ibid., p. 144; "U.S. Leaves Toxic Legacy at Military Bases", *Third World Resurgence*, Nos 29–30, 1993, p. 11.

135. Renner, "Assessing the Military's War", p. 144.

136. "U.S. Leaves Toxic Legacy", p. 11.

137. Myers, ed., *Gaia*, p. 87.

138. Cited in Kerry Richardson, "Report on the First Global Radiation Victims Conference and the Indigenous Uranium Forum (IUF)", Report No. 7, 1988, Indigenous Uranium Forum, 210 Columbus Avenue, Suite #428, San Francisco, CA 94133, USA.

139. US Department of Energy, "Human Radiation Experiments Associated with the U.S. Department of Energy and its Predecessors", Washington, DC, July 1995, pp. 176, 178, 186.

140. Renner, "Assessing the Military's War", p. 147.

141. Ibid., p. 149; Ecumenical Institute for Study and Dialogue, *Integrity of Creation*, p. 31.

142. T. LaBlanc, P. Guillory, Esq., and J. Redhouse, "First Executive Report of the Indigeneous Uranium Forum, IUF, First Global Radiation Victims Conference/Indigenous Uranium Forum", September and November 1987, p. 1; "Victims of Uranium Mining and Atomic Tests", The World Uranium Hearing, 1990, updated report published in cooperation with the Heinrich Böll Stiftung, The World Uranium Hearing, c/o International Action Center, 39 West 14th Street # 206, New York, NY 10011, USA.

143. LaBlanc et al., "First Executive Report of the Indigenous Uranium Forum"; "Growing Fight", *Akwesasne Notes*, p. 29; Hynes, *Taking Population Out*, p. 20.

144. Asoka Bandarage, "Global Peace and Security in the Post Cold War Era: A 'Third World Perspective'", in Daniel Thomas and Michael Klare, eds, *Peace and World Order Studies: A Curriculum Guide*, 6th edn, Boulder, CO and London: Lynne Rienner Publishers, pp. 31, 40.

145. Ecumenical Institute for Study and Dialogue, *Integrity of Creation*, p. 31.

146. Renner, "Assessing the Military's War", p. 150.

147. Seager, *Earth Follies*, p. 64; Glenn Alcalay, "Pax Atomica: US Nuclear Imperialism in Micronesia", in Peter Worsley, ed., *On the Brink: Nuclear Proliferation and the Third World*, London: Third World Communications, 1987, pp. 107–121.

148. Darlene Keju-Johnson, cited in Women Working for a Nuclear Free and Inde-

pendent Pacific, eds, *Pacific Women Speak: Why Haven't You Known?*, Oxford: Green Line, 1987, pp. 11–14; see also Seager, *Earth Follies*, p. 66.

149. "U.S. Burns Chemical Weapons in the Pacific", *Third World Resurgence*, No. 3, 1990, p. 6.

150. Chee Yoke Ling, "Nuclear Non-Proliferation Treaty: South Caves in to U.S. Pressure", *Third World Resurgence*, No. 58, 1995, pp. 36–37; see also Worsley, ed., *On the Brink, passim*.

151. Bandarage, "Peace and World Security", p. 30.

152. Madeline Drexler, "Casualty or Coincidence?", *The Boston Globe Magazine*, December 17, 1995, pp. 19–24, 28–31.

153. "The Scorched Afghan Earth", *The Economist*, June 4, 1988, p. 30.

154. Seager, *Earth Follies*, p. 17.

155. Ibid.

156. Ibid., p. 18.

157. Enloe, *Bananas, Beaches and Bases*, p. 88; see also Usher, "After the Forest", *passim*.

158. Joni Seager, "Making Feminist Sense of Environmental Issues", *Sojourner*, February 1991, p. 22.

159. Ibid.; Seager, *Earth Follies*, p. 18.

160. Drexler, "Casualty or Coincidence?", *passim*; "Pentagon Reveals Toxin Exposure", *Daily Hampshire Gazette*, June 22–23, 1996, p. 1.

161. Eric Hoskins, "Iraqi Children Suffer Radiation", *Third World Resurgence*, No. 31, 1993, pp. 8–9.

162. "The Military and the Environment", *The Defense Monitor*, Center for Defense Information, Washington, DC, Vol. XXIII, No. 9, 1994, pp. 4, 7.

7

Political Economy of Violence and Insecurity

Escalating global insecurity and violence is not attributable to 'overpopulation'. While population growth is an exacerbating factor, the global security crisis must be seen in relation to the deepening contradictions of capitalism and militarism and violent forms of repression and resistance engendered by those forces.

Inequality and Insecurity

Widening inequality, poverty and environmental collapse are accelerating the processes of dispossession, destitution and migration across the world. As subsistence economies, local cultures and communities are destroyed, people have no choice but to integrate themselves and attempt to survive in the global capitalist economy and competitive consumer culture.

In the past, it was mostly the upper classes in the Third World that sought to emulate the western lifestyle. But today, with the globalization of consumerism by the mass media, young people everywhere aspire to the same goal. As sociologist James Petras observes, cultural imperialism is vital to capitalist market expansion as well as political control:

> Imperial entertainment and advertisement target young people who are most vulnerable to US commercial propaganda.
> ...Cultural imperialism focuses on youth not only as a *market* but also for political reasons: to undercut a political threat in which *personal* rebellion could become *political* revolt against economic as well as cultural forms of control.... *Cultural penetration is the extension of counter-insurgency warfare by non-military means.* (emphasis in original).[1]

The modern ideals of democracy, freedom and equality kindle young people's desire to be 'somebody' in the world. Yet the hierarchy and inequality built into the global economy and society shut out most youth from occupations that provide self-esteem and dignity. In the absence of serious efforts to ease these global inequalities, the experience of young people around the world will be defined increasingly by scarcity, unemployment, anxiety, anger, despair and powerlessness.[2]

Increasing numbers of people struggling to survive in the informal economy by engaging in crime, prostitution and other forms of the skin trade have little or no stake in the status quo. In a world culture which glamorizes war and violence via Rambo movies and where weapons are easily bought and sold, angry and confused youth devoid of future prospects are easily lured into joining armies, armed insurgencies, gangs and other violent enterprises.

Violent and destructive behaviors are not inherent in the animal nature of human beings as assumed by the likes of Hobbes and Malthus (Appendix 2). Rather, such behaviors tend to occur where supportive social structures are absent and people are engulfed in fear and anxiety. Commodity production and the extension of techno-bureaucratic control over people's lives have undermined community, family and cultural integrity, resulting in greater competition and individualism.

Weakening family and community ties in the modern era have not been replaced with alternative modes of human commitment and social organization. As psychologist Mary Clark notes, the denial of human emotional needs such as bonding, trust, affection and a shared spiritual orientation to life in the modern world has resulted in a plethora of pathological behaviors ranging from "greed, dominance, wife-beating, child-abuse, drug abuse, callousness and violence to obsessive needs for attachment to sports teams, nations, and leaders who project an image of strength".[3] Indeed, the rootlessness and alienation produced by technological and capitalist expansion and human emotional need for acceptance and belonging underlie the popularity of extremely violent, often self-destructive sects, militias, ethnonationalist and religious fundamentalist movements in the world today.[4]

The global refugee problem is another manifestation of the insecurity and destitution created by the combined effects of militarism, poverty and environmental destruction. As noted in the Introduction, there are currently about 27 million refugees in the world. While millions of people remain displaced in their own countries, millions of economic, political and environmental refugees spill into other countries, contributing to the stresses and conflicts of international migration. Malthusian calls to halt migration into the rich North overlook the roots of the refugee problem situated in global political and economic structures.

It is estimated that by the year 2000 more than half the people in the world will be under the age of 20.[5] As Malthusians often point out, increasing numbers of young dispossessed and angry youth in the Third World constitute a great threat to global peace and security. Indeed, they are the ones carrying the guns and doing much of the actual killing in the world. Although a lowering of the size of the global population may ease the competition, it will not eliminate the inequalities, insecurities and the violence located in the global capitalist, patriarchal and white supremacist social system. To understand escalating global violence and insecurity and threats to democracy, we need to understand how this world order of domination is maintained by militarism.

Imperialism and Militarism

Psychological colonization was essential to the maintenance of white supremacy and imperialism, as articulated eloquently by writers such as Frantz Fanon and Albert Memmi.[6] Yet the sense of racial superiority achieved through western education, Christianity, the colonial state and the capitalist economic system could not have been maintained without the use of organized violence.

Superior military power as well as cunning and deception enabled the Europeans to colonize 85% of the earth by the end of World War I.[7] As a native of the Solomon Islands put it, "Nothing much is said about the sufferings on our side. Yet we fought with spears, clubs, bows and arrows. The foreigners fought with canons, guns and bullets".[8]

As noted in earlier chapters, like military superiority, collaboration with native elites was a precondition of colonial rule. Resistant native rulers were killed or their positions and titles given to others more amenable to colonial control. Indeed, not knowing the physical and social terrain, including the languages and customs of the natives, the foreign rulers were compelled to rely on a vast array of local administrators and to reward them amply for their services.[9] These features of imperialism have continued in the post-independence, neo-colonial period.

The Cold War and the Third World

Although Cold War ideology was formulated in terms of East–West competition, control of Third World resources and suppression of social revolutions were the major imperatives of western imperialism during the post-war, neo-colonial era as they had been during the era of classical colonialism.[10]

Already in the 1950s, foreign policy experts such as Henry Kissinger were arguing that US–USSR conflict was less likely to take place in Europe and that the greater risk to US power lay in the 'grey areas' of the Near East, Western Asia, Indo-China and Korea.[11] As noted in Chapter 6, almost all the 150 or so wars fought during the Cold War took place in the Third World. Except in Greece, no intense Cold War struggle took place in Europe, and of course none in North America.[12]

Even nuclear deployment was not an exclusively super-power issue. Not only was the hydrogen bomb first dropped on a 'non-white' people in

Japan in 1945, but, as political analyst Fred Halliday has pointed out, subsequent build-up of strategic nuclear weapons was designed primarily for use in Third World crises against people of color. Nuclear forces were placed on alert and the nuclear threat was used during a number of Third World crisis situations, as for example in: Uruguay in 1947; Korea in 1950 and 1953; Guatemala in 1954; the Middle East in 1956, 1958, 1963 and 1973; Cuba in 1962; Vietnam in 1969.[13]

Managing people

As capitalism expanded in the Third World, a huge infrastructure of dependency developed, spreading external control into state bureaucracies and universities and the managerial, technical and intellectual elites.[14] But techno-bureaucratic authority was not sufficient for managing people or the environment. Expansion of export production and market liberalization often required violent repression rather than democratic government. As Noam Chomsky and Edward Herman have argued in *The Washington Connection and Third World Fascism*, "U.S.-controlled aid has been positively related to investment climate and inversely related to the maintenance of a democratic order and human rights."[15]

Third World elites continued to be a collaborator class of imperialism in the neo-colonial period. But unlike in the earlier classical colonialist period, as the wielders of state power they had the right to use force against their populations. Without the support of outside military powers, however, most Third World dictatorships could not have survived against the opposition of local people. Both super-powers invoked Cold War ideology in seeking to extend their control and influence in the Third World through maintenance of client states, arms exports, armed intervention, as well as covert operations.[16]

In accordance with the Cold War national security doctrine articulated by George Kennan and others, the US provided arms, equipment and services to 'friendly governments'. Between 1950 and 1979, the United States provided foreign governments a total of $107.3 billion under military aid programs such as the MAP (Military Assistance Program), IMET (International Military Education and Training), FMS (Foreign Military Sales), EDA (Excess Defense Articles) and ESF (Economic Support Fund).[17] During this period, the US also trained nearly 500,000 foreign military personnel under the MAP and IMET programs.[18]

A good number of the thousands of Latin American military officers trained at the US Army School of the Americas during the last 50 or more years have been responsible for 'serious acts of lawless violence' against populations in their countries.[19] The United States was directly responsible for turning Third World regimes into brutal and corrupt military dictatorships, as, for example, in Nicaragua under Somoza, the Philippines under Marcos, Haiti under the Duvaliers. The United States also installed and maintained dictators in the name of anti-Communism after overthrowing the democratically elected regimes of Mossadeq in Iran in 1953, Arbenz in Guatemala in the same year and Allende in Chile in 1973 because they posed challenges to US corporate interests in those countries.[20]

Many of the armed conflicts in the Third World involved super-power military interventions in national liberation struggles. The United States intervened either overtly or covertly (through the CIA) in Korea, Guatemala, Cuba, the Dominican Republic, Iran, Vietnam, Angola, Nicaragua, El Salvador, Afghanistan, Libya and Grenada, among other countries. The Soviet Union intervened in Angola, Ethiopia, Korea, Yemen and Afghanistan (as well as in former Warsaw Pact countries).

For much of the Third World, the so-called 'Cold War' was not an "unprecedented half-century of global peace" as assumed by most Western analysts and the public.[21] Rather, it was a period of actual wars and tremendous violence, suffering and insecurity. Despite global fears of nuclear war, the arms build-up and the arms race during the Cold War primarily involved conventional weapons for use in the Third World. Defense analysts Michael Klare and Cynthia Aronson have described this vast trade in weapons as the "international repression trade".[22] As a result of this lethal trade, regions like Central America and the Horn of Africa, which are not weapons producers themselves, became some of the most militarized regions in the world.

In at least a few countries, such as the Philippines, Nicaragua and El Salvador, resistance took the form of left wing insurgencies seeking to overthrow repressive regimes and establish Communist or socialist states.[23] But even in the few instances where such movements came into power, as in Nicaragua after the overthrow of the Somoza regime, they did not succeed in establishing autonomous paths of development. Through the imposition of an economic embargo and continued military assistance to the pro-Somoza forces, the United States ensured that the Nicaraguan revolution did not succeed. As political analyst Holly Sklar has noted:

> Virtually all national liberation governments and movements from Angola to Zimbabwe, Jamaica to Nicaragua, have been co-opted or destabilized. Still strong movements like the South African ANC and Salvadoran FMLN have been forced to significantly lower their economic and political expectations.[24]

Counter-insurgency strategies were also used by the FBI and other US government surveillance institutions in domestic imperialist policies against Black, Native American, working-class as well as peace and justice movements in the US. In fact, many civil rights activists suspect that the Black American leaders Malcolm X and Martin Luther King Jr may have been killed with the knowledge of the FBI.[25]

Not all wars in the Third World during the Cold War were proxy wars of the super-powers. The global arms arsenal built up in the name of the super-power struggle militarized the Third World, encouraging all manner of armed conflicts by brutal military regimes and often equally violent opposition movements. In many Third World countries, repression has taken the form of "a systematic counter-insurgency strategy that is waged on a number of levels: ideological, social-psychological, political and military". The result has been widespread disappearances, torture, death squad activities, killings and other human rights violations.[26]

The full extent of the devastation caused during the Cold War by wars in the Third World, euphemistically referred to as 'low intensity conflicts', will probably never be known. According to official estimates alone, about 40 million people, over 75% of them civilians, died as a result of civil and international wars fought with conventional weapons in the so-called Cold War period. Between 25 and 30 million people were also turned into refugees by these wars.[27]

Anywhere from 1 million to 3 million people died at the hands of the Khmer Rouge in Cambodia between 1975 and 1979. Over a million people died in the decade-long Iran–Iraq war in the 1980s and over 100,000 people were killed and 40,000 disappeared in the Guatemalan army's counter-insurgency campaigns between 1970 and 1990. Land mines – a profitable part of the global arms trade – continue to kill and maim civilians long after the end of wars. According to 1994 UN estimates, in Cambodia, there is still one mine in the ground for every two people in the country and these kill or disable 300 people each month.[28] Indeed, casualties of war have never been restricted to the millions killed. As discussed in earlier chapters, environmental destruction, poverty and destitution are other major destructive outcomes.

As we discussed in Chapter 2, population control was a major plank of Cold War ideology and the global management strategy of the United States. Not only was Third World population growth seen as a major threat to US national security, but the initiative for international population control came from the military, particularly men like General William Draper, General William Westmoreland, General Maxwell Taylor and Vietnam war era Defense Secretary Robert MacNamara. It was MacNamara, subsequently the President of the World Bank, who initiated World Bank activism in global population control. Given this military connection, it is not surprising that, as discussed earlier, many population control programs have also been run on a military model as a war against Third World 'overpopulation'. They have used overt and covert psychological warfare to change Third World consciousness and the reproductive behavior of Third World women.[29]

Massive dumping of conventional arms by super-powers during the Cold War has been followed by political destabilization in many parts of the world at the end of the Cold War. Dismantling of nuclear warheads since the end of the Cold War could make available as much as 40,000 A-bombs' worth of plutonium in the coming decade, threatening efforts to curb nuclear proliferation.[30]

Global military expenditures and military expenditures of the 'developed' countries have dropped in the post-Cold War period of the so-called 'New World Order'. But arms production, arms exports and military intervention continue to be the ultimate basis for managing and controlling global resources and populations.

The New World Order

Many industrializing Asian countries now openly attack democracy and human rights as western concepts, endorsing political authoritarianism as being more conducive to competitiveness in the world market.[31] The US, on the other hand, increasingly justifies its trade relations with oppressive regimes such as China using the rationale of 'market democracy'. It claims that international trade alone will move these regimes towards greater democracy. But aggressive arms peddling and arms exports by the US and European countries belie alleged western commitment to global peace and democracy.

In 1993, the Clinton administration allocated $1.3 trillion to the US military for the next five years, which was only a 5% reduction of the allocation of the previous Bush administration.[32] This allocation represent about a $14,000 defense expenditure for every household in the US. As the US military continues to be the biggest 'public works program' in the world, providing regular paychecks to over 9 million people, the rationales, huge advertising budget, lobbying and of course arms production, exports, military construction, 'logistics support' and training around the world continue.[33]

In addition to maintaining existing weaponry, new weapons for international and domestic use are continuously being designed and marketed by the Pentagon and the defense companies. An example is a class of weapons known as 'mini-nukes', that is, nuclear weapons below 5 kilotons, designed to be used against developing countries. Thanks to the initiative of Congresswoman Elizabeth Furse, development of these was banned by the US Congress.[34] But there is no guarantee that the interest in producing such weapons will not be revived in the future, especially given the Pentagon's decision to continue building costly weapons such as the new nuclear-tipped submarine missiles and the multibillion dollar third *Seawolf* attack submarine.[35]

The Pentagon believes that efforts to stem the spread of weapons of mass destruction are unlikely to succeed and that US forces are increasingly likely to be attacked by 'Third World foes'. On these grounds, the Pentagon has launched several new initiatives to buy millions of dollars' worth of new vaccines to inoculate troops against germ warfare and to develop new bombs to incinerate chemical and biological weapons stocks.[36] As former Defense Secretary Les Aspin belligerently put it in a speech at the National Academy of the Sciences, "We cannot let future Saddams escape attack."[37] But just as the population question is unlikely to be resolved by inoculating Third World women with more effective vaccines, the global security crisis will not be resolved by developing protective vaccines for US troops or stronger and more sophisticated weapons that are designed to kill better.[38]

The growth of the global arms trade and massive arms build-up in the post-Cold War period cannot be approached from the supply side alone. On the demand side are long-simmering regional rivalries, persistent border and trade disputes, ethnic and class conflicts and growing political instability and insecurity. As in the Cold War era, many of these arms are being accumulated by anti-democratic regimes and resistance movements to repress populations.

Arms build-up

As noted in Chapter 5, the five permanent members of the UN Security Council and Germany are responsible for the spread of the most advanced and sophisticated weapons across the world (Tables 5.6 and 7.1)

The Clinton administration repeatedly asserts that "attention to human rights and democratic governance is a central tenet" of its foreign policy. Yet, as in the past, many countries such as Turkey identified by the State Department itself as severely violating human rights have been among the "top recipients of U.S. military aid and arms exports".[39]

While the US is claiming to 'bring peace' to the Middle East, it is simultaneously escalating the arms build-up in that region. Before the Gulf War, the Middle East absorbed more than $200 billion worth of weapons over a period of 10 years.[40] If post-Cold War trends in arms trafficking continue, these figures may well be exceeded before the end of this decade. The US government proposed $6.236 billion in foreign security assistance for fiscal year 1994 under the rubric of "Promoting and Maintaining Peace", of which 87% was to be allocated to Israel and Egypt.[41]

Saudi Arabia is planning to double the size of its armed forces, making its military "one of the largest engineering projects in the world".[42] While the purpose of this vast military complex is to safeguard Saudi oil reserves, they are already being threatened. Political control in Saudi Arabia could conceivably fall into the hands of a group inimical to western interests. Partly in response to such a potentiality, US military training and defense agreements with the Middle East states have been dramatically increased, along with weapons exports, since the Gulf War.[43] The insecurity and volatility in the Middle East, then, is not attributable so much to

Table 7.1   Quantity of weapons exported during 1994

	Battle tanks	Armored combat vehicles	Large caliber artillery	Combat aircraft	Attack helicopters	War-ships	Missile launchers
USA	702	1,036	121	82	5	0	316
Germany	181	1,170	546	24	2	9	1,020
Russia	30	328	129	2	0	1	436
UK	18	35	88	43	2	9	196
France	5	72	0	2	1	0	56
China	82	0	0	0	0	0	0

Source: United Nations General Assembly Document No. A/50/547, as cited in Federation of American Scientists Fund, *Arms Sales Monitor*, No. 31, December 5, 1995, p. 5.

population growth and the 'Islamic threat' as to the massive arms build-up in the region.

While the Middle East continues to be the most highly militarized region, Latin America and other regions are not excluded from the current frenzy of arms buying and selling. The threat of conventional and nuclear conflict in Asia is escalating in the post-Cold War era. As the Director of US Naval Intelligence observed in May 1994, "the overall technical threat and lethality of arms still being exported have never been higher".[44]

Finalizing a $1.6 billion arms deal with Britain in 1991, the Malaysian Defense Minister said, "The lesson that can be drawn from the Gulf War is that we need to be prepared. We need to build up our military hardware and to operate the equipment".[45] The accumulation of plutonium by Japan and nuclear activities by North Korea exacerbate the anxiety over nuclear proliferation among countries in Asia and elsewhere. Former Pakistan premier Benazir Bhutto affirmed her country's commitment to nuclear development, just as its rival, India, is pursuing its own nuclear activities.[46]

As discussed in Chapter 5, more and more 'developing' countries, especially those like the 'Asian dragons' with skilled work forces and industrial infrastructures, are moving beyond arms purchasing to domestic production. Many are requiring technology transfer or 'offset arrangements' as a condition for buying sophisticated weaponry from the Big Five suppliers. Once a country like South Korea fulfills its domestic needs for a weapon being produced, it will want to sell it to still other countries. As a Public Interest Report by the Federation of American Scientists has warned, in such cases it is unlikely that a licensing country such as the United States would be able to control sales by industries they have helped establish.[47]

Production of arms by Third World states as well as insurgent groups would further the glut in the global arms market, thereby driving down prices and magnifying arms proliferation and security concerns independent of demographic factors. Regional military powers are also increasingly following the example set by the global powers by militarily intervening in neighboring countries, as China has done in Tibet and India has in smaller neighboring countries like Sri Lanka.[48]

Despite the United Nations-sponsored Arms Trade Register to increase transparency in weapons sales, the global weapons trade is utterly un-regulated and booming.[49] Up to now, the arms trade in large expensive weapons has received most attention. But as Michael Klare points out, smaller arms and light weapons such as pistols, submachine guns, assault rifles and bazookas, which range in price from $500 to $2,500, became the basic arsenal of fighting in wars in places like Bosnia, Rwanda and Somalia.[50]

Illegal or covert arms sales involved only small arms and small quantities of explosives in the past. However, since the 1980s the illegal arms trade has greatly expanded in terms of value – to between $5 and $10 billion per year – as well as in lethality. The illegal arms trade has given rise to new types of arms dealers and buyers, for example to individuals who smuggle military supplies out of the former Warsaw Pact nations and sell them to governments that find it difficult to procure arms through legal channels, to criminal organizations like drug cartels and gangs, and to various insurgent and terrorist groups.[51] The recently murdered Colombian drug lord Pablo Escobar is considered an early prototype of the heavily armed 'new international gangster'.[52] As arsenals of conventional, chemical and nuclear weapons grow, tensions and the potential for armed conflict also rise. Then the arms exporters themselves have to intervene to curb the destructive capability of weapons arsenals they have helped build.[53]

Military intervention

The draft *Defense Planning Guidance* issued by the Department of Defense in March 1992 reveals that maintenance of economic and political hegemony in the world will guide US military intervention in the New World Order as it had during the Cold War. The document also presented the US vision of a world led by a single super-power:

> ...we still retain the pre-eminent responsibility for addressing selectively those interests which threaten not only our interests, but those of our allies, or which could seriously unsettle international relations. Various types of U.S. interests may be involved in such instances: access to vital raw materials, primarily Persian Gulf oil; proliferation of weapons of mass destruction and ballistic missiles, threats to U.S. citizens from terrorism or regional or local conflict, and threats to U.S. society from narcotics trafficking.[54]

Table 7.2 Military strength of nations, 1994–1995

Country	Defense expenditure (US$ billions)*	Troop strength (thousands)†	
		Active	Reserve
USA	254.0	1,650.5	2,048.0
Russia	63.0	1,714.0	20,000.0
Japan	54.0	237.7	47.9
France	41.0	409.6	339.8
UK	35.0	254.3	376.2
Germany	34.0	367.3	442.7
China	29.0	2,930.0	1,200.0
Italy	16.0	322.3	584.0
S. Korea	14.0	633.0	4,500.0
Saudi Arabia	13.0	n/a	n/a
Netherlands	9.0	n/a	n/a
Canada	8.0	n/a	n/a
India	8.0	1,265.0	300.0
Australia	7.0	n/a	n/a
Brazil	7.0	336.8	1,150.0
Israel	7.0	172.0	430.0
Spain	7.0	206.5	498.0
N. Korea	6.0	1,128.0	540.0
Turkey	6.0	503.8	952.3
Norway	4.0	n/a	n/a
Pakistan	4.0	587.0	313.0
Belgium	3.0	n/a	n/a
Denmark	3.0	n/a	n/a
Greece	3.0	n/a	n/a
Syria	3.0	408.0	400.0
Iraq	3.0	382.0	650.0
Iran	2.0	513.0	350.0
Portugal	2.0	n/a	n/a
Libya	1.0	70.0	40.0
Vietnam	1.0	572.0	3–4,000.0
Cuba	0.3	n/a	n/a

* Figures usually for 1995.
† Figures usually for 1994.

Source: Center for Defense Information, *The Defense Monitor*, Vol. XXV, No. 4, April/May 1996, p. 4; *The Military Balance, 1994–1995*, International Institute for Strategic Studies, published by Brassey's UK as cited in Robert Famighetti, ed., *The World Almanac and Book of Facts 1996*, Mahweh, NJ: Funk and Wagnells Corp., 1995, p. 164.

When Washington's plans to prevent the rise of military competitors in Western Europe and East Asia, as outlined in this document, came under criticism from abroad, the Pentagon quickly softened its stance. In a revised version of the document issued in May 1992, the Pentagon emphasized US commitment to collective military action and to developing "new tools in international relations", including "humanitarian aid, intelligence assistance, [and] measures to prevent the emergence of non-democratic aggressors in critical regions".[55]

While the United States has been reducing its forces in Europe, in 1988, even prior to the official end of the Cold War, the US National Security Council and the Department of Defense articulated the need for concentrating US military resources in fighting so-called 'mid-intensity' conflict (MIC) against emerging powers in the Third World.[56] The high-tech air war in the Gulf was a clear example of MIC in action.

US military strength is far superior to the military strength of Iraq, Iran and North Korea, identified as the potential enemies in the US government's "Bottom-Up Review: Forces for a New Era", issued in September 1993. US military strength far exceeds that of Cuba, Libya and Syria, also identified as opponents of the US, and all these six nations put together. With a military budget of $254 billion in 1995, the US far exceeded the second-ranking military spender, Russia, which allocated $63 billion (Table 7.2). Still, the US continues to justify its arms build-up by exaggerating the so-called Islamic threat and the military might of its Third World foes.

In its "Bottom-Up Review", the Clinton administration argues that US forces "must be able to fight and win two Major Regional Contingencies (MRCs) simultaneously and on short notice" and that "rapidly deployable, interventionary forces" are needed for this purpose. The Report cites Operation Just Cause in Panama, Operation Desert Storm against Iraq and Operation Restore Hope in Somalia as examples of the kinds of conflicts the US will face increasingly in the future.[57] As the *Arms Sales Monitor* points out, "In each of these cases, arms transfers directly enabled the aggression or fuelled the instability that necessitated the military operation." In the cases of Panama and Somalia, the arms were supplied primarily by the US.[58]

In the case of Iraq, which had become the largest retail buyer of arms in the late 1980s, arms came from many different suppliers, including the Soviet Union, France, West Germany, Brazil, the US, Britain, China and a dozen or so other nations.[59] In other words, many of the countries that fought Iraq in the Gulf War were also its weapons suppliers.

US arms sales to potential adversaries tend to be justified on both commercial and military grounds. As Rear Admiral John Snyder, Deputy Director of the US Navy International Programs Office put it at a Defense Trade Advisory Group meeting at the US State Department in September 1995:

I'd rather go to war against a country that has bought US equipment.... If they got equipment from the US, I know damn well what they got in their inventory, I know what their readiness is.... I also know what their tactics are, and I know how to defeat their weapons ... if a country's going to get technology anyway, let's make it US technology.[60]

It is the policies of the United States and other weapons suppliers that have turned the 'bottom' 20% of the global population, especially the youth, into an expendable 'surplus population' to be used as 'cannon fodder'. Clearly, arms suppliers and lobbyists like Admiral John Snyder in the US are far more responsible for global insecurity and violence than poor youth in the Third World.

Not only does the US military typically intervene in Third World countries, but US military interventions also use a disproportionate number of its domestic Third World population or youth of color in those interventions. For many lower-class youth in the US, joining the Army is one of the few avenues for relatively well paying work. Although African Americans constitute only about 12% of the US population, they, along with Hispanics, accounted for about 35% of the ground troops in Saudi Arabia during the Gulf War in 1991.[61] Some 11% of those troops were female, that being the highest employment of women in a US military intervention. Of those troops, nearly half were Black.[62] Even many feminists have called for combatant roles for women in the US as a form of women's liberation without looking at the race, class as well as ethical implications of US military intervention abroad.[63]

The increase of the number of women in the US Army does not necessarily represent a rise in support for militarism on the part of women as a group. Polls taken during the 1991 Persian Gulf crisis showed a large gender gap in support for US military action in the Gulf. Even before a single shot was fired, women were opposed by almost 25% more than men.[64] It is such factors as the rise in female-headed households, women's poverty and aggressive recruitment of women by the military that have contributed to an increase in women's search of military employment and associated material benefits. It is unlikely, however, that the military, which has historically been the bastion of male aggression, domination and conquest, will come to represent true freedom and liberation for women, or for gays or minorities for that matter. Rather, it represents integration of all social groups and sectors within the military–industrial complex.

The identification of new enemies – drug cartels, ecoterrorists, Islamic fundamentalists, and so on – is likely to increase US covert operations in the Third World. In 1991, the US Congress passed the National Security Education Act, which places foreign language, area studies and other international fields within the realm of US military and intelligence priorities and Department of Defense funding.[65]

Furthermore, despite its standing as the worst polluter of the environment, the US military has attempted to take on a green image in the post-Cold War era. But beneath the language of environmentalism is the objective of continued US access to the world's dwindling natural resources in the twenty-first century. For example, a huge project has recently been launched to direct US spy satellites towards studying and monitoring diverse and shifting natural habitats across the world.[66] The conversion of defense money into such intelligence operations will not entail a peace dividend. Instead, it will deepen the US military's control over the global environment and its permeation into civilian sectors of societies both in the US and abroad.

Militarization has given birth to the national security state, characterized by surveillance and subsumption of the media and information within the military. This was clearly evident in the United States during the interventions in Panama and the Gulf.[67] The corporate-controlled media succeeded in presenting the appearance of consensus on US military interventions abroad through manipulation of language, technology and adulation of military power. The sound-bite slogans of 'collateral damage' and 'smart weapons' helped present the Gulf War as a video game-deflecting public attention away from widespread death and suffering inflicted on the Iraqi people and the deaths of US troops themselves due to 'friendly fire'.[68] In this regard, the new emphasis on multilateralism and United Nations intervention also needs to be approached with caution.

Multilateralism

The overwhelming response of the western powers to escalating global violence and lawlessness is increased arms production and military intervention. The usual solutions advanced by western nations and the United Nations are armed intervention, break-up of nation states and redrawing of state boundaries. But these measures do not involve serious efforts to curb the arms trade and build social justice and democracy, which are the prerequisites for global peace and stability. Let us not forget that the five permanent Security Council members who possess veto power over global security matters are also the world's leading arms merchants. Indeed, as Albert Einstein once said, "We cannot simultaneously prevent and prepare for war."[69]

If the role of the United Nations in the Gulf War is the example of the New World Order, there is much to fear from manipulation of decisions in the Security Council by the United States. The United States used the UN to justify intervention in the Gulf, but once the war began the UN "vanished from the picture".[70] Like the World Bank, the IMF and other multilateral institutions, the United Nations is not a democratic institution. UN decisions and actions represent the interests of the dominant global powers which make the largest financial contributions (although the US still owes some $1.5 billion in dues to the UN).[71] For example, the UN has allowed Israel to defy Security Council resolutions repeatedly because of its alliance with the West, while it has enforced resolutions against countries like Libya and Iraq.[72]

Appproximately 100,000 people in Iraq were killed due to the military intervention sanctioned by the UN in 1991. But dictator Saddam Hussein still remains in power. According to a study commissioned by the FAO, since the end of the Gulf War, thousands of children have been subjected to malnutrition and sickness and as many as 576,000 children may have died due to the economic embargo imposed by the UN Security Council.[73] Hunger and disease generated by this embargo, like other economic embargoes against poor countries, cannot be blamed on the population explosion.[74] Instead, it should be asked whether economic embargoes by the North against the poor in countries in the South constitute a form of Malthusian population control.

The strategic importance of the Gulf region rather than humanitarianism was the underlying motivation for the allied intervention in the Gulf. Hardly any economic disruptions were felt by US, European or Japanese consumers during the Gulf War although their countries were at war with Iraq. In contrast, the poor in the Third World, especially in countries like Sri Lanka and the Philippines, suffered the effects of price hikes and loss of incomes from immigrant workers from the Middle East.[75]

Beneath a motto like "what is good for Mobil is good for America" lies a concrete material reality: the United States' disproportionate consumption of global resources. It is the maintenance of the American lifestyle based on systematic global inequality and exploitation that continues to guide US foreign policy. Militarism has always been the ultimate basis of imperialism.[76]

As political analyst Eqbal Ahmad has argued, recent world events further indicate that western interests rather than considerations of human rights, peace and international security seem to be "the chief determinants of which aggressions will be punished and who will be deemed to have violated international law."[77] Despite reports of hundreds of thousands killed, tortured, maimed, raped and displaced in wars in former Yugoslavia and Rwanda, the United States, the European Community and the United Nations vacillated for a long time "in a posture of complicity and appeasement".[78] As political scientist Richard Falk also states, the West has revealed its "moral decadence" and lack of compassion in relation to Europe itself.[79]

Women, Children and War

While arms producers, arms dealers, lobbyists, military and government officials, insurgent army and mafia leaders profit from the murderous arms trade, Third World youth are using imported weapons to kill each other, often for causes they hardly understand.[80] Countries such as Rwanda and Sri Lanka, which have suffered and continue to suffer greatly due to war, are not weapons producers themselves. One wonders whether arms exports are a form of population control coming from the North! Indeed, the same governments led by the United States that are pushing population control are pushing weapons into the Third World as well (Table 5.6).

As noted in the Introduction, children are the major victims of war.[81] They are also increasingly the perpetrators of wars as well. Lacking alternative means of employment and social status, it is often boys from the poorer classes who are compelled to join armed forces and lose their limbs and lives in wars which essentially benefit a small international and local elite. In today's global gun culture, the anger, idealism and naivety of the young are easily manipulated by arms traders and power-hungry men seeking recruits to bear arms for violent and extremist movements.

As armies and guerrilla forces exhaust the supplies of available men, they are turning more and more to children and young women to replenish their forces. Military leaders are finding children to be extremely pliable and effective soldiers: "In wartime, a commander wants total submission. You get that only from a child."[82] Girls are found to make especially obedient combatants. Of the 200,000 or so children involved as combatants in wars around the world today, about 10% are estimated to be girls.[83]

As UNICEF has pointed out, in many contemporary Third World war zones children do not voluntarily join armed factions; frequently they are forcibly conscripted.

...boys, 11 years old or even younger ... have been abducted and compelled to carry arms and others ... have been forced to kill members of their own family, or have been used as 'cannon fodder' to cross enemy lines or minefields.[84]

Quite often, children are drugged, as for example in Liberia, where teen-age gangs controlled by various war lords have apparently been roaming the country killing civilians indiscriminately.[85] In the more calculated killings by the Liberation Tigers of Tamil Eelam (LTTE), the separatist Tamil movement in Sri Lanka, both male and female children are conscripted, trained and widely deployed as suicide bombers. These children are also trained to wear cyanide capsules around their necks to be taken in case of capture.[86] Allegedly, the girls are made to wear two cyanide capsules instead of one, as a symbol of their greater patriotism!

In patriarchal societies, men unleash their aggression on children, considered to be their property, and on women, considered to be the weaker and more docile sex. In the contemporary period of generalized global violence and war, gender norms and sexual violence are taking more and more virulent forms.

Patriarchy and war

Male dominance in the family may have been the origin of war. In patriarchal culture, power is equated with aggression and masculinity; weakness with compassion and femininity. Women are supposed to bear male oppression silently and meekly. Where they fail to do so, they are branded as 'loud', 'hysterical', 'crazy' and frequently punished with rape and physical assault. As feminist analysts suggest, male desire to dominate and conquer may result from a deep psychological insecurity stemming from men's inability to give birth to life. The erotic fascination that many men have towards the hunt and war and their need to express their aggression could be derived from this primordial insecurity and fragility of the male ego.[87]

However, much of this weakness may also be culturally and historically created rather than biologically determined. For example, armed aggression has been used as a means for proving the power of the US by successive Presidents of the US. This was clearly visible in the case of the Gulf War, when President Bush vowed to "kick ass" in place of compromise or negotiation with Iraq. As political scientist Cynthia Enloe has written in her essay "The Gendered Gulf", "men's sense of their own masculinity, often tenuous, is as much a factor in international politics as the flows of oil, cables, and military hardware".[88]

Rape of the enemy's women has been a common aspect of war. As women become active in social movements, politically motivated rape is increasingly being used as a form of 'low-intensity warfare' against women. Many women in Chiapas, Mexico, have been attacked and raped by Mexican soldiers and other unknown assailants for alleged support of the Zapatista Army of National Liberation (EZLN) since the start of the rebellion in Chiapas in 1994.[89]

However, most women subjected to rape during wars are not necessarily political activists: their crime is often simply being women or belonging to an 'enemy' group, as has been the case of widespread rape of women in Bosnia and Rwanda. More than 250,000 women were raped during the civil war in Rwanda; many were also sexually mutilated and tortured. These traumatized women – mainly widows – and their children born of rape are now outcasts without any social or economic protection from their communities or the larger world.[90] Rape was a common occurrence during recent anti-Muslim riots in India as well. As an analysis published in the *Bulletin of the Committee of South Asian Women* states:

> ...after anti-Muslim riots following the demolition of the mosque at Ayodhaya, thirteen Muslim women were raped under flood-light in Surat and the rapes recorded on video. Seven of the women were then burnt alive. It is worth recalling that the Nazis also took pictures of their victims.[91]

What is also very disturbing is that many Hindu fundamentalist women reportedly applauded the rape of Muslim women, on the ground that "for hundreds and thousands of years Muslims have done the same to the Hindus".[92] The increasing identification of women with violent ethnic and religious fundamentalism portends not liberation but increased victimization of women.

In order to sustain conflicts, hatred has to be inculcated and enemies created even where they did not previously exist. The proliferation of weapons militates against the development of non-violent strategies for conflict resolution. In order to maintain and expand the military status quo, armed conflicts have to be continued. As the Communist enemy has now been defeated, the ethnic 'other' has become the main enemy in the post-Cold War world.

Ethno-Nationalism and Fundamentalism

While each nationalism gives itself a long history, the concept of the nation state is only a couple of centuries old; it is largely a phenomenon of the modern industrial capitalist age.[93] Ethnic and religious conflicts are not entirely attributable to primordialism. Colonial policies of divide and conquer exacerbated ethnic antagonisms, setting the stage for a large number of the contemporary ethnic and inter-state conflicts in the Third Word. Unequal incorporation of ethnic groups into the colonial economy, deliberate choice of certain ethnic minorities over ethnic majorities for colonial administrative positions and the drawing of colonial state boundaries without regard to historical relationships among neighboring groups are some examples.[94]

As Indian historian Romila Thapar has argued, religious fundamentalism emerged as a mode of resistance to the privatization of religion and the secularization of the polity in concurrence with capitalism and colonialism.[95] The main reason for the popularity and growth of fundamentalism today, whether it be Christian, Islamic, Hindu or any other, is increasing economic and political discontent stemming from unequal distribution of wealth and absence of political freedom. Underlying the appeal of religious fundamentalism as well as ethnic nationalism is a challenge to local elites and the global political-economic system.[96]

Indeed, cultural nationalism must be understood in the broader global and national contexts of deepening insecurity stemming from rapid social change. In regions such as the Middle East, religious nationalism is an expression of indigenous resistance to the homogenizing effects of western capitalist as well as Christian culture – globalization – and struggle for cultural survival and diversity – localization. In this regard, it is important to recognize that new GATT arrangements expanding trade in communication services would allow the corporate-controlled media to further penetrate Third World cultures, thereby increasing the threat to cultural diversity.[97]

Not all forms of resistance towards external domination and attempts to maintain local cultures can be equated with fanaticism and fundamentalism. As Palestinian scholar Edward Said has pointed out, "a scarf over the head, long-sleeved dress, a cap, a beard, frequenting mosques and prayer groups, paying homage to a local sheikh", simple ways of achieving emotional satisfaction for many people in the Middle East, must not be equated with "'fundamentalism' that encourages bomb-throwing and murder in the name of Islam" although they both stem from asserting Islamic identity.[98]

Still, in many places today, including the Middle East, ethnicity and religion are retreating into fundamentalism, that is, aggressive affirmations of a group's own beliefs through violent efforts to wipe out those identified as the enemy, and quite often those perceived to be allies of the enemy as well. Ethnic and religious nationalisms tend to lead to polarization and extremism; they know no middle ground. They force individuals to side with their ethnic group, blinding them to the complex realities of inter-group relations. In such a context, ethnicity or religion becomes an easy refuge and the ethnic or religious 'other' becomes an easy scapegoat for all of one's problems and frustrations. Nationalism is easily susceptible to manipulation by opportunistic politicians and ideologues seeking popular support to augment their own power.

As people are overwhelmed by the global economic system and feel powerless to resist and change it, many seek for enemies that can be more easily vanquished. In such a context, the extermination of the ethnic 'other' – 'ethnic cleansing' – capture of the state by one's own group or formation of a separate state become the strategies of liberation. Then, the transnational corporations, IMF, the World Bank and G7 governments that are the sources for much greater oppression remain relatively free from challenge. Economic manipulation, weapons sales and other policies of the dominant powers help extend religious and ethnic wars which keep the global masses fighting and killing each other. While nationalism based either on ethnicity or religion must not be reduced to the Marxist category of 'false consciousness', the contradictions of global capitalism and social class which underlie seemingly ethnic conflicts must be acknowledged. When these contradictions are not addressed, it is easy to simply attribute conflicts in places like Rwanda, Sri Lanka and India to primordialism, high population density or high population growth rates, as the case may be.

Ethnicity, capitalism and class

Most western analysts blame the tragedy in Rwanda on population and resource pressures and primordial, tribal sentiments of the poor, uneducated masses. But these analyses tend to overlook the fact that the massacres and war in Rwanda were planned, led and executed by political and military elites with foreign support for arming and training the regime's militia. They also ignore the fact that the silence and seeming lack of concern on the part of global powers actually enabled the carnage.[99]

In Sri Lanka, too, the framing of social discontent entirely in ethnic terms has undermined the common class experience of both the Sinhalese majority and the Tamil minority. Both groups have been oppressed by successive Sinhalese governments dominated mostly by westernized upper classes and by the forces of global capitalist development.[100] But in the case of the Sinhalese extremist group, the Janata Vimukti Peramuna (JVP) – People's Liberation Front – resistance came in the early 1970s and late 1980s in the form of a movement to take over state power, whereas in the case of the Tamil extremist group, the LTTE, resistance has taken the form of a protracted war to create a separate ethnic state.

However, what is often forgotten in the process of ethnic polarization is that, ultimately, both the Sinhalese and the Tamil youth want equal opportunities for education, employment, political participation and cultural survival. Yet the fuelling of ethnic hatred by opportunist politicians and intellectuals on both sides has created a situation of extreme nationalism where thousands upon thousands of youth of both groups are getting killed, maimed and traumatized and all of life is in danger.[101]

The Sikh movement in Punjab state in India, too, has been interpreted as largely an ethno-nationalist and secessionist struggle. But it is also a struggle stemming from the changes associated with the Green Revolution in that region. Many of the Sikhs fighting for a separate state have been angered by the central government's efforts to control their hard-won economic prosperity. The struggle in Punjab is not merely a religious conflict between Hindus and Sikhs; it is also a class conflict stemming from the contradictions of uneven and unequal capitalist development.[102]

The rise of Hindu violence against Muslims in India at the present time needs also to be viewed in the context of increasing western economic and cultural penetration, consumerism and resultant sense of alienation and powerlessness felt by the Hindu majority.[103] But in no way should this violence or any other form of violence be condoned.

Violence towards the 'other' is not separate from violence towards the self. Violence, like its opposite, peace, constitute a process – a continuum – rather than a separate and static category. This is clearly discernible in the treatment of women in fundamentalist movements.

Women and fundamentalism

As noted in the Introduction, cultural nationalism tends to rely on patriarchal authority to invoke a stable and secure past. In challenging the forces of modernization, right-wing fundamentalism attempts to restrict women to the private sphere and the wife and mother roles. In countries

such as Algeria and Afghanistan, women are being targeted and even as-
sassinated by fanatical male supremacist, Islamic groups for the 'crimes' of
simply working outside the home and not wearing the veil.[104]

Yet, frequently, nationalist and fundamentalist movements also rely on
women's participation in the public sphere for the achievement of their
objectives. The result is often contradictory expectations of women. An
example is the veiling of Islamic women. As Leila Ahmed and other scholars have shown, the veil has been both a symbol of anti-imperialism and
cultural self-assertion and an expression of women's subordination. It has
both been voluntarily adopted by women and been imposed upon them by
religious and state authorities.[105]

Despite their subordination in most nationalist movements, women have
been an important element in even in the more belligerent, fascist variants.[106]
The worsening global economic and social crisis is driving many women to
join the women's wings of such extreme movements. Thus women, who
have traditionally disavowed violence, are increasingly resorting to bomb-
throwing and murder as the only means of self-assertion and empowerment.

For young women joining such movements, as for their male counterparts,
carrying a gun and fighting for a cause provide a sense of dignity and self-
esteem they otherwise lack. As some observers have commented, it is often
women who come from lower social classes and who have experienced little
in the way of social status and self-esteem who tend to be the most militant
and virulent in dedication to their cause. As Sri Lankan journalist Rita
Sebastian has reported, participation in the violent struggle of the LTTE
has brought about a massive transformation of the roles of women.

> The woman suicide bomber responsible for the assassination of the Indian Prime
> Minister, Rajiv Gandhi, symbolises the extent of that transformation. Women on
> motor-bicycles, with automatic weapons slung across their shoulders, or at the
> wheel of heavy trucks are a common sight.... No different from their male
> counterparts, they have adopted the gun as the symbol of their liberation.[107]

Faced with a shortage of young and able-bodied men, the Sri Lankan
government is also seeking to increase recruitment of young women into
the armed forces.[108] However, ultimately the gun and the suicide bomb
symbolize not liberation but destruction of the 'other' as well as the self.
This is brought to light for example in a report on LTTE torture camps
issued by a human rights group in Sri Lanka. Based on information gath-
ered from escaped prisoners, it documents use of young Tamil women as
torturers of other Tamil women imprisoned for allegedly serving as in-
formants and accomplices for enemy groups. The utterly harsh and inhumane treatment meted out by young women, sometimes mere children,
to other women who could well be their mothers, sisters or grandmothers
bespeaks not women's liberation but delusion, insecurity and depravity.[109]

If more sane life-enhancing options are not made available to young men, women and children, the world will become an even more dangerous and insecure a place than it already is. Instead, Third World conditions are multiplying everywhere. The strategies of global free market authoritarianism make corporations increasingly "freer to exploit workers, consumers, and the environment, North and South, East and West".[110] As companies demand more labor repression, curtailment of environmental activism and punishment of terrorist activities and as social conflicts and turmoil increase, many people in the North are also succumbing to racism and fundamentalism as means to cope with uncertainty and fear.

Insecurity and Violence in the North

A recent report of the US Justice Department's Bureau of Justice Statistics shows that "even as the number of teenagers has declined" teenage violence with guns has steadily risen since 1985, thus making one question the Malthusian proposition that violence is inherently related to the increase in the number of angry young men. From 1985 to 1993, weapons-related arrests of juveniles more than doubled from 30,000 to 61,000. In 1993, 23% of all weapons arrests in the US were of juveniles and it is believed that if these trends continue, juvenile arrests for violent crime will double by 2010.[111]

Apparently, 135,000 students bring guns to school every day and there are over 200 million handguns in the United States today. For many young men without economic opportunities and who are lured by media violence, manhood is associated with joining a gang and carrying a gun. Much of inner city violence in the US is inter-personal and random. Teenagers kill each other at school and on the streets over petty rivalries and even over consumer items such as brand name sneakers and jackets. Every day, innocent bystanders are killed in crossfire and also because of police brutality. In the United States, inner city crime, drug- and gang-related deaths rival and sometimes surpass those of Third World 'low-intensity' conflicts. In 1987, the US had a homicide rate of 21.9 per 1,000 men aged 15–24, thus making the country "the unchallenged killing champion of the world". A young Black man from Harlem may be less likely to reach age 40 than a young man in Bangladesh.[112]

One in every three Black men in their 20s in the US today is imprisoned, on probation or on parole. A much greater proportion of Blacks are arrested, prosecuted, convicted and imprisoned than are whites in the US. The war on drugs in the United States has been waged largely against Blacks. Although Black men constitute 13% of all monthly drug users, they represent 35% of all arrests, 55% of all convictions and 74% of all prison sentences for drug possession. As many criminologists have pointed out, these racial biases in law enforcement explain the sharply divergent views of Blacks and whites on the acquittal in the O.J. Simpson murder trial.[113]

Everywhere women are the victims of sexual assault and family violence, these being the fastest growing crimes in the US. According to the
American Medical Association, in the US, 700,000 women are sexually
assaulted each year, one every 45 seconds. Some 61% of female rape victims are under age 18.[114] There seems to be little anguish that young boys
are raping women who could well be their own relatives. Often the victims
themselves are blamed for walking alone in the dark and castigated as a
prostitutes while the rapists brag about their manliness and sometimes even
their mothers defend them.[115]

Tired and angered by male violence frequently directed at them, many
young women are also seeking to assert themselves violently. Isolated acts
of violence and participation in armed gangs in inner cities such as Los
Angeles are increasing among young women. Films and advertising glori-
fying violence are making more women equate power and liberation with
aggression. Seeking new markets for guns, gun manufacturers and their
powerful lobby, the National Rifle Association, are promoting guns as the
symbol for women's liberation while companies in the fashion industry are
promoting clothes which allow women to carry concealed weapons.[116] What
is urgently needed in the US is not a domestic population control policy,
but a gun control policy.

Instead, the production of sophisticated weapons that kill more efficiently
is increasing. Winchester-Olin's new Talon bullet, targeted especially at the
domestic market, is an example. The superior performance capability of
this new bullet has been extolled in the *Handgunning Magazine*:

> ...the cuts made by the tips of the 'blades' promoted further tearing along the
> length of the wound. The actual measured surface area of the permanent wound
> channel is therefore hugely *greater than the mere tubular track left by any conventional
> hollow point bullet.* (emphasis in original)[117]

More and more states in the Unites States are also passing increasingly
lax policies for gun possession while at the same time they are building
more and more prisons to house criminals. The overwhelming response to
social turmoil in the US, as elsewhere in the world, continues to be calls
for population control, more weapons and 'law and order' rather than
justice and social change.

The number of prison inmates in the US has tripled over the past 20
years and prison building has emerged as one of the country's fastest growing 'industries'. The cost of building prisons rose from $6.8 billion a year
in 1980 to $30 billion a year in 1995, according to the US Justice Depart-
ment's Bureau of Justice Statistics. As the number of prison guards has
increased even faster than the number of prisoners, prison guards' unions
are emerging as a major political force in states such as California.[118] Where
prisoners are disproportionately people of color and the guards largely
white, racial tensions can easily be inflamed.

Racism and violence in the North

Ethnically based violence is on the rise in both the US and Europe. Much of this violence is directed against new immigrants, especially immigrants of color. In the US, the demands for limiting immigration are rising. An opinion poll carried out for *Time*/CNN showed that the percentage of US citizens favoring strict limits on immigration rose from 67% in May 1985 to 73% in September 1993.[119] Recent reports show that while much of Black violence is directed against Blacks themselves, 'hate crimes' by African Americans against Hispanics, Asians as well as whites are on the increase in the US.[120] Although hostility and conflict among communities of color are growing, it is the forces of white supremacy that are mostly responsible for hate crimes and racially motivated violence. such as the burning of Black churches now spreading across the US South. Feminist activists see a fundamental connection between the burning of Black churches and the bombing of abortion clinics in the US.[121]

In the North, as in the South, ethno-nationalism, religious fundamentalism and patriarchy are often interlinked and they take many forms in addition to violence against immigrants, people of color and women. In the US, right-wing Christian fundamentalism has championed their violent struggles against abortion and reproductive choice for women and social acceptance of gays and lesbians. Angry and desperate individuals, usually from economically depressed white communities, are also joining violent sects and militias to fight social groups, the government and other institutions they deem to be the cause of their economic and social problems. The bombing of a federal building in Oklahoma City in 1995 and populist support for the so-called 'Wise Use Movement', a creation of mining, fishing and timber industries against environmental protection efforts in the US, are just a few examples.[122]

In Europe anti-immigrant feelings and white supremacy movements are even stronger than in the US. In Germany as well as France and Britain, hate crimes are soaring. There are frequent reports, particularly from Germany, of residences of Turkish, Vietnamese and other immigrants and asylum seekers being set on fire and people getting hurt and killed.[123] While all barriers to trade are being lifted, the barriers to the movement of people are being tightened even against political refugees desperately seeking to escape from repressive regimes. As Jan Oberg, Director of the Amsterdam-based Transnational Institute observes,

> ...the new Maastricht Europe ... with a comparatively great potential to help those in need, is busy closing doors and building new walls.... Not even the millions of individual human tragedies in former Yugoslavia next-door seem to appeal to our European humanity...[124]

Neo-Nazism is attracting large numbers of disaffected punk, skinhead and other groups in Europe and the US.[125] As neo-fascists enter electoral politics in large numbers, it is well to remember that Hitler was elected into office not so long ago. It is also important to emphasize that, as in the South, fascism is not a peculiarly male phenomenon. Many women supported the Nazi state and many still support racism and political authoritarianism.[126] Increasing class polarization, global competition, unemployment, and so on, make many white people search for easy scapegoats. While racism, sexism, homophobia, and so on, have dynamics of their own, they are exacerbated by economic competition, insecurity and fear.

Although the genocide in ex-Yugoslavia is commonly attributed to ethnicity and primordialism, worsening economic conditions were a critical factor which made ethnic relations conflictual and violent. The excessive borrowing during the regime of the previous Yugoslavian leader, Marshal Tito, and IMF-imposed economic restructuring and cutbacks in social, education and health services created a situation where Serbs and Croats began to blame each other for their social and economic discontent. As social change activist Fran Peavey has observed, once the "wildfire of social hysteria caught on with the less educated, the rural populations, the more economically marginalized", the entire society was drawn into a war that no one seems to know how to end.[127]

The stresses and tensions associated with the breakdown of Communist authoritarianism have been compounded by spreading market forces, unemployment and class polarization throughout the former Soviet bloc. Young people in this region now share the same material expectations as their counterparts in the rest of the world. But like their global counterparts, they, too, are increasingly frustrated by lack of opportunities. Unless their growing insecurity, fear and anger are channelled in more positive directions, they, too, could become prey to the militant movements and neo-fascist organizations promising security and community, as have many youth in the South and the North.[128]

When the politics of fear and hate proliferate it is usually the weakest groups that suffer the most. An example is the millions of Gypsies or Roma people in Eastern Europe – Hungary, Romania and Czechoslovakia. Today, many of the problems of poverty and crime are being blamed on the Gypsies, their large families and welfare dependence by state officials, intellectuals and ordinary citizens alike. A return of the brutality and genocide visited on the Gypsies during the Nazi era cannot be ruled out. A survey of ordinary citizens conducted by a Bucharest daily newspaper found much support for 'ethnic cleansing' of the Gypsies. As one working class woman put it, "I'm sorry I don't have the power – I would exterminate them all."[129]

The racism people express towards each other cannot be understood merely at the demographic and psycho-biological levels. It needs to be examined in relation to the generalization of the militaristic model of conquest and domination into all sectors of life. As we have seen above, this model is not conducive to the preservation of life; instead, it moves inexorably towards its destruction. Historian E.P. Thompson called it the "exterminist mode of production".[130]

The confluence of the forces of technology, capitalism and militarism has alienated people from each other, from nature and the deeper aspects of self. It has bred pessimism and cynicism and an acceptance of poverty, ecocide, genocide, violence against women, children and ethnic others as inevitable. It encourages ignorance, greed, fear and hatred; not wisdom, generosity, courage and compassion.

Democracy or Fascism?

As discussed in Chapter 1, neo-Malthusian analysts see Third World population growth as threatening democracy and enlightenment in the West and giving rise to anarchy and fascism in the Third World. But our investigation reveals that the roots of global militarism and repression lie largely in the industrialized countries in the North where population growth rates are actually declining. Malthusian focus on Third World 'overpopulation' diverts attention from the intensification of fascistic tendencies in the North.[131] Moreover, as noted in earlier sections of this book, the collusion between population control interests and right-wing movements such as the anti-immigration movement encourage the spread of eugenicist and fascist ideologies of white racial and ethnic superiority.

Capitalism and right-wing fundamentalism may seem to be contradictory social forces: the former representing secular modernism; the latter religious tradition. But these two forces are increasingly converging to undermine democracy worldwide.[132] This is particularly the case with Christian fundamentalism in the US, which derives its power from the 'dictatorship' of the right represented by the merger of big business and the state.

Corporations and wealthy individuals in the US control the political candidates and agendas and policies of politicians in office, whether Republican or Democrat, making a mockery of democracy in the country. Large corporations, especially defense corporations, exercise a tremendous influence on politicians and the electoral process in the US (Table 7.3).[133]

The issue of abortion continues to separate most Democratic politicians from most of their Republican counterparts. Still, the 1996 US elections revealed increasing social class convergence of the two parties in upholding corporate business interests over the interests of the poor, the immigrants, the environment, and so on. Candidates who are the most skilled at fundraising and manipulating the media usually win. Once in office, staying in power seems to be the primary objective of most politicians in the US and everywhere else.

The alienation of ordinary citizens from electoral politics is so great that many do not vote at all in US Presidential, Congressional or local elections.

Table 7.3 PACs' (Political Action Committees') contributions, 1994 and 1996: 1994 and 1996 US Congressional elections

Top PACs	Total in 1993–94 elections (*US$ millions*)	Total in 1995–96 elections (*US$ millions*)*
Defense aerospace		
Lockhead Corp.	592,611	1,031,150
Martin Marietta Corp.	530,310	54,000
Textron Inc	356,810	265,250
Northrop Corp.	334,939	600,300
Rockwell International	282,969	249,050
Defense electronics		
Raytheon	279,655	265,350
Loral Corp.	273,759	299,600
Harris Corp.	182,500	141,738
Hughes Aircraft	181,780	251,100
TRW Inc	162,130	194,140
Misc defense		
General Dynamics	385,112	292,062
Tenneco Inc	310,600	585,475
General Atomics	134,920	238,750
BDM International	105,874	84,234
FMC Corp.	88,820	198,150
Oil and gas		
Exxon Corp.	495,875	476,390
Chevron Corp.	337,493	205,252
Coastal Corp.	292,369	130,700
Amoco Corp.	225,250	179,050
Atlantic Richfield	222,480	124,900
Mining		
National Coal Association	223,200	7,200
Cyprus Amax Minerals Co.	120,428	174,470
Peabody Coal	96,220	48,600
Phelps Dodge Corp.	72,750	68,240
Reynolds Metals	62,050	47,600
Electric utilities		
ACRE (Action Committee for Rural Electrification)	501,200	562,466
Southern California Edison	283,620	187,649
Pacific Gas and Electric	156,567	117,820
Detroit Edison	151,535	134,465
Carolina Power and Light	118,200	166,250

* Full data as yet unreleased: total for full cycle expected to be higher.

Source: Joshua Goldstein, *PACs in Profile: Spending Patterns in the 1994 Elections*, Washington, DC: Center for Responsive Politics, 1995, pp. 45–46; Federal Elections Commission Data released on 2 December 1996 compiled by Center for REsponsive Politics, Washington DC.

According to figures released by the Committee for the Study of the American Electorate, the percentage of eligible voters who voted at the Presidential elections declined from 55.2% in 1992 to 48.99% in 1996. Only 45.89% of eligible voters voted at the 1996 US Congressional elections. Voting is particularly low among the young and the minorities. According to US Census Bureau figures, only 16.5% of 18- to 20-year-olds, 46.9% of Blacks and 19.1% of Hispanics among registered voters voted at the 1994 Congressional elections.[134] The Republican 'Contract With America' does not represent a mandate by the majority of the country's citizens. It is ironic that many people in the US, a nation considered to be the exemplar of democracy and freedom, do not exercise the right to vote when so many people, especially in countries in the South like China, are sacrificing their lives for democracy and freedom of expression.

The media and the 'manufacturing of consent'

Thus far, psychological control has proven to be more powerful than direct force in managing people in the North and in maintaining the interests of the rich and powerful. It gives the appearance of choice and freedom even when they do not truly exist. Indeed, the media play a key role in the maintenance of what political scientist Bertram Gross and others have called the 'friendly' or 'soft' fascism' in the North, especially the United States.[135] It evokes a vision of the 'new totalitarianism' that Aldous Huxley described in *Brave New World* where people do not have to be coerced because they can be made to "love their servitude" by an army of propagandists and mind managers manipulating information.[136] The futurist scenario of human reproductive control that contemporary writer Margaret Atwood describes in *The Handmaid's Tale* needs also to be placed in this context of techno-bureaucratic authoritarianism and media manipulation.[137]

The goal of the media is not the dissemination of truth as much as the maintenance of the global status quo. The media are not independent entities but a global corporate enterprise with monopolistic, interlocking control over the collection and dissemination of what it constitutes as news. About 90% of the international news and information for newspapers around the world is filtered through four news agencies located in the North: API (Associated Press International), Reuters, Agence-France Presse and UPI (United Press International). Two television giants, Reuters Television and Worldwide Television, followed by CNN (Cable News Network) and the BBC (British Broadcasting Corporation) dominate the production and distribution of practically all the foreign news to television stations across the world.[138] Much of the news and information used in the local languages is also derived from these sources.

As critics point out, media domination is the North's most effective weapon in trying to persuade the South to embrace the capitalist model of development. When this media domination is combined with policies and aid programs from governments and institutions in the North such as the World Bank, Third World societies are left with hardly any room to determine their own paths of economic and cultural development.[139] Corporate control of the media has been instrumental in ignoring any serious discussions of radical transformation needed in the global status quo. For example, feminist critiques of the ICPD population agenda and Third World critiques of US and allied intervention in the Gulf War in 1991 were almost totally absent in the dominant media. The consensus on these events presented by the corporate media was largely their own creation.

Out of the world's largest 100 transnational communications industries, at least 30 have close linkages with military interests. As a result, choice of media techniques has been greatly influenced by military needs.[140] The Cold War was largely a media war of 'disinformation and propaganda'. Similarly, a media war of disinformation and propaganda is now being directed at the new Third World enemies in the post-Cold War period.[141] Indeed, as Noam Chomsky and Edward Herman have explained, the media "manufacture consent" where it does not authentically exist.[142] As we have seen earlier in relation to the creation of an alarmist fear of 'overpopulation', manufacturing of consent takes place in all arenas where important ideological and power differences exist.

The language of the New World Order is that of peace, democracy and human rights. This language shifts attention away from the widening and deepening structures of global inequality, militarism, authoritarianism and genocide. The disparity between language and reality has bred the kind of situation best described by George Orwell in *Nineteen Eighty-Four:*

> 'Reality control', ... Newspeak, 'doublethink'.... To know and not to know, to be conscious of complete truthfulness while telling carefully constructed lies ... to repudiate morality while laying claim to it, to believe that democracy was impossible ... to forget, whatever it was necessary to forget, then to draw it back to memory again at the moment when it was needed, and then promptly to forget it again, and above all, to apply the same process to the process itself that was the ultimate subtlety: consciously to induce unconsciousness, and then, once again, to become unconscious of the act of hypnosis ... just performed.[143]

Notes

1. James Petras, "Cultural Imperialism in the Late 20th Century", *Journal of Contemporary Asia*, Vol. 23, No. 2, May 1993, p. 139; see also Will Baker, "The Global Teenager", *Whole Earth Review*, Winter 1989, No. 65, p. 35.

2. Petras, "Cultural Imperialism", pp. 139–148.

3. Mary E. Clark, "The Backward Ones", *TRANET: A Bi-Monthly Digest for the A & T (Alternative and Transformational) Movements*, No. 85, November 1993, p. 8.

4. Ibid.; see also Special Issue on 'Fundamentalism' in *Turning Wheel*, Journal of the Buddhist Peace Fellowship, San Francisco, Fall 1995.

5. Baker, "Global Teenager", p. 3.

6. Frantz Fanon, *Black Skin, White Masks*, trans. Charles Markmann, New York: Grove Press, 1967; Albert Memmi, *The Colonizer and the Colonized*, Boston: Beacon Press, 1967.

7. Chee Yoke Ling, *How Big Powers Dominate the Third World: The Use and Abuse of International Law*, Penang, Malaysia: Third World Network, 1987, p. 3; Rosa Luxemburg, *The Accumulation of Capital*, New York: Monthly Review Press, 1968.

8. F. Bougotu quoted in John H. Bodley, "Demographic Impact of the Frontier", in Menard and Moen, eds, *Perspectives on Education*, p. 23; Hans Koning, *Columbus: His Enterprise*, New York: Monthly Review Press, 1976.

9. Bandarage, *Colonialism in Sri Lanka*, Chap. 7.

10. Rosa Luxemburg, "Militarism as a Province of Accumulation" in Gioseffi, ed., *Women on War*, pp. 129–130; Eqbal Ahmad, "At Cold War's End: A World of Pain", in *After the Cold War: The North/South Divide, Institute for Defense and Disarmament Studies*, Reprint 3, p. 4, (reprinted from *Boston Review*, Vol. 18, Nos 3–4, June–August 1993).

11. Eqbal Ahmad, "The Disarmament Movement: A Critique", in Worsley, ed., *On the Brink*, p. 52.

12. Fred Halliday, "Cold War, the Peace Movement and the Third World", in ibid., p. 95.

13. Ibid., p. 96.

14. Bertram Gross, *Friendly Fascism: The New Face of Power in America*, Boston: South End Press, 1980, p. 37.

15. Noam Chomsky and Edward S. Herman, *The Washington Connection and Third World Fascism*, Boston: South End Press, 1979, p. 44; Richard Falk, "Foreword", in Bello et al., eds, *Development Debacle*, p. xii.

16. David G. Stratman, *We Can Change the World; The Real Meaning of Everyday Life*, Boston: New Democracy Books, 1993, p. 158.

17. Michael Klare and Cynthia Aronson, *Supplying Repression*, Washington DC: Institute for Policy Studies, 1981, pp. 41, 48.

18. Ibid., *passim*.

19. Anthony Lewis, "Signals to Haiti", op.-ed., *The New York Times*, December 13, 1993.

20. Klare and Aronson, *Supplying Repression*, p. 57; see also Chomsky and Herman, *The Washington Connection*; Richard Falk, "Hard Choices and Tragic Dilemmas", *The Nation*, December 20, 1993; Halliday, "Cold War", p. 95.

21. Dankwart Rostow, "Democracy: A Global Revolution", *Foreign Affairs*, Vol. 64, No. 4, Fall 1990, p. 75.

22. Klare and Aronson, *Supplying Repression*, pp. 103–104.

23. Ligaya Lindio-McGovern, "The Philippines: Counter-Insurgency and Peasant Women", *Race and Class*, Vol. 34, No. 4, 1993, pp. 1–11.

24. Sklar, "Brave New World Order", in Peters, ed., *Collateral Damage*, pp. 25–26.

25. Howard Zinn, *A People's History of the United States*, New York: Harper and Row, 1980, pp. 452–455.

26. Lindio-McGovern, "The Philippines", pp. 1–2; see also *Human Rights World Reports*, 1991–1995, Human Rights Watch, New York.

27. "Code of Conduct on Arms Transfers Act of 1993", US House of Representatives 3538, introduced by Ms McKinney, November 18, 1993; Information Packet, International Working Conference on the Arms Trade, SANE/Freeze International, New York, November 1–2, 1991; UNDP, *Human Development Report 1994*, p. 56.

28. Agnes Black, "Carnage in Guatemala", Letter to the Editor, *The New York Times*, July 13, 1990; see also Michael Kidron and Dan Smith, *The New State of War and Peace: An International Atlas*, New York: Simon and Schuster, 1990.

29. Information Project for Africa, "Unconventional Warfare and the Theory of Competitive Reproduction", *passim*.

30. Michael R. Gordon, "Pentagon Fights Budget Officials Over $50 Billion", *The New York Times*, December 10, 1993, p. A1.

31. "Will East Beat the West? A Challenge from Two Asian Statesmen, *World Press Review*, Vol. 42, No. 12, December 1995, pp. 6–11.

32. Stephen Slade, "Emperor Bill", *War Watch Out Now*, No. 9, September–October 1993, p. 7.

33. Robert Borosage, "All Dollars No Sense", *Mother Jones*, September–October 1993, pp. 41–44.

34. Massachusetts Peace Action, *Monthly Update*, November–December, 1993.

35. Gordon, "Pentagon Fights Budget Officials".

36. Michael R. Gordon, "Pentagon Begins Effort to Combat More Lethal Arms in the Third World", *The New York Times*, December 8, 1993, p. A15.

37. Cited in ibid.

38. Cited in Julie Petersen, "This Bullet Kills You Better", *Mother Jones*, September–October 1993, p. 15; see also Klare and Aronson, *Supplying Repression*, p. 72.

39. *Arms Sales Monitor*, No. 20, April 30, 1993, p. 1; "Administration Proposes Year-End Missile Sale to Turkey", *Arms Sales Monitor*, No. 31, December 5, 1995, p. 1.

40. *Arms Sales Monitor*, No. 20, April 30, 1993, p. 3; US Arms Control and Disarmament Agency, *World Military Expenditures and Arms Transfers 1990*, Washington, DC: US Government Printing Office, 1991, p. 91.

41. *Arms Sales Monitor*, No. 22, September 30, 1993, p. 3.

42. Nicole Ball, *Briefing Book on Conventional Arms Transfers*, Washington, DC: Council for a Livable World Education Fund, August 1991, p. 19.

43. *Journal of the Federation of American Scientists (FAS)*, "Public Interest Report", p. 11.

44. Cited in *Arms Sales Monitor*, No. 28, February 15, 1995, p. 1.

45. Ball, *Briefing Book*, p. 19; "The U.S. Looks into Latin America", from *El Mercurio*, reprinted in *World Press Review*, September 1992, p. 16; "Asian Arms Binge", p. 34; Michael T. Klare, "The Next Great Arms Race", *Foreign Affairs*, Summer 1993, pp. 136–152.

46. "Pakistan Holds Firm to Nuclear Plan", *The New York Times*, November 21, 1993, p. 4.

47. *Journal of the Federation of American Scientists (FAS)*, "Public Interest Report", p. 8.

48. Barbara Crossette, *India: Facing the Twenty First Century*, Bloomington: Indiana University Press, 1993, Chap. 10; "Will East Beat the West?"

49. Ball, *Briefing Book*, p. 19; Michael T. Klare, "It's Business as Usual", *The Nation*, February 3, 1992, pp. 120–126; "Transparency Lacking in Exports of Small Arms", *Arms Sales Monitor*, No. 31, December 1995, p. 2.

50. Klare, cited in Fred Contrada, "Expert to Warn U.N. on Arms Trade", *Union News*, Springfield, MA, June 24, 1996, p. 1; see also Peace Action, "The Small Arms Trade", Fact Sheet, Education Fund, Washington, DC, August 1994.

51. UNDP, *Human Development Report, 1990*, p. 77; *Illegal and Covert Arms Transfers*, Center for Defense Information, Washington, DC, August 30, 1993, pp. 1–2.

52. "Death on the Spot: The End of a Drug King", Special Report, *Newsweek*, December 13, 1993, pp. 18–21; see also "Global Mafia", Special Report, *Newsweek*, December 13, 1993, pp. 22–24; 27–28; 30–31.

53. Quoted in "Potential Next Targets", in *War Watch Out Now*, No. 10, October 1991, pp. 4–5.

54. "U.S. Strategy Plan Calls for Insuring No Rivals Develop", *The New York Times*, March 8, 1992, pp. 1, 14.

55. "Pentagon Drops Goals of Blocking New Superpowers", *The New York Times*, May 24, 1992, pp. 1, 14.

56. "Downsizing Defence: From Swords to...", *United and Babson Investment Report*, November 30, 1992, p. 475.

57. *Arms Sales Monitor*, No. 22, September 30, 1993, p. 2; see also Gordon, "Pentagon Fights Budget Officials over $50 Billion", p. A28; "Far-Flung Frontiers of Security: The Clinton Administration's Two Year Strategy", *The Defense Monitor*, Vol. XXIV, No. 1, 1995, p. 3.

58. *Arms Sales Monitor*, No. 22, September 30, 1993, p. 2; Barbara Trent, Director, *Panama Deception* (video recording) – Rhino Home Video, The Empowerment Project, Santa Monica, CA, 1993; UNDP, *Human Development Report 1994*, p. 55.

59. Asoka Bandarage, "The Gulf War and the Crisis Facing Humanity", unpublished

manuscript (excerpted in *The Sunday Times*, Sri Lanka, February 10, 1991, p. 3); Peters, ed., *Collateral Damage, passim*.

60. Cited in "Military Sales Logic", p. 6.
61. Bandarage, "The Gulf War", p. 7; Sklar, "Brave New World Order", p. 34.
62. Sklar, "Brave New World Order", p. 34.
63. Cynthia Enloe, "The Gendered Gulf", in Peters, ed., *Collateral Damage*, p. 100.
64. Ibid., pp. 93–110; Bandarage, "Gulf War", p. 7.
65. National Security Education Act of 1991, signed by the US President, December 4, 1991 (PL 102–183); see also James K. Boyce, "The National Security Education Act of 1991: Issues and Analysis", in *The Bulletin of Concerned Asian Scholars*, Vol. 24, No. 2, 1992, pp. 85–88.
66. William J. Broad, "U.S. Will Deploy Its Spy Satellites on Nature Mission", *The New York Times*, November 27, 1995, p. 1.
67. Noam Chomsky, "What We Say Goes: The Middle East in the New World Order", in Peters, ed., *Collateral Damage*, pp. 49–92.
68. William Hoynes, "War as Video Game: Media, Activism, and the Gulf War", in Peters, ed., *Collateral Damage, passim*.
69. Bandarage, "Global Peace and Security", p. 37.
70. Hoynes, "War as Video Game", p. 309.
71. T. Rajamoorthy, "Double Standards are the Norm", *Third World Resurgence*, No. 31, 1993, pp. 19–20.
72. Thalif Deen, "Security Council Accused of Double Standards", *Third World Resurgence*, No. 31, 1993, pp. 21–22.
73. Sklar, "Brave New World Order", p. 13; Patrick E. Tyler, "Health Crisis is Said to Grip Iraq in Wake of War's Destruction", *The New York Times*, May 22, 1991, p. A16.
74. Barbara Crossette, "Iraq Sanctions Kill Children, UN Reports", *The New York Times*, December 1, 1995, pp. A6, 8.
75. Bandarage, "The Gulf War", p. 2.
76. Ahmad, "At Cold War's End", p. 6.
77. Ibid., p. 4.
78. Ibid., p. 5.
79. Falk, "Hard Choices", p. 758.
80. "Children in Bondage"; "A Pointless Conflict in Angola", *The New York Times*, Editorial, January 24, 1996, p. A18.
81. UNICEF, *State of the World's Children 1996*, p. 13.
82. "Children in Bondage", *passim*.
83. "Hunger, Hate and the Lure of Adventure", *World Press Review*, Vol. 43, No. 1, January 1996, p. 9.
84. Thalif Deen, "Children as Targets and Mine Sweeps: The 1990s", *Terra Viva*, IPS (Inter Press Service), June 19, 1993, p. 3; see also "Children of War", Special Issue of *Time/Newsweek*, 1992.
85. Thomas L. Friedman, "Heart of Darkness", *The New York Times*, January 21, 1995, p. E15.
86. Stephen Lambert, executive producer, *Suicide Killers: A Documentary on LTTE in Sri Lanka*, London: British Broadcasting Corporation, 1992; Crossette, *India*, p. 115.
87. Abouali Farmanfarmaian, "Did you Measure Up? The Role of Race and Sexuality in the Gulf War", in Peters, ed., *Collateral Damage*, pp. 129–30; see also Marti Kheel, "Ecofeminism and Deep Ecology: Reflections on Identity and Difference", in Diamond and Orenstein, eds, *Reweaving the World*; Carol Cohn, "Sex and Death in the Rational World of Defense Intellectuals", *Signs*, Vol. 12, No. 4, Summer 1987, pp. 687–718.
88. Enloe, "The Gendered Gulf", p. 101.
89. David Amdur, "Rape as Low-Intensity Warfare", *Peacework*, December 1995, No. 258, pp. 15–16.
90. Lucy Johnson, "Striking a Balance", *Terra Viva*, IPS (Inter Press Service), June 15, 1993, p. 8; Royte, "Outcasts", pp. 37–38.
91. Sucheta Mazumdar, "For Rama and Hindutva: Women and Right-Wing

Mobilization in Contemporary India", in *Committee on South Asian Women Bulletin*, Vol. 8, Nos 3–4, 1993, p. 7; Jyotsana Vaid, "On Women and the Hindu Right", ibid., p. 1.

92. Madhu Kishwar, "Warning from the Bombay Riots", in ibid., p. 23.

93. Dan Smith, "Nationalism: The Underside of World Politics", lecture sponsored by Five College Peace and World Security Studies Program, Amherst, MA, October 11, 1992.

94. Bandarage, *Colonialism in Sri Lanka*, Chap. 6; Stanley B. Greenberg, *Race and State in Capitalist Development: Comparative Perspectives*, New Haven: Yale University Press, 1980.

95. Romila Thapar, "Imagined Religious Communities? Ancient History and the Modern Search for a Hindu Identity", *Modern Asian Studies*, Vol. 23, No. 2, 1989, pp. 209–231.

96. "Seeing Green: The Red Menace is Gone: But Here's Islam", *The New York Times*, January 21, 1995, Section 4, p. 16.

97. David Arnott, "On Cultural Rights", *Third World Resurgence*, No. 33, 1993, p. 44.

98. Edward W. Said, "The Phony Islamic Threat", *The New York Times Magazine*, November 21, 1993, p. 62; also Edward W. Said, *Culture and Imperialism*, New York: Alfred A. Knopf, 1993, p. 65.

99. Jennifer Olson, "Behind the Recent Tragedy in Rwanda", *GeoJournal*, February 1995, pp. 217–222.

100. Bandarage, *Colonialism in Sri Lanka*, Chap. 8; Bandarage, "Packaging the Sri Lankan Conflict: Peace, Obstacles and Opportunities", *Samar*, No. 3, Summer 1994, pp. 18–21.

101. Ibid.

102. Shiva, *Violence*.

103. Thapar, "Imagined Religious Communities?"

104. Karima Bennoune, "Algerian Women Confront Fundamentalism", *Monthly Review*, Vol. 46, September 1994, pp. 26–39; see also Vaid, "Women and the Hindu Right"; John F. Burns, "Walled in, Shrouded and Angry in Afghanistan", *The New York Times*, October 4, 1996, p. 3.

105. Leila Ahmed, *Women and Gender in Islam: Historical Roots of a Modern Debate*, New Haven: Yale University Press, 1992; Nahid Toubia, ed., *Women of the Arab World: The Coming Challenge*, London: Zed Books, 1988; David C. Gordon, *Women of Algeria: An Essay on Change*, Cambridge, MA: Harvard University Press, 1968, pp. 56–57.

106. Claudia Koonz, "Mothers in the Fatherland: Women in Nazi Germany", in Renate Bridenthal and Claudia Koonz, eds, *Becoming Visible: Women in European History*, Boston: Houghton Mifflin, 1977.

107. Rita Sebastian, "Ethnic Conflict in Sri Lanka: Its Ecological and Political Consequences", in Shiva, ed., *Close to Home*, p. 125.

108. Semali Kallapatha, "We are Ready Even to Go into the Tiger's Mouth", *Silumina*, Sri Lanka, October 13, 1996, p. 26.

109. "Women Prisoners of the LTTE", The University Teachers for Human Rights, Jaffna, Sri Lanka, *Information Bulletin*, No. 5, March 1995, p. 4.

110. Sklar, "Brave New World Order", p. 29.

111. "Weapons Offenses Up Among Young, Study Says", *The New York Times*, November 13, 1995, p. A14.

112. Tom Wicker, "Violence and Hypocrisy", *The New York Times*, July 9, 1990, p. A17; see also John J. Diluio Jr, "Save the Children", *The New York Times*, November 13, 1993, p. 15; Don Terry, "A Graver Jackson's Cry: Overcome Violence", *The New York Times*, November 13, 1993, p. 1; Bob Herbert, "The 'Squash It' Campaign", *The New York Times*, December 8, 1993, p. A25..

113. Fox Butterfield, "More Blacks in their 20s Have Trouble With the Law", *The New York Times*, October 5, 1995, p. A18.

114. "Doctor Group Says Violence Imperils Nation", *The New York Times*, November 7, 1995, p. A15.

115. David Gonzalez and Garry Pierre-Pierre, "Little Sympathy or Surprise", *The New York Times*, November 21, 1993, p. 39.

116. Robert D. McFadden, "19 Injured: Student Sprays Acid in High School", *The New York Times*, November 20, 1993, pp. 16, 23; observation at Smith and Wesson gun

factory, Springfield, MA, October 1996.

117. Cited in Petersen, "This Bullet Kills You Better", p. 15.

118. Fox Butterfield, "Political Gains by Prison Guards: California Union Emerges as an Influential Power", *The New York Times*, November 7, 1995, pp. 1, 18.

119. Special Issue on Immigration – "The New Face of America", *Time*, Fall 1993, p. 10.

120. Peter Applebome, "Rise is Found in Hate Crimes Committed by Blacks", *The New York Times*, December 13, 1993, p. A12.

121. "Statement on Church Burnings by Abortion Providers and Women's Rights Activists", in *The Fight for Reproductive Freedom*, A Newsletter for Student Activists, Civil Liberties and Public Policy Programs, Hampshire College, Amherst, MA, Vol. XI, No. 1/2, Winter 1996, p. 7. See also publications of the Center for Democratic Renewal (PO Box 50469, Atlanta, GA 30302, USA) and Southern Poverty Law Center (PO Box 548, Montgomery, AL 36101, USA).

122. "The Narrowed Mind", interview with Denise Caignon, *Turning Wheel*, Special Issue on Fundamentalism, San Francisco, Fall 1995, pp. 16–17.

123. Frederic Clairmont, "Bonn: The Rising Tide of Nazidom", *Third World Resurgence*, No. 31, 1993, pp. 27–28.

124. Jan Oberg, "Many Global Wrongs, New Human Duties", *Terra Viva*, IPS (Inter Press Service), June 14, 1993, p. 4.

125. "Europe's Reborn Right", *The New York Times Magazine*, April 21, 1996, pp. 39–43.

126. Koonz, "Mothers in the Fatherland"; see also Andrea Dworkin, *Right Wing Women*, New York: Perigee Books, 1983.

127. Fran Peavey, "Taming the Wildfire: The Anatomy of Social Hysteria", *Turning Wheel*, Special Issue on fundamentalism, San Francisco, Fall 1995, p. 33.

128. Baker, "The Global Teenager", p. 29.

129. Henry Kamm, "In New Eastern Europe, an old Anti-Gypsy Bias", *The New York Times*, November 17, 1993, pp. A6, 12.

130. E.P. Thompson, "Notes on Exterminism: The Last Stage of Civilization", *New Left Review*, No. 121, May–June 1980, pp. 3–31.

131. "The Familiar Face of Fascism", cover story, *Utne Reader*, November–December 1995, pp. 54–55.

132. Benjamin R. Barber, *Jihad vs. McWorld*, New York: Random House, 1995.

133. "Who's Who of Money Moguls in '96 Race", *The New York Times*, January 12, 1996, p. A21.

134. 1996 electoral data obtained from the Committee for the Study of the American Electorate (421 New Jersey Ave. SE, Washington DC 20003, USA); US Bureau of the Census, *Statistical Abstract of the United States: 1995*, p. 289.

135. Gross, *Friendly Fascism, passim.*

136. Aldous Huxley, "Foreword", *Brave New World*, New York: Harper and Row, 1946, p. xv.

137. Margaret Atwood, *The Handmaid's Tale*, Boston: Houghton Mifflin, 1986.

138. Chin Saik Yoon, "New Global Trends Worsen N–S Information Imbalance", *Third World Resurgence*, No. 58, 1995, p. 17; Daya Kishan Thussu, "Lies, Damned Lies and 'Global News'", *Third World Resurgence*, No. 58, 1995, p. 26; see also Chandra Muzaffar, "Western Global Domination and Human Rights", *Third World Resurgence*, No. 33, 1993, p. 25.

139. Yoon, "New Global Trends", pp. 18–19.

140. "Interlocking Interests in the Communications Industry", *Third World Resurgence*, No. 58, 1995, p. 25.

141. "Disinformation and Propaganda:Lessons from the Cold War", *Third World Resurgence*, No. 58, 1995, p. 29.

142. Noam Chomsky and Edward S. Herman, *Manufacturing Consent: The Political Economy of the Mass Media*, New York: Pantheon Books, 1988.

143. George Orwell, *Nineteen Eighty-Four*, New York: New American Library, 1949, cited in Sklar, "Brave New World Order", pp. 4–5.

PART III

Paradigm Shift:
From Domination to Partnership

8

Towards Psycho-Social Transformation

Resistance against Domination

From the earliest of times, women and men have resisted the forces of domination and oppression in individual and collective ways. Even in feudal agricultural societies known for their extremely violent repression of resistance, some peasants refused to till the soil or pay taxes to feudal monarchs and aristocrats, just as some women sought to control their reproductive power to suit their own needs over that of men or dominant social classes.

With the emergence of the modern world order, resistance against the domination and oppression of capital, modern science and technology and the bureaucratic state has evolved and continues to evolve in many different directions. From the beginning, indigenous resistance to European conquest in the so-called 'New World' of the Americas constituted both anti-colonial and ecological struggles.

During the early period of industrial capitalist development in Europe, many peasants and artisans resisted the new ideologies and industrial management strategies such as private property rights, the Puritan work ethic and the Taylorist method of factory management imposed upon them. The challenges posed by the Luddites, who destroyed machines, and the Levellers, who attempted to create a community of independent citizens with basic civil rights for all, are examples of efforts to restore the right to work, and producers' control over their means of production and labor processes. Similarly, the resistance of women midwives and herbalists against the authority of male doctors and modern science represented women's efforts to maintain control over their bodies and biological reproduction.[1]

In the long run, working-class struggles, women's struggles and anti-technology movements were undermined by the joint efforts of capital, science and the state. As capital and technology expanded, dominating and centralizing control over more and more aspects of society, resistance to these forces became weaker and more reformist in character. Even the critics and dissidents came to be gradually integrated within the new social system, seeking only minor changes and compromises within it.[2]

The relatively higher living standards and racial privileges that imperialism bestowed upon white working classes in the metropolitan countries contributed to the thwarting of their revolutionary potential. Frequently, the divide and conquer strategies of the dominant forces resulted in fragmenting progressive social movements. For instance, in the early decades of this century, when the vote for women was pitted against the vote for Black men, many leading white suffragists in the US chose not to support the anti-abolition movement so that they could gain the vote for white women. In siding with the forces of white supremacy, they lost an opportunity to join Black women in a common struggle against slavery and the oppression of all women.[3]

Still, without continued but separate struggles by workers, women, people of color and other socially subordinate groups, social welfare programs, labor rights, women's rights and civil rights could not have been won and maintained at least to some extent in either the US or Europe. However, contrary to the predictions of Marx, it is in the Third World, where the exploitation and suffering of people have been the greatest, that the struggles between resistance to the modern world order and repression have also been the sharpest.

Third World struggles

In many colonized regions, peasants resisted the usurpation of their lands for export production and efforts to turn them into wage laborers. They continued to cultivate lands to which they had customary rights despite the new private property rights imposed by the colonizers. Many refused to become routine laborers on colonial plantations even though they had difficulty raising the cash to pay taxes to the colonial state. Quite often, peasants refused to register their marriages as required by colonial authorities, who were attempting to legalize patriarchal male-headed households and individual rights to property.[4]

Many local people also disregarded the efforts by European planters, administrators and Christian missionaries to inculcate the habits of impersonality, rationality and punctuality essential for modern technological and capitalist expansion. The mechanical clock and the western calendar introduced by the colonizers made living in accordance with the rhythms and cycles of nature increasingly difficult. Peasants and indigenous people used to treating the passage of time with a sense of submission without attempts to master or save it resisted the regimentation imposed by these artificial constructs as they resisted private property rights to land. As Pierre Bourdieu observed in Algeria, many peasants viewed the haste and acceleration of life that accompanied modernization "as a lack of decorum combined with diabolical ambition". Some even referred to the clock as the "devil's mill".[5]

In regions of Africa where women's pre-colonial rights to land, trade and other economic activities were severely curtailed by colonial policies, at least a few women dared to organize protests against colonial rule. As noted earlier, some slave women in the Caribbean and the Americas and women in Africa went on 'birth strikes' refusing to produce children for the colonial enterprise.[6] Many of these actions were not social revolutions; rather, they constituted what political scientist James Scott has called "every day forms of resistance" of the relatively powerless.[7]

Given the cultural and racial differences between colonizers and colonized, much of the resistance to capitalism and modern technological control was expressed as nationalist struggles against white supremacy and western culture rather than as social class or ecological struggles. Westernization did not guarantee equality between the colonizers and Third World elites. The second-class status experienced by westernized elites no doubt created tremendous insecurity and alienation. Perhaps Gandhi himself experienced these feelings before he gave up western ways to lead the Indian nationalist movement.[8] In other words, colonialism created the seeds of its own dissolution.

Post-World War period

Although the reins of state passed from the European rulers to local elites, in many colonial countries, from Algeria to India to Vietnam, independence was won only through national liberation movements involving mass participation of both men and women.[9] The Gandhian struggle which led to the independence of India and inspired national liberation movements worldwide was a movement of political, economic and cultural nationalism.

Third World liberation movements influenced the civil rights struggles of Blacks and other racial minorities in the US. Rosa Parks and other women played crucial roles in the origin and evolution of these struggles. These movements in turn inspired the rise of other liberation movements, notably the women's, gay and lesbian and environmental movements, setting the stage for a unified movement against all forms of social domination and oppression.[10]

Turning again to the Third World, it should be noted that in the 1960s and 1970s many countries struggled to strike out on paths of socio-economic development outside of the super-power struggle, seeking to develop indigenous forms of capitalism, socialism and cultural nationalism. Many Latin American and Asian countries emphasized import substitution as a means for national capitalist development, and countries like India experimented with 'mixed economies' of both public and private sector investment.[11] Peru, Jamaica, Tanzania, among others, sought to evolve indigenous forms of socialism, while many countries also sought to assert sovereignty over their natural resources and other means of production. Iraq and Libya asserted control over oil wells and oil assets; Sri Lanka nationalized plantations; Egypt nationalized the Suez Canal; and Panama sought unsuccessfully to gain control over the Panama Canal from the United States.[12] Some ex-colonies also sought to indigenize and democratize local cultures and education systems by greater use of native languages and pre-colonial cultural traditions. For example, in the early 1970s the Sri Lankan state tried to reintroduce the lunar calendar, but had to revert to the western calendar due to the exigencies of global trade.

Despite internal divisions and inter-state rivalries, Third World nations also attempted to develop collective movements to assert their autonomy and achieve global economic justice. The non-alignment movement, which sought political independence for Third World nations from the super-power struggle, the demands made by UNCTAD for a New International Economic Order (NIEO) with favorable terms of trade for the Third World, and the calls for a New International Information Order (NIIO) with greater Third World control of the global media are some examples.[13] Third World nations' opposition to the call for population control targets made by the United States at the World Population Conference in Bucharest in 1974 also exemplified Third World efforts towards autonomy and economic justice. However, as discussed in earlier chapters, rather than heed these demands, the West, and the United States in particular, continued to tighten its economic and political grip over the Third World.

Contemporary period

Both spontaneous outbursts and organized struggles against the joint forces of transnational capital and Third World states are increasing in the contemporary period, although they are given relatively little attention in the corporate-controlled global media. For example, in a number of countries, including Egypt and Venezuela, IMF-imposed price hikes in basic goods have resulted in riots, popularly referred to as 'IMF riots'.[14]

Despite legislation against unions and political organizing and increasingly violent forms of repression, indigenous people, peasants, workers, environmentalists, women and others continue to resist the dominant forces of global development. More than ever, local struggles today are simultaneously ecological and social struggles. Local struggles to stop deforestation and the building of massive infrastructural projects like dams and highways in regions such as the Amazon, India and South-East Asia constitute efforts to decentralize power and maintain local control over both natural resources and people's lives.[15]

Farmers' struggles against corporate efforts to usurp their lands and seeds are efforts to preserve local self-sufficiency and the integrity of both regional ecosystems and people's livelihoods. In Karnataka state in India, farmers have organized against the efforts of the agribusiness company

Cargills to wipe out local farmers through control of new hybrid seed varieties created by biotechnology. In Sri Lanka, farmers have organized protest rallies against agricultural policies imposed by the World Bank.[16] Twenty-five thousand plantation workers in 12 Third World countries affected by exposure to the fumigant DBCP are now suing Dow Chemical, Shell Oil – a unit of Royal Dutch/Shell Oil – and Occidental Petroleum as well as Del Monte Fruit, Chiquita Brands and Dole Fruit.[17] The rebellion in Chiapas, Mexico, is also an effort by local indigenous groups to wrest control away from global economic forces and the national state.[18]

Many of the contemporary women's movements in the South are grassroots struggles to ensure environmental sustainability as well as community rights and women's rights simultaneously. Many women around the world, especially indigenous women, are speaking out against big dams, forced population transmigration, structural adjustment and other policies supported by dominant world institutions such as the World Bank. The struggle of Chipko women against deforestation in India and the initiative taken by women of the Green Belt Movement to plant trees in Kenya demonstrate that poor women are frequently the leaders of environmental preservation. The demands of young women workers in the free trade zones of Asia and Central America for safer and improved working conditions; the campaigns of indigenous women against nuclear testing and toxic dumping in Micronesia; and the protests of Mothers' Fronts against 'disappearances' of their children and other human right violations in countries such as Argentina, Chile, Palestine and Sri Lanka are further examples of contemporary women's struggles.[19]

In fact, women are organizing against all forms of domination and violence, including the violence of top-down neo-Malthusian population control programs. Many local and national women's groups in countries like India and Brazil, as well as international networks like the Committee on Women, Population and the Environment and Women's Global Network for Reproductive Rights, are challenging the dominant population control paradigm, including the continued use of targets and economic incentives and experimental contraceptives in family planning programs (Appendices 1 and 4).

The widening of resistance, however, is leading to an intensification of repression of social change activists. This varies from attempts to silence and vilify radical thinkers and activists to outright killing of them. An example is the murder of the Ogoni human rights and environmental activist Ken Saro-Wiwa and eight of his associates – who had been organizing against the policies of the Shell Oil Company – by the Nigerian military regime. The killings of the Brazilian environmental activist Chico Mendes and the Jesuit priests in El Salvador; the long imprisonment of Aung San Suu Kyi, the leader of the democratic opposition in Burma; the suffering and resistance of Rigoberta Menchú and her family in Guatemala

and gang rape of Mexican-American human rights activist Cecilia
Rodriguez in Chiapas, Mexico – these are also some better known examples of human rights violations of countless people struggling for peace,
justice and democracy in the Third World.[20]

Struggles in the North

In the US, growing attacks against the environment and people by corporate interests and the Republican Party-led Congress are bringing grass-
roots environmental and social justice struggles closer together. This is
particularly evident in the growing environmental justice movement and its
challenge to environmental racism and the narrowly based white middle-
class environmentalism as represented by neo-Malthusian, corporate–scientific interests. Increased partnership between white people and people of
color and the development of a humane and broader approach to immigration are among the most important items on the agenda of the environmental justice movement in the US today (Appendix 4).

Although little reported in the mass media, many of the environmental
and social struggles in the US have involved working-class and minority
communities and leadership by women. For example, a working-class housewife, Lois Gibbs, initiated the environmental protection effort to stop toxic
dumping at Love Canal. Dolores Huerta, a Mexican-American woman, is
now leading the movement begun by Cesar Chávez to stop the exploitation
of immigrant and other farm laborers. Winona LaDuke, an Anishinabe
Indian from the White Earth Reservation, has organized to restore sustainable livelihoods for native communities threatened by casinos, toxic dumping, alcoholism and other effects of colonialism.[21]

The majority of progressive social change struggles in the North have
been relatively peaceful, being committed to legislative processes and non-
violent methods. However, if the global social crisis continues to worsen
and state repression increases, some of the contemporary social change
movements in the North could move in more violent directions, as have
some of their counterparts in the South. There are already signs of this
happening, the Mohawk Indian struggle in Canada for tribal sovereignty
over land being an example.[22] In the face of worsening poverty, police
brutality and other forms of violence against poor communities in the North,
spontaneous outbursts like the 1991 Los Angeles riots could also increase.

Challenges to social movements

From the outset, dominant social groups have sought either ideologically
and financially to co-opt or violently to suppress progressive social movements. As the authority of central governments weakens and NGOs increase their power to mobilize people, external institutions such as the

World Bank, the US government and national governments seek increasingly to control local organizations and people's movements such as environmental, human rights and women's groups.

Local activists in the South as well as the North are concerned that offers of large funds to resource-starved activists will 'professionalize' their services, making them vulnerable to the lures of money, travel and media fame, thereby separating them from the popular movements they have started out by serving.[23] As a result, the gap between the radical theories of many local groups and their daily practices could further widen. In such contexts, many well-meaning NGOs themselves tend to become focused on single issues and immediate concerns, thereby neglecting broader global political-economic analyses and wholistic visions for social change. Many Northern human rights and family planning NGOs functioning in the South, for example, have succumbed to narrow ethnic or gender analyses, failing to examine why many local people and organizations may bring the charges of white supremacy and imperialism against them.[24]

Despite the lofty language frequently uttered, fundamental social transformation is not on the global agenda as we move into the twenty-first century. It seems that even the most progressive organizations and movements are simply struggling for reforms that increase the scope for popular control and greater peace and justice in the world rather than bringing about social structural changes.[25]

At this time of ideological confusion and lack of direction, we need also to be cautious of quick-fix attempts at 'right' and 'left' political convergence. It is true that both the so-called 'left' environmentalism and right-wing libertarianism have historically struggled against the forces of techno-bureaucratic centralization and state control. In many ways, both left anarchist groups and right-wing militia and fundamentalist groups are seeking decentralization of power and local and individual autonomy.[26]

It is certainly true that Communism failed because it perpetuated many of the worst aspects of capitalism, such as centralization, technological dominance, militarism and human and environmental exploitation. Still, at a time when North–South, class, race and gender disparities are widening, we must not throw out left analysis and the promise of socialism altogether. Otherwise, liberal environmentalism and feminism could be further co-opted by dominant political and economic interests, leading to further exacerbation of class, race and gender oppression. A left–right political convergence in the North led by white males could also get directed against women, people of color, immigrants, gays and lesbians and other so-called 'minority' groups instead of being directed against corporate power.

In the face of efforts by the dominant interest groups to divide and conquer the forces of resistance and the rising popularity of right-wing religious fundamentalist and ethno-nationalist movements both in the North and in the South, it is necessary that progressive social change activists

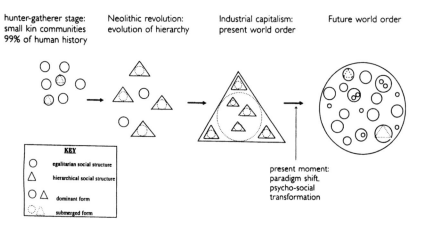

hunter-gatherer stage: small kin communities 99% of human history

Neolithic revolution: evolution of hierarchy

Industrial capitalism: present world order

Future world order

KEY

○ egalitarian social structure

△ hierarchical social structure

○ △ dominant form

submerged form

present moment: paradigm shift, psycho-social transformation

Figure 8.1 Global psycho-social revolution

develop an integrated analysis of the prevailing paradigm of domination as well as a clear vision of an alternative partnership paradigm. It is only then that we can begin to see the inherent connectedness between seemingly isolated issues and separate social change struggles and movements.

It is in the evolution of a new human and planetary consciousness and the coming together of local social movements for peace, ecology and justice and the women's movement that the integrity of local cultures, bio-regions and social groups can be preserved. It is in the development of non-violent struggles to resist the dominant world order that the hope for a global democratic and sustainable social order lies. Indeed, it is only by developing a wholistic, ecocentric philosophy on life that the reigning extremist ideologies such as Malthusianism and right-wing fundamentalism can be overcome. It is on the basis of non-violent strategies alone that politics can truly be integrated with spirituality.

From Domination to Partnership

It is the promise of freedom and democracy, more than materialist consumption, that makes people all over the world opt for capitalism over feudalism, Communism and other authoritarian social systems. The technological, capitalist world order holds within itself the basis of its own transformation. Modern science and technology allow people to see clearly the natural integration of the Earth and humanity. Mass communication

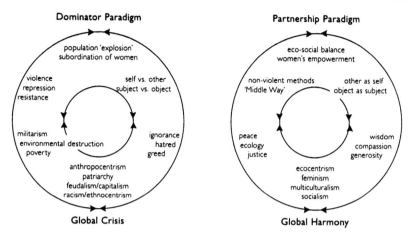

Figure 8.2 Paradigm shift: from domination to partnership

systems have the potential to help develop a global consciousness and interconnected social movements towards a harmonious and peaceful planetary community.

In order to solve the global crisis, we have to look deeply into the roots of violence and the processes through which domination has come to define human relationships with each other and the rest of nature. We must, in turn, examine the roots of peace and the processes through which peace and partnership can be established in all our relationships. In this regard, it is useful to contrast the pyramidal, dominator paradigm of global social organization with a circular, partnership paradigm towards which we must strive if, indeed, we are to create a more sane and livable world for ourselves and future generations (Figures 1, 8.1, 8.2, 8.3).

Dominator paradigm

As discussed in Chapter 3, the confluence of Judeo-Christian teleology and the rationalism of the scientific revolution in the seventeenth century led to the evolution of a linear, fragmented and mechanistic worldview and an aggressive technological approach to life. Much of modern western philosophy, including such ideologies as Malthusianism, is founded upon this worldview. Unfortunately, many social change philosophies and movements, including some branches of feminism, have also succumbed to the individualist, competitive ethic of the dominator paradigm. This book has focused on the social structures of domination and subordination that evolved in the course of industrial capitalist expansion. However, domination and subordination are not entirely attributable to the modern world order. As noted in earlier chapters, gender, race and class hierarchies predated industrial capitalism, violence being the organizing principle of patriarchal, feudal and caste based societies.

Violence, whether it be environmental destruction, poverty or militarism, is based on psychological structures of dualism (self versus the other and subject versus object) and social structures of domination and subordination: anthropocentrism (humans over nature); patriarchy (men over women); capitalism (capital over labor); imperialism (North over South); feudalism (lord over serf); white supremacy (whites over people of color); racism and ethnocentrism (races and ethnic groups over each other), and so on (Figure 8:2).

Dualistic thinking leads to ignorance of the dialectical nature of reality, encouraging greed, hatred and fear in people's minds. It upholds the mistaken belief in a separate self and the attitude that survival of the self requires domination over and even annihilation of the other. Such an approach leads to pursuit of extreme individualism, separation, control and permanence in life through relentless pursuit of technology, money and ultimately weapons of destruction (Figure 8.2). Despite its apparent arrogance, modern technological, capitalist expansion is driven by a deep fear and insecurity. Ultimately, it is the fear of death that drives science and technology in its vain and ultimately suicidal attempt to conquer death and the laws of nature.

Partnership paradigm

A revolutionary synthesis is now emerging among different intellectual and spiritual traditions, challenging the dominant dualistic and mechanistic paradigm. Elements of Buddhist, Native American and other indigenous teachings are being connected with feminism and social justice philosophies as well as elements of such monistic fields of western science as quantum theory and evolutionary biology. This synthesis is creating an ecocentric, wholistic approach that takes the entirety of nature rather than its separate parts as its point of departure. Like the Mother Goddess-worshipping prehistoric cultures, some contemporary scientists are also beginning to see the Earth – Gaia – as one living, breathing organism, indivisible and synergic.[27]

In contrast to the dominator paradigm, the ecocentric partnership paradigm accepts the inevitability of death as an aspect of the ever-changing cycle of nature – birth, decay, death, rebirth. It accepts the reality of impermanence, the constantly changing nature of all material and mental phenomena, *anicca*, in Pali, the language of the Buddhist scriptures. A grasp of this fundamental ecological principle of impermanence helps free the human mind from attachment to particular physical and mental entities, including the notion of a separate self. It allows the mind to see the organic unity of life and the interdependence of all phenomena, another basic principle of ecocentric thinking. It reminds us that humanity is not an entirely separate species, but a part of the animal system, which in turn is part of the plant system and the Earth organism, and ultimately of the ever-evolving universe. As such, humanity cannot be seen as an entity independent of and dominating over nature but must be regarded as a partner in the whole who must respect and preserve the complexity and integrity of the whole.[28]

To uphold the unity that exists in human and planetary life, variety and diversity must necessarily be honored. The illusion of a separate self must be replaced with ecological wisdom which recognizes that the 'other' is not an entirely separate entity but an extension of the 'self' co-existing within the constantly evolving cycle of nature. Indeed, the self is embedded in the other; it exists only in relation to the other (Figure 8.3).

The definition of the self that psychologist Gregory Bateson developed in *Steps to an Ecology of Mind*, as 'being-in-relation-to-others', is consistent with the ontological categories of being of many indigenous peoples of the Americas.[29] The Yanktonapais (Crow Creek Lakota) concept of 'as one with all my relations' (*mitakuye iyasin*) and the Highland Quich Maya 'you are my other self' (*in lak eck*) are examples.[30] Gandhi also wrote: "I believe in *advaita* (non-duality), I believe in the essential unity of man and, for that matter, of all that lives."[31] In other words, we must respect and protect, rather than conquer and destroy, nature and each other. The survival of the self depends on the survival of the other.

Perhaps nowhere else is the assumed dualism of self and other as fundamentally questioned as in the Buddhist concept of no-self (*anatta*), which considers the notion of a separate self as an illusion and ego attachment to this illusory self as the root of all human suffering (Figure 8.2).[32] In this sense, 'interbeing', the term coined by contemporary Vietnamese Buddhist scholar-monk Thich Nhat Hanh, is very helpful in taking the evolutionary leap that humanity needs to take at this time.[33] The concept of 'interbeing' allows us to move away from the hierarchical dualisms of the dominant world order towards an understanding of the inherent connectedness between such entities as subject/object, human/non-human, mind/body, male/female, heterosexual/homosexual, production/reproduction, white/people of color, North/South, capital/labor, nature/culture, and so on (Figure 8.2). The early teachings of Christ and of St Francis of Assisi, as well as some of the contemporary forms of Christian Liberation and Creation theology, take a more democratic, partnership approach to human and human–non-human relations, in contrast to the domineering approach upheld by orthodox Christianity.[34]

It is important that we focus our attention on changing ourselves rather than changing the other, over whom we ultimately have no control. We have to focus on common concerns we have with the other in order to transcend the us-versus-them mentality and to create unity amidst diversity.

Transformation of the self

We need to move beyond reform environmentalism, which touches on surface problems such as 'overpopulation' and immigration, to exploring the roots of our alienation from nature. The emerging philosophy of deep ecology, which draws upon the wisdom of earth-based peoples, calls for us to acknowledge the threat of planetary extinction created by our arrogant anthropocentric approach. Deep ecology sees an ecocentric consciousness which recognizes the common ancestry of all life as the foundation for planetary sustainability and harmony. Deep ecologist John Seed exhorts us to extend our sense of self to incorporate all of nature:

> As your memory improves ... there is an identification with all life. Then follows the realization that the distinction between 'life' and 'lifeless' is a human construct. Every atom in this body existed before organic life emerged 4000 million years ago. Remember our childhood as minerals, lava, as rocks? ... We are the rocks dancing. Why do we look down on them with such a condescending air? It is they that are the immortal part of us.[35]

Within the ecocentric worldview, power is equated not with domination and aggression but with partnership and compassion; it is not coercion of nature or of other human beings but a force within the self in connection with others. The partnership approach to power is based on respect and a deep sensitivity towards the oneness of all life and the necessity for cooperation and balance between the different parts and aspects of the whole. No narrow ideology based on economics and politics can overcome the wisdom and the reverence for nature embedded in the ecocentric approach to life.[36]

This wholistic, eco-psychological approach is also based on the acceptance of all aspects of knowledge and labor, not only rational, quantitative and left-brain learning but also intuitive, qualitative and right-brain learning. It particularly honors and values those aspects of wisdom and being associated with the feminine and seeks to restore harmony and balance between male and female. In "The Gaia Tradition and the Partnership Future: An Ecofeminist Manifesto", pioneer of partnership studies Riane Eisler writes:

> The real alternative to patriarchy is not matriarchy, which is only the other side of the dominator coin. The alternative, now revealed to be the original direction of our cultural evolution, is ... a *partnership* society: a way of organizing human relations in which beginning with the most fundamental differences in our species – the difference between female and male – diversity is *not* equated with inferiority or superiority. (emphasis in original)[37]

In contrast to rationalist, materialist approaches to feminism which encourage women to emulate the dominant male model, the ecological-cum-feminist approach – ecofeminism – upholds women's capacity to bear and nurture life as a form of power, encouraging men to develop the qualities of nurturance and caring as well. In this regard, ecofeminism draws inspiration from traditions of the earliest human societies such as the worship of the Mother Goddess and also from the Sanskrit concept of *shakti*, the primordial female energy of the universe, connecting the Earth as mother of all life with woman as the bearer of human life. Accordingly, ecofeminism sees the strengthening of the so-called 'female' principle of caring and peace and a weakening of the so-called 'male' principle of aggression and war as a necessary foundation for creating global psycho-social balance and harmony.[38]

The ecofeminist concept of power is based on an understanding of the fundamental equality of all people, as beings experiencing the same basic life processes of birth, growth, decay and death and the same basic survival needs for food, shelter and love. It calls on us to keep our focus on systems of exploitation that alienate people from each other and perpetuate violence rather than seeing individuals as our 'enemies'.[39]

We need to develop awareness of our own inflexibility and fundamentalism, whether it be red, green, Third World or feminist, instead of simply finger pointing at the dogmatism and extremism of the other. For example, progressive social change activists must see the common concerns for economic security and social stability we share with right-wing fundamentalists, militia members and others and seek to communicate and engage in dialogue with them without necessarily compromising our own ethical positions and commitment to social justice.[40] Feminist activist Sally Gearhart presents a transformational vision for the feminist movement, when she calls on us to move from anger and hatred to tolerance and compassion:

> ...my pain, anger and/or hatred accomplish nothing except to render me ineffectual and to increase the problem by adding to the pain, anger, and hatred that already burden the world. I've learned that whole parts of my identified 'enemy' are really my own self, walking around in different costume. And in the moments where we've found some joining space, I've learned that, though I still may not choose to spend time with him, I do feel kinship or love for that killer, that exploiter.[41]

The transformation required in the world now is not simply an intellectual one; it is primarily a shift of the human heart: from ignorance (*moha*), greed (*raga*) and hatred (*dosa*) towards wisdom (*panna*), generosity (*dana*) and compassion (*karuna*) (Figure 8.2).[42] It is only with wisdom and strong commitment on the part of more and more people to the basic values of compassion and generosity that the exploitation and domination of the present world order can be transcended and ecocentric, feminist, multi-

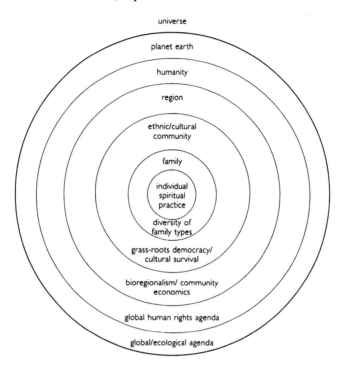

universe

planet earth

humanity

region

ethnic/cultural
community

family

individual
spiritual
practice

diversity of
family types

grass-roots democracy/
cultural survival

bioregionalism/ community
economics

global human rights agenda

global/ecological agenda

Figure 8.3 Levels and strategies of psycho-social transformation

cultural and socialist alternatives can be created. Solutions to the global crisis, including the population question, must be located within such a profound transformation in our consciousness and relationships – a psycho-social revolution (Figures 8.1, 8.2, 8:3).

Whereas haste and the achievement of ends and goals are the virtues within the mechanistic paradigm, the process and the means used to achieve ends are more important in the ecocentric paradigm. As we have seen, the dominant ideologies, including Malthusianism and ethno-nationalism, seek, to achieve freedom, peace, democracy and ecology through authoritarian, often violent and destructive, means. In contrast, the ecocentric approach exhorts us to be in each moment mindfully and to develop peaceful methods to achieve our goals. Aung San Suu Kyi, the leader of the democratic opposition to the military regime in Burma, who has been under house arrest for many years, speaks from personal experience when she calls on our capacity to change and to develop a non-violent approach to conflict resolution:

It is not enough simply to 'live and let live': *genuine* tolerance requires an active effort to understand the point of view of others; it implies broad-mindedness and vision, as well as confidence in one's own ability to meet new challenges without resorting to intransigence or violence.... The human race is not divided into two opposing camps of good and evil. It is made up of those who are capable of learning and those who are incapable of doing so. Here I am speaking of learning as the process of absorbing those lessons of life that enable us to increase peace and happiness in our world. (emphasis in original)[43]

Non-violence

Being accustomed to living within a competitive, mechanistic world, many people today are cynical about commitment to non-violent, participatory processes. They have been taught to see life as nasty and brutish and diversity and difference as leading inevitably to conflicts. Indeed, nature is not all peaceful and cooperative; conflict and violence are interwoven with harmony and interdependence. Like birth and creation, death and destruction are inevitable aspects of planetary evolution. Finding one's place in the hierarchy and fighting for it may also be a basic aspect of primate life.

However, recent studies and statements, such as the Seville Statement on Violence, issued by an international colloquium of scholars, help dispel the widespread belief that global violence and crisis are attributable to biologically determined aggression. The Seville Statement points out that aggression and war are not inevitable; they are socially and historically created (Appendix 2).

The ancient teaching of the Buddha – the *Dhamma* – helps us question the pessimism of the Hobbesian–Malthusian–Darwinian perspective which fails to recognize the capacity of the human mind for conscious transformation, the capacity which places humans above other species. Indeed, humans are not static, merely self-serving entities. Lacking a fixed nature, we are enormously variable, complex, creative and capable of change. The example of the Indian emperor Asoka, of the third century BC, is particularly relevant to our time and the United States, because it shows that a powerful ruler and a militarist state can change from conquering people by violence and war to 'conquering' them by compassion and peace. Asoka's example also teaches us that the attributes of good leadership are wisdom, compassion and generosity, not myopia, violence and greed.[44]

We have to move away from the reigning Darwinian principles of competition and 'survival of the fittest'. We must uphold the organic connectedness among humans and between humans and the rest of nature rather than increasing competitive, mechanical and market connectedness. Without the selfless love and nurturance of parents, especially that of mothers towards their children, life would not be continuing on the planet today. But the crisis facing the world requires that this familial love be extended as much as possible towards the rest of the planet and all its suffering human and non-human beings. As Buddhism, as well as other religions, tells us, hatred cannot be overcome by hatred; it can be overcome only with love. Indeed, to change the world, we have to change ourselves and our relationships to ourselves and to each other. It is in this sense that the crisis facing the world is fundamentally a moral and spiritual crisis: a crisis of our relationships.

We need to develop global visions and strategies that appeal to the highest moral and ethical values of human beings instead of our worst fears and insecurities. We need to strive to move away from stage one of moral development as identified by Lawrence Kohlberg, that is, the stage where the ideology of 'survival of the fittest' and physical power rule, towards stage six, where universal ethical principles and democratic principles prevail.[45] We need to develop an agenda for political action that is firmly grounded on universal, spiritual teachings that move us beyond narrow sectarianism and religious and ethnic fundamentalism. We need strong self-discipline based on spiritual practice, whether it be meditation, communion with nature or other voluntarily accepted methods. We need commitment to a universal ethical code of conduct such as that presented by Buddhist precepts and a non-violent methodology as experimented with by Mahatma Gandhi. Non-killing (*ahimsa*) must be the first principle of such a code of conduct.[46]

Non-violence must be regarded not as passive resistance but as an active power requiring creative confrontation and qualitative growth in all aspects of our lives. As Gandhi discovered, it is a power that lies in the process of discovering reality: it is a force of truth (*satyagraha*). As such, it is diametrically opposed to the power that comes from the barrel of the gun. The old model of revolution calling for immediate and violent transformation has failed. Instead, we need to develop new and alternative models of non-violent revolution that involve deeper processes of change leading to greater harmony and balance in our daily lives. Martin Luther King Jr used such an approach in the Civil Rights Movement in the US. We need also to learn from the examples of contemporary leaders like Aung San Suu Kyi who has used the power of meditation, compassion and non-violence in confronting the Burmese military regime, and the Dalai Lama, who has done the same in confronting the aggression of the Chinese government against the Tibetan people and their culture. The Dalai Lama speaks not as a Buddhist or a Tibetan, but simply as a human being when he points out that:

> 1) universal humanitariansim is essential to solve global problems; 2) compassion is the pillar of world peace; 3) all world religions are already for world peace in this way, as are all humanitarians of whatever ideology; 4) each individual has a universal responsibility to shape institutions to serve human needs.[47]

The identification of the self with the human body and mind obstructs the development of empathetic connections with the other. Only when we as human beings begin to transcend the numbing of our hearts and minds by technology, materialism and bureaucratic regimentation of modern society and begin to soften inside can we feel the pain of those destroyed by war, rape, poverty, and so on, as if it were our own pain. It is said that true love – compassion – is unconditional, not a dualistic emotion. The experience of compassion deepens as we release our separateness into the universal and begin to experience the essential oneness of life.

To move away from fear and despair towards courage and hope, and to develop the inner freedom, strength and peace we need for survival and sanity at this time, we need to open our hearts to the suffering of the other as well as to our own suffering. We need to develop respect and practice loving kindness towards ourselves as well. We must include ourselves in the cycle of compassion, as does the Buddhist loving kindness (*metta*) meditation:

> May all beings be free from sorrow
> May all beings be free from ill health
> May all beings be healed
> May all beings be free from anxiety
>
> May I be free from sorrow
> May I be free from ill health
> May I be healed
> May I be free from anxiety.

The global paradigm change needed at this time is not necessarily a final, utopian shift from domination to partnership. The forces of domination and authoritarianism and the forces of partnership and democracy are in a process of dialectical interaction. What is required for purposes of global crisis resolution is a strengthening of the democratic participatory processes and a weakening of the authoritarian ones (Figures 8.1 and 8.2). Revolution, in this sense, lies in the process of transformation itself: it lies in every moment, in the here and now, rather than in some distant future. Given the reality of impermanence, the processes of achieving ends are even more important than the ends themselves. Each individual can do only his or her part in global transformation. Each individual attempt to consciously move away from the dominator paradigm towards the partnership paradigm itself constitutes the psycho-social revolution. Such a theory of political action helps transform people from victimization to empowerment.

It is rarely, however, that dominant groups and individuals share their wealth and power voluntarily. Their resistance to the necessary changes is creating great suffering, social upheavals and violence in the world today. It is the dominant groups that need urgently to recognize the inherent interconnectedness between self and other, between wealth and poverty, between population decline in the North and population growth in the South, and other seeming social dichotomies.

It is the North, the wealthy classes, the white race and the male gender that need to change and to embrace the partnership paradigm the most.

Unlike in many parts of the South, it is in the North that the ideologies and institutions of domination can still be challenged in relative safety. Citizens in the North must become more honest in their analyses of the global crisis and more courageous in their actions to resolve it. The middle classes have a critical role to play in the global paradigm shift: they need to support the struggles of the so-called 'bottom' groups rather than identifying with the top elite.

Citizens in the US, in particular, bear a moral responsibility in leading the world from violence to peace. It is for this reason that strategies and movements for social change based in the US are highlighted in this chapter and in Appendix 4. In a talk given in the US entitled "The Source of Human Annhilation", the Venerable Nichidatsu Fuji, Japanese monk and the founder of Nipponzan Myohoji Buddhist Order, which leads inter-faith pilgrimages for peace around the world, said:

> The power to eliminate the war policy, the defense policy, the policy to increase military forces of the United States does not exist in other nations, but within the people of this country.... This country must be turned into a peaceful nation. This is the desire of the entire humanity. It is at the same time the responsibility of the people who live in this country.[48]

What is required now is not substitution of one form of authoritarianism and hierarchy with another form, but the development of what the Buddha called the Middle Path (*Majjhimā Patipadā*). The essential aspects of the Middle Path – ethical conduct (*sīla*), mental discipline (*samādhi*) and wisdom (*paññā*) – were explained in detail by the Buddha in his 45 years of teaching.[49]

The Middle Path is built on tolerance and equanimity, not fanaticism and violent emotional outburst. It is a path that avoids extremes of all forms, whether Malthusianism, right-wing fundamentalism, transnational capitalism or Communist authoritarianism. As Buddhist scholar-monk Bhikku Bodhi writes, the Middle Path "is not a compromise between the extremes but a way that rises above them, avoiding the pitfalls into which they lead".[50] It is this Path of balance and harmony that we need to pursue in seeking a democratic, sustainable model of development for the twenty-first century. Perhaps it is also on this Path that the alternative to both monopoly capitalism and authoritarian Communism can be found.

Towards Democratic and Sustainable Development

Sustainable development

The reproduction of the capitalist mode of production and the reproduction of human and planetary life are at odds with each other. Resolution of the global crisis calls for fundamental rethinking and transformation of the global economic system. The new partnership paradigm is most needed in the sphere of business.[51] A change from unbridled growth to sustainability calls for changes in both the technologies and social relations of production.

As economist E.F. Schumacher has shown in his book *Small is Beautiful*, 'Buddhist economics', or what others have called 'compassionate economics' and 'ecological economics', has great relevance in making the transformation towards rational allocation of natural resources, appropriate technology, balanced consumption, meaningful work, as well as sharing and redistribution of wealth.[52] While sectarian terms such as 'Buddhist' may be cast aside, the universal truths expounded in the Buddha's Middle Path should not be forgotten; they must be used creatively to grapple with modern dilemmas.

Ethical, social and ecological criteria must be introduced into economic decision making at the outset rather than after social and environmental degradation has already taken place. Production of negative use values – nuclear and conventional weapons, violent entertainment, the skin trade, and so on – must be transformed into production of life-enhancing goods and services. Right livelihood (*sammā ajīva*), that is, making one's living through non-violent and ethical means, is an essential aspect of the Buddhist way of life.

The health of the environment and people, the status of women and the well-being of children, rather than aggregate growth indicators like the GNP, should be the indices of socio-economic development. Social indicators must be reformulated to take into account the 'invisible labor' of women and children and the visible and invisible costs of economic growth and militarism on the environment.[53] Indeed, we need to question and change our very definitions of wealth, success, development and happiness.

Definition of sustainability must include people. Economic production must guarantee livelihood and the satisfaction of basic human needs of all. Profit and growth considerations should not override the need for gainful employment. Job sharing, shorter working weeks and other creative solutions need to be explored to alleviate the global unemployment crisis. Provision of jobs for more people would also lessen the burdens on those who already hold jobs, making their lives more compatible with needs of families and children.[54] Work must be organized not in order to exploit human beings but to foster their creativity, caring, joy and balanced development.

Instead of punishing women for bearing and nurturing families, social institutions, including the state and firms, must support both women and men who choose to become parents by making available good health care, child care, financial and other benefits. Transnational corporations should not use child labor for export production; instead, they must provide education, health and other basic amenities for children of employees, thus setting an example for local companies. Instead of pushing weapons and violent forms of entertainment on children and pauperizing women and experimenting on and exploiting their bodies, society must protect and nourish the women and children so that human life can continue on this planet (Appendix 4).

Sustainable development requires that the purpose of economic production be changed from short-term pursuit of growth and profit accumulation to reproduction of human beings and the ecosystem in the long term. In this respect, we have much to learn from traditional societies. In their Councils, the Iroquois and other Native American communities made each important decision by considering its impact on the seventh generation.[55]

It is not necessary to return to the stagnation that characterized many tribal societies or abandon economic and technological innovation and growth altogether. Buddhist societies like Ladakh which avoided the extremes of growth and stagnation and also the extremes of wealth and poverty were more sustainable environmentally and socially than modern industrial societies. They approached ecological, community and individual survival as inseparable. As Helena Norberg-Hodge has demonstrated in *Ancient Futures*, we need to apply the ecological and social wisdom of small-scale societies like Ladakh in shaping a sustainable and democratic future for the world. The *Sarvodaya* village awakening and self-help movement in Sri Lanka also attempts to apply the Buddha's teachings to the challenges of contemporary socio-economic development.[56]

Limits to economic growth

To restore both ecological and social balance and harmony, the extremes of globalization and individualization must be averted and local and intermediate economic and social structures strengthened. The road to planetary sustainability and global democracy lies in bioregionalism, living with respect for the limits and integrity of local ecosystems, and in decentralization and empowerment of local communities.[57] As ecologist Leopold Kohr put it:

> ...instead of centralization or unification, let us have economic cantonization. Let us replace the oceanic dimension of integrated big powers and common markets by a dike system of inter-connected but highly self-sufficient local markets and small states in which economic fluctuations can be controlled....[58]

Big and new are not necessarily better or beneficial. Economic production should be oriented primarily towards subsistence rather than commodity production for export. Technologies should also be small-scale, environmentally appropriate methods such as solar technology and organic agriculture rather than large-scale ones like nuclear technology, hydropower plants, dam building and agricultural technologies which involve massive ecological and social costs. As economist Herman Daly has argued, to maintain sustainability, the economy should not grow beyond the ecosystem's capacity to regenerate material inputs and to absorb waste materials and energy outputs.[59] In other words, use of renewable sources of energy and appropriate technology must come before economic growth.

The Middle Path does not call for a complete disavowal of quantitative growth and the state or a complete delinking of regions from the global market, technology or multilateral institutions. Rather, what the Middle Path calls for are greater possibilities for regional autonomy and for a plurality of socio-economic forms. Community economics is vital for the survival of local ecosystems, cultures, ethnic groups, communities and families (Figure 8.3) (Appendix 4). As futurist and economist Hazel Henderson has noted, the demand for bioregionalism and decentralization carries within it a critique of monopoly capitalism.[60] In other words, changes in technology and in social relations of production are necessarily interlinked.

Indeed, the long-term solution to the global economic crisis and immigration pressure on the North lies in preserving local ecosystems, in strengthening local economies and in empowering local producers. The basic human needs of all can best be met by ensuring local control over resources and livelihoods rather than through redistribution policies of welfare states or through regulation of transnational corporations and multilateral institutions pursuing the dominant industrial growth paradigm.

Still, given the reality of globalization, a global ecological agenda to protect tropical forests, oceans, biodiversity and the ozone layer is greatly needed just as a global human rights agenda is needed more than ever to protect the well-being and lives of all women, men and children. The conceptualization and implementation of such agendas and specific treaties and conventions cannot be left up to the dominant multilateral institutions which represent the interests of corporations and governments in the North. A democratization of multilateral institutions and drastic changes in their policies are urgently needed. The "50 Years is Enough" campaign which is demanding fundamental restructuring of the IMF and the World Bank, for instance, has called for greater transparency and democracy in decision making and a more balanced model of global development. It says:

> The World Bank and IMF must reorient their lending for economic reform to strengthen a wide variety of productive activity by the rural and urban poor, increase local self-reliance and broad-based local demand, promote equity for women and other marginalized groups, enhance workers' rights, ensure environmental sustainability and facilitate increased investment in physical and social infrastructure, especially investments in women's and girls' health, education and economic opportunities.[61]

Among other demands of the "50 Years is Enough" campaign are the establishment of a Global Environment Facility that is "legally, operationally and financially independent of the World Bank"; a moratorium on World Bank funding for large dams and support for projects involving forced settlement of people; a stop to World Bank and IMF structural adjustment programs as currently formulated; an immediate cancellation of the total outstanding debt owed to the World Bank and the IMF by severely indebted low-income countries and cancellation of 50% of the debt owed by severely indebted lower- to middle-income countries (Appendix 4).[62]

Denmark led the way towards debt cancellation by writing off $200 million in debts owed by six of the poorest nations at the Copenhagen Social Summit in March 1995. Other nations in the North should be pressured to do the same by concerned citizens in those countries. Mahbub-ul Haq, special advisor to the United Nations Development Programme, has suggested that all of the cancelled debts be spent on social services, the forgiven debt be matched with reductions in arms spending and the debt-forgiven countries be accountable for their spending.[63] Debt cancellation should also be tied to preservation of the environment. Debt-for-nature swaps must be extended and environmental gains made through such arrangements must be shared among the poorest people. Indeed, these actions need to be undertaken not to further extend the control of the North over the South and local elites over the masses, but to ease their suffering and the destruction of the environment.

A global, wholistic and compassionate approach to environmental sustainability must also recognize that immigration control in the North cannot be a quick-fix policy lever for environmental renewal. As the environmental justice movement in the US recognizes, the long-term, sustainable solutions to the immigration problem lie in such measures as reducing over-consumption in the North, blocking export of industrial degradation to the South, and improving standards for environmental, labor and reproductive rights in immigrants' countries of origin and in the US (Appendix 4).[64]

In the face of deepening globalization and centralization today, to act locally, we have also to think globally. In order to challenge the domination of global Goliaths such as Mitsubishi, Coca-Cola, CNN and the World Bank and to empower local communities, grass-roots struggles across the world must become better integrated. As activists from the Third World Gustavo Esteva and Suri Prakash point out, a global consciousness which informs and rallies behind local action is needed for confronting the tightly knit corporate control over the world.[65] Setting limits on the expansionary and centralizing power of transnational corporations and making them environmentally responsible and accountable to ordinary people must become central to the agenda of 'think globally, act locally'.

Much of the organizing and action needs to take place in the North, where corporations are located and where citizens can challenge them in relative safety. In exercising their power as stockholders in companies and as consumers of corporate products and services, concerned citizens in the North must join forces with citizens in the South who are largely the producers and the victims of transnational corporate expansion.

Regulation of TNCs

Halting of weapons production and the global arms trade must be a priority. The peace, justice and environmental movements and concerned citizens in the North, especially the US, must assume responsibility for combating weapons production and arms sales. Some important actions in this regard are: divestment of investments in defense corporations; lobbying for a ban on arms exports; collective tax resistance or refusal to pay federal taxes that support the military; conversion of defense production into civilian production; civil disobedience (Appendix 4).

Codes of conduct to regulate transnational corporations must be introduced and enforced. Global environmental regulations as well as labor regulations and means to enforce them are urgently needed. Those who hold stocks individually and collectively (for example, through investment of retirement benefits) must use shareholder resolutions and other mechanisms to move corporations towards environmentally and socially responsible investments (Appendix 4).[66] Divestment from apartheid South Africa is one of the most well-known and successful examples. Consumer boycotts, such as the Nestlé boycott undertaken some years ago to challenge unethical and harmful marketing of infant formula, must also be used more widely to make corporations environmentally and socially accountable.

More recently, citizen pressure in the US has led firms in the apparel industry like Levi-Strauss & Co, Liz Claiborne and Macy's to stop buying clothes made in Burma and to Eddie Bauer company leaving Burma altogether. The state of Massachusetts in the US has also passed a law boycotting business with Burma due to that country's massive human rights violations.[67] Levi-Strauss, Gap, Reebok and Nike have also declared publicly that they will no longer do business with manufacturers using child labor. Levi's is the first company to adopt a requirement that all its suppliers live up to a written code of ethics in labor practices. The Starbuck Coffee Company has also recently adopted a code of conduct to ensure minimum wage, health, safety and workers' right to organize.[68] These are only limited reforms; they still allow transnational corporations to place responsibility on local contractors or find other means to continue employing cheap Third World labor or violate environmental standards. Yet at a time when 'free trade' expands ruthlessly with hardly any regulation or accountability, these efforts must be acknowledged as important steps in the right direction. Ethical codes of conduct need to be adopted by other corporations and other sectors of production. Such codes are very much needed in the pharmaceutical sector to stop dumping of dangerous drugs in the South and experimentation with new drugs and contraceptives on the bodies of poor women (Appendix 4).

Equity and balanced consumption

Limits must be placed on the private appropriation of wealth (Appendix 3) and labor exploitation as well as on technological and material growth. The Buddha pointed out that equitable distribution of wealth among people is a prerequisite to peace, prosperity and security.[69] Equality and voluntary redistribution of wealth were cornerstones of the philosophies of latter-day Indian spiritual–political leaders Mahatma Gandhi and Vinoba Bhave also.[70]

In order to eradicate poverty and hunger among marginalized groups, overconsumption among the wealthy groups must be reduced and consumption among the poorer groups must be increased. For this purpose, an ethic of equity and simple living must be promoted.[71] To move towards simple living it is essential to make a wise distinction between basic human needs such as food, shelter, clothing and medicine and the plethora of artificially created human wants. It is also necessary to recognize human needs beyond the purely material ones, for example human needs for intimacy, connection to nature and spiritual fulfilment which cannot be satisfied through technology and the market.

Excessive materialism and technological usage are detrimental to wholistic and balanced development and the realization of our full human potential. Both human well-being and environmental sustainability are best achieved through simpler, more natural living. The Middle Path is helpful in moving us away from the extremes of material poverty and under-consumption, on the one hand, and material wealth and overconsumption of resources, on the other hand. Sri Lankan economist Patrick Mendis has demonstrated this through what he calls a 'Buddhist Equilibrium Curve' (Figure 8.4).

Excessive greed for material consumption has the tendency to decrease overall human happiness by contributing to natural resource depletion, social inequalities and conflicts as well as human alienation from each other and spiritual emptiness. Conditions of poverty and underconsumption also lead to decreasing levels of human well-being and social and environmental imbalances. In contrast to these two extremes, the optimum balance between human well-being and environmental sustainability can be achieved by following the Middle Path through rational use of natural resources and balanced and equitable consumption (Figure 8.4).[72]

To move towards the kind of psycho-social equilibrium discussed above, consumption of energy and natural resources in the North must be drastically reduced. New habits of food consumption based on the use of whole, organic foods must be popularized along with reduction in the consumption of expensively produced meat. In order to reduce problems such as the greenhouse effect and global warming, it is necessary to develop communally based living arrangements such as 'co-housing'. Individual use of energy-consuming technologies and products such as refrigerators, washers and dryers must be brought down through shared use in both the industrialized and industrializing countries. Indeed, the shift from a life-style of excessively individualist consumption to a lifestyle of shared consumption would take away a great deal of the ecological and social pressures that are generally attributed to population growth by the Malthusians. By

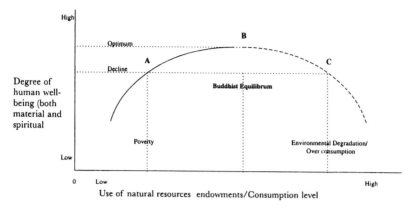

Figure 8.4 Buddhist well-being curve, equilibrium, and diminishing returns

Source: Patrick Mendis, "Buddhist Equilibrium: The Theory of Middle Path for Sustainable Development", Staff Paper P93-2, Department of Agriculture and Applied Economics, University of Minnesota, January 1993, p. 28.

helping to rebuild communities, sharing would also help relieve the social isolation and emotional deprivation felt by nuclear families and individuals in the North.

The development and promotion of efficient and inexpensive public transportation (such as trains, buses as well as bicycles) are absolutely essential for controlling the increase of automobiles, their negative effects on the environment and the separation created by individual use of cars. Much of urban congestion blamed on population growth could also be reduced through humane and ecological urban planning. Recycling and sharing of already available goods would also help reduce wasteful consumption and promote environmental education among children in affluent families in the North. It is necessary to change the annual consumerist capitalist orgy during Christmas into a more reflective experience of simple sharing in keeping with the true spirit of Christ. The women's movement in the North must take leadership in moving young women away from overconsumption towards alternative feminist values of women's empowerment, beauty and creativity.

Efforts should be taken towards voluntary redistribution of wealth (Appendix 3) as well as socially and environmentally responsible investing. This is an important strategy for averting possible violent change and forced redistribution in the future. At least a few individuals with inherited and earned wealth in the US have already begun to channel excess funds through progressive foundations to support national and international peace, justice and environmental efforts, including women's rights and cultural diversity.[73] Sharing of wealth among women and efforts to eradicate the feminization of poverty can be a focus for international feminist solidarity and the economic empowerment of women (Appendix 4).

The unequal and exploitative global economic order is maintained through violence and militarism. But this dominant world order cannot be overcome with further violence and militarism. To achieve economic democracy and environmental sustainability, a non-violent democratic political process that upholds both individual freedom and collective survival according to the principles of social justice is essential.

Participatory democracy

We are living in an extremely dangerous and volatile period in the history of humanity. Unless more and more citizens, especially citizens in the North and from the middle classes everywhere, begin to exercise their freedom of speech and speak out and act against widening and deepening inequality and militarism now, fascism, albeit in different guises, could envelop the entire world.

Currently, peace, justice and environmental groups in the US are fragmented into a myriad of single-issue campaigns, each struggling to fight the legislative onslaughts from the conservatives in the US Congress and state governments.[74] Perhaps a single strategy such as electoral campaign finance reform could provide a central focus and unity for all the different progressive groups.[75]

Campaign finance reform is essential for democratizing electoral politics in the US and for greater electoral participation of ordinary citizens. Ceilings must be placed on how much candidates can spend on their election campaigns and efforts must be taken to curtail corporate media control of the electoral process. This is vital for shifting governmental control from the representatives of wealth and corporate power to representatives of ordinary citizens. Such a shift of governmental power in the US is essential for non-violent social change and social justice both nationally and internationally (Appendix 4). Citizen pressure must also be used to make United Nations bodies, especially the Security Council, more democratic and accountable to the majority of the world's population.

Unlike representative democracy, participatory democracy requires that the means of power be socialized and that people's power take on a more dynamic, day-to-day partnership in social governance. As Brazilian scholar Leonardo Boff has written, the effect of such an approach to democracy should be to "increase the citizens' sense of responsibility as active agents of society and co-builders of their common history".[76] Decentralization of power calls for greater emphasis on small-scale, local, bottom-up approaches. Adaptation of older traditions of participatory democracy such as tribal councils of Native Americans, village councils of India (*panchāyat*) and feminist processes needs to be seriously tried wherever possible.[77]

We need a politics that can transcend rather than increase the polarization between subject and object, between producers and consumers of knowledge, and other such dualities. We also need participatory approaches to research and education that are committed to reducing inequalities and polarization between individuals and social groups.[78] As Indian political scientist D.L. Sheth has argued, the increasing disenchantment of qualified people with conventional professions and their growing participation in people's organizations could pose a threat to the political establishment in the years ahead.[79] From the vantage point of the Middle Path, what is required is not a complete renunciation of career ambitions but the bringing of individual career interests and political activism closer together. This means that the privileged classes have to take more risks with job security, material advantage and social status in exchange for honesty, emotional fulfilment and socially and environmentally meaningful work.

For participatory democracy to emerge, non-violent methods and a democratic partnership culture must be fostered within all human relations and human groupings, especially male–female and parent–child relations within the family; teacher–student relations within the school; relations among members of neighborhood communities, work settings and regional and global contexts (Figure 8.3).[80] Raising children in an ecocentric, partnership way must be given the greatest priority at each of these levels. Educational institutions, media and communications technology must be used creatively and wisely to raise consciousness towards the eradication of patriarchy, white supremacy and other forms of racism, ethnocentrism and oppressive thinking. We need to challenge the hegemony and homogenizing effects of western consumerist culture, institutional Christianity and the English language and preserve and develop the myriad of other cultures, religions and languages now threatened with extinction. Proselytizing efforts by the Catholic Church and evangelical Christian churches among poor communities around the world using economic incentives and psychological manipulation must be exposed and stopped. Rather than simply catering to a westernized English-educated audience, scholars and artists must attempt to work in and contribute to their mother tongues and their own cultural traditions wherever possible.

Creative forms of non-violent civil disobedience must be developed to delink ourselves from the oppressive social order of domination. In this regard, Gandhian strategies of withdrawing legitimation through non-cooperation and non-violence need greater exploration (Figure 8.2).[81] We must also create spaces in our lives where we can free ourselves from the tyranny of artificial constructs such as the linear calendar, the mechanical clock, mass media, private property and the cash nexus and relate to each other and nature in less frenzied and consciously organic and fulfilling ways. We need to adapt animist rituals of our earth-based, Goddess-worshipping ancestors and explore other ways to live more in harmony with the lunar calendar and the natural cycles and rhythms of nature.

The process of working for change must be a process of community building. It must be creative, wholistic and joyous as much as possible. It must appeal to human needs for emotional connection and the celebration of nature and life. Music, theater, dance and other forms of artistic expression are vital in the human struggle for freedom and happiness. Seeing the utter folly and suicidal nature of the dominant socio-economic system, we need to challenge it with both humor and a sense of detachment. And, in order to cultivate a lighter, freer and more forgiving human spirit, we must always remain in touch with the impermanence of all phenomena (*anicca*) and our own mortality – decay, death and rebirth as part of natural evolution.[82] As we develop greater awareness of impermanence, we will become less attached to 'I' and 'mine' and more connected to all.

We need to honor life, including our own short and precious lives as sojourners on this earth. Moving away from the extremes of narcissism and self-hatred, we need to develop respect and loving kindness towards ourselves as human beings and beings in nature. To eat whole and nutritious food, develop caring and nurturing relationships, to maintain psychological and physical well-being, we have to move away from the materialistic–mechanistic culture towards a more organic, simple way of life – a balanced Middle Path. This twin struggle for personal autonomy and social justice constitutes the global political and cultural revolution.

In reclaiming our lives, our cultures and dignity, we can take inspiration from women leaders in the South like Rigoberta Menchú. Reflecting on the devastating effects of the last 500 years of European imperialism on the masses of people of color and yet looking to the future with hope and determination, Menchú says:

> We must eliminate situations of usurpation, imposition, discrimination and marginalisation that generate these conflicts that cost our people so much.... [We must discover] the dignity of respect for life, for human rights, and our Mother Earth who belongs also to our children and grandchildren of tomorrow.... The common struggle of indigenous, mestizo, and black peoples – the common struggles of the poor ... is no longer a dream, it is a reality that our people are living.[83]

The strength of the feminine as represented by women like Rigoberta Menchú is essential for transcending the past half a millennium of European imperialism and moving towards a new model of democratic and sustainable development in the coming millennium. The empowerment of women, specifically poor women of color, is central to the psycho-social transformation needed in the world at this time.

Empowerment of Women

Economic and social empowerment of women is the key to breaking the cycle connecting women, population and global crisis (Figure 8.2). Women's empowerment requires changes in the patriarchal social order that subordinates women specifically as women. Matrilineal rights, including rights to property and custody of children, must be strengthened along with equal inheritance of family property between men and women. In addition to control over land and other natural resources, women need skills, training and access to credit; jobs with dignity; employment which provide a living wage for themselves and their families; equal wages; right to labor organizing; environmentally safe working conditions; maternity and health benefits; and safe and reliable child care.

Institutions like the Grameen Bank in Bangladesh have been successful in providing small loans to poor women and investing in their productive capacity. Their success shows the fallacy of the top-down World Bank corporate model of development based on mega-projects and large-scale foreign loans to governments and elites.[84] In the United States, too, where community development funds play a vital role in local survival, funds must be made more readily available to women (Appendix 4). Whether it be in the South or the North, credit to poor women must be available without the conditionality of family planning acceptance.

When the underlying causes of eco-social imbalances and poverty are alleviated, fertility will be voluntarily reduced. Eradication of poverty would also help curb the need for large-scale immigration and urbanization and the social unrest and conflicts associated with them. Long-term solutions to the population explosion and mass emigration do not lie in stringent population and immigration control, but in resource protection, employment generation, community survival and the empowerment of women at the local levels. Indeed, if the human 'caring capacity' in the world is increased, the problem of planetary 'carrying capacity' will take care of itself.[85]

The Middle Path teaches us that without redressing the extreme global economic inequality that now prevails, neither sustainability nor a democracy can be achieved. It shows us that we have to balance the quantitative approach obsessed with numbers with a qualitative approach which focuses on the improvement of social relations. The solution to the global crisis lies not only in transforming the sphere of economic production and class relations, but also in changing the sphere of human reproduction and gender relations. These transformations are also vital for shifting the focus of human reproduction from population control to birth control.

A new reproductive rights agenda

A democratic and sustainable approach to human reproduction must incorporate social, ethical and ecological criteria. The dogmatism and extremism of both pronatalist right-wing religious fundamentalism and antinatalist neo-Malthusianism must be avoided. To avert further strengthening of religious fundamentalism, to avoid Vatican interference in women's reproductive choice, and in fairness to other religions, the special status of the Holy See, as a Non-Member State Permanent Observer at the United Nations, must be revoked (Appendix 4).[86]

Appropriate technology and democratic, social relations must define the realm of human biological reproduction as they do the realm of economic production. Human well-being should be the guiding principle; not technological growth, profits for pharmaceutical companies or the neo-Malthusian goal of quick-fix population control. It is only with a fundamental shift in education and culture that the prevailing quantitative, Malthusian approach and narrow concept of population as an inanimate object can be replaced with a qualitative concept of people as powerful subjects/agents – individuals, families, communities – determining the course of our own lives. We need to shift from an approach which treats human beings as entities to be used and discarded, or, worse, used as cannon fodder for armies, to an approach which values each human being as a precious individual with enormous potential for creative contribution to society.

A paradigm shift from the hierarchical, techno-bureaucratic, pyramidal model of population control to a participatory, ecocentric, circular model of birth control is greatly needed. It is only with such a shift that the dualisms of subject/object, provider/client, and so on, of the neo-Malthusian model can be transcended and a partnership approach to health and reproduction achieved. Such a shift is essential for empowering women as subjects determining the course of their reproductive lives and for ending the victimization experienced by most poor women in family planning programs.

Numerical targets and economic incentives must be abolished from family planning programs in the Third World and they must not be extended to the US. Technological interventions that promote unnecessary fragmentation and domination must be used sparingly on women's bodies that bear life. In order to make family planning more democratic and safe, quality health care services and a range of safe contraceptives which help protect people against STDs are required. Development of safe male contraceptive methods is essential for greater male–female partnership in birth control.

Abortion should not be used as a contraceptive method, but safe and legal abortions should be available to women who choose to have them. Abortion is, almost always, a painful decision for women. Instead of punishing women for that difficult moral and emotional decision, society should develop compassion and support systems for women in making their own choices.

Women's biological connection to the rhythm and cycles of nature – the lunar cycle – needs greater appreciation. Local herbal methods and improvements on them must be placed before imported, costly, high-tech contraceptives and artificial reproductive technologies. So-called 'soft' contraceptive methods, especially the safe barrier methods and non-terminal methods which provide women with greater autonomy, should be made widely available along with necessary information and education to properly use them. Where needed, poor people must be given access to safe methods of infertility treatment, not only fertility control. The social and environmental causes of infertility need to be addressed rather than simply promoting new artificial reproduction methods such as embryo transplants, 'surrogate mothering', and so on.

Informed consent guidelines need to be strictly adhered to and good health care facilities must be available for the proper use of contraceptives. Only contraceptives that are proven safe over a long period of time should be made available. The health and ethical concerns raised by feminist health groups regarding hormonal and immunological contraceptives must be taken seriously. The charges made by the Campaign and Petition Calling for a Stop to Research on Anti-Fertility Vaccines must be considered carefully rather than shunted aside as an extremist anti-scientific stance (Appendix 4).[87] As feminist biologist Ruth Hubbard urges us, like the Luddites, contemporary women must exercise our right to choose as well as decide upon new reproductive technologies to be developed.

> Most of us who oppose some of today's technological 'advances' are not opposed to technology per se. We simply insist on exercising our right, if not civic obligation, to discriminate among technologies. And we must remember that, though the Luddites failed to stop the factory system, some of the regulations and improvements for which they agitated were put in place.[88]

In addition to appropriate technology, birth control requires a radical change of the hierarchical relationship between health care providers and clients. The services of traditional health care providers like village midwives and community leaders must not be appropriated for purposes of population control; rather, they must be supported in acquiring new skills to further their work on behalf of people. In other words, existing modes of community partnership, especially women's networks, need to be strengthened rather than weakened.

The definition of reproductive rights needs to be rescued from the narrow population control agenda and broadened to include a more enlightened vision of human life and a more liberating attitude towards human sexuality, an attitude which encompasses the human need for freedom, beauty, pleasure, creativity and solidarity with each other and nature.[89]

Human life cannot be reduced to the animal instinct to reproduce. Oppressive cultural traditions such as genital mutilation must be stopped so that women can have greater sexual freedom. To further ensure this freedom, women and girls must have legal protection against rape, wife battery and other forms of sexual and physical abuse. Women must not be forced into arranged marriages and abusive unions. They must have the right to remain single or develop alternatives to male-headed nuclear families and heterosexual relations, including close bonds and living arrangements with other women.

The concepts of family and community need to be enlarged to allow survival of extended families and the integration of destitutes and refugee children without negation of their cultures of origin. We must evolve a global culture which is child-centered and which makes loving care and nurturance of all children the highest priority.[90] Feminists must make the raising of future generations central to our reproductive rights agenda rather than leave it to be appropriated by the right wing. We need both a new feminist economics and a new feminist approach to child development. To have a truly 'new' reproductive rights agenda, a massive change is required in gender socialization.

The dominant–subordinate relations between men and women in all spheres of life need to be changed. Problems such as female infanticide, the spread of sex-selective abortions and the skewing of sex ratios against females cannot be stopped by legislation alone. Indeed, none of the global problems of global environmental destruction, poverty or war can be addressed without overcoming patriarchy.

The end of patriarchy

The quality of the male–female relationship bears on all aspects of life from child development to global policy making. To protect children and the environment, to have greater peace and harmony among races and nations, we need to overcome the 'gender weaknesses' that have been imposed on us by patriarchal socialization over thousands of years.[91] If men are genuinely to love women, they must attempt to understand, tolerate and respect them. In her Keynote address to the NGO Forum read at the UN Women's Conference in Beijing in August 1995, Aung San Suu Kyi pointed out:

> In societies where men are truly confident of their own worth, women are not merely 'tolerated', they are valued. Their opinions are listened to with respect, and they are given their rightful place in shaping the society in which they live....
> There are no gender barriers that cannot be overcome. The relationship between men and women should, and can, be characterized not by patronizing behaviour and exploitation, but by *metta* (loving kindness), partnership and trust.[92]

Men must liberate themselves from the association of masculinity with aggression and militarism; they need to become confident in their own self-worth without having to prove themselves through power over and conquest of others. In this regard, efforts of organizations such as Veterans for Peace in the US which challenge the identification of masculinity with war and aggression need to be widely supported (Appendix 4). Given that most women are also working outside the home, men must do their fair share of domestic work, including child rearing, cooking and cleaning. Men must take equal responsibility with women in the realms of sexuality, for example by maintaining sexual health and using birth control.

Women in turn must overcome the denial of agency, the self-doubt and self-denigration historically assigned to us by patriarchy. We must recognize that seeking greater acceptance within the dominant male model, whether it be in its Malthusian, right-wing fundamentalist or some other manifestation, will not bring us our empowerment. Instead, we must reclaim our power by asserting a partnership approach which allows both women and men to develop our full human potential. A position which offers the opportunity for change for both the sexes helps shift away from essentialism which reduces men and women simply to biologically determined characteristics.

Women need to apply strategies of non-violent confrontation in both the domestic and public spheres through work stoppages and other forms of non-cooperation. We need to challenge the subtle and blatant forms of sexism of individual men, workplaces and institutions, including transnational corporations, governments and the World Bank. To do so, we must strengthen ourselves individually and collectively. We have to remove the shackles of patriarchy that have bound our minds for millennia. We need to respect our minds and bodies, practicing loving kindness towards ourselves. We need to come together as women recognizing that our power lies not in aggression, hatred and greed but in our individual and collective wisdom, compassion and generosity.[93]

We need to find a Middle Path for women's liberation, a new model of feminism which transcends the patriarchy and extremism of both religious fundamentalism and professional careerism. We need to strike a balance between the traditional role of the self-sacrificing mother and the modern role of the individualist career woman. To find such a balance, women need to be supported by men, our families, communities, work places and the larger world. The opportunities for change and growth must be open to all women, not just an elite. It is only when the voices of the majority of women and men are heard that the world can move beyond crisis to an era of sustainability, peace and prosperity for all.

It is true that in recent times women have increasingly been pursuing the same model of aggression and domination as men, with many young women being misled to identify power and success with carrying a gun. Indeed, many current women leaders, including most feminists themselves, have not been able to make much progress in putting the alternative partnership model into practice. Still, we must remember that for thousands of years women have dedicated and continue to dedicate themselves to nurturing and caring for the human race as well as the environment. As

Aung San Suu Kyi's address to the Beijing Women's Conference stated, the age-old wisdom and ability women have gained especially in their role as mothers must be fully made use of at this critical time to create a more loving, just and peaceful world for all (Appendix 4).[94] But, as Aung San Suu Kyi has also reminded us, as women take on more of the teaching and leadership roles, we must remember that we, too, have much to learn and that we, too, need to be flexible in adapting to changing needs and circumstances.[95]

We are living in an extraordinarily challenging time as we move into the next century and the next millennium. Human and planetary survival requires that we break out of the cycle of violence and self-destruction in which we are caught in order to create a culture that honors peace and life. As Jungian analyst Jean Shinoda Bolen states, the incorporation of the sacred dimension of the feminine through the development of new archetypes and cultural myths is a major aspect of the paradigm shift needed at this time:

> ...the spiritual dimension is the last and the most significant wave of the women's movement, ... once the model of divinity having a feminine face is brought into the culture, the culture can change.... I see us generating new archetypes and cultural myths, with the image of Earth from outer space perhaps the most significant new symbol. The Earth is Mother, Gaia, matter, an icon that evokes emotion and imagination.... [It] evokes an enlargement of the archetype of Home, which in turn enlarges the notion of hearthkeeping and caretaking.[96]

The image of the Earth from outer space puts us in touch with our potential to develop a planetary consciousness and social movements towards global peace and unity. The solution to the global crisis does not lie in a narrow, quantitative approach to population size and natural resources that leads to wiping out poor women of color and their children. The solution to current dilemmas calls for healing and eco-social balance in relations between human and non-human life and between all aspects of humanity. In order to create healing and balance, we must try to deepen our wisdom and apply loving kindness and generosity in our social polities and daily lives as much as possible.

Notes

1. Thompson, "Time, Work-Discipline"; Kirkpatrick Sale, Rebels Against the Future: *The Luddites and their War on the Industrial Revolution: Lessons for the Computer Age*, Reading, MA: Addison-Wesley, 1995; G.E. Aylmer, ed., *The Levellers in the English Revolution*, Ithaca, NY: Cornell University Press, 1975; Ehrenreich and English, *For Her Own Good*.

2. Frances Fox Piven and Richard A. Cloward, *Poor People's Movements: Why They Succeed, How They Fail*, New York: Vintage Books, 1979; Ehrenreich and English, *For Her Own Good*, pp. 28–29.

3. Davis, *Women, Race and Class*, pp. 65–66.

4. Bandarage, *Colonialism in Sri Lanka*, pp. 193, 242–245.

5. Cited in Thompson "Time, Work-Discipline", p.59.

6. Judith Van Allen, "Sitting on a Man – Colonialism and Lost Political Institutions of Igbo Women", *Canadian Journal of African Studies*, Vol. 6, No. 2, 1972, pp. 165–182; Mies, *Patriarchy and Accumulation*, p. 99.

7. James C. Scott, *Everyday Forms of Peasant Resistance*, New Haven: Yale University Press, 1994.

8. Mohandas K. Gandhi, *An Autobiography: The Story of My Experiments with Truth*, Boston: Beacon Press, 1957.

9. See, for example, Arlene Eisen Bergman, *Women of Vietnam*, San Francisco: People's Press, 1975; Gordon, *Women of Algeria*.

10. Brad Erickson, ed., *Call To Action: Handbook for Ecology, Peace and Justice*, San Francisco: Sierra Club Books, 1990; see also Paul Ekins, *A New World Order: Grassroots Movements for Global Change*, London: Routledge, 1992; Robert Cooney and Helen Michalowski, *The Power of the People: Active Nonviolence in the United States*, Philadelphia: New Society Publishers, 1987.

11. Helen Desfosses and Jacques Levesque, eds, *Socialism in the Third World*, New York: Praeger Publishers, 1975.

12. Ibid.; Ling, *How Big Powers Dominate*, Chap. 3.

13. McGinnis, *Bread and Justice, passim.*

14. "Venezuela Will Receive IMF Loan", *Chicago Tribune*, March 30, 1989, Section 3, p. 2; Ian Black, "Jordan Prime Minister Resigns over IMF Unrest", *Guardian*, April 25, 1989, p. 24.

15. Aaron Sachs, "Eco-Justice: Linking Human Rights and the Environment", *World Watch Paper*, No. 127, Washington, DC: World Watch Institute, December 1995; see also publications of Rainforest Action Network (Appendix 4).

16. Martin Khor, "500, 000 Indian Farmers Rally Against GATT and Patenting of Seeds", *Third World Resurgence*, No. 39, 1993, pp. 20–22; "Sri Lanka Team Report", *Project Bulletin*, Peace Brigades International, New York, March 1995, p. 1.

17. Schemo, "U.S. Pesticide Kills Foreign Fruit Pickers".

18. Lynn Stephen, "Crackdown in Chiapas:Protests Nationwide", *Peacework*, No. 250, March 1995, p. 14.

19. Merchant, *Radical Ecology*, Chap. 8; Shiva, *Staying Alive*; Oxfam America, *The Impact of Structural Adjustment*, p. 13; Marguerite Guzman Bouvard, *Revolutionizing Motherhood: The Mothers of the Plaza de Mayo*, Wilmington, DE: Scholarly Resources Inc., 1994. For information on women's organizing in the manufacturing sector, see publications of Women Working Worldwide (Appendix 4); For information on support for rights of women and children worldwide, see publications of MADRE (Appendix 4).

20. Menchú, *I, Rigoberta Menchú*; Paul Lewis, "After Nigeria Represses, Shell Defends its Record", *The New York Times*, February 13, 1996, p. A1; Amdur, "Rape as Low-Intensity Warfare", pp. 15–16.

21. Hanlon "Supporting Our Front-Line Struggles", pp. 75–77; Merchant, *Radical Ecology*, pp. 192–193; for information on the environmental justice movement, see publications of the Political Ecology Group (Appendix 4).

22. Chris Hedges, "The Violent Debate Over Tribal Sovereignty", *The New York Times*, September 23, 1990, p. E5; Fred Langan, "Canada's Indian Protests Ignite Rights Movement", *Christian Science Monitor*, August 20, 1990, p. 4.

23. Joke Schrijvers, *The Violence of 'Development'*, Institute for Development Research, Amsterdam, Netherlands, 1993, p. 18.

24. Donaldson, *Nature Against Us*, p. 105; "Sri Lanka Project Report", *Project Bulletin*, Peace Brigades International, New York, January 1996, pp. 6–8.

25. Stephen R. Shalom, "Why the World Bank Can't Lead Us to a Just World Order", *Bulletin of Concerned Asian Scholars*, Vol. 27, No. 4, 1995, p. 49.

26. John McClaughry and Kirkpatrick Sale, "The History and Promise of Decentralism in America", Opening Keynote Address (unpublished), Decentralist Conference, The E.F. Schumacher Society, Williamstown, MA, June 28, 1996.

27. Bandarage, "In Search of a New World Order"; Eisler, *Chalice and the Blade*; see also Issac D. Balbus, *Marxism and Domination*, Princeton: Princeton University Press, 1982; Ken Jones, *The Social Face of Buddhism*, London: Wisdom Publications, 1989.

28. Leonardo Boff, *Ecology and Liberation: A New Paradigm*, New York: Orbis Books, 1995, pp. 41, 64.

29. Gregory Bateson, *Steps to an Ecology of Mind: Collected Essays in Anthropology, Psychiatry, Evolution, and Epistemology*, San Francisco: Chandler Publishing Co., 1972.

30. Devon G. Pena, "The 'Green' Marx: Capitalism and the Destruction of Nature", Colorado College, Colarado Springs, unpublished ms, September 1988, p. 18.

31. Gandhi, cited in Arne Naess, "Self Realization: An Ecological Approach to Being in the World", in John Seed, Joanna Macy, Pat Fleming and Arne Naess, eds, *Thinking Like a Mountain: Towards a Council Of Beings*, Philadelphia: New Society Publishers, 1988, p. 25.

32. Walpola Rahula, *What the Buddha Taught*, London: Gordon Fraser, 1978; William Hart, *Vipassana Meditation As Taught by S.N. Goenka*, San Francisco: Harper and Row, 1987.

33. Thich Nhat Hanh, *The Sun My Heart*, Berkeley: Parallax Press, 1988.

34. Boff, *Ecology and Liberation, passim*; Ecumenical Institute for Study and Dialogue, *Integrity of Creation*, Introduction.

35. John Seed, "Beyond Anthropocentrism", in Seed et al., eds, *Thinking Like a Mountain*, pp. 36 39; see also John Seed and Pat Fleming, "Evolutionary Remembering", in ibid., p. 47.

36. Seed, "Beyond Anthropocentrism", pp. 38–39.

37. Riane Eisler, "The Gaia Tradition and the Partnership Future: An Ecofeminist Manifesto", in Diamond and Orenstein, eds, *Reweaving the World*, p. 28.

38. Shiva, *Staying Alive*; Maria Mies and Vandana Shiva, *Ecofeminism*, London: Zed Books, 1993; Diamond and Orenstein, eds, *Reweaving the World, passim*; Merlin Stone, *When God Was a Woman*, New York: Harcourt Brace Jovanovich, 1970; Starhawk, *The Spiral Dance: A Rebirth of the Ancient Religion of the Goddess*, San Francisco: Harper and Row, 1986.

39. Sally Miller Gearhart, "Notes from a Recovering Activist", *Sojourner*, September 1995, p. 10.

40. "The Narrowed Mind", p. 17.

41. Gearhart, "Notes", p. 10.

42. Rahula, *What the Buddha Taught, passim*; Hart, *Vipassana Mediatation, passim*; Jack Kornfield, *A Path With Heart: A Guide Through the Perils and Promises of Spirtual Life*, New York: Bantam Books, 1993.

43. Aung San Suu Kyi, "Keynote Address", NGO Forum, United Nations Women's Conference, Beijing, August 31, 1995; see also Aung San Suu Kyi, *Freedom From Fear*.

44. Rahula, *What the Buddha Taught*, pp. 85–88; D.C. Ahir, *Asoka the Great*, Delhi: B.R. Publishing Corp., 1995.

45. Lawrence Kohlberg, "Development of Moral Character and Moral Ideology", in Martin L. Hoffman and Lois Wladis Hoffman, eds, *Review of Child Development Research*, Vol. 1, New York: Russell Sage Foundation, 1964, pp. 383–431; Ingolf Vogeler and Anthony de Souza, "Dialectics of Understanding the Third World", in Vogeler and Souza, *Dialectics of Third World Development*, pp. 3–27.

46. Gandhi, *An Autobiography*.

47. His Holiness Tenzin Gyatso, The Fourteenth Dalai Lama, *A Human Approach to World Peace*, London: Wisdom Publications, 1984, pp. 4–5; San Suu Kyi, "Keynote Address"; Cooney and Michalowski, *The Power of the People*, Chap. 8.

48. Nichidatsu Fuji, "The Source of Human Annhilation", in *Buddhism for World Peace: Words of Nichidatsu Fuji*, trans. Yumiko Miyazaki, Japan-Bharat Savodaya Mitrata Sangha, Tokyo, 1980, p. 139.

49. Rahula, *What the Buddha Taught*, p. 46.

50. Bhikku Bodhi, "Tolerance and Diversity", *Newsletter*, Buddhist Publication Society, Kandy, Sri Lanka, No. 24, Summer–Fall 1993, p. 1.

51. Michael Ray and Alan Rinzler, eds, *The New Paradigm in Business: Emerging Strategies*

for Leadership and Organizational Change, New York: Jeremy P. Tarcher/Perigee Books, 1993.

52. E.F. Schumacher, *Small is Beautiful*, New York: Harper and Row, 1989, pp. 56–66; H.N.S. Karunatilake, *This Confused Society*, Buddhist Information Society, Colombo, Sri Lanka, *passim*; Herman E. Daly and John B. Cobb Jr, *For the Common Good: Redirecting the Economy Toward Community, the Environment, and a Sustainable Future*, Boston: Beacon Press, 1994, p. 444.

53. Waring, *If Women Counted*; *Redefining Wealth and Progress: New Ways to Measure Economic, Social and Environmental Change – The Carcas Report on Alternative Development Indicators*, New York: Bootstrap Press, 1989.

54. Schumacher, *Small is Beautiful*, pp. 57–58; Lucy Anderson, "Work", in Simple Living Committee, American Friends Service Committee (AFSC), San Francisco, *Taking Charge: Achieving Personal and Political Change Through Simple Living*, New York: Bantam Books, Inc., 1978, pp. 149–167.

55. Robert Gilman, "Sustainability: The State of the Movement", *In Context*, No. 25, Late Spring 1990, p. 11.

56. Norberg-Hodge, *Ancient Futures, passim*; Joanna Macy, *Dharma and Development: Religion as Resource in the Sarvodaya Self-Help Movement*, West Hartford, CT: Kumarian Press, 1985; Jones, *The Social Face of Buddhism*, pp. 242–254.

57. Judith Plant, "Searching for Common Ground: Ecofeminism and Bioregionalism", in Diamond and Orenstein, eds, *Reweaving the World*, p. 158.

58. Khor, cited in Gustavo Esteva and Madhu Suri Prakash, "Editorial: From Global to Local Thinking", *The Ecologist*, Vol. 24, No. 5, September–October 1994, p. 163.

59. Herman E. Daly, "Achieving Development Without Growth", *Surviving Together*, Winter 1993, p. 44; see also "1994 in Review: Sustainable Communities", *TRANET: A Bi-Monthly Digest for the A & T (Alternative and Transformational) Movements*, No. 2, January 1995, p. 1; Sajed Kamal, "The Solar Revolution: Energy for A Sustainable Earth", unpublished ms, International Consortium for Energy Development, Boston, n.d.

60. Hazel Henderson, *Paradigms in Progress: Life Beyond Economics*, San Francisco: Berrett-Koehler Publishers, 1995.

61. Kevin Danaher, ed., *50 years Is Enough: The Case Against the World Bank and the International Monetary Fund*, Boston: South End Press, 1994, p. 187.

62. "Platform", World Bank/IMF: 50 Years Is Enough Campaign, n.d., pp. 1–8 (Appendix 4).

63. Barbara Crossette, "U.N. Parley Puts Focus on Africa", *The New York Times*, March 9, 1995, p. A4.

64. New World Foundation, Bastian and Alston, "An Update", p. 4.

65. Esteva and Prakash, "Editorial", pp. 162–163.

66. Peter D. Kinder, Steven D. Lydenberg and Amy L. Domini, *The Social Investment Almanac: A Comprehensive Guide to Socially Responsible Investing*, New York: Henry Holt and Co., 1992.

67. "Burma: Manerplaw Refuge Falls", *Peacework*, No. 250, March 1995, p. 9; Simon Billenness, "Waylaid in Rangoon: Junta Uses Investments to Block Democracy', *Investing for A Better World*, Franklin Insight Inc., Boston, MA, April 15, 1996, p. 1; Eddie Bauer, "News Release", February 1, 1995; Meg Vaillancourt, "Mass. Becomes First State to Boycott Burma Business", *The Boston Globe*, June 26, 1996.

68. McLaughlin, "Child-Labor Abuse"; "Nonviolent Action Leads to Coffee Victory at Starbucks", *Peacework*, No. 250, March 1995, p. 17.

69. Madihē Paññasiha Mahā Nāyaka Thero, "Foreword", in Karunatilake, *This Confused Society*, p. v.

70. Gandhi, *An Autobiography*; Lanza Del Vasto, *Gandhi to Vinoba: The New Pilgrimage*, New York: Schocken Books, 1974.

71. Duane Elgin, *Voluntary Simplicity: Toward a Way of Life That is Outwardly Simple, Inwardly Rich*, New York: William Morrow and Co., Inc., 1981; AFSC, *Taking Charge, passim*; Karunatilake, *This Confused Society*, p. 8; Wachtel, *The Poverty of Affluence, passim*.

72. Patrick Mendis, "Buddhist Equilibrium: The Theory of Middle Path for Sustainable Development", Staff Paper P93-2, Department of Agricultural and Applied

Economics, University of Minnesota, January 1993.

73. Christopher Mogil and Anne Slepian with Peter Woodrow, *We Gave Away a Fortune: Stories of People Who Have Devoted Themselves and Their Wealth to Peace, Justice And a Healthy Environment*, Philadelphia: New Society Publishers, 1992.

74. Bandarage, "In Search of a New World Order".

75. For information on Electoral Campaign Finance Reform in the US, see publications of Public Citizen and Common Cause (Appendix 4).

76. Boff, *Ecology and Liberation*, p. 83.

77. Bandarage, "In Search of a New World Order"; Charlene Elridge Wheeler and Peggy L. Chinn, *Peace and Power: A Handbook of Feminist Process*, Buffalo, NY: Margaret-daughters, Inc., 1984; Birgit Brock-Utne, *Educating for Peace: A Feminist Perspective*, New York: Pergamon Press, 1985; Asoka Bandarage, "Toward International Feminism", in *Brandeis Review*, Vol. 3, No. 3, Summer 1983, reprinted in Jo Whitehorse Cochran, Donna Langston and Carolyn Woodward, eds, *Changing Our Power: An Introduction to Women's Studies*, 2nd edn, Dubuque, IA: Kendall/Hunt Publishing Co. 1991, p. 232.

78. Paulo Freire, *Pedagogy of the Oppressed*, trans. Myra Berman Ramos, New York: Seabury Press, 1970; D.L. Sheth, "Alternative Development as Political Practice", *Alternatives*, No. XII, 1987, pp. 165, 169.

79. Sheth, "Alternative Development", pp. 155–171.

80. Gerald and Patricia Mische, *Toward a Human World Order: Beyond the National Security Straitjacket*, New York: Paulist Press, 1977.

81. Sheth, "Alternative Development", p. 159.

82. Cited in Bandarage, "Global Peace and Security", p.40; see also Menchú, *I Rigobeta Menchú*.

83. Stephen Levine, *Who Dies? An Investigation of Conscious Living and Conscious Dying*, Garden City, NY: Anchor Books, 1982.

84. Jessica Matthews, "Little World Banks", in Danaher, ed., *50 Years is Enough*, pp. 183–185.

85. Malini Karkal, "Why the Cairo Document", p. 19.

86. "Women's Groups Initiate Petition About Status of Holy See at UN", *Political Environments*, No. 3, Winter–Spring 1996, p. 32.

87. Campaign and Petition Calling for a Stop to Research on Anti-Fertility Vaccines (Appendix 4); "Canadian Resolution Against Norplant", The National Action Committee on the Status of Women, Canada, Toronto, *WGNRR Newsletter*, No. 48, October–December 1994, p. 13.

88. Ruth Hubbard, *Profitable Promises: Essays on Women, Science and Health*, Monroe, ME: Common Courage Press, 1995, p. 155.

89. Boff, *Ecology and Liberation*, p. 127.

90. Jean Liedloff, *The Continuum Concept: In Search of Happiness Lost*, Reading, MA: Addison-Wesley, 1977; MADRE (Appendix 4).

91. Aung San Suu Kyi, "Keynote Address".

92. Ibid.; Wheeler and Chinn, *Peace and Power, passim*.

93. Eisler, "The Gaia Tradition", p. 34.

94. Aung San Suu Kyi, "Keynote Address"; Sara Ruddick, *Maternal Thinking: Towards a Politics of Peace*, New York, Ballantine Books, 1989.

95. Aung San Suu Kyi, "Keynote Address".

96. Cited in Hanlon, "Living in a Liminal Time", p. 23.

Women, Population and the Environment: Call for a New Approach

The Committee on Women, Population and the Environment is an alliance of women activists, community organizers, health practitioners and scholars of diverse races, cultures and countries of origin working for women's empowerment and reproductive freedom, and against poverty, inequality, racism and environmental degradation. Issued in 1992, their statement "Women, Population and the Environment: Call for a New Approach" continues to gather individual and organizational endorsements from around the world.

We are troubled by recent statements and analyses that single out population size and growth as a primary cause of global environmental degradation.

We believe the major causes of global environmental degradation are:

- Economic systems that exploit and misuse nature and people in the drive for short-term and short-sighted gains and profits.
- The rapid urbanization and poverty resulting from migration from rural areas and from inadequate planning and resource allocation in towns and cities.
- The displacement of small farmers and indigenous peoples by agri-business, timber, mining, and energy corporations, often with encouragement and assistance from international financial institutions, and with the complicity of national governments.
- The disproportionate consumption patterns of the affluent the world over. Currently, the industrialized nations, with 22 percent of the world's population, consume 70 percent of the world's resources. Within the United States, deepening economic inequalities mean that the poor are consuming less, and the rich more.
- Technologies designed to exploit but not to restore natural resources.
- Warmaking and arms production which divest resources from human needs, poison the natural environment and perpetuate the militarization of culture, encouraging violence against women.

Environmental degradation derives thus from complex, interrelated causes. Demographic variables can have an impact on the environment, but reducing population growth will not solve the above problems. In many countries, population growth rates have declined yet environmental conditions continue to deteriorate.

Moreover, blaming global environmental degradation on population growth helps to lay the groundwork for the re-emergence and intensification of the top-down, demographically driven population policies and programs which are deeply disrespectful of women, particularly women of color and their children.

In Southern countries, as well as in the United States and other Northern countries, family planning programs have often been the main vehicles for dissemination of modern contraceptive technologies. However, because so many of their activities have been oriented toward population control rather than women's reproductive health needs, they have too often involved sterilization abuse; denied women full information on contraceptive risks and side effects; neglected proper medical screening, follow-up care, and informed consent; and ignored the need for safe abortion and barrier and male methods of contraception. Population programs have frequently fostered a climate where coercion is permissible and racism acceptable.

Demographic data from around the globe affirm that improvements in women's social, economic, and health status and in general living standards, are often keys to declines in population growth rates. We call on the world to recognize women's basic right to control their own bodies and to have access to the power, resources, and reproductive health services to ensure that they can do so.

National governments, international agencies, and other social institutions must take seriously their obligation to provide the essential prerequisites for women's development and freedom. These include:

1. Resources such as fair and equitable wages, land rights, appropriate technology, education, and access to credit.
2. An end to structural adjustment programs, imposed by the IMF, the World Bank, and repressive governments, which sacrifice human dignity and basic needs for food, health, and education to debt repayment and 'free market', male-dominated models of unsustainable development.
3. Full participation in the decisions which affect our own lives, our families, our communities, and our environment, and incorporation of women's knowledge systems and expertise to enrich these decisions.
4. Affordable, culturally appropriate, and comprehensive health care and health education for women of all ages and their families.
5. Access to safe, voluntary contraception and abortion as part of broader reproductive health services which also provide pre- and post-natal care, infertility services, and prevention and treatment of sexually transmitted diseases including HIV and AIDS.

6. Family support services that include child-care, parental leave and elder care.
7. Reproductive health services and social programs that sensitize men to their parental responsibilities and to the need to stop gender inequalities and violence against women and children.
8. Speedy ratification and enforcement of the UN Convention on the Elimination of All Forms of Discrimination Against Women as well as other UN conventions on human rights.

People who want to see improvements in the relationship between the human population and natural environment should work for the full range of women's rights; global demilitarization; redistribution of resources and wealth between and within nations; reduction of consumption rates of polluting products and processes and of non-renewable resources; reduction of chemical dependency in agriculture; and environmentally responsible technology. They should support local, national, and international initiatives for democracy, social justice, and human rights.

APPENDIX 2

The Seville Statement on Violence

The Seville Statement on Violence was drafted by an international committee of 20 scholars at the 6th International Colloquium on Brain and Aggression held at the University of Seville, Spain, in May 1986, with support from the Spanish Commission for UNESCO. The Statement's purpose is to dispel the widespread belief that human beings are inevitably disposed to war as a result of innate, biologically determined aggressive traits.

UNESCO adopted the Seville Statement at its 25th General Conference Session in Paris, October 17–November 16, 1989. The Statement has been formally endorsed by scientific organizations and published in journals around the world. UNESCO is preparing a brochure to be used in teaching young people about the Statement.

In August 1987 the Council of Representatives of the American Psychological Association voted to endorse the Seville Statement. The Board of Scientific Affairs emphasized that this is not a scientific statement on the issue of specific inherited behavioral traits. It is, rather, a social statement designed to eliminate unfounded stereotypic thinking on the inevitability of war.

Believing that it is our responsibility to address from our particular disciplines the most dangerous and destructive activities of our species, violence and war; recognizing that science is a human cultural product which cannot be definitive or all-encompassing; and gratefully acknowledging the support of the authorities of Seville and representatives of Spanish UNESCO; we, the undersigned scholars from around the world and from relevant sciences, have met and arrived at the following Statement on Violence. In it, we challenge a number of alleged biological findings that have been used, even by some in our disciplines, to justify violence and war. Because the alleged findings have contributed to an atmosphere of pessimism in our time, we submit that the open, considered rejection of these misstatements can contribute significantly to the International Year of Peace.

Misuse of scientific theories and data to justify violence and war is not new but has been made since the advent of modern science. For example, the theory of evolution has been used to justify not only war, but also genocide, colonialism, and suppression of the weak.

We state our position in the form of five propositions. We are aware that there are many other issues about violence and war that could be fruitfully addressed from the standpoint of our disciplines, but we restrict ourselves here to what we consider a most important first step.

It is scientifically incorrect to say that we have inherited a tendency to make war from our animal ancestors. Although fighting occurs widely throughout animal species, only a few cases of destructive intra-species fighting between organized groups have ever been reported among naturally living species, and none of these involve the use of tools designed to be weapons. Normal predatory feeding upon other species cannot be equated with intra-species violence. Warfare is a peculiarly human phenomenon and does not occur in other animals.

The fact that warfare has changed so radically over time indicates that it is a product of culture. Its biological connection is primarily through language which makes possible the coordination of groups, the transmission of technology, and the use of tools. War is biologically possible, but is not inevitable, as evidenced by its variation in occurrence and nature over time and space. There are cultures which have not engaged in war for centuries, and there are cultures which have engaged in war frequently at some times and not at others.

It is scientifically incorrect to say that war or any other violent behavior is genetically programmed into our human nature. While genes are involved at all levels of nervous system function, they provide a developmental potential that can be actualized only in conjunction with the ecological and social environment. While individuals vary in their predispositions to be affected by their experience, it is the interaction between their genetic endowment and conditions of nurturance that determines their personalities. Except for rare pathologies, the genes do not produce individuals necessarily predisposed to violence. Neither do they determine the opposite. While genes are co-involved in establishing our behavioral capacities, they do not by themselves specify the outcome.

It is scientifically incorrect to say that in the course of human evolution there has been a selection for aggressive behavior more than for other kinds of behavior. In all well-studied species, status within the group is achieved by the ability to cooperate and to fulfill social functions relevant to the structure of that group. 'Dominance' involves social bondings and affiliations; it is not simply a matter of the possession and use of superior physical power, although it does involve aggressive behaviors. Where genetic selection for aggressive behavior has been artificially instituted in animals, it has rapidly succeeded in producing hyper-aggressive individuals; this indicates that aggression was not maximally selected under natural conditions. When such experimentally created hyper-aggressive animals are present in a social group, they either disrupt its social structure or are driven out. Violence is neither in our evolutionary legacy nor in our genes.

It is scientifically incorrect to say that humans have a 'violent brain'. While we do have the neural apparatus to act violently, it is not automatically activated by internal or external stimuli. Like higher primates and unlike other animals, our higher neural processes filter such stimuli before they can be acted upon. How we act is shaped by how we have been conditioned and socialized. There is nothing in our neurophysiology that compels us to react violently.

It is scientifically incorrect to say that war is caused by 'instinct' or any single motivation. The emergence of modern warfare has been a journey from the primacy of emotional and motivational factors, sometimes called 'instincts', to the primacy of cognitive factors. Modern war involves institutional use of personal characteristics such as obedience, suggestibility, and idealism; social skills such as language; and rational considerations such as cost-calculation, planning, and information processing. The technology of modern war has exaggerated traits associated with violence both in the training of actual combatants and in the preparation of support for war in the general population. As a result of this exaggeration, such traits are often mistaken to be the causes rather than the consequences of the process.

We conclude that biology does not condemn humanity to war, and that humanity can be freed from the bondage of biological pessimism and empowered with confidence to undertake the transformative tasks needed in this International Year of Peace and in the years to come. Although these tasks are mainly institutional and collective, they also rest upon the consciousness of individual participants for whom pessimism and optimism are crucial factors. Just as 'wars begin in the minds of men', peace also begins in our minds. The same species who invented war is capable of inventing peace. The responsibility lies with each of us.

Seville, May 16, 1986

Correspondence concerning the Seville Statement on Violence should be addressed to David Adams, Psychology Department, Wesleyan University, Middletown, CT 06457, USA.

Correspondence concerning the American Psychological Association's endorsement of the Seville Statement on Violence should be addressed to Joan Buchanan, APA, Office of International Affairs, 1200 17th Street NW, Washington, DC 20036, USA.

APPENDIX 3

Responsible Wealth:
A Call to Action

Responsible Wealth is a group of people with wealth who feel called to speak out against growing economic injustice.

Who We Are

We are among our nation's wealthiest individuals and families. Among us are the founders and family members of some of the largest enterprises in America. We have earned or inherited substantial wealth in our lifetimes.

Why We Speak Out

We feel compelled to speak out, as part of the larger movement for economic justice, about the growing gap between the very rich and everyone else in American Society, and against the government policies and private corporate practices that are widening this gap.

Concentration of wealth

In 1976, the wealthiest 1% of the population owned 19% of all private wealth. The top 1% now owns almost 40% of all private wealth, which exceeds the wealth owned by the bottom 92% of the population combined. We believe this increasing concentration of wealth in the hands of the few deprives the many of good wages and the financial resources they need to live comfortably and securely.

Trickle up

In the 1980s, our nation enacted policies to relieve the tax burden on large corporations and the wealthy on the theory that they would use the additional money in ways that would benefit everyone. It is now generally recognized that this policy did not work. In fact, most income growth in the last 15 years has gone to the top income earners while most lower and middle income households lost ground.

As wealthy people, we personally benefited from the income tax cuts, the cuts in capital gains taxes and the policies that rewarded large asset-owners. But the majority of Americans did not benefit, and the nation is now saddled with an astronomical national debt and an annual budget deficit, due in part to the loss of income from the upper tax brackets. Between 1983 and 1989 alone, the combined assets of the richest 500 families in America increased from $2.5 trillion to $5 trillion; this increase was *three times* the increase in the national debt during that period.

Lack of fairness

We recognize that capital and assets play an essential role in building wealth and prosperity in our communities. However, we believe that there is an overemphasis on the rights and rewards of private capital. We are faced with a situation where those of us with large amounts of capital are able to pass on fortunes from generation to generation and multiply our wealth through passive investing, while around us, one in five children are born into poverty, and many in our economy have little hope of improving their financial situation.

We believe that in a healthy economy, workers should earn fair compensation, and all citizens should have the opportunity to earn, save and be economically secure. We believe that civil rights and economic rights are inseparable; we will never have one without the other.

Loss of community

We believe that the pursuit of the trappings of wealth has overrun the basic understanding of what American society is supposed to be about.

We believe that the extent of economic inequality and the scapegoating of welfare recipients and immigrants are dividing our nation and undermining our collective sense of community.

We believe that the ultimate effect of allowing the canyon between the wealthy and most Americans to continue to grow will be to destroy the basic unifying spirit of a democratic society, something that no amount of material goods can ever replace. By continuing to separate ourselves economically, we are contributing to a society in which people at one end of the economic spectrum are walled off in gated communities while many at the other end of the spectrum are behind bars.

For all of the above reasons, we feel called to speak out against the policies and practices which narrowly benefit only the few most affluent households and undermine the economic security of everyone else.

Our Call to Action

We call upon elected officials to squarely address the economic divide facing our nation and the rising economic insecurity facing more and more citizens. We ask that they investigate the dangerous consequences of further polarization of income, wages and wealth, and weigh each policy choice with a commitment to closing the divide.

The national debt now exceeds $5 trillion. In the effort to reduce the national debt, we urge that the largest burden of responsibility be placed on the wealthiest Americans, since we benefited the most from the regressive policy changes of the 1980s that fueled the debt.

We call upon elected officials to institute dramatic campaign finance reforms to buffer our democratic process from the undue influence of concentrated wealth, and return the control of our democracy to voters.

We call upon the media to tell the story of the costs and harm to our society of widening inequality, of the damage to our economy, our environment, our democracy, our sense of community, and our spiritual and civic lives.

We call upon other privileged US citizens and business leaders to join us in working for a stronger commonwealth, to strengthen the bonds of our nation and reduce inequality, and to remember that much of our wealth and privilege comes not from our own ingenuity and effort, but from the labor of others, and from the biased rules governing our economy.

We are people who value our privacy and do not wish to be subjected to great media attention. But we feel compelled to speak out because of concern for our fellow citizens and the future of our country. We believe that our best interests incorporate more than just our financial best interests, and that our country is capable of doing better.

APPENDIX 4

Networks and Organizations:
Peace, Justice, Ecology and Reproductive Rights

Only a few of the many different organizations and networks working for peace, justice, ecology and reproductive rights can be listed here. Given the book's focus on changes needed in the North, only organizations based in the North and especially in the USA are listed.*

The Boston Women's Health Book Collective

240 Elm Street, Somerville, MA 02144, USA
tel: (617) 625-2622
fax: (617) 625-0294
email: bwhbc@igc.apc.org

Campaign/Petition to Revoke the Status of the Holy See at the United Nations

c/o Catholics for Free Choice
1436 U Street, NW, #301, Washington, DC 20009-3997, USA
tel: (202) 986-6073
fax: (202) 332-7995
email: cssc@igc.apc.org

Campaign and Petition Calling for a Stop to Research on Antifertility Vaccines

c/o Women's Global Network for Reproductive Rights
NZ Voorburgwal 32, 1012 87 Amsterdam, The Netherlands
tel: 011-31-20-620-9672
fax: 011-31-20-622-2450

Children's Defense Fund

25 East Street, NW Washington, DC, 20001, USA
tel: (202) 628-8787
fax: (202) 662-3510
email: cdfinfo@childrensdefense.org

---

* The views expressed in this book do not necessarily represent the views of the organizations and networks cited in this appendix.

Committee on Women, Population and the Environment

c/o Population and Development Program, Hampshire College, Amherst, MA 01002, USA
tel: (413) 549-4600
fax: (413) 582-5620
email: bhartmann@hampshire.edu

Common Cause

1250 Connective Ave. NW, Washington, DC 20036, USA
tel: (202) 833-1200
fax: (202) 659-3716The Global Fund for Women
425 Sherman Ave, Suite 300, Palo Alto, CA 94306-1829, USA
tel: (415) 853-8383
fax: (415) 328-0384

The Global Fund for Women

2480 Sand Hill Road, Suite #100, Menlo Park, CA 94025, USA
tel: (415) 853-8305
fax: (415) 328-0384
email: gfw@igc.apc.org

Immigration and Environment Campaign

c/o Political Ecology Group
965 Mission, Suite 700, San Francisco, CA 94103, USA
tel: (415) 777-3488
fax: (415) 777-3443
email: peg@igc.org

Indigeneous Women's Network

Route 1 Box 308, Ponsford, MN 56575
tel: (218) 573-3049
fax: (218) 573-3060The Institute for Community Economics,
57 School Street, Springfield, MA 01105-1331, USA
tel: (413) 746-8660
fax: (413) 746 8862

Interfaith Center for Corporate Responsibility

475 Riverside Drive, Room 566, New York City, NY 10115, USA
tel: (212) 870-2295
fax: (212) 870-2023
email: info@iccr.org

Madre

121 West 27th Street, Room 301, New York, NY 10001, USA
tel: (212) 627-0444
fax: (212) 675-3704
email: madre@igc.apc.org

National Association of Community Development Loan Funds

PO Box 40085
Philadelphia PA 19106-5085, USA
tel: (215) 923-4754
email: nacdlf@aol.com

National Black Women's Health Project
1237 Ralph David Abernathy Blvd., SW, Atlanta, GA 30310, USA
tel: (404) 758-9590
fax: (404) 758-9661
email: nbwhpdc@aol.com

The National Network of Women's Funds
1821 University Ave., Suite 409 N., St Paul MN 55104, USA
tel: (612) 641-0742
fax: (612) 227-2213
email: wfn@wfnet.org

National War Tax Resistance Coordinating Committee
PO Box 774, Monroe, ME 04951-0774, USA
tel: (207) 525-7774
    (800) 269-7464
fax: (207) 525-3068
email: nwtrcc@igc.apc.org

New Road Map Foundation
PO Box 15981, Seattle, WA 98115, USA
tel: (206) 527-0437
fax: (206) 528-1120

Public Citizen
1600 20th Street NW, Washington, DC 20009, USA
tel: (202) 588-1000
fax: (202) 588-7799
email: publiccitizen@citizen.org

Rainforest Action Network
450 Sansome Street, Suite 700, San Francisco, CA 94111, USA
tel: (415) 398-4404
fax: (415) 398-2737
email: rainforest@ran.org

Responsible Wealth/Share the Wealth Project
c/o United for a Fair Economy
37 Temple Place, 3rd Floor, Boston, MA 02111, USA
tel: (617) 423-2148
fax: (617) 695-1295
email: www.stw.org/stw

Social Investment Forum
PO Box 57216, Washington, DC 20037, USA
tel: (202) 872-5319
fax: (202) 331-8166
email: ca@cais.com

Veterans Education Project
PO Box 416, Amherst, MA 01004, USA
tel: (413) 253-4947
fax: (413) 665-8260

The Women's Foundation
340 Pine Street, Suite 302, San Fransisco, CA 94104, USA
tel: (415) 837-1113
fax: (415) 837-1114

Women's International League for Peace and Freedom
1213 Race Street, Philadelphia, PA 19107, USA
tel: (215) 563-7110
fax: (215) 563-5527
email: wilpfnatl@igc.apc.org

Women Working Worldwide Centre for Employment Research
Room 3 St Augustine's Building, Lower Chatham Street,
Manchester, M15 6BY, UK
tel: 0161-247-1760
fax: 0161-247-6333

World Bank/IMF: 50 Years Is Enough Campaign
1025 Vermont Ave. NW, Suite 300, Washington, DC, 20005, USA
tel: (202) 783-7400
fax: (202) 783-0444
email: foedc@igc.org

Bibliography

Only works cited in the Notes are listed in this bibliography. It is classified alphabetically and/or chronologically under the following headings: (1) Books and Articles; (2) Works Published Without Author Name (listed under publication); (3) Governmental, Non-Governmental and Other Documents (listed under organization); (4) Newspapers; (5) Films.

Books and Articles

Adams, Patricia, "All in the Name of Aid", *Sierra*, January–February, 1987.

Afshar, Haleh, ed., *Women, Work and Ideology in the Third World*, New York: Methuen 1986.

Agarwal, Bina, "Gender, Environment and Poverty Interlinks in Rural India: Regional Variations and Temporal Shifts, 1971–1991", United Nations Research Institute for Social Development, Geneva, 1995.

———, "Rural Women, Poverty and Resources: Sustenance, Sustainability and Struggle for Change", *Economic and Political Weekly*, October 28, 1989.

———, ed., *Structures of Patriarchy: State, Community and Household in Modernising Asia*, London: Zed Books, 1988.

Agarwal, Anil, "Women Bear the Brunt of India's Eco-Catastrophes", *Habitat*, Australian Conservation Foundation, June 1988.

Ahir, D.C., *Asoka the Great*, Delhi: B.R. Publishing Corp., 1995.

Ahmad, Eqbal, "At Cold War's End: A World of Pain", *Boston Review*, Vol. 18, Nos 3–4, June–August 1993.

Ahmed, Leila, *Women and Gender in Islam: Historical Roots of a Modern Debate*, New Haven: Yale University Press, 1992.

Ainsworth, Diane, "Cultural Cross Fires", *Human Behaviour*, March 1979.

Akhter, Farida, "New Resources to Depopulate the Third World", *WGNRR Newsletter*, No. 42, January–March 1993.

Amdur, David, "Rape as Low-Intensity Warfare", *Peacework*, No. 258, December 1995.

Amin, Samir, "Moving Beyond Structural Adjustment", *Third World Resurgence*, No. 28, 1992.

Anderson, D., "Declining Tree Stocks in African Countries", *World Development*, No. 14, 1986.

Anderson, Elijah, "Sex Codes and Family Life among Poor Inner-City Youths", *The Annals of the American Academy of Political & Social Science*, Vol. 501, January 1989.

Angel, Brad, "Today's Conquistadors", *CrossRoads – Forward Motion*, Center for Democratic Alternatives, Jamaica Plain, MA, Vol. 11, No. 2, April 1992.

Anthony, Ian, "The Global Arms Trade", *Arms Control Today*, Vol. 21, No. 5, 1990.

Arditti, Rita, Renata Duelli Klein and Shelley Minden, eds, *Test Tube Women – What*

Future for Motherhood? London: Pandora Press, 1984.

Arnott, David, "On Cultural Rights", *Third World Resurgence*, No. 33, 1993.

Arrighi, Giovanni, "World Income Inequalities and the Future of Socialism", *New Left Review*, No. 189, September–October 1991.

Asad, Talal, *Anthropology and The Colonial Encounter*, Atlantic Highlands, NJ: Humanities Press, 1973.

Ashford, Lori S., "New Perspectives on Population: Lessons From Cairo", *Population Bulletin*, Vol. 50, No. 1, March 1995.

Atkinson, Jane Manning, "Review Essay: Anthropology", *Signs*, Vol. 8, No. 2, Winter 1982.

Atwood, Margaret, *The Handmaid's Tale*, Boston: Houghton Mifflin, 1986.

Aung San Suu Kyi, "Keynote Address", NGO Forum, United Nations Women's Conference, Beijing, August 1995.

———, *Freedom From Fear and Other Writings*, London: Penguin Books, 1991.

Aylmer, G.E., ed., *The Levellers in the English Revolution*, Ithaca, NY: Cornell University Press, 1975.

Baker, Will, "The Global Teenager", *Whole Earth Review*, No. 65, Winter 1989.

Balasubramanyan, Vimal, "Towards a Women's Perspective on Family Planning", *Economic and Political Weekly*, Vol. XXI, No. 2, January 11, 1986.

Balbus, Isaac D., *Marxism and Domination*, Princeton: Princeton University Press, 1992.

Ball, Nicole, *Briefing Book on Conventional Arms Transfers*, Washington, DC: Council for a Livable World Education Fund, August 1991.

Bandarage, Asoka, "Statement on Women, Population and the Environment", presented at the NGO Forum on the ICPD, Bureau for Refugee Programs, US Department of State, Washington, DC, April 29, 1993, reprinted in *Hunger Notes*, Issue on "Population: Broadening the Debate", Vol. 19, No. 4, Spring 1994.

———, "Packaging the Sri Lankan Conflict: Peace, Obstacles and Opportunities", *Samar*, No. 3, Summer 1994.

———, "The Gulf War and the Crisis Facing Humanity", unpublished ms, January 1991.

———, "In Search of A New World Order", *Women's Studies International Forum*, Vol. 14, No. 4, 1991.

———, "Women and Capitalist Development in Sri Lanka", *Bulletin of Concerned Asian Scholars*, Vol. 20, No. 2, 1988.

———, "Women of Color: Towards a Celebration of Power", *Women of Power*, No. 4, Fall 1986.

———, "From Universal Sexual Subordination to International Feminism: A Critical Assessment", unpublished paper, 1984, paper selected for presentation at session on Feminist Critiques of Gender Theory, American Sociological Association, Annual Meeting 1985.

———, "Women and Development: Liberalism, Marxism and Marxist-Feminism", *Development and Change*, Vol. 15, No. 4, October 1984.

———, *Colonialism in Sri Lanka: The Political Economy of the Kandyan Highlands, 1833–1886*, Berlin: Mouton, 1983.

———, "Toward International Feminism", *Brandeis Review*, Vol. 3, No. 3, Summer 1983.

Barber, Benjamin R., *Jihad vs. McWorld*, New York: Random House, 1995.

Barnet, Richard, "The End of Jobs", *Third World Resurgence*, No. 44, 1994.

——— and John Cavanagh, "The World the Transnationals Have Built", *Third World Resurgence*, No. 40, 1993.

Barry, Kathleen, *Female Sexual Slavery*, New York: New York University Press, 1984.

Basham, A.L., *The Wonder That Was India*, New York: Grove Press, 1954.

Basu, Alaka Malwade, *Culture, the Status of Women and Demographic Behaviour Illustrated with the Case of India*, Oxford: Clarendon Press, 1992.

———, "Birth Control by Assetless Workers in Kerala: The Possibility of a Poverty Induced Fertility Transition", *Development and Change*, Vol. 17, 1986.

Bateson, Gregory, *Steps to an Ecology of Mind: Collected Essays in Anthropology, Psychiatry, Evolution and Epistemology*, San Francisco: Chandler Publishing Co., 1972.

Bell, David and Michael Reich, eds, *Health, Nutrition and Economic Crises: Approaches to Policy in the Third World*, Dover, MA: Auburn House, 1988.

Bello, Walden, "Population Control: The Real Culprits and Victims", *Third World Resurgence*, No. 33, 1993.

———, David Kinley and Elaine Elinson, *Development Debacle: The World Bank in the Philippines*, San Francisco: Institute for Food and Development Policy, 1982.

Beneria, Lourdes and Shelley Feldman, eds, *Unequal Burden: Economic Crises, Persistent Poverty and Women's Work*, Boulder, CO: Westview Press, 1992.

Bennoune, Karima, "Algerian Women Confront Fundamentalism", *Monthly Review*, Vol. 46, September 1994.

Berelson, Bernard, "Beyond Family Planning", *Science*, Vol. 163, February 1969.

Berelson, Bernard and Jonathan Lieberson, "Government Efforts to Influence Fertility: The Ethical Issue", *Population and Development Review*, Vol. 5, 1979.

Bergman, Arlene Eisen, *Women of Vietnam*, San Francisco: People's Press, 1975.

Beulink, Anne-Marie, "Women and the Debt Crisis", *Development: Journal of the Society for International Development*, Vol. 1, 1989.

Bhat, P.N. Mari and S. Irudaya Rajan, "Demographic Transition in Kerala Revisited", *Economic and Political Weekly*, 1–8 September 1990.

Billenness, Simon, "Waylaid in Rangoon: Junta Uses Investments to Block Democracy", *Investing for a Better World*, Boston MA: Franklin Insight Inc., April 15, 1996.

Blauner, Robert, *Racial Oppression in America*, New York: Harper and Row, 1972.

Bluestone, Barry, *The Deindustrialization of America: Plant Closings, Community Abandonment, and the Dismantling of Basic Industry*, New York: Basic Books, 1982.

Bodhi, Bhikku, "Tolerance and Diversity", *Newsletter*, Buddhist Publication Society, Kandy, Sri Lanka, No. 24, Summer–Fall 1993.

Boff, Leonardo, *Ecology and Liberation: A New Paradigm*, New York: Orbis Books, 1995.

Bolles, A. Lynn, "Surviving Manley and Seaga: Case Studies of Women's Responses to Structural Adjustment Policies", *Review of Radical Political Economics*, Special Issue on Women in the International Economy, Vol. 23, Nos 3–4, Fall–Winter 1991.

Bookchin, Murray, *The Ecology of Freedom: The Emergence and Dissolution of Hierarchy*, Palo Alto, CA: Cheshire Books, 1982.

Borgstrom, Georg, *The Food and People Dilemma*, North Scituate, MA: Duxbury Press, 1973.

Borosage, Robert, "All Dollars No Sense", *Mother Jones*, September–October 1993.

Boserup, Ester, *Women's Role in Economic Development*, New York: St Martin's Press, 1970.

———, *The Conditions of Agricultural Growth: The Economics of Agrarian Change under Population Pressure*, Chicago: Aldine Publishing Co., 1965.

Bouvard, Marguerite Guzman, *Revolutionizing Motherhood: The Mothers of the Plaza de Mayo*, Wilmington, DE: Scholarly Resources Inc., 1994.

Boyce, James K., "The National Security Education Act of 1991: Issues and Analysis", *The Bulletin of Concerned Asian Scholars*, Vol. 24, No. 2, 1992.

Braudel, Fernand, *The Structures of Everyday Life: The Limits of the Possible*, Vol. 1, New York: Harper and Row, 1979.

Brezinski, Zbigniew, *Out of Control: Global Turmoil on the Eve of of the Twenty First Century*, New York: Charles Scribner and Sons, 1993.

Bridenthal, Renate and C. Koonz, eds, *Becoming Visible: Women in European History*, Boston: Houghton Mifflin, 1977.

Briggs, Vernon Jr, "Political Confrontation With Economic Reality: Mass Immigration in the Post-Industrial Age", *NPG Forum*, Washington DC, Negative Population Growth, February 1, 1990.

Brock-Utne, Birgit, *Educating for Peace: A Feminist Perspective*, New York: Pergamon Press, 1985.

Brown, Lester R., *Who Will Feed China? Wake-Up Call For a Small Planet*, New York: W.W. Norton and Co., 1995.

————, *Full House: Reassessing the Earth's Carrying Capacity*, New York: W.W. Norton, 1994.

————, "Facing Food Insecurity", *State of the World 1994*, Washington, DC: World Watch Institute, 1994.

————, "The New World Order", *State of the World 1991*, Washington, DC: World Watch Institute, 1991.

Bryceson, Deborah Fahey and Ulla Vurovela, "Outside the Domestic Labor Debate: Towards a Theory of Human Reproduction", *Review of Radical Political Economics*, Vol. 16, Nos 2–3, 1984.

Bumiller, Elisabeth, *May You be the Mother of a Hundred Sons: A Journey Among Women of India*, New York: Random House, 1990.

Buxamusa, Ramala, "The Price of Assistance: The Family Planning Programme in India", *Socialist Health Review*, March 1985.

Cahill, Kevin M., MD, ed., *Famine*, New York: Orbis Books, 1982.

Caldwell, John C., *Theory of Fertility Decline*, London and New York: Academic Press, 1982.

———— and Pat Caldwell, "Gender Implications for Survival in South Asia", Health Transition Working Paper, No. 7, The Australian National University, Canberra, 1990.

————, Indra Gajanayake, Bruce Caldwell and Pat Caldwell, "Is Marriage Delay a Multiphasic Response to Pressures for Fertility Decline?: The Case of Sri Lanka", *Journal of Marriage and Family*, Vol. 51, No. 2, May 1989.

Calhoun, Martin, "The Clinton Administration Plan for Future Military Spending", Center for Defense Information, Washington, DC, March 27, 1996.

Caplan, Patricia, *Class and Gender in India: Women and their Organizations in a South Indian City*, New York: Methuen, 1986.

Caulfield, Mina Davis, "Imperialism, the Family and Cultures of Resistance", *Socialist Revolution*, Issue 20, Vol. 4, No. 2, October 1974.

Cereseto, Shirley, "World Starvation: Causes and Solutions", *The Insurgent Sociologist*, Vol. 7, No. 2, Summer 1977.

Chase, Allan, "Health News Commentary", *Medical News*, January 8, 1979.

————, *The Legacy of Malthus: The Social Costs of the New Scientific Racism*, New York: Alfred A. Knopf, 1977.

Chaterjee, Pratap, "World Bank Failures Soar to 37.5% of Completed Projects in 1991", *Third World Economics*, No. 55, Third World Network, Penang, Malaysia, December 16–31, 1992.

Chomsky, Noam, "The Enemy is the Third World Itself", *Central American Reporter*, July–August 1990.

———— and Edward S. Herman, *Manufacturing Consent: The Political Economy of the Mass Media*, New York: Pantheon, 1988.

————, *The Washingon Connection and Third World Fascism*, Boston: South End Press, 1979.

Chossudovsky, Michael, "The World Bank Derogates Women's Rights", *Third World Resurgence*, Nos 61–62, 1995.

————, "The 'Third Worldisation' of Russia Under IMF Rule", *Third World Economics*, June 16–30, 1993.

————, "Feeding on Poverty: India Under the IMF Rule", *Third World Resurgence*, No. 28, 1992.

Clairmont, Frederic, "The G-7 and the Spectre of Job Destruction", *Third World Resurgence*, No. 44, 1994.

————, "Bonn: The Rising Tide of Nazidom", *Third World Resurgence*, No. 31, March 1993.

————, "The Dynamics of Beverage Imperialism", *Third World Resurgence*, No. 40, 1993.

———— and John Cavanagh, "The Rise of the TNC", Third World Resurgence, No. 40, 1993.

Clark, Mary E., "The Backward Ones", *TRANET, A Bi-Monthly Digest for the A and T (Alternative and Transformational) Movements*, No. 85, November 1993.

Cleland, John and W. Parker Mauldin, "The Promotion of Family Planning by Financial Payments: The Case of Bangladesh", Working Paper No. 13., World Bank, Washington, DC, 1990.

Cochran, Joe W., Donna Langston and Carolyn Woodward, eds, *Changing Our Power: An Introduction to Women's Studies*, 2nd edn, Dubuque, IA: Kendal/Hunt Publishing Co., 1991.

Cohn, Carol, "Sex and Death in the Rational World of Defense Intellectuals", *Signs*, Vol. 12, No. 4, Summer 1987.

Cole, Luke, "The Anti-Immigration Environmental Alliance: Divide and Conquer at the Border", *Race, Poverty and the Environment*, Earth Island Institute, San Francisco, Spring 1992.

Collins, Cate, "Havasupais Battle Against Uranium Mine to Preserve Their Land", *Navajo-Hopi Observer*, August 2, 1989.

Commoner, Barry, *Making Peace With the Planet*, New York: New Press, 1992.

———, "Rapid Population Growth and Environmental Stress", *International Journal of Health Services*, Vol. 21, No. 2, 1991.

Cooney, Robert and Helen Michalowski, *The Power of the People: Active Nonviolence in the United States*, Philadelphia: New Society Publishers, 1987.

Cooper, Mark, "Rain Forest Crude", *Mother Jones*, March-April 1992.

Cordell, Dennis D. and Joel W. Gregory, eds, *African Population and Capitalism: Historical Perspectives*, Boulder, CO: Westview Press, 1987.

Cornia, Giovanni Andrea, Richard Jolly and Frances Stewart, eds, *Adjustment with a Human Face*, Oxford: Clarendon Press and UNICEF, 1987.

Corrêa, Sonia, *Population and Reproductive Rights: Feminist Perspectives from the South*, London: Zed Books, 1994.

———, "The Rights of Reproduction in the Context of the Demographic Transition in Brazil", unpublished paper, 1992.

Croll, Elisabeth J., "Production versus Reproduction: A Threat to China's Development Strategy", *World Development*, Vol. 11, No. 6, 1983.

Crossette, Barbara, *India: Facing the Twenty-First Century*, Bloomington: Indiana University Press, 1993.

Cruz, Maria Concepción, Carrie A. Meyer, Robert Repetto and Richard Woodward, *Population Growth, Poverty and Environmental Stress: Frontier Migration in the Philippines and Costa Rica*, Washington, DC: World Resources Institute, 1992.

Cruz, Wilfrido and Roberto Repetto, *The Environmental Effects of Stabilization and Structural Adjustment Programs: The Philippines Case*, Washington, DC: World Resources Institute, 1992.

Dahlberg, Frances, ed., *Woman the Gatherer*, New Haven: Yale University Press, 1981.

Dalla Costa, Mariarosa and Giovanna F. Dalla Costa, eds, *Paying the Price: Women and Politics of International Economic Strategy*, London: Zed Books, 1995.

Dalsimer, Marilyn and Laurie Nisonoff, "The Implications of the New Agricultural and One-Child Family Policies for Rural Chinese Women", *Feminist Studies*, Vol. 13., No. 3, Fall 1987.

Daly, Herman E., "Farewell Lecture to World Bank", *Focus: Carrying Capacity Selections*, Vol. 4, No. 2, 1994.

———, "Achieving Development Without Growth", *Surviving Together*, Winter 1993.

——— and John B. Cobb Jr, *For the Common Good: Redirecting Economy Toward the Environment and a Sustainable Future*, Boston: Beacon Press, 1994.

Danaher, Kevin, ed., *50 years Is Enough: The Case Against the World Bank and the International Monetary Fund*, Boston: South End Press, 1994.

Darabi, Katherine F., Joy Dryfoos and Dana Schwartz, "The Fertility Related Attitudes and Behavior of Hispanic Adolescents in the U.S.", Center for Population and Family Health, Working Paper No. 9, July 1985, Columbia University, New York.

Dash, Leon, *When Children Want Children*, New York: Penguin Books, 1989.

Davidson, Basil, *The African Genius: An Introduction to African Social and Cultural History*, Boston:

Little, Brown and Co., 1969.

Davies, Susan E., ed., *Women Under Attack: Victories, Backlash, and the Fight for Reproductive Freedom*, Committee for Abortion Rights and Against Sterilization Abuse (CARASA), Boston: South End Press, 1988.

Davis, Angela Y., *Women, Race and Class*, New York: Random House, 1981.

Davis, Kingsley, Mikhail S. Bernstam and Rita Ricardo-Campbell, eds, *Below Replacement Fertility in Industrial Societies: Causes Consequences, Policies*, Cambridge: Cambridge University Press, 1987.

Davis, Kingsley, "Wives and Work: The Sex Role Revolution and its Consequences", *Population and Development Review*, Vol. 10, No. 3, September 1984.

Deen, Thalif, "World Bank Cash Exists for Population Projects", *Terra Viva* (Inter Press Service), ICPD Issue, September 7, 1994.

———, "Children As Targets and Mine Sweeps: The 1990s", *Terra Viva*, IPS (Inter Press Service), June 19, 1993.

———, "Security Council Accused of Double Standards", *Third World Resurgence*, No. 31, March 1993.

Degener, Theresia, "Sterile Without Consent", *Connexions*, No. 25, Winter 1987.

Deininger, Klaus and Lyn Squire, "A New Data Set Measuring Inequality", *The World Bank Economic Review*, Vol. 10, No. 3, 1996.

Del Vasto, Lanza, *Gandhi to Vinoba: The New Pilgrimage*, New York: Schocken Books, 1974.

Demeney, Paul, "Social Science and Population Policy", *Population and Development Review*, Vol. 14, No. 3, September 1988.

Demerath, Nicholas J., *Birth Control and Foreign Policy: The Alternatives to Family Planning*, New York: Harper and Row, 1976.

Desfosses, Helen and Jacques Levesque, eds, *Socialism in the Third World*, New York: Praeger Publishers, 1975.

Deval, Bill, Carrying Capacity Network, "Overpopulation and Deep Ecology", *Clearing House Bulletin*, Washington, DC, Vol. 3, No. 1, January–February 1993,

Dharamaraj, Daisy, MD, "Critical Review of Norplant", *Prepare*, India Rural Reconstruction and Disaster Response Service, 1993.

Diamond, Irene and Gloria Orenstein, eds, *Reweaving the World: The Emergence of Eco-feminism*, San Francisco: Sierra Club Books, 1990.

Diamond, Sara, *Roads to Dominion: Right-Wing Movements and Political Power in the United States*, New York: Guilford Press, 1995.

Diaz, Pablo, "Toxic Trade Remains Legal", *Third World Resurgence*, Nos 29–30, 1993.

DiConsiglio, John M., "Risks and Rewards: Family Planners Weight Quinacrine", *Family Planning World*, January–February 1994.

Divale, William Julio and Marvin Harris, "Population, Warfare and the Male Supremacist Complex", *American Anthropologist*, Vol. 78, No. 3, 1976.

Do Trong Hieu, Tran Thi Tan, Do Ngoc Tan, Pham Thi Nguyet, Pham Than and Dao Quang Vinh, "31,781 Cases of Non-Surgical Female Sterilisation with Quinacrine Pellets in Vietnam", *The Lancet*, Vol. 342, July 24, 1993.

Dogra, Bharat, "Tehri Dam Struggle at a Crucial Stage", 1995, paper available from *Southlinks*, United Nations Volunteers, Palais des Nations, CH-1211 Geneva, Switzerland.

Donaldson, Peter J., *Nature Against Us: The United States and the World Population Crisis, 1965–1980*, Chapel Hill: University of North Carolina Press, 1990.

——— and Amy Ong Tsui, "The International Family Planning Movement", *Population Bulletin*, Vol. 45, No. 3, November 1990, Washington, DC: Population Reference Bureau.

Drummond, Hugh, "And They Make House Calls, *Mother Jones*, May 1987.

Durning, Alan, *How Much is Enough? The Consumer Society and the Future of the Earth*, New York: W.W. Norton and Co., 1992.

———, "Asking How Much is Enough", *State of the World Report*, Washington, DC: World Watch Institute, 1991.

——, "Ending Poverty", *State of the World 1990*, Washington, DC: World Watch Institute, 1990.

Dworkin, Andrea, *Right Wing Women*, New York: Perigee Books, 1983.

Dyson, Tim, "Population Growth and Food Production: Recent Global and Regional Trends", *Population and Development Review*, Vol. 20, No. 2, June 1994.

Easterbrook, Gregg, *A Moment on the Earth: The Coming Age of Environmental Optimism*, New York: Viking, 1995.

Eberstadt, Nicholas, "Population Change and National Security", *Foreign Affairs*, Vol. 70, No. 3, Summer 1991.

Ehrenreich, Barbara and Deidre English, *For Her Own Good: 150 Years of the Experts' Advice to Women*, New York: Anchor Books, 1979.

Ehrlich, Paul R., *The Population Bomb*, New York: Ballantine Books, 1968.

—— and Anne H. Ehrlich, *The Population Explosion*, New York: Simon and Schuster, 1990.

——, Anne H. Ehrlich and Gretchen C. Daly, *The Stork and the Plow: The Equity Answer to the Human Dilemma*, New York: G.P. Putnam's Sons, 1995.

Eisler, Riane, *Chalice and the Blade: Our History, Our Future*, San Francisco: Harper and Row, 1987.

Ekins, Paul, *A New World Order: Grassroots Movements for Global Change*, London: Routledge, 1992.

Elgin, Duane, *Voluntary Simplicity: Toward a Way of Life That is Outwardly Simple, Inwardly Rich*, New York: William Morrow and Co. Inc., 1981.

Ellul, Jacques, *The Technological System*, trans. Joachim Neugroschel, New York: Continuum, 1980.

Elson, Diane, "How Is Structural Adjustment Affecting Women?", *Development*, Vol. 1, 1989.

Engels, Frederick, *The Origin of the Family, Private Property and the State*, London: Lawrence and Wishart, 1973.

Enloe, Cynthia, *Bananas, Beaches and Bases: Making Feminist Sense of International Politics*, Berkeley: University of California Press, 1990.

Erickson, Brad, *Call to Action: Handbook for Ecology, Peace and Justice*, San Francisco: Sierra Club Books, 1990.

Esteva, Gustavo, "Regenerating People's Space", *Alternatives*, Vol. 12, No. 198, 1987.

—— and Madhu Suri Prakash, "Editorial: From Global to Local Thinking", *The Ecologist*, Vol. 24, No. 5, September–October 1994.

Everett, Jana and Mira Savara, "Bank Loans to the Poor in Bombay: Do Women Benefit?", *Signs*, Vol. 10, No. 2, 1984.

Faber, Daniel, *Environment Under Fire: Imperialism and the Ecological Crisis in Central America*, New York: Monthly Review Press, 1993.

Falk, Richard, "Hard Choices and Tragic Dilemmas", *The Nation*, December 20, 1993.

Fanon, Frantz, *Black Skin, White Masks*, trans. Charles Markmann, New York: Grove Press, 1967.

Fargues, Philippe, "From Demographic Explosion to Social Rupture", *Middle East Report*, Issue on Gender, Population, Environment, Issue 190, Vol. 24, No. 5, March–April 1993.

Firestone, Shulamith, *The Dialectic of Sex: The Case for Feminist Revolution*, New York; Bantam Books, 1970.

Flavin, Christopher, "Slowing Global Warming", *State of the World 1990*, Washington, DC: World Watch Institute, 1990.

Folbre, Nancy, "Population Growth and Capitalist Development in Zongolica, Veracruz", *Latin American Perspectives*, Issue No. 15, Special Issue on Population and Imperialism, Vol. IV, No. 4, Fall 1977.

Forfeit, Karen F., Marcos Paulo P. de Castro and Elaine F. Duarte Franco, "The Impact of Mass Media Advertising on a Voluntary Sterilization Program in Brazil", *Studies in Family Planning*, Vol. 20, No. 2, March–April 1989.

Foster, Gregory D., "Global Demographic Trends to the Year 2010: Implications for U.S. Security", *The Washington Quarterly*, Spring 1989.

Foster, John Bellamy, "Global Ecology and the Common Good", *Monthly Review*, Vol. 46, February 1995.

———, *The Vulnerable Planet: A Short Economic History of the Environment*, New York: Monthly Review Press, 1994.

Franklin, John Hope, *From Slavery to Freedom: A History of Negro Americans*, 3rd edn, New York: Alfred A. Knopf, 1967.

Frazier, Franklin E., *Race and Culture Contacts in the Modern World*, Boston: Beacon Press, 1957.

Freire, Paulo Myre, *Pedagogy of the Oppressed*, trans. Berman Ramos, New York: Seabury Press, 1970.

Fried, Marlene Gerber, ed., *From Abortion to Reproductive Freedom: Transforming a Movement*, Boston: South End Press, 1990.

Fuji, Nichidatsu, "The Source of Human Annhilation", *Buddhism for World Peace: Words of Nichidatsu Fuji*, trans. Yumiko Miyazaki, Japan-Bharat Savodaya Mitrata Sangha, Tokyo, 1980.

Funiciello, Thérèse, "The Poverty Industry: Do Government and Charities Create the Poor?", *Ms. Magazine*, Vol. 1, No. 3, November–December 1990.

Gallagher, Sally K., "Economic Disarticulation and Fertility in the Periphery", Paper presented at American Sociological Association Meetings, Atlanta, GA, 1988.

Gallin, Rita S. and Anne Ferguson, eds, *Women and International Development Annual*, Vol. 2, Boulder, CO: Westview Press, 1991.

Gandł.i, Mahatma, *An Autobiography: The Story of My Experiments With Truth*, Boston: Beacon Press, 1957.

Gearhart, Sally Miller, "Notes from a Recovering Activist", *Sojourner*, September 1995.

Geertz, Clifford, *Agricultural Involution*, Berkeley: University of California Press, 1963.

George, Susan, "Debt as Warfare: Overview of the Debt Crisis", *Third World Resurgence*, No. 28, 1992.

———, *How the Other Half Dies? The Real Reasons for World Hunger*, Montclair, NJ: Allanheld Osmun and Co., 1977.

Germaine, Adrienne and Rachel Kyte, *The Cairo Consensus: The Right Agenda for the Right Time*, New York: International Women's Health Coalition, 1995.

Gerster, Richard, "Debt and the Environment – The Ecological Implications of the Debt Crisis in Developing Countries", *Third World Economics*, Penang, Malaysia, February 1–15, 1993.

Ghosh, Pradip K., ed., *Population, Environment and Resources, and Third World Development*, Westport, CT: Greenwood Press, 1984.

Gilman, Robert, "Sustainability: The State of the Movement", *In Context*, No. 25, Late Spring 1990.

Gingrich, Newt, *To Renew America*, New York: HarperCollins, 1993.

Gimbutas, Marija, *The Language of the Goddess*, San Francisco: Harper and Row, 1989.

Gimenez, Martha E., "Population and Capitalism", *Latin American Perspectives*, Issue 15, Vol. IV, No. 4, Fall 1977.

Gioseffi, Daniela, ed., *Women on War: Essential Voices for the Nuclear Age*, New York: Simon and Schuster, 1988.

Godelier, Maurice, "The Origins of Male Domination", *New Left Review*, No. 127, May–June 1981.

Goldsmith, Edward, *The Way: An Ecological World-View*, Boston: Shambala, 1993.

Goldstein, Joshua, "PACs in Profile: Spending Patterns in the 1994 Election", Washington, DC: Center for Responsive Politics, 1995.

Gordon, David C., *Women in Algeria: An Essay on Change*, Cambridge, MA: Harvard University Press, 1968.

Gordon, Linda, *Woman's Body, Woman's Right: A Social History of Birth Control in America*, New York: Grossman Publishers, 1976.

Gore, Al, *Earth in Balance: Ecology and the Human Spirit*, Boston: Houghton Mifflin, 1992.

Gould, Stephen Jay, "The Smoking Gun of Eugenics", *Natural History*, December 1991.

Greenberg, Stanley, *Race and State in Capitalist Development*, New Haven: Yale University Press, 1980.

Greer, Germaine, *Sex and Destiny: The Politics of Human Fertility*, New York: Harper and Row, 1984.

Gross, Bertram, *Friendly Fascism: The New Face of Power in America*, Boston: South End Press, 1980.

Gwatkin, Davidson, "Political Will and Family Planning: The Implications of India's Emergency Experience", *Population and Development Review*, Vol. 5, No. 1, 1979.

Gyatso, Tenzin, The Fourteenth Dalai Lama, *A Human Approach to World Peace*, London: Wisdom Publications, 1984.

Hancock, Graham, *Lords of Poverty*, London: Mandarin, 1992.

Handwerker, W. Penn, ed., *Births and Power: Social Change and the Politics of Reproduction*, Boulder, CO: Westview Press, 1990.

Hanh, Thich Nhat, *The Sun My Heart*, Berkeley: Parallax Press, 1988.

Hanlon, Gail, "Supporting Our Front-Line Struggles: An Interview with Winona LaDuke about *Indigenous Woman Magazine*", *Woman of Power*, No. 21, Fall 1991.

————, "Living in a Liminal Time: An Interview with Jean Shinoda Bolen", *Woman of Power*, No. 21, Fall 1991.

Hanna, Nick and Sue Wells, "Tourism Time Bomb", *New Internationalist*, August 1992, p. 9.

Hansch, Steven, "An Explosion of Complex and Humanitarian Emergencies", *Hunger Notes*, Vol. 21, No. 3, Winter 1996.

Hardin, Garett, *Living Within Limits: Ecology, Economics and the Population Taboo*, New York: Oxford University Press, 1993.

————, "The Tragedy of the Commons", *Sanctuary*, Vol. 27, No. 5, February–March 1988.

————, "Living on a Lifeboat", *Bioscience*, Vol. 24, No. 10, October 1974.

Hardon, A., "An Analysis of Research on New Contraceptive Vaccines", *Women and Pharmaceuticals Bulletin*, Health Action International, November 1990.

———— and Lenny Achthoven, "Norplant: A Critical Review", *Women and Pharmaceuticals Bulletin*, Health Action International, November 1990.

Harris, Donald J., "Capitalist Exploitation and Black Labor: Some Conceptual Issues", *Review of Black Political Economy*, Vol. 8, Winter 1978.

Harris, Marvin and Eric B. Ross, *Death, Sex and Fertility: Population Regulation in Preindustrial and Developing Societies*, New York: Columbia University Press, 1987.

Hart, William, *Vispassana Meditation as Taught by S.N. Goenka*, San Francisco: Harper and Row, 1987.

Hartmann, Betsy, "Dangerous Intersections", *Political Environments*, No. 2, Summer 1995.

————, *Reproductive Rights and Wrongs: The Global Politics of Population Control*, Boston: South End Press, 1995.

————, "Bankers, Babies, and Bangladesh", *The Progressive*, September 1990.

————, "International Update", *The Fight for Reproductive Freedom, Newsletter for Student Activists*, Civil Liberties and Public Policy Program, Hampshire College, Vol. V, No. 1, Fall 1990.

———— and Hilary Standing, *The Poverty of Population Control: Family Planning and Health Policy in Bangladesh*, London: Bangladesh International Action Group, 1989.

———— and Hilary Standing, *Food, Saris and Sterilization*, London: Bangladesh International Action Group, 1985.

Harvey, David, "Population, Resources, and the Ideology of Science", *Economic Geography*, Vol. 50, July 1974.

Hathi, Daksha, "Speaking Out on Norplant", *Political Environments*, No. 4, Summer–Fall 1996.

Hawken, Paul, *The Ecology of Commerce: A Declaration of Sustainability*, New York: Harper

Collins, 1993.

Heatley, Rachel, *Poverty and Power: The Case for a Political Approach to Development and its Implications for Action in the West*, London: Zed Press, 1979.

Hecht, S.B., "Environment, Development and Politics: Capital Accumulation and the Livestock Sector in Eastern Amazonia", *World Development*, No. 13, 1985.

Henderson, Hazel, *Paradigms in Progress: Life Beyond Economics*, San Francisco: Berrett-Koehler Publishers, 1995.

Herdt, Gilbert and Shirley Lindenbaum, eds, *The Time of AIDS: Social Analysis, Theory and Method*, Newbury Park, CA: Sage Publications, 1992.

Herrnstein, Richard and Charles Murray, *The Bell Curve: Intelligence and Class Structure in American Life*, New York: Free Press, 1994.

Herz, Barbara and Anthony R. Measham, "The Safe Motherhood Initiative", World Bank Discussion Paper No. 9, Washington, DC, 1990

Heyzer, Noeleen, *Working Women in South-East Asia: Development, Subordination and Emancipation*, London: Open University Press, 1986.

Hildyard, Nicholas, "Maastricht: The Protectionism of Free Trade?", *Ecologist*, Vol. 23, No. 2, March–April 1993.

Hodge, Merle, "Women and Structural Adjustment", in "Women and the Global Economy", *Global Exchange*, San Francisco, 1989.

Hoem, Jan M., "Social Policy and Recent Fertility Change in Sweden", *Population and Development Review*, Vol. 16, No. 4, December 1990.

Hoffman, Martin L. and Lois Wladis Hoffman, eds, *Review of Child Development Research*, Vol. 1, New York: Russell Sage Foundation, 1964.

Hofstadter, Richard, *Social Darwinism in American Thought*, Boston: Beacon Press, 1955.

Holmes, Helen Bequaert, ed., *Issues in Reproductive Technology: An Anthology*, New York and London: Garland Publishing Inc., 1992.

Homer-Dixon, Thomas F., Jeffrey H. Boutwell and George W. Rathjens, "Environmental Change and Violent Conflict", *Scientific American*, February 1993.

Hong Evelyn, "Women as Consumers and Producers in the World Market", *Third World Resurgence*, Nos 61–62, 1995.

———, "ICPD Under Fire for Sidelining Development Issues", *Third World Resurgence*, No. 50, 1994.

Hoskins, Eric, "Iraqi Children Suffer Radiation", *Third World Resurgence*, No. 31, March 1993.

Huang, Yukon and Peter Nicholas, "The Social Costs of Adjustment", *Adjustment with Growth: The Fund, The Bank, and Country Experiences*, IMF and World Bank, n.d.

Hubbard, Ruth, *Profitable Promises: Essays on Women, Science and Health*, Monroe, ME: Common Courage Press, 1995.

Hull, Terrence, "Recent Trends in Sex Ratios at Birth in China", *Population and Development Review*, Vol. 16, No. 1, March 1990.

Huntington, Samuel P., "The Clash of Civilizations", *Foreign Affairs*, Vol. 72, No. 3, Summer 1993.

Husson, Anna, "Integrated Development: Slum Resettlement and Sterilization Abuse in Visakhapatnam, India", *WGNRR Newsletter*, No. 34, January–March 1991.

Huston, Perdita, *Message from the Village*, New York: Epoch B. Foundation, 1978.

Huxley, Aldous, *Brave New World*, New York: Harper and Row, 1946.

Hynes, H. Patricia, *Taking Population Out of the Equation*, North Amherst, MA: Institute on Women and Technology, 1993.

———, "The Pocketbook and the Pill: Reflections on Green Consumerism and Population Control", *Issues in Reproductive and Genetic Engineering*, Vol. 4, No. 1, 1991.

Ingram, Paul, *Tibet: The Facts*, Dharamsala, India: Tibetan Young Women's Buddhist Association, 1990.

Isaacs, Stephen L., "Incentives, Population Policy and Reproductive Rights: Ethical Issues", *Studies in Family Planning*, Vol. 26, No. 6, November–December 1995.

———, "Incentives for Family Planning – Ethical Considerations", presentation at Expert

Round Table on Population Policy, UNFPA, New York, 1986.

Isbister, John, *Promises Not Kept: The Betrayal of Social Change in the Third World*, Hartford, CT: Kumarian Press, 1991.

Itzkoff, Seymour, 1994, *The Decline of Intelligence in America: A Strategy for National Renewal*, Westport, Connecticut, Praeger.

Jacobson Jodi L., Closing the Gender Gap in Development, *State of the World 1993*, New York: W.W. Norton and Co, 1993.

———, "Gender Bias: Roadblock to Sustainable Development", *World Watch Paper*, No. 110, September 1992.

———, "Women's Reproductive Health: The Silent Emergency", *World Watch Paper*, No. 102, June 1991.

———, "The Global Politics of Abortion", *World Watch Paper*, No. 97, July 1990.

———, "Anti-Abortion Policy Leads to ... More Abortions", *World Watch Paper*, May–June 1988.

Jaising, Indira and C. Sathyamala, "Bhopal: A Test Case of Toxic Industries for UNCED", Briefing Paper No. 7 for UNCED, *Third World Network*, Penang, Malaysia, n.d.

Jeffery, Patricia, Roger Jeffery and Andrew Lyon, *Don't Marry Me to a Plowman: Women's Everyday Lives in Rural North India*, Boulder, CO: Westview Press, 1996.

———, *Labour Pains Labour Power: Women and Childbearing in India*, London: Zed Books, 1989.

Jiggins, Janice, *Changing the Boundaries: Women-Centered Perspectives on Population and the Environment*, Washington, DC: Island Press, 1994

———, "Don't Waste Energy? Fear of the Future", *Conscience*, Autumn 1993.

John Paul II, *Crossing the Threshold of Hope*, New York: Alfred A. Knopf, 1994.

Johnson, Kay Ann, "Who is to Blame for High Death Rates in Orphanages", unpublished ms, Hampshire College, Amherst, MA, 1996.

Johnson, Lucy, "Striking a Balance", *Terra Viva*, (Inter Press Service), June 15, 1993.

Johnson, Stanley, "China, the United States and the United Nations", *Populi*, Vol. 15, No. 1, 1988.

Johnston, R.J. and P.J. Taylor, eds, *A World Crisis: Geographical Perspectives*, Oxford: Basil Blackwell, 1986.

Jones, Ken, *The Social Face of Buddhism: An Approach to Political and Social Activism*, London: Wisdom Publications, 1989.

Jones, Stephany Griffith, "Debt Reduction with a Human Face: The IDB and UNICEF Initiative", *Development: Journal of the Society for International Development*, Vol. 1, 1989.

Kamal, Sajed, "The Solar Revolution: Energy for A Sustainable Earth", unpublished ms, International Consortium for Energy Development, Boston, n.d.

Kane, Joe, *Savages*, New York: Alfred A. Knopf, 1995.

Kaplan, Robert D., "The Coming Anarchy", *Atlantic Monthly*, February 1994.

Karkal, Malini, "Patriarchal Demography: Tracing India's History", *Political Environments*, No. 4, Summer–Fall 1996.

———, "Why the Cairo Document is Flawed", *Third World Resurgence*, No. 50, 1994.

———, "Compulsion: Political Will and Family Planning", collection of documents, 4 Dhake Colony, Andheri (W) Bombay 58, India, n.d.

Karliner, Joshua, "Bhopal: Setting the Record Straight", *Third World Resurgence*, Nos 53–54, 1995.

Karunatileke, H.N.S., *This Confused Society*, Buddhist Information Centre Colombo, Sri Lanka, 1976.

Kaza, Stephanie, "Wise Use vs. The Green Menace", *Turning Wheel*, Journal of Buddhist Peace Fellowship, San Francisco, Fall 1995.

Kendall, Henry W. and David Pimentel, "Constraints on the Expansion of the Global Food Supply", *Ambio: A Journal of the Human Environment*, Royal Swedish Academy of the Sciences, 1994.

Kennedy, Paul, *Preparing for the Twenty-First Century*, New York: Random House, 1993.

Keyfitz, Nathan, "Population Theory", *International Encyclopaedia of Population*, Vol. 2, 1982.

Keysers, Loes, "Reflections on Reproductive and Sexual Rights During the ICPD", *WGNRR Newsletter*, No. 47, July–September 1994.

Khor, Martin, "Worldwide Unemployment Will Reach Crisis Proportions Says Social Expert", *Third World Resurgence*, No. 44, 1994.

———, "500,000 Indian Farmers Rally Against GATT and Patenting of Seeds", *Third World Resurgence*, No. 39, 1993.

———, "A Year After Rio the CSD Inches Forward...", *Third World Resurgence*, No. 36, 1993.

Kidron, Michael and Dan Smith, *The New State of War and Peace: An International Atlas*, New York: Simon and Schuster, 1990.

Kimbrell, Andrew, *The Human Body Shop: The Engineering and Marketing of Life*, San Francisco: Harper, 1993.

Kinder, Paul D., Steven D. Lyndenberg and Amy L. Domini, *The Social Investment Almanac: A Comprehensive Guide to Socially Responsible Investing*, New York: Henry Holt and Co., 1992.

King, Maurice, "Health is a Sustainable State", *The Lancet*, Vol. 336, September 15, 1990.

King, Timothy (coordinating author), *Population Policies and Economic Development, A World Bank Staff Report*, Baltimore: Johns Hopkins University Press, 1974.

Kishwar, Madhu, "When Daughters Are Unwanted: Sex-Determination Tests in India", *Manushi: A Journal About Women and Society*, New Delhi, India, No. 86, January–February 1995.

———, "Warning from the Bombay Riots", *Committee on South Asian Women Bulletin*, Vol. 8, Nos 3–4, 1993.

Klare, Michael T., "The Next Great Arms Race", *Foreign Affairs*, Summer 1993.

———, "It's Business As Usual", *The Nation*, February 3, 1992.

——— and Cynthia Aronson, *Supplying Repression*, Washington, DC: Institute for Policy Studies, 1981.

———, ed., *Peace and World Security Studies: A Curriculum Guide*, 6th edn, Boulder and London: Lynne Rienner Publishers, 1994.

Koblinsky, Marge, Judith Timyan and Jill Gay, eds, *The Health of Women: A Global Perspective*, Boulder, CO: Westview Press, 1993.

Kolko, Joyce, *Restructuring the World Economy*, New York: Pantheon Books, 1988.

Koning, Hans, *Columbus: His Enterprise*, New York: Monthly Review Press, 1976.

Kornfield, Jack, *A Path With Heart: A Guide Through the Perils and Promises of Spiritual Life*, New York: Bantam Books, 1993.

Kothari, Smitu and Rajni Bakshi, "On Dams and Protests", Editorial, *Lokayan Bulletin*, Vol. 7, No. 1, 1989.

Krishnan, T.N., "Population, Poverty and Employment in India", *Economic and Political Weekly*, November 14, 1992.

Kuhn, Thomas S., *The Sturcture of Scientific Revolutions*, Chicago: University of Chicago Press, 1970.

Kummer, David C., *Deforestation in Post-War Philippines*, Chicago: University of Chicago Press, 1992.

Kuznik, Frank, "Wasted", *American Politics*, March 1988.

LaBlanc, T., P. Guillory, Esq., and J. Redhouse, "First Executive Report of the Indigenous Uranium Forum, IUF, First Global Radiation Victims Conference/Indigenous Uranium Forum", September and November 1987.

LaNoue, George R., "The Demographic Premises of Affirmative Action", *Population and Environment: A Journal of Interdisciplinary Studies*, Vol. 14, No. 5, May 1993.

Lappe, Frances Moore and Joseph Collins, *World Hunger: Ten Myths*, San Francisco: Institute for Food and Development Policy, 1979.

Lappe, Frances Moore and David Kinley, *Aid As Obstacle: Twenty Questions About Our Foreign Aid and the Hungry*, San Francisco: Institute for Food and Development Policy, 1980.

Lappe, Frances Moore and Rachel Schurman, *The Missing Piece in the Population Puzzle*, Food First Development Report No. 4, San Francisco: Institute for Food and Development Policy, September 1988.

Leach, Penelope, *Children First: What Society Must Do – and Is Not Doing for Children Today*, New York: Vintage Books, 1994.

Leacock, Eleanor, *Myths of Male Dominance: Collected Articles on Women Cross-Culturally*, New York: Monthly Review Press, 1981.

Leghorn, Lisa and Mary Rood Kowsky, *Who, Really, Starves? Women and World Hunger*, New York: Friendship Press, 1977.

Leisinger, Klaus M. and Karin Schmitt, *All Our People: Population Policy With A Human Face*, Washington, DC: Island Press, 1994.

Lerner, Gerda, *The Creation of Patriarchy*, Oxford: Oxford University Press, 1986.

Lesthaeghe, Ron J., ed., *Reproduction and Social Organization in Sub-Saharan Africa*, Berkeley: University of California Press, 1989.

Levine, Robert A., Sarah E. Levine, Amy Richman, F. Medardo, Tapia Uribe and Clara Sunderland Correa, "Schooling and Survival: The Impact of Maternal Education on Health and Reproduction in the Third World", Working Paper Series, No. 3, May 1991, Harvard School of Public Health, Harvard Center for Population and Development Studies.

Levine, Stephen, *Who Dies? An Investigation of Conscious Living and Conscious Dying*, Garden City, NY: Anchor Books, 1982.

Lewis, Oscar, *Five Families: Mexican Case Studies in the Culture of Poverty*, New York: New American Library, 1959.

Lieberson, Johathan, "Too Many People", *New York Review of Books*, Vol. 33, No. 11, June 26, 1986.

Liedloff, Jean, *The Continuum Concept: In Search of Happiness Lost*, Reading, MA: Addison-Wesley, 1977.

Lindio-McGovern, Ligaya, "The Philippines: Counter-Insurgency and Peasant Women", *Race and Class*, Vol. 34, No. 4, 1993.

Lindsay-Poland, John, "Peru: On Desperate Terms", *Fellowship*, Fellowship of Reconciliation, December 1991.

Ling, Chee Yoke, "Nuclear Non-Proliferation Treaty: South Caves in to U.S. Pressure", *Third World Resurgence*, No. 58, 1995.

———, "Whither the GEF Restructuring?", *Third World Resurgence*, No. 29–30, 1992.

———, *How Big Powers Dominate the Third World: The Use and Abuse of International Law*, Third World Network, Penang, Malaysia, 1987.

Ling, Xiao, "No Red Eggs: China's One Child Policy", *Sojourner*, Vol. 12, No. 8, April 1987.

Little, Peter D. and Michael M. Horowitz with A. Endre Nyerges, eds, *Lands at Risk in the Third World: Local Level Perspectives*, Boulder, CO: Westview Press, 1987.

Lorde, Audre, *From a Land Where Other People Live*, Detroit: Broadside Press, 1973.

Lund, Ragnhild, "A Survey on Women's Working and Living Conditions in a Mahaweli Settlement Area with Special Emphasis on Budgets and Household Surplus", Colombo, Sri Lanka: People's Bank Research Department, 1978.

Luxemburg, Rosa, *The Accumulation of Capital*, New York: Monthly Review Press, 1968.

McDonnell, Kathleen, ed., *Adverse Effects: Women and the Phamaceutical Industry*, Toronto: Women's Press, 1986.

McGinnis, James B., *Bread and Justice: Toward a New International Economic Order*, New York: Paulist Press, 1979.

McLaughlin, Patricia, "Child Labor Abuse Gains Notice", *Plain Dealer*, Cleveland, May 13, 1993.

Macy, Joanna, *Dharma and Development: Religion as Resource in the Sarvodaya Self-Help Movement*, West Hartford, CT: Kumarian Press, 1985.

Magdoff, Harry, "Globalisation – To What End?", *Economic Review*, People's Bank Publication, Sri Lanka, Vol. 18, No. 5, August 1992.

Maine, Deborah, Murat Z. Akalin, Jyotsanamoy Chakraborty, Andres de Francisco and Michael Strong, "Why Did Maternal Mortality Decline in Matlab?", *Studies in Family Planning*, Vol. 27, No. 4, July–August 1996.

Makinson, Larry, "The Price of Admission: Campaign Spending in the 1994 Elections", Center for Responsive Politics, Washington, DC, 1995.

Malanes, Maurice, "Indigenous Women Victims of World Bank Policies", *Third World Resurgence*, No. 31, 1993.

Malthus, Thomas Robert, *An Essay on the Principle of Population*, ed. Philip Appleman, New York: W.W. Norton, 1976.

Mamdani, Mahmood, *The Myth of Population Control: Family, Caste, and Class in an Indian Village*, New York: Monthly Review Press, 1972.

Mann, Donald "A Negative Population Growth Position Paper", Negative Population Growth, Washington, DC, 1992.

Manning, Patrick, *Slavery and African Life: Occidental, Oriental and African Slave Trades*, Cambridge: Cambridge University Press, 1990.

Marcos, Sylvia, "Clergy, Goddesses and Eroticism", trans. Peter Bruce, *Conscience*, September–October 1991.

Marks, Donovan and N. Brown, "The Next Link in the Dumping Chain", in *We Speak for Ourselves: Social Justice, Race and Environment*, Washington, DC: The Panos Institute, 1990.

Martin, Susan Forbes, "Women Refugees Face Special Health Problems", *People*, IPPF, Vol. 18, No. 4, 1991.

Marton, Ruchama, "International Update", *The Fight for Reproductive Freedom: A Newsletter for Student Activists*, Hampshire College, Civil Liberties and Public Policy Program, Vol. VII, No. 3, Spring 1993.

Marx, Karl, *Capital*, New York: Modern Library, 1906.

Mass, Bonnie, *Population Target: The Political Economy of Population Control in Latin America*, Toronto: Women's Press, 1976.

Mazhar, Farhad, "Dumping Toxic Waste in Bangladesh as Fertiliser", *Third World Resurgence*, Nos 29–30, 1993.

Mazumdar, Sucheta, "For Rama and Hindutva: Women and Right-Wing Mobilization in Contemporary India", *Committee on South Asian Women Bulletin*, Vol. 8, Nos 3–4, 1993.

Mazur, Laurie Ann, ed., *Beyond the Numbers: A Reader on Population, Consumption and the Environment*, Washington, DC: Island Press, 1994

Meadows, Donnela H., Dennis L. Meadows and Jorgen Randers, *Beyond the Limits: Confronting Global Collapse, Envisioning a Sustainable Future*, Post Mills, VT: Chelsea Green Publishing Co., 1992.

——— and William W. Behrens III, *The Limits to Growth: A Report for the Club of Rome's Project on the Predicament of Mankind*, New York: Universe Books, 1972.

Mello, Fatima Vianna, "International Update: Sustainable Development For and By Whom?", *The Fight for Reproductive Freedom, Newsletter for Student Activists*, Civil Liberties and Public Policy Program, Hampshire College, MA, Vol. VI, No. 2, Winter 1992.

Memmi, Albert, *The Colonizer and the Colonized*, Boston: Beacon Press, 1967.

Menard, Scott W., "Inequality and Fertility", *Studies in Comparative International Development*, Spring 1985.

——— and Elizabeth W. Moen, eds, *Perspectives on Population: An Introduction to Concepts and Issues*, New York: Oxford University Press, 1987.

Mencher, Joan, "The Lessons and Non-Lessons of Kerala: Agricultural Labourers and Poverty", *Economic and Political Weekly*, Special Number, October 1980.

Menchú, Rigoberta, *I: Rigoberta Menchú: An Indian Woman in Guatemala*, London: Verso, 1984.

Mendis, Patrick, "Buddhist Equilibrium: The Theory of Middle Path for Sustainable Development", Staff Paper P93-2, Department of Agricultural and Applied Economics, University of Minnesota, January 1993.

Merchant, Carolyn, *Radical Ecology: The Search for a Livable World*, New York: Routledge, 1992.

———, *Death of Nature: Women, Ecology and the Scientific Revolution*, San Francisco: Harper and Row, 1983.

Merrick, Thomas W., "Recent Fertility Declines in Brazil, Colombia and Mexico", World Bank Staff Working Paper No. 692, Washington, DC, Population and Development Series No. 1, 1985.

Michaelson, Karen L., ed., *And the Poor Get Children: Radical Perspectives on Population Dynamics*, New York: Monthly Review Press, 1981.

Mies, Maria, *Patriarchy and Accumulation on a World Scale: Women in the International Division of Labour*, London: Zed Books, 1986.

———, *Lace Makers of Narsapur: Indian Housewives Produce for the World Market*, London: Zed Press, 1982.

——— and Vandana Shiva, *Ecofeminism*, London: Zed Books, 1993.

Millett, Kate, *Sexual Politics*, New York: Avon Press, 1969.

Minkin, Stephen, "Depo-Provera: A Critical Analysis", Institute for Food and Development Policy, San Francisco, 1981.

———, "Nine Thai Women Had Cancer... None of Them Took Depo-Provera: Therefore Depo-Provera Is Safe", *Mother Jones*, November 1981.

Mintzes, Barbara, Anita Hardon and Jannemieke Hanhart, *Norplant Under Her Skin*, Delft: Eburon, 1993.

Miringhoff, Marc L., *The Index of Social Health, 1990: Measuring the Social Well-Being of the Nation*, Fordham Institute for Innovation in Social Policy, Fordham University, Tarrytown, New York, 1990.

Mische, Gerald and Patricia Mische, *Toward a Human World Order: Beyond the National Security Straitjacket*, New York: Paulist Press, 1977.

Mogil, Christopher, and Anne Slepian with Peter Woodrow, *We Gave Away a Fortune: Stories of People Who Have Devoted Themselves and Their Wealth to Peace, Justice and a Healthy Environment*, Philadelphia: New Society Publishers, 1992.

Moore, Richard, "Confronting Environmental Racism", *Crossroads – Forward Motion*, Center for Democratic Alternatives, Jamaica Plain, MA, Vol. 11, No. 2, April 1992.

Moser, Caroline, "The Impact of Recession and Structural Adjustment on Women: Ecuador", *Development*, Vol. 1, 1989.

Muzaffar, Chandra, "Western Global Domination and Human Rights", *Third World Resurgence*, No. 33, 1993.

Myers, Norman, "Scientists Reinforce Population Policies", *WGNRR Newsletter*, No. 45, January–March 1994.

———, ed., *Gaia: An Atlas of Planet Management*, New York: Anchor Books, 1984.

Nag, Moni, ed., *Population and Social Organization*, The Hague: Mouton, 1975.

Nair, Sumati, "Imperialism and the Control of Women's Fertility", London and Amsterdam: The Campaign Against Long-Acting Contraceptives, 1989.

Nash, June and Maria Patricia Fernandez-Kelly, eds, *Women and Men in the International Division of Labor*, Albany, NY: State University of New York Press, 1982.

Norberg-Hodge, Helena, *Ancient Futures: Learning From Ladakh*, San Francisco: Sierra Club Books, 1992.

Norsigian, Judy, "Quinacrine Update", *Political Environments*, No. 3, Winter/Spring 1996.

Oberg, Jan, "Many Global Wrongs, New Human Duties", *Terra Viva*, IPS (Inter Press Service), June 14, 1993.

Obermeyer, Carla Makhlouf, "Women, Islam and Population: Is the Triangle Fateful?", Working Paper Series No. 6, Harvard School of Public Health, Harvard Center for Population and Development Studies, July 1991.

O'Brien, Mary, *The Politics of Reproduction*, Boston: Routledge and Kegan Paul, 1981.

Olson, Jennifer, "Behind the Recent Tragedy in Rwanda", *GeoJournal*, February 1995.

Paddock, William and Paul Paddock, *Famine – 1975! America's Decision: Who Will Survive?*, Boston: Little, Brown, 1967.

Palmer, Ingrid, *Gender and Population in the Adjustment of African Economies: Planning for Change*, Geneva: ILO, 1991.

Papanek, Hanna, "Class and Gender in Education–Employment Linkages", *Comparative Education Review*, Vol. 29, No. 3, 1985.

Papworth, John, "Community Population Control", *The Ecologist*, Vol. 23, No. 2, March–April 1993.

Patel, Vibhuti, "Sex-Determination and Sex-Preselection Tests in India: Modern Techniques for Femicide", *Bulletin of Concerned Asian Scholars*, Vol. 21, No. 1, January–March 1989.

Patterson, John G. and Nanda R. Shrestha, "Population Growth and Development in the Third World: The Neocolonial Context", *Studies in Comparative International Development*, Vol. 23, Summer 1988.

Peavey, Fran, 1995, "Taming the Wildfire: The Anatomy of Social Hysteria", *Turning Wheel*, Journal of the Buddhist Peace Fellowship, Special Issue on fundamentalism, San Francisco, Fall 1995.

Pena, Devon G., "The 'Green' Marx: Capitalism and the Destruction of Nature", Colorado College, Colorado Springs, unpublished ms, September 1988.

Pepper, David, *The Roots of Modern Environmentalism*, London: Routledge, 1986.

Percival, Debra, "EC Publicises Toxic Waste Trade", *Third World Resurgence*, Nos 29–30, 1993.

Peretz, Don, "Israeli Jews and Arabs in the Ethnic Numbers Game", *Ethnicity*, Vol. 8, No. 3, September 1981.

Petchesky, Rosalind Pollack, *Abortion and Woman's Choice: The State, Sexuality and Reproductive Freedom*, New York: Longman, 1984.

Peters, Cynthia, ed., *Collateral Damage: The 'New World Order' at Home and Abroad*, Boston: South End Press, 1992.

Petersen, Julie, "This Bullet Kills You Better", *Mother Jones*, September–October 1993.

Petras, James, "Cultural Imperialism in the Late 20th Century", *Journal of Contemporary Asia*, Vol. 23, No. 2, May 1993.

Piven, Frances Fox and Richard A. Cloward, *Poor People's Movements: Why They Succeed, How They Fail*, New York: Vintage Books, 1979.

Polgar, Steven, "Population History and Population Policies from an Anthropological Perspective", *Current Anthropology*, April 1972.

Pollitt, Katha, "A New Assault on Feminism", *The Nation*, March 26, 1990.

Pressat, Roland, *Population*, Baltimore: Penguin Books Inc., 1971.

Pritchett, Lant H., "Desired Fertility and the Impact of Population Policies", *Population and Development Review*, Vol. 20, No. 1, March 1994.

Purvis, Andrew, "A Pill That Goes Under the Skin", *Time*, December 24, 1990.

Quinn, Naomi, "Anthropological Studies on Women's Status", *Annual Review of Anthropology*, Vol. 6, 1977.

Raghavan, Chakravarthi, "Japan's Study on State's Role Refutes Free-Market Myths", *Third World Economics: Trends and Analysis*, May 16–31, 1993.

Rahula, Walpola, *What the Buddha Taught*, London: Gordon Fraser, 1978.

Rainwater, Lee and William L. Yancey, *The Moynihan Report and the Politics of Controversy*, Cambridge, MA: MIT Press, 1967.

Rajamoorthy, T., "Double Standards are the Norm", *Third World Resurgence*, No. 31, 1993.

Rao, Mohan, "The World Bank's Prescription for India's Family Welfare Program", *Political Environments*, CWPE Newsletter, Special Double Issue, Winter/Spring 1996.

Rao, Radhakrishna, "Illegal Kidney Trade Boom in India", *Third World Resurgence*, No. 17, 1991.

Ratcliff, Kathryn Strother, ed., *Healing Technology: Feminist Perspectives*, Ann Arbor: University of Michigan Press, 1989.

Ratcliffe, John, "Social Justice and the Demographic Transition: Lessons from India's Kerala State", *International Journal of Health Services*, Vol. 8, No. 1, 1978.

Ray, Michael and Alan Rinzler, eds, *The New Paradigm in Business: Emerging Strategies for Leadership and Organizational Change*, New York: Jeremy P. Tarcher/Perigee Books, 1993.

Raymond, Janice, "International Traffic in Reproduction", *Ms. Magazine*, May–June 1991.

Reilly, Philip, *The Surgical Solution: A History of Involuntary Sterilization in the United States*, Baltimore, MD: Johns Hopkins University Press, 1991.

Renner, Michael, "Assessing the Military's War on the Environment", *State of the World 1991*, New York: W.W. Norton and Co., 1991.

Repetto, Robert, *Economic Equality and Fertility in Developing Countries*, Baltimore: Johns Hopkins University Press, 1979.

Richardson, Kerry, "Report on the First Global Radiation Victims Conference and the Indigenous Uranium Forum (IUF)", Report No. 7, San Francisco, 1988.

Richter, Judith, *Vaccination Against Pregnancy: Miracle or Menace?*, London: Zed Books, 1996.

Rifkin, Jeremy, *The End of Work: The Decline of the Global Labor Force and the Dawn of the Post-Market Era*, New York: G.P. Putnam's Sons, 1995.

Roberts, Godfrey, ed., *Population Policy: Contemporary Issues*, New York: Praeger, 1990.

Robertson, Pat, *The Collected Works of Pat Robertson: The New Millennium, The New World Order, The Secret Kingdom*, New York: Inspirational Press, 1994.

Robey, Bryant, Shea O'Rutstein and Leo Morris, "The Fertility Decline in Developing Countries", *Scientific American*, Vol. 269, No. 6, December 1993.

Rogers, Barbara, *The Domestication of Women: Discrimination in Developing Countries*, New York: St Martin's Press, 1979.

Rollins, Judith, *Between Women: Domestics and their Employers*, Philadelphia: Temple University Press, 1985.

Rose, Stephen J., *Social Stratification in the United States: The American Profile Poster Revised and Expanded*, New York: New Press, 1992.

Ross, John A., "Sterilization: Past, Present, Future", Population Council Working Paper, No. 29, 1991.

Rostow, Dankwart, "Democracy: A Global Revolution", *Foreign Affairs*, Vol. 64, No. 4, Fall 1990.

Ruddick, Sara, *Maternal Thinking: Towards a Politics of Peace*, New York: Ballantine Books, 1989.

Ryan, John C., "Conserving Biological Diversity", *State of the World 1992*, Washington, DC: World Watch Institute, W.W. Norton and Co., 1992.

Sachs, Aaron, "Eco-Justice: Linking Human Rights and the Environment", *World Watch Paper* No. 127, Washington, DC: World Watch Institute, December, 1995.

Sachs, Wolfgang, ed., *The Development Dictionary*, London: Zed Books, 1992.

Sadik, Nafis, "Investing in Women: The Focus for the 90s", UNFPA, New York, n.d.

Safa, Helen I., "Women, Production and Reproduction in Industrial Capitalism: A Comparison of Brazilian and U.S. Factory Workers", New York: Women's International Resource Exchange Service, 1978.

Sagoff, Mark, "Playing the Numbers", *Conscience*, Vol. 14, No. 3, Autumn 1993.

Sahlins, Marshall, *Stone Age Economics*, New York: Aldine de Gruyter, 1972.

Said, Edward W., *Culture and Imperialism*, New York: Alfred A. Knopf, 1993.

St Hilaire, Colette, "Canadian Aid, Women and Development: Rebaptizing the Filipina", *The Ecologist*, Vol. 23, No. 2, March–April 1993.

Sale, Kirkpatrick, *Rebels Against the Future: The Luddites and Their War on the Industrial Revolution: Lessons for the Computer Age*, Reading, MA: Addison-Wesley, 1995.

Sanday, Peggy Reeves, *Female Power and Male Dominance: On the Origins of Sexual Inequality*, Cambridge: Cambridge University Press, 1981.

Sartika, Dewi, "Indonesia Goes for Tree Plantations", *Third World Resurgence*, Nos 29–30, 1993.

Sassen, Saskia, *The Mobility of Labor and Capital: A Study in International Investment and Labor Flow*, Cambridge: Cambridge University Press, 1988.

Saunders, John, ed., *Population Growth in Latin America and U.S. National Security*, Boston: Allen and Unwin Inc., 1986.

Sauvy, Alfred, "The World Population Problem: A View in 1949", *Population and Development Review*, Vol. 16, No. 4, December 1990.

Schneider, Cathy, "Chile: The Underside of the Miracle", *Report on the Americas*, NACLA (North American Congress on Latin America), Vol. XXVI, No. 4, 1991.

Schneider, Ingrid, "Anti-Pregnancy Vaccines", unpublished ms, Hamburg, Germany, September 1991.

Schnurr, Clare, "Family Planning or Population Control?", Shair: International Forum, Canada, March 1989.

Schrijvers, Joke, *The Violence of 'Development'*, Institute for Development Research, Amsterdam, Netherlands, 1993.

Schuler, Sidney Ruth, Syed M. Hashemi and Ann Hendrix Jenkins, "Bangladesh's Family Planning Success Story: A Gender Perspective", *International Family Planning Perspectives*, Vol. 21, No. 4, 1995.

Schumacher, E.F., *Small is Beautiful*, New York: Harper and Row, 1989.

Scott, Hilda, *Working Your Way to the Bottom: The Feminization of Poverty*, London: Pandora Press, 1984.

Scott, James C., *Everyday Forms of Peasant Resistance*, New Haven: Yale University Press, 1994.

Scott, Julia R., "Norplant: Its Impact on Poor Women and Women of Color", National Black Women's Health Project, Washington, DC, n.d.

Seabrook, Jeremy, "Re-examining the Lexicon of Development", *Third World Resurgence*, Nos 61–62, 1995.

Seager, Joni, *Earth Follies: Coming to Feminist Terms with the Global Environmental Crisis*, New York: Routledge, 1993.

———, "Making Feminist Sense of Environmental Issues", *Sojourner*, February 1991.

———, and Ann Olson, *Women in the World: An International Atlas*, New York: Simon and Schuster, 1986.

Seed, John, Joanna Macy, Pat Fleming, Arne Naess, eds, *Thinking Like a Mountain: Towards a Council of Beings*, Philadelphia: New Society Publishers, 1988.

Sell, Ralph R. and Stephen J. Kunitz, "The Debt Crisis and the End of an Era in Mortality Decline", *Studies in Comparative International Development*, Winter 1986–87.

Sen, Amartya, "Population: Delusion and Reality", *New York Review of Books*, Vol., XLI, No. 15, September 22, 1994.

———, "More than 100 Million Women are Missing", *New York Review of Books*, Vol. 37, No. 20, December 1990.

———, *Poverty and Famines: An Essay on Entitlement and Deprivation*, Oxford: Clarendon Press, 1982.

Sen, Gita and Caren Grown, *Development, Crises and Alternative Visions: Third World Women's Perspectives*, New York: Monthly Review Press, 1987.

Sen, Gita, Adrienne Germain and Lincoln C. Chen, eds, *Population Policies Reconsidered: Health, Empowerment, and Rights*, Cambridge, MA: Harvard University Press, 1994

Seneviratne, Kalinga, "Method Behind Dr. Mehta's Guinness Record", *Terra Viva*, ICPD, September 12, 1994.

Sen Gupta, Amit, "A Paradigm Shift", *Political Environments*, No. 4, Summer–Fall 1996.

Serron, Luis A., *Scarcity, Exploitation and Poverty: Malthus and Marx in Mexico*, Norman: University of Oklahoma Press, 1980.

Seshadri, B., "Male Infertility and World Population", *Contemporary Review*, Vol. 266, No. 1549, February 1995.

Shallat, Lezak, "Excerpts from: Business as Usual for Quinacrine Sterilization in Chile", *Political Environments*, No. 3, Winter/Spring 1996.

Shalom, Stephen R., "Why the World Bank Can't Lead Us to a Just World Order", *Bulletin of Concerned Asian Scholars*, Vol. 27, No. 4, 1995.

Shapiro, Thomas M., *Population Control Policies: Women, Sterilization and Reproductive Choice*, Philadelphia: Temple University Press, 1985.

———, William Fisher and Augusto Diana, "Family Planning and Female Sterilization in the United States", *Social Science Medicine*, Vol. 17, No. 23, 1983.

Sherbinin, Alex de, "Population and Consumption Issues for Environmentalists", Literature Search and Bibliography Prepared by the Population Reference Bureau for the Pew Charitable Trusts' Global Stewardship Initiative, October 1993.

———, "Population Issues of Concern to the Foreign Policy Community", Literature Search and Bibliography Prepared by the Population Reference Bureau for the Pew Charitable Trusts' Global Stewardship Initiative, October, 1993.

Sheth, D.L., "Alternative Development as Political Practice", *Alternatives*, No. XII, 1987.

Shiva, Vandana, "Beijing Conference: Gender Justice and Global Apartheid", *Third World Resurgence*, Nos 61–62, 1995.

———, "The Effects of WTO on Women's Rights", *Third World Resurgence*, Nos 61–62, 1995.

———, ed., *Close to Home: Women Reconnect Ecology, Health and Development Worldwide*, Philadelphia: New Society Publishers, 1994.

———, "North Blocks South in Biodiversity", *Third World Resurgence*, No. 28, January 1992.

———, *The Violence of the Green Revolution: Third World Agriculture, Ecology and Politics*, London: Zed Books, 1991.

———, "World Bank Cannot Protect the Environment", *Third World Resurgence*, Nos 14–15, 1991.

———, *Staying Alive: Women, Ecology and Development*, London: Zed Books, 1988.

———, *Biodiversity: A Third World Perspective*, Third World Network, Penang, Malaysia, n.d.

——— and Mira Shiva, "World Bank Role in Unsafe Contraceptive Promotion", *Third World Resurgence*, No. 50, October 1994.

———, "Was Cairo a Step Forward For Third World Women", *Third World Resurgence*, No. 50, October 1994.

Shostack, Marjorie, *Nisa: The Life and Words of a !Kung Woman*, New York: Vintage Books, 1983.

Silliman, Jael, "Women, Population and Development", *Conservation Digest*, Vol. 3, No. 1, February 1991.

Sills, David L., ed., *International Encyclopedia of the Social Sciences*, Vol. 3, Crowell Collier and Macmillan Inc., 1968.

Silva, Kalinga Tudor and W.D.N.R. Pushpakumar, "Suicide, Anomie and Powerlessness Among the Mahaweli Settlers in Sri Lanka", unpublished ms, n.d.

Silva W. Indralal de, "Ahead of Target: Achievement of Replacement Level Fertility in Sri Lanka Before the Year 2000", *Asia-Pacific Population Journal*, Vol. 9, No. 4, December 1, 1994.

Simon, Julian, *The Ultimate Resource*, Princeton: Princeton University Press, 1981.

Sivard, Ruth, *World Military and Social Expenditures 1989*, Washington, DC: World Priorities, 1989.

Sjoo, Monica and Barabara Mor, *The Great Cosmic Mother: Rediscovering the Religion of the Earth*, San Francisco: Harper and Row, 1987.

Slade, Stephen, "Emperor Bill", *War Watch Out Now*, No. 9, September–October 1993.

Slater, Jack, "Sterilization: Newest Threat to the Poor", *Ebony*, Vol. 28, No. 12, October 1973.

Smith, Andy, "Christian Responses to Population Control", *Political Environments*, CWPE Newsletter, No. 3, Winter/Spring 1996.

Smith, Dan, "Nationalism: The Underside of World Politics", lecture sponsored by Five College Peace and World Security Studies Program, Amherst, MA, October 11, 1992.

Smith, Joan and Immanuel Wallerstein, eds, *Racism, Sexism and the World-System*, New York: Greenwood Press, 1980.

Sobo, Elisabeth, "Crooning for Contraceptives in Nigeria", *The Progressive*, September 1990.

Souza, Anthony R. de, *A Geography of World Economy*, New York: Macmillan, 1992.

Spallone, Patricia and Deborah Lynn Steinberg, eds, *Made to Order: The Myth of Reproduc-*

tive and Genetic Progress, Oxford: Pergamon Press, 1987.

Srinivasan, Viji, "Death to the Female: Foeticide and Infanticide in India", *Third World Resurgence*, Vol. 29, No. 30, January–February 1993.

Stack, Carol B., *All Our Kin: Strategies for Survival in a Black Community*, New York: Harper and Row, 1974.

Standing, Guy, ed., *The New Soviet Labour Market: In Search of Flexibility*, Geneva: ILO, 1991.

Starhawk, *The Spiral Dance: A Rebirth of the Ancient Religion of the Goddess*, San Francisco: Harper and Row, 1986.

Stephen, Lynn, "Crackdown in Chiapas: Protests Nationwide", *Peacework*, No. 250, March 1995.

Stone, Merlin, *When God Was a Woman*, New York: Harcourt Brace Jovanovich, 1970.

Strange, Marty, *Family Farming: A New Economic Vision*, Lincoln: University of Nebraska Press; San Francisco: Institute for Food and Development Policy, 1988.

Stratman, David G., *We Can Change The World: The Real Meaning of Everyday Life*, Boston: New Democracy Books, 1993.

Stycos, J. Mayone, "The Second Great Wall of China: Evolution of a Successful Policy of Population Control", *Population and Environment: A Journal of Interdisciplinary Studies*, Vol. 12, No. 4, Summer 1991.

Summers, Carol, "Intimate Colonialism: the Imperial Production of Reproduction in Uganda, 1907–1925", *Signs*, Vol. 16, No. 41, 1991.

Teitelbaum, Michael S. and Jay M. Winter, eds, *Population and Resources in Western Intellectual Traditions*, Cambridge: Cambridge University Press, 1989.

———, *The Fear of Population Decline*, New York: Academic Press, 1985.

Thapar, Romila, "Imagined Religious Communities? – Ancient History and the Modern Search for a Hindu Identity", *Modern Asian Studies*, Vol. 23, No. 2, 1989.

Thomas, F.H., J.H. Boutwell and G.W. Rathjens, "Environmental Change and Violent Conflict", *Scientific American*, February 1993.

Thompson, E.P., "Notes on Exterminism: The Last Stage of Civilization", *New Left Review*, No. 121, May–June 1980.

———, "Time, Work-Discipline and Industrial Capitalism", *Past and Present*, No. 38, December 1967.

Thrupp, Lori Ann, "Sterilization of Workers from Pesticide Exposure: The Causes and Consequences of DBCP-induced Damage in Costa Rica and Beyond", *International Journal of Health Services*, Vol. 21, No. 4, 1991.

Thussu, Daya Kishan, "Lies, Damned Lies and 'Global News'", *Third World Resurgence*, No. 58, 1995.

Tibballs, Sue, "Northern Governments Hiding Behind the Cairo Agenda", *Terra Viva*, (Inter Press Service), ICPD Issue, September 12, 1994.

Timberlake, Lloyd, *Africa in Crisis: The Causes, the Cures of Environmental Bankruptcy*, Philadelphia: New Society Publishers, 1986.

Tobias, Michael, *World War III: Population and the Biosphere at the End of the Millennium*, Santa Fe, NM: Bear and Company, 1994.

Toffler, Alvin, *The Third Wave*, New York: Morrow, 1980.

Toubia, Nahid, ed., *Women of the Arab World: The Coming Challenge*, London: Zed Books, 1988.

Tsikata, Dzodzi, "Effects of Structural Adjustment on Women and the Poor", *Third World Resurgence*, Nos 61–62, 1995.

———, "Globalisation the Cause of Poor Women's Woes, Says Panel", *Third World Resurgence*, Nos 61–62, 1995.

Turk, Danilo, "How World Bank–IMF Policies Adversely Affect Human Rights", *Third World Resurgence*, No. 33, 1993.

Turner, Steve and Todd Nachowitz, "The Damming of Native Lands", *The Nation*, October 21, 1991.

Vaid, Jyotsana, "On Women and the Hindu Right", *Committee on South Asian Women Bulletin*,

Vol. 8, Nos 3–4, 1993.

Van Allen, Judith, "Sitting on a Man – Colonialism and Lost Political Institutions of Igbo Women", *Canadian Journal of African Studies*, 1972, Vol. 6, No. 2, 1972.

Vatsyayan S.H., *A Sense of Time: An Exploration of Time in Theory, Experience and Art*, Delhi: Oxford University Press, 1981.

Verano, J.W. and D.H. Ubelaker, eds, *Disease and Demography in the Americas*, Washington, DC: Smithsonian Institution Press, 1992.

Vickers, Jeanne, ed., *Women and the World Economic Crisis*, London: Zed Books, 1991.

Vicziany, Marika, "Coercion in A Soft State: The Family Planning Program of India: The Sources of Coercion", *Pacific Affairs*, Winter 1982–1983.

Vieira, Elisabeth Meloni, "Female Sterilisation", *WGNRR Newsletter*, No. 48, October–December 1994.

Viravaidya, Mechai, talk (unpublished) and slide show, Harvard Institute for International Development, Cambridge, MA, April 10, 1989.

———, "Community Development and Fertility Management in Rural Thailand", *International Family Planning Perspectives*, Vol. 12, No. 1, March 1986.

Vogeler, Ingolf and Anthony R. de Souza, eds, *Dialectics of Third World Development*, Montclair, NJ: Allanheld, Osmun and Co., 1980.

Wachtel, Paul L., *The Poverty of Affluence: A Psychological Portrait of the American Way of Life*, Philadelphia: New Society Publishers, 1989.

Wallace, Robert B., "Might Access to Credit for Poor Women Help Reduce Population Growth and Environmental Degradation?", *Conservation Digest*, Washington, DC, Vol. 3, No. 1, February 1991.

Wallerstein, Immanuel, *The Modern World-System II: Mercantilism and the Consolidation of the European World-Economy, 1600–1750*, New York: Academic Press, 1980.

———, *The Modern-World System: Capitalist Agriculture and the Origins of the European World Economy in the Sixteenth Century*, New York: Academic Press, 1974.

———, "The Rise and Future Demise of the World Capitalist System: Concepts for Comparative Analysis", *Comparative Studies in Society and History*, Vol. 16, 1974.

Ward, Kathryn B., "Toward a New Model of Fertility: The Effects of The World Economic System and the Status of Women on Fertility Behavior", Working Paper No. 20 in Women in International Development Series, Michigan State University, March 1983.

Ward, Sheila J., Ieda Poernomo Sigit Sidi, Ruth Simmons and George B. Simmons, "Service Delivery Systems and Quality of Care in the Implementation of Norplant in Indonesia", Population Council, New York, 1990.

Waring, Marilyn, *If Women Counted: A New Feminist Economics*, San Francisco: Harper and Row, 1988.

Warwick, Donald P., *Bitter Pills: Population Policies and their Implementation in Eight Developing Countries*, Cambridge: Cambridge University Press, 1982.

———, "Bullying Birth Control", *Commonweal*, Vol. 102, No. 13, September 12, 1975.

Wattenberg, Ben J., *Birth Dearth*, New York: Pharos Books, 1987.

Weber, Max, *The Protestant Ethic and the Rise of Capitalism*, trans. Talcott Parsons, New York: Charles Scribner and Sons, 1950.

Weston, Joe, *Red and Green: A New Politics of the Environment*, London: Pluto Press, 1986.

Wheeler, Charlene Elridge and Peggy L. Chinn, *Peace and Power: A Handbook of Feminist Process*, Buffalo, NY: Margaretdaughters Inc., 1984.

White, Lynn Jr, "The Historical Roots of Our Ecological Crisis", *Sanctuary*, February–March 1988.

Wickramasinghe, Anoja, "Forests in the Lives of Rural Women: A Case Study on a Fringe Community", in *Conference on Women, Environment and Development*, Ruk Rakaganno and Environmental Foundation Ltd, Sri Lanka, February 22, 1992.

Williams, Constance Willard, *Black Teenage Mothers: Pregnancy and Child Rearing From their Perspective*, Lexington, MA: Lexington Books, 1991.

Wilson, Christopher, ed., *The Dictionary of Demography*, New York: Basil Blackwell, 1985.

Wilson, William Julius, "The Underclass: Issues, Perspectives, and Public Policy", *The Annals of the American Academy of Political and Social Science*, Vol. 501, January 1989.

——, *The Truly Disadvantaged: The Inner-City, the Underclass and Public Policy*, Chicago: University of Chicago Press, 1987.

Wisner, Ben, "The Limitations of 'Carrying Capacity'", *Political Environments*, CWPE Newsletter, No. 3, Winter/Spring, 1996.

Wolf, Eric, *Europe and the People Without History*, Berkeley: University of California Press, 1982.

Wolfe, A.B., "Population Theory", *Encyclopaedia of the Social Sciences*, Vol. 12, 1934.

Wood, Charles H., "Infant Mortality, Trends and Capitalist Development in Brazil: The Case of São Paulo and Belo Horizonte", *Latin American Perspectives*, Issue 15, Vol. IV, No. 4, Fall 1977.

Worsley, Peter, ed., *On the Brink: Nuclear Proliferation and the Third World*, London: Third World Communications, 1987.

Wright, Nancy E., "Disastrous Decade: Africa's Experience With Structural Adjustment", *Multinational Monitor*, Vol. 21, April 1, 1990.

Yuki, Okuda, "A Move to Outlaw All Abortions – Revision of the Eugenic Protection Act", *Asian Women's Liberation*, No. 2, 1980.

Yoon, Chin Saik, "New Global Trends Worsen N–S Information Imbalance", *Third World Resurgence*, No. 58, 1995.

Zachariah, K.C., "The Anomaly of the Fertility Decline in India's Kerala State", World Bank Staff Working Paper, No. 700, World Bank, Washington, DC, 1984.

Zinn, Howard, *A People's History of the United States*, New York: Harper and Row, 1980.

Zopf, Paul E. Jr, *American Women in Poverty*, New York: Greenwood Press, 1989.

Works Published without Author Name

(listed under publication)

Akwesasne Notes, "Growing Fight Against Sterilization of Native Women", Late Winter 1979.

Alt-WID, "Reaganomics and Women: Structural Adjustment U.S. Style, 1980–1992: A Case Study of Women and Poverty in the U.S.", Washington, DC, n.d.

Arms Control Today, Vol. 21, No. 5, 1990.

Arms Sales Monitor, "Administration Proposes Year-End Missile Sale to Turkey", No. 31, December 1995.

——, "Military Sales Logic", No. 31, December 5, 1995.

——, "Transparency Lacking in Exports of Small Arms", No. 31, December 5, 1995.

——, "U.S. Approves Over $38 Billion of Exports in FY 1994", No. 29, March 1995.

——, "Surplus Arms Made for Export Only", No. 28, February 15, 1995.

——, No. 20, 30 April 1993; No. 22, 30 September 1993; No. 28, February 15, 1995.

Asian Women Workers Newsletter, "Call To Boycott Kader Products", Vol. 12, No. 3, Hong Kong, July 1993.

——, "Sri Lanka: Chemical Poisoning Among Women Workers", Vol. 12, No. 3, July 1993.

Atlantic Monthly, Advertisement by FAIR, June 1994.

Carcas Report on Alternative Development Indicators: Redefining Wealth on Progress: New Ways to Measure Economic, Social and Environmental Change, Bootstrap Press, New York, 1989.

Clearinghouse Bulletin, "Q: Will Family Planning Alone Stop the Population Explosion? A: No", Carrying Capacity Network, Washington, DC, Vol. 2, No. 10, December 1992.

Conservation Digest, "Easing Population Pressures: Key to a Sustainable Planet", Vol. 13, No. 1, February 1991.

The Defense Monitor, "Far-Flung Frontiers of Security: The Clinton Administration's Two Year Strategy", Vol. XXIV, No. 1, 1995.

———— "The Military and the Environment", Vol. XXIII, No. 9, 1994.

Earth Negotiations Bulletin, International Institute for Sustainable Development, Vol. 6, No. 33, September 14, 1994.

EarthWatch, "The Most Urgent Task of All", No. 41, 1991.

Economist, "The Scorched Afghan Earth", June 4, 1988.

———— "Conservative Economics", October 23–24, 1987.

Environmental Action, "Coming to America: The Immigrants and the Environment", Takoma Park, MD, Summer 1994.

Fax Bulletin, American Health Consultants, "American Study Says Progesterone Might Boost HIV Risk", Atlanta, GA, May 8, 1996.

The Fight for Reproductive Freedom: A Newsletter for Student Activists, "Statement on Church Burnings by Abortion Providers and Women's Rights Activists", Civil Liberties and Public Policy Program, Hampshire College, Amhurst, MA, Vol. XI, No. 1/2, Winter 1996.

Global Stewardship, "Administration Redefining 'National Security' says Wirth", Vol. 1, No. 3, Washington, DC, March 1994.

Greenpeace, July–September 1993.

————, July–August 1990.

Hastings Center Report, "Depo-Provera: Loopholes and Double Standards", October–November 1987.

Hunger Notes, "Microenterprise: On the Road to Success", Vol. 21, No. 2, Fall 1995.

————, "The Worst Global Unemployment Crisis", Excerpt from ILO, Vol. 20, No. 4, Spring 1995.

ICPD Special Issue, ICPD Secretariat, "UK Wants Democratic Decision in Cairo", August 1994.

ICPD Newsletter, ICPD Secretariat, No. 12, February 1994.

————, ICPD Secretariat, "Science Academies Urge 'Incisive Action' on Population and Development", No. 10, November–December 1993.

International Press Review, August 1991.

IPPF Briefing, "Population and Environment", London, June 1992.

Journal of the Federation of American Scientists (FAS), "Public Interest Report", Vol. 45, No. 6, November–December 1992.

Mother Jones, "This Bullet Kills You Better", September–October 1993.

Ms. Magazine, "Brazil: The Price of a Vote", January–February 1992.

Multinational Monitor, "'The Economics of Debt', An Interview with Lance Taylor", Vol. 11, April 1990.

————, "Marketing Abroad", Vol. 6, February–March 1985.

————, "'No Problem': Buying Depo-Provera in Mexico", Vol. 6, February–March 1985.

New Internationalist, "Keynote – Green Justice", No. 230, April 1992.

————, "Saints and Sinners", No. 230, April 1992.

Newsweek "Death on the Spot: The End of a Drug King", Special Report, December 13, 1993.

————, "Global Mafia", Special Report, December 13 ,1993.

————, "Bad Year for Girls?", April 16, 1990.

Open File, IPPF, London, May, July 1992, November 1994, January, March 1995.

————, "Reproductive Revolution Sweeps Developing World", April 1993.

Peacework, "Burma: Manerplaw Refuge Falls", No. 250, March 1995.

————, "Non-Violent Action Leads to Coffee Victory at Starbucks", No. 250, March 1995.

Planned Parenthood Bulletin, Family Planning Association of India, Vol. XXXIX, November 5, 1991.

Political Environments, "Joint Memorandum [by Women's Organizatios and Concerned Groups] to the Health Minister [Government of India] Against NORPLANT", No. 4, Summer–Fall 1996.

————, "SAPs and Women's Health in India", No. 3, Winter/Spring 1996.

————, "Women's Groups Initiate Petition About Status of Holy See at UN", No. 3, Winter/Spring 1996.

————, "News Briefs", No. 3, Winter/Spring 1996.

Population and Development Review, "The South Commission Report on Population and Population Policy", Vol. 16, No. 4, December 1990.

————, "The CIA on Youth Deficits", Vol. 16, No. 4, December 1989.

Population Bulletin, "Population and Water Resources: A Delicate Balance", Vol. 47, No. 3, November 1992.

Population Headliners, ESCAP, Economic and Social Commission for Asia-Pacific, No. 232, July 1994.

————, "Australia Plans Increase in Population Funding", No. 230, May 1994.

————, No. 219, June 1993.

Population Reports, "The Environment and Population Growth: Decade for Action", Population Information Program, The Johns Hopkins University, Series M, No. 10, May 1992.

The Progressive, advertisement by Negative Population Growth, December 1988.

Project Bulletin, "Sri Lanka Project Report", Peace Brigades International, January 1996.

————, "Sri Lanka Team Report", Peace Brigades International, March 1995.

Right to Choose, "W.H.O. Can You Trust?", No. 26, Autumn 1983.

Sojourner, "Immunological Contraceptives", The Women's Forum, March 1995.

Springfield Advocate, "Eco-Symposium", Massachusetts, October 31, 1991.

Terra Viva, Inter Press Service, International Conference on Population and Development Issue, Interview with Francis Kissling, September 6, 1994.

Third World Economics: Trends and Analysis, Nos 51, October 1992, 63, April 1993.

Third World Economics, Inter Press Service, "UNDP Cautions Against Indiscriminate Privatisation", 16–31 May 1993.

Third World Resurgence "The NGO Declaration of Indigenous Women", No. 61–62, Double issue, 1995.

————, "Disinformation and Propaganda: Lessons From the Cold War", No. 58, June 1995.

————, "Interlocking Interests in the Communications Industry", No. 58, 1995

————, Double Issue on Biotechnology and Genetic Engineering, Nos 53–54, 1995.

————, "Recent Developments in Southern Resource Flows", No. 46, 1994.

————, "Pacific Islanders Send Back Toxic Soil to US", No. 31, 1993.

————, "ITTO Promotes Deforestation Say Ecologists", No. 31, 1993.

————, "U.S. Leaves Toxic Legacy at Military Bases", Nos 29–30, 1993.

————, "Karnataka Farmers Ransack Cargill Seeds", Nos 29–30, 1993.

————, "GATT – A Four Letter Word", No. 28, 1992.

————, "Chile, A Success Story – But for Whom?", No. 28, 1992.

————, "An Indictment of the IMF and the World Bank", No. 28, 1992.

————, "Structural Adjustment Programmes (SAPS): Questions and Answers", No. 28, 1992.

————, Special Double Issue on the UNCED, Nos 14–15, 1991.

————, "U.S. Burns Chemical Weapons in the Pacific", No. 3, 1990.

Time, "The New Face of America", Special Issue on Immigration, Vol. 142, Fall 1993.

Time/Newsweek, "Children of War", Special Issue, 1992.

TRANET, Bi-Monthly Digest for the A & T (Alternative and Transformational) Movements, "1994 in Review: Sustainable Communities", January 1995, No. 2.

Turning Wheel, Journal of the Buddhist Peace Fellowship, "The Narrowed Mind", Interview With Denise Caignon, Special Issue on Fundamentalism, San Francisco, Fall 1995.

UBINIG, "The Price of Norplant is TK 2000! You Cannot Remove It", Bangladesh, n.d.

United and Babson Investment Report, "Downsizing Defence: From Swords to…", November 30, 1992.

U.S. News and World Report, "10 Billion for Dinner Please", September 12, 1994.
Utne Reader, "The Familiar Face of Fascism", November–December, 1995.
———, "Love for Sale", January–February 1992.
Vital Signs, "Norplant", Newsletter from the National Black Women's Health Project, n.d.
War Watch Out Now, "Potential Next Targets", No. 10, October 1991.
WGNRR Newsletter, "Canadian Resolution Against Norplant", The National Action Com-
   mittee on the Status of Women, Canada, Toronto, No. 48, October– December 1994.
———, "Indian Women's Groups Protest Population Committee's Attitude", No. 48,
   October–December 1994.
———, No. 47, July–September 1994.
———, No. 43, April–June 1993.
———, "A Critical Appraisal of the Women's Declaration of Population Policies", No.
   42, January–March 1993.
———, "Where are the Missing Chinese Girls", No. 36, July–September 1991.
———, "Campaign Against Sex Selection Continues in India", April–June 1989.
———, "Women's Group in Madras Criticized", April–June 1989.
———, "Norplant Trials Stopped in Brazil", July–September 1986.
WGNRR Third Campaign Report, "International Campaign for a Stop of Research on Anti-
   Fertility 'Vaccines'", November 1994.
Woman of Power, Issue on "Women of Color: A Celebration of Spirit", No. 21, Fall 1991.
———, "Building Coalitions for Our Earth", interview with Ellie Goodwin, No. 20,
   1991.
———, Issue on Women of Color: A Celebration of Power", No. 4, Fall 1986.
World Press Review, "Children in Bondage", Vol. 43, No. 1, January 1996.
———, "For Girls, Few Choices – All Bad", Vol. 43, No. 1, January 1996.
———, "Hunger, Hate and the Lure of Adventure", Vol. 43, No. 1, January 1996.
———, "Tragedy, Success and Precocity", cover story, Vol. 43, No. 1, January 1996.
———, "Where the Jobs Go and Why", Vol. 42, No. 12, December 1995.
———, "Will East Beat the West?: A Challenge from Two Asian Statesmen", Vol. 42,
   No. 12, December 1995.
———, "The US Looks into Latin America", Vol. 39, September 1992.
———, "Asian Arms Binge", June 1992.
———, "Poverty Dooms the Planet: Now is the Time to Act", June 1992.
World Rainforest Report, Vol. IX, No. 1, January–March 1993.
———, Vol. VII, No. 4, October–December 1991.

Governmental, Non-Governmental and Other Documents

(listed under organization)

African Development Bank, United Nations Development Programme and the World
   Bank, *The Social Dimensions of Adjustment in Africa*, 1990.
American Friends Service Committee (AFSC) Simple Living Committee, San Francisco,
   Taking Charge: Achieving Personal and Political Change Through Simple Living, New York:
   Bantam Books, 1978.
Association for Voluntary Surgical Contraception, *AVSC Technical Statement: Quinacrine Pel-
   lets for Nonsurgical Female Sterilisation*, September 1993.
Bank Information Center, "Sudan: Steady Economic Decline", in *Funding Ecological and
   Social Destruction: The World Bank and International Monetary Fund*, Washington, DC, 1989.
Bread for the World Institute, *Hunger 1995: Causes of Hunger. Fifth Annual Report on the State
   of World Hunger*, Silver Spring, MD, October 1994.
Canadian University Student Organization (CUSO, Education Department, *Here to Stay:
   A Resource Handbook Linking Sustainable Development and Debt*, Part 2, Ottawa, November
   1990.

Canadian Women's Committee on Reproduction, Population and Development, "A Canadian Women's Report on Canadian Policies and Practices in the Areas of Reproduction", issued in preparation for ICPD, August 1994.

Center for Defense Information, *Illegal and Covert Arms Transfers*, Washington, DC, August 30, 1993.

Center for Popular Economics, *Economic Report of the People*, Boston: South End Press, 1986.

Center for Reproductive Law and Policy, *Restrictions on Funding for Abortion Services*, New York, n.d.

Citizens for Tax Justice, *Inequality and the Federal Budget Deficit*, Washington, DC, September 1991.

———, *Annual Surveys of Corporate Tax Payers and Corporate Freeloaders*, Washington, DC, 1988, 1989.

Committee to End Sterilization Abuse (CESA), Helen Rodriguez-Trias, M.D. Testimony on Federal Financial Participation in Sterilization Funded by the Department of Health, Education and Welfare (DHEW), U.S.A., draft submitted by the Committee to End Sterilization Abuse (CESA), n.d.

Common Agenda Coalition, *Creating a Common Agenda: Strategies for Our Communities*, Executive Summary, A Citizens' Report on National Budget Priorities, Washington, DC, 1994.

Commonwealth Secretariat, *Engendering Adjustment for the 1990s*, Report of a Commonwealth Expert Group on Women and Structural Adjustment, London, 1989.

Ecumenical Institute for Study and Dialogue, *Integrity of Creation: How Humanity is Destroying the Environment*, Colombo, Sri Lanka, 1991.

E.F. Schumacher Society, "The History and Promise of Decentralism in America", Opening Keynote Addresses (unpublished), John McClaughry and Kirkpatrick Sale, Decentralist Conference, Williamstown, MA, June 28, 1996.

Federation for American Immigration Reform, *Backgrounder*, "Immigration Issues in Congress – 1993", Washington, DC, n.d.

———, "A Legislative Agenda for U.S. Immigration Reform", n.d.

Family Health International, "Selected Bibliography of Scientific Studies and Reviews on Hormonal Contraceptives and STDs", Research Triangle Park, NC, 1996.

FAO, "Rome Declaration on World Food Security and World Food Summit Plan of Action", November 13–17, 1996, Rome.

Global Exchange, "Women and the Global Economy", San Francisco, 1989.

Grassroots International, *Partnerships for Change: Mexico*, Cambridge, MA, n.d.

Human Rights Watch, *Human Rights World Reports*, 1991–1995, New York.

Information Project for Africa Inc., *Population Control and National Security: A Review of U.S. National Security Policy*, Washington, DC, 1991.

———, *Unconventional Warfare and the Theory of Competitive Reproduction: U.S. Intervention and Covert Action in the Developing World*, Working Paper No. 2, Washington, DC, 1991.

International Rivers Network, "Damning the World's Rivers: A Fact Sheet on World Bank Lending for Large Dams", World Bank/IMF: 50 Years is Enough, US Campaign, n.d.

International Women's Health Coalition, *Women's Voices '94: Women's Declaration on Population Policies*, New York, 1994.

Johns Hopkins Center for Communication Programs, Baltimore, MD, and Population Action International, Washington DC, "Population is a Food Security Issue", October 1996.

Massachusetts Human Services Coalition, "For the People", STAND, Boston, December 15, 1995.

Massachusetts Peace Action, *Monthly Update*, November–December 1993.

Ministry of Justice, Government of Cuba, "Working Women – Maternity Law", 1975.

National Audubon Society, *Population Newsletters*, Population Program, Washington, DC, 1994.

National Audobon Society and the Population Crisis Committee (PCC), *Why Population Matters: A Handbook for the Environmental Activist*, Washington, DC, 1991.

National Wildlife Federation, International Affairs Department, "Japan Supports Population Stabilization Program", *Beyond Just U.S. Newsletter*, Vol. 1, No. 2, Summer 1994.

National Women's Health Network, "The Depo-Provera Debate", March–April 1983.

Negative Population Growth, Inc., *Newsletters*, Vol. 18, No. 1, Fall 1992.

New Road Map Foundation, *All-Consuming Passion: Waking Up from the American Dream*, 2nd edn, Seattle, WA, 1993.

New World Foundation, "An Update on Developments in the Environmental Justice Movements", An Open Letter to Funding Colleagues by Ann Bastian and Dana Alston, New York, January 1996.

Oxfam America, *The Impact of Structural Adjustment on Community Life: Undoing Development*, Boston, April 1995.

Political Ecology Group (PEG), "Position Statement", Immigration and Environment Campaign, San Francisco.

Population Communications International, "Priority Statement on Population", 10 January 1991.

Population Crisis Committee, *Population Pressures – Threat to Democracy: Democratic Factors and Their Implications on Political Stability and Constitutional Government*, 1989.

——, "Country Rankings on the Status of Women – Poor, Pregnant and Powerless", Briefing Paper No. 20, 1988.

——, "Food and Population: Three Country Case Studies", Briefing Paper No. 18, Washington, DC, April 1987.

——, "World Population Growth and Global Security", Briefing Paper No. 13, September 1983.

Population Reference Bureau, *A Citizen's Guide to the Conference on Population and Development*, Washington, DC, 1994.

Rainforest Action Network, *Action Alert*, "Thailand Resumes Logging in Burma", No. 85, June 1993.

—— "World Bank Must Be Held Accountable", *Action Alert*, No. 80, January 1993.

SANE/Freeze International, International Working Conference on the Arms Trade, New York, November 1–2, 1991.

Sierra Club, International Population Program, *Population Stabilization – The Real Solution: Overpopulation, the Root of the Problem*, Washington, DC, n.d.

Survival International, "Banking on Disaster", *Index on Censorship*, Nos 6–7, 1989.

Third World Network, *Toxic Terror: Dumping Hazardous Wastes in the Third World*, Penang, Malaysia, 1989.

UNDP, *Human Development Report 1990–1996*, Oxford University Press, New York, 1996.

UNFPA, "Food for the Future: Women, Population and Food Security", New York, 1996.

——, *Population Growth and Economic Development*, Report of Consultative Meeting of Economists, New York, 1992.

——, *Women, Population and the Environment*, March 1992.

——, *Population, Resources and the Environment: The Critical Challenge*, New York, 1991.

——, "Pushing the Limits" (news feature distributed to media and journalists to promote the UNFPA *State of the World Population 1990* report), 1990.

——, INSTRAW, Joint Training Seminar on Women, Population and Development, May 22–26, 1989, Santo Domingo, Dominican Republic.

——, *State of the World Population 1990–1995*, New York.

—— and FAO, Report of the Expert Consultation on Women in Agricultural Development and Population in Asia, Penang, Malaysia, February 5–9, 1991.

UNHCR, *UNHCR at a Glance*, UNHCR Public Information, UNHCR Liaison Office, New York, December 30, 1995.

UNICEF, *The State of the World's Children*, Oxford University Press, New York, 1993, 1994, 1996.

United Nations, *The World's Women, 1995: Trends and Statistics*, Social Statistics and Indicators, Series K, No. 12, New York, 1995.

———, Fourth World Conference on Women, Beijing Declaration and Platform for Action, Beijing, China, September 4–15, 1995.

———, *World Economic and Social Survey*, Department for Economic and Social Information and Policy Analysis, New York, 1995.

———, World Summit for Social Development, Copenhagen, March 6–12, 1995.

———, Vienna Declaration and Programme of Action, World Conference on Human Rights, Vienna, June 14–25, 1993.

———, Report of the International Conference on Population and Development (ICPD, Cairo, September 5–13, 1994.

———, "Collective Declaration on Development and Economic Issues From the Cairo NGO Forum 1994", September 12, 1994.

———, Economic and Social Council, Report of the European Population Conference, Geneva, March 23–26, 1993.

———, Earth Conference, "Agenda 21: Programme of Action from Rio", United Nations Department of Public Information, New York, June 3–4, 1992.

———, Conference on the Environment and Development, "Alternative Treaty on Population, Environment and Development", Planeta Fêmea, Rio de Janeiro, Brazil, June 1992.

———, *World Economic Survey*, Department of Economic and Social Affairs, 1990, 1991.

———, *The World's Women, 1970–1990: Trends and Statistics*, Social Statistics and Indicators, Series K, No. 8, New York, 1991.

———, "World Population Trends and Policies: 1987 Monitoring Report", New York, 1988.

———, "The Relationship Between Disarmament and Development", Center for Disarmament, Disarmament Study Series, No. 5, New York, 1982.

———, "Proclamation of Teheran", in *United Nations Action in the Field of Human Rights*, New York, 1974.

United States Agency for International Development, J. Brian Atwood, 1994, Keynote Address, Meeting of the Office of Population Cooperating Agencies, Washington, DC, February 22, 1994.

———, "Preventive Diplomacy: Revitalizing A.I.D. and Foreign Assistance for the Post-Cold War Era", Report of the Task Force to Reform A.I.D. and the International Affairs Budget, September 1993.

———, "Revitalizing A.I.D.'s Role in the Post-Cold War Era", Report of the Task Force to Reform A.I.D Development Assistance, Draft No. 14, June 1993.

———, "Stabilizing World Population Growth and Protecting Human Health: USAID's Strategy", USAID Strategy Papers, Draft, May 10, 1993.

———, "Strategy for Sustainable Development: An Overview", USAID Strategy Papers, Draft, May 10, 1993.

———, Letter by James Shelton, MD, MPH, Chief Research Division and Cynthia Calla, MD, MPH, Medical Officer, Office of Population to Carlos Huezo, MD, Medical Director, IPPF, August 21, 1991.

———, "Norplant: Under Her Skin", letter regarding Norplant distribution from women attending the 6th International Meeting on Women and Health, to Duff Gillespie, November 1990.

———, "Blueprint for Development – The Strategic Plan of the Agency for International Development", n.d.

United States Arms Control and Disarmament Agency, *World Military Expenditures and Arms Transfers 1993–1994*, Washington, DC: US Government Printing Office, February 1995.

———, *World Military Expenditures and Arms Transfers 1990*, Washington, DC: US Government Printing Office, 1991.

United States Bureau of the Census, *Statistical Abstract of the United States: 1995*, 115th edn, Washington, DC, 1995.

————, *World Population Profile: 1994*, Report WP/94, Washington, DC: US Government Printing Office, 1994.

————, *Statistical Abstract of the United States, Projected Fertility Rates by Race and Age Group, 1994 and 2010*.

United States Department of Energy, "Human Radiation Experiments Associated with the U.S. Department of Energy and its Predecessors", Washington, DC, July 1995.

United States House of Representatives, 3538, "Code of Conduct on Arms Transfers Act of 1993", introduced by Ms McKinney, November 18, 1993.

United States Institute for Peace, "Sources of Conflict: Highlights from the Managing Chaos Conference", *Peaceworks*, No. 4, Washington, DC, August 1995.

United States National Academy of Sciences and the Royal Society, *Population Growth, Resource Consumption and a Sustainable World*, Washington, DC and London, 1992.

US President, "Remarks by the President to the National Academy of Sciences", The White House, Washington, DC, June 29, 1994.

————, National Security Education Act of 1991, signed December 4, 1991.

University Teachers for Human Rights, "Women Prisoners of the LTTE", *Information Bulletin*, No. 5, Jaffna, Sri Lanka, March 1995.

Women Working for a Nuclear Free and Independent Pacific, eds, *Pacific Women Speak: Why Haven't You Known?*, Oxford: Green Line, 1987.

World Bank, *Effective Family Planning Programs*, Washington, DC, 1993.

————, *Population and the World Bank: Implications from Eight Case Studies*, Operations Evaluation Department, Washington, DC, 1992.

————, "Safe Motherhood Initiative at Midpoint", *WIDLINE*, Population and Human Resources Department, No. 4, May 1992.

————, *WIDLINE*, Population and Human Resources Department, No. 4, May 1992, No. 5, August 1992.

————, Office Memorandum by Lawrence H. Summers, Chief Economist, December 12 1991 (reprinted in "Let Them Eat Pollution", *The Economist* (London), February 8, 1992).

————, *World Development Report*, New York: Oxford University Press, 1984, 1990.

————, *Sub-Saharan Africa: From Crisis to Sustainable Growth*, Washington, DC, 1989.

————, *Poverty and Prosperity: The Two Realities of Asian Development*, Address of Atilla Karaosmanoglu, Vice President for Asia.

World Bank/IMF: 50 Years Is Enough Campaign, "Food for Thought: Agriculture and the World Bank", n.d.

————, "Platform", n.d.

World Bank–IMF: 50 Years..., "Debt", Fact sheet, n.d.

————, "Bankrolling Homelessness: A Fact Sheet on Resettlement and the World Bank", n.d.

World Resources Institute, *World Resources 1990–1991* and *1994–1995*, New York: Oxford University Press, 1990, 1994.

The World Uranium Hearing, "Victims of Uranium Mining and Atomic Tests", The World Uranium Hearing, 1990, updated report published in co-operation with the Heinrich Böll Stiftung, The World Uranium Hearing, 100 West 12th Street, New York, New York 10011, USA.

Newspapers

Al-Ahram, September 8–14, 15–21, 1994.
Bangkok Post, October 13, 1991.
The Boston Globe, December 10, 1996.
————, June 26, 1996.
————, December 1, 1995.

————, June 26, 27, 1993.

————, July 29, 1992.

————, February 9, 1987.

The Boston Sunday Globe, June 16, 1996.

————, May 30, 1993.

The Boston Globe Magazine, December 17, 1995.

Chicago Tribune, March 30, 1989.

The Christian Science Monitor, May 23, 1995.

————, August 20, 1990.

Daily Hampshire Gazette, June 22, 23, 1996.

————, July 14, 1993.

Guardian, April 25 1989.

The Island (Sri Lanka), December 17, 31, 1995.

The New York Times, January 5, 1997.

————, November 12, 17, 1996.

————, October 4, 1996.

————, August 20, 1996.

————, July 11, 1996.

————, June 11, 1996.

————, March 7, 31, 1996.

————, February 13, 16, 1996.

————, January 6, 11, 12, 13, 18, 21, 24, 1996.

————, December 1, 6, 11, 15, 1995.

————, November 7, 13, 27, 1995.

————, October 15, 21, 31, 1995.

————, September 16, 1995.

————, August 8, 20, 21, 1995.

————, June 6, 1995.

————, April 2, 7, 17, 1995.

————, March 9, 17, 22, 1995.

————, February 2, 1995.

————, January 21, 22, 1995.

————, November 15, 1994.

————, October 6, 1994.

————, September 6, 8, 11, 13, 14, 23, 29, 1994.

————, August 30, 1994.

————, June 26, 29, 1994.

————, May 17, 1994.

————, March 6, 1994.

————, January 2, 1994.

————, December 6, 8, 10, 13, 1993.

————, November 17, 20, 21, 1993.

————, June 4, 12, 1993.

————, May 24, 1992.

————, March 8, 1992.

————, February 7, 1992.

————, January 16, 1992.

————, December 19, 1991.

————, November 5, 9, 1991.

————, October 8, 1991.

————, September 9, 23, 1991.

————, August 11, 15, 1991.

————, June 16, 1991.

————, May 22, 1991.

————, September 23, 1990.

————, July 9, 13, 1990.
————, October 7, 1989
————, November 21, 1989.
————, August 7, 1987.
————, January 5, 1979.
New York Review of Books, 7 April 1996.
————, October 15, 1995.
————, October 5, 1995.
New York Times Magazine, January 19, 1997.
————, May 19, 1996.
————, April 21, 1996.
————, January 2, 30, 1994.
Silumina (Sinhala newspaper/Sri Lanka), October 13, 1996.
Seattle Times, December 4, 1993.
The Sunday Times (Sri Lanka), February 10, 1991.
Tico Times, November 27, 1987.
Union News, Springfield, June 24, 1996.
Wall Street Journal, April 22, 1993.
Washington Post, June 4, 1993.
————, January 16, 1990.
————, July 5, 1985.
Washington Star, June 22, 1980.

Films

Antibodies Against Pregnancy, Ulrike Schaz and Ingrid Schneider, Bleicherstr. 2 D2267, Hamburg.
The Burning Times, Video Studio D, National Film Board of Canada, 1993.
Panama Deception, Rhino Home Video, The Empowerment Project, Santa Monica, CA, 1993.
Something Like a War, D.N. Productions, India, in association with Equal Media Ltd, London, 1991.
The Suicide Killers: A Documentary on LTTE in Sri Lanka, British Broadcasting Corporation, 1992.
Ultimate Test Animal, New York: The Cinema Guild, 1985.

Index

abortion(s) 8–10, 336
    sex-selective 98–100, 101
Adé, King Sunny 90
advertising, global 234
Agarwal, Anil 243
Agarwal, Bina 242
agricultural societies, emergence of 118–22
agriculture, capitalist
    and the environment 241–2, 243–8
    establishment of 127–8
    see also food production
Ahmad, Eqbal 284
Ahmed, Leila 290
Allende, Salvador 274
alternative statements on population 18
Amin, Samir 199
Amsterdam Declaration (1989) 66
Anchthoven, Lenny 85
Antrobus, Peggy 202
Arbenz 274
Arendonk, Dr Joseph von 75
Arms Sales Monitor 205, 281
arms trade 204–8, 275, 277–9, 281–2,
    328–9
    see also military expenditures
Aronson, Cynthia 274
Asiyo, Phoebe 169
Asoka, Emperor 321
Aspin, Les 277
Atlantic Monthly 44
Atwood, Margaret, The Handmaid's Tale 297
Aung San Suu Kyi 311, 320, 322, 338, 340
Auto Immune Deficiency Syndrome
    (AIDS) 144, 220
automobiles, ownership of 230–31
Aveden, John 79

Bacon, Francis 122
Bahuguna, Sunderlal 247
Bangladesh 42–4, 72–4
Barrett Brown, Michael 128
Barnet, Richard 150
Bartleet Microdevices 254
Basel Convention on the Control of
    Transboundary Movement of

Hazardous Wastes and their
    Disposal 256
Basu, Alaka 159, 177
Bateson, Gregory, Steps to an Ecology of Mind
    317
beef and meat production 194, 229, 241
Beijing Women's Conference, see World
    Conference on Women
Belcher, Martha 249
Berelson, Bernard 35, 86
Bertell, Dr Rosalie 259
Beulink, Anne-Marie 198
Beyond the Limits (1992) 31, 41
Bhave, Vinoba 330
Bhopal disaster 252–3
Bhutto, Benazir 278
biodiversity, ownership of 245–6
bioregionalism 326–7
biotechnology 245–6
birth control
    vs population control 63–4, 103–4,
        336–7
    receptivity to, and social class 161, 168
Black, Dr Tim 88
Bodhi, Bhikku 324
Bodley, John 130
body parts, sale of 221
Boff, Leonardo 332
Bolen, Jean Shindoa 133, 340
Borgstrom, George 134
    The Food and People Dilemma 129
Bourdieu, Pierre 308
Boutwell, Jeffrey 44
brain drain, South–North 210–11
Braudel, Fernand 134
Brazil 71, 249
breast-feeding rates, in Third World 167
Brezinski, Zbigniew 50
Brown, Lester 11, 39
Brundtland, Gro Harlem 34
Buddhism 316, 317, 323, 324, 325
Bulletin of the Committee of South Asian
    Women 286
Bumiller, Elizabeth 76, 77
Bush, George 286

Caffentzis, George 135, 144
Caldwell, John 157, 160, 173
Caldwell, Pat 173
Calla, Cynthia 93
capitalism
    and domination 307–12
    and the environment 238–57
    and global crisis 13–19, 123–4
    and population growth 11–16, 124–8,
        135–46, 149–52
    see also corporate restructuring;
        economic growth
caring and nurturance, ethic of 7–8, 123
carrying capacity
    concept of 30–31, 127–8
    export of 233
Carrying Capacity Network 36, 37–8
Chavez, Cesar 312
chemicals, agricultural and industrial
    244–5, 253–4
child adoption industry 220
child labor 159, 160–63, 169, 196
child mortality 172–4, 202
children
    attitudes towards 158, 159, 164
    as economic assets 160–63
    impact of global crisis on 2, 151
    as priority 338
    as soldiers 284–5
China
    population control in 78–80
    protest against family planning in 102
Chinese Medical Journal 99
Chomsky, Noam, and Edward Herman 298
    The Washington Connection 273
Chossudovsky, Michael 202
Christianity 122, 131–2, 317
Clairmont, Frederic 150
Clark, Mary 271
class, social
    analysis of 15, 18
    and consumption patterns 228–34
    and demographic transitions 124–6
    and fertility rates 157–70
    see also poverty
Clinton, Bill 34
Cold War, and Third World 261–3, 272–6
Committee on Women, Population and the
    Environment 180, 311
    Call for a New Approach 18, 345–7
Commoner, Barry 140, 238
Communist regimes, and environment 239
Conservation Digest 54
Constanza, Robert 37
consumer boycotts and pressure 329
consumerism 234–7, 270–1
consumption
    balance in 329–32
    inequalities in 32–3, 228–37
Contemplacion, Flor 219
contraception
    and human welfare 63, 336–7

methods of, and population control
    68–92
    see also population control
contraceptive revolution 65, 81, 101
    'second' 91–2
Contraceptive Social Marketing (CSM)
    90–91, 92
corporate restructuring, since 1970s 15–16,
    211–27
Correa, Sonia 71

da Silva, Ignacio Lula 202, 251
Dalai Lama 322
Daly, Gretchen, *The Stork and the Plow* (with
    Anne and Paul Ehrlich) 33
Daly, Herman E. 37, 191, 326
dam building 246–8
Darwin, Charles 129
    The Origin of Species 29
Dash, Leon 139, 164
Davis, Kingsley 101
Dawson, Marc 138
de Silva, Indralal 176
death, attitudes towards 316–17, 334
debt, international
    cancellation of 327–8
    crisis of 197–203, 251–2
debt-for-nature transactions 251–2
deep ecology 318
deforestation 32, 240–41, 242, 243, 251
democracy
    and global crisis 151–2
    participatory, idea of 332–4
    and population control 101–4
    threats to 295–8
    and US military 276
demographic imbalance, fear of 48–51
demographic targets, use of 66–8, 70–80
demographic transition(s)
    and social class 124–6
    theory of 64
    and the Third World 140–49, 176,
        177
Depo-Provera 83–4, 91
depopulations, co...... 129–31, 134
Descartes, René 122
Deval, Bill 37
development
    indigenous forms of 309–10
    and population growth 40–44, 143,
        162–3, 175–81
Development Alternatives with Women for
    a New Era (DAWN) 203
Dhanraj, Dheepa 77
dictatorships, Third World 273–4
disaster ethic 35–8
Divale, Julio 121
dominator paradigm 18, 102–4, 314–16
    origins of, in agricultural societies
        118–19, 122
    see also partnership paradigm
Draper, General William 275

drug companies, and contraceptive
  research 80–88 *passim*, 92
dualistic thinking 316, 317
Duden, Barbara 28
Duke, David 86
Durning, Alan 228, 229, 231, 232
Duvalier, Jean Claude 210, 274
Duvalier, Michele 210
The Dying Rooms (film) 100
Dyson, Tim 193

Easterbrook, Greg 11
Eberstadt, Nicholas 48
ecocentric thinking 316–20
ecofeminism 122, 318–19
economic growth
  and environmental damage 32–3, 34–5,
    238–9
  as ideology 11–12, 191
  limits to 326–7
  see also capitalism
economic incentives, in population control
  programs 68, 70–79, 89
economic inequality
  between men and women 217–18
  and demographic crisis 151–2
  and fertility rates 175–82
  global, level of 12–15, 187–91
  and imperialism 128
  North–South 191–2, 195, 233–4
  and population growth 40–41, 50–51,
    140–43
  and restructuring of global economy
    211–17
economic system, transformation of 324–32
ecosystem
  and capitalist production 127–8, 228,
    238–57
  collapse of 1, 228
  damage to, and North–South
    divide 233–4, 239–41
  Malthusian analysis of 30–38
  and military activities 257–63
  protection of, and social struggles
    310–11
  and sustainable development 326–7
  see also nature
education and fertility 174–5, 178–9
Egypt, population growth in 138
Ehrlich, Anne 30
Erlich, Anne and Paul
  The Population Explosion 33, 37
  The Stork and the Plow (with Gretchen
    Daly) 33
Ehrlich, Paul 11, 30, 75
  The Population Bomb 51
Einstein, Albert 283
Eisler, Riane 122, 318
elderly, and 'resources' 151
electoral politics
  and campaign finance reform 332
  corporate control of 214, 295

elites, Third World 35, 158, 272, 273–4,
    309
  and development aid 209–10
Ellul, Jacques 236
Elson, Diane 218
emigration, Third World
  of female labor 218–19
  of skilled labor 210–11
emissions trading 256–7
Engels, Friedrich 121
Enloe, Cynthia 286
Enter-Educate program 90
environment, *see* ecosystems
environmental groups, *see* social movements
equity and simple living, ethic of 329–32
Escobar, Pablo 279
Esteva, Gustavo 328
ethnic groups, and differential fertility
  rates 48
ethnic nationalism and violence 118–19,
    287–90, 293–5
eugenics 11, 29, 63–4, 78–9, 85–6
Europe
  ethnic violence in 293–4
  restructuring in 215–17

Falk, Richard 284
family and community 271, 338
famines, causes of 193
Fanon, Frantz 272
farmers' struggles 310–11
fascism, rise of, in Europe 293–4
Fathalla, Mahmoud F. 92
FAIR (Federation for American Immigrant
  Reform) 36, 38
Federico, Silvia 143
feminism
  and analysis of global crisis 17–18
  and Malthusianism 7–8, 29, 35
  and partnership 318–19
  and patriarchy 122
  and WID programs 96–7
  see also social movements
fertility decisions, control over 171–2
fertility rates
  in North and South 48–9, 50–51,
    146–9
  social determinants of 157–82
Folbre, Nancy 162
food, consumption of 228–9, 330
food production
  global rates of 192–5
  and monocrop agriculture 128, 137–8,
    243–4
  and poverty 39
foraging communities, *see* hunter-gatherer
  societies
Foreign Affairs 49
Foster, Gregory 50
Foster, John Bellamy 238
Francis of Assisi, St 317
Frazier, Franklin 139

'free trade' 191–5, 253
fuel consumption 257–8
Fuji, Nichidatsu 324
Fursee, Elizabeth 276

Gandhi, Indira 74, 75, 102
Gandhi, Mahatma 309, 317, 322, 330
Gearhart, Sally 319
Geertz, Clifford 138
Gender and Development programs 97
gender dynamics, and reproduction 115–22
    see also women
General Agreement on Tariffs and Trade
    (GATT) 13, 35, 193, 221, 245
George, Susan 194, 198
Gerster, Richard 251
Gibbs, Lois 312
Gimbutas, Marija 122
Gingrich, Newt 11
global crisis
    effect of, on youth 270–72
    nature of 1–19
Global Environment Facility 246, 327
Godwin, William 28
Goldman, Emma 63
Goldsmith, Edward 244
Gore, Al 11
    Earth in the Balance 34
Gouri Parvathi Bai, Queen of
    Travancore 179
Green Revolution 244
Greer, Germaine, *Sex and Destiny* 159
Gross, Bertram 297
Gulf War 262–3, 283–4
guns, proliferation of 292
Gwatkin, Davidson 74
gypsies 294

Halliday, Fred 273
Hancock, Graham, *Lords of Poverty* 209
Handgunning Magazine 292
Handwerker, Penn 119, 160, 168
Hardin, Anita 85
Hardin, Garret 35–6
    Living Within Limits 36
Harper, Ida Husted 64
Harris, Marvin 115, 121, 124, 126
Hartmann, Betsy 10, 72, 74
Hawken, Paul 11
health care
    and population control 93–6
    and women 337
Henderson, Hazel 327
Herero people 136–7
Herrnstein, Richard, and Charles Murray,
    The Bell Curve 11
Heyzer, Noeleen 217
Hitler, Adolf 293
Hobbes, Thomas 27, 271
Hoem, Jan 149
Holzhausen, Walter 73, 79
Homer-Dixon, Thomas 44

Hoskins, Eric 262
households, female-headed 218
Hubbard, Ruth 337
Huerta, Dolores 312
Huezo, Carlos 93
Hull, Terrence 98, 100
Human Genome Project 148
human relationships
    crisis of 322–4
    quality of, and consumerism 235–7
hunter–gatherer communities, population in
    116–18
Huntington, Samuel 49
Hussein, Saddam 284
Huxley, Aldous, *Brave New World* 297
Hynes, Patricia 33

immigration
    and global inequality 328
    hostility to 38–9, 46, 48, 293
imperialism
    and ecology 239–41, 243–8
    and fundamentalisms 287–9
    and militarism 204, 272
    and population dynamics 126–43
    resistance to 308–12
    see also Cold War; Third World
India
    and child labor 161
    ethnic nationalism in 289
    fertility reduction in 42, 95–6
    protests against population control
        in 102
    sterilization programs in 74–8
    see also Kerala
indigenous peoples
    and colonial depopulations 129–31
    and uranium mining 260–61
    see also Native Americans; World
        Conference on Women
Indonesia, *see* Java
infant mortality, and poverty 167–8, 215
infanticide, female 100, 101, 117, 121,
    172
information–education–communication, *see*
    promotion of family planning
Ingram, Paul, *Tibet: The Facts* 79
injectable contraceptives 83–4
'interbeing', concept of 317
intergenerational wealth flows 157, 160–63
internal colonialism 139
International Conference on Population
    and Development (Cairo, 1994)
    and demographic targets 66
    and economic growth 11
    and fertility rates 5
    and immigration 38, 46
    and media management 10, 298
    and reproductive rights 7, 9, 29, 53–5,
        92
    see also Committee on Women,
        Population and the Environment

International Monetary Fund 198–200, 327
International Tropical Timber Organization 240
Intra-Uterine Devices (IUDs) 82
investment, North–South 197, 198
see also World Bank
Iraq, and Gulf War 262–3, 281, 284
Isaacs, Stephen 71
Itzkoff, Seymour, *The Decline of Intelligence in America* 11

Jacobson, Jodi 169
Janata Vimukti Peramuna 289
Java
    and colonialism 137–8
    and population transfers 248–9
Jeffrey, Patricia 76, 174, 181
Jeffrey, Roger 174, 181
Jesus Christ 317
John Paul II, Pope 11
Johnson, Darlene 86
Johnson, Kay Ann 100
Jolly, Richard 209

Kader Company 253
Kaplan, Robert 44–5, 47
Karkal, Malini 95
Keju-Johnson, Darlene 260, 261
Kendall, Henry 39
Kennan, George 6, 273
Kennedy, Paul 49, 50
    Preparing for the Twenty First Century 47
Kenya, fertility in 138
Kerala, fertility reduction in 176, 177–80
Kerr, Dr Blake 79
Keswani, Raj Kumar 252
Keyfitz, Nathan 45
Khandawala, Dr S.P. 76
Kimbrell, Andrew, *The Human Body Shop* 221
King, Martin Luther, Jr. 274
King, Maurice 36
Kishwar, Madhu 100
Kissinger, Henry 272
Klare, Michael 274, 279
Kohlberg, Lawrence 322
Kohr, Leopold 326
Krishnan, T.N. 180
Kummer, David 240

labor
    exploitation of 120, 123, 124
    migration of 210–11, 218–19
    and population growth 149–50
    reproduction of, and colonialism 135–9
LaCheen, Cary 91
Ladakh society 142, 326
LaDuke, Winona 250, 312
Lancet, The 88
Lappe, Frances Moore 162, 176, 180, 194
Lerner, Gerda 122

Lesthaeghe, Ron 182
Liberation Tigers of Tamil Eelam (LTTE) 285, 289, 290
Lieberson, Stanley 35
Limits to Growth (1972) 31, 41
Lovins, Hunter 37
Lund, Ragnhild 250
Lyon, Andrew 174

McDaniel, Ed 83
McNamara, Robert 75, 275
Magdoff, Harry 128
Mahaweli River Project (Sri Lanka) 249–50
Mahbub-ul Haq 328
Malcolm X 274
Malthus, Thomas 4, 5, 271
    Essay on the Principle of Population 27–8
Malthusianism 4–12, 28–55, 101–104
Mamdani, Mahmood 161, 162
Manning, Patrick, *Slavery and African Life* 134
manufacturing
    economic inequalities in 195–6
    and the environment 252–7
    see also technology
Manushi 100
Marcos, Ferdinand 210, 274
Marcos, Sylvia 132
marine ecosystems 241, 251, 259
marketing of contraceptives 90–91, 92
Marx, Karl 124, 238, 308
Masih, Iqbal 196
maternal mortality 94–5
Mathews, Jessica Tuchman 49
Mazumdar, Vina 95
meat eating, and resource depletion 229
media
    control of, during war 283
    corporate control of 297–8
    management of 10–11
    use of, for contraceptive promotion 89–90
Mehta, P.V. 76–7
Memmi, Albert 272
men and masculinity 338–9
Mencher, Joan 161
Menchú, Rigoberta 312, 334
Mencken, H.L. 69
Mendes, Chico 311
Mendis, Patrick 330
Merrick, Thomas 162
Middle East, militarization of 277–8
Middle Way 324, 326–7, 330, 33, 334, 335, 339
Mies, Maria 122, 237
military activities
    and environmental destruction 257–63
    see also violence; wars
military expenditures 2, 205–9, 212–13
    see also arms trade; nuclear weapons production
'missing women' 97–101, 174

Mitra, Asok 160
Mobutu, Sese Seko 210
Morris, Leo 42
mortality rates
  in agricultural societies 119
  in Europe 27
  Third World 140, 143–6
  working class 124
Mossadeq, 274
Moser, Caroline 181
Moynihan, Patrick 214

Nader, Ralph 212
Nair, Sumati 80
national liberation movements 309
National Wildlife Federation 34
Native Americans
  depopulation of 129, 136
  and toxic dumping 255
natural resources, depletion of, and
  population growth 30–34
  see also ecosystem
nature
  'dispensability' of 245
  as object of domination 122–4
  as unified 316–18
Net-En 83, 84
'New World Order' 276, 279–84
Non-Governmental Organisations
  (NGOs) 6, 18, 312–13
non-violent strategies 314, 320–23, 333
Norberg-Hodge, Helena, *Ancient
  Futures* 142, 326
Norplant 85–6
Norsigian, Judy 88
North American Free Trade Agreement 35,
  195
nuclear weapons production 2, 259–61,
  272–3, 278

Oberg, Jan 293
Obermeyer, Carla Makhlouf 169
oil production 239–40
orphanages, and abandonment 100–101
Orwell, George, *Nineteen Eighty-Four* 298
overconsumption, *see* consumption
Overseas Development Aid 209–10

Palacios, Chailang 131
Palmer, Ingrid 170
paradigm shift 19, 314–24
Parks, Rosa 309
partnership paradigm 102–4, 314–24
patriarchy
  creation of 120–23
  end of 338–9
  fertility rates 170–75
  and violence 286, 291–2
Patterson, John 137
peasantry, resistance of, to capitalism 308–9
Peavey, Fran 294
Petchetsky, Rosalind 80

Petras, James 270
Philadelphia Inquirer 85
Pierce, Clovis 69
pill, contraceptive 81–2
Pimentel, David 39
Piotrow, Phyllis 90
Polgar, Steven 129, 137
Polonoreste Colonization Scheme 249
population control
  as approach to global crisis 5–12, 30,
    50–51, 52–5
  and democracy 101–104, 295
  and the environment 33–8
  global institutions of 10–11, 65–8
  and health care 93–6
  methods of 68–88, 91–2
  and poverty 39–44, 52–3
  in pre-capitalist societies 117–18,
    119–22
  promotional activities for 88–91
  resistance to 102, 311
  and US military 275
  and women's rights 92–101
population dynamics 115–52
population growth
  and capitalism 14–15, 140–46, 149–52
  and development 162–3, 177–81
  and imperialism 128–43
  and Malthusianism 4–7, 27–55, 345–6
  and political instability 44–51
  in pre-capitalist societies 118, 119
  and social class 124–6
  and women 51–3
population momentum 148
Population Services International 89–90,
  91
population transfers 248–50
Potts, Dr Malcolm 84
poverty
  and the arms trade 204–9
  and debt crisis 197–203
  feminization of 17, 136, 214–15, 217–
    19
  and fertility 137–9, 159–70, 175–82
  global, level of 1–2
  and informal economy 219–21
  and levels of consumption 228–9
  Malthusian analysis of 28, 39–44, 52–3
  and mortality 95, 143–6
  political economy of 187–221
  and sterilization 72–8
  and toxic dumping 255
  in US 214–15
  and welfare spending 215–16
  see also economic inequality
PPE Spiral 33
Prakash, Suri 328
prescription, and contraceptives 90–91
Pritchett, Lant 168
privatization of state enterprises 199
promotion of family planning 88–91
prostitution 126, 219–20

as child labor 162
and Vietnam War 262
psycho-social revolution 319–24
Puerto Rico 138

Qian Xinzhong 75
quinacrine 87–8

racism 46–7, 64, 133–4, 291, 293–5
Rao, Dr Mohan 95
rape, as warfare 286–7
see also sexual violence
Ratcliffe, John 177, 179, 180
Rathjans, George 44
Ravenholt, Reimer 65
raw-material consumption 231–2
refugees 2, 271
see also immigration
religious fundamentalism
and population control 8–11
as resistance 287–8
and women 289–90, 293
and US politics 295
Renner, Michael 258
Repetto, Robert 175, 180
repression, of activists 311–12
reproductive disorders 262
reproductive rights 7–11, 53–5, 335–8
resistance, forces of 307–14
Rifkin, Jeremy 150
Rio Earth Summit (UNCED – 1992) 11,
35, 235, 246
Alternative Treaty on Population,
Environment and Development 18
Convention on Biological
Diversity 245–6
Robbins, Dr Frederick 82
Robertson, Pat 11
Robey, Bryant 42
Rodriguez, Cecilia 312
Ross, Eric 115, 124, 126
Russia
mortality in 144–5
poverty in 216–17
Rutstein, Shea O. 42
Rwanda 288–9

Sadik, Nafis 52, 73, 79
Safa, Helen 163
Safe Motherhood Initiative 94–6
Sagoff, Mark 140, 143, 148
Sahlins, Marshall, *Stone Age Economics* 116
Said, Edward 288
Sale, Kirkpatrick 37
Sanger, Margaret 64, 69
Sankaracarya 179
Saro-Wiwa, Ken 311
Saudi Arabia 277
Sawhill, Sybil 86
Schumacher, E.F., *Small is Beautiful* 325
Schurman, Rachel 162, 176
Scientific American 42

Scudder, Thayer 248
Seager, Joni 262
Sebastian, Rita 290
Seed, John 318
Sen, Amartya 173, 179, 192, 193
Seville Statement on Violence 321, 348–50
sex ratios 98–9
sexual relations, and social class 124–6
sexual violence 171
see also rape
Shelton, James D. 93
Sheth, D.L. 333
Shiva, Mira 7
Shiva, Vandana 7, 245
Shockley, William 69
Shrestha, Nanda 137
Sierra Club 34, 39
Simon, Julian 8, 11
Singh, Gurudev 161
skin trade 219–21
Sklar, Holly 274
Sklar, Leonard 248
slave trade 134
slavery and reproduction 139
Smith, David 46
Snyder, Rear Admiral John 281–2
social justice
and environmental justice, struggles for
312
ethic of 18–19, 180
and Malthusianism 28
social movements
co-optation of 12, 312–14
liberal, and Malthusianism 34–5, 37–9
Northern 312
Third World 310–12
socialism 239
Sojourner Truth 18
soldiering, as employment 221
Solow, Robert 245
Something Like a War (Dheepa Dhanraj,
1991) 77
Somoza, Anastazio 273, 274
son preference 171–2
South Korea, fertility decline in 175
Spencer, Herbert 29
sperm count, decline in 146
Sri Lanka 180
fertility decline in 176–7
resettlement in 249
war in 285, 289
Srinivasan, Viji 101, 172
Standing, Hilary 72, 74
stepladder approach 35
sterilization 68–80, 181
Stoller Chemical Company 256
Stone, Jonathan 36
structural adjustment policies (SAPs)
198–203
and the environment 251–2
and fertility 169–70
and mortality 143–4, 202

Stycos, J. Mayone 79–80
subsistence production
  undermining of 127–8, 242
  and women 203, 243
Summers, Carol 135
Summers, Lawrence 254
surrogate mothering 220–21
sustainable development 324–32
Sweden, fertility increase in 149

Taiwan, population growth in 138, 175
Talwar, Dr G.P. 87
Taylor, General Maxwell 275
technocapitalism 123
technology
  and alienation 236
  and capitalism 15
  and the environment 32–2, 123
  and the skin trade 220–21
  and Third World population
    growth 140–42
  see also capitalism
teenage pregnancy 163–4, 171
Thapar, Romila 287
Thich Nhat Hanh 317
Third World
  and arms trade 207–9, 277–9
  food production in 193–5
  maternal and child health in 94–6
  missing women in 97–101
  political conflict in 44–5, 47–8
  population collapses in 182
  population control programs in 65–9,
    80–91, 96–7
  population growth in 4–6, 48–51, 64–5,
    140–48
  and resistance to modern order 308–12
  sterilization abuse in 70–80
  super-power military interventions in
    261–3, 271–7, 279–84
  toxic dumping in 254–5, 256–7
  see also economic inequality; elites;
    imperialism
Thompson, E.P. 123, 295
Thurow, Lester 151
Tibet, sterilizations in 79
time, commodification of 236
Tito, Marshal 294
Toffler, Alvin 11
toxic dumping 254–7
trade, international 191–5
Transmigration Project (Indonesia)
  248–9
transnational corporations
  and environmental degradation 239–41,
    252–7
  power of 13–14, 194–5
  regulation of 328–9
  and unemployment 150
transportation, inequalities in 229–31
triage 36–7
Tropical Forest Action Plan 240

underpopulation crisis
  in Europe 135
  in US 139
unemployment 1, 124, 150–51, 196
Union Carbide 252–3
United Nations, and imperialism 283–4
United Nations Fund for Population
  Activities 10, 31–2, 40, 54, 73
  reports by 31–2, 40, 42, 52, 53, 54–5,
    231
United Nations Population Conference, *see*
  World Population Conference
United States
  arms trade of 205, 277–8, 281–2
  control of politics in 295–7
  corporate restructuring in 211–15
  interventions by, in Third World 273–4,
    276–7, 279–84
  military bases of 258–9
  overconsumption in 230, 232
  and partnership paradigm 324
  and population control 6, 8, 9–10, 37,
    44, 45, 65
  social justice struggles in 312
  sterilization abuse in 69–70
  teenage pregnancy in 163–4
  toxic dumping in 255–6
  violence in 291–3
  wealth inequality in 189
US Agency for International
  Development 12, 42, 81, 82, 90
uranium mining 260
urbanization 45, 124

'vaccines' 87
Vatican 8, 9, 10, 11
Vatsyayan, S.H. 236
Vicziany, Marika 74
Vietnam, effects of war in 262
violence
  causes of 270–72, 348–50
  and dualistic thinking 316
  in feudal societies 118–19
  in the North 291–3
  and population growth 44–5, 47–8
  and Third World 273–91
  see also wars
Viravaidya, Mechai 89
voting, in US 295–7

Wachtel, Paul 237
Wallace, Robert B. 55
Ward, Julie 64
Ward, Kathryn 169
Ward, Martha 171
wars
  causes of 348–50
  and patriarchy 121, 286
  and population growth 121, 146
  proxy, in the Third World 261–3,
    272–6
  since 1945 2

see also violence
Weber, Max 123
Weindling, Paul 64
welfare, social
  expenditure on, decline in 208–9, 215–16
  and fertility rates 163, 179–80
  and SAPs 200
  and women 203, 208–9
Wessman, James 138
Westmoreland, General William 275
White, Benjamin 163
White, Lynn, Jr 122
Williams, Constance Willard 164
Willson, Dr Robert 82
Wilson, William Julius 164
Wisner, Ben 128
witchcraft persecutions 122
Woman, The 88
women
  attitudes of, to childrearing 158–9
  and birth control 63
  and consumerism 237
  control over, in agricultural societies 120–23
  effect of environmental degradation on 242–3
  effects of SAPs on 202–3
  empowerment of 335–40, 345–7
  and fundamentalism 289–90
  and global capitalism 2, 17–18, 187, 193, 195–6, 217–19, 252–4
  hours worked by 217–18
  in hunter-gatherer societies 117
  and imperialism 133, 136–7
  position of, and fertility rates 169–79
  and research into contraceptives 81–8
  and resettlement programs 249–50
  and skin trade 220–21

struggles by 307, 308, 309, 311
  as target of population control 51–5
  and US military 282
  and violence 292
  and war 285, 286–7, 290
  and welfare expenditure 203, 208–9
Women in Development (WID)
  programs 96–7, 174
women's rights
  agenda for 345–7
  and population control 7–8, 29, 92–101, 103
working conditions 252–4
Working Women's Forum (Madras) 96–7
World Bank
  development projects 244, 246–50
  and population control 42–4, 54, 65, 89, 93–5
  reform of 327
  reports by 160, 181
  and sterilization studies 73–4, 77–8
  and SAPs 198–200
World Conference on Women (Beijing, 1995) 9, 11–12, 54, 338
  Declaration of Indigenous Women 18
  NGO Declaration 18
World Population Conference (Bucharest, 1974) 41, 142–3, 192, 310
World Population Conference (Mexico City, 1984) 8
The World's Women (UN) 208
World Trade Organization 13

youth
  as soldiers, in Third World 284–5
  and violence 47, 270–71, 291
  and US military 282
  see also children

Zapatista Army of National Liberation 286